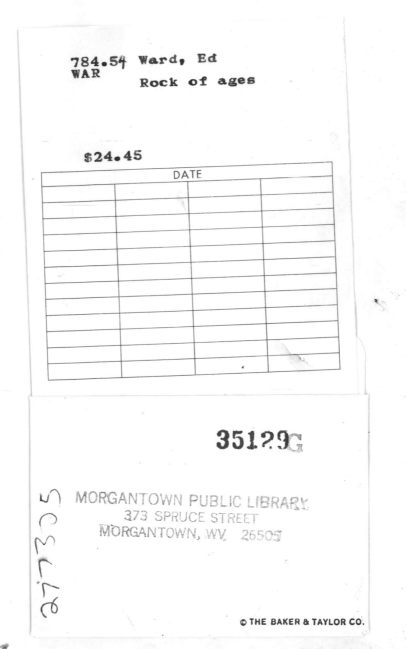

ROCK
OF AGES

THE RollingStone
HISTORY OF ROCK & ROLL

by
ED WARD
GEOFFREY STOKES
KEN TUCKER

with an introduction by
JANN S. WENNER

Rolling Stone Press / Summit Books
NEW YORK

(Continued on page 622)

Copyright © 1986 by Rolling Stone Press

All rights reserved
including the right of reproduction
in whole or in part in any form
Published by SUMMIT BOOKS
A Division of Simon & Schuster, Inc.
Simon & Schuster Building
1230 Avenue of the Americas
New York, New York 10020

SUMMIT BOOKS and colophon are trademarks of
Simon & Schuster, Inc.

Designed by Stanley S. Drate/Folio Graphics Co. Inc.

Manufactured in the United States of America

10 9 8 7 6 5 4 3 2 1

Library of Congress Cataloging in Publication Data

Ward, Ed, date.
   Rock of ages.

   Includes index.
   1. Rock music—History and criticism.   I. Stokes,
Geoffrey, date.   II. Tucker, Ken.   III. Rolling
stone.   IV. Title.
ML3534.W33   1986   784.5'4'009   86-14553
ISBN: 0-671-54438-1
       0-671-63068-7 (Pbk.)

Acknowledgments

The editors of *Rolling Stone* thank Mary Astadourian, Phil Bashe, Stephanie Franklin, Holly George, Sarah Lazin, Tim McGinnis, Jay Merritt, Michael Ochs, Marcia Peterson, Elisa Petrini, Lynne Richardson, Patty Romanowski, and Arthur Samuelson for their help in seeing this book through to completion.

The authors are grateful to the following for their contributions to the individual sections:

ED WARD: This book took a phenomenal amount of research and work, and I'd never have done it without the help of a lot of people who kept my spirits up, graciously took time for me, and volunteered information or other resources out of the blue. And I'd never have wanted to do it if it hadn't been for people all along who made me realize that my enthusiasms were shared by others who were occasionally crazier than I was about them. The list that follows is surely not complete, but it'll go a long way toward repaying the debt I have to an awful lot of people.

In the past, I'd like to thank my parents for getting me the transistor radio with the earplug so I didn't have to keep them awake with my nocturnal scanning of America's airwaves in the late fifties; Jeffrey Schlossberg for forcing me to listen to rock and roll so that his big brother wouldn't beat us up; the great disc jockeys who made all the difference: Alan Freed, Jocko Henderson, Dick Clark, Murray "the K" Kaufman, Scott Muni, B. Mitchell Reed, and the others at WINS, WMCA, and WLIB; and the men and women of the *Billboard* staff from 1944 to 1960, who, although I was never aware of them back then, were astute enough to see what was happening and report on it so that I could follow the exciting story I had already lived when I read their work on microfilm decades later. In that number, I would particularly like to thank Paul Ackerman, Ren Grevatt, and Bill Simon.

In the present, my work took me—live and over the telephone—all over the place. In Los Angeles, John Breckow gave me an unforgettable tour of the ghosts of Central Avenue and its landmarks that only somebody deeply in love with the rhythm and blues of postwar Los Angeles could have given. The Reverend Johnny Otis was just as helpful and full of memories as I'd been led to believe, and the late Lloyd Glenn was gracious and giving during a very trying time for him: I regret that we never got to spend enough time together but need to thank him anyway. Michael Ochs's enthusiasm for all of this music frequently spills over so that others may catch some of it, and I've had my share. Tom Vickers was a gracious host despite his growing doubts about my sanity. Also in L.A., much thanks to Lucinda Williams, Susan Clary, Hudson Marquez, Dick Blackburn, Bob Merlis, Gene Sculatti, Texas Terri Laird, and Jonathan Zimmerman.

5

I also had plenty of help from Northern California, in the Bay Area, where Down Home Music and Village Music, the two best record stores in the world, saw to it for years that I had just as much great music as I could afford and then some, and the folks who have worked at both places over the years turned me on to more superb stuff than I'd even known was out there. Major thanks in the Bay Area also go to Greil and Jenny Marcus, Bob Watts, Lee Hildebrand, Bruce Schmeichen, the great Charles Brown, Rick and Marty—sorry, *Rico* and Marty—from Solid Smoke Records, John Goddard, Adam Block, and Dawn Holliday.

In New York, Dave Marsh put me on to so much good info it hardly fit in the book, including an invaluable tape of actual radio shows by some of the great radio pioneers of rock and roll, a treasure and a half in these days of Radio Bland. He also put me in touch with Bob Rolontz, another ex-*Billboarder*, who not only inspired me with his writings but helped me clarify a few questions of social attitudes and gave me some context in which to place some of the events that appear here. Rolontz, in turn, put me on to Mike Stoller, who endured what must have seemed like some painfully obvious questions on several occasions like the gentleman he is. Tim McGinnis was a huge help in the manuscript's early stages, Elisa Petrini helped whip it into shape once it was written, and Sarah Lazin made sure it was there on time. Elsewhere in New York, A. J. Bernstein, Bob Christgau, Carola Dibbell, John Rockwell, David Browne, Dan Doyle, John Swenson, Brian Cullman, Joel Webber, Mark Josephson, Mark and Laurie Weeks, RJ Smith, M Mark, and Tonice Sgrignoli helped out.

Around the country and around the world, help and encouragement came from Stanley Booth, who raised the ghosts of Beale Street one unforgettable night, Bill Holdship, Pete Frame, Simon Frith, who helped me get a handle on teenagerhood in the late forties and early fifties, Gill Frith, James Osterburg, Charles Shaar and Ruth Murray, Ben Mandelson, Andrew Lauder, Jake Riviera, Tom Miller, Dickie Landry, Marc Savoy, Mike Doucet and Beausoleil, Jean Callahan at *New Age*, Bunny Matthews, and Ted Carroll.

Most of this book was done in Austin, and there is where most of the help was rendered. The staff at the University of Texas's Fine Arts Library went out of its way to be helpful and provided much more than an air-conditioned place to read microfilm. The staffs of *Third Coast*—notably John Talliaferro and David Stansbury—and the *Austin Chronicle*—Capt. Nick Barbaro, Louis Black, Sylvia Bravo, Marge Baumgarten, Roland Swenson and Martha Grenon—always made sure I had too much work to do, which was fine by me. Around town, thanks go to Jim and Jessica Shahin, John and Ada Peterson, Joe Nick Patoski and Kris Cummings, Kevin Phinney, John Morthland, Mike Buck for surfacing with a copy of "I Wonder" and memories of working with Johnny Carroll, Jon Emery for reminiscences with Kenneth Threadgill, Robert Draper and Judy Frels, Jay Trachtenberg for setting me on the trail of L.A.'s riches, Lin Sutherland, Bob Simmons, Margaret Moser, Rollo Banks, Mary and Sophie McNeill, Hank Vick and Lorraine Russo, Gary Rice, Jungle Bruce Sheehan, Mac Hruska, Ann and Marilyn, Michael Corcoran, Chris Walters, Zigy Kaluzny, Mike Sullivan, David Gordon and everyone at Tower, Louis Meyers, Mark Pratz, Jeannette Ward, Lloyd Goad and the rest of the Lunch Bunch, Bill and Nancy Booth, Brad First, Nels Jacobson, Tim Hamblin, Peter Butcher, Kent Benjamin, Clyde Woodward III, Don Davis, the Wild Seeds, Glass Eye, Zeitgeist, True Believers, the Dharma Bums, Doctor's Mob, Timbuk 3, Joe "King" Carrasco y las Coronas, Dan DelSanto, Ray Benson, Keith Ferguson, David Lord and the Austin Chamber of Commerce, the Austin Police Department for helping to deliver the final draft, Lewis Karp and the Waterloo crowd, Sam Hurt, Debi Martin, Deborah Davidson, Pete the Pup for making sure I didn't work *all* the time, and all the folks on West 9½ Street.

GEOFFREY STOKES: Like any historian, I'm standing on a lot of shoulders. I've attempted to identify the books and periodicals I used in the text, but two publications, *Rolling Stone* and *Zigzag*, deserve special mention. In their interviews, and in Pete Frame's lovingly researched family trees, they are primary sources for anyone who wasn't at every concert, every party, everywhere (though I tried, lord knows I tried). And even when I haven't quoted them directly, the way I think about music has been shaped by the rock critics who first made their mark (who, indeed, invented themselves) during this period—even the ones who will disagree with much that I've written.

Finally, however, my debts are personal: to my sons, who not only played a lot of music with me over the years but whose generosity in caring for their ailing grandmother gave me added time to work on this book; to my daughters, who (mostly) didn't play in my office; and above all to my wife, who (an imperfection, let's face it) values Cream more highly than I do, but who seems to love me anyway.

KEN TUCKER: To Anne, with all love and thanks.

CONTENTS

9

The Seventies and Beyond
by Ken Tucker

INTRODUCTION
by Jann S. Wenner

Whenever some enterprising cultural excavator attempts to pinpoint the origins of rock and roll, he or she soon discovers there's a bewildering array of fossil records to examine. Just like artifacts from an archaeological dig, some have survived; some are known to exist but are lost and unrecoverable; and others are simply hypothesized from circumstantial evidence—the proverbial missing links. As to the hard facts of rock and roll's first appearance—name, date, title, label, and so on—there are any number of defensible candidates.

But who's to say precisely where rock and roll began, anyway—does it date back to the "hillbilly" and "race" records issued by the nascent music industry in the 1920s? Was it born from the blues movement of the post–World War II era, in songs like Wynonie Harris's "Good Rockin' Tonight"? Perhaps it was a hard-rocking ode to a then-current car ("Rocket '88' ") by an Ike Turner sideman, Jackie Brenston, that turned the corner from blues into rock and roll. Or did Elvis Presley, Scotty Moore, and Bill Black stumble onto it in Sun Studios while goofing around between takes with an Arthur "Big Boy" Crudup number, "That's All Right (Mama)"?

If this were a test question, then the answer "all of the above" would have to be deemed acceptable. And that is by no means the whole picture. Into the melting pot you can add other seminal influences—jazz, folk, country, western swing, ragtime, gospel, ethnic balladry, and Broadway pop. Simmer for four decades and through two world wars. At some time in the early fifties, rock and roll emerged as an entity quite distinct from its antecedents. Nurtured during an era of affluence by a generation that would find its voice and vocabulary through music, rock and roll set off on its headlong, reckless course.

Rock of Ages attempts to track rock and roll—as music, as culture, as headline maker, as business—from its hazy origins through to the present day. As much as anything, the book is a celebration of the durability of this protean music form. Without question, rock and roll—like America itself—

11

is a great cultural assimilator, drawing upon myriad influences, integrating them into an ever-expanding inventory and yet maintaining that connective thread to the spirit that set it off in the first place. The adaptability of rock and roll in an era of blinding changes in the way we live is nothing short of a miracle.

Documenting this rapid evolution on its many fronts is no simple task. Because of the constantly changing face of the charts, contemporary music is widely and wrongly regarded as disposable. After a record has had its day—and, in some cases, that can literally mean *day*—it returns to anonymity—out of sight, out of mind, out of print—unless, perchance, it is revived years later as nostalgia (as the 1983 film *The Big Chill* has done for, or to, the music of the sixties). Records enjoy a vexingly short life span. One type of rock and roll deposes another. Today's star is tomorrow's where-are-they-now item. With pop music, it often seems as if there is too much input to completely make sense of as it's unfolding, and too little time to look back and analyze, assess. This is the nature of rock and roll.

Rock and roll is, yes, the music of the moment, but there is also plenty that qualifies as timeless art. While the pop-culture mandate insists we keep our eyes on the road ahead of us, some thirty-odd years of rock-and-roll history have piled up in the rearview mirror. And since the past constantly informs the present, preservation of this rich legacy ought to be a high priority. It is this sort of thinking that led to the establishment of the Rock and Roll Hall of Fame in 1986, as well as to the compiling of books like *The Rolling Stone Illustrated History of Rock & Roll* and, now, *Rock of Ages*.

Rock of Ages was written by three fine chroniclers—Ed Ward, Geoffrey Stokes, and Ken Tucker—each of whom tackled a particular decade. Intrepid journalists all, they faced up to the task of distilling voluminous material into a coherent, comprehensive narrative. History written from this short distance, of course, poses problems, namely, that it is difficult to find the proper perspective when one is standing so close to the subject. But, rising to the task, they've combined formal scholarship and sound judgment with their own fan's enthusiasm to animate and document the rock revolution.

And, thus, *Rock of Ages* sorts out the tangled thread of rock and roll as it weaves its way through three and a half decades of change. Survival is one of the principal subthemes. Not only has rock and roll been under constant attack from without, by an always hostile establishment; it has periodically run afoul of its own self-destructive tendencies. It was silenced, for a spell, by death and scandal in the late fifties, and ran aground of its utopian ideals at the violence-scarred festivals of the late sixties. In the middle seventies, much of what passed for rock was mere product, made complacently by pampered "superstars." And in the eighties, video has been threatening to turn rock and roll into harmless visual fodder while, on another flank, a group of politicians' wives has attempted to censor it into submission.

Still, rock and roll has a marvelous capacity for regeneration and renewal. Now well into its fourth decade, it is a multibillion-dollar industry that is still growing. Its very tenacity poses fundamental questions that are considered herein. Namely, does rock and roll survive from decade to decade on the strength of gifted, groundbreaking artists, like the Beatles, who revitalize the idiom? Or does its momentum derive from the sheer accumulation of material, upon which the tens of thousands of bands extant at any given moment continue to build?

Rock of Ages perhaps doesn't provide a final answer, though it sets forth plenty of evidence. Ambitiously, it attempts to give shape to the development of rock and roll and provide the causal linkages from musician to musician, year to year, city to city. It is a chronological history of an ineluctable phenomenon—the rise of rock and roll—as recounted by three writers who know it from the inside.

Each contributor has his own voice, which suits the personality of the decade he's written about. Ed Ward writes of the fifties with the same brash insouciance of those pioneering rockers who kicked it to life: Buddy Holly, Chuck Berry, Jerry Lee Lewis, Elvis Presley, and a slew of others who would be King. Geoffrey Stokes charts the turbulent changes of the sixties, from the simple beat-crazed fun of the British invasion and Motown through to the bohemianism of the San Francisco bands and the serious stabs at "art rock" near decade's end. The seventies, documented by Ken Tucker, find rock shaped less by the unity and social conscience of the previous decade than by the ever-surer corporate hand of the record industry. During this often unmemorable decade, glam-rock and disco thrived alongside singer/songwriters and California country rockers—until the punks interrupted and changed all the rules once again. And now we find that the eighties are yielding their own formulators and rule-breakers.

Along the way, there have been a multitude of forgotten hits and brilliant misses. There are major figures and minor heroes, and many who died in the line of duty. Within its pages, *Rock of Ages* offers a wealth of intriguing facts—did you know that Keith Moon was in a surf band called the Beach Combers before joining the Who?—that have been culled, combed, and carefully laid in place.

The end result is a fascinating cruise through the age of rock. When all is said and done, the story of rock and roll is the story of a sound. It is the sound of rural blues and folk instruments and voices, disseminated through the technologies of radio and records and eventually electrified. Various indigenous regional styles are absorbed into the mix. The sound comes to life as a vehicle to express a generation's restlessness. Rock and roll becomes a teenager's sanctuary from the adult world, a badge of identification with its own lingo. And it continues to grow and evolve, hybridizing with jazz, folk, rhythm and blues, country and western, and even classical.

By the mid-sixties, it no longer echoed only the carefree side of youth but became a unifying voice of protest as well. And it became an industry, too, although often the industry of rock and roll has been at odds with the spirit of the music. Rock and roll has never completely made its peace with the industry that sponsors it, or with the society it inhabits, though there have been periods of concession and co-optation on both sides.

In a sense, rock and roll has lately come full circle. Though the world has changed radically since the halcyon days of the fifties and sixties—in music no less than in any other sphere—waves of nostalgia have lately made the songs of both decades popular again. Some sense of the altruistic spirit of sixties rock and roll has lately resurfaced in the eighties, via rock charity balls like Live Aid and Farm Aid. And the music constantly feeds on its traditions, though in moments of revolt, it may disavow them.

It is something of a shock, however, to realize that rock and roll—this modern passion of ours—is nearly forty years old. And while it continues to insist upon absolute currency as a strategy for survival in a changing world, its roots are deep, buried in decades that are now far away in time and memory. *Rock of Ages* reaches back into the past and embraces the present, telling the story of a music form that is both ageless and old enough to have a significant history.

THE
FIFTIES
AND BEFORE

by

ED WARD

1

ALL-AMERICAN MUSIC

E pluribus unum: "out of many, one." That's what it says on the dollar bill, and it's as good a motto as you can find for the way popular music developed in this country. Until very recently, Americans took great pride in their differences and wore them proudly, as befits a nation of people who nearly all came from somewhere else, bringing with them the musical traditions of their old homelands. Even the dour Scottish Calvinists who prohibited musical instruments as the devil's technology had their "mouth music," in which the sounds the instruments might have made were replaced by sung and chanted syllables like *diddley diddley dum dum.* Violins—or fiddles, when played in a folk context—were integral to the music of the Irish, the British, and the Swedes, who first settled the New World. African slaves introduced drums, which were banned when slave owners realized that they were a means of passing messages, and also reed pipes, panpipes, and *banjars*, guitarlike instruments with a stretched skin that served as a resonator. And so the pieces were in place long before the American Revolution, ready to be combined and altered in ways the Founding Fathers and their contemporaries could never have dreamed.

With the rise of industrialism in the mid-nineteenth century, America soon gained a large middle class with a lot of leisure time on its hands. Urban upper-class people had long had access to European music, with local orchestras under their patronage performing the latest compositions and itinerant opera troupes performing new and old favorites. It was a sign of breeding to study music, especially for young ladies, who were expected to learn to sing or play the piano or the spinet, a smaller, more parlor-worthy cousin of the piano. Outside major cities, musicales became a

17

popular form of entertainment, with friends and neighbors gathering to play off the sheet music that was rapidly becoming less expensive and more varied. They used whatever instruments were handy—most often members of the string family—but the basic requirement was that the music they played be simple. And so it was these amateurs, as much as any considerations of taste, who wound up bringing about the start of what became known as popular music. Despite the existence of the British music hall and street entertainers of all stripes in Europe, it was in America that a kind of music was born that had no pretensions of being anything other than what it was.

At first, it was a body of music that combined the depth and drama of the classics with undemanding technique, eschewing complexity in favor of direct expression. If it was vocal music, the words would be in English, despite the snobs who declared English an unsingable language. In a way, it was part of the entire awakening of America that happened after the Civil War, a time in which American painters, writers, and "serious" composers addressed specifically American themes.

Perhaps the best-known composer of popular music in the United States was Stephen Collins Foster, who won fame writing about the mysterious, romantic South—which he had never seen when he penned some of his greatest "Southern" songs. His melodies were clear and direct—both in his piano-and-voice settings and in his "social orchestra" works intended for cotillions, or semiformal dances—but nonetheless allowed for a variety of interpretations, whether melancholy and nostalgic, uptempo and optimistic, or somewhere in between. Competent amateur musicians could master them easily after a few runthroughs. Moreover, his orchestral arrangements could accommodate a wide range of instruments, to meet a town's on-hand inventory. With some simple substitutions, an orchestra could play waltzes, quadrilles, and the ever-popular "Old Folks at Home."

Sadly, being a popular-music composer in the 1850s was no way to get rich, for until copyright laws were enacted in 1909, composers were never paid royalties. Publishers were the ones who profited from the sales of sheet music, which, in the days before recordings, was the medium of disseminating music. So, although he had won widespread recognition, Stephen Foster died a pauper, succumbing to pneumonia and alcohol at the age of thirty-eight, in 1864.

The Civil War brought many changes to this country; from a musical standpoint, one thing it did was popularize brass band music. After the war, with less marching going on, fewer marches were played, and eventually the military band evolved into something called the concert band, performing more refined pieces that often featured a cornet virtuoso such as Jules Levy or Herbert L. Clark, who could dispatch the remarkably fast sixty-fourth notes in Jean Baptiste Arban's "Fantasie and Variations on 'The Carnival of Venice.'" Among the other instruments some of these bands featured were the now-forgotten saxhorn, invented by Adolphe Sax in the late 1840s, while he was still flushed with the success of his reed instruments, the saxophones; the serpent, a snakelike brass instrument with holes to be covered by the player's fingers; the ophicleide; and the spectacular double-belled euphonium. No matter that these various brass instruments didn't sound too different from one another. They looked good, and they could make a good noise if enough of them were gathered in one place. In the late nineteenth century, mandolin orchestras also enjoyed a great vogue; transcriptions of light classics were performed by collections of several dozen musicians playing mandolins, mandolas, mandocellos, and bass mandolins, the latter surely one of the most cumbersome fretted instruments ever made.

Another postwar development, the musical theater, provided repertoire for both the bandstand and the parlor. Musical theater had been around for a while, but only as a sort of variety show: blackface minstrels singing Stephen Foster's and lesser composers' songs, or as a species of the British music hall, where variety acts performed one after another, a form that later became known in the United States as vaudeville. It was on "Broadway," which was more a genre than an actual location, that, late in the 1800s, the pop music industry as we know it today was born. Originally the shows were a series of skits tenuously connected by the thinnest of plots; and, with scantily clad chorus girls and risqué lyrics, they weren't as high-toned an entertainment as operetta, which required a full orchestra, if not the vocal skills of grand opera. The Broadway show was something more than vaudeville, something less than operetta. Musical plays required actors to act speaking roles and then burst into song, accompanied by a small pit band or orchestra. The intended audience was the middle class, and they loved it. By the early 1900s, the first certified Broadway hits, with the first Broadway hit songs, appeared.

But this was city music. Outside the big towns, things were very much as they'd been since the Revolution. Over time, old folk tunes and ballads had eroded, since oral transmission is a notoriously inaccurate method of passing stories along, but, particularly in Appalachia, there were plenty of people who were untouched by the changes the United States was experiencing. Some of them even spoke Elizabethan English. But just as the railroads opened up the West, the U.S. mail opened up the farthest corners of the hills. Mail-order houses like Sears, Roebuck & Co. sold not only the plows and stoves these people needed, but the 1900 catalog offered violins for between $2.50 and $9.60, guitars for between $2.70 and $10.80, and banjos for anywhere from $1.75 to $25.00; the only piano offered cost a flat $98.00; and all prices were F.O.B. Chicago. All of a sudden, people with no access to a music store could obtain well-made, affordable instruments. It is worth noting that Sears did not sell sheet music.

When these inexpensive musical instruments found their way into the most remote areas of the nation, they inalterably changed centuries of musical traditions. The English/Scottish people of Appalachia, whose ballads had mostly been sung unaccompanied and who used the fiddle as a lead instrument for dancing, began to adapt their traditional melodies to fit the intonation of the readily available guitar, with its fixed frets. Soon they started playing guitar chords behind the modal dance melodies that squeezed around them like a tight pair of shoes.

Afro-American music, too, changed. Black folk music had captured white America's attention from the time of Stephen Foster's phony Negro minstrelsy. After the Civil War, whites mimicking blacks, such as the Christy Minstrels, with black skin created by the application of burnt cork, became a fad on the stages of America; and European-trained black composers like Louis Moreau Gottschalk and Edmond Dédé achieved a measure of fame by presenting very highly "refined" versions of black music on the concert stages of New York and New Orleans. One of Gottschalk's most famous pieces was based on the "cakewalk" that was so popular in the late nineteenth century, in which couples were required to walk a short distance in as silly and complex a fashion as possible, with the winners taking home a fine cake. These men's music didn't sound at all like its models, however, although their use of minor chords slightly approximated the black musicians' microtonal pitches. Even in such a genteel fashion, they were preparing ears raised on European tonality to accept something different.

The most popular Afro-American innovation around the turn of the century was ragtime, a piano-based music with strongly syncopated rhythms and chromaticisms. Ragtime's genius was Scott Joplin, whose career began in the piano parlors of St. Louis's whorehouses before he refined his technique and signed a very lucrative deal with Joseph Stark, a music publisher who employed him to write music and demonstrate pianos in his music-store showroom. Like Foster, Joplin orchestrated a number of his compositions for brass band, in *The Red-Back Book*, and was so cheered by his success that he wrote a ragtime opera, *Treemonisha*, which died after one costly performance. The opera's total failure demoralized Joplin and, along with a case of syphilis he'd picked up earlier, contributed to his death in 1917 at the age of forty-nine.

It was around this time—scholars usually place the event in the first decade of this century—that the guitar, played in both standard and nonstandard ways,* and the piano, once found mostly in churches but by now a standard piece of recreational equipment, gave birth to the Afro-American song form known as blues. The lament in the lyrics and the so-called blue scale, with its flatted or indeterminate third as its most crucial element, had existed previously; but the blues as a codified form—most frequently with the lyrics taking an A A B structure, for example, "Woke up this morning, blues all around my head / Woke up this morning, blues all around my head

---

*Often a guitar was tuned to an open chord instead of its usual tuning; it was not uncommon to bend strings or to slide a knife blade or wine-bottle neck along the strings.

/ It's the worst old feeling, I swear I've ever had"—is a twentieth-century invention. However, in its early years, blues was restricted to rural areas and played no role in the music black Americans played for white audiences.

Forming the link between the country and the city were the black vaudevillians, professional black entertainers (some of whom actually wore the burnt cork of the Christy Minstrels) who played in minstrel and medicine shows and on steamboats. Chief among this new professional class of blacks was W. C. Handy, who went on from vaudeville to become one of America's top music publishers and, later, record executives on the strength of having introduced a cleaned-up (harmonically, metrically, and lyrically) version of the blues that was suitable for white audiences. Handy was ideally situated in Memphis, a city that continues to receive black immigrants from the rural South, and it was from them that he undoubtedly heard this new music. Most white people had never heard the blue third in the scale being bent, the tension between major and minor that produces the *frisson* that was to revolutionize twentieth-century music. In compositions like "St. Louis Blues" and "Memphis Blues," Handy produced hit songs faithful enough to the roots music they are derived from that they have gone on to be accepted into the canon of jazz standards, something few other pop tunes of this era can claim.

In New Orleans, a parallel development was taking place as an excellent public school music system encouraged youngsters of all races—which in New Orleans meant white, black, and the ambiguous designation for combinations of the two known as creole—to take up instruments that had been donated to the schools after the Spanish-American War. Brass bands became a rage there, as they had earlier with white people in the rest of the country, but there was a difference in the way the New Orleans bands approached the rhythm, something that made it simultaneously lazier and yet insistent: swinging, as it would come to be called. In 1902 or thereabouts, someone improvised a countermelody against the one the rest of the band was playing, and the seed of an all-new indigenous American music, jazz, was planted. *

Of course, this music was beneath contempt for people of quality, no matter what race, but even some of the more genteel dance orchestras found they had to "rag" their music in order to be accepted by younger people. The idea of jazz spread quickly, and it became one of the dominant popular music forms of the 1920s and 1930s, slacking in popularity only when its practitioners became so adept that they took the music off to realms where it was no longer suitable for dancing and became, like classical music—which, in a way, is what it was—something to sit and listen to. The

*Legend has it that the person who did this was the great Buddy Bolden, a cornet player given to heavy drinking and fits of violence who spent most of his life institutionalized as a psychotic and, much to the regret of historians of American music, never recorded.

conventions of jazz informed mainstream popular music through the 1950s, however, and many players continue to pass back and forth over the gray line that separates jazz and pop.

W. C. Handy died rich, and Stephen Foster did not. There are, of course, dozen of reasons for this, but one of the most important is the fact that in 1909, Congress passed a copyright law to protect written and printed materials, including music. For the first time in history, composers and songwriters had protection, and in 1914, a group of them formed the American Society of Composers, Authors, and Publishers (ASCAP), to help them collect fees from cabaret performers, hotel orchestras, and sheet-music salesmen.

In the days before records, sheet music was the big money-maker, and public performances were what sold sheet music. The idea was to get the star singers at cabarets frequented by show-biz types to perform one's material so it would filter down to the mass of home musicians and provincial semipros. To do this, music publishers employed song pluggers, whose descendants, the promo men, are still all-important to the music business today. Song pluggers used all kinds of ruses to get their material noticed. Often a plugger would slip a bribe to the pianist at a fashionable cabaret, along with the sheet music, and then, when the pianist played the introduction to the song, the plugger would stand up and start singing. It was a good way to get thrown out of the cabaret, but it must have worked a little bit, because it became a standard ploy. Young Israel Baline, who later changed his name to Irving Berlin, started out this way, and was inspired by the low quality of the material he was plugging to start writing himself. Few of these early pop songs stayed in the repertoire of American popular singers much past the early 1930s, because they were not very jazzy and because many of them were sentimental in a way that didn't go over too well with succeeding generations.*

World War I brought Americans to Europe in quantity, not only as soldiers but, later, as musicians. The 369th Infantry Regimental Band, under the leadership of James Reese Europe, was probably the most noticed of the bands that made the journey with their black regiments. After the Armistice, they played a concert tour of France. They were followed by the Scrap Iron Jazz Band, apparently a bunch of Europe's men moonlighting, who also never recorded, much to the dismay of historians. This was not real jazz, nor was the music made by the Original Dixieland Jazz Band, an all-white ensemble from New Orleans that was the first to record and tour under the word *jazz*. But what is important for our purposes is the fact that after World War I, jazz became the crucial element in American popular music. Even though the 1920s are now known as the Jazz Age, it was

---

*None of which precluded their being picked up even later: Tommy Edwards's 1958 hit, "It's All in the Game," comes from this era and was co-written by Charles Dawes, who later became Calvin Coolidge's vice-president.

jazz-*influenced* music that was played at those F. Scott Fitzgerald flappers-and-bathtub-gin parties.

Small groups like Louis Armstrong's Hot Five live on as the most artistically significant bands of that era, but the vast majority of Americans—even the ones who considered themselves jazz fans—never heard them or their records.

Most of the top songs of the day had their origin in Tin Pan Alley, the name that was given to the professional songwriting industry, particularly the part of it that thrived around certain parts of Broadway in midtown Manhattan, where music publishers had their offices and the sound of songwriters pounding away on half-dead pianos created a cacophony not unlike a tinworks. This was where people like Irving Berlin, Sammy Cahn, and, later, George and Ira Gershwin worked. Often the songwriters were classically trained men who had fled the Russian Revolution and the anti-Semitism of Eastern Europe and who found it easy to write the kind of songs Americans liked. More than one of them has made the connection between the cantor's song in a Jewish temple and the blue notes of jazz and the blues.

In time, the popular bands grew big enough that they could legitimately claim the title of orchestra, and they fell into three categories: sweet, corn, and swing. Sweet bands played their Tin Pan Alley numbers straight and were considered "refined," suitable for a debutante party or a sophisticated night on the town, creating a background for fox-trots and similar dances. Corn bands were more for entertainment, in that they played sweet material but leavened it with cut-up behavior and comedy, often featuring novelty vocalists or hillbilly skits. Corn bands were very popular with collegians. Swing bands, however, wound up with the most enduring place in American popular music, both because they were the most "musical" and because they produced some of the most memorable jazz virtuosos. They also created the climate in which the great black jazz orchestras—most notably those of Duke Ellington, Count Basie, and Fletcher Henderson—could thrive, and it is these bands that made the 1920s and 1930s jump. They also helped lay the groundwork for rock and roll by emphasizing instrumental solos, particularly saxophone solos, and massed groups of horns (saxophone and/or brass instruments) riffing, or playing a short phrase over and over, while the soloist constructed a coherent improvisation above the riff.

Even though swing band leaders often wrote a lot of their own material (and always made their own arrangements if they could possibly afford to keep an arranger on staff), swing didn't do away with Tin Pan Alley. If anything, it gave professional songwriters a boost, since several different versions of a song could coexist in the marketplace at once: a "straight" pop rendition done by a sweet band and a couple of jazz or swing interpretations, each of which could be bought by the same consumer.

But the biggest boost for all areas of the popular-music business after

World War I came from a new technological development: the phonograph record. As early as 1900, Sears, Roebuck and Co. had offered a panoply of record players, some with multiple stethoscopelike earpieces snaking from them, that played Edison cylinder recordings of music or such light classics as those done by the Sousa Band. But the wax cylinders were very fragile and never really caught on. Instead, Emile Berliner's invention, the flat phonograph record playing at seventy-eight revolutions per minute, became the popular format after the war. It was introduced to the public at "phonography parlors," where you could rent a headset and have the proprietor play your selection.

Although some authentic singing cowboys had made cylinder recordings, as had the Fisk Jubilee Singers and other purveyors of whitened-up Negro spirituals, it wasn't until the 1920s that the first country and blues records were made. Country offerings came into being with the decision of a couple of fiddling Confederate veterans, A. C. "Eck" Robertson, of Amarillo, Texas, and Henry Gilliland, of Virginia, to hop a train to New York in 1922. They showed up at Victor Records' office, one dressed in a Confederate uniform and the other in a cowboy suit, carrying two fiddles, demanding to be recorded. To get rid of them, some Victor person sat them down in front of an acoustic microphone and recorded their versions of "Sallie Gooden" and "The Arkansas Traveler." For some reason, the record was issued, although the music is primitive and alien-sounding today, with its odd-metered Indian-style drone and scratchy bowing technique, and it could hardly have sounded less alien to city ears back then. But it wound up selling well enough for the company to send talent scouts to the South, looking for other "hillbillies" to record.

Blues got its recorded start on February 14, 1920, when Mamie Smith, a black vaudeville performer (and not so much a blues singer as a black pop stylist) took advantage of another singer's cancelled session to record something called "Crazy Blues," which sold phenomenally and started the record companies beating the bushes for any black woman who could sing—a surprising number of whom were named Smith, including, of course, the great Bessie Smith. But none of the artists who were recorded as blues singers in the early days were people who had invented the form. Whereas the great majority of blues songs were performed with a simple guitar or piano accompaniment, the accompaniment on these early discs tended to be a small jazz band, with piano, horns, and soloists. Still, as Mamie Smith undoubtedly knew, calling a recording blues would help sell records to black people, who had followed Handy's lead and turned blues into the fad of the day. And with Mamie Smith's record selling as well as it did, record companies told the talent scouts who were already down South scouting hillbillies not to ignore the commercial possibilities of what they called race music, and soon some of the more countrified blues artists found themselves before the microphone.

A funny thing happened to American folk music as a result of the race and hillbilly record lines: It was simultaneously preserved and destroyed. Each native performer, as he or she stepped before the microphone, was delivering a rendition specific to the area he or she was from. Eck Robertson's fiddle style was Texan, Blind Willie McTell's finger-picked guitar style showed how they played the blues in Georgia, and the murder ballad "Omie Wise" that Clarence Ashley recorded concerned a sex crime committed near his North Carolina home. "Ragtime" Henry Thomas came from the Texas Gulf Coast with his panpipes and guitar and preserved for us a rare pre-blues Afro-American song style, while "Dock" Boggs's Virginia gothic song "Oh, Death" invoked the darker side of the hills and Robert Johnson's moaning bottleneck guitar style could have come from no other place than the Mississippi Delta. Today we can sit at our expensive stereos, correct the primitive recording with our graphic equalizers, and hear this as fact. Then people in Georgia bought Robert Johnson's records and people in Mississippi bought Blind Willie McTell's; Carolinians essayed Texan and Virginian fiddle styles, and Texas bluesman Blind Lemon Jefferson could play gigs across the country on the basis of a dozen bestselling records, even though his style was very much that of the place where he grew up.

Soon there were mutant voices, made stronger by the hybridization of already strong stock. "Dock" Boggs was a coal miner who recorded songs in a very traditional style, along with some, like "Mean Mistreater Blues," that he could only have learned from a record of a black woman singing the blues. Texas fiddler Bob Wills picked cotton side by side with black people in West Texas and dreamed of the day when he could meld the fiddle tunes, the blues, and pop songs into an idiosyncratic whole—a day that, thanks to the radio, was soon coming his way. White Jimmie Rodgers recorded black-derived blues, accompanied by his guitar, with both the Carter Family, whose roots were Appalachian but who employed a black man to seek out black tunes for them, and with Louis Armstrong, who occasionally indulged in a passion for white pop while he was reinventing jazz cornet playing. This stuff was still "American traditional music," because it was constructed from traditional materials—blues, hymns, Elizabethan ballads—but whether it could be called pure folk music is certainly open to question.

But it was a substratum of popular music that was just profitable enough that the companies kept recording it—and recording it fairly indiscriminately, since record executives in New York couldn't tell what would sell well in the Mississippi Delta or the hills of Kentucky. These recordings have preserved the musical America that preceded the onslaught of the mass media, in its ethnic and regional diversity. It was these race and hillbilly strains that, after World War II, would be the seedbed for rock and roll.

The cross-fertilization process that began with records exploded with the advent of radio. By the time commercial broadcasting entrenched itself, after World War I, a crystal set* was within the means of almost everyone. Radio's function in its early days was to present a community with news and entertainment, to serve as a nexus for activity, and to bring all the listeners in the scope of its range together. From the cream of the town's piano students to dramatic readings and comedy, from the farm report to the parson's sermon, each small radio station had its choice of talent. If it was affiliated with a network, it could bring the dance orchestras of New York and Chicago to its listeners, as well as dramatic programs, such as the early soap opera "Guiding Light," and the comedy of such stars as Jack Benny and Burns and Allen. Radio didn't feature records at first, simply because there was too much else to broadcast, but their advantages were just too numerous to keep them off entirely. They were a cheap source of ready music in case a network feed went bad or the baseball scores hadn't come over from the newspaper yet, or whenever time needed filling. More important, they made it possible for a local station to play big stars anytime they wanted to, regardless of whether they owned rights to a network's broadcast of that star and regardless of how far out in the sticks the station might be.

Of course, record companies felt threatened by the radio boom, fearing that free airplay would compete with sales. Initially they opposed the new jukeboxes as well: Instead of spending seventy-five cents or a dollar on a record, a customer could hear it for a nickel. But eventually companies realized that jukebox play stimulated rather than diminished record sales— and besides, old 78-rpm records wore out fast in jukeboxes.

But they held the line when it came to radio, and soon records began to carry notices that they were not for broadcast—a hard-to-enforce prohibition that was at least partially ignored. But radio threw down the gauntlet in July 1926, when the first disc jockey appeared on WCRW in Chicago.† The station's owner, Clinton R. White (hence the call letters), put his wife, Josephine, on the air with his new machine, the Vibrophone, which allowed the mechanical vibrations of the records to trigger electrical impulses that could then be broadcast. The head of the Chicago musicians' union, James C. Petrillo, was irate, and eventually he succeeded in having White hauled up before the Federal Radio Commission, which issued a desist order. Not that this stopped any of the smaller stations. They just neglected to announce that it was a record they were playing. They were also neglecting to pay ASCAP, and ASCAP was stumped when it came to collecting from radio stations.

Since the controversy applied only to commercially available phonograph records—though many sponsors made available electrical transcriptions that could be used as shows and were not available in stores—

---

*A lump of galena (lead ore) with a coil and a "cat whisker" wire to run along the coil, to tune in stations, along with a set of earphones.

† The term disc jockey itself seems to have been coined in a Variety headline in 1941.

the smaller stations began exposing more jazz, hillbilly, and blues records, especially in rural areas. Surely nobody could object to the broadcast of records whose issuing companies barely knew they existed. With the popularity of hillbilly and blues music today, it should be emphasized that even in rural areas, this was minority music for people on the social and economic fringes. Back then, nobody thought of Robert Johnson or Uncle Dave Macon as geniuses. If anything, they were embarrassments.

Then, in 1925, a station in Nashville began broadcasting a live show called the "WSM Barn Dance," featuring hillbilly talent from the Nashville area (and, later, all the major hillbilly recording artists), which became an immediate hit. In 1927, WSM changed the name to the "Grand Ole Opry." Broadcasting on a "clear channel" station—one that could be heard without interference from other stations competing for the same frequency—the "Opry" became a major factor in spreading American roots music to households that might never have heard or tolerated it otherwise—especially black households, where it was a very popular show. But although a significant number of people were becoming aware of black and hillbilly music through radio and records, they tended to treat the players and audience as charming, primitive people and kept them at a distance. Soon similar programs sprung up, most notably Chicago's "WLS National Barn Dance" and the "Louisiana Hayride" on KWKH in Shreveport, Louisiana, which, like the "Opry," served an audience unmoved by real hillbilly music.

As for black music, some white audiences felt comfortable with black jazz, even if it wasn't always easy to see it in person. Whites-only nightclubs such as Harlem's famous Cotton Club usually featured crack black jazz orchestras, like Chick Webb's or Duke Ellington's, playing the absolute latest in sophisticated arrangements and featuring the best soloists of the day. But these clubs were very expensive, and the fact that blacks were excluded (the Cotton Club did make a few exceptions for well-off, light-skinned blacks and black celebrities) meant that this music was more often experienced on the radio than live. Orchestras like Ellington's and Webb's, nonetheless, were feeding ideas into the pop mainstream, since even the most conservative bandleaders and arrangers could tell that they were making people dance.

Sweet bands that flirted with jazz, like Paul ("The King of Jazz") Whiteman's, began to attract substantial numbers of young people, particularly of college age. Benny Goodman, a well-educated clarinet player, went Whiteman one better by adopting Fletcher Henderson's arrangements as Henderson's band was folding. Goodman was also a pioneer of multiracial music, employing black musicians like pianist Teddy Wilson and the electric guitar player who virtually invented interest in that instrument, Charlie Christian, to play in the smaller band that performed between sets.

It was Goodman, in fact, who ignited the first contemporary example of what later became thought of as "teen hysteria" at his legendary Carnegie

Hall concert of 1938. As the band swung into its showcase number for drummer Gene Krupa, "Sing Sing Sing," hundreds of young white "jitterbugs" jammed the aisles, ignoring the pleas of ushers, and danced like mad as the band built in intensity, chorus after chorus.

There had been youth phenomena before Goodman sent 'em bopping into the aisles, of course. First Rudey Vallee and then Bing "the Groaner" Crosby were pop stars with 1930s college kids, but their reception by their fans looks pretty pale to us today—not that that kept their parents and other members of the older generations from deploring the swooning, the idolatry, and other evidences of the "pash" the kids had for these singers. But they were singers with sweet bands, and Goodman carefully walked a tightrope between swing pop and real jazz. The mass audience, and even the average jazz fan, was still not aware of what black Americans were singing and playing.

John Hammond turned things around. At the height of the swing era, Hammond, a Vanderbilt heir, was sitting in his car in Chicago late one night listening to his car radio—a radio in his car? He must have been a Vanderbilt!—and heard something unlike anything he'd ever heard before: the Count Basie Orchestra, broadcast from Kansas City. Hammond was an inveterate record collector and avid jazz fan, and he'd been assembling acts for a concert that would showcase the entire spectrum of black American music. He'd even journeyed South to find his favorite country bluesman, Robert Johnson, whose eerie, doom-filled records represented the summit of the Delta blues style, with its irregular rhythms and screaming bottleneck guitar. There is some evidence that Hammond wanted Johnson to sign a contract with him, but before it was signed Johnson was murdered (or, as local legend had it, the devil came back to collect on an old debt, since some believed that Johnson, whose technique had started off poorly, had sold his soul for his prowess on the guitar). So Hammond drove down to Kansas City to see if the Basie Orchestra would be interested in playing his show.

While he was there, he also heard Big Joe Turner, the singing bartender whose rough blues-shouting would prove so influential in the 1940s, accompanied by Pete Johnson's superb boogie-woogie piano (basically a rhythmic style emphasizing a repetitive run in the bass). The pieces fell into place, and in 1938, when the first of Hammond's two "From Spirituals to Swing" concerts was mounted at Carnegie Hall, it was both a summing up of the era of black popular music that was passing and a stage-clearing for the new era to come.

In the Hammond show, jazz fans could see an old-time New Orleans band, featuring many of the pioneers of that city's jazz tradition, and they could also hear the jazz of the future. The concert gave the Basie band, in both large and small setups, its first New York gig (which must have made Basie feel good, since he'd grown up in Red Bank, New Jersey, but had to get marooned in Kansas City in order to reach any sort of prominence), showcasing Lester Young, whose saxophone style and harmonic ideas would influence jazz for the next twenty years. A little closer to the roots was a trio of boogie-woogie pianists, Meade "Lux" Lewis, Pete Johnson, and Albert Ammons, who jammed away with great abandon, lighting the first sparks that would ignite quite a fad during the next decade. Countering the urban blues of Big Joe Turner and Pete Johnson were the country blues of Sonny Terry and Big Bill Broonzy, a last-minute substitution for the late Robert Johnson.

It was the city blues style, especially the boogie-blues style of Turner and Pete Johnson, that would lay the foundations of what would be known as rhythm and blues after the Second World War. Among the other practitioners, it was Louis Jordan, an alto saxophonist of no particular distinction as an instrumentalist, who led a band called the Tympany Five that rapidly got a reputation for showmanship. With Jordan's pop-eyed stare, wild dancing, and hot rhythms (derived from swing but peppier, so that they became known as jump), he was a natural entertainer. Although performers like Jordan and Turner were considered crude by jazz fans, their work did bring the idea of blues to the attention of the cognoscenti, even if many of them still regarded it a novelty, a sort of primitive, backwoods sort of expression from which such giants as Lester Young had grown. (Imagine what these sophisticates would have thought of the *real* backwoods music of blues primitives like Robert Johnson's teacher, Son House.) Fans were familiar with acts like Bessie Smith—who, having recorded in the 1920s, had passed into the category of "classic jazz"—and with the other blues women who belted out lyrics over fairly sophisticated backing, but the guitar- and piano-based country blues styles of the time were virtually unknown to all but a few jazz collectors.

Nonetheless, these blues performers enjoyed fairly good careers catering to the Southern market and to displaced Southern blacks in cities like St. Louis, Chicago, and Detroit. Robert Johnson is supposed to have toured much of the country on the basis of his records, often riding in boxcars and hitching rides to get to his destinations. During the 1930s, RCA's "race" subsidiary, Bluebird, extensively recorded a generation of blues singers, including the guitarist Tampa Red and the pianist Big Maceo Merriweather, who were developing a distinct Chicago blues style that would really flower in the early 1950s. It is a shame that jazz fans were hip enough to pick up on Louis Armstrong's astonishing Ornette Coleman–like "free" introduction to "West End Blues" and missed the odd session of May 17, 1930, at 4 P.M., probably in Memphis, at which Tennessee guitarist "Sleepy" John Estes, mandolinist Yank Rachel, and pianist Hammy Nix recorded a song for Victor titled "Expressman Blues" that is eerily prophetic of rock and roll. Its crisp 4/4 time, swirling piano, and simple but effective mandolin soloing, relying on many of the same techniques Chuck Berry would use on electric guitar, put it way outside the blues mainstream (and outside Estes's usual work) and into another dimension entirely. All it lacks is bass and drums to put it squarely in contention for the title of first rock and roll record ever.

For hillbilly musicians, too, the late 1930s were a time of innovation, inspired by Jimmie Rodgers, with his seamless mixture of country and blues elements. Rodgers's career was cut short by the tuberculosis he sang about so often, but he was a hard act to follow. Most chose to do it by imitation, including the lanky young Texan named Ernest Tubb, whose heartfelt tribute to Rodgers earned him the singer's guitar, given Tubb by his widow. Tubb broke with tradition in the noisy honky-tonks and oil-camp bars he played in Texas by adding first an electric guitar, then drums. But even these innovations paled next to what fellow Texan Bob Wills was doing with his fiddle band, the Texas Playboys.

Wills, a fiddler from west Texas, was clearly taken with black jazz orchestras. As a band member later recalled, every time they hit a big city with a well-stocked record store, Wills would run in and see what Count Basie had released recently. Although his own fiddle playing remained rooted in the Anglo-Irish style of his birthplace, Wills assembled a band that at times had a large horn section; several other fiddlers capable of "takeoff" solos—jazzy improvisations on the melody and harmony, similar to, say, a Basie sideman's solo—and a pianist and guitarist (Al Stricklin and Eldon Shamblin) who could essay anything from a waltz to a swinging extravaganza like the Playboys' recording of Benny Goodman's "White Heat." Wills accurately dubbed his music western swing, and it remained too eccentric for the mainstream of hillbilly and jazz record buyers. Still, it became one of the dominant styles in Texas and Oklahoma, producing at least one pop standard, "New San Antonio Rose," which was a big hit for Bing Crosby, and continued to inspire country musicians even after Wills's death in 1975.

But all this was esoteric stuff, and throughout the Great Depression regional music was not exactly in the forefront of people's minds. By the late 1930s, the mainstream of pop music was dominated by sweet bands and crooners. It was the heyday of these performers, the era in which many of the foremost American songwriters—the Gershwins, Cole Porter, Irving Berlin, and the other Tin Pan Alley greats—were at the peak of their songwriting powers. Despite the staying power of these writers' best songs, however, their sound had little to do with the musical forms that would arise in the late 1940s, except as something to rebel against.

It was this time that saw the rise of the first pop idol to get the really young teenagers—high school kids instead of collegians—riled up: Frank Sinatra. As a teenager in Hoboken, New Jersey, Sinatra had won a "Major Bowes Original Amateur Hour" contest with his group and had parlayed that into a series of dates in various New Jersey roadhouses and saloons. Incredibly confident of his own talent, he talked swing bandleader Harry James into hiring him in 1939. Although James wasn't too well known with the public, musicians paid attention to him, admiring his young vocalist's way with even the slightest piece of Tin Pan Alley fluff. Sinatra slid around notes before settling on them, and he had a breathiness to his singing that was expressive, for sure, but expressive of things parents would rather not think their children were experiencing, even vicariously. Six months after he'd signed with James, Sinatra left to join Tommy Dorsey's band, which was one of the top organizations in the country. There his star rose so fast that he was able to launch a solo career two years later, and by early 1943, he had a top radio show, emceeing the popular "Lucky Strike Hit Parade." Sinatra unleashed a torrent of teen sexuality that parents—no less than the surprised teens themselves—were at a loss to understand. He drew the first screamers and fainters, the first girls who fought for a piece of his bed sheets and wore his cigarette butts in lockets near their hearts. The hysteria culminated on Columbus Day, 1944, when 30,000 fans showed up at the Paramount Theater in New York to claim 3,600 seats per show, six shows per day, interspersed with a movie. After the first show, only a few fans left, and a riot developed outside the theater. It was the first really violent pop music confrontation the world had ever seen.

By the early 1940s, with the experimentation going on in jazz, the golden era of Tin Pan Alley, and the cross-fertilization of genres and styles that was occurring in country and blues, the creative ferment in American music was reaching critical mass. Throughout the previous decade, problems among publishers, radio, and the American Federation of Musicians had grown, leading the National Association of Broadcasters to form a new performing rights organization that wouldn't be as Tin Pan Alley– and Broadway–oriented as ASCAP. Broadcast Music, Incorporated (BMI), was formed in 1940 to provide for the needs of the minority or special-interest songwriters and performers whom ASCAP wouldn't touch. As a result of ASCAP's elitism—which continued into the 1950s and would wind up costing it a lot in royalties once this music became popular—there came a point when a number of stations, including the CBS and NBC networks, wouldn't sign an agreement with ASCAP.

And then disaster struck, at least from a historian's viewpoint. James C. Petrillo, by now president of the national American Federation of Musicians and still just as leery of mechanically reproduced music, called a strike early in 1942 that would prevent AFM musicians from recording for record or jukebox play. Performers like Sinatra, with his radio sinecure, were relatively safe, since they didn't rely exclusively on records for exposure. But the ban would virtually silence less prominent musicians, and the trouble intensified with the coming of World War II, when shellac, which was largely imported from Southeast Asia, now under Japanese control, became very scarce. With the double problem of limited shellac and musicians forbidden to record, the documentation of innovations all but stopped.

Among other things, Petrillo's strike ensured that the early efforts of jazz musicians to forge the new sound that would become bebop by the war's end never got recorded, forcing jazz historians to rely exclusively on the memories of the musicians involved for information on this crucial development in American music. Fortunately the ban didn't extend to records on hand (although a lot of prewar records are lost forever because people donated them to shellac drives), but it meant that new releases weren't forthcoming once a brief fad for a cappella songs (performed without accompaniment) waned. Petrillo's strike lasted until late 1943, by which time the nation had other things—like winning the war—on its mind.

This war drew people together in a way that the previous World War hadn't. As dozens of clichéd war movies show, men of wildly disparate backgounds were thrown together in the common good, although the armed forces remained for the most part racially segregated until the Korean War. Hillbillies and New York Jews fought side by side, as did blacks from the city and the country. The way Americans thought about each other would never be the same again, and the sound the land made was taking on a newer and more direct tone. It was as if people were raising their curtains and seeing their neighbors for the first time. After the war, they would invite them over. Or they would come over to visit anyway.

2

SWINGING INTO PEACETIME

By the end of 1944, the mainstream of American pop was dreary indeed by today's standards. Bing Crosby had had the year's biggest hit with "Swinging on a Star"; and Dinah Shore, Harry James with vocalist Dick Haymes, Jimmy Dorsey, and the Andrews Sisters with Bing Crosby, again, were in the top ten tunes. So were the slick black Mills Brothers, with "You Always Hurt the One You Love." Wacky novelty singer Louis Jordan released his most famous record, "Caldonia." Zippy upbeat messages were beamed to a war-weary nation, encouragement to "Ac-Cent-Tchu-Ate the Positive." Youngsters liked Sinatra, but it was no coincidence that Japanese soldiers lured Americans into battle with cries of "To hell with Roy Acuff!" The army's *Yank* magazine surveyed 3,700 GIs in the European occupation zone and found that they preferred folk artist (the new industry term for *hillbilly*) Roy Acuff to Sinatra by a margin of 600 votes.

In fact, a folk boom was building. If Jimmie Rodgers had been the first great synthesizer of traditional and commercial elements, people like Ernest Tubb and Roy Acuff represented his legacy. Acuff, for instance, was a talented fiddler who fronted a group that combined traditional instrumental techniques with custom-written, often sentimental songs that Southerners loved. This commercialized music was now selling well enough that record-industry trade magazines like *Billboard* and *Cashbox* started listing the top ten "folk" records each week. It was to the folk charts, rather than to the "race" charts, which also started up around this time, that big-name vocalists would go for offbeat material like "Don't Fence Me In," "San Antonio Rose," or "Smoke! Smoke! Smoke! (That Cigarette)." A survey of jukebox operators revealed that the names they wanted more of were Acuff, Ernest Tubb, Tex Ritter, Al Dexter (all highly commercialized and highly successful "folk" artists), and Bob Wills, whose patriotic "Smoke on the

33

Water" was an anthem that drooled over the doom that would occur "when our Army and Navy overtake the enemy" in vivid terms.*

Most of the folk music on live radio and records was "western" in its most sentimental and synthetic form, Tin Pan Alley–written songs played by cowpeople on accordians, just like the range riders in the movies which provided more than a little of this material. It is not insignificant that one of the folk centers was Philadelphia—not exactly sagebrush central, but it was there that the young Bill Haley got to sit as a "Down Homer" on WLBR in nearby Lebanon, Pennsylvania, during the war while regular Down Homer Kenny Roberts was off in the service. Haley got so fired up about it that he agitated for his own show, which he finally got late in 1947.

Of course, not all this folk music was terrible. Jack Guthrie, whose cousin Woodrow Wilson "Woody" Guthrie was a folk musician of another type, caught the right nostalgic feeling for all the transplanted Okies in the Los Angeles area with "Oklahoma Hills," and turned it into a smash hit. The Sons of the Pioneers, the prototypical "western" group, released "Cool Water"; and their fiddler and guitarist, the Farr brothers, built a sizable reputation with jazz fans, who saw their resemblance to the guitar-and-fiddle jazz of Stephane Grappelli and Django Reinhardt of the Hot Club of Paris. Other western stars included the gravel-voiced Tex Ritter and the smoother Al Dexter and Tennessee Ernie Ford, although for many, western music was epitomized by Spade Cooley's ludicrous take on Bob Wills's band. Not to be outdone by some fiddler from Turkey, Texas, Cooley featured lots of accordian playing and had a harp in *his* western swing band, even if he didn't have half of Wills's talent.

This was the era of Bob Wills's last great band, which was based in Fresno, California, so as to have easy access both to Hollywood, where they were making movies, and the hot spots of the San Fernando Valley, where they were playing their big-money gigs. Wills's music differed from today's country music in that it drew lots of inspiration from black music—blues and Count Basie in particular. From listening to Wills and the Farrs and, to a lesser extent, Spade Cooley and the bluesy fingerpicking guitar pyrotechnics of a new whiz named Merle Travis, it might be assumed that the racial scene was fairly enlightened. But the armed forces were still segregated, and despite the talk of tolerance that was bruited about to show how much we differed from Hitler's Germany, there was much racial animosity. In 1943, Harlem and Detroit erupted with racial tension, and in 1945, Chicago followed.

Segregated stages were still the rule, not only in the deep South but in such cosmopolitan areas as Kansas City and Washington, D.C. Not all performers acquiesced to this situation. Earl "Fatha" Hines refused to lecture on jazz at the University of Louisville because, ironically, the lecture was closed to black students. When students in Gary, Indiana,

*Cowboy Copas would revive the song during the Korean War, with an additional verse in which we smote 'em with "that great Atomic Bomb."

staged a walkout to protest what they considered excessive black enroll-
ment, Frank Sinatra visited Gary in an effort to cool them down. He talked
to student leaders, finally addressing a mass meeting of five thousand
striking students, and accused two local men, an undertaker and a custo-
dian at City Hall, of using the students to further their own racist goals.
(They threatened to sue for libel.) Sinatra, who had just released a record
with the black vocal group the Charioteers backing him, was one of the
leading proponents of tolerance on the white side, just as Nat "King" Cole
became the leading voice on the black side.

A typical incident, unfortunately, took place in Kansas City, where the
noted bandleader Cab Calloway tried to get into the Pla-Mor Ballroom. He
had tickets, but the manager refused to admit him—he later said Calloway
was drunk—and Calloway pushed him. After he had been soundly pistol-
whipped, Calloway was booked for public intoxication. Although the
NAACP threatened to blacklist the ballroom, Calloway sued, but he lost the
case. It was clear that as far as mainstream American show business was
concerned, a black man's place was on the bandstand, unless he was
waiting on tables.

Nonetheless, when they made music, white people did listen. In February, *Billboard* reported that Negro music grosses for 1944 had hit a new
high, with the Cab Calloway Orchestra making $750,000, Duke Ellington
$600,000, and the Ink Spots with Ella Fitzgerald and the Cootie Williams
Orchestra $500,000. Bands were asking for a $750 guarantee and getting it,
even in the impoverished South. The Count Basie Orchestra was averaging
between $1,350 and $1,750 for a one-nighter. Louis Jordan, with a much
smaller band but equal crossover appeal, announced in mid-January that he
would be opening at the New York Paramount in February for a seven-week
run, grossing $3,500 a week. The King Cole Trio, which flirted with jazz in
between silken-smooth ballads, were all over the charts, helping to keep the
biggest independent label, Capitol, afloat.

Nor were bands the only ones making it. Private Cecil Gant, for example,
came to prominence accidentally in 1944 when he walked up to the
bandstand at a war bond rally in downtown Los Angeles and asked if he
could play a couple of numbers on the piano. His boogie-woogie style slew
the crowd, and the rally's organizers sought his commanding officer to ask
permission to keep Gant available for future rallies. Then, following another bond rally, he was approached by one Richard A. Nelson, who offered
him a chance to make a record for his brand-new label, Gilt-Edge. Where
Nelson was getting his shellac was anybody's guess, since even the major
labels, like RCA and Columbia, had been short since Pearl Harbor Day. But
Nelson got his shellac, and Gant got his record, "I Wonder," a wistful song
about someone "a million miles away" wondering how his sweetie was
doing, all delivered in a nasal but palatable voice accompanied by some
solid piano work. The other side was "Cecil's Boogie," a perfect indication
of why the crowds loved him so. Although *Billboard* said it sounded like

"something picked up with a machine hidden under a table in a smoky back room," it nonetheless put Gant, a country boy from Nashville, on the map—and, more important, on the "Harlem Hit Parade" chart in the trade magazine. But Gant was stuck in the army and couldn't tour, couldn't play the clubs, and couldn't really reap the benefits of his new-found fame.

Nelson's Gilt-Edge label was only the latest of the new crop of independents that were swinging up on the West Coast. *Billboard,* in an article headlined IT MUST BE THE $$, noted that "indie record companies [are] poppin' up, with every Tom, Dick and Harry getting into the business," although a glance through its pages showed very few of the labels hitting even the Harlem or "folk" (country) charts. But Los Angeles was a boomtown during the war. Thousands of poor people, white and black, had settled there to work in war industries, which were notoriously egalitarian: If you could put in a day's work, you could get a job. Whites and blacks moved from Texas, Louisiana, Oklahoma, and Arkansas, and soon divided the turf, with whites settling in the San Fernando Valley and Bakersfield, and blacks in Watts and Compton. While the valley rocked to the western swing sounds of Bob Wills and his Texas Playboys and the Spade Cooley Orchestra, the black Central Avenue scene gave birth to rhythm and blues.

A cornerstone of the L.A. black music scene, Johnny Otis was, in fact, Greek. He had been born John Veliotes, the son of a couple of shopkeepers in Berkeley, but he had moved south in his teens. With his drumming and bandleading skills, he soon became known in L.A. for his fairness and keen eye for talent. With the connections he had picked up while playing in others' orchestras, he found no trouble securing a gig at the Club Alabam and, later, at the Barrelhouse, which he co-owned. With its swinging arrangements and emphasis on the blues, the Otis Orchestra played music that had one foot in black pop's past and the other foot in its future.

Part of what attracted Otis and many other musicians to L.A. was the René brothers, Otis and Leon. In the late 1930s, these two enterprising black men started Excelsior and Exclusive, two independent record labels,* and bought their own plant when they had trouble booking time at plants the majors used. With that end of it wrapped up, they started looking for talent. "Here," says Johnny Otis, "if we were in a little club somewhere, we might get recorded. There's an underground telegraph, and everyone from Mississippi to Maine knew that Los Angeles is where you'd go to get yourself recorded."

Central Avenue, which stretched from near City Hall downtown all the way south through Watts, and Avalon Boulevard, which paralleled it for much of the way, were the hot spots. "The Club Alabam was a little Cotton Club," Otis remembers, "except that it was owned by a black man, Curtis Mosby. It was at Central and Forty-second Street. The audience was a black audience, although of course there would be whites here and there, but

---

*These were not the first black-owned labels: W. C. Handy's Black Swan label holds that distinction.

they were musicians and entertainers, people who appreciated black art, and who came and were delighted with what they saw." Other big clubs included Shep's Playhouse, downtown on First Street in Little Tokyo, where a black hotel owner had taken over a Japanese hotel after the Japanese were interned and turned it into a nightclub complex with four floors of entertainment. The Plantation, in Watts, was a warehouse-sized dance hall that catered to touring orchestras. But the real action occurred after hours, when the musicians would get together after their regular gigs and engage in cutting contests or simply sit back and watch. Spots like Blacktop McGee's, Johnny Cornish's Double V, Stuff Crouch's Backstage, Alex Lovejoy's and Jack's Basket Room—which Otis says had the last legal after-hours license granted in Los Angeles County—saw to it that the street jumped until the sun came up. So great was the demand for entertainment that even the most marginal avant-garde performers, like the king of bebop, Charlie Parker, could get gigs playing their own music—although keeping them was quite another matter.

On February 28, 1945, the War Manpower Commission put a damper on all this by ordering a midnight curfew for all entertainment places—a curfew that lasted until mid-May and hurt the live music business nationwide while it was in effect. But people could still enjoy the radio, at least as long as they had mainstream taste in orchestras and singers, and, of course, there were records. Some were by vocal groups like the Mills Brothers and the Ink Spots, who had been around for a while, but their sounds were very stylized, not much more than a somewhat colored version of the Andrews Sisters. Nat "King" Cole, the first of the "sepia Sinatras"—really just a crooner in the Crosby/Sinatra mold—was popular with blacks and whites, and he had some competition from Johnny Moore's Three Blazers, whose "Drifting Blues" featured a young, slightly bluesier crooner named Charles Brown. Other records, like those of Wynonie Harris and Bull Moose Jackson, were rough, with more primitive songwriting, and were occasionally blue in another sense of the word, as with Jackson's "Big Ten-Inch (Record of the Blues)" and Harris's "Lovin' Machine." It might have taken *Billboard* nearly six months to get around to reviewing Bull Moose Jackson's "Who Threw the Whiskey in the Well?" because no white band had recorded it, but Joe Liggins's "Honeydripper," a simple instrumental based on a shuffle rhythm, with broad tenor sax work over all, wound up with well over a million copies in print and conclusively proved that black music was selling to whites.

Joe Liggins played piano, and his Honeydrippers had a huge following at the Samba Club near downtown L.A. The curfew was in effect when they were at their height, so they would start "The Honeydripper," exactly fifteen minutes long, at quarter to midnight, and finish at lights-out. "Leon René [of Exclusive Records] came down at eight o'clock to hear this thing," Liggins told Charlie Lange. "So he said, 'I'm Leon René, I'm Exclusive Records, and I'd like to hear your "Honeydripper."' I said, 'Well, fine.' He said, 'When can I hear it?' I said, 'Quarter to twelve.' So he fumed a little bit, but he sat back there." René was impressed by the amount of original material Liggins's group had and came to a rehearsal the next day, where he got to hear even more, as well as an encore of the song he'd come for in the first place. "He says, 'Man, how we gonna get all that on a three-minute record? Can you cut that down?' I says, 'We don't know. We don't cut "The Honeydripper" down.' He said, 'But you've got to get it on a record.' So I thought, well, maybe we can cut some of it out. Let us know when three minutes is, we'll hit a long note and hold it right there. I said, 'My idea is to have a two-sided record, call it part one and part two.' He said, 'I never heard of that, nobody's doing that.'"

But he did it, and he was glad he did. "We recorded 'The Honeydripper' April 20, 1945. April 21, Leon René took it to Sybil's Drugstore at Fifty-fourth and Central and put it on the jukebox that morning around eight o'clock. He went back that night around seven o'clock to see if it had played. It had only played 135 times. So he knew he had a hit." That's an understatement. By the end of the year, the three top records on *Billboard's* race charts were recordings of "The Honeydripper" by Liggins, Jimmie Lunceford, and Roosevelt Sykes, until Louis Jordan's "Buzz Me" knocked it off. Although Exclusive never got another megahit on the order of "Honeydripper" out of Liggins, he made another inadvertent contribution to our history in June 1946, when *Billboard*, reviewing his latest record, "Sugar Lump," pronounced it "right rhythmic rock and roll music"—the first time that phrase had appeared in print.

As it turned out, small combos like Joe Liggins's Honeydrippers and Louis Jordan's Tympany Five were the wave of the future. By September 1946, *Billboard* noted that box office receipts for music had declined 50 percent, and by year's end, record stores were reporting poor sales. In one three-week period late in 1946, Benny Goodman, Woody Herman, and Charlie Ventura all folded their orchestras, for with the postwar demand for such things as tires and gasoline far outstripping the supply, touring a large band was a nightmare. People still didn't have much money to spend, and anybody who charged as much as two dollars for admission to a dance was either crazy or courting the Park Avenue crowd. Bandleaders were slashing salaries. Gene Krupa, for instance, closed his business office and paid $100 salaries across the board.

Louis Jordan, however, was quick to point out that his $1.50 shows were selling out everywhere. He credited this to his unbroken string of hits, as well as to a very unusual promotional device—he was making short films of his songs. His short of "Caldonia," for instance, was available for between $25 and $50 to theaters, and not only was it moving copies of the record, but the film itself was making money through rentals. Jordan even spliced several of these shorts into his short Western feature *Lookout*, which, with its shots of Jordan riding horseback with his alto sax slung over his shoulder, is surely one of the weirdest Westerns ever made. It also offers living proof of the audacity that made Jordan as popular as he was.

But even bigger changes loomed, not only in music but in the entire entertainment industry. Jordan's short films were the ancestors of music videos, though black cowboys with alto saxophones slung across their shoulders were the furthest thing from the minds of those who were choosing what Americans would be seeing on the new entertainment medium, television. During the immediate postwar years, the pages of *Billboard* were filled with amusing speculation as to the nature of programming for TV. It would be culturally enriching, there was no doubt about that: There was already enough trash on the radio and in the movies. There was debate as to whether it would broadcast in color or black and white, with many experts favoring color. Dr. Peter Goldmark, a research scientist at CBS, reported in October 1945 that experimental color video progress "exceeds all expectations, and represents highly gratifying results of sweat and luck. Anyone seeing the true-tone color images on the screen would never again be content with plain black and white reception." And the Federal Communications Commission (FCC) was seeing "virtually complete replacement of standard broadcasting by FM during the first postwar decade." They also noted that television, for all its cultural uplift, would be commercial just like radio.

Innovations were also coming in recording technology. In September, Vogue Records started pressing color discs, which were regular ten-inch 78 rpm records made of expensive vinylite, with a color picture illustrating the song sandwiched between two transparent layers. (Sadly, Vogue, although its records were very eye-catching, never recorded any music of merit.) In July, the army declassified documents pertaining to an interesting machine they'd seized in Germany in the war's last days: the tape recorder. The Germans had used this device on radio, making it possible for Hitler to "broadcast" from a given location while he was actually hundreds of miles away. The machine used one-inch cellophane tape that was said to be able to record for up to eight hours on a spool and to be durable enough to last through a thousand plays without loss of fidelity. Like the silly expensive vinyl Vogue was using, and like the "unbreakable" children's records Cosmopolitan introduced in October (which would result in a $2 retail price, it was thought, because the raw materials were so expensive), this development was ignored by the music industry, although it was hailed as a boon for actors studying their lines. No, it was much more likely that the music business would go for wire recorders. Already Sears had one on the market for $169, and pundits were predicting the eventual replacement of records by wire recordings. That the magnetized wire was fragile, had poor fidelity, and tended to rust bothered them not at all.

Clearly, we were fast approaching an age when mankind could do anything it wished. Once the war was over, there would be plenty of free time to discover just what that might be.

3
MUSIC OF A
NEW WORLD

Although, by today's definition, rock and roll hadn't yet been born, by the late 1940s, all its elements were lining up. Sometime in 1946, a young bluesman named Riley B. King drifted into Memphis from his boyhood home of Indianola, Mississippi, with his guitar in a gunny sack. Unable to duplicate the bottleneck guitar sounds of his cousin Booker "Bukka" White's style, young King had found a way of radically stretching the strings with his powerful fingers to get what he figured was basically the same effect. King came to Memphis determined to succeed, but there were more than a few guitar players to conquer first.

Up in Chicago, another Mississippian from around the same area, McKinley Morganfield, had been trying to get established since 1943, but he wasn't having much luck. Blues in Chicago seemed to be dying out as its prewar audience grew older. Morganfield, who billed himself as Muddy Waters, was a typical Delta acoustic blues picker, expert at the use of the bottleneck, who found his way around the rent-party circuit but wanted something more. His uncle gave him an electric guitar in 1945, and he cut a couple of sides for Columbia (they weren't released until 1981). Then a talent scout for a Chicago indie label, Aristocrat, heard him and told Aristocrat's owners, Leonard and Phil Chess, that they should record him. They did, but the records didn't do very well.

Maybe it took longer for guitar players. Aaron "T-Bone" Walker was a black guitarist from Dallas whose lean, forceful single-string lines, played on his electric guitar, had been getting him attention for some time. He'd

40

played acoustic with Les Hite's band, but work with small combos was his bread and butter, whether back in Texas on the legendary Jacksboro Highway, outside Forth Worth, where black and white honky-tonks alternated along the road for a mile or more; up in Chicago, where he had a following; or in Los Angeles, where he finally got lucky and snared a record deal with Black and White Records. His first record for them, "Bobby Sox Blues," made the *Billboard* race charts and prompted Black and White to take out ads that said, "Here's one T-Bone that's not rationed."* But it wasn't until 1948 that Walker found the right formula, with an old blues song that he turned into his signature tune, "Stormy Monday."

Not that the more primitive blues stopped being recorded, of course. RCA kept recording Sonny Boy Williamson in Chicago, and Arthur Crudup was a big favorite, although his label misjudged the record he released in April 1947, calling "That's All Right" the B side. *Billboard* liked it better than the other side and said he "shouts it joyously," an impression that would soon be shared by a young man named Elvis Presley, who had just turned twelve.

But there were other black idioms waiting to be tapped, such as the call-and-response singing of gospel. It would be popularized by a most unusual song, the Yiddish novelty number "Mahzel," picked up by a black group, the Ravens. This group had stumbled onto a strange style in which their bass singer, Jimmy "Ricky" Ricks, sang lead, supposedly the result of an accident on the stage of New York's Apollo Theatre, when he was so nervous that he came in too early on one of the group's Mills Brothers–style arrangements. It was a radical new style, this bass lead with the rest of the singers just humming chords or occasionally singing along, instead of the Mills Brothers/Ink Spots sort of barbershop style. And it caught on, although the strain of the Yiddish humor and the black bass singer was too much to produce a hit out of "Mahzel." The Ravens really hit it big with "Old Man River" from the hit show *Showboat*, and after that were regular visitors to the charts with songs like "Write Me a Letter" and "Send for Me If You Need Me." These hits paved the way for their greatest triumph: their seasonal 1949 hit of "White Christmas," which was later copied virtually note for note by Billy Ward and the Dominoes and the Drifters.

The Ravens' success bred more success. It's anybody's guess why the Ravens were called the Ravens (unless it was simply because they were black), but the Orioles called themselves the Orioles because they were from Baltimore. About all the Orioles had in common with the Ravens was the birdiness of their name, their popularity in Baltimore, and the fact that they, too, were tearing up the charts. Their first record, "It's Too Soon to Know," was a smash practically from the moment in August 1948 that it was released. Written by the group's manager, a teenaged department store salesclerk named Deborah Chessler, it featured not one but two lead vocals,

---

*Actually Walker's nickname came not from the steak but from T-Bow, a corruption of his French middle name, Thibeaux.

by silky tenor Sonny Til (whose real name was Earlington Tilghman) and by second tenor George Nelson. The rest of the group hummed quietly in the background, instead of singing the words like the Ravens did, and an unobtrusive guitar and bass whispered just loud enough to keep everybody on key. It is an ethereal, stunning recording, and it definitely touched a nerve, selling 86,000 copies within a week of its release.

The group had appeared on Arthur Godfrey's "Talent Scouts" television show, and had lost, but Chessler had successfully gotten them onstage at the Apollo Theatre. After that not even the cover versions of "Too Soon" by the Ravens, Ella Fitzgerald, and Dinah Washington could dislodge them from the black record-buyers' hearts. Black music was definitely changing, and 1948 saw the release of one song that was, in title and performance, a definite portent of the music to come. Wynonie Harris, that tall, lean blues shouter, had one of the year's biggest records with "Good Rockin' Tonight." Listeners raised on Elvis Presley's and subsequent recordings may find Wynonie's version tame, but the message was very definitely there. The drumming wasn't quite as on-the-beat crisp—the legacy of swing was very definitely still present, which meant a more relaxed attitude to the drummer's placement of the 2 and 4 beats—and the tempo seems downright dirgelike by today's standards, but it was a wild and woolly record in its day. Perhaps just as important, it and Roy Brown's cover version sold enough copies to ensure that the song would be a standard wherever blues shouters fronted a big band for the next half-dozen years. Similar "hard" beats can be heard on a number of other 1948 rhythm-and-blues hits: "Sneaky Pete" and "I Want a Bowlegged Woman," by Bull Moose Jackson— whom *Billboard* called a "rhythm blues shouter"—and T-Bone Walker's "Stormy Monday," for instance.

White music was changing, too, although it's fruitless to look on the pop charts, which listed tuneful but insipid songs like "Near You" and "Far Away Places," for the evidence of rock and roll's birth. The folk charts, however, were rife with change. In February 1947, Sterling, a tiny independent label, released "Calling You" b/w "Never Again (Will I Knock at Your Door)" by a young Alabaman, Hank Williams, who, *Billboard* noted, "sings in true backwoods fashion, with a tear in his voice." The record never showed up on the folk charts, though, so Sterling tried again with "Wealth Won't Save Your Soul" b/w "When God Comes and Gathers His Jewels," which *Billboard* found "entirely funereal." When that died, they came back with "Honky-Tonkin'." Like most folk records released that year, it was eclipsed by Tex Williams's "Smoke! Smoke! Smoke! (That Cigarette!)." A month later, MGM picked up Hank's contract, announcing his new release, "Move It on Over," with a badly laid out trade ad trumpeting " 'Hank' Williams, the 'country boy' that's different!" There were those who felt that this nasal, whining music would never sell and that folk artists would be better off courting the jazz market. Bullet Records, Nashville's first indie, decided to play it both ways with their hot young guitar-picking star,

Chester Atkins, and released "Guitar Blues" on one side of his initial single and "Brown Eyes a-Cryin' in the Rain" on the other.

Western swing had been a major trend ever since Bob Wills had abandoned the Light Crust Doughboys to form the Texas Playboys in the mid-1930s, and its swing beat, like the swing beat played by black musicians, had been an important ingredient of the "western" end of country-and-western music. Emphasizing virtuosity in its take-off solos, it was, as somebody has latterly called it, hillbilly jazz. Yet there was another tradition at work alongside it, one that also came from Texas. Although it would be awhile before anybody christened it honky-tonk music, that was the sound that Ernest Tubb and the Texas Troubadours had been delivering since the 1930s. Honky-tonk music required a smaller band, "squarer" rhythms, and lyrics that were either rougher or more sentimental than those usually found in western swing. Tubb had been purveying it pretty much single-handedly, carving out a very comfortable place for himself in the business, but after the war, he began to be joined by others.

Among them was Floyd Tillman, who had played with swing bands around Houston and San Antonio and who had a real flair for pop-style melodies with uncompromising lyrics and a definite country feel. A song like "I Love You So Much It Hurts" had a strange whole-note opening (based on the top four strings of the guitar) that soon turned into a beautiful waltz, but it was "Slippin' Around" that cemented Tillman's reputation. Based on a scrap of conversation he overheard in a truck stop one night, it scandalized and titillated the country with its plaint of a man who has to slip around to be with the one he loves. The reason, he explains, is that he is tied up with someone else, as is the object of his affections. This was pretty stark stuff for a nation that spent most of its time humming silly novelty songs like "Woody Woodpecker" and "Doo Doo Doo on an Old Kazoo," but it portended a new lyrical honesty, one that was a bit crude for "refined" tastes, that would be a mark of country music in the years to come.

Between honky-tonk and western swing lay a number of other country-and-western styles. Brother acts had been a mainstay of this genre since the late 1930s, when the Blue Sky Boys (Bill and Earl Bolick) hit with "I'm Here to Get My Baby Out of Jail," but the Delmore Brothers, Alton and Rabon, were the new wave. Featuring brilliant take-off work on Rabon's four-string tenor guitar, they pioneered "hillbilly boogie," a red-hot predecessor of rockabilly. The Delmores' recordings, like "Freight Train Boogie," "Blues Stay Away from Me," and "Pan American Boogie," are as hot as western swing at its best. They feature sweet harmonies patterned after the Bolicks and often include harmonica work by Arkansas whiz Wayne Raney (who also hit in 1949 with the swingish "Why Don't You Haul Off and Love Me") that was clearly based on the work of black instrumentalists like Sonny Terry.

Closer to swing, but with a definite honky-tonk affinity, was Hank

Thompson, an Oklahoman who took over as his home state's singing representative when Jack Guthrie died suddenly in early 1948. Songs like "Humpty-Dumpty Heart," "Whoa Sailor!," and "Green Light," with its tricky rhythmic gimmick in the first line, were easy to dance, and easy for a small combo like Thompson's Brazos Valley Boys to play—big bands weren't the only dance bands having trouble staying afloat in the postwar era. Although Thompson's voice tended to be flat and not too expressive, his Merle Travis–inspired guitar-picking style, in which bass runs were played by the thumb, with a melody picked out by the first two fingers on the treble strings, turned his big Gibson into a virtual orchestra.

But the big star of the day, whom even such a brilliant and idiosyncratic talent as Hank Williams had trouble displacing from the charts, was Eddy Arnold, the Tennessee Plowboy, and His Guitar. Arnold's smooth voice very likely attracted a steady following of people from the pop side of the tracks, and there were weeks when his songs would command eight of *Billboard's* fifteen top country slots. He toured constantly, and it is a mark of his popularity that when Hank Williams finally hit big in 1950 with "Lovesick Blues," a monster seller that got phenomenal airplay and jukebox attention, the song played tag with Arnold's "Don't Rob Another Man's Castle" for the entire time it was hovering at or under number one. He played the industry as well as he played his guitar, thanking disc jockeys for their help and showing up at trade conventions that may have bored him silly but improved his visibility among jukebox operators, disc jockeys, and fair bookers.

Arnold was usually accompanied by his manager, a stout, cigar-chomping veteran of the county-fair circuit who bought full-page ads in all the trade magazines—another thing no other country artist did—and made sure that at the bottom the all-important words appeared: "Exclusive Management by Thomas A. Parker, Madison, Tennessee." His real name was Andreas Cornelius van Kuijk, but Tom Parker was a lot easier to say. Of course, Parker was learning the business as he went along, but he was remembering everything: how publishing deals worked, and how to get his act a movie deal, for instance. When the points (based on *Billboard* charts) were totted up at the end of 1948, Eddy had 843, against Jimmy Wakely's second-place showing of 132, and Hank Thompson's third-place 105.

In fact, the folk fad was attracting many pop-music fans, and Arnold was definitely in front, since his smooth vocals and light hillbilly backing weren't nearly as rustic as that of many of the other folk stars of the day. When pop stars slummed, they slummed in the country, and Margaret Whiting cut several duets with Jimmy Wakely, including a sanitized version of "Slippin' Around." Probably the weirdest combination for this era was Ernest Tubb trying to mesh his nasal, somewhat flat and toneless voice with the Andrews Sisters' precision harmonizing on an Eddy Arnold tune, "Don't Rob Another Man's Castle." It charted, but it would be hard to claim that it and its follow-up, "I'm Biting My Fingernails and Thinking of You," were among Tubb's better achievements.

Equally profound changes were taking place in the recording industry. To begin with, there was the problem of radio. Disc jockeys were becoming more popular, and nearly everybody in the broadcast industry considered them pests, the lowest of the low, not performers or entertainers or talents, but egotists filling the air with aimless talk, singing along with records, and ad libbing during commercials, which sponsors didn't appreciate at all. To the industry's chagrin, the public, especially outside the big cities, thought disc jockeys were wonderful. The American Federation of Musicians and the American Federation of Radio Artists (which represented "real" talent, people with their own transcription shows) also deplored the trend, and in mid-1947, the unions started grumbling about the possible need for legislation curbing jockeys. On the other side of the fence was New York air personality David Garroway, a self-styled "intellectual" disc jockey who felt that the term was demeaning and mounted a campaign for a better sobriquet. He got plenty of them, and a couple were even printable.

As the talk grew louder, Congress once again called in James Caesar Petrillo. Much of the music industry was based in Southern California, and a young congressman from there named Richard M. Nixon headed up the inquiry. Petrillo, who had been making a lot of noise about barring radio chains from sending out transcriptions to their affiliates (presumably because one transcription could be played on dozens of stations, whereas Petrillo would prefer that each station hire dozens of musicians) and record-making by union musicians (because nobody was doing anything to rid the air of those disc jockeys), was his usual contentious self during the hearings. But Nixon was impressed enough with the union chief's behavior to say, late in July, that he'd delay further hearings for two months to give Petrillo "a chance to be a good boy. If Petrillo calls a general strike against record companies just because he doesn't like canned music—as he testified—he might be charged with violation of the antitrust laws for joining in a conspiracy in restraint of trade." A week later, Petrillo had named a date: December 31, 1947. The gauntlet had been thrown.

The ban started out on a humorous note, as Mercury Records folk artist Art Gibson delivered a ditty called "No More Records," which immediately slid into well-deserved obscurity. But in the first week of January, a fire destroyed New York's International Studios, a recording studio in which many independent companies recorded and mastered their records. Damage was estimated at around $500,000, and the master tapes of King artists Wynonie Harris, Bull Moose Jackson, and Ivory Joe Hunter were all lost—at a time when they could not be rerecorded.

Naturally everybody tried to find a way to beat the ban. It did seem to be helping record sales—people were stocking up on discs at an unprecedented rate—but it wasn't helping the companies stay one step ahead of public taste. As in 1942, the first dodge that they tried was recording a cappella selections, eliminating the need for instrumental backing. This enabled King, for instance, to record Swan's Silvertones and Nashboro to get in some masters by the Fairfield Four, but they were black gospel artists, hardly suitable for the big time, and big-timers who tried to sing a cappella found it limiting. Plus, the public couldn't dance to it, and Petrillo eventually banned it as well.

The next dodge was recording with backing that the AFM didn't consider real musical instruments—and so at first singers fronted harmonica orchestras, then Philadelphia mummers' string bands. Such novelties palled almost as soon as they were pressed, but they were doomed anyway—Petrillo howled that these recordings were still illegal.

Imperial Records president Lew Chudd announced in May that he would try to record and sell his discs in Mexico and Central America, but Petrillo got to the Mexican musicians' union and put a stop to that, too. Chudd grumped that when he ran out of masters, he would record hillbilly and race artists anyway. The difference between him and his fellow label owners was that he was willing to come out and say it, while the others kept silent.

Some artists, such as the Andrews Sisters and Dinah Shore, sailed to England to record, until Petrillo nixed this practice. London Records tried to bridge the gap by interesting Americans in British stars, but there was something corny and old-fashioned about most English entertainers. As the ban continued, Majestic Records, one of the first postwar indies, went bankrupt and sold off its masters in October. Senator Hartley (of Taft-Hartley bill fame) interviewed Petrillo in some subcommittee and asked gingerly, "Apparently you didn't mean [the ban would go on] forever?" Petrillo grinned and replied, "At the moment, we mean forever." It was beginning to look like that would be the case.

Petrillo did relent on one point early on: He allowed AFM musicians to work on radio and television. By midyear, there were reportedly 225,000 television sets in American homes, and the industry was predicting that there would be 600,000 by year's end. But there would be none of that "canned music" if Petrillo had anything to say about it; which, of course, he did.

Then Columbia Records threw the industry for a loop by announcing that they had developed new record technology—microgroove high-fidelity vinylite discs that played at an ultralow speed of 33⅓ rpm, and so could contain an entire symphony. A complete opera could fit on only three or four discs. The new records required a smaller needle—the grooves were much smaller than those of a standard 78—and a slow-moving turntable, but Columbia was willing to share the technology with whoever wanted it, as long as they could hang on to the LP trademark. As people began to wonder just how they were going to slow down their turntables, one manufacturer started offering a gizmo that slipped onto the turntable like a record, equipped with a set of gears that would make it revolve more slowly than the 78-rpm turntable under it.

Soon RCA Victor developed a competing slow-speed disc—a 45-rpm, seven-inch record with a hole in the center over an inch wide! True, Victor said, it wasn't long-playing like the Columbia system, and it wouldn't fit on standard record-player spindles. But with their hot little changer you could hear a new record only twelve seconds after the final note of the last.

Both 33 and 45 rpm had a big advantage over 78: They offered a much broader sonic spectrum, since wartime technology had yielded equipment that could reproduce the entire range of human hearing with no noticeable distortion. LPs did tend to distort a little toward the inner grooves, so 45s sounded better, even if they could only fit five or six minutes of music on a side. And both the record industry and network radio were discovering that music sounded better still when it was recorded on tape. By the end of 1949, all the networks would routinely be sending their shows out to affiliates on tape, eliminating the cumbersome sixteen-inch transcription discs that could erode, ruining the sound quality, or easily shatter.

Before the record-speed battle could really heat up, James Caesar Petrillo gave the industry a swell present for Christmas 1948: After getting some major concessions about payments to musicians from the networks and record labels, he rescinded the ban. Literally within hours of the repeal, everybody from Moon Mullican, "King of the Hillbilly Piano Players," to Wynonie Harris to Charlie Parker was back in the studio celebrating.

Although Columbia was hard at work transferring their classical catalog to LP, they largely ignored popular music. In fact, when they unveiled the first releases in the new format, there was only one popular selection, *The Voice of Frank Sinatra* (CL 6001). This was probably an effort to placate the unpredictable young star, who was very unhappy with the material Columbia chose for him, rather than a bid for the popular audience.

The rest of the industry remained very perplexed about this speed battle, with some taking the conciliatory but potentially ruinous step of pressing everything at all three speeds. RCA stumped hard for the 45 system, color coding their releases by genre—country-and-western records were pressed on green plastic and rhythm and blues on cerise. Still, in February 1949, Columbia announced that they'd already sold 766,023 LP changers. In July, a *Billboard* survey of record dealers showed that the great majority of them felt LPs were selling very well, but half of them were disappointed in 45 sales.

There were a couple of other surveys that helped give a picture of the pop world in 1948 and 1949. A 1948 survey of college students showed that 122 respondents first heard records on disc-jockey shows on the radio, 95 first heard them on the jukebox, and 70 on their home phonographs. As many as 117 felt that disc jockeys—who, even at this late date, were still plenty controversial—encouraged record buying, and only 25 felt they discouraged it. And collegians took their music seriously: 181 college papers had record-review columns and 60 had columns that discussed bands.

In 1949, the Palmer College of Business surveyed record retailers to define the new shape the business was taking. They found that 71 percent of the retailers felt that the life of a hit was three months, and 85 percent of them said that disc jockeys were the biggest help in selling records. Teenagers, or people under twenty-one, made up 33 percent of the record-buying public, those aged twenty-two to thirty-five comprised 45 percent, and those over age thirty-five were 21 percent. Already, teens were gaining an edge.

So let us gather around the Christmas tree in 1949, slip on a few endangered 78s of Charles Brown singing "Merry Christmas, Baby" with Johnny Moore's Three Blazers, the band he left that year, and of the Ravens singing "White Christmas"; let us drink a toast to the passing decade. In a week, the 1950s will be upon us, and we will never be the same again.

4

DECLARATION OF INDEPENDENCE

The artisans of change would be new kinds of record companies, already hard at work finding the music that would become rock and roll. As early as 1949, *Billboard* printed an article headlined INDIES' SURPRISE SURVIVAL that more or less equaled a detailed campaign map for the years ahead. While major labels like RCA, Decca, and Columbia lumbered on, topheavy with executives and pluggers, recording large ensembles with choruses behind solo voices, the small labels were going where the action was.

According to *Billboard*, the indies had the jump because, to start with, each company was usually just one person, who acted as talent scout, recording director, business manager, promotion man, receptionist, and mailroom clerk. Because he had to capture a share of the market nobody else was getting, he had to keep a fairly open mind about material, often going to the areas where majors weren't even looking: namely country, rhythm and blues, Latin, and Polish music. Costs were low because few of these labels hired union musicians—and in any event, the number of musicians on a session would be small. Usually there was no such thing as a royalty agreement with the artist, who would feel happy to get even a small flat fee. Another reason the indies were often profitable was that the label head didn't have to know the entire record market in order to do business; he could concentrate on, say, selling blues in Los Angeles and cover his whole territory—record stores, radio stations, and wholesalers—in a day or two with his car.

Of course, since the majors were always looking for good material, the indie man could also shop a record there, hoping they'd decide a tune

49

would work for one of their artists. Publishing—*that's* where the real money was for an indie label. From the start of the pop music industry in this country, it was the song that counted, because the artist almost never wrote his or her own material. Even as great a composer as Duke Ellington was pitched songs, and in old trade magazines, the Top Ten would feature songs, not particular versions, which would be turned out by a dozen different artists, including all the major vocalists of the day.* Jukeboxes would carry the most popular songs in three or four renditions. It's hard to grasp this, in the post-Beatle era, this age of writer-composers, but it was the way the business worked until the early 1960s, when writer-composers, not the industry, first came to control their own material.

And not only control it, but profit from it. In the first half of this century, anybody who expected to make money from a hit song naturally had to copyright and publish it, but that person was very rarely the artist or songwriter. In independent companies, usually the label head gave himself songwriting credit to maximize his profits, even if sometimes he'd list his wife or girlfriend as the author so he didn't look *too* greedy. Then he'd usually have to sell his copyright to a major New York publisher for exploitation if the song was going to wind up in the hands of a big orchestra. It's important to remember, then, that it wasn't only poor, ignorant bluesmen who got the five-dollars-and-a-bottle-of-whiskey treatment for their musical labors—everyone from polka orchestras to Mexican crooners got the same treatment. Of course, that might have seemed like perfectly reasonable payment not only to the artist but also to the record man, who could scarcely expect a crooner like Vaughn Monroe to cover a record like Little Sam Davis's "Goin' Home Blues," with its memorable couplet "Tell me mama, where do you eat / Makes your breath smell just like your feet."

Still, such seemingly marginal records were doing better and better. Raw, gutbucket blues records by John Lee Hooker and Lightnin' Hopkins showed up on the rhythm-and-blues charts, which proved that not all black buyers wanted jump blues with a saxophone-heavy orchestra behind them. Hooker is a Mississippian with an insistent, if occasionally monotonous, guitar style that often sits on one chord for the entire song, and he sings in a deep, menacing growl that often frightens first-time listeners with its intensity. Usually recording with minimal accompaniment or none at all, he showed up consistently at the bottom of the race charts and had a major hit in 1951 with "Boogie, Chillen." Hopkins was even more primitive. Hailing from Houston, his primitive electric guitar playing, his irregular meters, and his stream-of-consciousness lyrics, usually made up on the spot at the session, somehow captured listeners, particularly in the South, although he never had as big a hit as Hooker. Both men recorded with a truly astonish-

*Bestselling record charts, of course, were also included but were not yet considered important.

ing frequency and often had five or six records out simultaneously under different names.

Hillbillies, too, had money to spend, and toward the start of the 1950s, acoustic music featuring a banjo—dubbed bluegrass by its founder, Bill Monroe—began to sell to rural audiences. Rich-R-Tone, a label in Campbellsville, Kentucky, the very heart of the bluegrass country, sold nothing but bluegrass and prospered. Wade Mainer hit with his slightly updated versions of prebluegrass string-band music, and the Stanley Brothers, who deftly mixed the two styles, caused Bill Monroe to get out of his Columbia Records contract because he thought they sounded too much like him. Monroe was always a hard guy to get along with, and two of the best musicians who had ever played with him, a guitar-and-banjo duo named Lester Flatt and Earl Scruggs, exited his band to make a more modern, streamlined form of bluegrass music fueled by Scruggs's unusual three-finger banjo-picking style.

The commercial success of such heavily folk-tinged music notwithstanding, the real dollars, as *Billboard* noted, were in the more sophisticated rhythm-and-blues and country styles, where independent labels (particularly rhythm and blues–oriented ones) were dominating the market: Labels like Aladdin, King, Atlantic, and Savoy came up with records that sold incredibly well for indie releases, with Savoy reporting sales of 500,000 on a saxophone instrumental, "The Hucklebuck," and Atlantic claiming 200,000 copies of Stick McGhee's "Drinkin' Wine, Spo-Dee-O-Dee." Somebody named Mr. Goon Bones had recorded a novelty version of the old standard "Ain't She Sweet?" and done nearly half a million, and Atlantic, still very much a fledgling firm, said they anticipated moving 950,000 records in 1949. In the country field, it was the same story with slightly smaller numbers, with King claiming 250,000 sales for Wayne Raney's "Why Don't You Haul Off and Love Me?" despite the competition from several other versions on the market, and the Delmore Brothers' King recording of "Blues Stay Away From Me" doing 120,000 copies in six weeks.

Not that ownership of an indie record label was necessarily a ticket to riches and leisure, either. Black & White Records folded in 1949 and sold all their T-Bone Walker masters to Capitol; and early in 1950, pioneering black record-executive Leon René shut down his Exclusive label but couldn't find anybody to pick up his masters, which constituted a treasure trove of Central Avenue rhythm-and-blues artists, for any money whatever.*

---

*This kind of buying and selling, incidentally, is one of the reasons it's so very hard to find reissues of this music today. Ownership of the masters is clouded by the way companies absorbed each other and, most often, the reissues available in this country are unauthorized pressings made in Europe, in countries where 1,000-edition bootlegs are legal. But since access to the masters is impossible, these records are made from the best available copies of the original records, which are usually in Europeans' collections.

But oh, lucky you if you could find the formula. Take, for instance, Syd Nathan, who founded King Records in Cincinnati in 1945. By the time he started the label, Nathan was already middle-aged, a portly Jewish man with very thick glasses who had been advised by his doctor to switch to a less stressful occupation so that his blood pressure would go down. For some reason, Nathan chose the record business, but at least he got the location right: Cincinnati, located on a bend in the Ohio River, is a gateway city where the East meets the Midwest and, more important, the North meets the South. Across the river is Kentucky: the small city of Covington, a wide-open town in those days, with nightclubs, speakeasies, whorehouses, and gambling dens aplenty. It also had WCKY, one of the most influential radio stations in the area, broadcasting hillbilly and blues music (on separate programs, of course) with a strong signal that could be heard as far away as New York when atmospheric conditions were right.

Nathan waded into the business with what seems in retrospect to be an incredible naiveté, recruiting a lot of his talent from WCKY's live broadcasts and issuing the hillbillies on King and the blues shouters on Queen. Black bands backed white singers, white bands backed black singers. If an act seemed to be slipping, or his A&R* department (such as it was until 1951, when he hired Ralph Bass to start his own label, Federal) was having trouble finding material for it, Nathan would dip into the Lois Music catalog (owned by him, named for his wife, containing hundreds of songs credited to his pseudonyms) and find a hillbilly song for a rhythm-and-blues artist—hence Bull Moose Jackson's recording of "Why Don't You Haul Off and Love Me?" which was a big success—or a rhythm-and-blues song for a country artist, such as the Stanley Brothers' disastrous bluegrass recording of Hank Ballard and the Midnighters' "Finger Poppin' Time."

What Nathan couldn't discover, he bought. The Delmore Brothers, who sang sweet country harmonies over a boogie-woogie beat, came from WCKY; Wynonie Harris seems to have sought him out; but Nathan bought Roy Brown's catalog from DeLuxe Records in 1950, sensing that he could do more than they could for the so-called Solid Sender, and later he acquired the whole label; and he wooed the Stanley Brothers away from Columbia, where they were hopelessly lost in the hillbilly department. He also wasn't above buying up masters of successful artists that had been cut before they were famous, and advertising them as if he had the artist under contract.

King was one of the first rhythm-and-blues and country labels to release albums on 33⅓, as well as one of the first to release four- or five-song extended-play 45s. He employed one of the most lurid art departments in the history of records, and King's album covers—some, according to legend, done by his teenage daughter—and trade ads featured liver-lipped darkies and hillbillies in patched overalls smoking corncob pipes. All his efforts

---

*A & R (artists and repertoire) departments match talent with material.

placed King among the top ten rhythm-and-blues labels every year between 1948 and 1960, usually hitting the top spot or at least being among the top three. He was rewarded decently—albeit not as richly, since the competition was greater—in the country field.

Few of the independent labels started out with any clear idea of what they were going to do, except that presumably all of them intended to make money. Atlantic Records was to become one of the powerhouses of rhythm and blues as the 1950s progressed, but its origins certainly didn't point in that direction. The label was the brainchild of Ahmet and Neshui Ertegun, who were the sons of the Turkish ambassador in Washington, and great jazz fans. They formed Atlantic in 1947, after their father died, because, as Ahmet put it, "I didn't want to go into the army, and I didn't want to work." So, to raise money he auctioned off his tremendous record collection and made a nice profit, then headed for New York, where his friend and fellow jazz-fanatic Herb Abramson lived. Abramson was no stranger to record production, having scored a huge hit in 1947 with his recording of comedian Dusty Fletcher's "Open the Door, Richard" routine and having done a few other successful projects. Together, Ertegun and Abramson produced some sessions for the indies Quality and Jubilee Records, but Ahmet was so naive that he immediately checked into a suite at the Ritz and waited for the royalty checks to start rolling in.

It didn't take him long to blow all his money, living like that, so he headed back to Washington and visited his dentist, Dr. Vahdi Sadit, who he knew was something of a risk-taker, and borrowed $10,000 in installments. Then he went back to New York, corraled Abramson, and set about signing some talent: Eddie Safranski, Melrose Colbert, Bob Howard, Tiny Grimes, the Joe Morris Orchestra, the Harlemaires, Phyllis Brand, Toni Mego, various gospel acts, and a number of pop-oriented jazz performers. They also had extravagant plans to record entire Shakespeare plays on 78s, and to start a hillbilly division. They could dream, couldn't they? Especially considering the fact that the entire operation was run out of Abramson's living room at the Jefferson Hotel on Fifty-sixth Street, where the hotel switchboard would take their messages, saving them the unaffordable cost of employing a secretary.

All it took to establish an independent record label was one big hit, and it is indicative of the confusion surrounding ownership of masters that Atlantic's first major record was one that they, scrupulous blues fans that they were, didn't even record or produce, at least not originally. As Ertegun later told Charlie Gillett, "One day I was on the phone to our New Orleans distributor. He was normally very cool, and would rarely even accept my calls, and when he did, it would be to order five of this, ten of that—we were a meaningless company to him. But this time he took my call, and while I was trying to get him to take a few of at least one of our latest releases, he said, 'There's a record out, on a label based either in Cincinnati or Harlem, called "Drinkin' Wine," by somebody called Stick McGhee. If you can find me five thousand copies of it, I'll really work on your record.' So I said, 'Send me a copy,' so I would know what to look for.

"He sent it up, and I listened to it, but I didn't know how to begin to look for five thousand copies of a cut-out record on a label I'd never heard of before, so I decided to do the record again, to copy it. The only guy I knew of in New York was Brownie McGhee, so I called him and said, 'Brownie, I'd like you to make a record for me; all you have to do is copy another record exactly.' He said, 'What's the song?' I said, 'It's called "Drinkin' Wine."' He said, 'But that's my brother's record.' "*

Atlantic scored a smash with Stick McGhee's "Drinkin' Wine Spo-Dee-O-Dee," even though Decca quickly bought up the rights to the original Harlem Records version and tried to beat Atlantic's head start. Fortunately for Ertegun and Abramson, none of the other versions did nearly as well. And they certainly needed the break—at the time, the act they were counting on to make the company's fortune, Ruth Brown, was flat on her back in a Chester, Pennsylvania, hospital room.

Brown had been singing her entire life, first in church, then as a teenager, with various bands on the Virginia coast where she grew up. A club owner in Petersburg, Virginia, heard her and recommended her to Al Green, a fellow club owner in Detroit, who gave her a booking. While she was there, she was discovered by the guitarist from Lucky Millinder's band,† and before she knew what was happening, she was sharing the stage with Bull Moose Jackson and Millinder's other vocalist, Ernestine Allen. But Millinder fired her capriciously one night in Washington, refusing to pay her, claiming she owed him for rent and food. In tears as she watched the band's bus pull out, she met an old high school acquaintance, who took her to meet Blanche Calloway, sister of bandleader Cab Calloway and owner of the Crystal Caverns club. She hired Brown on the spot, and after disc jockey Wills Conover caught her Crystal Caverns show, he introduced Brown to Abramson and Ertegun. She and Blanche Calloway were on their way to New York for her first Atlantic session when they were involved in an automobile accident that laid up Brown for a year.

But when Ruth Brown finally started recording for Atlantic, she received a full dose of the care that made the label so attractive to artists. As with any other singer, she was backed by a pickup band, but, since Ertegun and Abramson were such jazz fans, what a pickup band it was! It was the all-star ensemble of Eddie Condon, a long-time New York jazz favorite, and when the drummer, Big Sid Catlett, heard Brown's voice, he made sure the

*This is the way Ertegun tells the story; Abramson says they already knew that Stick was Brownie's brother and that he felt he hadn't been fairly treated when he'd been paid ten dollars for the original, so he was happy to work with Atlantic, which was known to be fairer to their artists.
†Millinder was a very popular black bandleader who backed many of King's blues shouters, in particular Wynonie Harris, and who gave young John Coltrane his first professional experience.

band took extra care with the arrangement. "So Long," the song that came out of the session, established Ruth Brown as a major talent, but it also affirmed that Atlantic was a label that took chances, since the record straddled the area between blues and pop. Along with the rest of Ruth Brown's work, "So Long" would lay the foundation for the music later known as soul.

King and Atlantic were successful national independent labels, but in the dawning of the rock and roll era, some of the most important work was being done on a regional level. After all, part of the way an independent label stayed on top was by covering territory the majors ignored.

Lew Chudd, for example, had decided that Mexican music was an undiscovered turf when he founded Imperial Records in 1947. He figured that there were enough Mexican-Americans in California to keep his label afloat, and he may have been gambling on a fad for their music among Anglos, who, after all, were going wild for the rhumba and other Cuban rhythms. He kept an eye as well on the hillbilly field and had a young singer with a pencil-thin mustache, Slim Whitman, making records that were going nowhere in particular; he also watched rhythm and blues, which just about every indie tried to some extent or other, with, naturally, varying degrees of success. But Imperial was foundering, and having once tasted success—first as producer of the show that brought Benny Goodman to prominence in the 1930s, then as an executive at NBC—Chudd was very likely growing impatient with his new label's failure.

Then Roy Brown happened—but not to Chudd. Brown, a big man who crooned the blues a little harder than Charles Brown but not nearly as crudely as Wynonie Harris, was big news on the rhythm-and-blues charts in 1948 and 1949. He'd gained a great reputation touring Texas and was welcome in Los Angeles, too, but when it came to recording, he preferred to do it in New Orleans, his home town. There he cut his records for DeLuxe, a label owned by David and Julian Braund, two brothers from New Jersey who had come to the so-called birthplace of jazz, quite logically, to look for artists. They found a young man named Cosimo Matassa who knew something about sound engineering, and using the auditorium of Booker T. Washington High School on Earhart Boulevard (very near the present site of the Superdome) as a studio, they cut Roy Brown's version of "Good Rockin' Tonight," as well as records by bandleaders Paul Gayten (with vocalist Annie Laurie) and David Bartholomew. Suddenly Brown's record took off, and Syd Nathan swooped down from Cincinnati and bought up the whole DeLuxe catalog, Roy Brown's contract, and all the unreleased masters.

It may very well be that the DeLuxe coup prompted Chudd to head down to New Orleans, to see if there were some artists the Braunds had missed. He had a contact there, the aforementioned David Bartholomew, a trumpet player whose medium-size band was a fine collection of virtuosos and whom he had met at the Bronze Peacock, a Houston nightclub owned by

Don Robey, a fair-skinned black man who also ran an indie, Peacock, recording local blues artists. Bartholomew spread the word, and Al Young, a record store owner whose Bop Shop was one of the hipper places in town, set about finding talent for Chudd. He arranged a session with Matassa engineering at the J & M Studio on Rampart and Dumaine, with Bartholomew arranging and leading the pickup band (which contained members of his own band and Paul Gayten's outfit), featuring two singers, Jewel King and Tommy Ridgley. Nothing came of Ridgley's record, but Jewel King had a hit with "3 x 7 = 21" before she disappeared from sight.

Chudd was encouraged and asked for some more recommendations. Bartholomew knew the city was fairly crawling with piano players, and introduced Chudd to a twenty-seven-year-old "professor" named Archibald. Archibald, whose real name was Leon T. Gross, obliged him with a rollicking traditional ballad about murder in which one gambler shoots another during a dispute and in turn gets shot to death by the police, after which he goes to hell and chases the other man's soul, much to the consternation of the devil. Set against a bouncy boogie-woogie bass, "Stack-a-Lee" soon joined "3 x 7 = 21" on the charts.

But Chudd's greatest find was a twenty-year-old kid, sort of heavyset, who played with Billy Diamond's band at the Hideaway Club. Since he was five feet five inches and 224 pounds, it was easy to see why people called Antoine Domino "Fats," but it was his stomping piano playing and unusual voice that attracted Chudd on the night in December 1949 that he heard the kid singing "Junker's Blues," a song about heroin.

Once again, Bartholomew assembled some musicians, and they cut eight songs. What better song to introduce the young singer than the one he opened with, the one that said, "They call, they call me the Fat Man/ Because I weigh two hundred pounds"? And so "The Fat Man" it was. At first Imperial pushed the other side, "Detroit City Blues," but "Fat Man" took off, winning Imperial some prominence in the rhythm-and-blues world and, more important, on its charts.

Next they released what may be Fats's worst record ever: "Korea Blues," with Bartholomew's manic bugle-blatting threatening to drown out a perfectly ordinary blues song that starts with an old Big Joe Turner line, "Uncle Sam ain't no woman, but he sure can steal your man." This record, too, was quickly turned over to "Every Night About This Time," which introduced Fats's signature piano triplets, a style he'd gotten from an obscure pianist named Little Willie Littlefield and made his trademark.

Chudd found one more classic in New Orleans, Amos Overton Lemmon, who preferred to be known as Smiley Lewis. Lewis is something of a tragic figure, since he was easily as good a singer as Domino and had as distinctive a voice, but never really found the winning formula. Despite minor successes with songs like "I Hear You Knocking" and "One Night," which would become hits in later versions by Dave Edmunds and Elvis Presley, respectively, Lewis himself never met with commercial success during his lifetime, although his records are highly prized today.

Lew Chudd might have come to New Orleans in search of talent because he'd missed out on signing the cream of the postwar L.A. rhythm-and-blues acts, but the reason the Bihari brothers, Jules and Saul, began to cast abroad was that they were on top and intended to stay there. Sons of a Lebanese grain merchant from Oklahoma, they'd established their company, Modern Records, in Watts in 1945. At first, their best selling artist had been Hadda Brooks, a gimmicky piano player who made her name boogying up the classics, but soon they were lucky or smart enough to find an urban market for down-home blues, and "Boogie, Chillen," by John Lee Hooker, was one of the best selling rhythm-and-blues records of 1948. Before long, their roster also included bluesmen Lightnin' Hopkins, Jimmy McCracklin, Jimmy Witherspoon, and Pee Wee Crayton; and they did very respectably in the year-end tallies of label action that *Billboard* published. If Modern had a style, it was funky.

Thanks to a third Bihari brother, Lester, they wound up making history. Lester had gone to Memphis to see Sam Phillips, formerly of Florence, Alabama, who had built a studio in a converted radiator repair shop at 706 Union Avenue especially to record the blues. Sam's studio, naturally, was a magnet for the musicians who had swarmed into Memphis after the war. They got exposure through Rufus Thomas's radio show on WDIA, "the mother station of the Negroes," and on Dewey Phillips's late-night stint on the white station WHBQ, as well as by performing live on amateur nights at the Palace and Handy theaters. One performer in particular was a standout: Riley B. King, who had released a couple of records on the Nashville indie label Bullet in 1949 that had been panned in *Billboard* and didn't sell well. But now, calling himself the Beale Street Blues Boy, he was even gaining a radio audience with his "Sepia Swing Club" and "Heebie Jeebies" shows on WDIA. Soon his fans shortened the Blues Boy moniker to B. B. Although he was getting famous, King still wasn't rich. At the Palace, amateur contestants would get a dollar for each performance, and Rufus Thomas remembered that "B. B. used to come with holes in his shoes, his guitar all patched up, just to get that dollar."

Another young guitarist who came to Memphis early in 1950 was Ike Turner, bringing his band, which performed under the name the Kings of Rhythm or the Delta Cats, up from Clarksdale, Mississippi. One of his band members, Jackie Brenston, cut a hard-rocking blues record called "Rocket '88'" at Sam Phillips's studio, sold it to Chess Records in Chicago, and wound up with a number-one hit in mid-1951. After his success Brenston took off with the Delta Cats to live and work in Chicago, leaving Ike stranded in Memphis. There Lester Bihari found him and came to his rescue by making him the label's talent scout. Ike would drive with them all over the Deep South, carrying a Magnecord tape recorder and using any old room in a house, school, or YMCA as his recording studio.

Seeing the value of Sam's connections, the Biharis cut a deal with him to gain the right of first refusal on any artists he recorded. Although Phillips agreed to it, he continued to sneak recordings to Chess in Chicago and to Duke, a small local label. But with the cachet of being the man the record companies came to for Memphis-based hits, he was able to record such notables as Howlin' Wolf, Bobby "Blue" Bland, Johnny Ace, and Roscoe Gordon—some of whom he passed on to the Biharis. Soon the Biharis would add Junior Parker and B. B. King to their list as well. By 1952, Modern's RPM subsidiary, which they'd started to issue records by some of these artists, was munching its way up the charts, thanks to B. B. King's remake of Lowell Fulson's "3 O'Clock Blues." (B. B. would later score a hit with another Fulson song, "Every Day I Have the Blues.") Overall the Biharis were doing very well.

So were the Mesners, Eddie and Leo, who were the Biharis' toughest competition for a while. Like the Biharis, the Mesners had started their label in 1945, calling it Philo at first but changing it to Aladdin soon thereafter. Jazz fans, the Mesners hit pay dirt almost immediately with a record by Count Basie's vocalist Helen Humes. "Be-Baba-Luba" was the same, for all intents and purposes, as the various other records based on some bop nonsense syllables hung on a catchy riff: "Be-Baba-Leba," "Hey Ba-Ba-Re-Bop," and "E-Bop-O-Lee-Bop." However you spelled it, it made enough money for the brothers to record other jazz favorites, like the King Cole Trio and Lester Young, who made some of his greatest recordings for Aladdin.

The Mesners, too, were aware of the rhythm-and-blues scene coming up on Central Avenue in Los Angeles and quickly signed a young piano-playing Texan, Amos Milburn, who seemed capable of great things in that field. "Chicken Shack Boogie" became one of 1948's biggest rhythm-and-blues hits, and he virtually owned the charts in 1949, 1950, and 1951. Milburn, it might be said, owed his career to whiskey—not that he had to get loaded in order to perform, but because his audience liked those drinking songs. "Bad, Bad Whiskey," "Thinking and Drinking," "Let Me Go Home, Whiskey," "Just One More Drink," "One Scotch, One Bourbon, One Beer," and others rode the charts and helped put Aladdin in the indie picture. (Just in case you were wondering, Milburn told Nick Tosches, "I practiced what I preached," although he stopped drinking for several years before his death in 1980.)

The Mesners depended on people with good ears across the country to keep them up to date. Milburn had come to them courtesy of a Houston dentist's wife, Lola Anne Cullum, who did a little booking and promoting on the side. Somebody else pulled the Mesners' coat to the scene in New Orleans, where they paid a visit to Cosimo Matassa, who, in his expansive way, started talking about how he had the weirdest people coming in to make tapes for him. For instance, a group of kids, literally thirty of them, had come in and recorded an interminable song that could obviously never be released. But they'd come up with the recording fee of two dollars, and there was actually something sort of catchy about it. He played the song, and the Mesners listened, fascinated, to the boy and girl who sang lead. That's how fifteen-year-old Shirley Goodman and seventeen-year-old Leonard Lee became Shirley and Lee, and a shortened version of that same song, "I'm Gone," became a big hit for them in late 1952. They were billed as "The Sweethearts of the Blues," and much of their recorded output from then on chronicled the rocky romance (on vinyl only—both became involved with others off stage) of Shirley and Lee.

Aladdin's third big act hailed from Newport News, Virginia, and was very definitely a glimpse of the future. The Five Keys were the first truly modern vocal harmony group. Rejecting the polite song stylings of the Ravens and the Orioles, they went for full jazz harmonies, trading off two strong lead voices but allowing the "blow" harmonies (so called because the singers went *hooo* when singing the note instead of humming it or singing *ahhh*) to cut through and be far more than mere accompaniment. In 1951, they were a bit ahead of the times, but they won enough amateur-night contests to wind up with a week's booking at New York's Apollo Theatre, where the Mesners first spotted them. Their second record for Alladin, "Glory of Love," was an old hit from the 1930s, modernized enough to make it virtually unrecognizable, and it took them to the top of the charts.

If anything assured Alladin's success, it was the way the Mesners kept their talent roster diversified. Amos Milburn's boogie blues, Shirley and Lee's teen pop, and the Five Keys' vocal harmony represented three different slices of the same market, and when they got the very popular crooner Charles Brown, who had left Johnny Moore's Three Blazers, and started issuing his smooth records, the Mesners had succeeded in amassing a portfolio that was to pay dividends throughout the 1950s.

And, of course, there was Chess, which had broken the classic "Rocket '88'." The Chess brothers, Leonard and Phil, probably had the best understanding of what was available to them in the Deep South, thanks to the fact that they were based in Chicago instead of New York or L.A. Polish immigrants, they had arrived in Chicago in 1928 and had gone into the nightclub business, and by the war's end, they were proprietors of one of the South Side's most prestigious black clubs, the Macamba Lounge at Thirty-ninth Street and Cottage Grove, in the middle of what was to become one of the hot centers of Chicago blues. The Chesses' club, however, was a little tonier than the Tick Tock and Pepper's, its near neighbors, and it presented sophisticated high-dollar people like Billy Eckstine, Ella Fitzgerald, and Louis Armstrong.

Still, as the brothers' booking policy changed to reflect changing tastes in the black community, they started presenting some of the new popular black acts and, as a result, began attracting some indie record talent scouts.

One day they noticed some scouts buzzing around a singer they'd booked named Andrew Tibbs, so they decided to take a chance on recording Tibbs themselves. The record stiffed, but, like the Mesners, the Biharis, and hundreds before them, they were hooked. They began scouting around the South Side, and in doing so, made a very important discovery. There had been a thriving blues scene in Chicago during the 1930s, and RCA's subsidiary, Bluebird, was still recording some of the big names from that era; but the postwar migration had brought with it a formidable number of younger men, like McKinley Morganfield, or Muddy Waters, as he was known. They recorded him on their Aristocrat label but didn't do very well. In fact, Aristocrat itself wasn't doing very well.

They solved that problem in 1948 simply by changing the name of the label to Chess, an obvious choice. Success didn't come overnight: 1950 saw them score a decent hit with saxophonist Gene "Jug" Ammons's "My Foolish Heart," and they almost saw some action with Muddy Waters's "Rollin' Stone" and Jimmy Rodgers's "That's All Right," and of course, 1951 brought them Jackie Brenston's "Rocket '88'," courtesy of Ike Turner and Sam Phillips. By this time, they'd taken to making twice-yearly trips to the South, visiting wholesalers, retailers, and radio stations; lugging around a huge old Magnecord tape recorder run by a gasoline-powered generator, and sometimes walking right out into the middle of a cotton field to record a musician on his lunch break. On one of the 1952 trips, they took Muddy Waters along, both as a talent scout and as proof to the undiscovered blues musicians in the Delta that the man who'd scored with "Louisiana Blues," "Long Distance Call," and "She Moves Me" was living well as an artist for Chess. And once the Chess brothers had resolved the contract dispute that Sonny Boy Williamson (Sonny Boy II—Rice Miller) had with Trumpet and that Chester Burnett (Howlin' Wolf) had with the Mesners' RPM subsidiary, and then had issued a rompin', stompin' harmonica instrumental, "Juke," by Muddy's harmonica player, Little Walter (Marion Walter Jacobs), who played the instrument like a saxophone through a microphone, they had all but cornered the market in Chicago in the mean, electrified, defiant modern Chicago blues.

This music howled, it moaned, it brought the spirit of the most elegant and haunting Delta blues into the city, electrified it, and turned its boasting sexual power loose among people who were simultaneously homesick for the old land and trying hard to forge a new life in a place that allowed a black man lots of opportunity—within bounds, of course. Muddy Waters played the same kind of bottleneck guitar that Robert Johnson had played, but it was electric guitar, turned up so high you could hear the bottleneck scraping against the wire wound around the strings. Little Walter played the same sort of single-note harmonica the Mississippi Sheiks had played, only he breathed into a cheap Electro-Voice harmonica that distorted its tones way out of the instrument's normal timbre. And heaven knows there had never before been a place for the dark visions of Howlin' Wolf, who had grown up trying to yodel like Jimmie Rodgers and had resolved his total inability to do so in an eerie *aaah-oooo* that became his trademark the day Sam Phillips recorded his "Moanin' in the Moonlight" for the Mesners. Leonard and Philip had found something unique, something that worked, and they would soon find out that success bred success, and that people would come looking for them—people who would really be changing things around.

There were other indies that would play a major role in the development of rock and roll, but for the most part, they hadn't really started rolling as of 1952. But the indies that had, became the cradle of rhythm and blues, now beginning to emerge as a distinct new musical idiom. They also spawned the occasional "obscene" record, which Congress was trying to ban through 1950 and 1951. *Billboard*, which doubtless was carrying advertising for the offending records, reported on the legislating process and the sporadic raids without printing the titles or types of the records seized. A clue might have come from the testimony of an indie record man who "was concerned with the possibility that some bigots might rule against 'genuine Negro folk expressions simply because they felt that all Negro music is "dirty."'" Certainly there was a reason that rhythm and blues seemed to appear almost solely on indies, for whom daily existence was a struggle, while majors like Columbia were willing to take chances on minority-interest hillbilly music and even hillbilly music like that of the Stanley Brothers and Bill Monroe, which appealed to a small segment of the hillbilly market. Not that the majors ignored rhythm and blues: RCA's race label, Bluebird, in particular had been good about issuing old-time Chicago-based artists like Big Maceo, Tampa Red, Arbee Stidham, and especially John Lee "Sonny Boy" Williamson. Williamson's career was doing very well until the morning of June 1, 1948, when he left the Plantation Club at 328 East Thirty-first Street in Chicago and somebody decided to relieve him of his night's pay. His body, riddled with ice-pick wounds, was found after sunup, but his pioneering harmonica style had already become part of Chicago's growing blues vocabulary—so much so that another bluesman, Rice Miller, took his name after Williamson's death.

RCA also took tentative steps to record more modern artists, although they were awfully behind the times. On October 16, 1951, for instance, after the Five Keys and the Orioles, not to mention Wynonie Harris and Amos Milburn, had started pointing rhythm and blues in a new direction, RCA recorded some blues at Atlanta's WGST radio studios by a young kid named "Little" Richard Penniman. But the songs Penniman brought to the session were old-fashioned, and he seemed to lack both the self-confidence and the vocal power ever to become much of a star. So the label eventually dropped him.

But still, RCA was an exception. Decca had Louis Jordan, but the rest of their pitch to the "sepia" market, as they persisted in calling it, was on the level of Sister Rosetta Tharpe, an evangelist from the 1930s who sometimes went secular, and Louis Armstrong, who was playing less trumpet and cutting more novelty vocals. Capitol barely bothered; Mercury made tentative efforts with poor-quality artists; and although Columbia announced the formation of a rhythm-and-blues department on April 1, 1950, a year later they had yet to appoint anyone to work in the new division, let alone sign any artists. With responses like that from the majors, no wonder T-Bone Walker got out of his contract with Capitol (who had his old Black and White masters) and signed with Imperial. At least Lew Chudd knew how to sell records to black people.

The thing was, at the majors, it was the hillbillies who were getting radical, with many seminal releases in 1950. One was a very curious instrumental by Hank Penny, "Hillbilly Be Bop," an instrumental hybrid that showed some avant-garde jazz chops on the part of steel guitarist Speedy West—something nobody expected from a hillbilly. Flatt and Scruggs recorded "Foggy Mountain Breakdown," a very modern bluegrass instrumental that would show up later as the theme music for the film *Bonnie and Clyde.* "Little" Jimmy Dickens, much wilder and more rhythm oriented than most of his peers, came up with "Hillbilly Fever." (Dickens is considered by some to be one of the earlier performers of rockabilly.) There was Hank "The Singing Ranger" Snow's "I'm Movin' On," Tennessee Ernie Ford's rocking "Shotgun Boogie," as well as Lefty Frizzell's "If You've Got the Money I've Got the Time." All these records show a distinct drift away from sentimental themes, traditional instrumentation, and traditional rhythmic schemes, and toward more realistic lyrics, electric instruments, and more blues influence.

In July 1950, Capitol Records announced that they were going to relocate their hillbilly operation to Nashville, Tennessee—the first major record company to move South. Nashville had had a record label, Jim Bulleit's Bullet Records, ever since the end of the war, but though it did record some hillbilly music, it preferred to stick to straight pop. Nashville, of course, was the home of WSM's "Grand Ole Opry," and since it was a live show, that meant that the "Opry" regulars, who included such popular stars as Ernest Tubb, had to be there every week for at least one day. Tubb, in fact, had made his day in town very profitable. First he opened the Ernest Tubb Record Shop just a block or so from the Ryman Auditorium, where the "Opry" was staged, and never hesitated to plug it when he took his show on the road. Then he erected a small stage in the shop and began the "Midnight Jamboree," a show that came on the radio just after the "Opry" and starred Tubb; it became a very important launching point for new talent like Loretta Lynn and the Wilburn Brothers.

The fledgling music business in Nashville in the early 1950s consisted of two recording studios, Castle and Brown Brothers, and a powerhouse music publishing firm, Acuff-Rose, started by the popular hillbilly entertainer Roy Acuff, and Fred Rose, a professional songwriter and publisher. Rose's expertise helped the firm place songs by their songwriting star, Hank Williams, with pop artists like Kay Starr, who turned them into pop hits. Acuff's connections with the "Opry" stars helped attract new writers like Felice and Boudleaux Bryant, who became the first professional country music songwriters when they settled in Nashville in 1950. The Bryants' song-plugging techniques were a bit more primitive than those used in New York, but they worked: Boudleaux would stand in the wings and catch "Opry" performers as they came offstage, regaling them with the latest effort he and his wife had come up with, and this would very likely lead to an invitation to a recording session. "They'd ask if I had anything new," Bryant remembers, "and I'd always say yes. I figured I could always write 'em some in the car on the way down to the session."

Among Bryant's friends were the new crop of studio musicians, people like Chet Atkins and Hank "Sugarfoot" Garland, two guitarists who played country but studied every kind of guitar there was so they could invent some kinds that there weren't and use them as the basis of what later became known as the Nashville sound.

By 1952, this crowd would have a place to congregate when two other musicians, Owen and Harold Bradley, opened the Bradley Film and Recording Studio at Second and Lindsley. Unlike Castle and Brown Brothers, this was a studio whose owners were interested in every technical innovation that came along, and technical innovations were becoming increasingly important. In fact, the big hit of 1951 was a hillbilly number, "The Tennessee Waltz," and its most popular version was described on the record label as a duet with Patti Page and Patti Page. Using a two-track recorder, the thrush had laid down the melody and then gone back to sing the harmony herself! And it sounded so natural and the song was so pretty, it really didn't seem like a gimmick.

By 1952, the final groundwork had been laid: The industry structures that would sustain new forms and support innovative artists were in place. Continuing musical advances were providing the raw materials to create rock and roll. Now it was time to tell the teenagers.

5
TEENAGE NATION

If America was forging a new kind of music, it was also seeing a change in the makeup of the audience that consumed it. Before the coming of automation, families had two kinds of people in them: infants and adults. Once an infant was old enough to be integrated into the family's daily routine, it quickly set about learning whatever elements of the family trade (farming, weaving, metalwork) small hands could master. Boys worked with their fathers, girls with their mothers, and it was a rare child indeed who ever broke the mold of this way of life.

When industrialization became part of the life of the towns, things changed somewhat. Boys and girls rarely worked in mills or mines until they were ten years old or so, which meant that the period of infancy for working-class children was extended by several years. The middle classes, whose work was of a different kind and who came into prominence during the Industrial Revolution, used their children as showpieces for their affluence, dressing and educating them in the finest style they could afford. In the reformist atmosphere of the nineteenth century, public education and child-labor laws extended infancy into the teen years.

The child was, by the mid-nineteenth century, the object of rather romanticized idealism. Children were innocent, possessors of a wisdom that adults would never know again, in touch with the truest perceptions humans were vouchsafed during their time on earth. This, for instance, was the thinking behind Lewis Carroll's *Alice* books and so much other late-Victorian children's literature, as well as the educational philosophy of Rudolf Steiner, whose Waldorf Schools continue to be a popular type of alternative education. Nor did these attitudes change too much during the early years of this century, even among progressive thinkers. High school graduation became a milestone of maturity, the point at which a child was, finally and irrevocably, on its way to becoming an adult.

Traces of this can be seen in the popular culture of the 1920s and 1930s. Harold Teen was a comic-strip character whose life was supposed to echo middle-class white kids' experiences, and it is illuminating to note that although his creators used the word teen, his behavior was that of an older child. He had his pals, but any dating or other relating to the opposite sex was reserved for his older sister. At least this was the case early in his career; but because situations of that sort made for funny reading, Harold was sent to college, where a freshman was expected to behave with the gawkiness and fear of girls that is the hallmark of much younger children today. Similarly, Henry Aldrich, a character who walked out of a successful 1938 Broadway play, What a Life, into his own radio series, a series of movies, and a later (and, as a hallmark of the times, very unsuccessful) television series, was a character who was probably a high school senior. Although he had a girlfriend, she was as much a member of the gang as an object of courtship or sexual objectification. As the rise of the middle class made college a possibility for increasing numbers of young people, childhood extended even longer. Kids were "teens" right through their college years, and the sociological limbo they inhabited, as neither adult nor child, neither mature nor kidlike, was not really recognized as such by anyone besides the teens themselves. What was dawning—although it wouldn't really arrive until the 1950s—was a sense of a separate teenage identity, with teen idols, like Frank Sinatra, and teen fads, like writing silly slogans on the outside of a beat-up car.

World War II wrought a lot of changes in teenagers' daily lives. To begin with, as during the early Industrial Revolution, they were integrated back into the work force, but with the crucial distinction that they were being educated at the same time. Pre-draft-age kids did war work or held down part-time jobs to help cover the expenses of a family whose head of household was off at war. They found themselves being taken seriously as people, their opinions solicited and heeded—valuable to adults, probably for the first time in their lives. When the war was over, there was a newfound cohesion to teenage life and society.

Postwar prosperity kept the momentum going. Wartime manufacturing plants retooled to produce an avalanche of consumer goods previously unknown in any society. The money to buy them was there, too, and that money was shared among the members of the family, with even the youngest getting allowances. By the time teenagerhood arrived, a child had had experience with money, and now the desired goods increased in magnitude, quantity, and cost. Cars became essential tools of a teenager's social life, especially for boys. Parties became a principal mode of teen entertainment, a chance to meet the opposite sex. Both sexes threw them often, girls more than boys, with girls spending $432 million on party foods in 1959.

The entire teenage market was estimated to be a $10-billion pool of consumers. Considering that General Motors took in only $9 billion in 1959, that's impressive. According to figures delivered by Sigana Earle, an editor of *Seventeen* magazine, in a talk at Michigan State University in 1960, young women under the age of twenty had $4.5 billion to spend, with $20 million going to lipstick, $25 million to deodorants, and $9 million to home permanents. The record business was taking in $75 million on the sale of 45 rpm single records, and the vast majority of them were sold to teenagers, predominantly girls. And since a third of all eighteen- and nineteen-year-old girls were already married in 1959, the teenage market also embraced all sorts of consumer durables, such as furniture and appliances, as well as radios and record players.

Once teenagers realized that they constituted a bloc and that the money they were spending could change the goods made available to them, they began influencing the marketplace heavily. Before the war, the years between twelve and sixteen were known to mothers of girls as the awkward years, because the girls' maturing bodies and the childish clothes they were expected to wear were so clearly out of phase. With the rise of the teenager, girls got what they demanded: clothes that were uniquely teen, from the same designers who were making clothes for older women or from designers who specialized in teen-only fashions. They even got clothes for which they had no earthly use—the "training bra," for example. Earle estimated that in the sixty-day "back-to-school" sales period, girls spent $889 million on clothes each year.

It should be noted that these figures overwhelmingly apply to the middle classes, especially the children of the baby boom, growing up in the newly developed suburbs where their parents had purchased homes with GI loans. But youth would become the message of the advertisers, edging out that old standby, sophistication. Pepsi would be "for those who think young," and after older adults stopped smoking during the first wave of reports linking cigarettes and lung cancer, tobacco companies would aim their advertising squarely at youth, causing a huge upsurge in teenage smoking. America would suffer its first wave of youth mania; although no figures exist to show how much teen taste steered the economy toward some trends and away from others, there is absolutely no question of its influence.

Teens certainly had an impact on music. A survey of New York City teenagers taken in 1951 (as an attempt to determine what their tastes might be like when they went to college and had some real money to spend on entertainment) revealed that they preferred bands that didn't stray too far from the melody, didn't play too much jazz in the course of a set, and made it easy to dance. Girls bought most of the records, and boys did most of the listening, and when they bought a record, it was first for the song and second for the artist performing it. It took five or six exposures by a disc jockey to prompt the purchase, and jukebox exposure didn't seem to matter too much. As for the music they liked, swing and jazz were out, and mambo and square dancing—as a result of the folk craze that was sweeping the cities and bringing success to artists like Burl Ives and the Weavers—were in.

But that was in the East. Elsewhere, the picture was changing. Throughout the South, for example, the radio reflected the postwar boom in minority music. There were no all-black stations to speak of—WDIA, with Rufus Thomas and the Beale Street Blues Boy, B. B. King, was definitely an anomaly, and anyway, it was owned by white people—but radio in those days, particularly the small stations, was a very different proposition from what it is today. There were no three- and four-hour air shifts or monolithic programming. All it took to be a dj was a sponsor and an idea for a show, and shifts ran fifteen minutes—or thirty, for really popular personalities. In country music, the "Grand Ole Opry" was only the biggest radio show of its type; almost every major performer in country music had his own show. The formula was standard: Open with a hymn, a fiddle tune, and the band's latest hit; include plenty of commercials for the sponsoring flour or feed company; and close things out with another hymn. Even Hank Williams, who was certainly at the top of the heap, did these shows, sponsored by Duck Head Work Clothes, for one. Nor was the practice limited to country artists: Howlin' Wolf had a show on station KWEM in West Memphis, and Rice Miller's "King Biscuit Time" show on KFFA in Helena, Arkansas, made him famous enough that he began using the name of the dj who'd originated the show, Sonny Boy Williamson. Ironically, it's Miller whom people remember now when the name Sonny Boy Williamson is mentioned.

Blues and country programming tended to be shoved into the times of the day when the fewest people would be offended by them. It was customary to have the country shows right after sign-on, sometime between five and six A.M., because that was when farmers, who were presumed to be their largest audience, were eating breakfast and had time to listen. Blues programming was broadcast either early in the morning or late at night. Since there were plenty of well-produced transcription programs to choose from, offering mainstream fare, the days and early evenings consisted of news, sports, soap operas, variety shows, and big-name orchestras "direct from Hollywood" on sixteen-inch discs.

This was the way it worked on stations big and small—on the tiny 250-watters that barely reached the city limits and the powerhouse 50,000-watt "clear-channel" stations that kept the truckers awake on America's highways. Of course, another thing about AM radio was its unpredictability, thanks to the ozone skip. On a good clear night when conditions in the ionosphere were just right, you could pick up stations that had "skipped" like a flat rock across the water of a clear pond. Mysterious accents introduced records with bizarre sounds. Sometimes they chattered in Greek or Spanish, or you'd intercept a French broadcast from Quebec. Mexico didn't have nearly as many regulations limiting transmitter power as the United States had, so monster stations like XERF and XERB could be heard nearly everywhere in the country on some nights.

And bit by bit, America's youngsters were getting their own radios. Television had caused the market to cave in anyway, and radios had gotten cheaper. Some of them even came with earphones that cut off the speaker so you could listen all night, going slowly through the dial waiting for the static to resolve into . . . what? There were records played late at night that you just couldn't find at your local record shop—wild, primitive records that you could order from, say, Stan's Record Shop in Shreveport. Stan might not have owned KWKH, but the disc jockeys who did "Stan's Record Review" late at night on that station sure knew how to lay on the hard sell to the "late people," as the disc jockeys would call you.

"Late people"—what a concept! Here you were, an insignificant teenager, bumbling your way through school, filled with teenage anxieties and problems and fears of the opposite sex, and here was this guy—a white guy, at that—playing weird records with sort of dirty lyrics, talking into your ear, like a co-conspirator. He knew who you, all of you, were—the "late people" who stayed up to hear that show, to groove on this weird stuff. It was your own secret society!

Blacks, of course, had always had their own secret society, one forced upon them by racism and segregation. It is hardly surprising, then, that youngsters in search of a change would seek out black music. It is something that has always happened when American music is going through a change, since the black musical world has been the source of many of the ideas that pump new blood into popular music in this country. This happened in the thirties with swing, in the forties when young jazz fans turned to bebop; and it was happening all over again.

In postwar Los Angeles, one of the most popular programs was "Huntin' With Hunter," on KGFJ, featuring Hunter Hancock, a wild disc jockey in the style blacks liked best. Mixing jazz, blues, and spirituals just like all the other rhythm-and-blues disc jockeys did, Hancock was a real fixture on the hipster scene, his Texas accent making many of his listeners, who'd migrated during the war, feel right at home. He was *the* man when it came to breaking a record in Watts, and Johnny Otis was a good friend of his. Together they'd discovered the fourteen-year-old blues singer Little Esther, and Hancock's constant spins of "Double Crossing Blues" made people flock to Otis's club, the Barrel House, deep in Watts, to see her sing with his band.

Hancock kept his personal appearances to a minimum, however. It wasn't necessarily a good idea for his fans to discover he was white. Not that they'd guess from the show: Hancock growled, shook his voice, used the latest hip slang, and generally carried on like any wild man; and he kept emphasizing that his program featured "the latest and greatest Negro performers and entertainers." His mad, mile-a-minute style caught on in a big way, and before long, "Huntin' With Hunter" was made available on transcription to radio stations across the country every week. More than a few of the kids who were tuning in to his program and to his friend Art LaBoe's "Teentimes Matinee" on the same station were white.

There was no way to measure this, of course, just as there was no way to prove whether the whites who listened to KWKH in Shreveport were listening to Groover Boy and "Stan's Record Review" or to the "Louisiana Hayride," a program that wasn't quite the "Opry" but that certainly had a knack for picking up on country-and-western artists well in advance of their becoming popular. But when storekeepers started noticing a run on rhythm-and-blues records by white kids in a place like Cleveland, well, there was something happening, all right.

The man who was detailed to take care of the phenomenon was doing a classical show on WJW in Cleveland in August of 1951. Alan Freed was something of a troublemaker. A classically trained musician with a particular affection for Wagner (he had named one of his daughters Sieglinde), Freed had had one of the top pop shows on WAKR in Akron in the late 1940s, but it got him into trouble. He'd gone from a $43-a-week air shift in New Castle, Pennsylvania, to being one of Akron's top jocks. In early 1950, when his contract with WAKR was about up, he decided that he was worth a substantial raise in salary. WAKR disagreed, so he packed his things, walked across the street, and offered his services to WADC. The trouble was, his contract with WAKR hadn't expired yet, and the station took him to court, where the judge issued an injunction prohibiting Freed from broadcasting within seventy-five miles of Akron for a year.

Freed was only chastened for a moment, and he showed up next in Cleveland, where he tried doing his "Request Review" show on television on WXEL. It bombed. His other dj stint on WJMO didn't go so well, and his combative personality and drinking problem didn't endear him to management there, either. He found his way to WJW, playing classics in the evening, nipping from a bottle of Scotch in defiance of FCC rules.

Leo Mintz had one of the biggest record stores in Cleveland, the Record Rendezvous, and it was he who noticed the hordes of white teenagers coming in and requesting rhythm-and-blues records. To Mintz, it looked like a trend, not the tail end of a hipster fad. One day he cornered Freed and told him about the phenomenon. It would be something to pull Freed's career out of the doldrums if he tried a late-night show that played nothing but Negro music, Mintz thought. Freed wasn't sure, but Mintz kept after him. He'd advertise on the show, and he'd help him get other sponsors. After all, WJW wasn't doing much after ten—why not give it a shot?

So in June of 1951, remembering Mintz's advice that "the beat is so strong that anyone can dance to it without a lesson" and figuring that could mean quick popularity, Freed debuted "The Moondog Show" on WJW, with its 50,000 clear-channel watts waiting for the ozone skip to bring the beam of liberation to moondog daddies and crazy kittens throughout Ohio and

Pennsylvania. On the air, the cultured Freed went wild. Todd Rhodes's "Blues for Moondog," a wailing sax solo, would start things off, with Freed, his mike open, howling like a demented coyote, and then he'd slide into the program with his patented gravelly voice, introducing the first record and getting ready to read a commercial. He kept a thick Cleveland phone book within easy reach, not far from his ever-present bottle, and over a particularly wild saxophone instrumental, he'd begin beating the rhythm out on the phone book, wailing "Go! Go! Gogogogogogogo! *Go! Go!*" and screaming. It was crazy, it was close to anarchy. It was just what a very large number of teenagers had been waiting all their lives to hear.

Still, Freed realized that simply spinning the records was not the road to the really big money. If teenagers liked the records, imagine how they'd feel about seeing the shows live, safe in the company of the Old Moondogger himself!

Freed was on solid ground getting into concert promotion. Earlier in 1952, a Los Angeles promoter, Ben Waller (who represented Roy Milton, Joe Liggins, Percy Mayfield, Jimmy Witherspoon, B. B. King, and others on a long list that read like a Who's Who of rhythm and blues) had tried an experiment: He booked a revue of some of his top acts into a club in Phoenix, Arizona, for a three-night run, but segregated the three nights into white-, Mexican-, and black-only. To his evident surprise, the whites-only evening outdrew and outgrossed the other two.

So in June, Freed took a week off to visit New York, where he began looking for talent to use on his rock-and-roll dances. He'd already set up the first three-show tour, featuring the Swallows, Edna McGriff, and the Buddy Lucas Orchestra, three minor rhythm-and-blues acts, and at the end of the weekend, he'd drawn 1,000 people to Vermilion, Ohio; 2,342 to Akron; and 1,522 to Youngstown, doing remote broadcasts from each over WJW. In August, he tried again at the Summit Beach Ballroom in Akron with the talent he'd picked up in New York: Charles Brown and the red-hot vocal group the Clovers. He had 3,007 paid admissions, and *Billboard* reported that "several thousand" were turned away. Freed was ecstatic. Not getting that raise looked like it was the luckiest thing that had ever happened to him.

Now rhythm-and-blues programs started showing up on lots of radio stations, particularly the small foreign-language stations that abounded in cities like New York and Chicago, catering to the immigrant populations. WLIB in New York, for instance, had Bettelou Purvis with her "Spinner Sanctum," and Philadelphia's WHAT lured the Baltimore-based madman Doug "Jocko" Henderson to the City of Brotherly Love to drive Philly teens crazy with his "Jocko's Rocket Ship" program. Gene Nobles and John "John R." Richbourg broadcast out of Nashville; Atlanta had Zenas "Daddy" Sears; Ken "Jack the Cat" Elliott and Clarence "Poppa Stoppa" Hamman, Jr., kept New Orleans jumping; while the professorial-sounding George "Hound Dog" Lorenz hipped the teens in the Buffalo–Niagara Falls area.

They howled, they screamed, or they made deadpan an art. They played records that you thought you could get only on the wrong side of town and told you where you could get them on the right side of town. They stirred up hormones and caused brain cells to misfire in interesting configurations. Pioneers and pied pipers, they were the ones who began the process of bonding the secret society of teenagers, gave them the passwords and the identity cards, told them that being separate didn't mean being lonely, and helped them find each other, the army of the ozone skip, brethren of bop 'n' babble, the chosen people who heard the news: There's good rockin' tonight.

Jocks like Freed and Hancock were very lucky. They were where the action was when it really started to happen. Pop was moribund, overloaded with novelty and sentiment; jazz had gone off on an undanceable intellectual tangent that would deny it a place as truly popular music from then on. Although hillbilly music was going through a golden age, with songwriter-performers like Hank Williams and William Orville "Lefty" Frizzell virtually ruling the charts, it wasn't the sort of dance music that teenagers, who were very definitely becoming strong consumers of popular music and records, wanted to hear, even in the South.

Some of the sharper hillbilly performers, in fact, were seeing that there was gold in rhythm and blues. In April 1952, a young disc jockey from Chester, Pennsylvania, Bill Haley, figured things out in a way that had been eluding him since his earlier attempt at a country/rhythm-and-blues fusion, a pallid cover of Jackie Brenston's "Rocket '88'," which sold only 10,000 copies. His new "Rock the Joint" was truly wild and crazy, a record way ahead of its time, and sold 75,000 copies. Haley thought he was simply updating western swing. Others probably figured he'd been listening to too many of the rhythm-and-blues records WPWA got sent.

But if there was innovation going on in popular music, it was in the field of rhythm and blues. *Billboard* hired a young man named Bob Rolontz to take over the "Rhythm and Blues Notes" column, and he began noticing trends right off the bat. In his column of September 15, 1951, he noted that vocal groups had virtually taken over the rhythm-and-blues field, both in terms of number of records sold and dollars taken in at the box office when these performers appeared. Then, less than six months later, he was noting the success of so-called Southern blues, of the John Lee Hooker–Lightnin' Hopkins style, which was selling well in New York and Chicago as well as in the traditional centers like New Orleans, Dallas, Atlanta, and Los Angeles.

And there it was: the first part of the formula that would give us rock and roll.

6

SUNRISE IN THE SOUTH

In Memphis, Sam Phillips was not unaware of all this activity. It didn't take long, in fact, for him to start feeling downright left out. Here he was with an up-to-date studio and a plethora of great black artists practically lining up on the sidewalk waiting to record, and he was selling the records he cut to the Bihari brothers and Phil and Leonard Chess up in Chicago. Truly, he was taking bread out of his own mouth. He'd let Howlin' Wolf slip out of his hands; he'd recorded Jackie Brenston's number-one record and sent it to the Chess brothers; he'd had that monster singer and guitar player B. B. King in his studio and let the Biharis have "3 O'Clock Blues," which subsequently raced out of the stores so fast it left skid marks. No, it was about time for Sam Phillips to start looking out for Sam Phillips. After all, down in Jackson, Mississippi, Lillian McMurray and Johnny Vincent were recording the very same artists on their Trumpet label that Sam was recording.

So in February 1952, Sam Phillips approached Nashville label owner Jim Bulleit for some capital. "I thought I could maybe make a go of a company that just recorded R&B numbers," he later recalled, "so I quit my announcing job and opened my record company. I had a wife and two children, and it was a big move, but I was sure that I could do it. Everybody laughed at me for recording black people, but those were great artists. . . . I never fooled with anyone who had recorded before I found them." Or so he said. But in fact, the first record he tried, "Blues in My Condition," backed with "Selling My Whiskey," was by "Jackie Boy and Little Walter"—actually Jack Kelly and Big Walter Horton, the latter of whom was known as Shakey from

72

his quavering harmonica style—who had recorded in Phillips's studio for the Biharis the year before. Still, although both artists were very well known around Memphis, the disc jockeys Phillips approached rejected the record, so he didn't bother pressing more than a few of them.

He called his new record company Sun, and had an old high school friend design him a beautiful label: On the upper half of it (where all the design is, since the lower half of the circle is for the artist and title information), a sun rises, sending off rays that reach to the label's perimeter. Standing in front of the sun is a rooster, crowing at the word SUN that bursts forward from the rays. The rooster is standing on a bar with the words record company on it, and the entire circle is bounded by a five-lined staff with musical notes on it, except at the very bottom of the label, where the words Memphis, Tennessee appear. The label was yellow-orange, with brown printing. It didn't even matter that there were already two other Sun labels in existence, one in Albuquerque that had come into existence at virtually the same time as Phillips's, and one in New York that issued Yiddish records. Sam won a lawsuit against the New Mexicans, and the fate of the New York label is unknown.

Sam wasn't daunted by the failure of Jack and Walter's record, and he plunged right back into the fray with a saxophone instrumental—they were big sellers then—called "Drivin' Slow," by Johnny London, and a blues number, "Dreary Nights," by a local group, Walter Bradford and the Big City Four. Sam's brother Judd, who was a solid professional, having worked with Roy Acuff and with Jimmy Durante on the West Coast doing radio-station promotion, joined as promotion director. Of course, promoting Walter Bradford for Sam was a little different from having cocktails with executives from KGO at the Top of the Mark and discussing Jimmy's latest project. Judd loaded the back of his car with heavy 78s and hit the road, going to every podunk town in the South. So did Sam: "I recall leaving on a Sunday afternoon to visit distributors and radio stations. I'd sleep in my car. No one drove more in a three-year period than I did." Nobody, that is, except the dozens of other independent-record men who combed the territories, simultaneously seeking record sales and new artists, just as Sam was doing.

The Biharis, the Chesses, Lew Chudd, Art Rupe, and the others trod the same ground Sam Phillips did, except in the fall of 1952, when they were different from him in an important respect: They were successful. No matter how much Sam loved the music, no matter how meticulously he recorded it, one thing stood out—he couldn't get it on the radio or off the racks in the record stores. The new label wasn't getting anywhere. But Sam knew he had the ear—hadn't he fed the competition some of their best artists? He continued his custom recording business ("A Complete Service to Fill Every Recording Need," said the card. "Combining the NEWEST and BEST EQUIPMENT with the LATEST and FINEST SONOCOUSTIC STUDIOS") and kept listening to WDIA and looking to Beale Street for talent. He needed a break badly, and he spent the better part of a year before he issued another record.

Meanwhile, the competition was reaping the harvest in the South, and for Lew Chudd and Art Rupe, it would come in New Orleans. It's typical of the way things were done down there—in a word, loosely—that the two top New Orleans records of 1952, Fats Domino's "Goin' Home" on Imperial and "Lawdy Miss Clawdy," by Rupe's new discovery, Lloyd Price, on Specialty, had just about the same people playing on them. Both were recorded at Cosimo Matassa's studio, because it was virtually the only place in town, and both featured members of Dave Bartholomew's band, because they seemed to have the hit formula—but the surprise was, the piano that gave the Price record its easygoing quality was played by Fats Domino. "Lawdy Miss Clawdy" had a medium-tempo bounce to it that defied you to forget it, and it wasn't long before black teenagers had invented a dance, the stroll, to go along with the song. It was becoming more evident every minute that New Orleans was a gold mine for independent rhythm-and-blues labels.

But Memphis was, too, and Sam Phillips must have been seething with frustration. He'd recorded a great record for Roscoe Gordon, one of the Beale Street singers, and playing both ends against the middle, he'd sold one take of "Booted" to the Biharis and another to Chess. In the tangle of lawsuits that followed, RPM wound up with Gordon under contract while the Chess version of the record scored the hit. The Biharis saw this as the last straw and worked exclusively with Ike Turner in Memphis from that day forward. Sam probably saw "Booted" as just one more hit record he could have had for himself but had had to sell.

Then, to pique Sam still more, along came Johnny Ace. A devilishly handsome youngster from the Beale Streeters group, Ace sang in a mellow, expressive tenor that caused mass heartthrob everywhere. He recorded a smooth ballad, "My Song," against chord changes (I-VI-IV-V) that came from the jazz standard "Blues in the Night" and would start showing up again and again in the next couple of years. Ace was backed by a sleepy saxophone and a piano that could have used tuning, with a drummer shushed away in the background. It was utterly convincing, sexy as hell, and sold well enough to come in second to "Lawdy Miss Clawdy" as the year's top rhythm-and-blues song. Ace was on Duke Records, a small Memphis indie, and it was probably the success of "My Song" that induced Don Robey to come to Memphis from Houston and buy the label outright; from then on, his company was known as Duke-Peacock.

It was time for Sam to gear up. Memphis was obviously a hotbed of talent, and they'd been calling it the home of the blues since the days of W. C. Handy. Help, as it turned out, was as close as his radio and WDIA dj Rufus Thomas. Thomas was not exactly teen-idol material like Johnny Ace, but he was a born entertainer. He'd been in the Rabbit Foot Minstrels, the same troupe that the 1920s blues queen Ma Rainey had sung with at one time, and he'd assimilated the whole history of black entertainment in the South into his act. He'd been a tapdancer, and since 1940, he'd been emceeing the "Amateur Show" at the Palace Theatre, where he'd discovered B. B. King, Bobby "Blue" Bland, Johnny Ace, and plenty of other famous Memphians. Apart from his radio show on WDIA—one of the most popular on the station because he played all kinds of music—he'd also recorded some of the blues songs he was constantly writing. Some of them were made at the Memphis Recording Service, and Sam had sent the masters off to Chess, although they hadn't done anything much in the marketplace.

It was right at this time that the fad in rhythm and blues was the answer record: Willie Mabon recorded "I Don't Know," and Linda Hayes responded with "Yes! I Know (What You're Putting Down)," while Ruth Brown's smash hit on Atlantic, "(Mama) He Treats Your Daughter Mean" had Gloria Irving replying, "Daughter, That's Your Red Wagon," Bennie Brown recording "Pappa!," Scatman Crothers defensively noting "Papa (I Don't Treat That Little Girl Mean)," and Wynonie Harris suggesting, "Mama, Your Daughter's Done Lied on Me." There was some question as to the legality of these discs, which were usually no more than the original song, the original arrangement, and a new set of words, but everybody was doing them, and anyway, it was only rhythm and blues.

The hottest single in the country at the moment was "Hound Dog," which had been written by two twenty-year-olds in Los Angeles, Jerry Leiber and Mike Stoller, and recorded by a big, gruff blues-singing woman, Willie Mae Thornton, whom Johnny Otis had taken into his troupe after hearing her in Houston. They recorded the song for Peacock, and it took off like a rocket. Released in early March 1953, in two weeks Peacock claimed it had sold 96,000 copies and was back-ordered for 55,000 more. Thornton was touring the country with Johnny Ace, and "Hound Dog" was sitting atop the charts in no time. It was such a phenomenon that it spawned four country-and-western versions—by Billy Starr, Eddie Hazelwood, Jack Turner, three unknowns; and by former Bob Wills vocalist Tommy Duncan—but they flopped terribly. After all, it just wasn't the sort of song a white performer could do convincingly.

But "Hound Dog" was ripe for parody, so Sam Phillips grabbed Rufus Thomas, and on April 4, Sun released "Bear Cat" as an answer record. All of a sudden, Sun Records was on the map. The record took off, making the number-three spot on the rhythm-and-blues charts, two slots down from Willie Mae Thornton, and stimulating people to start looking into Walter Horton's "Easy" and other Sun records by Memphis bluesman Joe Hill Louis and Willie Nix.

It also stimulated Don Robey to sue Sun—a surefire indication that Sam was big time, since there didn't seem to be a hit on the pop charts that wasn't tied up in litigation for at least part of its history. Robey was evidently going for a test case, something that would settle once and for all the legal status of an answer record. It took until August for the United

States District Court to rule that it was an infringement. BMI, representing the publisher, denied Sun rights to the song, whereupon Sun settled by agreeing to pay a two-cents-per-record royalty to Lion Music, Robey's firm, plus court costs, and Lion agreed to let Sam keep the record in print instead of forcing him to take it off the market. As for Leiber and Stoller, who'd written "Hound Dog" in the first place, they had to name their mothers as legal guardians so they could collect their royalties on the song, and when Robey eventually got around to writing them a check, it bounced, so they had to sue him.

Sam Phillips, meanwhile, was on his way. Rufus Thomas cut "Tiger Man," complete with jungle noises and a killer band-track courtesy of Joe Hill Louis. Sam's success with Rufus's records attracted "Little" Junior Parker, one of the Beale Street crew and one of the most talented blues singers in town. Under the name Little Junior's Blue Flames, they cut "Feelin' Good," a masterful record and an instant classic, with the small band laying down an insistent boogie beat and Junior's voice soaring above it, only allowing itself to touch down and ride the rhythm at the very last instant. It was heavy on the guitars, a Southern record, no doubt about it, not nearly as sophisticated as the jazzier blues being cut in the cities, but it was successful nonetheless. Parker cut one more record for Sun, "Love My Baby" and "Mystery Train," before he got snatched up by Don Robey and cut a string of classics for Duke. Neither side of his last Sun single sold too well, although "Mystery Train" at least survived locally.

Sam was encouraged, and he stretched out. He found a gimmick—five convicts in the Nashville State Penitentiary who called themselves the Prisonaires, and sounded more than a little like the Orioles. They had a good song in "Just Walkin' in the Rain," so Sam negotiated to bring them to Memphis, where armed guards surrounded them as they performed it. Just in case anybody missed the point, their subsequent records were labeled "Prisonaires Confined to the Tennessee State Prison, Nashville, Tenn.," and some of the discs were pressed on red plastic with black bars in it.

But Sun's real bread and butter was local bluesmen, whose records sold to local blues fans. Ike Turner's band backed Billy "The Kid" Emerson, their pianist, on a number of songs, and Sam recruited a session guitarist from Trumpet Records, Little Milton Campbell, to cut some sides, the first Milton had ever done by himself. Another sideman on the local scene whom Sam encouraged was a young harmonica player, James Cotton, who'd grown up imitating Sonny Boy Williamson. Cotton had been in Howlin' Wolf's band and had played with practically every major blues-man, so Sam had him assemble a band and recorded some sides, of which "Cotton Crop Blues" did well locally.

By now, Sam Phillips knew what Alan Freed was discovering—that his R & B records weren't just selling to the blacks of Memphis, but to cats. Not furry four-legged house pets, but the increasing number of Southern kids— white kids—who were finding rhythm and blues irresistible. The cats tended to be poor white kids who lived in slum neighborhoods with blacks and worked side by side with them at various bottom-of-the-barrel jobs. Although few of them thought of the blacks as their equals and most were happy to be segregated from them in movie theaters and at school, the cats somehow related more to black culture than to hillbilly culture, yearning for the sophistication they heard in rhythm-and-blues songs. Being cats meant they could stand out in a world that offered them precious little in the way of a chance to be somebody.

And they were becoming a marketing target. As an Atlantic Records executive told *Billboard* in April 1954, when Atlantic launched its Cat Records subsidiary, they chose that name specifically to attract Southern white teens, to let them know that the releases were suitable for the sort of dancing the cats (who often dressed in clothes bought at stores that catered primarily to blacks, like Lansky's in Memphis) and their kittens liked to do.

Sam recognized these kids' untapped potential. As he often remarked to his secretary/assistant, Marion Keisker, "If I could find a white man with the Negro sound and the Negro feel, I could make a billion dollars." That was hyperbole, of course; the entire record business grossed only $205 million in 1953, and that included Patti Page as well as Howlin' Wolf. But Sam had a point. An artist who could appeal to the cats and who actually was one of them would be a godsend for any record maker. So many more doors were open to whites, and the exploitation would be so much easier. Touring would be less troublesome without Jim Crow laws to worry about, and there might even be a loyalty among the cats to such a performer, an identification, that would lift him up out of the ordinary. He would be a pioneer. If only Sam could find him!

That person existed right there in Memphis, but, unfortunately for Sam Phillips, in the summer of 1953, he was knocking on Lester Bihari's door. Elvis Presley was a white-trash teen who had recently graduated from Humes High School and was now driving a truck for Crown Electric for $1.25 an hour. He'd moved to Memphis from Tupelo with his parents when he was a young child, shortly after his father had been released from jail for kiting checks. Elvis had grown fascinated with the city. With his cousin, he would hit Beale Street, looking for women and music, dressed in their cat clothes from Lansky's. Cat clothes tended toward the flamboyant, to put it mildly. The color combination Elvis was known to favor was pink and black, and it became widely copied. Huge winged collars, imitation exotic skins and leathers on shoes, pegged pants, and synthetic fabrics that shone were all favorites. If a jacket was called for, it would be double-breasted, in some loud tweed or woolen fabric, with padded shoulders. And for every-day wear by both sexes, there were blue jeans bought too long and folded several times to make a cuff. Elvis and his cousin also collected rhythm-and-blues records, which was how Elvis knew that Lester Bihari could help him record his music.

Fortunately for Sam, Lester knew just what to do with pests—every record man had to learn out of self-preservation, especially in the poor South, where everybody wanted the lift out of poverty that a hit record could give. Modern recorded some hillbilly music, but Elvis was too much. He had long hair, clothes that looked like he'd bought them at Lansky's on Beale Street (he had), and he was nervous. Besides, no one could just walk in off the street and make a record with Lester Bihari. No, he told the boy, "I think Sam Phillips can do a better job for you than I can. Why don't you go see Sam?"

The trouble was, seeing Sam cost $3.00, so it wasn't until August or September that Elvis could get down to Union Avenue. On the day he finally made it, Sam wasn't there. Instead, he had to deal with Marion Keisker, who was one tough lady.

She remembers that there was a real separation between his flashy dress and his deferential, almost apologetic manner, so she asked him, "What do you sing?" "I sing all kinds," he replied. "Well, who do you sound like?" "I don't sound like nobody." He told her he was making a record for his mother, whose birthday was coming up soon—that was the first lie he told her, because his mother's birthday was seven or eight months away. What he really wanted was to hear if he sounded at all like the men on the records he collected at home.

Finally, his turn came, and he went into the tiny studio and sang two Ink Spots numbers, "My Happiness" and "That's When Your Heartaches Begin." Keisker heard something, and while Elvis was singing into the machine that cut the song directly onto the acetate disc, she turned on a tape recorder so Sam would have a copy. Elvis wasn't too happy with what he'd done that afternoon ("Sounded like someone beating on a bucket lid," he said later), but Marion insisted that he leave his name and his phone number with her. He didn't have a phone at home, so he left the number of the rabbi who lived downstairs.

Eventually she got around to playing the tape for Sam, and Sam wasn't overwhelmed. But in January, when Elvis came back, this time with two obscure country songs, "Casual Love Affair" and "I'll Never Stand in Your Way," Sam started paying attention. All these recordings are lost, so there is no way of knowing what got Sam's interest this time, but he took down the name and phone number again.

Then, as so often happened to successful recording executives, Sam got pitched a song. Called "Without You," it was a beautiful ballad sung by some young black artist on the acetate demonstration record that the publisher sent Sam. What a record, Sam thought, a pop smash just as it was on the demo! He called the publisher to ask who'd recorded the song, but no one knew—the singer had vanished. Seeing Sam's frustration, Marion suggested that he call Elvis Presley. She got him on the phone, and Sam asked, casually, if Elvis would like to come down to Sun and see about making a record; later, both would remember what happened the same way: Elvis came through the front door of 706 Union Avenue before Sam hung up the phone. Did he want to make a record? Had there ever been anyone who wanted to make a record more?

Unfortunately, although Sam really wanted "Without You" on record, and Elvis really wanted to put it there, it didn't seem to work. Time and again, they'd try to duplicate or even to approximate the feel the unknown black Nashville singer had put into the song, and time and again, they'd fail. Midnight came and went, and after the umpteenth playback of the demo, after they'd tried and tried to figure out where things were going wrong, Elvis heard the kid's sweet voice as if it were mocking him. "I hate him! I hate him!" he cried, and Sam must have been close to feeling the same way himself. He called a break.

Elvis, Sam, and Marion were alone in the still of the night in the tiny studio. Finally Sam broke the silence. "What can you do?" he asked. "I can do anything," Elvis replied. "Do it," Sam commanded.

"So he started playing," Marion Keisker remembered years later. "Just snatches of anything he knew—religious, gospel, western, everything. Real heavy on the Dean Martin stuff. Apparently he'd decided, if he was going to sound like anybody, it was gonna be Dean Martin. We stayed there I don't know how many hours, talking and playing. Elvis said he was looking for a band. Sam said maybe he could help him, he wasn't sure."

But something came of all this: Sam realized that Elvis had just the sort of talent that he'd been looking for. Elvis knew it, too, and yet, although he was burning with ambition, he didn't let it take him over completely. "He tried not to show it," Sam told Robert Palmer some years later, "but he felt so inferior. He reminded me of a black man in that way. His insecurity was so markedly like that of a black person."

After all those fruitless hours in the studio, Sam probably felt indebted to Elvis, so he mentioned his request for a band to Scotty Moore, who was playing with a local country group, the Starlight Wranglers. Scotty was hungry for work, so although he thought "Elvis sounded like a name outta science fiction," he invited him over to play. The next afternoon, when Elvis arrived at Scotty's wearing his cat clothes—pink slacks, pink shirt, white buck shoes—"I thought my wife was going to go out the back door," Scotty said. But they soon settled down in the living room and started picking a mélange of popular country and blues tunes of the day.

Bill Black, a bass-playing friend of Scotty's who lived down the street, dropped in to watch for a while. Later Scotty asked Bill what he thought of Elvis, and Bill replied, "He didn't impress me too damned much." But Scotty knew that Sam had seen something, so he called him up to give him his impressions: The kid had a good voice, but he didn't think he'd exactly improved on the songs they'd done. Sam still thought it was worth pursuing, though, so he told Scotty to bring Bill for a rehearsal at the studio the next evening, Monday. "We'll put down a few things and we'll see what he sounds like coming back off the tape recorder."

What was intended to be an audition soon turned into a workshop, a laboratory. Every day when the three men got off work, they'd head to Union Avenue and hammer away, circling something that refused to emerge, something that would be unique and worth recording. Sam wanted confirmation of his suspicion that Elvis was a major talent, and Scotty and Bill very likely realized that as country musicians, they were a dime a dozen. If they'd managed to keep in Sam's good graces this long, it was worth thrashing around with a hillbilly upstart so Sam would consider them professional and keep them in mind for future sessions. So they kept at it, night after night, for months, even having Elvis do a guest set with the Starlight Wranglers at a local honky-tonk. But Elvis's style didn't work with the sound of the full band. Maybe Sam, with his constant adjurations to keep it simple, was right.

Finally one night Sam threaded a reel of tape into the machine and announced, "Okay, this is the session." He entered it in the studio log: July 5, 1954. They started out with "I Love You Because," a nice ballad that didn't really require much from Scotty and Bill, who stayed in the background, followed by a few indifferent country numbers. Then, as Scotty Moore told Jerry Hopkins, "Little while later we were sitting there drinking a Coke, shooting the bull, Sam back in the control room. So Elvis picked up his guitar and started banging on it and singing 'That's All Right.' Jumping around the studio, just acting like the fool. And Bill started beating on his bass and I joined in. Just making a bunch of racket, we thought. The door to the control room was open, and when we was halfway through the thing, Sam came running out and said, 'What in the devil are you doing?' We said, 'We don't know.' He said, 'Well, find out real quick and don't lose it. Run through it again and let's put it on tape.'"

Admittedly, the final version didn't sound very much like Arthur Crudup's original, although Elvis was faithful to the chorus melody and the *dee-dee-dee-dee-dee-dee-dah* scat verse at the end. He left out a verse and changed another one—the line about women being the death of you—and of course Scotty's guitar playing bore no resemblance to Crudup's, although he may well have been familiar with the original. But it didn't matter. Elvis had finally cut a record.

One side of a record, anyway. Unfortunately, they had to come up with something for the flip side, and it took them the next few nights to find it. They tried song after song, with such unspectacular results that Sam just sat there at the controls, waiting. Then once again, in the boring studio atmosphere, the group started acting silly. They began making fun of bluegrass singer Bill Monroe, who was enjoying a modest success at the moment with "Blue Moon of Kentucky." As Scotty recalled it, "Bill jumped up, started clowning with his bass, and singing 'Blue Moon of Kentucky' in falsetto. . . . And Elvis started banging on his guitar. And the rhythm thing jelled again." Sam taped it, even though it was only a jam, with Scotty figuring out the guitar part and Elvis blowing some of the phrasing. But they had it. Sam came out of the control room, saying, "Fine, fine, man. Hell, that's different. That's a pop song now, little 'Vi. That's good." They did one more take, just to make sure it was straight.

"Blue Moon of Kentucky" should never have worked, but it did. Once again, the boys had taken liberties with the subject matter, using a chugging rhythm that was miles away from the strict meter of bluegrass, with Elvis pouring on the bluesy inflections like sorghum syrup over hotcakes. Sam labeled the cut Sun 209 and had an acetate made as soon as he could. He just had to get it tested out on the radio.

The natural man to approach was Dewey Phillips (no relation), whose "Red Hot and Blue" show on WHBQ was tops with the cats in Memphis. Dewey must have been confounded with the record—with a bluegrass tune on one side and an ancient Arthur Crudup song on the other—but he sat there while Sam spun both sides for him, and he decided he'd play it on the show. Sam gave the news to Elvis, who must have realized that he was about to be exposed to the world, a poor-white-trash kid doing something weird. The night Dewey was going to debut the record, Elvis tuned the Presley family's radio to WHBQ and bolted to a movie theater, where he sat, trembling, as the images splayed across the screen. He hid there until his parents came to haul him out. The cats were jamming the station's telephone lines, demanding to hear Elvis Presley again. Dewey Phillips wanted Elvis on the radio for an interview.

Elvis stumbled into the studio, scared and out of breath. "Sit down," the dj commanded Elvis. "I'm gonna interview you." Elvis swallowed hard and said, "Mr. Phillips, I don't know nothing about being interviewed." And Dewey replied with one of the oldest lines in the dj book: "Just don't say nothin' dirty." Dewey told Jerry Hopkins what happened next: "He sat down and I said I'd let him know when we were ready to start. I had a couple of records cued up, and while they played, we talked. I asked him where he went to high school and he said Humes. I wanted to get that out because a lot of people listening had thought he was colored. Finally I said, 'All right, Elvis, thank you very much.' 'Aren't you going to interview me?' he asked. 'I already have,' I said. 'The mike's been open the whole time.' He broke out in a cold sweat."

Sam had already placed his usual small order with the pressing plant, but all of a sudden he had requests for five thousand copies of the single, and then they were up to seven thousand. On July 19, Sam finally took delivery of the first shipment and sent it out. It took a while to get started, especially with radio people; most couldn't figure why a colored artist would be singing Bill Monroe, and the country jocks couldn't fathom the Crudup side at all. Finally a promotion man named Alta Hayes, who worked for Big State Record Distributors in Dallas, got the record going in Texas, and it began to sell. Sam was excited, but the rest of the country wasn't particularly. *Billboard*, for instance, ignored the release in its review columns, and Elvis didn't really appear in the trade magazine until its regional country charts showed him with the number two and three records (each side) in October.

And by the time he appeared on the *Billboard* charts—as well as in a gossip item in the "Folk Talent and Tunes" column mentioning that he'd played the "Opry," Texas Bill Strength's nightclub in Atlanta, and, on October 16, the "Louisiana Hayride"—Elvis, Scotty, and Bill had already stood in front of Sam Phillips's microphones again and asked that all-important question: "Have you heard the news? There's good rockin' tonight."

W.C. Handy

Paul Anka

Hank Ballard and the Midnighters

Chuck Berry

Ruth Brown

Ray Charles

Dick Clark at the Second Anniversary of "American Bandstand"

The Coasters

Sam Cooke

Bo Diddley

Fats Domino

The Drifters—far left, Ben E. King

The "5" Royales

Alan Freed

Bill Haley and His Comets

Buddy Holly and the Crickets—Joe Mauldin and Jerry Allison

Mike Stoller, Elvis Presley, Jerry Leiber

Little Richard

Jerry Lee Lewis

Frankie Lymon and the Teenagers

Clyde McPhatter

The Orioles

Carl Perkins

Elvis Presley

The Ronettes—Ronnie Spector, Nedra Talley, Estelle Bennett

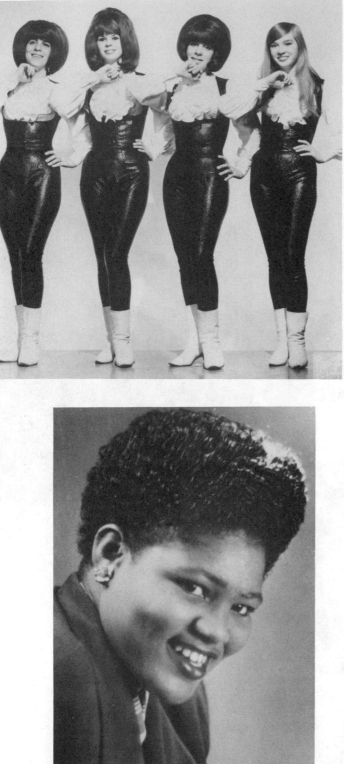

The Shangri-Las

Phil Spector

Willie Mae Thornton

Ike and Tina Turner

Muddy Waters

Joe Turner

T-Bone Walker

Bob Wills

7

STREETCORNER SYMPHONY

Long before Elvis Presley visited Sun Records for the first time, the Korean War had come and gone. President Truman had ordered U.S. forces into Korea on June 30, 1950, and the end came about a year and a month afterward. The Korean conflict, unlike World War II, didn't make a distinct mark on pop music, apart from a few records like Fats Domino's "Korea Blues." There were no wartime emergency measures like rationing to make funny songs about, and no soldier-superstars like Cecil Gant (who died on February 4, 1951, in Nashville, broke, drunk, and despondent).

But the war wrought one lasting change in American life that would have profound implications for American popular music: President Truman had signed an executive order integrating the United States Armed Forces. That meant that the boys who were being drafted would share quarters and duty not only with people from different ethnic and economic backgrounds, but with people of other races as well. Although there is no way to prove it, it would not be at all surprising to learn that the rise of the poor Southern white cat in this era might have had something to do with exposure to more sophisticated urban blacks.

And for blacks, there was certainly an air of increasing freedom that can be traced back to Central Avenue, but very probably also to the liberating experience of integration and equality as cannon fodder. There was a feeling that anything was possible for black people, all of a sudden. Now rhythm-and-blues artists began to release material that spoke to a shared experience, not just to black (usually rural black) life—the kind of rhythm and blues that could become a truly biracial popular music in this country.

83

Sex and booze were certainly part of this shared experience. Pop musicians of all sorts had been singing about both subjects since the 1920s, but now there was a new candor about them, especially in rhythm and blues. In May, 1951, King's Federal subsidiary, under the leadership of Ralph Bass in Los Angeles, released a record called "Sixty Minute Man" by the Dominoes, which had a Ravens-style bass lead describing his sixty-minute lovin' program in some detail. It didn't sound very revolutionary, but the lyrics were funny and a bit off-color, and it became a big hit. The Dominoes were under the iron hand of Billy Ward, a classically trained pianist with an eye for young talent and a particularly stern disposition that could result in heavy fines or dismissal for members of the group who went against his orders. In 1950, Ward had hired a seventeen-year-old singer with a phenomenal voice, Clyde McPhatter, away from a gospel group, the Mount Lebanon Singers, in New York. Although he didn't sing on their first big hit, it was evident that, novelty aside, McPhatter had the energy the Dominoes needed, and his plaintive tenor voice ringing out on "Have Mercy, Baby" brought it to the top of the rhythm-and-blues charts in 1952. It was a new sound, the sound of contemporary black gospel, radically different from the Orioles or the Five Keys, with the urgency of the church coupled with the urgency of awakening sexual need. It was a hot sound, a blacker sound.

It was copied by a number of other groups around the same time. In Washington, D.C., the Clovers picked up on it right away and were grabbed by Atlantic, a label that wouldn't ordinarily court that sound. Starting with "Don't You Know I Love You" and "Fool, Fool, Fool" in 1951, they started off a string of hits that would continue unabated until 1959. In Winston-Salem, North Carolina, a spiritual group called the Royal Sons got noticed by Bess Berman of New York's Apollo Records, one of the biggest gospel labels in the country, thanks to its star, Mahalia Jackson. Berman usually liked to have a clause in her contracts stipulating that artists could, at her discretion, be asked to record secular material if their sacred music wasn't profitable. The Sons were willing to secularize,* and in 1952, they changed their name to the "5" Royales, producing hits almost immediately. Like most former gospel groups, the Royales learned early in their careers that a certain amount of mischief onstage, combined with some overtly sexual behavior, could cause audiences to go wild, and guitarist/songwriter Lowman Pauling was one of the first guitarists to sling his guitar down to crotch level and swing it around suggestively.

The Royals were another group entirely, led by Detroiter Hank Ballard, and dedicated to outrageous behavior. "Moonrise," their first record, was indication of talent aplenty, but they had an unscrupulous manager who figured that he could ride his group to fame on the coattails of the North Carolinians, so early in 1953, the "5" Royales had to file suit against the

---

*Mahalia Jackson definitely refused to abandon gospel, something that may have contributed to her decision to leave for Columbia later.

Royals, claiming that the latter were being booked as and identified with the Royales, even using the Royales' pictures and song titles on their advertising posters. They asked for $10,000 in damages as well as a restraining order, but the judge simply barred the Royals from using the pictures and song titles and sent them on their way. Still, it hardly seems likely that anybody could mistake Hank Ballard's sinuous tenor for Johnny Tanner's sandpaper baritone.

Soon the Royals wouldn't have to resort to such tricks, for they cut three of the wildest records of 1954. "Work with Me, Annie," was a pretty unambiguous tune, with lyrics that did not seem to indicate that Ballard needed help around the office. If anybody was still confused, the follow-up record, "Annie Had a Baby," spelled things out, explaining she "can't work no more," as a result. Rounding out the Annie trilogy was "Sexy Ways," on which Ballard choked out a lust-filled vocal leaving little to the imagination when he said he loved her (gasp) sexy ways. Federal Records lost no time releasing a newfangled EP record, which was like a 45 with four tracks on it, featuring "Moonrise" and the Annie songs, and Ballard tried one more time with "Annie's Aunt Fannie," but the charm wasn't quite as strong. And to combat any more cries of riding on the "5" Royales' coattails, they changed the name of the group to the Midnighters.

The Annie records were hot stuff, and they sold way beyond the usual boundaries of black neighborhoods to whites who considered them "party records." Other such novelties, like "Drunk," "One Scotch, One Bourbon, One Beer," "Let Me Go Home, Whiskey," "Wild Wild Young Men," "Big Ten-Inch (Record)," "Such a Night," and the legendary "Baby Let Me Bang Your Box (I Love to Play Your Piano)" by the Toppers were tracked down by curiosity-seekers, some of whom undoubtedly liked the music as much as the lyrics and began opening up to rhythm and blues. Not that any of this music was too hard to find: Even the Annie records were played on rhythm-and-blues radio stations, presumably because nobody thought that anybody but black people paid attention to them.

And they contributed to the growing ascendancy of rhythm and blues. By 1953, Alan Freed was going great guns in Cleveland, Hunter Hancock's taped show was being heard all over the place, and eventually Freed, too, sent out a taped show. New York itself may not have had a rhythm-and-blues outlet of any size, but over in Newark, New Jersey, WNJR was blasting eighteen hours a day of jazz and R&B by the end of 1953. It featured disc jockeys Hal Jackson, Charlie Green, Ramon Bruce, and Hal Wade, and had a daily Alan Freed show on tape. Soon more and more stations began playing this music: in 1953, 25 percent of all the stations Billboard surveyed were programming some R&B, with an average of 2½ hours a week. To compare, pop was programming 31 hours a week and country 11½, the rest of the time being filled with news, sports, and dramatic shows.

By then, stations could afford to be selective in what they played. Whereas once, not too many years previously, they mixed old and new, sacred and secular, now they could concentrate exclusively on hits of the day. In July 1953, the Orioles, who hadn't seen a major hit for several years, scored again with "Crying in the Chapel," a quiet showcase for Sonny Til's voice that told of a lover's disappointment and was hung on the sort of sad, beautiful melody that all the brokenhearted people in the country could relate to. And they did: There were several simultaneous pop versions, and although several of them outsold the Orioles' original, still the Orioles managed to climb to the number eleven spot on the pop charts.

As whites began to follow rhythm and blues and as more black people had the money to spend on records and nightclubs, rhythm and blues was becoming big business. Bob Rolontz reported in *Billboard* on May 23, 1951, that labels were appearing on the order of two or three per week, even though rhythm and blues accounted for only 5.7 percent of the entire record business. Over a hundred labels were slugging it out in the marketplace, even though the rewards were slim—over 40,000 copies was considered a hit, and 100,000 a big hit. If there was a Holy Grail to shoot for, it was the rare, elusive record that sold over 250,000, and they were few indeed.

For the most part, these new companies were fly-by-night. They could record a singer or a group with minimal accompaniment, pay the artist a one-time session fee, take the publishing, and cut the record, and if one in ten releases did decently, they were in business. At least on the blues scene, artists exploited this situation in the same way the record companies exploited them: John Lee Hooker, for instance, recorded under several other names throughout the 1950s—among them John Lee and John Lee Booker—and other artists followed his lead.

Still, these new companies were such shoestring operations that airplay was achieved in many cases through out-and-out payola, although at the beginning that didn't mean minks and Cadillacs. According to *Billboard*, one label spent $40 a month in New York, $25 in Newark, $55 in Philadelphia (there were three jockeys involved there), and $10 in Detroit when there was a special project. In addition, their Washington distributor was given 150 free records, with which they bought ad time. Not huge sums of money—certainly not enough for even a down payment on a Cadillac.

Despite all this activity, the major labels continued to be blinkered, and try as they might, even big ones like Decca couldn't seem to compete in the new market. So it was no surprise (although something of a shock) when pop/R&B star Louis Jordan announced, late in 1953, that he was leaving Decca for the independent Aladdin. One sign of hope from the majors was Columbia's reactivating its Okeh subsidiary, a major blues label from the 1930s, to record the new rhythm and blues, but its major success so far had come from a fragile, almost effeminate boy named Johnnie Ray, who took his own advice every time he performed his smash hit "Cry." Some thought Ray's voice not unlike Billie Holiday's, but that wasn't the point: Okeh was lagging way behind the indies in the R&B field, even if it was ahead of the rest of the majors. And Johnnie Ray was white, after all.

Maybe it was the attraction black popular music has always held for white ears—maybe it was the fact that Alan Freed and the other disc jockeys who played R&B were slowly changing America's ears—but the "cat" scene was growing, spreading out of the South, and in 1953, rhythm-and-blues record sales reached an all-time high of $15 million. *Billboard* ascribed the phenomenon to the same teenage quest for music with a beat—dance music—that had created the swing era. After all, all that youthful energy needed an outlet. And now teenagers were pressuring jukebox operators and record dealers into stocking their favorites, and were doing their part by buying the records and keeping them spinning on the jukes.

From this phenomenon, then, it was only a short step to tailoring records specially to teenagers, black and white. The men who would raise this commercial impulse nearly to the level of an art form were already at work in Los Angeles. Jerry Leiber and Mike Stoller had moved to L.A. from Baltimore and New York, respectively, in 1950, when they were both seventeen years old. Stoller, the musician of the duo, had graduated from high school and was attending Los Angeles City College and playing with some dance bands, when a drummer offered to introduce him to an aspiring young songwriter, Jerry Leiber. "When he told me on the phone that he wanted to write songs, I envisioned some kind of song I didn't like," Stoller remembered, "because I was into Charlie Parker and Lester Young, and also had developed an interest in serious music, and I thought he had in mind something that I would find saccharine and uninteresting. But when he came over, I could see that a lot of his stuff was blues, and I had always liked blues."

In 1950, this definitely set Jerry, who was still attending Fairfax High in a predominantly Jewish section of the city and working at a record store there after school, apart from the crowd. "I wouldn't say that we were the only Caucasians interested in the blues," Stoller said, "but generally speaking, it was unusual for teenage white kids to be involved, knowledgeable, and interested in black popular music."

Leiber and Stoller spent the entire summer writing songs together, and then fate, in the person of Modern Records' national sales manager Lester Sill, walked into the record shop where Jerry was working. "Jerry sang him some songs and Lester took us under his wing. He introduced us to various people, including the Biharis, of course, and Gene Norman, who had a big blues jamboree. In fact, our first performance was in December 1950, at Gene Norman's Blues Jamboree at the Shrine Auditorium. Jimmy Witherspoon sang our song."

Suddenly the two were launched into the world of professional songwriting. "The following year, Lester took us to New York and Philadelphia and introduced us to the A&R men who were involved with the East Coast record companies." These men were all-important since they matched the artists (A) with the repertoire (R) in the days before the majority of performers wrote their own material. "We met Ralph Bass and Bobby Shad (who was with Mercury), and then Ralph Bass headquartered himself the following year in Los Angeles [working as head of King's subsidiary Federal], so he would call upon us to write for recording sessions. He'd call us and say, 'We're doing Little Esther Tuesday up at Radio Recorders, so bring some of your songs to the studio,' and we would. I guess the most usual thing that would happen would be that we'd bring three songs and we'd teach the songs to Little Esther or Little Esther and Bobby Nunn as a duet, or [singer] Little Willie Littlefield, teach them the song at the session, teach it to the band—if [arrangers] Johnny Otis or Maxwell Davis were on the session we'd give 'em the idea of what was going on to the band and then they'd make a head arrangement. Between takes on maybe the last tune, we'd go off in the hallway and write another tune. That was pretty typical.

"On other occasions we would write something and go right out. I remember going off to Charles Brown's house to teach him 'Hard Times' and to Maxwell Davis's house when Little Willie Littlefield was coming up for a date to teach him a song that we called 'Kansas City,' but Ralph Bass didn't think the title was hip enough and he retitled it 'K.C. Lovin'.' And then sometimes Johnny Otis would call us over to his house to hear some of the singers who worked with him, like Willie Mae Thornton." She impressed them enough to get them to write her—and their—biggest record to date, "Hound Dog."

But Leiber and Stoller weren't quite the canny marketing specialists they might seem from today's perspective. Stoller denies that they were crafting songs specifically for the new teenage market. "We wrote to amuse ourselves. I guess we were talking over ideas some, but you're influenced by everything that goes on around you, and I don't think we ever made any conscious decision about what to write or how to write or what direction to write in. In fact, I know that we didn't. . . . If we were amused, if we really liked what we did, we had a pretty darn good shot at having a hit, because we were our audience, and we were, on some level or another, typical of the people who bought our records. Not necessarily that we were the same as they, but we were not that far removed. There was something universal about the humor, or the emotional content, that caught the teens."

The universality didn't extend to the other professional songwriters on Tin Pan Alley, most of whom felt that this music was utter junk. They soon began to change their tune when a group called the Chords put a song called "Sh-Boom" on the flip of their debut for Atlantic's Cat label, "Cross Over the Bridge." The Chords had gotten past the door at Atlantic in the first place by singing the song a cappella, and the song did have a nice skipping rhythm to it, as well as silly, optimistic lyrics and a tricky chorus, all delivered with tight, almost barbershop-style harmonies. It's a little amazing that they got to cut it, since Jerry Wexler, another jazz fan and a former *Billboard* rhythm-and-blues reporter, had joined the label, and he considered the majority of vocal groups sloppy musicians at best.

After its release in May 1954, "Sh-Boom" immediately started making waves. A summer is nothing without a silly song, and "Sh-Boom" filled that need, climbing aboard the pop charts at number sixteen on June 23. But then a week later, the Crew Cuts, a group that was just as white as their name implied, hit the pop charts with their version on Mercury, identical in every way (except for a certain lack of feeling in the vocal) to the Chords' original. The Crew Cuts debuted at eight, while the Chords struggled to keep up with them. Throughout July, the Chords' version stayed five or six points below the Crew Cuts', and on August 7, the week the Crew Cuts finally hit number one, the Chords' version had already started to slip. On the sales charts, anyway: *Billboard* also carried disc-jockey charts showing the most-spun platters, as well as jukebox charts listing the cuts that garnered the most nickels. On these charts, the Chords ruled throughout the summer.

The Chords' pop success wasn't unprecedented, although the other major smashes achieved on the pop charts by vocal groups had all been ballads. What was unusual was that the cover version, as the industry calls a record that copies an original (often one from another genre, like pop singer Joni James's covers of Hank Williams songs), used the same arrangement, vocal, and instrumental. With "Sh-Boom," the pop establishment had found itself a potent weapon to use against R&B records—whiten them up and use the corporate might of a major record label to get them to places a hapless indie caught with a hit on its hands could never reach.

Hot on "Sh-Boom"'s heels came a cover of another Atlantic hit, and this one was even more insidious. Bill Haley had made some noise in 1953 with his self-penned "Crazy Man, Crazy" on Philadelphia's small indie Essex—enough so that Decca took a chance and signed him. His first release on Decca, "Rock Around the Clock," failed to gain attention at first, but his track record was strong enough that *Billboard* spotlighted his second Decca single, a cover of Big Joe Turner's "Shake, Rattle and Roll." Nobody could claim that Haley's record exactly copied the original. Some of Turner's gamier lines (comparing himself to "a one-eyed cat peepin' in a seafood store," admiring the woman's "dresses the sun comes shinin' through" and declaring her "the Devil in nylon hose") were rewritten; and Haley's band, which originally played western swing, was quite incapable of reproducing the sound of Turner's big band of jazz veterans, assembled by Ahmet Ertegun. They relied instead on guitars and a more swing-oriented rhythm section. Haley, a moon-faced twenty-nine-year-old with a weird spitcurl on his forehead, was an unlikely teen idol, but his face was clean and white, unlike the gigantic leering visage of Joe Turner, a man given to pronouncements like "All I want to do is drink and sing the blues." But even though nobody expected much for Haley despite his being on Decca, "Shake, Rattle and Roll," a radical departure for America's pop music, shot up to the Top

Ten—not only in the United States but also in England, where teenagers were apparently awaiting this blast of new music just as avidly as Americans were.

Atlantic was undaunted. They had a few more young artists ready to go, and the first had already arrived. Ahmet Ertegun was a huge fan of Billy Ward's Dominoes, and one night he found himself at Birdland in New York for one of their shows. After the first set, Ertegun noticed Clyde McPhatter wasn't singing with the group, so he went backstage and casually asked Ward where his singer was. Apparently Clyde had run afoul of one of the numerous regulations Ward laid down for his group, because the leader snarled at Ertegun, "I fired his ass,"—despite all the great records McPhatter had sung lead on, from "Have Mercy Baby" to the bizarre "The Bells," in which Clyde performed with near-psychotic intensity as a man watching his girlfriend's funeral. He sobs, screams, and wails throughout the entire record, a very hard song to listen to, but riveting.

Needless to say, Ertegun lost no time cabbing it to Harlem and, finding McPhatter in a furnished room, took him out to dinner and convinced him to sign with Atlantic. Clyde told Ahmet that "he had some friends who would form a group," as Ertegun recalled to Charlie Gillett, "and he collected them together and brought them in for a session. We taped some stuff, but they weren't much good, not what I was looking for, which was a gospel sort of sound, which was how Clyde sang naturally. So he said he had another group of friends who were really good, gospel singers called the Thrasher Wonders, one of them could sound just like the bass of the Dominoes." This group, composed of Bill Pinkney and Andrew and Gerhart Thrasher, Clyde dubbed the Drifters. Atlantic hated the name. A handle like Clyde McPhatter was bad enough—Ahmet likened it to that of a Western-movie sidekick—but "Drifters" had a real cowboy ring. Still, it was a minor point; they'd nailed down one of the great voices of the time, so if "Drifters" was what he wanted, "Drifters" was what he would get.

The first record the new group made was 1953's biggest R&B hit, "Money Honey." While the group hooted out "blow harmonies" (*ha-oooo* instead of humming), Clyde went through a litany of troubles his landlord, girlfriend, and others could easily solve with an infusion of cash, something he was currently short of. It was a bluesy, funny song, and its socially-conscious humor presaged some of the great Leiber and Stoller hits and voiced a universal concern. Next came "Lucille," a fair success, and "Such a Night," which may not have been as explicit as the Annie records but raised the hackles of the censors just as much. After all, the reason Clyde remembered the night so well was that they did more than just kiss, if the lyrics weren't lying. Even Johnnie Ray, who covered it, found his version of the song getting banned. "Honey Love" was just as lascivious, and it went to the top of the charts. The sincerity of Clyde McPhatter's voice was irresistible and so gospel-tinged it was absolutely impossible that he would get covered this time. The year 1954 saw three Drifters records in the R&B Top Forty: Atlantic was on another roll.

But early in 1954, a group of R&B disc jockeys on the East Coast had formed a club to "combat smut and racial derogation," according to *Billboard*. With the ascent of such releases as the Annie records, it was now clear that the rhythm-and-blues market was getting a little raw. The story continued: "Tunes that the club hopes to stop play on are those that deal with sex in a suggestive manner, those that deal with drinking, and those that hold the Negro up to ridicule. The club is not against blues records as such, but it is against a record in which 'rock,' 'roll,' or 'ride' doesn't deal with the rhythm and meter of the tune."*

Some weeks later, WXYZ in Detroit banned "Such a Night," after a campaign by local mothers who were outraged that such "suggestive trash" was being played for teenagers. However, the jockeys noted that the ban didn't stop teenagers from calling in and requesting the song. In July, R&B was banned outright from the airwaves in Boston, where jocks started feeding teens mambo records as a sort of musical cold shower. In September, the sheriff in Long Beach, California, banned an unspecified "spicy R&B disc," and in Memphis, they were confiscating jukeboxes with off-color records on them.

Of course, everybody likes a scapegoat, and the disc jockeys were the scapegoats in this controversy. Unwitting scapegoats, perhaps, but they had the blame placed on them. "I don't like to feature blues," Bill Laws of KLX in Oakland told a reporter, "but the requests keep coming in." And Don Sherman at WLYN in Lynn, Massachusetts, added, "I've found it necessary to start including some of the less offensive R&B records on my pop show. The teenage crowd seems to know nothing else."

Ah, the teenagers! Were they the misguided dupes of the low-life disc jockeys, or were they the actual culprits? Certainly the R&B stations seemed to be policing themselves: In October, WDIA in Memphis banned the Annie records, "Honey Love," the Bees' "Toy Bell" (later known as "My Ding-a-Ling"), and ten other records.

The teenagers! Would the censors have been so vigilant if it were adults hearing these songs? Given the tenor of the times—don't forget that *Playboy* was only a year old when all this was happening, and while it was relatively timid compared with its present state, the magazine was considered the rawest pornography—the censors would have been upset if adults (or white adults, at any rate) had been buying the "bluer" R&B records.

A worse blow to Atlantic came on May 7, 1954, when Clyde McPhatter was drafted. Fortunately, that wasn't going to happen to the other two stars Atlantic was counting on: One was blind and the other was female.

---

*Ironically, this club was originally founded the same week the Royals/Midnighters released "Work With Me, Annie."

Ray Charles Robinson was probably the ideal Atlantic artist. Born in Albany, Georgia, he went blind in late childhood and was educated in schools for the blind in Florida. While very young, he had shown a formidable talent at the piano, and since blind kids in the South became either musicians, broom makers, or beggars, this stood him in good stead. He soon became a big attraction on the Southern honky-tonk circuit, playing piano and trying to croon like Charles Brown or Nat "King" Cole, and at one point playing with a country band that was all white except for him. Somewhere along the way, he dropped his last name so as not to be confused with boxer Sugar Ray Robinson, and early in 1949, he came to the attention of Jack Lauderdale, who had a small indie label in Los Angeles called Swing Time. Lauderdale figured he had another sepia Sinatra on his hands and signed up Charles, recording him extensively, sometimes with jazz players and sometimes with members of Johnny Moore's Three Blazers.

The Swing Time records were modestly successful, but they were very derivative of Brown and Cole, very genteel and overpolished. Swing Time started having financial difficulties (it finally sputtered to a finish in 1953), and Lauderdale offered masters to anyone who'd take them. In Charles's very last recordings for the label, some of his most successful until then, another voice had started breaking through—rough, strong, and dripping with a complex emotion that people began to call soul. "Baby Let Me Hold Your Hand" was one of these records, and it got some substantial airplay during 1951. So, when Ahmet Ertegun and Herb Abramson heard that Lauderdale was so strapped that he'd let the singer go for $2,500, they bought out the contract without hesitation.

This was the old days at Atlantic, when the partners would conduct business during the day, then pile the furniture in the corner and bring in some microphones, along with a young recording wizard named Tom Dowd. Dowd was one of the first engineers to take great pains with the sounds he was recording, to make sure that every nuance of an arrangement got onto the tape and that the balance of performer and backup was perfect.* Still, Ray Charles's first session proved frustrating, since he was hard for the musicians, the arranger (Jesse Stone), and the producer (Ahmet) to get along with; and he insisted on singing in his smooth, Charles Brown style. A second session, on May 10, 1953, proved more fruitful, as Charles laid down six tracks, including the growling "Mess Around," a dance-craze number, and "It Should Have Been Me," the tale of a man who just can't win. "Mess Around" didn't make much noise, but "It Should Have Been Me" reached number seven on the R&B charts in 1954. Then, in a session on November 18, 1954, Ray really hit the jackpot. He was fooling around with an old gospel number, one that goes "I've got a Savior, Way over Jordan, He's saved my soul, oh, yeah." Charles changed the savior

---

*Since Atlantic was one of the first labels to get into LP albums, as well as the burgeoning high-fidelity craze, Dowd was worth his weight in platinum.

to a woman, Jordan got changed to across town, and of course, the nature of the relationship was changed. On the song, Ray pulled out every trick in the gospel book and not a few from the blues side, too, as he wailed, sailed into falsetto, and curled melismatically around the melody. "I Got a Woman" became one of 1955's greatest hits, and Ray Charles was on his way to inventing a whole new kind of music—or maybe to reviving a great old one.

Atlantic's other ace in the hole, La Vern Baker, had been performing through the late 1940s as Little Miss Sharecropper (taking off from the already popular Little Miss Cornshucks), but by 1950, she had bounced off several labels, and her recording career looked moribund. Certainly she had the voice to be a success: big, bold, but not unfeminine, capable of anything from a growl to a lilt. She wasn't quite adept enough technically to sing jazz, but neither was she a blues shouter like Willie Mae Thornton; her style was closer to that of Ruth Brown, which may have been the reason Atlantic signed her in 1953. Her first few records, typically, sank fairly soon, but early in 1955, she hit her stride with a sly, sexy number called "Tweedle Dee." It was irresistible, and started climbing the pop charts fast, heading into the Top Ten. It seemed certain to revitalize Baker's flagging career.

But then, all of a sudden, Georgia Gibbs moved in with a cover version so close to the original of Baker's song that it seemed she'd actually been able to record a new voice over the old backing track.* It was painful competition: La Vern Baker estimated that Georgia Gibbs's cover of "Tweedle Dee" cost her a shocking $15,000 worth of royalties. After she'd ascertained that arrangements weren't copyrightable and that Gibbs was well within the law in her cloning of the song, she wrote her congressman to see whether she could spark some legislation. All she got back was an envelope full of reelection materials.

But if Atlantic was spearheading the movement of quality rhythm and blues into the pop marketplace, they were nonethless hardly typical of a rhythm-and-blues label of this period. They cared about recording quality, they worked with their artists and developed their careers, and they were turning out records that were far more sophisticated than those of the competition. Jerry Wexler derides the majority of these early rock and roll hits from the rhythm and blues field as "the most incredible crap," explaining that "we were making records in tune; they sounded like beautiful gospel records."

Wexler is too harsh about a type of music made by people who did not share his ambitions and esthetic, not to mention Atlantic's resources in both personnel and cash. For many label owners, rhythm and blues was

---

*In fact, as Tom Dowd recalled, "Mercury . . . called me up after I'd engineered 'Tweedle Dee' and said that they were going to cut the song again with Georgia Gibbs, and that they had the same musicians, the same arranger, and they wanted the same engineer." Dowd, a good company man, stood pat.

still a gamble that might yield a huge return on a very small investment; and there were artists, too, who didn't share the perfectionist impulses of the Clovers or have a charismatic leader like the Drifters did.

Still, it was a time of incredible innovation. Take, for example, the Skylarks, who started out singing in the schoolyard of Wadley Junior High School at 115th Street and Seventh Avenue, in the heart of Harlem. They did it for fun, but they were also very aware that just a few blocks away stood the mighty Apollo Theatre, with its Amateur Night. Every Wednesday people from all over came to the Apollo to try for the prize in front of the toughest panel of critics in America: the audience. Apollo audiences were not shy about expressing their feelings about an act, and the theater had an emcee, dressed in rags, named Porto Rico, who carried a cap pistol and would come out and "shoot" an act that needed to be put out of its misery. To get applause at the Apollo meant honor and adulation for weeks to come. To get shot by Porto Rico meant abject humiliation. Like hundreds of other groups that bravely trod the boards, the Skylarks suffered being booed off stage by the crowd.

Undaunted, they started hanging around a record store that specialized in vocal groups, both on record and as customers. Soon they convinced the owner to help them cut a demo record that they could use to get a contract. Again, the Skylarks failed; the record was so bad nobody would listen to it all the way through.

Some of the Skylarks got disgusted, and others got drafted. Eventually they came across Raoul J. Cita, also in his late teens, who wrote songs and played the piano. Talented and capable of crafting vocal arrangements, Cita took the dispirited Skylarks under his wing and started custom-writing songs for them. Then another young man who had worked with vocal groups in Virginia, Willie Winfield, moved to New York's Lower East Side, where he assembled a group he called the Harps. Through an incredibly complex series of groupings and regroupings, the Harps and the Skylarks merged, with Winfield being lead singer and Cita the piano-playing arranger.

Refortified, they tried the Apollo again, venturing their strongest song, a stunning reworking of a 1930s hit from the film *Holiday Inn*, "A Sunday Kind of Love." The audience went wild this time, and as they left the stage, a man from MGM Records handed them his card, telling them to come to his office. Nervous about making a good impression, they were rehearsing the song in the hallway when along came a man named Leo Rogers, who worked for a wing-and-a-prayer label called Bruce, after its co-owner Monte Bruce. Somehow he talked the Harps into going to his office instead, and before long, the group had inked a contract, although not as the Harps. It turned out that another group with Virginia roots living in New York and recording for Savoy across the river in Newark already had that name, so Cita suggested changing it to the Harptones, and the name stuck.

Their natural first release was "Sunday Kind of Love," and they must have been nervous about this, too, because the record opens with a corny organ before bassist Bill Brown leads the group in the intro, and in the second bar of the organ's chording, a bottle can clearly be heard shattering on the studio floor. But Willie Winfield sounds perfectly confident once the song gets underway, and the group sings sweet, if slightly avant-garde, jazzy harmonies around his lead, adding some truly unconventional cadences at the song's end. Possibly because it was Bruce's first release and the label had not picked up the sort of major-league distribution it needed, or possibly because this was not a type of music that appealed to older or more rural blacks, the record didn't sell nearly in proportion to its influence, which was immense. For the next decade, "Sunday Kind of Love" was one of the songs to beat, one of the numbers any vocal group would use to show off its chops. It didn't hurt that it was a slow, sensual number, a "grind," as some called it, essential for dances.

Yet, despite the kind of harmonies it introduced, "Sunday Kind of Love" was still an old-fashioned number. There was another style being perfected on the streetcorners, one that was a little more complex and a little more silly simultaneously. The key was the use of nonsense syllables, very often in the bass but occasionally in other parts and sometimes even as a major feature of the song. Nonsense syllables began to abound in 1954: The Crows had had a smash in 1954 with "Gee," which started out with the group chanting the chords to the syllables *dit-dit-duh-dit-dit*. Clyde McPhatter and the Drifters sang "Bip Bam." Shirley Gunter and the Queens, one of the first girl groups, sang "Oop Shoop," and the Chords tried to follow "Sh-Boom" with "Zippity Zum." And then there was the way Otis Williams belted out the *no no no no no no no* part of the Charms' "Hearts of Stone," which under Syd Nathan's ministrations became 1954's second-biggest-selling rhythm-and-blues record.*

Vocal group music was sweeping all the large Northern cities. New York was probably the biggest source, but Chicago had the Moonglows, a stupendously talented group that had caught Alan Freed's ear and signed with him for management; as well as the Spaniels, whose "Goodnite, Sweetheart, Goodnite," with its *di-di-dih, di-dah* bass hook, became a huge hit in 1954. Detroit boasted Nolan Strong and the Diablos, whose specialty was far-out harmony and mood pieces like "The Wind." Los Angeles had the Penguins, who released a simple ballad, "Earth Angel," on newcomer Dootsie Williams's DooTone label in October 1955. "Earth Angel" was a nice, relaxed ballad, a perfect slow-dance song, and it became the first

---

*There is a wonderful legend about "Hearts of Stone" that has Syd Nathan, who has just heard the song from a plugger, wandering over to his office window to mull over which King act should record it, when he spies a bunch of black kids at the baseball diamond across the street. In no time, the story continues, he goes out and recruits them to sing it. A famous story, but a false one: Williams had sung on demos and was pestering Nathan to record him as a country singer, a wish he was finally granted in the late 1960s.

rhythm-and-blues record on an indie label to hit the pop charts, reaching number eight early in 1955.

None of this surprised Alan Freed, of course. In May 1954, he had drawn over 10,000 moondoggers to the Newark Armory for a gala show with a fairly high ticket price of $2 and had had to turn thousands away. According to *Billboard*, most of the attendees were between fifteen and twenty years old—teenagers!—and about 20 percent of them were white. Shortly thereafter, Freed announced that he'd had it with the hassles of armory shows and would present his next New York–area concert at Ebbets Field in Brooklyn, home of the Dodgers. The show would feature the Clovers, the Dominoes, the Orioles, Count Basie's Orchestra and Buddy Johnson's Orchestra (partially for accompaniment and partially because teen taste wasn't all slanted toward the new music), and six "combos," or self-contained acts, including Fats Domino, Muddy Waters, and Little Walter.

Then, in July, Freed made his most daring move of all: After toying with the idea of offering his services to the networks,* he signed a contract with an independent radio station, WINS, 1010 AM in New York City. The deal included a salary of around $75,000, plus Freed got to keep his syndication rights. It was the largest sum ever paid to an R&B jock by an indie station, and he would be working six nights a week from 11 P.M. to 2 A.M., howling, beating an even thicker Manhattan phone book, and probably able to afford an even better brand of Scotch. His farewell show in Ohio, at the Akron Armory, the site of his early triumphs, drew a capacity crowd of 3,100, a third of whom were white teenagers, to see Joe Turner, Faye Adams, Al Savage, the Joe Morris Orchestra, the Five Keys, Joe Cooper, and the old Moondog himself, broadcasting live on WJW from the giant rhythm-and-blues party for the last time in the state where he rose to fame.

Freed's move to New York proved that rhythm and blues had gone big time, and it would also give the music a new name. It came about because of Louis Hardin, a six-and-a-half-foot-tall blind white street musician, who dressed like a Viking and wrote serious compositions that chamber groups played in New York—compositions he had copyrighted under his pseudonym, Moondog. When Alan Freed came to WINS, Hardin/Moondog was outraged, and he filed suit to keep Freed from using the name. In December 1954, Hardin won his case, and so Freed changed the name of his air shift from "The Moondog Show" to "The Rock and Roll Show," and his big holiday special became the "Rock and Roll Jubilee." Freed then set about trying to copyright that term, but he found out quickly that he couldn't and would just have to make sure people associated it with him.

Rock and roll. It was perfect. It was a way of distinguishing the new

*Freed very likely discarded the idea after investigating the state of network radio: A survey later that year concluded it'd be gone by 1956, and that the only reason the networks stayed alive was that their television affiliates were pumping in the desperately needed cash.

rhythm and blues from just plain blues and the old, corny Mills Brothers style. After all, rock and roll didn't fit into any of the old categories, and it was a way of saying that Fats Domino had more in common with Bill Haley than he did with Wynonie Harris, that Elvis Presley had more in common with Ray Charles than he did with Ernest Tubb. As 1954 drew to a close, the old guard stood puzzled, trying to figure out what was going on. And since the explosion of new styles was so unprecedented, they can be forgiven their confusion.

At this point in its evolution, it was really a lot easier to say what rock and roll was *not* than to say what it *was*, although a lot of teenagers might have been willing to try. However indefinable it seemed, the groundwork had been laid for a teen-oriented, rhythm-and-blues-based music with country elements. If it met those criteria, the chances were good that it was rock and roll.

8

ROCK AND ROLL IS BORN

As 1955 dawned, a solitary figure stood looking out the second-floor window of his home in Oak Park, Illinois. Dr. Charles A. Lauhead had been dismissed from his teaching position at the University of Michigan by colleagues who refused to believe that he had heard voices from outer space, telling him that a giant tidal wave would sweep over the Midwest, engulfing it and ending life there, and that the world would be destroyed shortly thereafter. What he didn't know was that there would be a wave, but it would not be of water, and that far from destroying life on Earth, it would enhance it for many. But as the year progressed, parents across the country would come to regard some of their children as if they were space aliens, so strange would their behavior become.

The shift may have begun sometime during the night that changed 1954 to 1955, when Don Robey got a phone call from the great New Year's Eve extravaganza at Houston's City Auditorium. The show was loaded with Duke and Peacock blues artists, including Willie Mae Thornton and Johnny Ace. Johnny Ace was backstage waiting to go on, showing off to the ladies like any twenty-five-year-old who'd had eight straight hits on eight straight releases and knew that the world was his for the taking. Johnny liked guns, and he traveled with some all the time. He wasn't afraid of them, and to prove it, he took one of his favorites, a cheap and gaudy .22 made in Italy, stuck it in his mouth, and pulled the trigger. Apparently he realized there was one bullet in the gun, but he may not have known where it was. As the news of his death spread through the auditorium, hysteria broke out, especially among the women. In the months to come, a cult would develop, an eerie, almost pathological devotion to the memory of the late singer. These teenagers almost celebrated death.

Then, nine months later, a young actor named James Dean would die, and since the phenomenon would occur among white teenagers, it would get some attention in the press. To have achieved death became something of an honor, a point of fascination, among teens. There wasn't anything particularly ghoulish about it, either; death, being inevitable, became somehow "cool," for after all, two of the hippest people around, Johnny Ace and James Dean, had already crossed to the other side.

There were those who said that Johnny Ace was riding high and would never have committed suicide, or even taken such a risk. There were rumors that he had gone off, cocky, and signed a contract with another record company, since Don Robey was known to be less than meticulous when it came to contracts, and more than likely, Ace's would have been easy to break. There was one particularly appalling story that had a hired assassin squeezing in through the bathroom window in the backstage area, walking out of the bathroom toward a group of people playing cards—a group that included Willie Mae Thornton and Johnny Ace—grabbing Ace from behind, sticking a gun in his mouth, firing it, and wrapping the corpse's fingers around it, confident that although the other card players recognized him, they knew better than to squeal and that the irregular death of a black man would hardly warrant notice by Houston police. These stories circulated because of other, more easily documented irregularities concerning Don Robey and his treatment of the artists who toiled on what was basically a plantation named Duke-Peacock Records, where a contract—unlike those signed at Atlantic or Aladdin—could be a lifetime thing.

The stories also made the rounds because Johnny Ace had died leaving a glorious song in the can, "Pledging My Love," that would very likely have been his greatest moment. It was a classic ballad with a simple melody and minimal arrangement—the perennial hit formula. Within a few days of Ace's death, "Pledging My Love" was firmly entrenched on top of the rhythm-and-blues charts and was being covered by a veritable swarm of pop artists.

Cover versions were very definitely the ants at the increasingly sumptuous rhythm-and-blues picnic. "Earth Angel," for all its pop success, was chased up and down the charts the whole time by the Crew Cuts' version, which briefly outranked it.* Some thought the covers vogue was a fad, among them Hugo and Luigi, as the duo who ran Mercury's East Coast A&R operation called themselves, probably figuring that nobody could pronounce their last names. They announced in March that after "Dance With

---

*The Crew Cuts' version did better on the record sales charts, that is; the Penguins more than held their own on the jukebox charts, which were more likely to show what the teens were listening to.

Me Henry (Wallflower)," Georgia Gibbs's cover of an Etta James tune that was itself a cleaned-up version of "Work With Me, Annie," her Nibs would record no more R&B covers because the trend was dying. La Vern Baker, at least, was probably relieved.

But other rhythm-and-blues indie labels considered covers a life-threatening menace. After all, it had been predicted that records were going to gross $325 million in 1955, and it was discovered that $25 million of the record sales in 1954 had been R&B records. And by mid-March 1955, thirteen of the top thirty pop songs were either R&B records or covers of R&B material. If those covers, on labels with much bigger promotional budgets, got better sales and airplay than the originals, the indie geese laying those particular golden eggs were going to starve to death. Short of enacting legislation—and that didn't seem too likely—the solution would have to lie in coming up with hit music that people like the Crew Cuts and Georgia Gibbs couldn't possibly copy.

Atlantic Records, with its remarkable chart success, was a particular target for raids. Over at King, Syd Nathan had even ordered Carl Lebow, his A&R head, to spare no effort to find the Atlantic songwriter who seemed to have the winning formula—how many Nugetres could there be in New York, anyway? So Lebow called Atlantic, where some patient soul suggested he spell Nugetre backward, and Lebow probably spent the rest of the afternoon wondering how he could break the news to Syd without losing his job.

Phil and Leonard Chess, while not immune, were not as troubled by cover problems. For them, 1955 had started with "Sincerely," a medium-tempo number chasing "Earth Angel" around the charts, both in the Moonglows' rhythm-and-blues hit on Chess and the McGuire Sisters' cover on Coral—but then, they owned part of the publishing rights, the other part belonging to "co-author" Alan Freed. The Chess brothers knew that they had a gold mine as long as Southern people loved blues and kept emigrating to the North, where their homesickness made them buy records and their good jobs ensured that they could afford them in quantity. Hardly a week had gone by in *Billboard* when Muddy Waters or Little Walter didn't have an R&B chart item, and even the records that didn't chart—by artists like Howlin' Wolf and Sonny Boy Williamson, who were a little too raw for the New York and L.A. stations, except late at night—sold respectably. Chess had raided a mediocre R&B group, the Big Three Trio (which had recorded unsuccessfully on Columbia since 1945), for its rotund bassist, Willie Dixon, who became the label's chief songwriter. Dixon created a pool of excellent material Chess could offer to its artists, all owned by the brothers' publishing firm, Arc Music.

And they maintained a very admirable open-door policy when it came to aspiring stars. Take Ellas McDaniels. Born in Mississippi, he'd moved to Chicago as a child, where he became a boxer in his teens. Despite his size, success eluded him in boxing, and he soon quit to get married and start hustling in his other big interest, music. As a boxer, he'd gone by the nickname he'd picked up years before, Bo Diddley,* but when he went to Okeh Records, Columbia's on-again, off-again rhythm-and-blues subsidiary, he'd presented himself as Ellas McDaniels. There he'd brought in talent from the streets of Chicago and had even produced some of it; but he couldn't interest his bosses in his own alter ego, Bo Diddley.

Finally, when Okeh closed for the umpteenth time, McDaniels as Bo Diddley approached the Chess brothers. This giant man with the huge, thick glasses must have impressed them, because in the spring of 1955, they put him in the studio with his friend Jerome Green on maracas, "Lazy" Lester Davenport on harmonica, Otis Spann from Muddy Waters's band on piano, and Frank Kirkland on drums, and let Bo Diddley loose on a rampage: *chunk-a-chunka-chunka-chunk, chunka-chunk-chunk* went the band, while McDaniels sang a "play party" tune he remembered from the South and everybody sang, "Hey, Bo Diddley" on the chorus. For the other side, they recorded a stop-time blues number loaded with sexual braggadocio and seething with menace that declared "I'm a Man," and even spelled it out—M-A-N—for those who didn't get the message. People were probably scared not to buy it, and it quickly shot onto the R&B charts.

The Chesses also valued their artists' opinions of other performers. One day in 1955, Muddy Waters walked in with an artist from far left field: Chuck Berry, a country-and-western-singing black cosmetician from St. Louis who played blues guitar. Sure, he'd done three years for armed robbery in the 1940s, but when Muddy heard him in Chicago, he knew Berry had a future in music. Fortunately, too, he was no threat to Muddy's superiority as a bluesman; indeed, Chuck Berry was as unlike Muddy Waters as he could be. Like Muddy, he was rather dark-skinned, but his features showed that he had Indian in his background. And when he was asked to play, he whipped out an old fiddle tune, "Ida Red," which had been recorded by everybody from Bob Wills to one of King's most commercial country stars, Lloyd "Cowboy" Copas.

It was Copas's version, in fact, that Berry's "Ida Red" most closely resembled, the version recorded when Copas was playing swing and hot licks, the period that produced his hit "Jamboree." But Berry had revised the song, putting Ida Red into a car and adding lyrics to the verse so that he could spit them out rapid-fire to simulate the car chase that was the song's central action. It was a freakish mixture—no wonder Capitol and Mercury had already rejected Berry—but there was something about the song that the Chesses liked. The main problem was that "Ida Red" was p.d.—public domain—it couldn't be copyrighted, and that meant no royalties. So they asked Berry to think of another title, another name for the girl in the car,

---

*The nickname came from the term for the string Mississippi children would nail to the wall and to a broomstick, plucking it and improvising rhymes as they varied the pitch by stretching and loosening it.

and his mind went back to the beauty shop in St. Louis and came up with "Maybellene."

Then the brothers dubbed a copy of "Maybellene" and gave it to Alan Freed,* who liked it enough to attach his name to the credits, along with the name of one Russel D. Fratto and—oh, yes, Charles Edward Berry. Chess released "Maybellene" in July, and in exactly four weeks, it had hit the top of the rhythm-and-blues charts—at a time when people in the industry were complaining that the glut of records had made the rhythm-and-blues market sluggish.

But that was just the beginning: Soon the record broke into the pop charts at thirteen and it hovered in the Top Ten for weeks! Cover versions—if you can imagine a cover version of "Maybellene"—by the Johnny Long Orchestra and the Ralph Marterie Orchestra, among others, sat choking on Chuck Berry's dust.

Even if Berry had had only one song, he would have been an important coup for Chess, and they needed coups, since there was a new Chicago indie challenging their turf—literally, from across the street. Vee-Jay Records was Vivian Carter Bracken, the Vee; James Bracken, her husband, the Jay; and Calvin Carter, Vivian's brother, who soon developed into a fine record producer. One advantage these three had over the Chess brothers, at least in the eyes of some, was that they were black, which made Vee-Jay not America's first black-owned indie, but certainly one of the first successful ones. What got Vee-Jay off the ground was doo-wop, the new style of harmony singing; and the Spaniels, a group they'd discovered back when the Brackens owned a record shop in Gary, Indiana, had the label's first success. Their "Goodnite, Sweetheart, Goodnite" attracted a McGuire Sisters cover but more than held its own in the marketplace, and although the Spaniels never topped that 1954 hit, they remained steady sellers.

Next came the El Dorados, a Chicago group from Englewood High who started out as the Five Stars but changed their name when they became a six-piece band. The Brackens found them at an amateur show and released a couple of not-so-successful but definitely soulful records before the uncharacteristically up-tempo "At My Front Door," which told of a "crazy little mama doll" who craved the singer so much that she was banging on his door night and day. It was a frantic workout, a perfect fast-dance record for the summer of 1955. Although it, too, got a few covers, the original made the Top Twenty pop charts easily. Like the Spaniels, the El Dorados never eclipsed their early success, but they also continued to release worthy records.

Vee-Jay acquired their third major threat by truly poaching on Chess

---

*Perhaps at the bar mitzvah of Leonard Chess's son Marshall in April, which was attended by 325 of the top names in the R&B business community, including the heads of every major label, most of the top djs, distributors, and even a couple of journalists. The Flamingos, another Chess vocal group and recent discovery, performed.

territory. Jimmy Reed was one of the scores of Mississippians transplanted to Chicago. How he eluded the Chess net is a mystery, for he was an extremely popular club attraction, hailed for his skeletal guitar work and sinuous harmonica playing, which he performed on simultaneously, thanks to a rack mount for the harmonica. The antithesis of Muddy Waters's dread, Jimmy Reed's blues were laid back and sort of happy, and when he hit in 1955 with "You Don't Have To Go," he started an unbroken string of hits for Vee-Jay that would last well into the 1960s.

As for Art Rupe, who had been concentrating on blues, he was lucky to have a stake in the new music at all. Lloyd Price was his entree into the rock-and-roll sweepstakes, and Guitar Slim's "The Things That I Used To Do" was unbluesy enough to hit the charts. But by looking at those charts, Rupe could see that his personal taste was outdated, and that if he wanted to stay in business, he'd have to cultivate some of the younger rock and roll artists. He knew who could help him—Robert "Bumps" Blackwell, who'd gone to UCLA to learn composition and then had taken a job with Specialty, producing their gospel artists and gaining the label a preeminent place in that small but important black market. Fired with Ray Charles's success—after all, Rupe had known Jack Lauderdale, and he could have bought out Charles's contract if he'd been thinking—he asked Blackwell to come up with a Ray Charles for him.

There was already a pile of tapes from various hopefuls at Specialty, and Blackwell set about going through them. "One day," he remembered nearly thirty years later, "a reel of tape, wrapped in a piece of paper looking as though someone had eaten off it, came across my desk. . . . The voice was unmistakably star material. I can't tell you how I knew, but I knew. The songs were not out-and-out gospel, but I could tell by the tone of his voice and all those churchy turns that he was a gospel singer who could sing the blues."

At first, Rupe waffled when Blackwell came raving into his office, urging him to sign "Little" Richard Penniman, but finally Bumps wore him down. Richard was still under contract to Peacock—where he'd cut some truly somnolent records with both his own band, the Tempo Toppers, and with Johnny Otis's orchestra—and going head to head with Don Robey was hardly what a struggling entrepreneur like Art Rupe wanted to do. But the singer himself approached Robey, who never knew there was another interested party, and got his contract price down to $600. Rupe wired him the money.

It was not until the first recording session, at Cosimo Matassa's J&M Studios in New Orleans, that Rupe or Blackwell ever laid eyes on their new artist. As Bumps recalled, it was a shock. "There's this cat in this loud shirt, with hair waved up six inches above his head. He was talking wild, thinking up stuff just to be different, you know? I could tell he was a mega-personality." Richard liked Fats Domino, which was encouraging, since Fats was hot, so Bumps set him up with Domino's band: Lee Allen on tenor sax, Alvin "Red" Tyler on baritone sax, Earl Palmer on drums, Edgar Blanchard and Justin Adams on guitars, Frank Fields on bass, and Huey "Piano" Smith and James Booker taking turns on the piano.

And then Richard froze. Well, not completely; after all, he was a seasoned performer at twenty-two, and he'd been making records since he was eighteen. But now it was like pulling teeth. Bumps was paying serious money for studio time and only got one keeper, "I'm Just A Lonely Guy," by Dorothy La Bostrie, a writer who had been hounding him forever. "The problem was that what he looked like and what he sounded like didn't come together," Blackwell recalled. "If you look like Tarzan and sound like Mickey Mouse it just doesn't work out . . . I didn't know what to do. I couldn't go back to Rupe with the material I had because there was nothing there that I could put out, nothing to merchandise."

Lunch break! Maybe they could get him drunk or something—anything to loosen him up. So they walked down the street to the Dew Drop Inn, a musicians' hangout, and Richard was transfigured the moment he entered the door. "We walk into the place, and the girls are there and the boys are there and he's got an audience. There's a piano, and that's his crutch. He's on stage reckoning to show Lee Allen his piano style. So *wow!* He gets to sing. He hits that piano, *dididididididididi* . . . and starts to sing, 'Awop-bop-a-loo-mop a good goddam—Tutti-Frutti, good booty. . . .'"

It was just what Blackwell had been waiting for—something that matched the image—a hit song, although filthy, that the singer had picked up somewhere along the road people travel when they're very young, homosexual, and black in the Deep South. Blackwell knew that Dorothy La Bostrie was probably still hanging around the studio, waiting to pitch yet another set of lyrics, and so they rushed back to find her. There was hardly any time to rewrite the song and then get the whole band to rehearse it and cut it—and then Richard got embarrassed to play it in front of her. Bumps explained that La Bostrie was over twenty-one, a consenting adult, she needed money to raise her kids, and finally Richard turned to the wall and pounded out the song. "Fifteen minutes before the session was to end," Blackwell recalled, "the chick comes in and puts these little trite lyrics in front of me. I put them in front of Richard. Richard says he ain't got no voice left. I said, 'Richard, you've got to sing it.'" So they reset the mikes so that Richard could sing and play simultaneously, and fifteen minutes later, they were listening to the playback:

"*Awop bop a loo mop a lop bam boom! Tutti frutti! Aw rootie!*" It sounded like Dr. Lauhead's space people had landed, and it was outrageous enough that it spent twenty weeks on the rhythm-and-blues charts, getting as high as number two, and had enough momentum to blast onto the pop charts, landing at number seventeen. Something about this weird singer's voice was affecting teenagers, that was certain.

Amazingly there were still those who thought that rock and roll was nothing but a momentary craze, something the teens would grow out of, like the Davy Crockett fad that had swept the nation in 1955. It had sprung from one of Walt Disney's "Disneyland" television shows, which, unlike his kiddie-aimed "Mickey Mouse Club," had a little something for everybody. Each week "Disneyland" would be focused on a theme—Adventureland, Fantasyland, Tomorrowland, Frontierland—and Frontierland had featured the saga of Davy Crockett, the trailblazer from Tennessee who fought bears and Indians, got elected to Congress, and went down fighting at the Alamo. A previously unknown actor named Fess Parker, clad in buckskin fringe and coonskin cap, carrying a long rifle, drawled his way through the heavily fictionalized biography, and something about the story galvanized America's children.

Soon "The Ballad of Davy Crockett," forged by authentic folk songwriters in the employ of Disney's Buena Vista Music, raced up the charts in a half-dozen versions, most bearably by Tennessee Ernie Ford. And suddenly lots of little boys got air rifles and BB guns, Davy Crockett lunch boxes, T-shirt iron-ons, and sets of action figures made out of plastic—as well as the essential Davy Crockett coonskin cap. Now, those coonskin caps were expensive, and so was much of the other merchandise that Disney licensed with Parker's picture on it. During the life of the fad, which was about six months, there were literally millions of dollars pouring into the stores to buy Davy Crockett trappings.

But there were others who continued to see rock and roll as an ominous symptom of decay. In Chicago in April 1955, fifteen thousand teenagers bombarded djs (at stations that were playing mostly pop records, if the truth be known) with letters patterned on a suggested model printed in a Catholic high school newspaper, accusing them of playing dirty records. In Boston, six djs formed a censorship board to screen new records, with the help of newspaper writers and religious leaders. In Bridgeport and New Haven, the police announced a ban on rock-and-roll dances. Bridgeport Superintendent of Police John A. Lyddy claimed his department was merely responding to the pleas of hundreds of concerned parents and noted, "Teenagers virtually work themselves into a frenzy to the beat of fast swing music" at the dances. Disc jockey Marc Jennings, at WCMI in Huntington, West Virginia, announced that "tunes like . . . 'Hearts of Stone,' 'Ko Ko Mo,' and 'Tweedle Dee' are products of the mass hysteria prevalent in our world today." That the hysteria should have reached Huntington was certainly food for thought. No doubt about it, the rock-and-roll mania was becoming an epidemic.

Even *Life* magazine devoted a few pages—albeit not as many as for the Davy Crockett fad—to the latest bit of teenage craziness. Readers were treated to pictures of a dance that spontaneously erupted (in front of a *Life* photographer, conveniently enough) in the parking lot of a suburban Los Angeles supermarket; Alan Freed with some fans; San Francisco teenagers dancing on television; Herbert Hardesty of Fats Domino's band writhing on the floor, tenor sax afly; an integrated audience in the balcony of the

Brooklyn Paramount at Alan Freed's first spectacular show, which broke all house records for attendance; New Haven's Police Chief Francis McManus warily eyeing a program for a rock-and-roll dance he'd just banned; and, as a last shot to show people it wasn't anything serious, two pictures of Arthur Murray learning how to do the dance and then teaching it to one of his classes. "Rock and roll," the text said, "is both music and dance. The music has a rhythm often heavily accented on the second and fourth beat. The dance combines the Lindy and Charleston, and almost anything else. In performing it, hollering helps and a boot banging the floor makes it even better. The overall result frequently is frenzy."

Frenzy—yes, there had been a bit of that. *Life* had reported on a new movie, *The Blackboard Jungle,* based on a novel by Evan Hunter, in which a new teacher at a high school in a "bad" section of town is taunted and abused by a group of his students (including a black one, portrayed by Sidney Poitier). Among the terrible things they do to one of his fellow teachers is mock his taste in music when he tries to reach them through playing some jazz records in class. They laugh and throw the priceless discs around the classroom as the teacher stands frozen with fright, watching his collection being smashed to bits. This disgusting bit of behavior was not lost on a lot of the teenagers who flocked to see *The Blackboard Jungle.* When the theme song, Bill Haley's not-too-successful record of 1954, "Rock Around the Clock," came on at the start of the movie, they'd dance on the seats, which were frequently not up to the chore and collapsed. Then the teenagers would throw the broken seats at each other.

This movie and others addressed to the insatiable teenage audience fed public fears of "juvenile delinquency," the disease that had teens committing senseless crimes, indulging in alcohol and cigarettes and premarital sex, riding motorcycles or driving hopped-up cars, and listening to rock and roll. First there had been *The Wild One* in 1953, in which Marlon Brando and a gang of thugs on motorcycles terrorized a town, something that had really happened in the mountains above San Bernardino, California, where a group of war veterans who had formed a motorcycle club named after a war movie, *Hell's Angels,* had just taken over for a weekend. At least the *Blackboard Jungle* kids were from the slums, so there was an excuse for their behavior. But the 1955 *Rebel Without a Cause,* based on a real case history from California psychiatrist Robert Lindner, featured teen idol James Dean sympathetically portraying a screwed-up kid who just didn't seem to care, no matter how his parents tried to steer him right. The film blasphemously seemed to be placing the blame for Dean's antisocial behavior on his parents and on society at large! It was a stretched-out exposition of Marlon Brando's famed line in *The Wild One,* when he is asked what he's rebelling against. "Whaddya got?" he replies. And teens were eating up these movies, seeing them literally dozens of times. It did no good to explain to parents that teenagers like Brando and Dean were a distinct minority, or, as President Eisenhower once put it, that "teenagers are like airplanes: You only hear about the ones that crash."

And in May 1955, it was discovered that class distinctions had nothing to do with rock and roll's ability to incite the baser passions: at Princeton University, it was reported, a student fired up "Rock Around the Clock" in his dorm room, and was answered right afterward by another student doing the same thing. Soon a mob had formed in the courtyard, chanting and stamping their feet, setting fire to trash cans as they moved beyond the halls of Old Nassau into the streets at midnight, until finally a dean was found to quell the boiling blue blood, reminding them of the dire consequences of being thrown out of Princeton.

That was the week Haley's record entered the Top Ten—*The Blackboard Jungle* was giving it new life. Down in Nashville, where Randy Woods's Dot Records was emerging as *the* pop indie to beat, Pat Boone, a young singer who had married the country star Red Foley's daughter, let himself be talked into doing a cover version of the song, and, perhaps in sympathy, black record-buyers flocked into record stores and walked out with enough copies of Haley's "Rock Around the Clock" to push the song to the number fourteen slot on the rhythm-and-blues chart. Decca Records was ecstatic: in thirteen short months, Haley had sold an incredible 3 million records. It looked like rock and roll might turn out to be bigger than Davy Crockett after all.

Now more and more black teens began harmonizing in stairwells and bathrooms at school, or on streetcorners while the early evenings were warm enough, because they suspected that if they could get good enough, there'd be a record company out there that could make them stars—and often there was. As for white Southern kids, the cat was prowling as never before. Blue jeans with the cuffs rolled up, shirts with the collars turned up, and a high-maintenance haircut with sideburns all conspired to tell the world they meant business.

In New York, there was Alan Freed's back-to-school show at the Brooklyn Paramount the week of September 2, featuring Tony Bennett, the Harptones, Nappy Brown, the Moonglows, the Red Prysock band, and for the first time anywhere outside the blues circuit in the Midwest, Chuck Berry. What an amazing thing it must have been to see Berry for the first time, with his pencil-thin mustache and elaborately curled hair, his full drape jacket and tight slacks, take his guitar (slung at crotch level, as all the rhythm-and-blues guitarists had been doing in imitation of Lowman Pauling of the "5" Royales), point it out at a right angle to his body, and, while he played a tricky but repetitive riff, execute a strange walk across the Paramount stage, bobbing his head and squatting, looking for all the world like a duck!

That week Freed sailed way past his previous house record at the Brooklyn Paramount, grossing $154,000, netting $125,000 for him to split with the promoter, Morris Levy, and WINS. Figuring that the cost of renting the theater for a week and the salaries of all the theater employees came out of the $29,000 left over, one can only guess at the pittance paid to the performers. No wonder rhythm-and-blues package shows were on the road all over America, all the time!

And not just rhythm-and-blues shows, either. Elvis, Scotty, and Bill were touring, too, trying to capitalize on the success of their second Sun single, "I Don't Care If the Sun Don't Shine" b/w "Good Rockin' Tonight," which *Billboard's* reviewer noted was somewhere between country and rhythm and blues and pop, and probably headed for great things. The record didn't sell very well, actually, but it ensured Elvis a spot as a regular on the "Louisiana Hayride," and it was a big enough hit in Texas to warrant a stop. The tour started out fine: they conquered Dallas at the Sportatorium and were treated like heroes, but a few nights later, they were at Dessau Hall, just northeast of Austin, playing to a much more traditionally oriented audience, and the crowd hated them. Between sets, Kenneth Threadgill, a local filling-station owner who liked to pick Jimmie Rodgers tunes on his guitar and yodel, was in the parking lot going to his pickup truck when he heard an odd sound. He followed the sound to its source, and found Elvis sobbing his heart out. "What's the matter?" the older man asked. The youngster looked at him pitifully and said, "They don't *like* me, sir. I don't know what to do." Mr. Threadgill pointed his bottle at Elvis, offering him a sip, but the young singer declined. "Well, now, you've got something a little different, son, and sometimes it takes people a little time to get used to it. But keep it up. I think you'll do all right." Elvis thanked the old man and headed back into the hall to do the next set.

Threadgill's speech may have had a heartening effect on Elvis, because he certainly played with a fury when he hit Lubbock a few nights later. The Cotton Club, Lubbock's only real nightclub, booked everybody from Duke Ellington and B. B. King to Bob Wills, and among the fans who turned out for Elvis was Charles Hardin "Buddy" Holley, a bespectacled young singer and guitarist, and his partner Bob Montgomery, who, as Buddy and Bob, played plenty of R&B in their "western and bop" act. Holley thought Elvis was great, and when they saw that between the sets, Elvis was just sitting in a corner nursing a Coke, Buddy and Bob went over to tell him how much they liked his music and how often it was requested at their live shows.

Buddy was impressed with Elvis's politeness, telling his manager, Hipockets Duncan, "You know, he's a real nice, friendly fellow." And he asked Duncan to get the Buddy and Bob act added to the grand opening of a Pontiac dealership the next day because Elvis was going to play it. Elvis probably had to: the Cotton Club gig netted him, Scotty, and Bill a total of $35, and on the way out of the club, Elvis was confronted by a few Lubbock lads who didn't like the way the Memphian had stirred up their girlfriends. It's still a matter of dispute whether blows were traded, but it was not a friendly encounter.

But incidents like that were becoming less frequent. By July 1955, Elvis Presley would settle in for a long stay on the country charts with "I'm Left, You're Right, She's Gone" and "Baby, Let's Play House," which was joined shortly thereafter by "Mystery Train" and "I Forgot to Remember to Forget." By the end of the summer he had gone big-time, touring on a package show with Hank Snow, the Louvin Brothers, and Cowboy Copas and clearly dominating the proceedings. As promoter Sherrif Tex Davis, who also had a radio show on WCMS in Norfolk, Virginia, wrote to *Billboard*, "The whole gang was great, as usual, but the teenagers went wild when Elvis went into his act. The girls mobbed him afterward and literally tore him apart for souvenirs." It was Hank Snow's manager, "Colonel" Tom Parker, who engineered this genius bill, and a month after that tour ended, he assembled another involving Hank Snow and Bill Haley, with Hank's son, Jimmie Rodgers Snow, and Elvis joining for the last leg of the tour. Elvis and Bill Haley on one stage? It's likely the Colonel had no problem selling out those shows.

But the real product was records. By 1955, it was becoming clearer that Americans were enjoying entertainment as never before; that they were spending more money on it than ever; and that for the first time, the home was becoming a major entertainment venue. Television, a novelty three short years before, had become an appliance as common as the refrigerator, with variety shows like Jackie Gleason's and Ed Sullivan's presenting the talent that network radio used to provide—only now you could see the performers. And nearly every home had a phonograph, whether it was a little fold-up child's model, a record changer that attached with a jack to the television set, or a large console. Some people—people with money—were indulging in the new "high-fidelity" craze, which required an investment of thousands of dollars in amplifiers, preamplifiers, FM tuners, and speakers with funny names like woofers and tweeters, as well as tape recorders. There was no denying that sound had made a quantum leap in five years, especially considering the advances being made with microgroove recording and long-playing records. By 1955, although most manufacturers were still making 78s for customers who hadn't changed over or wouldn't change over, they were becoming more expensive specialty items, and by June 1955, the ten-inch LP was on its way out, too, as Columbia shifted completely to albums, along with 45s, and the other majors soon followed suit.

Despite these new scientific advances, most R&B labels stuck to the singles format, and by 1955, that meant 45s. Most—but not Atlantic. Atlantic was going like a house afire, with Ray Charles, the Clovers, the Drifters, Ruth Brown, and La Vern Baker having at least one record on the charts at all times, and the hyperactive imaginations of Wexler and Ertegun finding new creative outlets. They'd recorded New Orleans jazzman Wilber de Paris in "binaural" sound, even though there weren't many record players capable of handling this two-channel innovation, and captivated by the idea of albums, they set the industry on its ear by announcing that they would actually release some rhythm-and-blues albums in the fall. A lot of their steady accounts wouldn't touch the idea: except for items like Duke's *Johnny Ace Memorial Album*, rhythm and blues was a singles market only, they insisted, and anyway, it might be a dying trend. But the Atlantic albums sold respectably.

Then Atlantic came up with another nutty plan: They broke up their most successful group. Clyde McPhatter had been stationed near enough New York that he could visit Atlantic and cut records with the Drifters, but Atlantic also experimented with recording him solo and doing duets with Ruth Brown. These collaborations worked, so Atlantic pulled him from the group and set about finding a replacement in Little David Baughan, a singer from Harlem who sounded uncannily like Clyde. When McPhatter came out of the army in 1956, they'd have his solo career mapped out for him.

Next up was reorganizing the company to welcome Herb Abramson home from his two-year stint in the Army Dental Corps. The Cat label hadn't been particularly successful lately—the Chords had changed their name to the Sh-Booms, proof positive that the public was beginning to forget about them—so Atlantic took that label and the skeleton of a structure for another label they'd been thinking of starting and dubbed it Atco. Atco was an ideal niche for the returning soldier who had missed out on Atlantic's rise to glory, and Wexler and Ertegun turned it over to him to run. For dessert, Atlantic took over the masters from Leiber and Stoller's Spark label, since they'd scored a hit with the young songwriters' "Smokey Joe's Café," a rollicking tale of chili beans and lust south of the border that the Robins had recorded, and nothing else on Spark had amounted to much. Leiber and Stoller seemed to be coming into their own, so it was good to have them aboard.

Maybe the rock and roll phenomenon *wasn't* going to disappear as fast as some people thought. Ed Sullivan, respected columnist for the New York *Daily News*, with his own television program "The Toast of the Town" (the same name as his column) drawing a huge viewing audience on Sunday nights, had begun inviting these acts onto his show. Not only that, he hired Tommy "Dr. Jive" Smalls to give the audience a fifteen-minute taste of the shows he'd been doing in Harlem. Dr. Jive was up to the challenge and got some hard-core entertainment into his segment, too: La Vern Baker, Bo Diddley, the Five Keys, and tenor honker Willis Jackson's Orchestra.

The show came off well, but there was one hitch: Sullivan's producer had spotted Bo Diddley and thought, aha! A guy with a guitar! The fastest rising song in the country—in fact, the fastest-rising song in the history of the American record business—was "Sixteen Tons," which had been written in the mid-1940s by the fingerpicking guitar whiz Merle Travis and had just been recorded by Tennessee Ernie Ford. Sullivan hadn't been able to corral Tennessee Ernie for an appearance on the show, but the producer figured Diddley would do—like the rest of the entertainment establishment, he still thought it was the *song*, not the performer, that mattered. At first, Mr.

Diddley insisted that he didn't know "Sixteen Tons." So the producers sat down with some members of the studio orchestra and the production crew and went over it with him. Just to make sure he got it right, they wrote the words down on big cue cards in big letters, in deference to his bad eyes. Everything was set for the live broadcast, and Dr. Jive introduced the guitar slinger, who blithely strolled onstage and performed—"Bo Diddley." As he strutted offstage, he was met by the production staff en masse, who demanded an explanation. "Man, maybe that was 'Sixteen Tons' on those cards," he drawled, "but all I saw was 'Bo Diddley!'" Coke-bottle lenses, you know . . .

Those unpredictable rock and rollers! Why would anybody want to work with them? The answer came along the first week of December 1955.

DOUBLE DEALS HURL PRESLEY INTO STARDOM, screamed the front page of *Billboard*. THE BIG TIME AT 19. "In practically all of 1955 there were negotiations of some sort going on," Elvis's manager during the Sun years, Bob Neal, told Jerry Hopkins. "Some people thought I had an interest in Sun, and I'd get a call from some company asking, can we buy the Presley contract, how much is it? I'd say, 'Let me see, I'll check with Sam Phillips and let you know.' I know when it started off we would have taken only four or five thousand dollars, but I recall one time later when Mitch Miller, who was with Columbia, called me. We were out on a tour in Texas and he said, 'How much is the contract?' I said I'd check. By that time Sam was asking eighteen or twenty thousand. I called Mitch back and he said, 'Forget it. No artist is worth that kind of money.'"

Then Ahmet Ertegun stepped in with an offer of $25,000. "That was everything we had, including my desk," he told Hopkins. But Colonel Parker, who had induced Elvis's parents to sign a document allowing him to negotiate on Elvis's behalf—something Neal didn't quite feel up to, since he'd gone overnight from being a country disc jockey in Memphis to being the manager of the biggest artist since World War II—was holding out for something like $45,000, a ridiculous, totally unprecedented figure.

Setting up shop at the Hotel Warwick in New York, Parker started talking to some of his old friends at RCA Victor, whom he knew from his days of managing Eddy Arnold and Hank Snow, both Victor artists. After all, if anybody had the money, it would very likely be RCA. The company was in the virtually unique position of being affiliated with a giant corporation, of which the record division was only a small part—and RCA Whirlpool was selling a lot of refrigerators in 1955. But Parker was even cannier than that: He also began negotiations with Hill & Range, a publishing company that was buying up the catalogs of many country and western songwriters, in an effort to get Elvis his own publishing deal, independent of the record deal, which was even more unusual than the $45,000 asking price for his contract.

It was a huge gamble, and the Colonel had set it up as an all-or-nothing situation. Either they'd wind up on RCA Victor with an independent publishing deal or they'd be on Sun—which was having problems, even then, getting Elvis Presley records into the stores. But the Colonel was a gambling man, and this time he hit the jackpot. Sam Phillips flew up to New York for the final rounds of negotiations and flew back to Memphis with $35,000 in cash for Elvis's unexpired Sun contract, the rights to all his previously recorded material, and a $5,000 bonus when Elvis signed. Sun could fill back orders for records until January 1956, after which they had to turn over the master tapes to RCA Victor, who would renegotiate the deal three years hence. In addition, Hill & Range agreed to establish Elvis Presley Music, which would split publisher's royalties fifty-fifty on anything Elvis recorded for a period of five years. As a topper, Hill and Range bought Hi-Lo Music, a publishing house Sam had started to publish Sun artists' works, including several of Elvis's hits, and agreed to publish a portfolio of Elvis's sheet music as soon as they could set the type—if that couldn't pull the sheet-music business out of the doldrums, nothing could.

The industry was agog. When the amazing deal was struck, Elvis had just been voted Most Promising Country and Western Artist by the annual Country and Western Disc Jockey Convention, and the fan magazine *Country And Western Jamboree* had named him Best New Male Singer. But the word from RCA was nothing short of revolutionary: whereas Sun had pushed Elvis as a country artist, RCA announced they were going to break him as an all-market performer—pop, country, R&B—even though Steve Sholes, who would oversee the recording process, said they'd be using the same instrumentation as had been on his Sun hits: electric lead guitar, Elvis on acoustic rhythm guitar, string bass, and drums.

The very fact that RCA thought they could sell Elvis to everybody meant that they were thinking along the same lines as Sam Phillips: that the day had finally arrived when an artist who combined elements from each field would appeal to everyone—urban and rural, black and white—embodying a fusion that had been building since the days of Jimmie Rodgers (himself an RCA artist), Bob Wills, and Nat "King" Cole. But to the industry at that time, it seemed clear that this bumbling giant, this major label that had been ignoring the rhythm-and-blues and rock-and-roll explosion, had lost its corporate mind.

But then again, maybe everybody had. Alan Freed announced that he was going to star in a movie called *Rock Around the Clock* and lead an eighteen-piece band in the sanctum sanctorum of New York jazzdom, Birdland. He would be featured on trombone. His uptown counterpart, Dr. Jive, bought Small's Paradise, the legendary Harlem nightclub, from owner Edwin Smalls (no relation) and announced an all-R&B booking policy, even though he must have realized that teenagers couldn't drink and rarely frequented nightclubs. Decca went ahead and ignored cooler heads by releasing Bill Haley and His Comets' album *Rock Around the Clock*, which seemed as foolish as Atlantic's R&B album release. Sun Records, in its second coup of the year, won a lawsuit against Don Robey for inducing

Junior Parker away from them despite a legally binding contract, and the judge made Robey pay not only the amount of the unexpired contract but damages as well. And at the year-end BMI awards, the publishing organization noted that sixteen of the twenty-eight songs cited for generating the most income over the year were R&B tunes, and two of them, "Sincerely" and "Maybellene," were co-written by Alan Freed.

The statisticians were out in force, analyzing the year's developments. An outfit called Teen-Age Surveys, Inc., reported that teenagers still liked rock and roll, and that the slight decline in popularity of R&B detected in their poll was "insufficient to justify any claims that it is waning in popularity." They also advised America's churches to get hip and put some rock and roll into their programs for teenagers, since the teens were beginning to perceive church as, well, a little square. Kay Starr released something called "Rock and Roll Waltz," and any radio that wasn't exhorting you to buy early for Christmas was screaming "*A wop bop a loo mop a lop bam boom!*" Maybe Dr. Lauhead's space people had landed after all.

9

Don't Lose That Kid

RCA's huge expenditure and radical marketing plans for Elvis had two immediate major effects on the industry. First, they sent a signal to everyone that a major label thought it had found a rock and roll singer who had the potential to become as large a popular-music phenomenon as Perry Como or Frank Sinatra, and that they were willing to invest heavily in such a person. Second, it proved to a whole generation of young performers with country backgrounds but an interest in rhythm and blues that they, too, had a chance to be heard.

In the wake of Elvis's signing, country music essentially split into rockabilly—the name that was eventually applied to the mutant rock-and-roll hillbilly music—and straight country. Rockabillies followed Elvis's lead, and the straight country singers followed Hank Williams and the other classic performers. Of course, that's oversimplifying things a bit: There were plenty of shades of gray in between.

For example, the mutated country-and-western way Buddy Holley and Bob Montgomery played was completely different from what the cats in Memphis were evolving. Most of the songs Buddy and Bob sang (and wrote—Montgomery was and is a prolific songwriter) were patterned on the country-and-western "brother" style that had been around since the Blue Sky Boys started recording in the 1930s, and that was reaching its apogee in the early 1950s with Johnnie and Jack, the Delmore Brothers, and the Louvin Brothers. From what we can hear under the horrible overdubbing that was later imposed upon the recordings Buddy and Bob made in Wichita Falls and Lubbock in 1954 and 1955, their guitar work was pretty much four-square country picking, with little flash and a good deal of solid

114

chording, with their friend Sonny Curtis helping out with some typical West Texas fiddle work.

Buddy and Bob sang in thirds, with Buddy taking the solo leads, but it was not their country sound that made them so popular with the teenage crowd in Lubbock, Texas. Lubbock was a city set out in the middle of absolutely nowhere, a place so ordinary that it could be anywhere. And their anybody-from-anywhere quality gave Buddy and Bob their edge in the record business.

They were discovered in Lubbock by Eddie Crandall, talent scout for Decca Records, on October 14, 1955, performing on the Hank Snow/Bill Haley tour that Elvis would join later. The act Crandall caught featured their rock and roll sets, with less of Bob's country sounds, and he saw them again two weeks later, when an act he managed, Marty Robbins, played Lubbock.* When they all headed over to the Cotton Club for an all-night picking session, Crandall stayed in the background, watching; and finally, in December, when he got back to Nashville, he wrote KDAV's owner, Dave Stone, a letter that said: "I'm very confident I can do something as far as getting Buddy Holly a recording contract. It may not be a major, but even a small one would be beneficial to someone who is trying to get a break." He'd misspelled Buddy's last name (originally Holley)—something Buddy would have to get used to—but he followed up with a telegram asking Stone to cut four demo tapes at the station, where their manager, Hipockets Duncan, was a dj. Most important, on the telegram, he counseled Stone: "Don't change his style at all."

Armed with demos, Crandall started hitting the few record companies that had Nashville offices. RCA was occupied with Elvis, so they were out; Columbia was concentrating on mainstream country acts like Carl Smith and Lefty Frizzell and didn't need anything left field; so that left Decca, where Paul Cohen knew that if a thirty-year-old fat guy with a spitcurl could sell two million records, probably an eighteen-year-old with glasses could, too. Crandall left the negotiations to Jim Denny, an "Opry" booker, and before long Buddy got a phone call. It left him with mixed emotions, because Denny had told him, when he'd inquired about Bob Montgomery, "Well, you can bring him along if you want, but he can't sing on the records. We want one singer, not two." Since Buddy had been responsible for most of the rock-and-roll numbers in the set, that couldn't have been much of a surprise, but they'd been together for a long time, and for a while, Buddy considered refusing the contract if Bob wasn't included. Finally he talked it out with Bob, who said, according to Buddy's mother, "You've got your chance—now go ahead!" Contrary to their mean-spirited depiction in the 1978 movie *The Buddy Holly Story,* Buddy's parents always completely supported their son's musical aspirations.

---

*Robbins recorded "That's All Right" a few months after Elvis, with guitar work that copied Scotty Moore's pretty carefully.

So, in January, Buddy went off to Nashville, and on the twenty-sixth, he cut four tracks at Decca's studio with his friend Sonny Curtis helping out on second guitar. One cut was the latest in the "Annie" songs—although one the Midnighters had probably never heard—"Midnight Shift," with the shocking opening lines, "If you see ol' Annie, give her a lift/Cuz Annie's been a-workin' on the midnight shift."

It was a flat-out rockabilly song, although the term was about a year away from becoming common currency. But it typified the fact that the lines dividing pop, country, and rhythm and blues had been blurring for a long, long time, and now the industry was trying to puzzle it out. Addicted to labels, industry pundits had been confused when "Crying in the Chapel" did well in both country and R&B versions. In November 1955, *Billboard* had editorialized about the increasing fusion between country and rhythm and blues—and not only the fusion, but the very real empathy that supposedly country performers had for rhythm-and-blues material. There were also anomalous black performers who drew inspiration from country music—Chuck Berry was the best example—although at this point the most noticeable fusion was in the country field.

Elvis, of course, was the foremost example of country boy playing R&B. Now he was making his television debut on Tommy and Jimmy Dorsey's CBS-TV variety program, "Stage Show." It was being produced by Jackie Gleason, who had decided to steal a march on the competition, "The Perry Como Show," by booking Elvis Presley, whom Gleason saw as "the guitar-playing Marlon Brando."

But on January 28, when the Dorseys presented Elvis, nobody noticed. Although Elvis's sales had been very healthy so far, they had been largely in the South and Midwest, and sophisticated New York teens probably couldn't be bothered with this greasy hillbilly singer. The theater was less than half-full, and although Elvis's name was on the marquee outside, teenagers walked right past it to get to a nearby skating rink. Onstage, Elvis was a little nervous, especially when dj Bill Randle introduced him as "a young fellow who, like many performers, Johnnie Ray among them, come up out of nowhere to become, overnight, very big stars," and went on to opine, "We think tonight he will be making television history for you: Elvis Presley, and here he is!"

And there he was, first singing a medley of Joe Turner songs, "Shake, Rattle and Roll" and "Flip Flop and Fly," during which Scotty Moore fluffed the entire guitar part so badly that you can almost hear him melting with embarrassment, and then "I Got a Woman," the Ray Charles hit. It's obvious that the applause was turned way up during the instrumental breaks (Scotty did better on the second song) and that it largely came in response to the lit-up "Applause" sign. Two songs, and then off. Elvis must have been relieved. But the torture wasn't over: He'd be back next week, and the week after that.

He'd come to New York to start recording for RCA Victor at their studios, to produce enough material so that Victor could release an LP if they should deem it necessary. He'd already cut his next single over the Christmas holidays in Nashville, a gruesome ditty called "Heartbreak Hotel," which schoolteacher and songwriter Mae Boren Axton had composed after a friend had showed her a newspaper story about a young man who had killed himself, leaving only a note that read, "I walk a lonely street." He also cut "I Want You, I Need You, I Love You" and "I Was the One" at that session; and the Monday after the first Dorsey show, he recorded Carl Perkins's "Blue Suede Shoes," something called "So Glad You're Mine," and another Arthur Crudup tune, "My Baby Left Me." Later in the week, he added three hot rhythm-and-blues numbers, "Tutti-Frutti," "Lawdy Miss Clawdy," and "Shake, Rattle and Roll." Elvis had brought the South with him like a basket of his mother's fried chicken—he knew where he was coming from, even if nobody could imagine where he was going.

And as "Heartbreak Hotel" climbed the charts and Elvis peered out from black-and-white televisions across the country, was Sam Phillips wringing his hands and crying tears of bitter regret? "If I've been asked once," he said to Robert Palmer on one occasion, "I must have been asked a thousand times, did I ever regret it? No, I didn't, I do not, and I never will." It wasn't a matter of altruism. A blockbuster could kill an independent label—for instance, the Beatles would sink Vee-Jay some fifteen years hence. The whole economic structure of a record company is based on distributor payments, and in order to get major distributors like Sam's, Big State in Dallas, a label had to offer them attractive terms, such as allowing them to return unsold records for credit and letting them hold on to wares for up to ninety days without paying a cent. Meanwhile, the label would need money to keep pressing and shipping records, and if a record got hot, that could mean a huge sum. Of course, many distributors were less than honest about sales figures, and during the 1950s, some even pressed and sold bootleg or counterfeit copies, sending the legitimate records back, especially but not solely to indies. By the time the big profits started rolling in, a label owner could very well have sold everything he owned to amass the capital to keep pressing—literally starving his company to death with success.

So the $40,000 RCA paid for Elvis assured that Sun had a future, that Sam could afford to experiment and fail. Even better, the Presley phenomenon had put Sun on the map, and Sam had ambitious cats crawling in the windows. Now he was beginning to record some more left-field country material, like "Cry Cry Cry" and "Hey Porter" by a gravel-voiced baritone from Arkansas named Johnny Cash, whose minimal instrumentation — muffled guitar, bass, and light drums—served as a perfect foil for his deep voice. But Cash was straight country.

Closer to his original vision was a performer Sam signed from Tennessee who looked to outcat all the cats: Carl Perkins. Talk about a white man with a colored sound! Carl Perkins and his brothers had grown up as sons of a sharecropper near Tiptonville, Tennessee, right where Arkansas, Missouri, and Tennessee twist around each other in the state's northwest corner. It was definitive white-trash country, hillbilly, even, and yet Perkins and his brothers had grown up being the only white kids on the farm. Carl listened to the "Opry" like everybody else, white and black, and, fascinated, started playing on a homemade guitar as a child. Pretty soon his brothers Clayton and Jay B. took up playing, too, and the Perkins Brothers Band became a triple threat at local dances and on their show on WTJS in Jackson.

Soon they added a drummer, W. S. "Fluke" Holland, and they began working steadily, playing country music, of course. But none of them could shake the environment of their youth. Carl admitted that he "liked Bill Monroe's fast stuff and also the colored guys, John Lee Hooker, Muddy Waters, their electric stuff. Even back then I liked to do Hooker's things Monroe-style, blues with a country beat and my own lyrics." And after Carl heard Elvis, he realized, "It was identical to what our band was doing and I just knew that we could make it in the record business after that."

Of course, nobody in the record business seemed to agree, but that didn't bother Carl. The band approached a series of country labels with no success, so they started in on the blues labels, beginning with Sun. After the usual screening by Marion Keisker, they finally got to audition for Sam in December 1954 with a song, "Movie Magg," Carl had won an amateur-night contest with in 1945, and Sam signed him to a two-year contract in January 1955. Unfortunately, the records kept stiffing: "Movie Magg" and "Turn Around" were supposed to inaugurate Sam's new Flip label, but they were virtually ignored. A few months later, Sam released "Let the Juke Box Keep On Playing" and "Gone, Gone, Gone" on Sun, and even though the A side was classic country in just the mold that was selling well, it, too, went nowhere.

That made Sam consider some of Carl's more unusual numbers, and he certainly had a strange one saved up. "Blue Suede Shoes" was a cat anthem if there ever was one, a song of pride in ownership of a pair of garish shoes that invited slander, physical violence, and theft of one's whiskey but threatened—what? The song doesn't say, but it makes clear that the singer's blue suede shoes are not to be trodden upon. A symbol of having come from the farm into the city, with enough money to buy something purely for show, those blue suede shoes, like the pink rayon shirts Elvis bought at Lansky's on Beale Street, cat central, were a declaration of independence as impudent as anything that had ever been thrown in George III's face. And just to make sure that this third-time charm worked, Carl also recorded "Honey Don't," a boogie-based tune with some of the slinky Perkins pickin' that drove them onto the dance floor during his stage shows.

This time Perkins clicked, and in mid-February, after the record had been out only three weeks, it was on the country charts. Just a few weeks later, it was number fifteen on the pop charts and had broken onto the R&B charts as well. It was a bona-fide hit, finally going to number two on all the charts.

The success earned Carl his biggest break yet: a chance to appear on "The Perry Como Show." But when he was driving up to New York with his band, their car collided with a pickup truck and overturned. The pickup's driver was killed, Jay B. had spinal injuries and several broken ribs and lay in a coma for some time, and Carl also had spinal injuries and numerous cuts on his face and body that would keep him in the hospital for six months. "I was just a poor farm boy," he commented later, "and with 'Shoes' I felt that I had a chance, but suddenly there I was in the hospital. But Elvis had the looks on me. The girls were going for him for more reasons than music. Elvis was hitting them with sideburns, flashy clothes, and no ring on that finger. I had three kids. There was no way of keeping him from being the man in that music, but I've never felt bitter, always felt lucky to be in the business. Most kids from my background never get to drive a new car."

Although Elvis had recorded "Blue Suede Shoes," he wouldn't release it as a single because he liked Perkins's work and wanted to see him do well. And he could afford to be generous. By March, Elvis had six of RCA Victor's twenty-five top-selling singles—not bad for somebody who'd only been on deck for three months—and by mid-April, he was selling $75,000 worth of records a day. His first album, *Elvis Presley*, had sold 155,000 copies in two and a half months, his singles were selling at the rate of 50,000 a day, the album and EPs were selling 5,000 copies a day, and Elvis Presley accounted for exactly 50 percent of RCA Victor's popular record business.

All of which began to panic the old-timers, especially in the country field. Afraid that the music they had loved all these years was about to be mongrelized by R&B, some forces in the country industry pressed *Billboard* to stop listing R&B-influenced singles on its country charts. The magazine laughed off the suggestion with the caution that R&B had made fools out of many people in the pop field, and now it seemed to be doing the same for country. Then, in the early summer, the magazine editorialized again, this time attempting to lay the fears of the entire industry to rest. Pointing out that music was a business, the editorial, headlined DON'T LOSE THAT KID reminded readers that it was the consumer, characterized as "the kid with the 89 cents in his pocket," who called the tune, and that if the industry was going to survive, they'd have to dance to it. When the kid with the 89 cents looked elsewhere, so would the industry. It was as simple as that.

By now, every label was scrambling to find the next Elvis Presley. Decca had Buddy Holly, of whose debut waxing, "Love Me," *Billboard* commented, "If the public will take more than one Presley or Perkins, as it well may, Holly stands a strong chance." Sun was certainly keeping its hand in, with Carl Perkins's remarkable "Boppin' the Blues," and releases by Warren Smith, a good-looking singer from Mississippi who scored nicely with a Johnny Cash composition, "Rock 'n' Roll Ruby," and Roy Orbison, who was not so handsome but whose high, haunting voice recalled the wide open spaces of West Texas, where he had grown up on the flatlands, in a tiny burg called Wink. Orbison's voice wasn't really suited for the odd rhythm novelty he recorded for his debut, but "Ooby Dooby" might have sold as well as it did because it sounded so peculiar.

Capitol got into the "next Elvis" sweepstakes with Eugene Vincent Craddock, a sailor from Virginia with a thin, craggy face; a penchant for motorcycles, black leather, and drinking; and a crippled leg that caused him great pain and was a souvenir of a motorcycle accident. He might not have seemed appealing from a written description, but his voice had a smoldering sexuality that was hard to beat, and he had a band, the Blue Caps, that made Haley's Comets sound like the old men they were. Craddock, renamed Gene Vincent, had come up with a song called "Be-Bop-A-Lula"— its title was inspired by a Little Lulu comic book, easily the most innocent thing about it—that featured him muttering, growling, and breathing heavily while the Blue Caps laid down a backing of menace and lust, screaming in abandon when Gene sang, "She's the one who gives me more, more, more!"

The Decca subsidiary Coral had entered the race with the Johnny Burnette Rock 'n' Roll Trio, featuring guitar madman Paul Burlison. Burnette's records didn't gain much recognition in 1956, but after his death in 1964, songs like "Tear It Up" and "Train Kept a-Rollin'" would be rediscovered by record collectors and the band would finally get the belated recognition it deserved.

Meanwhile, the current Elvis was having a busy year. In April, he received his first gold record, an award RCA invented especially for him.* But even now "Heartbreak Hotel" would prove a better address than the New Frontier Hotel in Las Vegas, a burgeoning resort town in the middle of the Nevada desert. Since the end of the war, wealthy speculators, including some gangsters, had been developing the former army air-base town and promoting it as an entertainment mecca. Gambling and prostitution were legal, it wasn't far from L.A., and it would become a lavish, sophisticated American Monte Carlo—or so said the tourist brochures.

Colonel Parker made the first huge mistake of his career managing Elvis when he booked him into the Frontier for a week. On opening night, Elvis headlined and the mostly adult crowd gaped, scratched its collective head, paid the bill, and went back to the gambling tables. A few nights later, Elvis was moved below comedian Shecky Greene on the bill, reduced to a novelty warming up for some good, clean, all-American borscht-belt

---

*Real gold records, representing one million verified copies sold, were not yet presented by the music industry. The Recording Industry Association of America, the body that awards them today, had only just been established, and had announced plans for some sort of standardized record-sales award in March 1956.

humor. UPI had sent its top gossip columnist, Aline Mosby, to interview the young sensation, and he stood her up to go see a Randolph Scott Western. The stint was a total fiasco, and mercifully, the Colonel decided not to exercise his option to renew for seven nights. But the misjudgment was easily forgotten after RCA released "My Baby Left Me" b/w "I Want You, I Need You, I Love You" and reported sales of 653,219 in the first ten days. The Colonel got back on the phone, and soon he'd pulled off another coup: Elvis was booked on the granddaddy of all television variety shows, Milton Berle's.

The critics were lying in ambush. Elvis did "Heartbreak Hotel" and "Blue Suede Shoes" on the telecast from San Diego on April 3 to surprisingly little reaction, but the June 5 show from Hollywood set off the heavy artillery. The *New York Times*'s Jack Gould called the performance "a rock and roll variation on one of the most standard acts in the business, the virtuoso of the hootchy kootchy," and the New York *Journal-American's* Jack O'Brien assured himself a place in rock and roll history with his review: "Elvis Presley wiggled and wriggled with such abdominal gyrations that burlesque bombshell Georgia Southern really deserves equal time to reply in gyrating kind. . . . He can't sing a lick, makes up for vocal shortcomings with the weirdest and plainly planned suggestive animation short of an aborigine's mating dance." Fretted disc jockey Jerry Marshall on WNEW, "I think that Elvis and the people handling him should be interested in his future and building his popularity into something more lasting than a current-day craze. If the future is important, Elvis will have to drop the 'hootchy kootchy' gyrations or end up as 'Pelvis' Presley in circus side shows and burlesque, where he will not find the biggest crowds and financial rewards."

The negative press prompted Ed Sullivan to declare that an act so suggestive would never appear on his show, "Toast of the Town." Aha, said Steve Allen, whose variety show competed with Sullivan's and had never beaten it in the ratings: Operator, get me the number of Colonel Tom Parker in Memphis! On July 1, when Elvis headlined the show, Steve Allen buried Sullivan in the ratings for the first time ever, and Sullivan, confronted with "the most controversial entertainer since Liberace" (in *Billboard's* words), had to reverse his stance. He offered Elvis a whopping $50,000 for three appearances, the first of which would air in September.

Summer 1956 saw the release of a spate of novelty records, some of which were absolutely repulsive. One of them, "Transfusion," seemed to have been conceived with the express purpose of disgusting people. Nervous Norvus (aka Jimmy Drake, a middle-aged character who drove a truck for a living, which was absolutely all he had in common with Elvis) warbled the tale of a man who just couldn't stop having automobile accidents, over the sound of a ukelele and dubbed-in car-crash sounds, after which he'd request a transfusion with lines like "Shoot me some juice,

Bruce" or "Pass the claret, Barrett." To the glee of America's teenagers, Norvus, who recorded for Dot, was unanimously censored, giving rock and roll's not-so-secret society a new under-the-counter hit.

But now the radio and television networks united behind a code of ethics, banning "songs which are profane, ridicule physical deformities, contribute to juvenile delinquency, are offensive to minorities [and] songs which are lascivious." One of the first victims of this code was the World War I chestnut "K-K-K-Katie," because of its stuttering gimmick; and then several songs from the 1940s hit musical *Showboat* had to be rewritten to eliminate the references to "darkies."

After "Transfusion" came "The Flying Saucer," by Buchanan and Goodman (actually, they called themselves John Cameron Cameron, as a takeoff on the deadpan newscaster John Cameron Swayze), and although nobody publicly seemed to know who they were, all of a sudden they had the hottest-selling—and hottest, as in "illegal"— record in the United States. Framed as a broadcast of a rock-and-roll station interrupted by a news bulletin that flying saucers had shown up "downtown," the record featured snippets of about a dozen hit songs that moved the story along.

For instance, when asked what they'd do if the saucer landed, Little Richard replied, "Jump back in the alley," Fats Domino replied, "What I'd do is hard to say," and Elvis opted for saying "I'll take a walk down Lonely Street." From time to time, an Alan Freed–soundalike would announce the record wrong ("That's Pa Gerkin's record, 'Shoes!'"). As stupid joke piled on top of stupid joke (the space people's first words to Earth—naturally— were "A-wop-bop-a-loo-mop-a-lop-bam-boom") at rapid-fire speed, the primitively made disc kept listeners laughing. By the time the spaceman's voice said "Good-bye, Earth pee-pul" at the end, lawyers in the music business around the country were adding up the copyright violations.

The word that they were wanted men got out quickly to Buchanan and Goodman, and record dealers could never tell whether, when they placed an order, they'd be getting a genuine Luniverse label Buchanan and Goodman record, a cheaply manufactured counterfeit, or a summons from feared and powerful music-business attorney Julian Abeles, who was filing the infringement-of-copyright suit on behalf of the publishers through the Harry Fox Agency, the publishers' watchdog. Of course, Buchanan and Goodman hadn't gotten the clearances, but they may never have intended this to be anything but a joke for disc jockeys. On the other hand, the record was a boon for some. One publisher admitted—oh, but don't print my name!—that "If you're not on the 'Flying Saucer,' you're nowhere!" and Dootone noted a decided upturn of sales in "Earth Angel," which had died months ago. *Billboard* coyly noted that "attempts to reach Buchanan by phone were impossible, but he was last seen in Hanom's Drug Store," a well-known Tin Pan Alley and music-industry hangout, "taking orders."

Naturally a flock of imitations ensued, most notably one on RPM, which didn't have to worry about clearances because the Biharis owned the publishing on everything they released, but it was only Buchanan and Goodman who were selling. Lawyers spent the summer tearing their hair out waiting for a decision, and teenagers spent it saying "Good bye, Earth pee-pul" to each other. (Unless they were saying "See you later, alligator" and "In a while, crocodile," phrases made famous by Bill Haley's cover of a record, on Chess, by Robert Charles Guidry, a Cajun kid from Louisiana who recorded as Bobby Charles.)

These records provoked a new barrage of protests that rock and roll was not "good music," but America's teenagers continued voting with their allowances and the money they were making from after-school jobs. As the class of 1956 graduated, Scholastic Magazines' Institute of Student Opinion found that there were 13 million teenagers in America, with an income of over $7 billion *a year*, 26 percent more than they had in 1953. The average teenager had a weekly income of $10.55, with boys saving twice as much money as girls and spending about a third more. Junior high school girls bought most of the records, with 61.7 percent of them buying at least one a month, as opposed to 46.6 percent of junior high school boys, 48.9 percent of senior high girls, and 41.9 percent of senior high boys. The average buyer bought two records a month, but among the ones who bought over twelve a month, the boys took the lead. Everybody overwhelmingly voted for pop music—which included rock and roll, but was not limited to it—as their favorite kind, swamping semi-classical, classical, and folk music. And for some reason—Elvis?—teens overwhelmingly preferred RCA-brand radios and phonographs.

RCA had been the first to capitalize on a new scientific advance, the transistor, in a radio that ran on regular flashlight batteries, weighed only a couple of pounds, and was small enough to fit in a woman's purse. By the summer of 1955, a daring consumer with between $24.95 and $49.95 to spend could pick up an RCA portable radio to take to the beach or on a picnic. But by 1956, both GE and Emerson had gotten into the act with new, all-transistor pocket radios. GE had one outfitted with nickle-cadmium batteries that were rechargeable and capable of giving ten thousand hours of play. It only weighed 20 ounces and sold for $49.95 with regular batteries and $64.95 with the rechargeable ones. Emerson's was a garden-variety pocket radio with regular batteries, and sold for $58. That may have been too much for a teenager to spend except in the more affluent suburbs, but surveys had shown that nearly 100 percent of America's teenagers had at least one radio in the house.

And science had been breaking other ground, too! In May 1955, the Sarnoff Labs in Princeton announced the creation of the "synthesizer," which they claimed was capable of duplicating any sound and any voice, based on the shape of its sound waves, and of producing some heretofore unheard sonorities as well. The possibilities were awesome to contemplate, although "electronic music" wasn't really new. The development of the tape recorder after the war had attracted a group of young composers in

Paris to the idea of taking natural sounds and playing them backward, or using them as sonorities the same way you'd use an instrument. They claimed this *musique concrète*, as it was called, would become the music of the future. The early experiments of these composers—most notably Karl-heinz Stockhausen, John Cage, Vladimir Ussachevsky, and Otto Leuning—were greeted with such howls of outrage from established "good music" circles that it quickly became obvious that they were on to something.

But for now, what America's teenagers needed was a rallying force, a song that would tell them that they were together, united, that they had some-thing that was theirs alone, and that this banner was rock and roll. They got that song in May, from the pen and guitar of Chuck Berry. "Roll Over Beethoven" was a manifesto, a battle cry that had Berry contacting his favorite disc jockey and telling him to take off the classical music because he'd heard a rockin' record on the Rhythm Revue and wanted to hear it again. "Roll over, Beethoven, and tell Tchaikovsky the news!" Chuck or-dered, and backed it up with some furious guitar playing. There it was! There was the song that said it was okay to be a teenager, okay to have your own music, and that nobody could tell you what was "good" music and what was "bad." Still, it only dented the bottom of the pop charts and performed in mediocre fashion on the R&B charts, finishing up in the number thirty-seven slot at year's end, way down there. Eventually it would be hailed as a classic, but somehow it got lost when it was new.

Still, the teenage mandate was becoming a powerful force. New York's Roxy Theatre had an annual ice show, and for 1956, it was "Rock 'n' Roll Ice Revue, the hottest production ever staged on ice." Camel cigarettes were sponsoring the Alan Freed network show, and Pall Mall had already re-corded a radio commercial with a rock-and-roll beat. Columbia Pictures was putting big money into *Rock Around the Clock*, a film with Alan Freed and Bill Haley. But the greatest rock and roll picture of 1956—indeed, of the whole era—was *The Girl Can't Help It*, a film so unlike the ones that preceded and followed it that it might have fallen out of Buchanan and Goodman's flying saucer.

To begin with, it had real actors (Tom Ewell, Edmund O'Brien, and Jayne Mansfield); a real plot; a good director (Frank Tashlin, who went on to fame making Jerry Lewis films, but don't judge him too harshly for that); color; Cinemascope; stereophonic sound; and performers like Fats Domino, Gene Vincent and His Blue Caps, the Platters, Little Richard, Julie London, and Eddie Cochran. O'Brien plays a gangster who hires Ewell, a press agent with a drinking problem, to turn his girlfriend, Mansfield, into a rock-and-roll star, using his song (written while on an enforced vacation), "Rockin' Around the Rock Pile." Naturally Ewell and Mansfield fall in love while he's trying to develop her nonvoice, and along the way, they get to hang out in nightclubs and rehearsal studios where Little Richard and Gene Vincent and the rest just happen to be playing. The Vincent scene, with the Blue Caps all throwing off their blue caps in unison, goes a lot further than mere words ever could to explain Vincent's charisma, and the scene of Mansfield twitching down the street, clutching two milk bottles to her ample breasts while Richard belts out the theme song, is a classic of some sort.

The summer and fall of 1956 also saw some of the dreamiest vocal-group records yet released. Somebody figured out that there were 25 million plays a day on the nation's jukeboxes, and in places where teens danced to the jukeboxes, they were guaranteed to play the slow records like the Five Satins' "In the Still of the Nite" with its memorable sho-doe-ten-doe-bee-doe background chant; or the Platters' "The Great Pretender," propelled by Tony Williams's high tenor; or the Heartbeats' "A Thousand Miles Away," poorly produced, but with an unforgettable melody and arrangement; or "Oh What a Night," by the Dells on Vee-Jay, with its ultraromantic lyrics and fine harmonies, launching the group on a career that is still going strong; or the Clovers' "Devil or Angel" on Atlantic, with its tricky oh-oh-oh-oh break. "Devil or Angel" was one of Atlantic's few vocal group offerings, because Jerry Wexler considered the style unsophisticated and crude—which made sense, given his jazz background. It *was* unsophisticated and crude, which is just what appealed to the teens who bought it—it was a style anyone could attempt. And lots of the songs were built, like "In the Still of the Nite," on the I-VI-IV-V-I chord progression (same as "Earth Angel," one of the progenitors of this noble doo-wop family), a chord progression that seemed to cry out for emotive tenor work and the sort of slow dancing where you and your partner just draped yourselves across each other and shuffled.

There were fast records, too, much to the chaperones' relief: the Cleftones' "This Little Girl of Mine," which rattled along with the group doing a complicated chant in the background while the lead singer effortlessly spun the lead vocal; the Cadets' "Stranded in the Jungle," in which the group made jungle noises as the lead singer told the story of how he had to escape from hungry natives to keep a date with his sweetheart ("meanwhile, back in the States . . .")—one of the records people pointed to as an example of how degenerate rock and roll really was; Bill Doggett's mid-tempo instrumental "Honky Tonk," one of those stupidly simple riffs that can only be removed by surgery once you've heard it twice, which turned out to be the year's number-one R&B release; and Shirley and Lee, who had been spinning out a fictitious soap opera of romance, betrayal, reconciliation, and joy, urging everyone to "Let the Good Times Roll" against a honking, pumping background that could only have come from New Orleans. In fact, New Orleans was on the rise, with Fats Domino coming in with four of the top thirty R&B hits of the year, including two of the top five, "Blueberry Hill," an old 1930s standard, and the double-sided monster "I'm In Love Again" b/w another rocked-up classic, "My Blue Heaven."

The attraction of rock and rollers to standard Tin Pan Alley songs of yore was one of the most frustrating facts critics of the new music had to face:

How could they condemn vocal groups as degenerate when the two big showpieces every group had to learn were "Sunday Kind of Love" and "Stormy Weather"—two gilt-edged classics—and when everybody from Elvis to Fats Domino was enriching copyright holders who hadn't seen a nickel since the War? But not everybody was jumping on the rock-and-roll bandwagon. Somebody named Patty Andrews released a "polka novelty" called "Too Old to Rock and Roll," and Pearl Bailey informed everybody, "I Can't Rock and Roll To Save My Soul." You could understand why when you heard Little Richard's "Rip It Up," b/w "Ready Teddy," which seemed to be competing with each other for fastest record alive.

Little Richard had created a funny incident earlier in the year on the March 9 edition of NBC Radio's "National Radio Fan Club" show. Specialty had given the show a copy of his new record, "Slippin' and Slidin'" b/w "Long Tall Sally," so that "Sally" could be tested live before the teenage audience. The only thing that stood in the way was NBC's notorious network censor, easily the most conservative, and the fact that Richard's song dealt with Uncle John cheating on Aunt Mary with Sally, who was not only long and tall but bald-headed as well. The whole thing was delivered rapid-fire in Richard's gritty scream, and the network censor listened to it several times, then handed it over to the show's producer, Parker Gibbs, with the comment, "How can I restrict it when I can't even understand it?" The kids understood, and voted it the number-one record of the week's show; before long, it was selling like one, too.

A similar misunderstanding occurred in Cincinnati when Syd Nathan walked into a room at King because he thought a record somebody was playing had gotten stuck. He'd been roused from his office by the word "Please!" being screamed over and over. Nathan opined that this was the worst record he'd ever heard, the sort of song that gave ammunition to people who thought R&B singers were gibbering baboons. "But Syd," the man at the desk said, "that's our fastest-moving record in a year," and suddenly Nathan heard its beauty. It was the debut of another weirdo, a Georgia singer with the unspectacular name of James Brown. He'd been a boxer, a shoeshine boy, and of course a gospel singer, had done time for stealing cars, and for a few years had been playing drums and organ in a band called the Famous Flames. The Flames weren't particular. They'd do R&B or gospel. What mattered to James Brown was pride, and pride was what some people heard when they heard him sing "Please, Please, Please," begging his woman to stay because he loved her so. There had never been a record that sounded anything like it before.

Naturally, Brown's song didn't take off immediately because it was so unusual, but eventually it would; and when James Brown made it to mecca—the Apollo Theatre—with his ragtag group of Famous Flames, he performed in a borrowed jacket in front of a group of people who also felt pride in having escaped the red-dirt poverty he obviously still had one foot in, and conquered them totally. No question about it, he would be back.

Uptown from the Apollo, in the secton of Harlem known as Sugar Hill, a more innocent sound was developing. Up at 164th Street and Edgecomb Avenue, Sherman Garnes, Herman Santiago, Jimmy Merchant, Joe Negroni, and Frankie Lymon hung around harmonizing, like so many of their friends did, but the five had a gimmick that the racial tenor of the times, even in Harlem, made unique: Santiago and Negroni were Puerto Ricans and the rest of the group was black. Little Frankie, especially, only twelve years old, was a natural performer, guaranteed to steal the spotlight. Yet he never suffered from stagefright or balked when it came to changing one of his ideas for an arrangement. It was as if he had been born a total professional.

But it was the Puerto Rican members who wound up getting the group noticed. The quintet had been singing around Harlem as the Premieres and the Ermines and the Coupe deVilles; and one night Richard Barrett, a neighborhood scout for George Goldner, owner of the nascent Latin music labels Tico and Rama, heard them rehearsing at a community center. Barrett told Goldner that he'd discovered a group that sang R&B vocal music with a Spanish accent (Herman Santiago had been taking most of the leads), and Goldner, distracted, told him to book an audition. When five kids arrived, Goldner was confused. If they were a Latin act, where were their instruments? Barrett urged him to wait, to reserve judgment until he heard them sing.

History is divided as to what happened next. One version of the story has Herman coming down with a bad cold and handing the lead vocals to Frankie. Another version has Goldner recognizing that while the group was good, the little singer was incredible, and assigning him the lead. But there was no doubt whatever that their song, "Why Do Birds Sing So Gay?" had hit potential even if the lyrics needed work. At the time, a tale circulated that Frankie had written the words out of unrequited love for a teacher, but the truth seems to be that the original poem came from a neighborhood crony who had gotten it from his girlfriend and thought it would make a good song lyric.

At any rate, by the time the Teenagers, as the group had renamed themselves, released it, the song was called "Why Do Fools Fall in Love." Frankie was now thirteen, and George Goldner was established in the R&B business. The small *t* teenagers had taken the group straight to their hearts, captivated by the simplicity of the *ooh-wah, ooh-wah* opening and Frankie's soaring falsetto. The record went straight into the pop top ten and stayed on the R&B chart for weeks, leaving only when "I Want You to Be My Girl," the Teenagers' next record, came along to take its place.

The Teenagers' success touched off another wave of vocal group fever, especially among younger singers, and a surprising number of these acts got recorded. It was a buyers' market—a fact not lost on record company executives, who depended on the kids' utter lack of business savvy to help them make a profit. In a typical deal of the time, a group of youngsters signed a contract that gave them a penny per record sold, with no royalties paid until the full cost of the recording session was recouped. All the songs written by the group were assigned to a publishing company owned by the record label, and the label head got half the writer's credit, although he didn't contribute a line. Obviously the record company would be the only winner in such a deal—unless the group wised up, as the Penguins did, declaring the contract invalid because they had been minors when they signed it. But such rebellions were infrequent, since the prestige of releasing a record, for many of these groups, outweighed the benefits of their meager royalties.

One of the big things that sold the Teenagers was their wholesomeness. It would be hard to look at Frankie Lymon and think of him as a degenerate in the same class as Little Richard. The two were obviously worlds apart, with one a screaming queen from the back alleys of rural Georgia and the other a sweet-faced junior high school student from a good neighborhood in Harlem. Late in 1956, Frankie Lymon even released a song called "I'm Not a Juvenile Delinquent," with lines like "It's easy to be good / It's hard to be bad / Take this tip from me / And you'll be glad." It sounded almost exactly like "Why Do Fools Fall in Love," though.

But rock and roll was developing other kinds of apologists. Associated Booking announced that their new rock-and-roll package tour was a "refined one, with specially screened acts." This was directly to mollify the horror-stricken theater owners, who wanted the teenagers' bucks but not their teenage behavior. Associated could, with this package, offer absolute assurance that "our new, sedate version of r&b will . . . keep audiences under control." Acts on the bill were the Chuckles, the Penguins, Eddie Fontaine, Shirley Gunter, and Arnold Dover and the Blockbusters. The Penguins, of course, were famous, and Shirley Gunter was the leader of the Queens, the only significant all-girl doo-wop group at this point, who had scored a hit with "Oop Shoop," but the others must have been too sedate to make much impression.

Still, none of them was as sedate as Pat Boone, who, with his all-American features and gleaming smile, was Nashville's pop answer to rock and roll, its perfect antidote, with his uncanny ability to make even the most exciting material seem bland. He was the kind of teenager—except, of course, he hadn't been a teenager in a decade—that parents wanted their own adolescents to be. No one seemed to notice that his celebrated virtues, including good church attendance and respect for his elders, could just as easily be found in Elvis.

But in the face of the juvenile delinquency threat, even Alan Freed was joining forces with Buck Ram, whose production was responsible for the Platters, a smooth vocal group who weren't really rock and roll but still attracted teen dollars, to combat the small minority of teenagers who were giving rock and roll a bad name. Ram's immediate contribution to the cause would be a record by his new duo, Sugar and Spice, called "Don't Be a

Bunny." A bunny, he explained, was a wise guy or troublemaker. Freed, for his part, very likely figured he'd just keep staging his shows, and that teenagers would behave well at them, and he would make money proving the kids were good.

But people hadn't given up the campaign to get rid of rock and roll. It was getting banned in Boston by the Board of Education after a record hop at MIT, of all places, ended in a riot. Norman Furman, the head of WBMS, had forbidden his disc jockeys to play record hops; and Samuel Marcus, president of the Boston Musicians' Association, noted that "Live musicians play dignified rock and roll, which is much more sensible for teen-agers." The music played at record hops, on the other hand, he characterized as "jungle rhythms," and he denounced in no uncertain terms the disc jockeys who thought teens actually liked it. Down in Helena, Arkansas, KXLJ disc jockey Gene Hogan sought to meet these criticisms halfway by suggesting that rock-and-roll artists should put anti–juvenile delinquency messages on their records. And one especially virulent response had come from Birmingham, Alabama, where the White Citizens Council had tried to ban rock and roll entirely. Having failed at that, a few of its members attended a show by Nat King Cole, and a little way into his set, stormed onto the stage, dragged him off his piano stool, and beat him to a fare-thee-well. Cole was hardly a rock and roller, but he was black, which was convenient.

But rock and roll had found some defenders, if rather surprising ones, after an incident at Alan Freed's show at the State Theatre in Hartford, Connecticut. Although Freed denied that anything untoward had happened, the police claimed they'd arrested eleven teenagers for various offenses during the show's three-day stand, and tried to revoke the State's license. The first voice for the defense came from Sammy Kaye (of "Swing and Sway With . . ." fame), the very epitome of squaredom, who, while admitting that teens who broke the law should be arrested, begged, "Please do not injure the millions of nice, respectable youngsters who like rock and roll music by automatically putting them in the same class as the wrong-doers. Some years ago when the teenagers began to Lindy Hop there were persons—among them perhaps you—who called them lunatics and delinquents. I have no doubt that the same reception greeted those who first danced the fox trot years ago."

Freed had also gotten invitations to compare notes from both Benny Goodman and the aging white "King of Jazz," Paul Whiteman, who had elicited similar comments from bluenoses during their heydays, with Whiteman recalling with nostalgia the Sunday on which the bishop of Iowa had declared, "Jazz is leading our youth down the primrose path to hell!" Freed was also muttering that the movement to combat rock and roll was a conspiracy. "If a stageshow is well policed and well presented, they won't have riots," he claimed. "Music has nothing to do with it." He remembered the worst riot he'd ever seen, in Youngstown, Ohio, in 1944, which erupted to the jungle rhythms of Guy Lombardo and his Royal Canadians.

But the moralists kept after Freed, underestimating his devotion to this music, a devotion born as much out of a true feeling that he was providing a service for America's youth as out of his increasing financial involvement.* Finally, on Eric Sevareid's April 15 television show, Freed got to blast back at the critics who had been shelling his position. Sevareid showed film clips of rock-and-roll shows, with interviews of the teens in attendance, who all said variations of "It's keen," backed up by opinions from several psychiatrists that perhaps the rioting kids had something wrong in their home environments, rather than being whipped up to destruction by the music. Next, Mitch Miller—who, in his capacity as head of A&R at Columbia, was certainly doing his best to keep rock and roll off the label—paid Freed a left-field compliment by saying, "You can't call any music immoral. If anything is wrong with rock and roll, it is that it makes a virtue out of monotony." Then Freed appeared, trying to take on both the New York *Daily News* and an industry trade paper that had scourged him, as well as Monsignor John B. Carroll, head of the Catholic Youth Organization of the Archdiocese of Boston, who railed, "There is no doubt but that the by-product of rock and roll has left its scar on youth."

Freed was outraged, and he let loose with all the dignity at his command. First, he noted that there had been no press coverage—nor had he sought any—on the rainy Saturday afternoon when he and eleven thousand rock and roll fans had distributed cards for the foundation fighting childhood nephritis, a kidney disease. Then, thanking all the people who had written to him to express their support during the time the *Daily News* was spreading its bile, he brought forth his credo: "As long as there are radio stations like [WINS] in America, and as long as there are people who like me around, we're going to rock and roll until you don't want to rock 'n' roll any more, and then, when you don't want to rock and roll any more, I'll give you what you want!"

What most people wanted was Elvis, and in September 1956, his cover of the old Willie Mae Thornton song, "Hound Dog," with its hiccuping B side, "Don't Be Cruel," conquered the radio. "Hound Dog" was the Elvis song that got the most exposure the fastest, shooting to number one almost immediately. With it came a vast merchandising scheme from Colonel Tom Parker and H. G. Saperstein and Associates, licensing manufacturers, to put Elvis's picture on items like Heartbreak Pink, Hound Dog Orange, and Tutti Frutti Red lipstick. By the end of September, they'd granted eighteen licenses for thirty products, including hats, T-shirts, black denim jeans, handkerchiefs, bobby sox, canvas sneakers, skirts, blouses, belts, purses, billfolds, wallets, charm bracelets, necklaces, magazines, gloves, mittens,

---

*Apart from his shows, Freed's name kept cropping up in composer credits on hit records—as well as on would-be hit records—and more than a dozen releases had borne his name in less than a year. Taking composer's credit was standard practice among record-company owners, but it wasn't so common among djs.

statues, bookends, guitars, cologne, stuffed hound dogs, stuffed dancing dolls, stationery, greeting cards, sweaters, and a soft drink (this last possibly never manufactured). There was also a glow-in-the-dark picture of Elvis that radiated for two hours after the lights were doused, so that he could burn his way into teenage dreams.

By the time this merchandising bonanza was announced, there had already been 4 million charm bracelets, 120,000 pairs of jeans, and 240,000 T-shirts sold, and Saperstein was confident that over $20 million worth of Elvis memorabilia would be moved by the end of 1956—only *three months away!* His confidence was probably bolstered by the fact that Elvis Presley was finishing up his first motion picture under a multifilm deal the Colonel had spent the summer negotiating. And Elvis was going to perform on the Ed Sullivan show.

The night Elvis first appeared on "The Toast of the Town," civilization threw in the towel. Sullivan didn't appear that night, and he'd handed the emcee duties to one of the most incongruous people imaginable, Charles Laughton. For the benefit of those who felt a moral obligation to protect the virtue of America's teenagers by his third appearance on Sullivan, Elvis was shown only from the waist up. On television, that is. Live, if they could have made him stand in a waist-high box, they would have, but they couldn't. On that first show, America was treated to the sound of girls in the audience shrieking hysterically while Elvis performed "Don't Be Cruel," "Love Me Tender"—which, he let everybody know, was the title tune from his forthcoming movie—"Ready Teddy," and, of course, "Hound Dog."

The next week Jack Gould of the *New York Times* wrote a long editorial chiding the network, reminding it of its responsibility to the tender youngsters who might be watching. "When Presley executes his bumps and grinds, it must be remembered by the Columbia Broadcasting System that even the twelve-year-old's curiosity may be overstimulated," he pontificated, then added, on an oddly sensible note, "In the long run, perhaps Presley will do everyone a favor by pointing up the need for early sex education so that neither his successors nor TV can capitalize on the idea that his type of routine is somehow highly tempting yet forbidden fruit."

Religious leaders weighed in as well. The Reverend William Shannon, writing in the *Catholic Sun*, proved to be one of the few people who could remember who else was on the program when he wrote, "Presley and his voodoo of frustration and defiance have become symbols in our country, and we are sorry to come upon Ed Sullivan in the role of promoter. Your Catholic viewers, Mr. Sullivan, are angry; and you cannot compensate for a moral injury, not even by sticking 'the Little Gaelic Singers of County Derry' on the same bill with Elvis Presley." And Billy Graham, always willing to grab a headline despite the fact that he admitted not knowing a lot about Presley, commented that "From what I've heard, I'm not so sure I'd want my children to see him."

Even in radio land, the reaction would be negative: one disc jockey announced that he didn't much care for Elvis and was so overwhelmed by the fans' indignation that he set aside two fifteen-minute sections of his program, one for all-Elvis programming and the other a segment titled "Music for People Who Don't Much Care for Elvis." Dave Pringle at WPAG in Ann Arbor issued membership cards in the I Hate Elvis Presley! Club, which bore the inscription, "He makes me feel surgical—like cutting my throat," and had a razor blade attached. Just down the road in Detroit, Robin Seymour of WKMH, who had banned Elvis's records after the June appearance on Milton Berle, got five hundred letters from teens boycotting his segment. Seymour backtracked after the Steve Allen Show, saying that Presley's more modest behavior on that telecast had changed his mind. Terry McGuire of WCMC in Wildwood, New Jersey, blithered that "as a Christian I could not morally justify playing the music of Mr. P. I would like to begin an organization [of djs] to help eliminate certain wreck and ruin artists," while Bob Day of WNIX in St. Johnsbury, Vermont, sermonized, "Although we must cater to the public's musical likes to a great extent, we in this business should not, nevertheless, praise and foster what we truly believe to be obviously poor taste."

Of course, there were plenty of pro-Elvis djs as well, especially among those who wanted to keep their jobs in large urban areas. Bob Rickman, for example, of WPGC in Washington, D.C., founded a Society for Prevention of Cruelty to Elvis Presley, and Norman Prescott of WBZ in Boston offered six authentic hairs from Elvis's sideburns as contest prizes.

It was enough to make a man go ape, and that's what happened to songwriter Joie Bruno of Penn Township, just outside of Pittsburgh. Bruno climbed a tree at the end of August and vowed not to come down until his song "Bolder and Bolder," recorded by Dorice Brown on MGM, sold a million copies. He had a phone up there and a mattress, and his friends sent food up in a bucket three times daily. "The idea," he told *Billboard*, "is to call attention to the need for good music. The kids are gonna hold a corn roast under the tree tonight. They're gonna play rock and roll music to kid me. They're gonna carry pickets reading 'Bruno Is Unfair to Rock and Roll,' but I'll stay right up here." Rock and roll aside, it seems that "Bolder and Bolder" never charted, let alone sold a million copies. Bruno may still be up there.

That same week RCA issued seven—count 'em, seven—Elvis singles, fourteen tracks from his album, and EPs that had never been released on singles before, including "Blue Suede Shoes." It put those songs at last within the reach of any kid with 89 cents. And by September 15, "Hound Dog" was the number-one song on the R&B jukebox charts as well.

Then came the movie. Originally titled *The Reno Brothers*, it told the story of three Civil War–era Confederate brothers, two of whom went off to fight the war, and one of whom, Clint (Elvis), stayed home. When word came that the eldest had been killed, Elvis married his sweetheart (Debra Papet), and together they helped Mom keep the farm going. When the two brothers, very much alive, returned to the farm, a conflict was ignited and the story started sinking, but by then it hardly mattered; Elvis and writer Vera Matson had collaborated on four songs, which Elvis performed, complete with gyrations, when the plot started bogging down. Realizing that Elvis's contribution was a plus in a film that was basically a minus, the producers retitled it *Love Me Tender* and targeted the title song as Elvis's next single. A week before it was released, RCA had received 856,327 orders for the new record, and they had over a million by the time they started shipping it. "Love Me Tender" became the first record ever to debut as number two on the *Billboard* charts.

As bad as the movie was, eager fans packed the houses. Imagine the tension teenage girls felt in the film's opening sequence, in which a group of Confederate soldiers ride past the camera, their faces showing one by one: Was that him? Was that? He had to be next! But he wasn't. He showed up about fifteen minutes into the film, strapped behind a plow. Movie houses echoed to the screams of his fans as he performed, and in the ending, he got shot—dead!—by one of the villains. It was the answer to a teenager's mother's prayer, perhaps, but he emerged in ghostly montage at the end, singing "Love Me Tender" again as his film family walked away from his grave.

On September 26, after his screen debut, Elvis returned to Tupelo, where he'd spent his boyhood, to attend the Mississippi/Alabama Fair and Dairy Show; there, as a child, he'd won an amateur contest singing a bathetic song about a boy's dead dog, "Old Shep." The Colonel gave the promoters a break: two shows at only $5,000 each, a thousand times what Elvis had won at the amateur show, and Elvis gave Tupelo a break, handing the money over to the city. There was a parade (which Elvis did not attend because of the city's concern for his safety) under the huge banner strung across Main Street, and local merchants had Elvis-oriented sales and specials, like "hound dogs" and sauerkraut at a local coffee shop. The entire Tupelo police force, county sheriffs, forty highway patrolmen, and a detachment of the National Guard that was on call (and needed for the evening show) maintained a semblance of order. Elvis was presented with a guitar-shaped key to the city by Mayor James Ballard as the governor of Mississippi read a proclamation ". . . welcoming home America's Number One entertainer in the field of popular music, its own native son, Elvis Presley."

Fans came from as far away as New York and Philadelphia to see Elvis perform, and 20,000 people attended the shows—in a town of 22,000 residents. Nipper, the RCA dog, was represented by a statue at one side of the stage, but Elvis respectfully refrained from addressing him when he sang his recent hit. Between songs, he reminisced, "I've been escorted out of these fairgrounds when I was a kid and snuck over the fence, but this is the first time I've been escorted in." The town had never seen anything like it.

* * *

By now the secret teenage society was large enough to splinter into camps—you could love Elvis or hate Elvis, but you stood behind rock and roll. A significant number of college radio stations were programming the music, and even the military was beginning to realize that American fighting men wanted rock-and-roll performers and records on their jukeboxes and at dances. Gary Kramer, *Billboard's* new rhythm-and-blues columnist, wrote that "it may be questioned whether the youngsters who have been brought up on rock and roll these last few years are going to turn 'naturally' to blander varieties of pop music as they pass into their twenties. This music may be making a deeper and more permanent influence on musical tastes than many adults realize."

Part of that was undoubtedly due to disc jockeys, who reached a new peak of ascendancy in 1956. The gentlemen of the turntable now commanded 68 percent of the airtime, a two-thirds increase in one year. The average jock was playing 16.4 records an hour over the land's 2700 AM station, which worked out to 500,000—a half-million—spins a day. Nor was it just here: Alan Freed's syndicated show was being played over Radio Luxembourg, an English-language station located in the tiny principality, with a mighty signal that not only reached many homesick Americans working or stationed in continental Europe but a good part of England as well.

England, in fact, was rocking. They'd been rocking over there since *The Blackboard Jungle*, and "Rock Around the Clock" had been a smash hit, along with "Why Do Fools Fall in Love." On September 21, 1956, the *New Musical Express*, a jazz and pop paper, devoted a four-page supplement to the rock-and-roll phenomenon. The paper noted that thirteen of Britain's top thirty tunes were rock and roll, and that although teenagers were rioting at screenings of the Bill Haley–Alan Freed movie *Rock Around the Clock*, the riots were the work of a bad element who would have been fighting somewhere anyway. The Queen had even invited Bill Haley and His Comets to do a command performance, which he accepted graciously on the same day that his hometown hall, Pittsburgh's Syria Mosque, banned him. Editorialists had a field day with that one.

Then in November, Johnny Brandon, a long-time BBC performer known as the King of Zing, cut Britain's first rock-and-roll record, "Do You Love Love Love Me," for London Records. But it must have been a pathetic effort indeed, since no rock historian seems to remember it. No self-respecting British teen thought that the homeland could produce a rocker, anyway. "It was the films that gave everybody a chance to congregate," wrote Ian Dury, who rose to some fame there twenty years later. "Before there were many concerts, Sunday afternoon was when we used to sit round the big screen, telling jokes, singing songs and spoiling the film. Mad Ron Cordry took a pigeon to the pictures under his jacket and let the poor fucking thing go during the flick. Flapping and shitting. Also he once let off a rocket in Upminster Gaumont. Bouncing along the ceiling. The manager never used to walk out to do his sprout in front of the curtain in his bow tie on Sundays. Not likely." It would seem that a certain universality of teen-agerhood was emerging.

Alan Freed had taken to the movie screen again in Rock Rock Rock, released shortly after Rock Around the Clock—just in time, in fact, for him to feature it in his now-legendary annual Brooklyn Paramount Holiday Show. Although the new film, starring Tuesday Weld, would hardly give the rising Swedish director Ingmar Bergman sleepless nights, it did have some wonderful performances in it: Lymon singing "Juvenile Delinquent," Chuck Berry doing another car-chase song, "You Can't Catch Me," and La Vern Baker singing "Tra La La," as well as songs by the Moonglows, the Flamingos, and the Johnny Burnette Rock and Roll Trio. The movie proved such a success that Chess, which had a number of artists in the picture, released an album featuring songs from it. It was the first rock-and-roll sound-track album, and it is a rare item today—although not as rare as the real sound-track album, with all the songs from the movie, that was dis-tributed to disc jockeys as a promotion for the film.

Christmas was coming, and it was obvious what kind of Christmas it was going to be when Atco and Regent both released a tune (sung by Little Lambie Penn and Marlene Paula, respectively) called "I Wanna Spend Xmas With Elvis." They might have had to settle for a genuine Elvis Presley Autograph Victrola, with a four-speed manual version selling for $32.95 and an automatic 45-rpm version for $44.95. Both were covered in simu-lated blue denim, and both came with a free Elvis record to get you started.

As for Elvis himself, there was never any doubt in his mind where he was spending Christmas. He went back to Memphis, bought a new home near Audubon Park and a couple of Cadillacs for his parents,* and invited Marilyn Evans, a girlfriend of his from Las Vegas, to spend the holidays. One afternoon—December 4, to be exact—he and Marilyn dropped by 706 Union Avenue to see how the group at Sun was doing. They surprised his old buddy Carl Perkins, now back on his feet singing hymns around a piano, at which sat Sun's latest backwoods wild man, a youngster from Ferriday, Louisiana, named Jerry Lee Lewis. Jerry was thrilled to see Elvis, and Carl was excited, too. Elvis, who had had dreams of joining the Blackwoods, one of country gospel's oldest and best-loved groups when he was a child, joined right in with the singing. They harmonized nicely, and Sam, seeing what was going on, sent out for a photographer and for his newest star, Johnny Cash. Engineer Jack Clement kept the tapes rolling, Marion Keisker and Marilyn sang along. And then they switched to some country songs, with Elvis doing imitations of Hank Snow and Bill Monroe and chatting about Pat Boone's new record, "Don't Forbid Me." Elvis said,

---

*Still, his mother, Gladys, never learned how to drive, which is why there's no registra-tion of license plates on the green 1956 Cadillac that is parked behind Graceland, the mansion Elvis bought later.

"It was written for me and sent to me over to my house and it stayed there for ages. I never did even see it. Y'know, so much junk lyin' around and all." The contempt in his voice was palpable, and then he picked up his guitar and roared into a ferocious version of the song that would have left Pat Boone gasping for breath. Elvis and Carl and Jerry Lee knew which side of the fence they were on. It was a good thing they did, because battle was about to be pitched. On the other hand, there were reinforcements coming, too.

10
WHOLE LOTTA SHAKIN'

F irst, though, would come a retrenchment. At the start of 1957, it looked as if teens were beginning to get tired of the rock-and-roll fad. For one thing, the jockeys were hearing a different tune over the telephones: Bud Arkell at WNDB in Daytona Beach, Florida, said the requests were running three to one for pop ballads over rock and roll. His "What I Like Best About Elvis Presley" essay contest got more entries on what they *didn't* like about him. Cal Zettmayr at WNGS in Tifton, Georgia, said his Presley requests had declined from 80 percent to a mere 15 percent of total calls in only one month, and Slim Jim Stephens of WLLH in Lowell, Massachusetts, said his listeners were asking to hear rhumbas, polkas, and Frank Sinatra.

For another thing, both the rhythm-and-blues and country charts were showing a decided emphasis on more traditional music, and country, especially, was entering a real golden age. Ray Price, a singer from the Dallas area, was coming into his own with a slow but insistent rhythm called the Texas shuffle that he had made his signature; and he ruled the country charts and airwaves throughout 1956 with a song called "Crazy Arms," which featured that beat—fine for two-stepping—and an instantly memorable melody sung by a voice that just poured out a song like an oil well pumps crude, except that Price's voice was much too smooth to be crude. From East Texas came another incredible voice, that of George Jones, who smashed into the charts in late 1955 with "Why Baby Why," the first song in a career that would virtually define what country music in the 1950s and 1960s was about—drinking, divorcing, and deep, deep sorrow, onstage and off.

137

Now Jim Reeves was back in action, as was a newcomer named Sonny James, whose ballad smash "Young Love" not even Presley could unseat. And early in 1957 came the astonishing Patsy Cline, tough yet vulnerable, whose ballad "Walkin' After Midnight" was a pop as well as a country smash, and Bobby Helms's sweetly sentimental song "Fraulein," which must have brought back memories to World War II veterans whose marriages might have grown lukewarm. Sam Phillips was represented on the country charts by Johnny Cash, who must have seemed like an insurance policy for him, since the best his other records did was sell well locally. Even his new hope, Jerry Lee Lewis, with his nervous, fidgety, piano-based version of "Crazy Arms," wasn't really prospering.

Over on the rhythm-and-blues side, it was ballad and roots time, too. Atlantic had gambled well in acquiring Chuck Willis from Okeh, with his ballad smash "It's Too Late" going pop as well as R&B. Then they'd resurrected another old bluesman, Ivory Joe Hunter, who scored with "Since I Met You Baby," a virtual rewrite of his 1950 hit, "I Almost Lost My Mind." Syd Nathan had found a young singer from Detroit who promised to become the next Johnny Ace. Little Willie John (real name: William J. Woods) had a sinuous high tenor that he could wrap around a ballad or use to belt an up-tempo number, and he had first hit in 1955 with a stoptime big-band blues number, "All Around the World." But he really triumphed in 1956 with two ballads, "Need Your Love So Bad" and "Fever," which crossed over to the pop charts and inspired a cover two years later by Peggy Lee. Although he was only eighteen at the time of his first hit, Willie John had worked with the Duke Ellington Orchestra and was more of an adult attraction than teen bait.

Even Fats Domino was out with a two-fisted ballad attack, "Blueberry Hill," followed by "Blue Monday," both featuring his patented Domino triplets on the piano, but slower. And from time to time, old-time blues made new, by B. B. King or by a twenty-year-old Chicago sensation, Otis Rush ("I Can't Quit You, Baby" was a 1956 hit), or by the redoubtable Muddy Waters, would hit the charts. As for black pop artists, the Platters were the group who were welcome on the turntables of most white homes.

The reasons for this shift are hard to guess. Maybe that first wave of rock-and-roll fans was growing older, beginning to settle down. It's also possible that sometimes the cultural fabric gets too strained by the onslaught of innovation, and people need time to catch their breath. Possibly a steady diet of innovation doesn't nourish, and a brief period of looking back provides strength for the future. But for a while, it looked as if rock and roll was over, and with a sigh of relief, the nation's pundits and conservative disc jockeys started looking for the next big thing.

All the wild antics of the rock and rollers pointed to a taste for something more exotic. Capitol hoped it would be found on its new album, *Legends of the Jivaro*, by Yma Sumac. Sumac and her husband had just spent some time in South America, where they had risked their lives to observe the songs and dances of fierce headhunters whose music was an integral part of the mysterious Sumac's cultural heritage. Back from the jungle, she and her husband arranged these exotic melodies for vocal, choral group, and drums. But they proved to be *too* exotic for the hit parade.

Even Elvis Presley's own record company had hopes for exotic music. Harry Belafonte was a young singer of West Indian extraction and folksinging bent whom RCA had signed a few years before, no doubt attracted by his clean-cut appearance, fine voice, and unusual choice of material. He languished for a while until somebody hit on the brilliant idea of having him record calypso. Now, calypso was hardly anything new, having existed since the late nineteenth century in Trinidad, but it had never really caught on in the United States. Nobody had really ever tried to exploit it, though, outside of a few efforts in the 1930s and then in the early 1950s to sell a singer named Wilmouth Houdini. But it certainly met the exotica requirements—it had a catchy rhythm, the lyrics were in English and in some cases very literate, and Belafonte was a salable enough performer to spearhead the new movement.

Sure enough, his very first effort, "Jamaica Farewell," did very nicely on the pop charts, and the slightly more daring "Banana Boat" did even better,* cracking the R&B charts—no mean feat. Calypsomania! It hardly mattered that the rhythms behind Belafonte were more Latin than Caribbean, or that when *Billboard* dispatched a reporter to Jamaica to find out what kind of calypso the natives listened to, the clerk at the record store smiled and said, "We only stock that for tourists"—and, presumably, others who couldn't tell Jamaica from Trinidad—requesting more Fats Domino records. Fats and, for that matter, the rest of the New Orleans crew were huge heroes in Jamaica, thanks to the powerful clear-channel radio stations beaming from New Orleans and Miami; and Jamaican entrepreneurs like Clement Dodd and Prince Buster were already trying to imitate their rhythms on homemade records.

But the other calypso tunes by American pop artists were stiffing, and when companies tried releasing Trinidadian records by Lord Nelson and the Mighty Flea, nobody wanted to hear them, either. There was talk of a "rock-calypso fusion" in *Billboard*, which pointed to recent releases by Chuck Berry ("Havana Moon," a stiff) and the Gladiolas ("Little Darlin'" which would be a bigger hit when a white Canadian group, the Diamonds, got hold of it) as harbingers of a trend. But American blacks have a traditional dislike for their West Indian brethren, and the West Indian presence in the United States isn't strong enough for calypso to have been part of our ambient noise, the way blues and country are. So, finally, American record companies just had to break down and admit it—it wasn't calypso that was selling records, it was the charismatic Harry Belafonte.

*The song was known to many as "Day-O," to distinguish it from a similar song that was a hit at the same time for the Tarriers, a folk trio that included Alan Arkin.

By spring, the last vestiges of the fad were appearing: a Los Angeles group, Richard Berry and the Pharaohs, released an attempt at calypso (titled "Louie Louie"), backed with a reading of the country standard "You Are My Sunshine," which various R&B companies were inexplicably trying to turn into a hit. *Billboard* gave "Louie Louie" a 70. And by the time the Loews Metropolitan Theatre in Brooklyn tried to go head-to-head with Alan Freed's annual Easter show at the Brooklyn Paramount down the street, it was possible to stand on the right corner and watch the crowds literally turn toward rock and roll and away from calypso.

Rock and roll was certainly thriving abroad, and January 1957 saw lucky La Vern Baker, Bill Haley and His Comets, and Big Joe Turner escaping the cold by touring Australia, selling out every show they played. In February, the Teenagers were booked at Carnaval in Panama, where they took the place by storm, came back long enough to pack some warmer clothes, and flew off to London. The British press was not on their side, and reviews ranged from tepid to outright hostile. There was bickering in the group, much was made of a voluptuous tutor who had come along to make sure Frankie did his schoolwork (after all, he wasn't a juvenile delinquent!), and members of the group muttered in front of the eager English reporters that success seemed to have gone to Frankie's head, that he seemed to think that he *was* the show. Frankie told reporters that he preferred progressive jazz, by artists like Stan Kenton, Dave Brubeck, and Ted Heath, to rock and roll.

Bill Haley followed Frankie over to Britain and also died the death. Part of his problem was undoubtedly his appearance, since looks have always been critical in British pop music; but another significant factor was that in order to get him, the promoter of the tour had overpaid, so his shows were extremely expensive. Still, he was scheduled to tour Jamaica in June, and West Indian fans seemed excited, even though he wasn't Fats Domino. In fact, Fats Domino was virtually the only major rock-and-roll performer who refused to tour abroad—not because he had throat cancer, as one of those wildfire rumors held, but because, as the Fat Man said, "It's a long way from New Orleans."

But there is no doubt that in early 1957, rock and roll's power was slightly diminished. The Top Ten on March 9 was all male, and almost all pop: Tab Hunter, Elvis, Pat Boone, Sonny James, Harry Belafonte, Terry Gilkyson, Tommy Sands, the Hilltoppers, Frankie Laine, and Fats Domino. Elvis and Fats Domino were proven big sellers, but where was the rest of rock and roll?

Learning a little about capitalism, that's where. There was a glut of records on the market, a lot of them very good, but the Presley juggernaut had obscured the fact that rock and roll was still the province of indie labels and that they were regional. As Casey Casem, a Detroit disc jockey who has since become one of the most prominent announcing voices of American pop music, noted, "In those days, you made your reputation by discovering and breaking a record"; and finding one in the stock of local favorites, which then would grow bigger and become a national hit, was a very difficult task. There were so many records, and teen tastes were so unpredictable. How could a middle-aged man reach into a stack of records, come up with something called "Swing-Bop-Boogie" b/w "Sleep, Rock-a-Roll Rock-a-Baby" by Alvis Wayne from Corpus Christi, Texas, and know whether it was gold or trash? Among the records released in late 1956 and early 1957 that never made it big were the Johnny Burnette Trio's "Train Kept A-Rollin'," Jimmy Murphy's "Grandpa's a Cat," Chuck Berry's "You Can't Catch Me," Jerry Lee Lewis's "Crazy Arms," Warren Smith's "Rock 'n' Roll Ruby" and "Ubangi Stomp," Charlie Feathers's "One Hand Loose," Sonny Burgess's "We Wanna Boogie" b/w "Red Headed Woman," Buddy Holly's "Modern Don Juan," Johnny Horton's "I'm Comin' Home," Billy Lee Riley's "Flyin' Saucers Rock & Roll," Bobby Marchan's "Chickee Wah Wah," Muddy Waters's "Got My Mojo Workin'," Bo Diddley's "Hey, Bo Diddley" b/w "Mona," Carl Perkins's "Matchbox," and, as noted, Richard Berry and the Pharaohs' "Louie Louie." Those are eighteen classic slabs of rock and roll, and some of them were played in Memphis, others in Chicago, still others in New Orleans, Dallas, Shreveport, and Seattle—but there wasn't a single station that played them all, except maybe in heaven.

Even the hippest dj (and they existed) had problems making good records heard. With the advent of network-radio broadcasting rock and roll, and with network outlets usually in possession of the most powerful transmitters, big-label records—which, even in 1957, were usually pop songs or covers—had the advantage. Jockeys were much more receptive to telephone requests then, and they'd play what their listeners asked to hear. Live record hops, hosted by local radio djs who provided turntables and either broadcast live or simulated a broadcast (without commercials) at a teen club or high-school gym, were also very useful in figuring teen tastes as well as boosting ratings for the jockeys. If a local performer cut a deal with a popular dj, either giving him a percentage of his record or letting him manage the act, the artist could appear at a hop and get attention that way. Other stations in the area would take notice as fan clubs grew and phone requests came in, and soon a record would spread to a big city nearby, where the pop stations and jukebox operators reported to *Billboard* or another trade magazine. From there, disc jockeys in other cities would adopt the record and, if it proved successful, could brag that they'd broken so-and-so in Minneapolis or Cleveland. Pretty soon the whole Midwest would be humming, and from there, with a little bit of luck, the artist would get national recognition.

The trouble was, the process could take months, and that lag time could kill the label. As the market heated up, many small indies—even successful ones—sold themselves outright to larger, better capitalized companies that could weather out the wait. In January, Paramount Pictures, one of the growing number of studios looking for a hedge against the losses that television might inflict on motion pictures, bought Randy Woods's massively successful Dot outfit in Nashville, adding it to a stable which already contained the nascent ABC-Paramount label, used mostly for sound-track music. But not exclusively: in February, ABC-Paramount, after seeing how a Washington, D.C., label was selling Lloyd Price's "Just Because," bought the master from the label, which was having trouble meeting the demand. A week later, Dot zoomed in on the tiny Pittsburgh label Fee-Bee and purchased one of vocal music's all-time classics, "Come Go With Me," by the Del Vikings, an integrated group that had formed on a Pittsburgh air force base and was now going to be able to hit the Top Ten with ease.

But there were several independent labels that had acquired sufficient muscle over the past couple of years to be fairly secure in their positions in the marketplace. Chess was one of them. They had moved into spanking new quarters on the South Side of Chicago, at 2120 South Michigan Avenue, and at the beginning of the year, they announced that they'd soon be releasing their first album, a set by Chuck Berry. An album was very definitely a prestige move for a rhythm-and-blues record company,* but Chess was not only working on the Berry project (which was easily assembled from tracks on hand, old hits and their B sides, and so on), but also announced a sophisticated "Moonglows with strings" album, no doubt to cash in on the ballad craze, although it seems never to have been released. Fats Domino had one album out, and another on the way; in March, Art Rupe released *Here's Little Richard!*; and the Biharis, spearheading a trend the majors were just beginning to follow, inaugurated the Crown Records line of $1.98 albums with releases by B. B. King, the Teen Queens, and some sax-honking instrumentals. Atlantic, for their part, printed a mass of technical information on the back of their records, including types of microphones used, so their albums cost $4.98—but, being by people like Ray Charles, they were worth it.

The glut, calypso, and ballads notwithstanding, rock and roll would eventually prevail. Of course, some people still didn't like it—a little old lady was arrested in Indianapolis for making repeated trips to a local record store so she could smash their stock of Elvis Presley 78s with her cane—but by the spring of 1957, great records again abounded. La Vern Baker sang of "Jim Dandy" to the rescue; and Mickey "Guitar" Baker and his wife, Sylvia Robinson, showed off their picking and singing prowess with "Love Is Strange," a sprightly R&B cha-cha number that made pop waves and spawned the oddly titled flop follow-up, "Love Will Make You Fail In School." Fats Domino came on with a boogie-woogie rocker, "I'm Walkin'," that Pat Boone tried to cover; and Buddy Knox, the pride of Happy, Texas, blazed in with "Party Doll," a full-tilt rocker from left field.

Not as far left field as Screamin' Jay Hawkins, however, who had gotten blind drunk in the studio while trying to recut a mild-regional-hit ballad, "I

---

*At the start of 1957, only about twenty-five rhythm and blues albums existed, several of which were quickies that Syd Nathan had released to capitalize on Bill Doggett's success with "Honky Tonk."

Put a Spell On You," and wound up gargling, screaming, grunting, and—only incidentally—singing. Still, Okeh released the recording and advertised it as a novelty: "D.J.'s—Be brave . . . Put a spell on your fans . . . Tie up your switchboard—it happened in New York, Chicago, Philadelphia and Hartford!—If you get fired, we'll get you a job."

But the song was enough of a novelty that nobody got fired—or nobody but poor Bob Friesen, all the way up at CHWK in Chilliwack, British Columbia. In February, he lost his job because his station's management was outraged by the song, and as requested in the ad, appealed to Okeh-Columbia for employment. The company passed the buck until a worthy soul at one of its pressing plants got Friesen's story into *Billboard*, where, presumably, some station contacted him, out of pity as much as out of publicity value.

And it was in the spring of 1957 that Chuck Berry finally produced the anthem he'd had in him all along, "School Day (Ring Ring Goes The Bell)." Its premise was simple: Berry enumerated the travails of school in short, chopped-off lines of verse, and punctuated each line with a machine-gun burst from his guitar. He made school sound as oppressive and stifling as he had made the menial jobs sound in his earlier "Too Much Monkey Business." The teacher was ugly, you couldn't find a place to sit in the cafeteria, the kid behind you was pestering you. You were living for that three o'clock hour to come around, so you could go straight to the "juke joint," as Berry put it, drrrrrrop the coin into the jukebox (Berry rolled the r with delight), and dance with the one you loved. Berry repeated the verse about the jukebox and dancing twice, and then, just in case anybody still didn't know that there was a single, specific cure for what school put you through, he added these words:

> Hail hail rock and roll!
> Deliver me from the days of old
> Long live rock and roll
> The beat of the drums is loud and bold.
> Rock! Rock! Rock and roll!
> The feeling is there, body and soul!

Naturally the song was an immediate smash hit, topping the pop charts for weeks and riding solidly on the R&B charts as well. It was played on the radio and on jukeboxes, and teens sang that last verse in the halls. It was something really *theirs*, this rock-and-roll music. The teacher couldn't have it. It was freedom. It was an assertion of power.

And why shouldn't it be? It was beginning to dawn on people—and not just teenagers—that this was a new age. The American standard of living had never seemed higher, and after two major wars, America was asserting its place in the world. American scientists were asserting their technological superiority by taking the lead in the International Geophysical

Year celebration, in which sixty-six countries around the world cooperated for scientific advancement and mutual benefit. American auto makers were asserting their products' virtues of speed and power, turning the 1957 models into rocketship fantasies with nose cones, chromed grills, and razor-sharp fins; Ford's new model, the Edsel, had a design so futuristic that, what with the oval grille and the winglike rear, it really looked capable of interplanetary travel. American Negroes were winning rights back from entrenched interests of the past, with a Civil Rights Act barring discrimination by federal law.

Not everybody saw the American dream in the same way. Jack Kerouac, a French-Canadian ex-college football player, published his novel *On The Road*, telling of his drug-fueled coast-to-coast automobile journeys, searching for what he called kicks. His pal Allen Ginsberg, a former marketing researcher and a self-acknowledged homosexual, looked around at this great postwar world and saw "angelheaded hipsters burning for the ancient heavenly connection to the starry dynamo in the machinery of night" in a poem called *Howl* that stood trial for obscenity; and flat out said, in a poem he dared call *America*, "Go fuck yourself with your atom bomb." The media called them the beat generation, and they were tracing a bigger rip in the moral fabric of America than anybody had imagined.

But far more than the beats, a mild-mannered recluse named J. D. Salinger was influencing the older teens and college kids with *The Catcher in the Rye*, a novel he'd written in the late 1940s and published in 1951, which was just beginning to circulate, thanks to the rise of new paperback books. Some of its popularity came from its spectacular obscenity trial, but it was the protagonist, Holden Caulfield, with his disdain for the phonies and the stodgy attitudes of those around him, who was attracting Salinger admirers. *Catcher* showed its readers a different world from the one they'd been brought up to expect, but one they recognized as their own—a world of loneliness and alienation that adults couldn't begin to understand. That, for those who read the book, was as revolutionary as what Chuck Berry was saying.

That spring Nashville began responding to the rock-and-roll slump with a new kind of music. It was slow getting off the ground, probably because country music was doing very well crossing over to pop and not doing too badly on its own. What really got Nashville's rock-and-roll era going was an independent label that was hungry to the point of starvation. Archie Bleyer had risen to fame as Arthur Godfrey's musical director in the early 1950s, when the rotund ukelele-playing announcer was king of the airwaves. Bleyer may have thought he could lure Godfrey away by starting Cadence Records, but he was soon disappointed. Living from semi-hit to near-miss like the hundreds of other indies, Bleyer slowly built up a stable of artists, most of whom were undistinguished. He did have Andy Williams, a young crooner in the great tradition, who was a fairly consistent seller, and the Chordettes, four girls who chirped in a style similar—too similar, probably—to the McGuire Sisters and the other female pop groups. But in 1957, Bleyer needed a new sound, and so he looked to Wesley Rose, head of Acuff-Rose, Nashville's most popular publishing company, for help.

Through Rose, Bleyer met Don and Phil Everly, two brothers from Kentucky who had grown up singing brother-style country music on their parents' radio show on KMA, in Shenandoah, Iowa, where father Ike's peripatetic country career had settled his small family. The two had naturally drifted to Nashville and had achieved a bare success: a hit for Kitty Wells called "Thou Shalt Not Steal," and one single on Columbia, "The Sun Keeps Shining," that was a major flop. Still, for beautifully textured harmonies, the Everly Brothers were unparalleled.

But they had recently begun to suspect that their own songwriting wasn't strong enough, so they had turned to Nashville's odd couple, Felice and Boudleaux Bryant, who had also just signed a songwriting deal with Acuff-Rose. "I knew Ike Everly," Boudleaux remembers, "because he'd been my barber, and Felice had been on television with the boys but didn't remember them because she was so concerned with her own act." Bleyer, meanwhile, was on a signing binge and had written out contracts for Gordon Terry and Anita Carter as well as for the Everlys.

As Bryant recalled, "We had appointments with all of Archie's new artists, and I was supposed to show Gordon Terry songs before lunch and the Everly Brothers after lunch. I played Gordon a song called 'Bye Bye Love,' and he said, 'Don't you have anything stronger?' I'd been showing that song to everybody and his brother"—thirty people and brothers, to be exact—"because I thought it was a hit. Well, the Everlys liked it immediately." Wesley also slipped the song to Webb Pierce, just in case Bleyer's version failed, but it turned out that wasn't necessary. "Bye Bye Love," with one of the most soulful and haunting brother-style songs ever recorded, "I Wonder If I Care As Much," on the reverse, stomped up the pop and country charts, unseating Pierce handily on the latter and showing the land that yet another of its ancient musics, pure Appalachian harmony singing, could be bent gently to rock and roll.

"Bye Bye Love" was not a one-shot success. As Bryant tells it, "Don was wandering around our office one day, and hit some chords on the guitar, and I sat up and said, 'That's an intro!' We changed the same lick around and came up with 'Wake Up Little Susie.' We recorded it that night, did it on the Friday night 'Opry,' and everybody said 'That's a hit!' After that, we started writing songs specifically for them. We did ten for every session." "Susie" was a little daring, a song about two teenagers who go out on an innocent date at the drive-in and see a movie that is so boring that they fall asleep. The singer pleads with Susie to wake up, realizing that coming home so late will arouse the suspicions of their families and friends. Teenagers responded to it because it was a perfect picture of the way life really was for them, just as "School Day" had been. And its guitar lick was extremely catchy, too.

But there were some people for whom the country-leaning-toward-rock-and-roll idea didn't seem to work. Jerry Lee Lewis, Sam Phillips's new young singer, had failed miserably with his reading of "Crazy Arms," even though it was sincerely performed. Probably the drubbing was as much due to the fact that Ray Price had already laid claim to the song as it was to Jerry Lee's slightly itchy performance. *Itchy*, in fact, was a good word for the young blond dynamo from Ferriday, Louisiana. Conflicting emotions were his stock in trade, which is why he made such a good country singer; he seemed really to feel the songs of cheating and drinking and losing that were the necessary components of a country performer's repertoire.

But in his youth, along with his cousins Mickey Gilley and Jimmy Swaggart, he used to sneak behind Haney's Big House, a black honky-tonk in Ferriday, and watch the bluesmen who came to play there, paying particular attention to the piano players. Jerry Lee's family had bought a battered old piano, and all the kids used to practice on it, playing hymns or, when the adults weren't looking, the music they heard at Haney's. White-trash juvenile delinquents all, they were smart enough to realize that the gospel circuit was a way out of the dead-end life Ferriday presented. And good as Jimmy and Mickey were, the consensus was that it was Jerry Lee who was the major talent. Jerry Lee, never meek and retiring, tended to agree; and although the gospel world rejected him after he was thrown out of the Southwestern Bible Institute in Waxahachie, Texas, for his blasphemous pianistics, he took to country music. That road led him to Memphis, where Sam Phillips needed a session pianist who could play country and rock and roll. So Jerry Lee accompanied Carl Perkins and then Warren Smith around the beginning of 1957. It is his piano powering Billy Lee Riley's "Flyin' Saucers Rock & Roll" and Riley's most famous record, "Red Hot," with its famous exchange between Riley and his band that goes "My gal is red hot!" "Your gal ain't doodly-squat!"

But Sam realized that his pianist could do more than studio work and kept letting him record whenever he had time. Jerry Lee had been working on a tune called "It'll Be Me," a funny song about a lover who never let his girlfriend out of his sight, and during a break in one session, somebody suggested he play a song he had performed with a singer named Johnny Littlejohn, called "Whole Lotta Shakin' Goin' On," which Webb Pierce's piano player, Roy Hall, had brought out on Decca in 1955. After taking a minute to recall the words—it'd been a while since he'd done it—Jerry Lee started pounding out a savage boogie-woogie bass line and, when the band fell in behind him, started singing. It was the story of a party in a barn, where a whole lotta shakin' was goin' on, and two minutes and some seconds later, the fun was over and they got back to work on "It'll Be Me." But when they played back the tapes, the diversion seemed stronger than the song they'd been recording.

Sam wasn't convinced, but he arranged another session, determined to get a hit single out of Jerry Lee, in whom he correctly perceived a lot of the same qualities that had made Elvis a star. At the second session, they tried "Shakin'" again, and this time, partly because the musicians were different, the song was completely transformed. Guitarist Roland Janes, who had sounded like he was auditioning for a polka band on the first take with his off-the-beat chords, was mixed down this time, and probably most important, Jerry Lee's regular drummer, Jimmy Van Eaton, was on board, attempting homicide on his set of skins. It was molten fury tempered with heavy sexuality, when Jerry Lee told the band to get "real low" and, leering, instructed the dancer to stand in one place and shake it and then the band swept up into a howling chorus and the song ended. One take. Jerry Lee Lewis was on his way.

His success was sealed with his midsummer stint on "The Steve Allen Show." Stuck on at the very end, he got five minutes and he took full advantage of them. Swinging into "Whole Lotta Shakin'," he slowly stood, riding the piano like a madman, kicking the piano stool out of his way so he could get a better purchase on the keyboard. Caught up in the spirit of the moment, Steve Allen threw the stool back at him and then sent a hail of other objects after it. Undaunted, Jerry Lee started playing with his foot. It was scandalous, and it gave Jerry Lee his big break. Recognizing the debt, he later named his son Steve Allen Lewis.

After seeing Jerry Lee on television, Otis Blackwell, the black songwriter who'd penned "Don't Be Cruel" and "All Shook Up" for Elvis, sent Sam Phillips a demo called "Great Balls of Fire." During the recording session, some alcohol was making the rounds, and as it sometimes will, it began to raise something from Jerry Lee's conscience. Back in the booth, Sam's faithful engineer, Jack Clement, decided to record the tumult that ensued as Jerry Lee began to argue with Sam. Nick Tosches, in his biography of Jerry Lee, *Hellfire*, transcribed the argument:

"H-E-L-L!" Jerry Lee loudly spelled.
"I don't believe this," Sam Phillips muttered.
"Great Godamighty, great balls of fire," James Van Eaton proclaimed mockingly.
"That's right!" hollered Billy Lee Riley, right behind him.
"I don't believe it," Sam repeated.
"It says make merry with the joy of God *only*," Jerry Lee yelled. "But when it comes to *worldly* music, rock 'n' roll . . ."
"Pluck it out!" Billy Lee Riley shouted.
". . . anything like that," Jerry Lee went on, fast, driven. "You have done brought yourself into the world, and you're in the world, and you're still a sinner. You're a sinner and unless you be saved and borned again and be made as a little child and walk before God and be holy—and brother, I mean you got to be *so* pure. No sin shall enter there—*no sin!* For it says *no sin.* It don't say just a little bit; it says *no sin shall enter there.* Brother, not one little bit. You got to *walk* and *talk* with God to go to heaven. You got to be *so* good."

"Hallelujah," Riley said,

"All right," Sam said. "Now look, Jerry, religious conviction doesn't mean anything resembling extremism. All right. Do you mean to tell me that you're gonna take the Bible, that you're gonna take God's word, and that you're gonna revolutionize the whole universe? Now, listen. Jesus Christ was sent here by God Almighty—"

"Right!" said Jerry Lee.

"Did He convince, did He save all of the people in the world?"

"Naw, but He tried to!"

"He sure did. Now, wait a minute. Jesus Christ came into this world. He tolerated man. He didn't preach from one pulpit. He went around and did good."

"That's right! He preached everywhere!"

"Everywhere!"

"He preached on land!"

"Everywhere. That's right, that's right."

"He preached on water!"

"That's right, that's exactly right. Now—"

"Man, He done everything! He *healed!*"

"Now, now, here's the difference."

"Are you followin' those that heal? Like Jesus Christ did? Well, it's happenin' every day!"

"What d'ya mean . . . you . . . what . . . I, I . . . what—"

"The *blind* had eyes opened. The *lame* were made to walk."

"Jerry, Jesus Christ—"

"The crippled were made to walk."

"Jesus Christ, in my opinion, is just as real today as He was when He came into this world."

"Right! Right! You're so right you don't know what you're sayin'!"

"Now, I will say, more so—"

"Aw, let's cut it," Riley interrupted disgustedly.

"It'll never sell, man," Van Eaton said to him. "It's not commercial."

"Wait, wait, wait just a minute," Sam said, throwing his arms up, "we can't, we got to—now, look listen, I'm tellin' you outta my heart, and I have studied the Bible a little bit—"

"Well, I have too," said Jerry Lee. "I studied it through and through and through and through, and I know what I'm talkin' about."

"Jerry, Jerry. If you think that you can't do good if you're a rock and roll exponent—"

"You can do good, Mr. Phillips, don't get me wrong."

"Now, wait, wait, listen. When I say *do good—*"

"You can have a kind heart!"

"I don't mean, I don't mean just—"

"You can help people!"

"You can save souls!"

"No! No! No! No!"

"Yes!"

"*How can the Devil save souls? What are you talkin' about?*"

"Listen, listen . . ."

"Man, I got *the Devil* in me! If I didn't have, I'd be a Christian!"

After some more talk in this vein, they cut the tune, with Jerry Lee pouring his torment out into the lyrics, which were those of a simple I-love-you-but-you-drive-me-crazy sort of love song, and utterly transforming them, creating an explosion the equal of anything happening in the Nevada desert.

It was a time for madmen at the piano, in fact: Little Richard was firing them off and burning them down one after the other. He started 1957 with "The Girl Can't Help It," followed it up with the screaming "Lucille," and the same week in May that Jerry Lee released "Whole Lotta Shakin' Goin' On" saw "Miss Ann" and "Jenny, Jenny." "This was my richest time," Richard wrote in his autobiography, "with all my hit records selling over the country and me and my band working every night. The river was running. The river of loot. And I was on the bank at that time. At the height of my career, our initial guarantee had risen to about $2,500 a night, plus 50 percent of the take over double the guarantee amount. Most often we would walk out with maybe $10,000 or $15,000 as our part of the total gate receipt. And understand that during that era the price of a concert ticket was at the maximum $3.50."

Those were huge sums in the 1950s, and it was all in cash—cash Richard carried in satchels or just loose in the back of his car. Bobby Byrd, of James Brown's Famous Flames (who were flagging because somebody, insisting that James was the next Little Richard, was having him cut record after record in a conservative rhythm-and-blues style) remembers being broken down on the highway when Richard's car came along. Richard opened the trunk, extracted a fistful of money, and drove off into the night.

It was a good thing Richard was making a substantial income on the road, though, since his arrangement with Art Rupe didn't make him a lot from his records. Rupe owned his publishing, for one thing, so he was the one who profited when Elvis or Pat Boone recorded a Little Richard cover. But Richard was happy to perform, happy to be recognized after all those years of hiding his light under a bushel. Rupe had more or less stopped looking for other talent, since besides Richard, he had signed up nearly every major gospel talent of the day and they sold very steadily, providing him with a cushion that would probably last long after the rock-and-roll fad had faded.

He'd found new gospel talent, and he'd also sought out older artists like Chicago's famous Soul Stirrers, who'd recorded for Lew Chudd. They were suddenly becoming the hottest property in the gospel world, thanks to their new lead singer, Sam Cooke, whose good looks and sensational, melismatic singing affected young women the way Elvis Presley's did, only Sam did it in the service of the Lord. Unfortunately, Cooke was rebellious and kept trying to record pop records. He'd released "Lovable" in 1956, under the name Dale Cooke, but Rupe wasn't happy with this development and warned him not to try it again.

Of course, the gospel/rock-and-roll conflict was hardly news in the rhythm-and-blues field. Richard himself suffered twinges of guilt from time to time, since he was perfectly well aware how much of his show and his style came from the black churches of his childhood. It must have hurt him deeply to see his music decried as a thing of the devil, or to hear comments like those of disc jockey Noble Gravelin of WAMM in Flint, Michigan—the censors were still out there—who piously told *Billboard's* Vox Jox columnist, "I banned Little Richard's 'Lucille' because I feel the lyrics advocate immoral practices. I'm happy to say that the general consensus of my listeners—teenagers and adults—is that I did the right thing." Gravelin must have gotten a different version of the song from the one most people are familiar with, because the song deals with a girl who's married somebody else, leaving Richard pleading for her to come back. Maybe that was advocating adultery, but there was nothing in the song to indicate that she would return. Soon there were rumors that Little Richard was getting evangelical in his stage shows.

Elvis, too, had been touched by the spirit, releasing an EP called "Peace in the Valley," which featured the title song and three other spiritual numbers. *Billboard* noted its "commendable reverence," and the Jordanaires, the sometime-gospel group RCA had given Elvis as backup singers, enjoyed this return to their past. But even though it was sacred music, this record, just like all the rest of Elvis's RCA releases, started shooting up the pop charts.

By June, Elvis was coming off his latest hit, "All Shook Up," and was ready to release his next movie, *Loving You.* This was no black-and-white quickie with songs dropped in at odd moments like *Love Me Tender.* It was a Technicolor extravaganza featuring Elvis as Deke Rivers, an unassuming hillbilly kid with a job delivering beer and a talent for riling up the girls when he sang the occasional song. Discovered by a publicist (Lizabeth Scott) who was working for a failed bandleader trying to make a comeback as a country musician (Wendell Corey) and hating every minute of it, Deke rose to the top touring with Corey's band, finally entirely eclipsing his mentor. (Not that "Tex" minded too much; he hated country music and only stuck with it when Scott lectured him, saying, "Don't knock country music—it's the voice of the nation. Folk music's big and getting bigger. If you make it to the top again—*if*—it's the route you'll take."

Along the way, Elvis/Deke delivered nearly an album's worth of songs, including a medley sung over a montage of performances and clips of the road going by that's right out of a rock video; Ray Charles's "Mean Woman Blues"; a Little Richard–inspired "Let's Have A Party"; and Elvis's next chart-topper, "(Let Me Be Your) Teddy Bear." Deke also got to trounce an opponent in an argument in Amarillo, the big city for Tex and the band, where the kids dressed in top-notch cat clothes. The wild thing was, despite a plot that was occasionally too corny for its own good, Elvis jumped right in and *acted*—and did a fine job of it! Without question, he was the star of the film.

Movies and, of course, television appearances had brought many musicians hits, but in 1957, a hit television show actually created a musician. "The Adventures of Ozzie and Harriet" was a long-running situation comedy built around the family life of Ozzie and Harriet Nelson and their sons, David and Ricky. Ricky, especially, kept the show high in the ratings, with his cute face, good haircut, and fair simulacrum of the Presley sneer. He was sixteen years old and, like many modern teenagers, wanted to cut a record. So Ozzie, a bandleader in the 1930s, turned to jazz guitarist Barney Kessel, who'd just signed on as A&R chief with Norman Granz's Verve Records. Barney, who hadn't come near releasing a hit since he'd joined the label, agreed, and they chose a proven tune, Fats Domino's "I'm Walkin'." It was released with little fanfare, but Ozzie, never one to miss a trick, soon worked it into the show as "a rhythm-and-blues tune" young Ricky had recorded. Three weeks later, it was a hit. Ozzie, sensing that there was more here than just a way of saving face, began to entertain offers from various record companies (the deal with Verve was very loose; it was just a favor to Ozzie), and before long, Ricky was signed to the same label as Fats, Imperial. Of course, once the record started selling, suits and countersuits began to fly between Verve and Imperial, but in the end, Lew Chudd would up with his first bona-fide pop hit maker.

What was important about a lot of the new acts that were emerging in 1957—the Everly Brothers and Ricky Nelson, in particular, but also Chuck Berry and even Pat Boone in many respects—was that they seemed (even if they weren't) teenage. Their music was aimed exclusively at teenagers, a strategy that their producers, A&R men, and record labels took seriously. Atlantic Records liked to imply that their music was more sophisticated and that their nonjazz offerings were aimed at adult rhythm-and-blues fans, who could go to a nightclub instead of a malt shop, but they weren't fooling anybody when, in early 1957, they signed Leiber and Stoller to an A&R deal along with their production deal. Now all that remained was to find a way to reach the teens that Ertegun and Wexler didn't feel compromised them.

The answer seemed to be the Robins, the group that Atlantic acquired from Leiber and Stoller's Spark label, and who had recorded their story songs, "Smokey Joe's Café" and "Riot in Cell Block No. 9." Neither song was particularly teen oriented, but the funny stories had potential. Unfortunately, the Robins' manager didn't want the group to record on Atlantic, so Leiber and Stoller talked to lead singer Carl Gardner and to Bobby Nunn, the comic bass singer, and suddenly the Coasters (so called because they were operating out of the West Coast, unlike most vocal groups) were born. Their first record, "Down in Mexico," sold fairly well, though it was really just a rewrite of "Smokey Joe's Café," but in May, their second release blew the lid off things.

"Searchin'" b/w "Young Blood" was the first monster Herb Abramson's Atco subsidiary had come up with, and it was the most teenage record the Atlantic family had yet released. On its A side, the singer is searching for his runaway girlfriend, vowing to track her down with the tenacity of a Northwest Mountie or a Bulldog Drummond, as the group executes a fiendishly tricky vocal arrangement built around the chant of "Gonna find her." But "Young Blood" was dangerous. In some ways, it is the opposite of "Searchin'," in that it tells about finding The One, the girl who unhinges a boy and dominates his dreams. In simple, direct language, it describes him meeting her, being tongue-tied when he tries to talk to her, and finally encountering her father, who tells him to get lost. The last verse finds the singer tossing and turning till sunrise; and the song ends with the words "Can't get you out of my mind" swooping up to a surprising and beautiful major-chord resolution that seems to imply a subtle and wonderful surprise, that the story will have a happy ending anyway. Each line is punctuated by a lubricious saxophone smear, and each verse but the last is capped by being repeated by each group member in a comic fashion: "Looka there! Looka there! Looka there! Uh, looka there!" (this last by the bass). Funny, true, sexy, and innocent, it captured the entire teenage experience in just over two minutes, established the Coasters as major talents, and gave Leiber and Stoller the capital to move their operation to New York, where they set up in the Brill Building with all the other professional songwriters. "Searchin'" and "Young Blood" reminded America that teenagers could be black, and that adolescence forged a bond of desires and concerns that even transcended race.

Teen dollars ruled the market in the summer of 1957 with a Top Ten that included Pat Boone's "Love Letters in the Sand," Elvis's "All Shook Up," Jimmy Dorsey's "So Rare," Marty Robbins's "White Sport Coat (And a Pink Carnation)," Gale Storm's "Dark Moon," the Everly Brothers' "Bye Bye Love," the Diamonds' cover of the Gladiolas' "Little Darlin'," the Coasters' "Young Blood," Chuck Berry's "School Day," the Coasters' "Searchin'," and Ricky Nelson's "I'm Walkin'"—four slots more than rock and roll had claimed in January. The ballads that made dancing close so much fun despite the summer heat were appearing: Lee Andrews and the Hearts' "Long Lonely Nights," which Chess bought from Philadelphia's Main Line label, and the Five Satins' "To the Aisle," carrying the vaguely upsetting message that "each step draws you closer to the aisle"—that marriage was, in fact, the only proper solution to romance. But there were up-tempo songs, too, with Little Richard *whooooing* away about "Jenny, Jenny"; the Bobbettes, an all-girl vocal group on Atlantic, singing "Mr. Lee," a tribute to a hip high school teacher, and a weirdo from New Orleans, Huey "Piano" Smith, recording with the same musicians Little Richard was using, who declared that he had "The Rockin' Pneumonia and the Boogie-Woogie Flu."

But what the summer really needed was a fresh face or two, a new song to brighten it up. One came along at the end of August: "That'll Be the Day"—the same Buddy Holly song that he recorded for Decca in 1956. But now it was recorded by the Crickets, one of whom was Buddy Holly, and it emerged while Buddy's relationship with Decca was falling apart. His band had been treated poorly by producer Owen Bradley at their second recording session (Sonny Curtis remembers that Bradley was in a hurry to get it over so he could go water-skiing), and Decca didn't even bother to promote the single, "Modern Don Juan," put out at the end of 1956. At the end of the year, Holly was given his release, and he realized that he had to make a living. To do that, he had to assemble a working group, since Sonny Curtis had left because he and Buddy didn't get along, leaving only drummer Jerry Allison. There were plenty of musicians in Lubbock, and, as an almost-successful western-and-bop star, Buddy easily found a bassist, Joe Mauldin, and a guitarist, Niki Sullivan.

The next step was to make some more records. Buddy knew that Decca hadn't realized his potential, so he looked west instead of east, to Clovis, New Mexico, the home of Norman Petty. With Petty's wife, Vi, on piano, Petty on organ, and Jack Vaughn on drums, the Norman Petty Trio had somehow gotten a recording deal that, by 1957, thanks to a couple of hits, he had parlayed into a deal with Mitch Miller at Columbia. The profits from these low-overhead hits he had plowed into a publishing company, Nor Va Jak Music, as well as recording studio, which brought him in contact with musicians. Soon he produced two cuts for a band called The Rhythm Orchids, led by Buddy Knox and Jimmy Bowen. The band owned the rights and sold them to Morris Levy at Roulette. Released separately, Knox's "Party Doll" and Bowen's "I'm Stickin' With You" helped establish Roulette as a successful label and made Petty's name golden among the hopefuls of West Texas.

On February 25, 1957, the Crickets went into Petty's studio and re-recorded "That'll Be the Day," along with another tune Buddy had written called "I'm Looking for Someone To Love." The rerecorded song was peppier than the earlier Decca version, so Buddy sent off a copy to Morris Levy, naively expecting the contract to arrive by return mail. Meanwhile, the band got a chance to audition for Arthur Godfrey's "Talent Scouts" show in Amarillo, which proved disheartening; according to Joe Mauldin, the Godfrey scout simply stared at them and said, "Oh my gosh, what is music coming to?" And when Roulette eventually responded, it was even more distressing—the label suggested having Buddy Knox record the songs. But Petty remembers Buddy as "a person ultra-eager to succeed," who wouldn't let a few more setbacks stop him. He turned to Petty and asked him to go to New York and use his contacts to get them a deal.

Petty turned to his friend Murray Deutch of the Peer-Southern publishing house, and Deutch set up a meeting with Bob Thiele, the A&R director of Coral Records, a Decca subsidiary. Thiele liked the song, but he realized that on a label that had the McGuire Sisters and Lawrence Welk, a band like the Crickets would be hard to sell. After Jerry Wexler, Mitch Miller, and Joe Carlton (at RCA Victor) passed on the record, Thiele got an idea: Coral controlled the old Brunswick label and used it as a dumping ground for masters they were obligated to release. He got the Crickets a deal with Brunswick and prepared "That'll Be the Day" for release, deciding to press just a thousand so that the publishing deal between Nor Va Jak and Peer-Southern could be activated. Petty returned from New York with the Brunswick deal, and the Crickets celebrated by going into the studio and recording fifteen more songs. Meanwhile, Thiele called and said he'd gotten Buddy a separate deal with Coral. It was complicated, but it was made a bit easier by the fact that the flow of tapes was controlled by Petty and the Crickets, who made all the artistic decisions and delivered finished tapes to Thiele. This is a rather commonplace arrangement these days, but Buddy Holly and the Crickets were among the first artists to get a deal like that.

The record that had been issued to get Peer-Southern its deal suddenly started getting reorders—then more reorders. From an unprepossessing start in late May, it really got moving in July, when *Billboard* gave it a pop pick. It was doing well enough on the pop charts that the Ravens, of all the unlikely groups, cut a cover on Argo, one of the Chess Brothers' new subsidiaries. But, surprisingly enough, it was the Crickets who scored the R&B hit with the song, which reached number two in August, as well as the pop hit, of course.

They would follow up with "Oh Boy!" and "Not Fade Away," "Every Day," and then "Peggy Sue," under Buddy's name. At least Coral had taken the trouble to identify Buddy as "One of the Crickets" in their trade ads for "Peggy Sue," the record that established Buddy's hiccupping vocal style over Jerry Allison's rolling drums as the Crickets' sound. "Peggy Sue," incidentally, was a real person. Buddy had written the song as "Cindy Lou," but Jerry Allison thought it would be better if it were named after a real person: his girlfriend. Buddy agreed, and another rock and roll classic was born.

All during the summer of 1957, Colonel Parker had been denying rumors that Elvis was going to tour Britain or America. Elvis was too busy making movies, he said, plus he needed a vacation. There was another reason, too, one that didn't surface until the late sixties: the Colonel was not only not a colonel, but as Andreas van Kuijk, the son of illegal Dutch immigrants. He'd never become a United States citizen, and he didn't want to be found out. Meanwhile, Elvis was working on his latest movie, *Jailhouse Rock*, which featured a great title song by Leiber and Stoller and some of the best singing and dancing he had ever done. It was announced that the film would debut in Memphis on October 24, at the Loew's State, where Elvis had once been an usher. All his old friends would be there except one, Marion Keisker. Without warning, she had announced that she was joining the air force and was reporting to active duty at Lackland Air Force Base in San Antonio.

Summer also brought Chicago its first rock-and-roll show. Hosted by Howard Miller, it grossed $16,000 at the Chicago Opera House with a lineup that included Tab Hunter's first-ever appearance,* along with Charlie Gracie, Chuck Berry, Eddie Cochran, and the Everly Brothers. Tab was so nervous that he had to sit down for his entire performance, and he soon abandoned vocalizing for an acting career. And starting in July, ABC television decided to try to rescue its summer ratings by giving Alan Freed his own television show, the first all–rock and roll experiment. It was a complete success—so much so that in August, ABC picked up another show from its Philadelphia affiliate WFIL, "American Bandstand," which debuted as a daily program in the afternoons from 3 to 4:30.

Its host was twenty-seven-year-old Dick Clark, who'd long been a radio personality around Philadelphia, but who looked as young as the teenagers who appeared on his program. The show was modeled on a record hop: the majority of the airtime was spent with the camera following dancers as they bopped to the records Clark played. Since the dancers were drawn from local high schools, talent costs were minimal (they even lined up outside the studio for the privilege of being on the show). Clark would have feature dances, interview couples (always making sure to get the names of their high schools for viewer identification), and deliver ads for teen-oriented products. He did a top record countdown and solicited the audience's response to newly released records, which were judged on danceability, lyrics, and performance, which is where the famous phrase "It's got a good beat and you can dance to it: I'll give it a 92" was born. Of course, this was also an invaluable consumer-research ploy for record companies, and Clark made sure his contacts within the industry were solid. And on each and every show, one or more acts would perform, or, rather "perform," since they only mimed the song to the record—lip synching, it was called.

Even more than Freed's show, Clark's "American Bandstand" had hit on a perfect formula for teen identification: The kids in the audience looked like typical teens (and for the most part, they were), the songs were rock and roll, and the ambience was loose. But more important, by going national, it was giving American teens a standard, a ritual that was performed every day to confirm their membership in the secret society. Dick Clark's dancers became celebrities in their own right. They set fashion. They did the latest dances, so that teens and their friends could try them before they went to record hops and wowed everybody with their up-to-the-minute stepping. Hairstyles, slang, tie widths—all those critical concerns of adolescence—the "Bandstand" regulars set the tempo.

Not that Alan Freed was worried about the competition from "American

---

*"Since February, Norm Prescott, who was close enough to Elvis in 1956 to be giving away hairs from his sideburns over his show on WBZ in Boston, had been predicting that Tab would replace Elvis.

Bandstand." He was, as the name of the movie he had just contracted to appear in announced, *Mr. Rock and Roll.* Nor was he worried about the all-black "Bandstand"-like show Doug "Jocko" Henderson had just been signed to do by WATV in Newark. Jocko was one of the most popular R&B djs in the country, thanks to his ten-to-midnight slot on New York's WOV, his four-to-six p.m. slot on WDAS in Philadelphia, which he did by wire, and now his television show, which was called "Jocko's Rocket Ship." (Being black, Jocko, of course, would never go nationwide.) He was a wild man, talking jive as easily as most people talked English, which some of the hipper white teens preferred to Clark's safe image, and his dancers had spectacular moves. Like Freed, Jocko also had his stage shows, held at the Apollo, and he had his own crazy repertoire. For instance, he'd rewritten the Ten Commandments, including the original Top Ten but adding five more: attend classes, do your homework, help with household chores, go places and do things with your parents as well as your friends, and be home every night before the Jocko show.

Despite all this activity, people had begun to wonder whether teenagers were really all that important to the music business itself. When radio researchers looked at the mid-season Pulse and Nielsen ratings, they got a dose of reality: The teens they'd been catering to were in school six hours a day, and according to the surveys, in the four-to-six p.m. slot, when the teenagers were listening the most, they still only comprised 12 percent of the total audience—which is not to say that they were not a crucial market. *Billboard* took a hard look at the situation and concluded that rock and roll was enough a part of the musical mainstream by now that adults were used to it—after all, if Elvis was selling 5 million copies of "Don't Be Cruel," not all of those records had gone to teenagers. But the magazine also questioned the wisdom of forcing the entire listenership to endure music aimed at 12 percent of the audience, just because that 12 percent bought the most records and made them "popular." Did advertising warrant this programming? Not always, *Billboard* noted, reporting several cases in which large teenage listenership had fooled a station into raising its ad rates, only to find that the increase was unmatched by a subsequent rise in the advertisers' business. In the end, *Billboard* cautioned that it was extremely difficult to determine what mixture of adult and teen music to play and that stations should be very careful in tailoring their programming. What that meant was that the secret society would stay secret—or at the very least, underground—a little while longer.

But perhaps only a little while, because the debate was as much over format as over content. Earlier in 1957, a new form of radio had been born in a bar somewhere in the Midwest. Todd Storz, owner of a large Midwestern chain of radio stations, had been drinking with his station manager, Bill Stewart, and they noticed that the bar patrons seemed to play the same forty songs on the jukebox over and over. Then, at the end of the evening, the waitresses, who had been hearing them all during their shifts, took some of their tip money and played the same songs as they cleaned up and closed the bar. Storz and Stewart decided this might be a workable formula for a radio station, and so KOWH in Omaha began featuring what they called the Top Forty format.

Soon Storz stations in Minneapolis, Kansas City, and New Orleans were beaming Top Forty and enjoying high ratings along with it. In Fort Worth, station owner Gordon McLendon came up with his own version of the formula and started feeding it to his chain of stations. Then the disc jockeys started quitting: Ed Scott at KYMR in Denver and Leo Leonard at WCOL in Columbus, Ohio—no way management was going to tell them what to play. Many disc jockeys felt like mini-Freeds, friends to the teenagers and closely tied to the industry by their ability to break a record. Many of them, in fact, were taking money overtly from companies that hoped that a special push, an extra bit of exposure, would help recoup some of the costs of making and promoting the record.

But the djs weren't the only ones having trouble coping. Many old-timers had begun to suffer during the 1957 drive for teen dollars. Louis Jordan bounced off yet another label and onto a smaller one. Billy Ward and the Dominoes bowed out of a booking at Zardi's Jazzland in Hollywood, saying that the club "rocks too much," and that "we aren't a rock and roll group any more and have been singing and playing a different type of music for the last three months." They had recorded the ballad "Blue Velvet," but their new lead singer, Jackie Wilson, couldn't tolerate Billy Ward, so, with Nat Tarnopol, his twenty-five-year-old manager/discoverer, he went solo with a record that had been co-written by the owner of a Detroit record shop, Berry Gordy, Jr. "Reet Petite" never charted R&B but it helped establish Jackie on his peripatetic singing career.

Other older acts, of course, could adapt with grace: the "5" Royales released their first hit in years—four years, to be exact, which, considering all that had happened in between, was virtually a millenium—with "Think," featuring a hand-clapping chorus, some of Lowman Pauling's inspired guitar work, and a great Johnny Tanner vocal.

By fall 1957, the package tours were crisscrossing the land again, hitting even the smaller towns. The hottest one was called the "Biggest Show of Stars for 1957," featuring Fats Domino, Clyde McPhatter, La Vern Baker, Frankie Lymon (who had parted company with the Teenagers in a bid for solo success), Chuck Berry, the Crickets, young teen crooner Paul Anka (who was expected to be a draw during the show's five dates in his native Canada), the Everly Brothers, the Spaniels, the Bobbettes, Johnnie and Joe, and the Drifters. Booked for an eighty-day run, it was more like a military operation. It was announced, for instance, that when the tour hit the West Coast, the Bobbettes, the Spaniels, and Johnnie and Joe would leave, and Eddie Cochran, Buddy Knox, and Jimmy Bowen with the Rhythm Orchids would take their places. Then, when they got to the Deep South, the Everly Brothers, the Crickets, and Paul Anka would not perform in Chattanooga, Tennessee; Columbus, Georgia; Birmingham, Alabama; New Orleans or Memphis; because those communities had laws strictly forbidding white and black performers to appear on the same stage. The plan served to point up the real difference between the "Biggest Show of Stars for 1957" and the R&B package tours that had been a fact of show-biz life since the end of the war: This one, like rock and roll itself, was integrated.

It was one of the smaller of these package tours, in fact, that gave birth to one of the worst/best rock-and-roll movies of this era. J. G. Tiger was a Dallas wrestling promoter who decided that a rock-and-roll package might be another good way to make quick money, so he assembled one around local star and Decca recording artist Johnny Carroll, who sounded a lot like Elvis and sported a haircut with a sort of Beatle fringe in front that flopped up and down when he got excited. To round out the tour, he recruited a Dixieland band, the Cell Block Seven; the singing group the Five Stars; Sun blues star Roscoe Gordon; Fats Domino–inspired Preacher Smith and the Deacons; and Everly-like singers the Belew Twins.

What happened next is not clear, but it appears that Tiger ran out of money somewhere along the road and raised funds to make a movie to recoup the losses. For heavies, he used his stable of aging Texas wrestlers, and for heroes, he enlisted Carroll and some local teens. Romantic interest (for somebody) was supplied by Kay Wheeler, a not untalented dancer, and Dallas locations were used. Although the "plot" and "acting" are appalling even for 1950s rock-and-roll cinema, the resultant movie, *Rock, Baby, Rock It*, is a complete success in showing what the nonstar stratum of rock and roll was like in 1957. All the performances were recorded live—which was more than could be said for Freed's movies, Elvis's movies, or even *The Girl Can't Help It*—and except for the Dixieland sequence, there aren't even any performances that would make a rock-and-roll fan squirm (once again, unlike the movies of Freed, Elvis, etc.). Although none of the acts is great, on the level of Jerry Lee Lewis or Little Richard, they're good enough to make a fan pause and reflect on how many first-rate performers have slipped through the cracks of rock-and-roll history.

And no wonder so many got lost: According to a *Billboard* headline in August, NEW LABELS TAKE DISK BUSINESS FLING AT THE RATE OF ONE A DAY. The initial investment was small, the risk was great, but the potential payoff was huge. The trouble was, more and more distributors were refusing to settle with indie label owners until they produced a second hit. This way, the distributors argued, they knew a label was worth the investment of warehouse floor space, that it would stay in business. The indie men howled; often it wasn't possible to make a second record until they'd been paid for the first. But the indies still dominated rock and roll: On September 30, *Billboard* ran a chart analysis, showing that twenty-three of the top thirty records were from indies. And on September 9, they'd noted that there were twelve R&B chart items on the pop chart and that eleven of them were in the top fifteen, which certainly showed an improvement in indies' fortunes since the beginning of the year. Since R&B still meant indies, it was clear that investing in a marginal musical form could still pay off for a smart indie man. If only he could get paid!

Then, too, stereo was coming. In July 1957, Capitol became the first big company to enter a new phase of the high-fidelity industry by introducing a line of stereo reel-to-reel tapes. They also introduced a line of machines to play them on and declared that they were going to spend a million dollars on a merchandising drive to bring this new phenomenon to the public ear. It worked with the hi-fi bugs; pretty soon there were other companies getting on the bandwagon.* Still, everybody knew that stereo as a mass consumer item was a pipe dream until a means of making records in stereophonic sound was invented. It would be a bonanza for the electronics industry. Everybody in America would have to get a new record player. On the other hand, the new system would have to be compatible with mono playback so that even if there was only one speaker at the end, it would produce the information from both channels of a stereo record.

In September, a company called Westrex introduced a stereo record system, but in October, George Marek of RCA told the press that stereo was still far off in the future. After all, there were still 78s around. The big old slabs of shellac were the record business's longest-dying actors, although by the summer of 1957, 78s comprised merely 5.7 percent of total record sales. King, one of the few companies still making them, raised the retail price to $1.15 just to make it worthwhile to press and distribute them. The 78 took even longer to die outside the United States: copies exist of an Indian Parlophone 78 of the Beatles' "Paperback Writer" b/w "Day Tripper," a 1966 release.

But the greatest technological advance in 1957 came from Russia. In October, the Russians, as their contribution to the International Geophysical Year, launched Sputnik I, the first artificial satellite. Scientists at the Pentagon and at major universities shamefacedly admitted that it was a technological coup, and as such, it raised an immediate cry from the nation's educators for more science in the curriculum. It also inspired Buchanan and Goodman (of course!), and brought forth a flock of Sputnik novelty records.

It had another effect on rock and roll, too: At the time of Sputnik's launch, Little Richard was on tour in Australia. He'd been acting strangely recently, and the Russian launch seemed to crystallize everything. As he says in his autobiography, remembering the momentous night in Sydney,

*Of course, since the early 1950s, when Patti Page introduced the first multitrack vocal, showing its possibilities, many companies had been routinely recording their sessions on four-track equipment, and it was easy enough to remix the master tapes from four tracks to two channels.

"That night Russia sent off that very first Sputnik. It looked as though the big ball of fire came directly over the stadium about two or three hundred feet above our heads. It shook my mind. It really shook my mind. I got up from the piano, and said, 'This is it. I am through. I am leaving show business to go back to God.'" The next day he and his band were leaving Sydney on the ferry, after a press conference at which Richard had announced, "If you want to live for the Lord, you can't rock and roll too. God doesn't like it." His saxophonist, Clifford Burks, doubted the sincerity of Richard's decision,* and Richard showed him just how much he meant it by whipping off a ring valued at $8,000 and hurling it into Sydney Harbor. The cancellation of the tour, which also featured Gene Vincent and His Blue Caps and Alis Lesley, the "Female Elvis Presley," cost Richard thousands in lawsuits from promoters and from Art Rupe, but he really did mean it. As if to drive home the wisdom of the move, after Richard came home, he noted that the plane on which he and the band had been scheduled to return crashed into the Pacific Ocean, killing all on board.

But rock and roll itself was certainly alive and well. Within just a couple of months, "American Bandstand" had conquered the country, beating out all competition in its time slot. Raymond Hunsicker, representing the Record Dealers of Greater St. Louis, called it "the greatest stimulant to the record business we as dealers have ever known. Many dealers have installed TV sets in their record departments and extend teenagers an invitation to see the show in their stores," he told *Billboard.*

And Chuck Berry was back with another anthem, "Rock & Roll Music," that spoke for most of his teenage audience. Systematically denying all the other styles as vehicles for dancing, Chuck swung his way through a series of vignettes punctuated by chancy rhymes ("rockin' band" and "hurrican," for instance), as Lafayette Leake's piano swirled around a top-notch rhythm section of Willie Dixon and Fred Below, and Berry's guitar playing understated fills. It was odd that teenagers would accept Berry's idiosyncratic, Deep South view of the music, with his references to drinking home brew and black people holding a "jubilee," just as the odd reference to a "juke joint" in "School Day" was a little off-center, but probably most teens stopped listening to the lyrics after agreeing to that first line: "Just give me rock and roll music!"

And they were getting it: Jerry Lee's "Great Balls of Fire," Larry Williams's "Bony Maronie," Elvis's "Jailhouse Rock," Buddy Holly's "Peggy Sue," and Little Richard's rewrite of a whorehouse classic, "Keep a Knockin'," which was one of the sides Art Rupe still had in the can. Ricky Nelson was singing about his "Be Bop Baby" and "A Teenager's Romance," and a couple of teenagers from Forest Hills, a wealthy section of Queens in New York,

---

*Little Richard's decision had actually been some months in the making, thanks to the evangelical efforts of saxophonist Joe Lutcher, who had been an R&B figure in the late 1940s until he had a similar conversion.

released "Hey, Schoolgirl." Tom and Jerry, as they were called, "sound like a cross between the Everly Brothers and the De John Sisters," said *Billboard*, but they had more potential than people thought. Certainly Tom and Jerry was a much better name than their real names, Paul and Artie, or their last names, Simon and Garfunkel, which sounded like a law firm.

It didn't look like rock and roll would fade anytime soon: Howard Miller set a third show in Chicago to top his other Opera House successes and blew the lid off the place once again with acts ranging from Sam Cooke, the Rays, and Jerry Lee Lewis to Pat Boone's kid brother, Nick Todd. Vic Gale, a long-time rock-and-roll promoter, said that he was swamped clear through July of 1958, "which," he wryly noted, "is no indication that the bubble is bursting." Far from it—Gale predicted that rock and roll would grow "because each year a new crop of kids is converted to it, and they help build new attractions making their debut."

It was becoming part of the scenery, to the point that Leonard Bernstein, a young composer and conductor of some fame, could write and have staged a Broadway musical, *West Side Story*, about juvenile delinquents who, for the most part, were essentially good-hearted. True rock and rollers scorned the show, with its slick recasting of the Romeo and Juliet story as Italians versus Puerto Ricans, Sharks versus Jets, but there were many teens who were happy just to see some of their thoughts and actions, however co-opted, actually represented onstage. The original cast records sold about as fast as a rock-and-roll album usually did.

Meanwhile, Mode Records, an indie in New York, featured real juvenile delinquents: the Juveniles, with "Beat in My Heart" b/w "I've Lied." Once members of rival street gangs, this quintet had been assembled by social workers at the New York City Youth Board and would have been a poignant success story if the record hadn't stiffed.

Then came the fall crop of movies: Freed's *Mr. Rock and Roll*, followed by *Jailhouse Rock*, arguably Elvis's finest film, spangled with Leiber and Stoller songs, and finally, in November, Warner Brothers released *Jamboree*, which all but dispensed with a plot, just jamming one group or singer's performance up against another. And what a lineup it was: Jerry Lee Lewis, Fats Domino, Buddy Knox, Jimmy Bowen, Charlie Gracie, the Four Coins, Carl Perkins, Frankie Avalon, Lewis Lymon and the Teencords (led by Frankie's little brother), and more. Furthermore, the film was customized so that a locally prominent disc jockey would be featured wherever the film was shown; some half-dozen djs cut special footage to be dropped in as needed. There were some bad performances, and the "plot" kept intruding, but it was almost worth sitting through *Jamboree* for the sight of Jerry Lee Lewis coming to terms with "Great Balls of Fire."

By the end of the year, it began to look as if rock and roll had conquered the radio and record businesses completely. The Top Ten in *Billboard's* December 23 issue was nearly all rock and roll: "You Send Me," by Sam Cooke; "Jailhouse Rock," by Elvis Presley; "Raunchy," an instrumental by

Bill Justis on Sam Phillips's Phillips International subsidiary label; "April Love," by Pat Boone; "Peggy Sue," by Buddy Holly; "At the Hop," by Danny and the Juniors, one of the first made-in-the-studio groups and not a streetcorner sensation, as many thought; "Silhouettes," the Rays' silly melodrama with its catchy melody; "Rock and Roll Music," by Chuck Berry; "Great Balls of Fire," by Jerry Lee Lewis; and "Wake Up Little Susie" by the Everly Brothers. An incredible list! An incredible time to be a teenager with your ear to the radio!

But still opponents raged, and still the target was Elvis. In Los Angeles, supposedly a more sophisticated American city, the police department dispatched their vice squad to his performance at the Pan-Pacific Auditorium and issued him a warning to "clean up the show or else." People seemed to be waiting for Elvis to fall, but now he was back on top. In November, Don Bell, at KIOA in Des Moines, held an "Is Elvis Presley Slipping?" essay contest and drew four hundred no answers to one hundred yes answers. Dick Clark ran a contest to name America's first artificial satellite and got plenty of votes for "Elvis," since people seemed to think it was American enough that nobody would mistake it for Sputnik.

In the holiday spirit, RCA released *Elvis' Christmas Album*, mostly traditional songs, with a smattering of new ones thrown in. It was quickly banned throughout Canada (although one disc jockey who aired it got nearly all positive responses, including some from priests and ministers), and in Portland, Oregon, Al Priddy was fired from KEX for playing Elvis's version of "White Christmas," with management explaining that "the treatment of the song was in poor taste." Elvis got some relief: Two weeks before Christmas, New York Federal Court Judge Archie O. Dawson dismissed a suit brought by Johnny Otis against Elvis Presley Music and Leiber and Stoller in which Otis contended that he'd co-authored "Hound Dog" with the then-teenage songwriters and so was entitled to some of Elvis's royalties. Dawson couldn't find any proof that Otis had done anything but sign his name to the papers, and he sent everybody home.

Worse, there was a legal-size envelope sitting at Elvis's home back in Memphis, along with the fan mail (Elvis had moved to Graceland, a mansion just outside of town, in March). Inside was the order: "To Elvis Aron Presley, selective service number 40 86 35 16, Mailing address Graceland Highway 51 South, Memphis Tennessee, GREETINGS: You are hereby ordered for induction into the Armed Forces of the United States and to report at Room 215, 198 South Main Street, Memphis Tennessee, at 7:45 A.M. on the 20 of January, 1958, for forwarding to an armed forces induction station." It was signed by Grace F. Morton, clerk of the local board. There was more than a little vindictiveness abroad during this Christmas season. As the head of the Memphis draft board said, "After all, when you take him out of the entertainment business, what have you got left? A truck driver."

Well, this truck driver had a movie to finish, and he asked for a sixty-day deferment so that Hal Wallis wouldn't have to abandon the footage of *King*

Creole that was already shot. Knowing that they had Elvis by the short hairs, the draft board kindly granted the request. Meanwhile, Colonel Parker announced that no special favors would be sought for Elvis; nor would he try to get him into the Special Services, where Clyde McPhatter, for instance, had served.

Throughout 1957, despite his 1-A classification, Elvis had personally turned down all the special offers he'd gotten, including one from the navy, which suggested establishing an Elvis Presley Company for him to serve in, made up of Memphis boys. No, he would be just like everybody else. "If they want him to entertain the troops," Parker said, "that's fine with us. While we're in the service, anything we can do to help those boys we'll be glad to do." But the Colonel insisted that if Madison Avenue, working with the army, wanted Elvis to do recruiting drives or make television commercials for the army, they'd have to pay his full fee, because that was the sort of work Elvis got paid—and paid well—for. And anyway, the Colonel said, "We don't want to hurt his career by overexposure."

Elvis himself was telling the press, "I'm kinda proud of it," though he'd miss his mom and dad, of course. "It's a duty I've got to fill, and I'm gonna do it. My induction notice says for me to leave my car at home. Transportation will be provided. They tell me just to bring a razor, toothbrush, toothpaste, a comb and enough money to hold me two weeks."

Hate mail poured into the Memphis draft board office. Teenagers sobbed: "White Christmas" indeed! This was surely one of the blackest ever. It is significant that more than twenty-five years after the induction, Dave Marsh was still wondering just how innocent the government's move was. "Military conscription was an effective weapon against uppity new celebrities," he writes in *Elvis*, "as had already been proven with the unconventional World Series heroes, Billy Martin and Johnny Podres, who were immediately drafted after their moments of glory. Even though Elvis had become famous, there was nothing to prevent the draft from being used as a weapon to put him back in his place. . . . The government's intention in drafting Elvis was to rob him of everything—not just fame but also his wealth and whatever new dignity he had acquired. . . . Certainly, the least the draft board expected was that making Presley an infantry grunt would eliminate his unholy arrogance." It's true that draft boards are usually comprised of an area's wealthier or more important citizens, and it is very probable that people troubled by Elvis's amazing popularity would think that keeping him out of the public eye for a few years might cool him off. Whatever the intent—or lack thereof—Elvis was on his way into uniform.

Still, there was a record called "Jingle Bell Rock" climbing up the numbers—was it possible that rock and roll could be *bigger than Elvis?* What if Alan Freed disappeared, the army had Elvis, and something happened to Chuck Berry—would this music survive?

It was too much for an old man to consider. Rock and roll had been very good to Al Green, the manager of the Flame Show Bar in Detroit, who had nurtured the careers of Johnnie Ray and La Vern Baker and who had at last become her personal manager, helping out young Jackie Wilson along the way. Green had done very well by rock and roll, and it returned the favor. Green was in New York to visit Atlantic Records, staying at a midtown hotel, when a terrible pain ripped through him. That was it. If, as he slumped to the floor, his whole life passed before his eyes, he probably died with a smile on his face, tapping his foot. Good-bye, Al; the old ways are passing, even within rock and roll. It's a younger man's game now, Al. Rest in peace. The rest of us have 1958 to contend with.

11

IT'S ONLY MAKE BELIEVE

T in Pan Alley isn't really a place, it's more of a state of mind; and by 1958, that particular state was in turmoil. It was clear that rock and roll had infiltrated the deepest recesses of the songwriter's trade and that most of the veterans on Tin Pan Alley didn't have a clue how to write a rock-and-roll song, not even one of those sentimental slow ones *Billboard* had taken to calling "rockaballads." Rockaballads were often written by black vocal groups, and their "I love you, why did you leave me, please come back" bare-bones simplicity and lack of subtlety caused veteran cleffers' skin to crawl. True, the pop market hadn't entirely succumbed to rock and roll: Disc jockeys across the land swore their allegiance to "good music" and adult-oriented programming, but a rock-and-roll hit could bring in more money faster. Think, just for a minute, how much could be made from an Elvis Presley song, even if it was on the B side of his single! Of course, Hill and Range took half for the privilege of getting it to Presley, but half a monster was better than a whole mouse.

It was the industry's consensus that Tin Pan Alley had missed the boat, and that if the traditional songwriting industry was to survive, rock and roll would have to be factored in. It wasn't enough for rockers to cut the occasional standard; they would have to be given well-crafted, profession-ally written pop songs that had a rock-and-roll feeling. And this, it was beginning to occur to some of the brains on Tin Pan Alley, would mean that the kids would have to be fed some new pop idols—which didn't seem that hard, really. It was already a truism that kids would buy anything, and the Wham-O company had proved it. Late in 1958 they had started a craze for a length of plastic tubing stapled into a circle, marketed under the name

Hula-Hoop. Millions sold, and then Hula-Hoops vanished as quickly as they came, but Wham-O had learned a valuable lesson to be applied to its other products, Silly Putty and the redoubtable Frisbee.

The salvation of Tin Pan Alley had begun late in 1957 when three performers, one from Canada and the other two from the streets of Philadelphia, appeared on the scene. Paul Anka was a chunky, vaguely ethnic sort from Ottawa who aspired to a career as a professional songwriter. Being a teenager, he figured he could sing the songs he wrote, too; and in 1957, after his unsuccessful debut single, with backing by the Cadets (of "Stranded In the Jungle" fame), he was signed by ABC-Paramount, one of the new movie studio–affiliated labels hungry for new talent, and released "Diana," which did well in the United States and spectacularly in Canada. Anka could sing, and his songs were the sort of pop that any broad-minded Tin Pan Alley man could accept.

Frankie Avalon was another story. He was handsome in a way that Anka certainly wasn't, but the reedy, nasal voice that came out of that pretty face was hardly the stuff of legends. His song, "Dede Dinah," was so cute, so cloying, so perfectly made up and synthetic that it had to be a hit— especially after Dick Clark, happy to see a local boy trying to make it big, plugged him relentlessly on "American Bandstand." And later in the year, Chancellor Records, the same Philadelphia machine that produced Frankie Avalon, would spew forth Fabian. He was a very clever, very calculated product created by Bob Marcucci and Pete DeAngelis, who together owned Chancellor Records. They'd started out a few years before as just another struggling indie (at one point mailing hundred of parakeets to djs to promote a woof-woof called "Calypso Parakeet"), but after experiencing the ups and downs of the industry for a while, they got businesslike.

"We now run a school where we indoctrinate artists into show business," Marcucci told *Billboard's* Ren Grevatt. "We may sign them and spend three months schooling them before they cut their first record. We teach them how to walk, how to talk, and how to act onstage when they're performing. We worked with Frankie Avalon for three months before making 'Dede Dinah.'

"It was Frankie who introduced me to Fabian, a sixteen-year-old high school kid who likes to play football. Somehow I sensed that here was a kid who could go. He looks a little bit like both Presley and Ricky Nelson. I figured he was a natural. It's true that he couldn't sing. He knew it and I knew it. . . ." And so did everyone else when his single was released: "I'm in Love" b/w "Shivers." But boy, was he handsome! Handsome enough, in fact, that with enough exposure, he finally started having hits.

By now, Dick Clark, Philadelphia's hottest export, was coming to dominate televised rock and roll. "American Bandstand" was by far the top-rated daytime television show, and ABC was so captivated by the twenty-eight-year-old Philadelphian that in February 1958, they gave him a Saturday-night show that was like Sullivan's without the trained dog acts: all rock and roll. The first show, which aired on February 15, featured Pat Boone; Jerry Lee Lewis; Connie Francis; and the Royal Teens, a white group from Long Island that was scoring heavily with a song called "Short Shorts" that came out "Shawt Shawts" when they sang it. That was certainly an acceptable mix of talent: two middle-of-the-road-but-young performers (Boone and Francis), a novelty act (the Royal Teens), and an out-and-out rock and roller (Jerry Lee). They all lip synched their tunes; the crowd chewed mountains of Beech-Nut Spearmint Gum (the sponsor); and Dick grinned and looked clean and wholesome.

But it was on "American Bandstand," at the beginning of 1958, that Clark broke a very different kind of record, the Silhouettes' "Get a Job." Even though it had a funny *Sha-da-da-da* hook, a Coasters-like bass intoning "Get a job," and a really silly *yip-yip-yip-yip-yip-yip-yip-yip* mum-mum-mum-mum-mum turnaround, it was stark social realism when the group sang, over fairly radical harmonies, "I come back in the house / Hear my mother's mouth / Screechin' and a-cryin' / Tellin' me that I'm lyin' / About a job / That I never could find." The song definitively proved that rock and roll could tell the truth about more than simple teen love. There was a recession mounting in America, and the Silhouettes, who were black, were feeling its effects first.

"Get a Job" must have touched a nerve, because it rocketed to the top. Originally released on the Junior label, it had been picked up by Herald Ember, a national label, soon after it sold nine thousand copies with virtually no distribution. As Ember's Al Silver remembers, "Unbeknownst to me, the record was lying on Dick Clark's desk for two weeks. Dick wanted to play it in the worst way, but he wouldn't because the Junior label had no national distribution. Dick smelled a smash hit. Anyway, in a few days, I had finished pressings and air-mailed several copies to Dick Clark. As soon as he saw that it was on Ember, a label with national distribution, he programmed it. When I walked into the office the morning after he played it, there were telegrams with back orders for about 500,000 records underneath the door. . . . It was unbelievable. The first record wasn't shipped yet. Eventually, that record sold a couple million."

Given its success, "Get a Job" naturally spawned imitations and answers, like the one on George Goldner's End label by a Detroit group, the Miracles. "Got a Job" told of the travails of a kid who was hired by a tyrannical grocer, and it was very well sung and well written (that rhyme of "basement" and "replacement" was undoubtedly the work of lead singer William "Smokey" Robinson, collaborating with Berry Gordy, who had been writing songs for Jackie Wilson), but it was terribly recorded and sank like a stone.

Goldner had more luck with another group that scored early in 1958. The Chantels were five girls in their early teens whose combined vocal sound was almost choral. Arlene Smith, the fourteen-year-old lead singer, had an amazing voice, capable of soaring over the other four girls' voices, and she had written a wonderful song of unrequited teen love called "Maybe."

Goldner loved it,* and he set about getting it recorded. The story goes that he produced the session himself, urging and coaxing and terrorizing poor Arlene for take after take until her voice reached the correct degree of desperation, pleading with her dream lover to take notice of her. She sings with a noticeable sob in her voice, and nearly three decades later, "Maybe" remains a riveting performance.

It was also a first. There had been plenty of vocal groups before, and even a few made up of girls, like Shirley Gunter and the Queens and Atlantic's vanished Bobbettes. Decca had actually bought the master of "I Met Him On A Sunday," by the Shirelles, from the tiny Tiara label, but, in characteristic Decca fashion, had completely failed to sell it to the R&B market, and it would be 1960 before the real pioneers of this genre got heard. So the distinction of being the first big girl group would fall to the Chantels.

But then the face of rhythm and blues was changing in other ways, too, epitomized by the rise of Sam Cooke. Cooke wasn't a blues singer particularly; neither was he a Nat "King" Cole type of cocktail singer. His voice was smooth and mellow, although rougher than Columbia's new answer to Nat Cole, Johnny Mathis. Unlike Cole or Mathis, Cooke's background was in gospel music, which had begun to flower in its modern sense in the early 1950s. Cooke had been a member of one of the oldest yet most progressive gospel quartets, the Soul Stirrers, who recorded for Specialty, and with his good looks and dreamy voice, he had lowered the age of the average female attendee of a gospel program by about thirty years. With his growing teen following, he began to consider crossing over to pop. Art Rupe was terrified of endangering the sales of his top gospel group, so Sam's 1956 hit, "Lovable," had been released under the name Dale Cooke. Sam cut more sides with Bumps Blackwell (who had just lost Little Richard to the gospel life) and then because Rupe refused to issue the pop records, he took the discs and Blackwell to his own label, Keen.

The first Keen record was "You Send Me," one of 1957's top R&B songs, but after that, Cooke wisely stuck to standards for a while, getting bookings in top nightclubs. He was clear about his esthetics—"I think Frank Sinatra's phrasing and intonation are the greatest. La Vern Baker and Billie Holiday are both wonderful to hear, and I'd say that Presley is a real terrific performer"—but his style was straight out of gospel. For him, the shift to pop didn't present a conflict, for as he told a reporter, "Gospel and blues, after all, are very close together, and you can't help being influenced by them when you have those feelings in your soul."

Soul—it was the very word Jerry Wexler was using to describe the way Ray Charles sang. Gospel fans heaped derision on Cooke for defecting, which upset him, but he continued to attend gospel shows and stayed friendly with many performers, including some of the brightest stars in the

*Goldner liked it so much that he copyrighted it, assigning the rights to Alan Freed's Figure Music; ever the diplomat, he assigned the rights to "Every Night (I Pray)," the follow-up, to Dick Clark's Sea Lark Music.

gospel firmament. In November 1958, he was in an automobile accident that claimed the life of his chauffeur, Edward Cunningham, and also injured Cooke and his passenger, Louis Rawls of the Pilgrim Travellers, a popular gospel group. Gospel was Cooke's bedrock, a touchstone he would never completely abandon. Cooke knew that gospel music would always be part of what he did, and he knew that there were others in the field who wanted a taste of his pop success, like Rawls, who later became a secular star. For those raised in the church, however, this is a terrible conflict, and one that is not easily resolved—if it ever is.

Performers like Cooke and the girl groups were broadening the vocabulary of popular music, and as Danny and the Juniors were announcing, "Rock and Roll Is Here To Stay," Alan Freed concurred in a *Billboard* interview and went on to explain that "there will be trends set within the field which no one can predict. But the power of the music is now showing up at the college level. Kids have been exposed to it for four or five years. Now they're carrying their taste right into colleges, and it looks to me as though the colleges will be completely saturated with rock and roll. On my tour, we'll do shows at various college towns, including Columbus and Toledo, Ohio, and Madison, Wisconsin.

"I've dealt with kids for sixteen years, and I believe that rock and roll has a good influence on them. And I don't think they grow out of it just because they reach eighteen or nineteen or twenty. Sure, their tastes expand. They begin to like many other kinds of music, but that doesn't mean they stop liking rock and roll at all."

In a separate discussion, Dick Clark agreed, adding, "As a matter of fact, years ago in the days of the Glenn Millers and the Benny Goodmans, tastes were a lot narrower than they are right now. Take a look at any top-fifty or top–one hundred charts today. There's never been a time when so many different kinds of music were popular at one and the same time, and the kids who are being so often attacked for being all kinds of terrible things should be given credit for liking many different styles. Sure, there are always a few in any group in society who make the total group look bad. But what's wrong with being enthusiastic in a rock-and-roll theater show or dance at something you like? Opera lovers whistle and shout like crazy when they like a performance."

Indeed, so many good records were coming out that it seemed that this golden era would go on forever. Not even disappearance could shake fans' loyalties: Little Richard had achieved a big hit with "Good Golly, Miss Molly" even as he sat at divinity school, publicly renouncing such worldly music. The Crickets and Buddy Holly scored a one-two punch with "Maybe Baby" and "I'm Gonna Love You Too," respectively, as it became more apparent that Norman Petty's strategy was to keep the Crickets' records closer to out-and-out rock and roll and Holly's to a more pop sound. Little Willie John courted the Sam Cooke fans with the sensuous "Talk to Me, Talk to Me," and Larry Williams, whom Art Rupe had discovered playing piano on various Specialty sessions, had a double-sided threat with the Little Richard-ish "Dizzy, Miss Lizzy" and the more ominous "Slow Down." Bobby Freeman emerged from San Francisco singing one of the year's more infectious party sides, "Do You Wanna Dance?" And these were only a handful of the indie offerings.

The masters were at it, too: Chuck Berry's first record of 1958 changed his focus a little, concentrating on the teens who were buying rock and roll instead of on the music itself. "Sweet Little Sixteen" was that teenage ideal, the girl who lived for rock and roll, existed to dance and get autographs from her favorite rock and roll stars, dressed in tight dresses, wore lipstick (this Berry attributed to her having the "grown up blues"), and put pictures of her idols on her wall. Best of all, she existed all over the country—deep in the heart of Texas and by the Frisco Bay, anywhere teenagers rocked. Yet for all her early-budding maturity, when the morning came, she would be found behind her desk in school, sweet little sixteen once again. The song was simple, but Berry's intricate guitar work and especially Lafayette Leake's swirling piano, which sounded like Jerry Lee Lewis riding a roller coaster, made it possible to listen to it repeatedly and always find new things to like—and new hope, if you were a teenager—every time.

But certainly Jerry Lee would never let Berry or Leake steal his thunder! His first record of the year was his sexiest ever, as its title, "Breathless," suggests. Another great Otis Blackwell song, it carried for its stunning tag line: "You have left me [long exhalation of breath] Buh-reth-less-ahhhhh!" It, too, was a hit, and Sam Phillips must have been glad: Columbia Records (probably out of its Nashville office, since it's hard to imagine Mitch Miller going along with this idea) raided Sun early in 1958 and walked away with both Carl Perkins and Johnny Cash under contract. Jerry Lee would have to sustain the label, at least until Sam could develop some new artists to stand alongside him. Fortunately, he was so popular that he had just signed a contract for a British tour.

The record business had been good to Sam and to a lot of other people as well. Atlantic Records was ten years old in January 1958, and a few months later, Ahmet Ertegun traded in his trademark Jaguar for a Rolls—there was still a fortune to be made in R&B for the determined label owner. For instance, in late January, a record blew out of New Orleans by way of Jackson, Mississippi, where Johnny Vincent, a former producer for Specialty Records, had set up shop. He'd labored in New Orleans for Art Rupe, and then, realizing that he was the one spotting the hits, he went into business for himself. He scored a few regional blues hits, and he also developed connections to some maniacs in New Orleans who played with the house band at Cosimo's studio and called themselves Huey "Piano" Smith and the Clowns. Since they were basically the A team of New Orleans cats (in fact, some of them had provided backing for Little Richard and Fats Domino), and not strictly a group, they weren't really set up to tour, but they liked having Johnny record their occasional efforts. They gave

Johnny's Ace* label one of its first national hits, "Don't You Just Know It," a raucous bit of New Orleans foolery studded with nonsense syllables (like *gooba-gooba-gooba*) and a basic rhythm that owed as much to the cockeyed rhumbas of Professor Longhair as it did to marching music.

As soon as the record hit, Vincent was deluged with offers for the master, but rejected bids as high as $25,000. "I don't need to sell masters to make money," he told *Billboard*. "I make out pretty well selling records."

He wasn't alone in his adamant refusal to sell out: Lew Chudd kept fending off offers for Imperial throughout 1958, saying, "Imperial is having the biggest grosses in its history. . . . Imperial is not sold, and still wants to retain its position as the leading independent label in the industry." For this attitude, he was featured in *Fortune* magazine, which chronicled the growth of the company and marveled at the huge profits Chudd was reaping from recording Fats Domino and Ricky Nelson.

Everybody was trying to get a piece of the action. A raid on one of the largest Chicago record distributors, Lormar Distributors, which also supplied many jukebox operators with records, uncovered thousands of counterfeit records with labels virtually indistinguishable from the real releases. Significantly, all the records seized were on indie labels: Cadence, Roulette, Brunswick, Ember, Keen, Vee-Jay, Chess, and Checker. Lormar had already been under investigation for alleged strongarming of local jukebox operators to buy strictly from them, and the whole operation seemed to be linked to a racketeer with the colorful name of Joey Glimco, who headed the Chicago taxicab union and ran the Automatic Phonograph Distributing Company. Evidently the operation was airtight, making its own copies of hit records and distributing them to their own jukeboxes, netting a 100 percent profit. In Washington, Robert F. Kennedy, a young lawyer with federal connections, announced that the Lormar/Glimco affair had started the federal government thinking about investigating the jukebox industry nationwide.

Not that a few gangsters in the jukebox trade in Chicago were going to stop rock and roll now. Nor was the management of KWK in St. Louis, which banned rock and roll in January and smashed every rock-and-roll record in its library after giving it a farewell spin. (The station's president, Robert T. Convey, said it was "simply a weeding out of undesirable music.") Nor would the Iranian and Egyptian governments, who banned rock and roll in their countries, with Walter Cronkite reporting that the decision "was made with the advice of Iranian doctors, who reported that many young rock and roll dancers had injured their hips in extreme gyrations." Nor would Phil Burgess of WCFR, Springfield, Virginia, who auctioned off the "worst" rock-and-roll records for the benefit of the March of Dimes. ("Hound Dog" was bought by a local merchant who sent it to the Kremlin.)

---

*One theory on label naming holds that the higher up in the alphabetical listings you are, the sooner you'll get paid by your distributor.

Nor would attitudes like that of Thomas P. Chisman, president of WVEC in Norfolk, who told a panel discussion on the rise of Top Forty programming, "Screening rock and roll tunes for my station is a very simple matter. First we keep a wastepaper basket handy and as the new releases come in, we just dump them in. We have the same screening procedure for the so-called modern jazz, hillbilly, and other fad music—down the drain. Believe it or not, we still have a fine audience that likes good music—and I mean music."

And there were new kinds of records coming out that would stoke the fires higher, even though they were mild enough to appeal to teens who might be straddling the fence between pop and rock and roll. Two big trends began to manifest themselves as 1958 got going: instrumentals and novelty records. Disc jockeys always loved instrumentals, because they could put one on and talk over it to fill in extra seconds that would otherwise be dead air, but these weren't the kind that could bridge the end of the hour going up to the news. The Champs' "Tequila," the year's biggest instrumental hit, had a melody, a very catchy saxophone line played over a Latin-style rhythm, and a release that approximated swing. At the end of the chorus, everybody shouted "Tequila!" and repeated the pattern. It was just annoying enough to merit another hearing. Of course, the freak hit of "Topsy II" by veteran swing drummer Cozy Cole was the opposite, a monotonous drum solo that begged for a jock to yak over it, but it, too, sold very well. Orthodox cha-chas also flourished, with Perez Prado's "Patricia" and the Tommy Dorsey Orchestra's "Tea for Two Cha Cha" both making the year's list of top records, thanks to the emerging fad for this new Latin dance that adults had imported from Cuba via Miami. And there were the records that had started it all: Moe Koffman's "Swingin' Shepherd Blues," which set off a brief search for the next hot flutist, and Bill Justis's "Raunchy," a simple saxophone wail over an insistent guitar riff, by one of Sam Phillips's A&R men, that Sam released on the new Phillips International label he'd started for more sophisticated talent.

There were several reasons for instrumentals' sudden vogue, not the least of which was that people kept waiting for the rock-and-roll fad to pass and the bands to come back. And, too, with the rise of teenage culture, there were more dances, record hops with local disc jockeys, and shows like "Bandstand" to keep teens innovating on the dance floor. Uncomplicated by the demands lyrics make on melody, instrumentals were a perfect excuse just to dance.

One of the best instrumentals of 1958, by a young American Indian named Link Wray, wasn't about dancing. "Rumble," which (as many of the people who banned the record noted) was slang for a teenage gang fight, was too slow—menacingly slow, in fact—and it was mostly about playing guitar so loudly that it made horrible noises. Executed by an all-electric band, "Rumble" helped popularize the Fender electric bass guitar, which featured four strings like a bass fiddle and frets like a guitar, all on a solid body like the Fender Stratocaster and Telecaster guitars the rockabillies preferred to the semi-hollow body Gibson 335 that Chuck Berry used. It would prove to be a formidable influence on later rock and roll.

Novelty records were another matter entirely. The term *novelty* is hard to define exactly. After all, for some, Little Richard was a novelty—and not a very pleasant one, at that—while for others, the nasally chanted nonsense syllables of the vocal groups like the Silhouettes seemed to be novelties because they weren't exactly music. But both appealed to adolescent sensibilities, and that's where Ross Bagdasarian came in. Bagdasarian had been around since the early 1950s, doing arrangements and issuing the odd Armenian-tinged instrumental record, but early in 1958, he threw his good taste to the winds, changed his on-record name to David Seville, and with the help of some amusing tape recorder tricks, produced "Witch Doctor," in which he details his troubles with his girlfriend and goes to his friend the witch doctor for advice. The advice, rendered in a speeded-up tape voice, is *"Ooh, eeh, ooh ah ah / Ting tang walla-walla bing-bang."* Naturally, a record so calculated to inflame parents had to be a hit, and "Witch Doctor" stayed on the charts until an even odder novelty was created to supplant it—Sheb Wooley's "Purple People Eater," the tale of a man-eating creature that was one-eyed, one-horned, and flew. Amazingly, the song sold even better than "Witch Doctor" had.

These new developments incensed Mitch Miller, since the growing number of Top Forty stations chose their playlists from the *Billboard* sales charts, and because novelty records sold, they got a lot of airplay. Miller, speaking to a collection of disc jockeys at a convention sponsored by Todd Storz, said the programming was being abdicated to "the eight to fourteen-year-olds, to the pre-shave crowd that make up twelve percent of the country's population and zero percent of its buying power. You used to play a record because you liked it; it was part of the personality of your show. Now you play it for Sam, Joy, Flo, Sal, Mickey and Joyce loves Shorty and will he please meet you after three at the sweetshop, second booth from the rear."

But the tide continued unabated. In Philadelphia, local TV horror-movie-show host John Zacherle recorded a macabre recitation to capitalize on teens' increasing interest in horror movies. "Dinner With Drac" was gruesome, and in almost no time, the powerful WERE in Cleveland banned the record. In response, Cameo Records, Zacherle's label and an up-and-coming Philadelphia indie, put the old ghoul back in the studio and rush-released a more conservative version.

Actually this was just a new flare-up of an old problem, since teens had been fascinated with the macabre even before the James Dean cult developed. In the early 1950s, a slew of comic books issued by Educational Comics—EC to fans—with titles like *Tales from the Crypt, Vault of Horror,* and *Weird Science* had published well-illustrated, graphic horror stories featuring dismemberment, mutilation, and torture, albeit in a somewhat tongue-in-cheek way, and arguably in the tradition of such masters as H. P. Lovecraft and Edgar Allan Poe. Before there was really enough rock and roll around to blame juvenile delinquency on, EC Comics caught the flak, and a congressional subcommittee told the entire industry to start regulating itself, leading to the birth of the Comics Code Authority under the aegis of John Goldwater, whose comic *Archie* dealt with squeaky-clean 1950s teens. EC suspended publication of its horror titles in 1955 and concentrated on its satire comic, *Mad*.

The outcry over the new novelty records brought another round of attacks on rock and roll. Bestselling author Vance Packard, whose *Hidden Persuaders* had lately shocked the public with its exposé of how Madison Avenue used sex to sell soap, testified before the Senate Subcommittee on Communications that rock and roll had been foisted on "passive" teenagers by conniving disc jockeys and didn't really reflect the teens' own taste. Packard maintained that broadcasters were "manipulated" to keep "cheap music" on the air, and when asked to amplify on what he meant by cheap music, he said rock and roll, hillbilly, Latin American, and rhythm and blues—all musics that were cheaply obtained and easy to record. Not only did he not have any statistics to back up his arguments, but he also aroused a howl of outrage from Southern senators who represented hillbillies, Floridians who were affronted by his insensitivity to Latin music, and record trade people from across the country who resented his hostile attitude. Naturally, in the American spirit of fair play, rebuttals were called for on the record, so Lew Chudd hied himself to Washington to declare that "there is no evidence of allied businesses attempting to force records on the public," and Don Owens of WARC in Arlington, Virginia, noted that "the strongest condemnation of rock and roll and country music comes from people who have never spent five minutes paying attention to it. The same people who screamed and rioted when Sinatra sang in 1943 are now calling such actions 'horrifying' today."

But underneath this debate lay a much more volatile issue: the teenagers' right to a voice on the airwaves—not from the standpoint of free speech, but from a capitalistically oriented, pragmatic standpoint: Did kids spend enough money to make it worthwhile for advertising agencies to spend thousands of dollars courting them? The debate begun in 1957 continued to rage through much of 1958. Firing the first shot was Teen-Age Survey, Inc., which, in its report at the end of March, stated that the nation's 19 million teens were now spending $9 million a year and furthermore "have an important say in the purchasing of auto accessories, toothpaste, shampoo, automobiles, furniture, bread, canned food, syrups, television sets, phonographs, entertainment, sports, watches, clothing, cigarettes, and homes."

Not that this sat well with Madison Avenue. "This means the average teenager is spending $500 annually," snorted a media buyer at a major ad agency to an inquiring *Billboard* reporter, "or about one-fifth the spending of the average adult radio-listener. It's still a drop in the bucket and still a minor target." Maybe so, acknowledged Teen-Age Survey's Sidney H. Ascher, but "the reason advertising on disc jockey shows with primarily a teenage audience is not productive with many items is because the commercials are way off base." The opposition presumably slunk back, but the fight wasn't over yet.

By now, it was spring, time for the next edition of the big package shows to start hitting the road. Alan Freed had been preparing his "The Big Beat," buoyed by the success of his New Year's show at the Brooklyn Paramount, which yet again had shattered all house records. The bill had featured Fats Domino, who used the forum to announce that he'd gotten over his fear of flying, the real reason he hadn't toured abroad, and Jerry Lee Lewis, predictably enough, walked away with the show, prompting Sam Phillips, beaming with pleasure, to tell a reporter that Jerry Lee was "the most sensational performer I've ever seen, bar none." Freed had signed Jerry Lee for the new show and booked the Crickets as well. He was so confident that he poohpoohed the doomsayers who pointed out that his tour would conflict with Irving Feld's 1958 edition of the "Biggest Show of Stars"—they'd both be on the road, sometimes in the same territories, at the same time.

Then, more optimistic than ever, Freed announced in April that he would open a nightclub in Miami Beach, Alan Freed's Sugar Bowl, catering exclusively to teenagers, and that he was considering franchising the idea elsewhere. As if the market weren't saturated enough with Freed's and Feld's shows, Universal Attractions threw its hat in the ring with the "Big Rhythm and Blues Cavalcade of 1958," starring the Midnighters, the Original Little Richard Band, the "5" Royales, Bo Diddley (who had just been presented with a square guitar by the Gretsch company), Tiny Topsy, Etta James, Al Jackson, Little Willie John, and more.

The promoters should have listened more closely to their radios: "Get A Job" could still be heard. In the April 28 issue of *Billboard*, the Biggest Show of Stars promoters were saying, "you could flip a coin as to whether we're making money," and Freed's spokesmen said they were "not losing yet, and maybe a few dollars ahead." "The Big Rhythm and Blues Cavalcade" was yanked off the road after barely a week, according to Universal, because it needed fine-tuning. "Don't kid yourself," a "tradester" was quoted as saying in *Billboard*, "there's a lot of hardship today. Unemployment is serious and many have been hit. The entertainment part of the pocketbook is the first to suffer. The kids are the primary market for these shows and in tough times their allowances for shows and dates get cut out fast." Dick Clark, no doubt after consulting his broker, decided to postpone his own package show until the situation got clarified.

And then disaster struck. On May 3, the Freed package pulled into Boston to play a date at the Boston Arena. The show went on as usual—or so it seemed at first. Since after the fact, emotions ran so high, it is nearly impossible to know for certain what actually happened, but a Boston television station covering the show for the news caught the moment when the powder keg exploded. Apparently a vocal group was onstage and a white girl rushed the stage in a frenzy, jumped up to the lip of the stage, and grabbed a black singer by the genitals. A Boston policeman saw this and flipped out, pushing his way forward and wading into the crowd, which panicked. Seeing this, and fearing the worst, the rest of the security forces moved in, and the crowd was driven out of the auditorium and into the streets. Outside, the cops were waiting for them, and a pitched battle ensued.

Freed claimed to know nothing of the riot when the media finally caught up with him. "I stood on a streetcorner signing a few autographs for a half hour or so, then [manager] Jack Hooke and I went to the Hotel Statler, where we slept till noon Sunday. At two o'clock we got on a plane for Montreal. At no time did we get a phone call from the police or anyone else before we left Boston to tell us anything was wrong. Sunday night during our show in the Montreal Forum we got a phone call from the New York *Journal-American* asking us what happened in Boston. That's the first we knew of any trouble."

That wasn't strictly true. At one point, Alan Freed took that stage and declared, after the house lights had been turned on, "The police don't want you to have any fun here." And Hooke admitted that a Boston cop had pushed Freed, saying, "We don't like your kind of music here," before the show.

Certainly Boston was not known as a paradise of racial tolerance, and Freed's show was integrated, which must have irritated some of the conservative members on the force. Rumors immediately started flying about what had really happened. Gangs of reefer-smoking youths had been prowling the area outside the arena and several girls had been raped, some said. Weeping teens, hopped up on who knows what, had been herded into black marias by the score, said others. Boston's worst nightmares of teenage anarchy had been loosed upon the city, and a cry of hysteria went up in the press; the tales grew with each retelling in a North End barroom.

When the smoke cleared, though, it was only Alan Freed who was indicted. No teenagers had been arrested for rape, narcotics violations, or even jaywalking. Within days, Freed had been indicted by the Suffolk County Grand Jury for inciting to riot, and immediately his lawyer was in Boston scouting for witnesses. The end of the tour, with shows in Troy, New York, New Haven, and Newark, was canceled. And then Freed, blinded with self-righteousness and deeply hurt by the suspicion that his vision of rock and roll uniting America's teenagers would never be realized, quit WINS, angrily denouncing the station for failing to "stand behind my policies and principles." Jock Fearnhead, general manager and vice president of WINS, straightfacedly told the press that "Alan Freed's resignation last night came as a complete surprise to WINS. In cases of this kind, the public usually assumes that a person has been fired—but such was definitely not the case with Alan Freed and WINS. The station's policy has been one of a third party and a separate entity because the incidents involved the nonradio activities of Mr. Freed. WINS sincerely wishes Mr. Freed the best in his future activities."

But Rick Sklar, who was a disc jockey at the station at the time, offers a different account. According to Sklar, Boston was the final straw for Elroy McCaw, the eccentric owner of WINS. Freed's contract was up for renewal, and McCaw, sickened by Freed's flamboyance and the bad publicity he saw Freed bringing to the station, decided not to renew. Freed walked into this situation with an already sold-out show waiting in Newark. Says Sklar, "The acts would perform only if Freed could play their records. Without a radio station, there would be no concerts. Elroy was unmoved. Freed called the arena and tentatively canceled the concert while he bargained with McCaw. Freed was still in McCaw's office when the concert promoter burst in the rear door to the station (next to the record library), gun in hand, looking for Freed. My pregnant wife, Sydelle, and Inga Freed (who was a secretary at WINS), who were standing at the Coke machine, took one look and dashed into the record library, locking the door and barricading themselves inside. The promoter left the station frustrated, unable to find Freed, who was still meeting in McCaw's office. By nine p.m., when the meeting ended, Freed was still alive, but he was finished at WINS."

Dick Clark lost no time in canceling his "Caravan of Stars" "temporarily," because of Boston and "other reasons."

The melee had long-reaching consequences. For one thing, it spelled the end of the big rock-and-roll tours for a while. For another, it once again made theater owners squeamish about booking small rock-and-roll shows. And it definitely encouraged radio station owners to think twice before engaging the services of a flamboyant personality jock like Freed. Wasn't it better, in the final analysis, to have somebody who was more easily controlled, who wouldn't whip up those teenage hormones, who would avoid those more extreme kinds of rock and roll in favor of something that nice teens, the kind who never rioted and who behaved themselves, really liked? To their credit, the folks at WABC in New York didn't think so,* and they proudly announced that Freed would start an evening airshift from 7:15 to 11 each night, starting June 2.

But the tours continued abroad. Buddy Holly and the Crickets had covered Britain in March, playing twenty-five nights in a row; and while they'd made more money on the road and had more leisurely tours, they were overwhelmed by the enthusiasm and friendliness that greeted them everywhere they played. They boosted guitar sales in Britain noticeably and attracted a large coterie of devoted fans. The British were certainly warming to rock and roll: The group had even played some television shows in addition to their concert dates, and when *Billboard* noted that

---

*Their decision may have been influenced by the fact that the network that owned the station was also carrying Freed's television show.

fifteen of the top twenty records in Britain were American, they were talking about rock-and-roll records, for the most part, and about Buddy Holly and the Crickets.

The next rock and roller to head overseas was Jerry Lee Lewis, and Britain's emerging audience of rockers awaited his arrival with bated breath. On May 22, he landed at Heathrow Airport outside London with a retinue from home, one of them his sister and the youngest one his new wife.

Jerry Lee Lewis was married? He had been since December, it developed, but both Sam and Judd Phillips had urged him to keep it a secret. For one thing, as they had already discovered with Carl Perkins, marriage could be the kiss of death to a rock and roller's career. For another thing, Jerry Lee's somewhat irregular life included two other marriages in his past, and Sam and Judd still weren't certain whether they were legally over. And for a third thing, Myra Gale was Jerry Lee's third cousin, and she was only fifteen. Judd knew that there was a press conference scheduled at Heathrow as they landed and begged Jerry Lee to have Myra Gale wait with his sisters and her mother, but Jerry Lee told him, "Look, people want me, and they're gonna take me, no matter what."

The press descended on them as they got off the plane. Jerry Lee's new manager, Oscar Davis, tried to hustle off Myra Gale, but Jerry Lee clung to her. Somebody asked who she was. "This is my wife, Myra," he announced. She looked awfully young. How old was she? "Fifteen." Well, gee, Mrs. Lewis, isn't that a little young to be getting married? "Oh, no, not at all," Myra chirped. "Age doesn't matter back home. You can marry at ten if you can find a husband." And off they went to the hotel.

The British had always suspected that American rock-and-roll stars were degenerates, but they hardly expected to have the evidence served up to them on a silver platter, and that's what Jerry Lee and Myra had just done. The news hit the wire services and traveled back to America as fast as the electrons could carry it, and when it ticked out in the newsroom of the Memphis *Press-Scimitar*, a reporter did a little more digging and found out that the marriage had occurred five months before Jerry Lee's divorce became final, and that Myra Gale Lewis was not fifteen at all, but thirteen (well, almost fourteen).

Meanwhile, in Britain, as gigantic headlines started to appear, there was a sold-out house awaiting Jerry Lee at the Regal Cinema in Edmonton. Two thousand British teenagers, many of whom were probably willing to give Jerry Lee the benefit of the doubt, sat through opening acts, confident that he would redeem himself the moment he put finger to piano. But, although he put on a raging performance, he only gave them ten minutes. The audience was stunned, betrayed, and they started to boo and hiss. The next morning's papers mixed contemptuous reviews with stern editorializing about Jerry Lee's morals, and the next night, when the show played at the

Kilburn State Theatre in the London suburbs, the house was only a quarter filled.

The morning papers continued to howl, calling for deportation, and at the Monday-night show at the Granada Theatre in Tooting, Jerry Lee was heckled with cries of "Cradle-robber!" and "Sissy!" when he combed his long blond hair. The next day the British promoter met with the Rank Organisation, which owned the theaters where the show was booked, and they mutually agreed to cancel the tour. Reporters followed the disgraced Americans to the airport, and Jerry Lee delivered some straight-from-the-hip opinions. "You British are nice, on the whole," he told a reporter, "but some of y'all are jealous, just plain jealous." Would this scandal hurt his career? "Back in America, I got two lovely homes, three Cadillacs, and a farm," he said. "What else would anyone want?" Photographers blocked him as he tried to make his way onto the plane, and he aimed a kick of his two-tone loafers at one of them who was flashing his bulbs at his sister, Frankie Jean, and Myra Gale.

Back home, more trouble and more reporters were waiting for the plane. Jerry Lee insisted that he hadn't been deported—and he hadn't—and said instead that he'd just gotten homesick. And when one raised the question about Myra's age, Jerry Lee came close to losing his temper. "You can put this down," he snarled. "She's a woman." Sam Phillips must have been reeling: Perkins and Cash were gone, it was beginning to look like Jerry Lee was ruined, and he had nobody waiting in the wings. So he called Jack Clement and a Memphis disc jockey named George Klein, who had been a high school friend of Elvis's. With Klein as announcer, they put together a little "Flying Saucer" type of record called "The Return of Jerry Lee," using some of Jerry Lee's records to answer the interviewer's questions. Said Sam, "We think it's a cute record. It makes light of the whole British episode, which is the way we think the whole thing should be treated anyway." It was cute, but it was a dangerous thing to do to an artist's career, mocking the established morality like that.

Sam also bought a full page in *Billboard*, and Jerry Lee and he composed an open letter to the public. "I have in recent weeks been the apparent center of a fantastic amount of publicity and of which none has been good," it began. "But there must be a little good even in the worst people, and according to the press releases originating in London, I am the worst and am not even deserving of one decent press release. Now this whole thing started because I tried and did tell the truth. I told the story of my past life, as I thought it had been straightened out and that I would not hurt anybody in being man enough to tell the truth. I confess that my life has been stormy. I confess further that since I have become a public figure I sincerely wanted to be worthy of the decent admiration of all the people, young and old, that admired or liked what talent (if any) I have. That is, after all, all that I have in a professional way to offer. If you don't believe that the accuracy of things can get mixed up when you are in the public's eye, then I hope you never have to travel this road I'm on. . . ."

The wound was clearly visible, and it would grow worse. Dick Clark got a phone call urging him not to book Jerry Lee anymore, and Clark later wrote, "In a very cowardly act I decided to hold off further bookings for Jerry Lee on the show, for which I've been very sorry ever since." Still, Jerry Lee had a hit, "High School Confidential," the theme song to a spectacular and sensational film about a dope ring in a suburban high school, starring Russ Tamblyn and Mamie Van Doren, and it was a swinging piece of wax, with the immortal opening line, "Open up honey it's your lover boy me that's a knockin'." It was decided to book him into the Café de Paris, a swank New York nightclub that was in financial trouble and trying anything to stay afloat. The opening-night audience was appalled by his act, and the booking contract was terminated at the end of the evening "by mutual consent," according to the club. The Café de Paris went broke the next week, but it would take Jerry Lee several more years to hit bottom.

With Jerry Lee in trouble and Elvis in the army, it might seem like the summer of 1958 was a particularly dark one for rock and roll. In some ways it was, both because hucksters were beginning to move into the field in greater quantity and because their interest in making money outweighed their ability to think creatively. *Billboard* noted in July that instead of covering a song outright, now A&R men were copying sounds in a frank play for the market. The example they used was a good one: the scores of rockabilly records that, good as any one of them might be, had begun to sound like hundreds of Elvis imitations, without the spark that set Elvis apart. Not to mention the triplet-laden "rockaballad" formula that was emerging, all set to the same chord pattern: I-VI-IV-V. "In the Still of the Nite" had been one of the first of this genre, but hundreds—perhaps even a thousand—were to follow, and it is a real testimony to the inventiveness of the harmony group singers that those changes could be rung so many ways and so successfully so much of the time.

But this was also still a very fertile time for rock and roll. In April 1958 Chuck Berry released the record that became the capstone of his career: "Johnny B. Goode" b/w "Around and Around." The B side itself would have made a hit single, with its stop-time description of a dance that went on all night long, powered by the greatest rock and roll band of all time. But it was eclipsed by the story of the young man who carried his guitar in a gunnysack and swore that someday he would rise to fame as the leader of a great band. Autobiographical, mythic, and propelled by one of the great Chuck Berry choruses of all time—"Go! Go, Johnny go!"—while hammering away at the strongest of the limited but unforgettable Chuck Berry guitar licks, "Johnny B. Goode," the story of rock and roll Everykid, gave hope to all those who knew that rock and roll had given them a new way out of the miseries of teenagerhood, poverty, and any and all dead-end situations.

And there were more great records. The Everlys had now perfected their formula, and nearly everything they released went right to the top. Spring saw "All I Have To Do Is Dream," on which their harmony was just too pure for the song to have been about sexual fantasizing. They followed it up later in the summer with a song that seemed actually to threaten, "Bird Dog," in which they sneered at an oily character who used his wiles to steal somebody's girlfriend, contrasting his good behavior ("He's a bird") with his sneakiness ("He's a *dawg!*") in spoken asides. Buddy Holly also got tough with "Rave On," which rocked about as hard as anything he ever released and on which the mild-mannered West Texan actually seemed to snarl at times. Dion and the Belmonts, some young Italian singers from Belmont Avenue in the Bronx, proved that black vocal groups didn't have any monopoly on soulful singing when they debuted on the charts with the tricky "I Wonder Why," which may have suffered from their dese-does accents but was made instantly memorable by a simple but effective vocal arrangement. And Leiber and Stoller hooked up with the Coasters again to make yet another teenage classic of social commentary, yet another record that would set parents and school authorities against rock and roll: "Yakety Yak." Its hero was a poor kid bedeviled by his parents. They fire off order after order at him—do the laundry, clean up your room, take out the garbage, bring in the dog, put out the cat—and each intricately structured verse ends with the words "Yakety yak—don't talk back!" The kid doesn't even get a chance to have fun: If the work's not done, he doesn't go out to the show, and his mother warns him, "Tell your hoodlum friends outside / You ain't got time to take a ride." As frosting on this teen-rebellion cake, Leiber and Stoller got King Curtis, a Texas-born tenor saxophonist, to play a distinctive, almost hillbilly-tinged sax line that yaketied in counterpoint to the mother's orders. Like "Get a Job," it touched a nerve, and it became the bestselling rhythm-and-blues record of 1958.

Part of the reason for the success of "Yakety Yak" was that it walked the line between novelty record and vocal-group record. That quality also contributed to the success of three other summertime hits of 1958. The Olympics' "Western Movies" was the best record the Coasters never made, with the singer complaining that his girlfriend's passion for oaters exceeded her passion for him, while crudely dubbed in sound effects from Westerns clopped and kapweenged around him. And if the Edsels hadn't sung "Rama Lama Ding Dong," it would have been necessary to have invented the song to prove how silly vocal-group rock and roll could get. The singer pours out his heart passionately, declaring his love for a girl he claims is named Rama Lama Rama Lama Ding Dong—and yet he is strangely convincing. The Monotones were a group of Chicago high school students who were trying to combine a current toothpaste commercial ("You'll wonder where the yellow went / When you brush your teeth with Pepsodent") with a half-formed idea they had called "Book of Love," with each line being a chapter. Rehearsing in the school's band practice room, which stood near the playground, they were trying to figure out how to phrase the line "I wonder wonder who-who-who-who-who" when a bas-ketball hit the window at just the right time, and one of the most unforgetta-ble hooks in rock and roll was born. Recorded first on a small Chicago indie, "Book of Love" became another of the year's best sellers when the Chess subsidiary Argo picked it up.

Not all the vocal groups had such whimsical material: Summer snugglers could moon to the Danleers' "One Summer Night," a ballad in the great tradition, which they sang every bit as skillfully as the Platters but were too underproduced to rival. George Goldner made a tremendous discovery, Little Anthony and the Imperials, whose "Tears on My Pillow" sounded like it was sung by a girl but struck home with its tearful story of betrayal by a heartless female. In fact, ballads were there in force. Peggy Lee, of all people, had a big hit with her cover of Little Willie John's "Fever"; the Elegants' "Little Star," delivered with New York diction ("Dere you ah, little stah,"), combined vocal-group mooniness with an infectious mid-tempo dance beat; Johnny Vincent found Jimmy Clanton somewhere in the South and recorded "Just A Dream," a doom-laden bit of nasality that seemed to answer the needs of the same girls who were buying the Poni-Tails' "Born Too Late," the theme song of every junior high schooler in love with the football captain.

For those whose hormones were a bit more stable, a young singer from Mississippi finally justified MGM Records' faith in him when "It's Only Make Believe" became a big hit for Harold Jenkins, who recorded under the unforgettable name Conway Twitty.* This ballad really smoldered, starting out low and soft and rising bit by bit, both in intensity and pitch, until Twitty sobbed out the title. And speaking of teen urges, a wonderful little canon by a group of Massachusetts teens who called themselves the Jamies, "Summertime, Summertime," was described by a *Billboard* writer as "an exciting blend of medieval polyphonic structure with the modern hor-monal sound," a description that may herald the first awakening of modern know-nothing rock criticism.

The other seasonal song, Eddie Cochran's "Summertime Blues," told of a kid so tormented by his parents and his summer-job boss that he decides to appeal first to his congressman ("I'd like to help you, son, but you're too young to vote") and finally to the United Nations. Although, as in "Yakety Yak," the problem was presented humorously, Cochran's gravelly voice and urgent guitar playing subverted the humor somewhat. After all, teens were still subject to adult restraints. Not Cochran himself, of course: Although he was a true rock and roller, he also epitomized a coming trend in that, along with songwriter Jerry Capehart, he was truly professional in his approach to rock and roll, producing songs that, like "Summertime Blues," were calculated in their effect. He also was one of the first rock-and-roll perform-

---

*In an odd publicity campaign in 1957, they had taken out ads in *Billboard* reprinting negative comments about Twitty from djs and fans.

ers to take advantage of multitrack studio technology and performed all the parts on "Summertime Blues" himself.

But then, American technology seemed to be zooming ahead, the Sputnik gap notwithstanding. In January, the new Recording Industry Association of America announced that the Westrex stereophonic record system seemed to meet all the criteria of compatibility and technical excellence in separation of channels, and so now America had a stereo record system that the industry could sell. A month later, RCA almost revolutionized the stereo tape business when it introduced a tape cartridge that you just popped into the player, selected the track you wanted to hear, and played.* Once the Westrex stereo system was approved, the floodgates of stereo opened, and dozens of recorded Ping-Pong games and "provocative percussion" records, not to mention live recordings of the Le Mans speedway and various steam railroad engines, hit the hi-fi market. There were 19,830 LP records in print, *Billboard* announced in March, and at the end of that month, the first Westrex albums arrived in the stores, many of them catalog items—but recorded on multitrack equipment—that had simply been remixed and mastered in stereo. By the end of August, a consumer survey revealed that consumers were eagerly accepting the new system, and jukebox operators began speculating about the possibility of pressuring record companies to start pressing singles and EPs in stereo so that stereo jukeboxes (at ten cents a play: they were determined to double the cost) could become commonplace.

The summertime records brought a new wave of reaction. Predictably, *Contacts,* the Catholic Youth Organization's newspaper, urged pious teens to "smash the records you possess which present a pagan culture and a pagan concept of life. Check beforehand the records which will be played at a house party or at a school record dance. Resist the pressures created by the money-mad record hucksters and popularity-hungry disc jockeys. . . ."

More unexpected trouble came from NBC Spot Sales, the division of the radio network that was responsible for soliciting advertising from agencies, which issued an album, *Music to Buy Time By,* that was sent to agencies across the country. One side featured music and commentary that was an example of what WRC, Washington, D.C., the station selected to epitomize NBC, deemed acceptable. The other side was a flat-out attack on rock and roll, the people who played it, and the stations that programmed it. So virulent were the attacks against the four records played—"Rave On," "Yakety Yak," "Breathless," and something called "Slam Bam Thank You Mam" by Paul Hampton—that the labels involved considered legal action against the company. For example, the commentary for "Yakety Yak" went: "Well, let's see what other garb—uh—rock and roll music we have. This one

---

*This development foreshadowed an innovation that Holland's Phillips Industries would patent about eight years later, the compact cassette, except that it was much bigger and failed to capture the public's imagination.

is by the Coasters, four fugitives from the hog caller seminar and they've come up with an ear-caressing little dandy. . . . [plays record] Well, now, I don't know who wrote that little opus, but I bet six months' pay against the chance of an ice cube in you-know-where that it wasn't Cole Porter or Gershwin."

True, said Ahmet Ertegun, when he was apprised of the slam. "That little opus was written by Jerry Leiber and Mike Stoller, who penned many of Elvis Presley's biggest RCA Victor hits, including 'Hound Dog,' and who are currently under contract to produce records for RCA Victor." In fact, Ertegun noted, not a single one of these records under attack was on RCA, of which NBC was a wholly-owned subsidiary; and the name of Elvis Presley, an RCA recording artist responsible for selling 16 million records for the label, was never even whispered.

Even in the army, Elvis was still visible. Almost immediately after his induction, a group called the Threeteens came out with a song called "Dear 533010761," addressing Elvis by his new serial number, and some enterprising soul pressed up counterfeit dog tags with the number, blood type, and portrait of the new soldier etched on them. But when the Colonel found out, he quickly took over rights to the souvenirs himself, making several thousand dollars' royalties in just a couple of weeks. The dog tags became very popular charms.

And in May his fans received an even better souvenir: Elvis's fourth movie, King Creole, and it was a monster. Adapted from a Harold Robbins novel, A Stone for Danny Fisher, it dealt with a poor-but-good boy growing up in New Orleans' French Quarter with a talent for singing but absolutely no affinity with luck. The story was strident, the emotions fairly garbled, and the tacked-on happy ending incongruous, but once again, Elvis rose above the material seemingly without effort and virtually singlehandedly carried the movie. The film was a hit all summer long, and RCA made sure that there were singles to follow it up (including "Hard Headed Woman" from the Leiber and Stoller sound track, a tricky selection because it was only partially heard in the movie) as well as an album, Elvis' Golden Records.

After his induction at Fort Chaffee, Arkansas, Elvis entered basic training at Fort Hood, Texas, in March. Once there, he rented a trailer in nearby Killeen and installed his parents in late June, since a soldier with dependents in the immediate area was allowed to live off the base. It was a great solace to Elvis (who, in order to be what he wanted to be in the army—one of the boys—had to take a great deal more ribbing than the average recruit) to be able to visit his parents and let off steam. Vernon and Gladys were perhaps the only human beings on earth whom Elvis didn't have to prove anything to. But during July, Gladys started to fade. Something was sapping her of her energy, her attentiveness, her ability to get around; and Elvis and Vernon decided it was time she went back to Memphis for a checkup. A few days later, the doctors called the Presley men and told them that she had hepatitis, and that the prognosis was poor, so they left for Memphis as soon as Elvis could arrange compassionate leave. Elvis and Vernon took turns sitting with Gladys in her room at Methodist Hospital, but she continued to sink rapidly. In the early morning hours of August 14, while Elvis slept at Graceland, Gladys died.

Elvis was torn apart. There had been and would be other women in his life, but none of them would ever measure up to the forty-six-year-old woman who lay dead in Memphis. She had given him so much, starting with the will to make something of himself and, sadly, ending with a congenitally weak heart that, stressed with pharmaceuticals, would give out the way hers had, nearly nineteen years to the day from the hour of her death. He would later say of her, "She was very close, more than a mother. She was a friend who would let me talk to her any hour of the day or night if I had a problem. I would get mad sometimes when she wouldn't let me do something. But I found out she was right about almost everything. She would always try to slow me up if I ever thought I wanted to get married. She was right."

After her death, Elvis and his father returned to Fort Hood, where he prepared to ship out to Germany. The final souvenir he would leave his fans was a recording of his dockside press conference, "Elvis Sails." Predictably the first question was stupid: "What's your description of the ideal girl?" Elvis fielded it with aplomb: "Female." Other questions about his love life were gently deflected, although he joked that "When I get to Europe, the first place I want to go when I get a pass is Paris. I'd like to look up Brigitte Bardot. No, I don't speak any French or German, but I guess I'll learn enough to get around."

Then, on a more crucial matter: "I haven't had a chance to make any new records. I've been spending my time soldiering. But the record company has eight sides they haven't released." Eight sides to last two years. Would that be enough to keep rock and roll alive? What if rock and roll died while Elvis was gone? "I'd probably starve to death. If it ever did happen—and I don't think that it would—I'd make a serious try to keep on top in the movies. That would be my best chance." Not that Elvis was keeping rock and roll alive in his own personal record collection. "What songs do I like best? One of my favorites has been 'Padre,' that record by Toni Arden. And 'I'll Never Walk Alone' has always been a favorite of mine. Sure, 'Volare' was a great record.* I went out and bought it right away."

There's no doubt that that fall the words *rock and roll* were becoming poison. Even Alan Freed, in the wake of the Boston riot, suddenly became a paragon of virtue. His new television show, which premiered in July, was called "The Big Beat," eschewing the mere mention of rock and roll and avoiding some of the more raucous acts. *Billboard* viewed the new look

---

*The Italian ballad was inescapable in the summer of 1958, sung in its most popular version by Domenico Mondugno.

with amusement: "Freed's fans may go along with the gag for a few weeks. . . ." it wrote in a review of the premiere. "However, polite rock and roll isn't Freed's forte and chances are 'The Big Beat' won't really start rocking, rating-wise, until it stops trying to sell two generations and concentrates on the one 'beat.'"

Nor was Freed the only one trying to downplay rock and roll. A State Department-sponsored tour by several American disc jockeys, who went overseas to stage American-style record hops in foreign countries, was forbidden to play any rock-and-roll records, a ban that the head of the group, Murray Kaufman, said they'd all honor.*

Kaufman was another odd figure, the first truly conservative rock-and-roll disc jockey. A morning man on WINS, he larded his program with Como and Sinatra but played enough rock and roll to keep his teen audience. When Atlantic Records decided to jump into the pop world with a New York crooner named Bobby Darin, they had little luck until he recorded a tune, "Splish Splash," that he'd written in twelve minutes and that had half its publishing assigned to someone named Jean Murray. Murray turned out to be Kaufman's mother, and the publisher, Portrait, a company owned by Kaufman. Of course, in light of the entanglements of Freed and Clark, it was merely business as usual.

But it was that very kind of business that was beginning to come under scrutiny. The mechanics of getting a record on the right radio programs, so the right people would hear it and decide they wanted to buy it, have always been very complicated. No amount of research or planning can make a record a success if it's not in the grooves. Not that people don't try. Payola, the practice of paying a disc jockey to play a record, had long been part of the rhythm-and-blues scene and of the pop scene to a certain extent. In fact, hearings were being held in Washington to examine the allegation that records from BMI, which had close ties with radio stations, were getting more than their fair share of airplay, possibly through corrupt means.† And in 1958, these means might have been wrong, but they weren't actually illegal. All the interconnected business deals that disc jockeys like Kaufman, Freed, and Clark, and many others established may have been unethical, but since they'd never been tried in a court of law, they hadn't been banned. As long as you reported your income, you were safe.

Bob Horn had never been safe. At WFIL, he'd preceded Dick Clark as host of the "Bandstand" show, and his brash, crazy manner was something teenagers loved and management tried to pretend didn't exist. He was one of those personalities like Alan Freed who was tolerated because he

---

*Considering that Russian teens were bootlegging Elvis records by pressing them on X-ray plates, rock and roll could have been a much more potent weapon against the Communist threat, looming so large in the 1950s, than the pop the djs were playing.

† Of course, what the ASCAP people who made the charges conveniently forgot was that ASCAP had for years refused to admit hillbilly or blues songwriters, and now that music based in these two traditions was selling, the old-time Broadway and Tin Pan Alley types who were members of ASCAP were out in the cold.

brought in the ratings, but whom management privately wished would go away. In 1956, the station found its excuse: In the middle of a WFIL campaign against drunk driving, Horn was involved in a spectacular auto accident while he was drunk. The next day he was fired, Dick Clark took over "Bandstand," and his career was on the skids.* He drifted from station to station, and in April 1958, he was rumored to be at some tiny place near Houston. Then, that month, a Philadelphia grand jury indicted Horn for income tax evasion for failing to report $30,000 of payola income, and once he was tracked down and extradited, he was found guilty.

Most djs were a little more circumspect than Horn. There were many other ways of being courted by a record company than bald-facedly snaring cash. Drop a hint here or there and you might wind up with a nice piece of clothing, maybe a dinner and drinks on somebody's account at a good restaurant, or if you were really important, you might find that somebody'd picked up the plane fare for your Miami vacation. More likely, though, you'd get cooperation from a record company when you needed an artist to appear at your record hop, and you'd get it for way below the asking price: union scale for union members, or free if circumstances allowed. This practice offered much more direct benefits to all concerned: The artist got exposure, the record company sold records, and the jockey gained favor with the fans.

But as the record business grew more cutthroat, some of these under-the-turntable dealings grew more serious. *Billboard* straightfacedly reported on one record company taking several "New York models" on the road to promote a record, and tales of artists providing sexual favors for jockeys were not unknown. One colorful Texas figure was famous for his spiel whereby he'd extract a hundred-dollar bill from his pocket, explain that he knew a particular jockey couldn't be bought, pontificate that money was trash, and then wad up the bill and throw it in the wastebasket. It is extremely unlikely that this gimmick made many radio-station janitors rich.

Of course, this sort of payola was predicated on the theory that the jockeys made the hits, and that's where Todd Storz and his Top Forty format made the difference. Storz admitted that he didn't let jocks pick the records because their personal preferences made for dangerous programming. A dj's IQ and his income were above average, Storz claimed, and that meant he couldn't relate 100 percent to the average person's taste. Storzites argued for science, which, in those post-Sputnik days, was certainly a sexier argument than art. Over and over again, management took the Top Forty line, and djs—at least the ones who'd been in the business for a while—decried it. Said Ted Collins, who produced Kate Smith's successful radio show, "I'm against Top Forty on two counts. Number one—it would mean

---

*A further bit of trouble was a statutory rape charge that emerged around the same time as the accident; it made headlines, but Horn was found innocent.

programming about 75 percent rock and roll. Number two—by sticking only with proven top records, you are doing a disservice to the entire music industry by not giving a showcase to as many new songs as you possibly can. I would sooner quit radio than adhere only to a Top Forty formula. Personally, I think the only way out of the current musical mess would be to abandon all Top Forty shows, and let all kinds of music get an equal chance to be heard. That way, maybe rock and roll would disappear."

George "Hound Dog" Lorenz, the man whose Niagara Falls show helped bring rock and roll to Canada, echoed Collins's second point, noting, "A lot of the stations are programming twenty-four hours a day with no more than fifty records. Maybe that's okay, but when it's the same records every day for a week and they change only ten or so a week, then it begins to get pretty monotonous. . . . With this kind of programming, it's harder than ever for an artist to get off the ground, because it's only hits the stations play, and practically nothing else. It's a lousy situation." So lousy, in fact, that he'd quit his job in Buffalo, where he'd been since the early 1950s, and was now working out of WHAY, Hartford, Connecticut.

It was, in fact, getting harder and harder for a new artist to get a break. According to a *Billboard* study, fewer than 10 percent of the records released became hits—that is, sold between 100,000 and 1 million copies—and the true number was closer to 5 percent. Sixty percent sold between 2,000 and 3,000, 20 percent sold up to 25,000, and only 10 percent sold in excess of 50,000. In fact, 80 percent of the records released caused losses for the record labels and for distributors, who often went unpaid when a record flopped. The industry was now churning out over a hundred singles a week, which, at an average of three minutes each, was five solid hours of A sides and five more of B sides to listen to. No jockey or program director had that kind of time.

By October, it was becoming evident that singles sales were down, and Teen-Age Survey, Inc., found four reasons for the slump. First, there were so many records available that consumers were confused. Second, the recession was hitting youngsters hard. Third, the lack of an exciting trend made record buying less urgent; and fourth, fewer teens were visiting record stores on their weekly shopping trips. Also, the LP was cutting into singles business, since it only cost four times as much as a single and had six times as much music on it. People would wait for a hit to come out on an album before they made their buy.

Still, if live music was packaged well enough, people would go to see it. At the Hollywood Bowl, 11,800 people came out for a "Salute to Dick Clark," featuring some of the best talent Philly had to offer. Alan Freed, after rejecting the idea of a Labor Day show, later changed his mind, even though the Brooklyn Paramount, chary after the Boston fiasco only four months before, refused to rent him the theater. Freed shrugged and booked his show into the Brooklyn Fox, down the street, announcing a lineup of Chuck Berry, Frankie Avalon, the Kalin Twins, the Elegants, the Poni-Tails,

Larry Williams, Jimmy Clanton, the Danleers, Bo Diddley, Jo Ann Campbell, Teddy Randazzo, Jack Scott, the Royal Teens, Bobby Freeman, the Everly Brothers, and more. In retaliation, the Paramount mounted its own rock-and-roll show, but Freed had clearly scooped them on the talent end, and he wound up setting a new record for a show in Brooklyn, grossing over $200,000. Equally important, Freed's show proved (according to a thank-you ad the Fox management placed in *Billboard*), "that rock and roll can go in theaters without unpleasant incidents."

Individual musicians were preparing to tour, too. Buddy Holly mentioned his new tour on Alan Freed's television show and wound up giving an interview that, in light of subsequent events, is positively chilling. Freed was reminiscing about his last package tour, which had included the Crickets. "Buddy, we had a lot of fun, we did a lot of *flying.*" "Yeah," Buddy replied, laughing, "we sure did. Y'know, I was just in a town the other day, Cincinnati. Remember we landed there that day and the helicopter had just crashed that day when we got there? When we took the ride in from the airport there it reminded me." "Buddy, we played, I think we rode every kind of airplane imaginable." "We sure did." "Those DC-3s were really something." Buddy laughed some more and moved his hand in an undulating motion, going "*Wmmp, wmmp, wmmp.*" "Oh, boy," Freed said with a laugh. "Without those seat belts, we'd have been right through the top of the plane."

This would be Buddy's first tour after taking the summer off to marry Maria Elena Santiago, a receptionist at Peer-Southern Music whom he'd met at lunch during a visit to New York and proposed to at the table. Nobody took him seriously at the time, especially not Maria Elena, but he'd gotten serious that evening over dinner (after Maria Elena had waged a war with her conservative, traditional aunt over whether she should go out with an entertainer, even to dinner), and she'd accepted. They honeymooned in Acapulco a few weeks later with Jerry Allison and Peggy Sue. As Holly's current record said, "It's so easy to fall in love."

Buddy was growing up, and so, perhaps, was rock and roll. His next record was "Heartbeat" b/w "Well All Right"—both rockers but very gentle rockers. Encouraged, Norman Petty began thinking that Buddy and the Crickets, plus the artists they were developing, like "Ivan" (Jerry Allison) and Waylon Jennings, who was now playing bass with Buddy, would become the sort of sinecure that would give him a steady income. In October, consequently, when his own contract with Columbia ran out, Norman declined to renew, planning to gamble on releasing future Trio records on his Nor Va Jak label. By now, Buddy had had an offer to record with a string section, and Paul Anka had pitched him a song, "It Doesn't Matter Anymore." They held the string session in October, and Norman was excited by the results. Buddy was going to be a pop artist, the first rock and roller to make the leap into the mainstream.

But Maria Elena had been talking to Buddy, and Buddy had begun to realize that he and the Crickets didn't need Norman anymore. After all, they frequently toured without him, and they'd learned how to get money out of recalcitrant promoters (Buddy even carried a gun, a pretty standard precaution in those days). So, with Maria Elena, he went back to Lubbock and confronted Petty, demanding that they work out a split. Norman protested, but the young couple was adamant. Meanwhile the Crickets—Jerry Allison and Joe Mauldin—were already in Clovis, New Mexico, waiting to record. Given the odds, they elected to stay with Norman, so Buddy moved back to New York with Maria Elena. Time was running out, he'd been telling people; he had to push for success while he was young. So far he only had one hit record, "Peggy Sue," under his own name.

Was rock and roll really growing up? That depends on your definition of rock and roll. Certainly the old masters were getting more sophisticated. In the fall of 1958, Chuck Berry released "Sweet Little Rock and Roll" (best known as "Sweet Little Rock and Roller"), who never got any older and was Everyfan. The song was weak musically next to his best efforts, but his myth making was stronger than ever. Eddie Cochran came out with "C'Mon Everybody," another multitrack rocker that was sophisticated technologically even if it was at heart a simple rock and roll tune. Cochran sold better abroad than he did in America and was one of the first rock and rollers to see possibilities in the overseas market. He probably agreed with British bandleader Ted Heath, who said, "The British people will never really accept British jazz or for that matter popular rock and roll, either. Nor do the Germans and Scandinavians accept the same thing from their own countrymen. They all see jazz and blues and rock and roll as purely American and they feel the Americans are the only ones who can really perform in those veins." Fats Domino, whose career had been in a slump for a year and a half (on records; his tours still did well), came back strong with "Whole Lotta Loving," which was a little different from his usual fare—the patented Domino triplets were exchanged for a sort of *ooom-pah* rhythm—if not radically new.

Even rhythm-and-blues performers were experimenting with less teen-oriented stylings. James Brown, whose career had stalled even longer than that of Fats (two and a half years to be exact), erupted with the pleading ballad "Try Me," which was so slow that in spite of its 6/8 meter it sounded like a waltz (in 3/4). Jackie Wilson, the Detroit singer who had bailed out of Billy Ward's Dominoes, released a sophisticated record, "Lonely Teardrops," that mixed blues and gospel into a basic pop tune by Berry Gordy, Jr., and Tyran Carlo, who seemed to have a knack for writing him hits. Lloyd Price took Archibald's old New Orleans folk tale about the legendary murderer, "Stagger Lee" and turned it into a hit that nonetheless conveyed the myth's ambivalence about its central character; having a haikulike opening—"The night was clear/And the moon was yellow/And the leaves came tumblin' down"—didn't hurt, either. And the Platters completed their leap into pop standards territory with a reading of "Smoke Gets in Your

Eyes" that must have made even the staunchest "good music" fan cry tears of joy.

On the other hand, there were records like the Playmates' "Beep Beep" and David Seville's "The Chipmunk Song," numbers that were clearly aimed at the very youngest record-buying audience. The Playmates were a male trio who started out as a comedy act but began incorporating more music during their tours, and finally wound up with a record on Roulette. "Beep Beep" was the story of a car race, with a "little Nash Rambler," one of America's first compact cars, sprinting to beat a Cadillac as the tune got faster and faster. In "The Chipmunk Song," David Seville was back with his speeded-up tapes, which he presented as chipmunks to whom he was attempting to teach a cute Christmas tune. They performed it well, except for Alvin, the troublemaker. It became a tremendous hit, and throughout the Christmas season, the chipmunks' trilling voices could be heard everywhere. The other juvenile favorite was little Brenda Lee, singing "Rockin' Around the Christmas Tree," written by Johnny Marks, who had forged a nice career by writing Christmas songs, including the perennial "Rudolph the Red-Nosed Reindeer." These two year-end records were probably responsible for keeping one of rock and roll's truly great Christmas songs obscure: Chuck Berry's "Run Rudolph Run," in which Rudolph, with the speed of a Sabre jet, runs Santa down the freeway to deliver a doll to a girl and a "rock and roll record guitar" to a boy.

Despite these bids to the very youngest teens, it was difficult to disagree with the veteran disc jockey Bill Randle at WERE in Cleveland, who said, "Rock and roll is being integrated into popular music. It's no longer a novelty. Rock and roll was an earthy, virile influence, but the authentic artists were destroyed by the gimmick imitators. . . . There's a point to which you can't cater to the mediocre any longer." Randle went on to say that Sputnik had saved America's youth from isolation and despair, from being torn between the draft and the bomb, and that now rock and roll was not the only available outlet for teen frustrations. "Now they track sputniks, build rockets," he explained. "They read. It's no longer smart to be dumb. Elvis Presley's setting an example now. He's in the Army. . . . He's a genuine culture hero."

And anyway, rock and roll had existed for roughly five years by now. People had grown accustomed to a good backbeat and had by now lost their fears about "jungle rhythms" with their powers to inflame and corrupt. Wildness was out. Respectability was in. Tin Pan Alley was getting a few new faces now, younger ones. The rebels were being tamed, and there was only one year to go until a whole new decade brought fresh promise. Why rebel? The future was bright. Ah, but school wasn't out quite yet.

12

TRAGEDY

I t was January 1959, and Ritchie Valens knew his year had come. He was a Mexican-American, and proud of it, too, even if on his records he had had to change his name from Valenzuela so that the disc jockeys could pronounce it. Mexican-Americans had been rock-and-roll fans from the start, providing Johnny Otis with some of his hottest audiences, both at the Barrel House, back when Watts was as much brown as black, and when he started staging shows especially for them at El Monte Legion Stadium in the heart of brown L.A. First jump blues and then vocal group music formed the sound track for the pachucos—"bad boys"—cruising Whittier Boulevard in the cars they'd so lovingly restored and polished. But there had never been a Mexican-American rock-and-roll star, and now Ritchie Valens—seventeen years old, good-looking, if a bit chubby, and possessed of a fine high tenor voice and a natural, fluid songwriting ability—was the obvious candidate.

Bob Keene recognized his potential. Keene had helped Sam Cooke get established when he left Specialty for pop, recording him on Keen Records; and Ritchie would be the first major artist on Del-Fi, Keene's new label.

Ritchie's debut, "Come On, Let's Go" was a perfect first single. It sounded like a folk song, but it was as light and danceable as the best of Buddy Holly. But for his second record, Ritchie mined his Mexican heritage for a more ambitious song, which was released toward the end of 1958. "La Bamba" was almost a pan-Latin folksong, based on an incredible riff that a guitarist would play over and over as the singer improvised verses—usually nonsense lyrics, but sometimes sly satires. (Perhaps there was a double meaning to the lines "Yo no soy marinero / Soy capitán," meaning, "I'm not a sailor/I'm a captain.") All Ritchie did was add a killer rhythm section and a fine electric lead guitar, and "La Bamba" became the biggest foreign-language smash since "Volare." And to clinch his success, the B side was a tribute to all the late-night dances he'd ever played. "Donna" would never win any prizes for lyrics, but nobody would be listening to its words. It had the perfect creeping tempo for slow, passionate dancing.

Now he needed exposure, not so easy to achieve in the winter as it was in the summertime, when the big package tours went out. But there was one tour, sponsored by GAC, called the "Winter Dance Party" and headlined by Frankie Sardo; the Big Bopper, J. P. "Jape" Richardson;* Dion and the Belmonts; and Buddy Holly, performing without the Crickets for the first time. Ritchie filled the package out nicely, and the tour set off in January.

It was odd that Buddy Holly was on it. He was really just beginning his solo career, and his latest record, "It Doesn't Matter Anymore" (that song with the strings by Paul Anka b/w "Raining In My Heart"), hadn't been out long enough to start selling. Furthermore, his life was stabilizing. He'd been taking acting lessons at the Lee Strasberg Acting School, and Maria Elena was pregnant. He still maintained the hope that if he waited long enough, he would reunite with the Crickets, but for now, apparently, Buddy needed money.† The GAC jaunt was short enough—only two weeks—and it offered ready income.

The first step Buddy had to take was to assemble a band for the tour. Tommy Allsup was ready to play guitar, and Buddy's crazy disc jockey friend at KLLL, Waylon Jennings, had already played bass with Buddy and was eager to come along. Buddy called Niki Sullivan a few times, hoping he'd join them on drums, but they missed connections and so Charlie Bunch took over. Even so, the name *the Crickets* was used in all the advertising, although it may not have been legal.

The morning Buddy left, he and Maria and Tommy Allsup had breakfast together, and Buddy and Maria related that they'd both had strange dreams. "The night before Buddy left," Maria remembered years later, "I dreamed I was with Buddy, and then there was a lot of commotion—people were scared and running every which way, and then I found myself alone in a big, empty prairie or desert. Then I heard shouts and screams, and saw hundreds of people running towards me shouting, 'Look out, it's coming!' They all passed by me and I turned to watch them go, and when I turned back, I saw this big ball of fire coming through the air. It passed by me and fell a few feet from where I was, and made a deep hole in the ground. Then I

---

*A disc jockey from Beaumont, Texas, who'd scored a hit after jockeys turned over his record "The Purple People Eater Meets the Witch Doctor" to find a funny recitation called "Chantilly Lace."

† There is still a controversy today over whether Norman Petty had been shorting him, but no doubt feeling abandoned, Petty was disinclined to hurry any payments due to the newlyweds in New York.

woke up, and I must have screamed because I woke Buddy up, too. And then he told me about the dream he had been having.

"He had been dreaming that he was in a small plane with [his brother] Larry and me. Larry didn't want me to be there, but Buddy told him, 'Anywhere I go, Maria comes with me.' They kept arguing about it, and Larry kept landing the plane because he wanted me to get off, and Buddy wouldn't agree, so they'd take off again. Finally, Larry won the argument, and they landed on the roof of a tall building and left me there. And Buddy said, 'Don't worry, just stay put—I'll come back and get you.' And then he flew off."

The dreams were ominous, and the reality was grim as well—two weeks in what turned out to be drafty, ill-heated buses touring the northern Midwest. Once a bus broke down and it got so cold that Charlie Bunch developed frostbitten feet and had to be hospitalized while the tour went on without him. On February 1, they played two dates, an afternoon show in Appleton, Wisconsin, and an evening show in Green Bay. Then everybody piled onto the bus and headed 350 miles over frozen highways to Clear Lake, Iowa. The bus broke down again, and they got in at six for an eight o'clock show. Because the heat in the bus was so bad, everybody was dressed in stage clothes—and everything else they could pile on—and they were beginning to stink. Buddy figured that as the star, he could rectify the situation, and he promised his band that after the show in Clear Lake, they would charter a plane and fly to Moorhead, Minnesota, where they could take time to rest, get their laundry done, and be relaxed for the next night's show. Tommy and Waylon agreed, so the manager of the ballroom in Clear Lake (called, for some unknown reason, the Surf) called Dwyer's Flying Service, the local charter outfit. Jerry Dwyer, who owned the service, was out of town that afternoon, but they reached Roger Peterson, a young pilot who worked for Dwyer, and he agreed to fly them from the Mason City Airport to Fargo, North Dakota, which was just across the river from Moorhead.

Naturally, the word got around, for Buddy and his band weren't the only ones who were tired of the ordeal of touring. J. P. Richardson approached Waylon, saying that his size made riding on the bus uncomfortable, and anyway, he had a cold. Would Waylon mind giving up his seat on the plane? Waylon graciously agreed. Then Ritchie Valens asked Tommy Allsup, who refused to part with his seat. Ritchie kept at him, and finally Tommy agreed to flip a coin with Ritchie, with the loser staying on the bus. Tommy lost the toss.

The show was as good as anyone could expect from tired, frostbitten rock and rollers. Since some of their number had left the tour, Buddy wound up playing drums behind Dion and the Belmonts, and the bass-singing Belmont, Carlo Mastrangelo, played drums for Buddy; and Buddy, J. P., and Ritchie sang some trio numbers as a joke. During his time offstage, Buddy called Maria, telling her that the tour was near mutiny and outlining his plans; and at 12:40 that night, he, Ritchie, and J. P. arrived at the airport. Roger Peterson was thrilled to have such big stars as passengers, and Buddy insisted on sitting up front to watch him pilot the red four-seat Beechcraft Bonanza. He loved planes and had been taking flying lessons behind Maria's back.

Peterson had filed his flight plan, but for some reason, the airport traffic controllers had neglected to tell him that there were two special advisories out for the route, parts of the journey he'd have to fly on instruments instead of visually. The whole Dwyer Flying Service was only licensed for visual flying, and Peterson had flunked his instrument certification a year before.

Almost as soon as they took off, Peterson had to switch to instruments and immediately lost his bearings, because the gyroscope was set up in the opposite way from the one he usually used. He got so confused that he forgot to file a final flight plan, and Dwyer, on the ground, could tell that the plane was acting oddly. He got on the radio, but there was no answer. He tried again later, again without results, and the Fargo airport reported that they hadn't seen the plane. A nasty storm was brewing, so Dwyer checked the map for alternate airports where they might have been forced to land. Just before dawn, an alert was sounded. The Beechcraft was missing.

As Dwyer later told investigators, "I just couldn't sit there, and decided I would go fly and try to follow the same course that I thought Roger would have taken. I was only approximately eight miles northwest of the field when I spotted the wreckage." It was in a cornfield, smashed up against a fence. The right wing had hit the ground and ripped off, and the rest of the plane had thumped and bounded five hundred feet before a fence had stopped it, careening J. P. Richardson forty feet over the fence. Buddy and Ritchie were thrown twenty feet in the opposite direction, and Peterson was tangled in the wreckage. All were dead on impact.

Ironically, the night before, the Crickets had held a meeting at Jerry Allison's house in Lubbock. They'd decided Buddy was right, and that they'd break with Petty. Maria gave them the number of the next ballroom in Moorhead, and they'd been trying to call him there. When the Clear Lake troupe reached Moorhead, they heard the news, and, after they'd cried, decided to go on with the show. The producers held a talent contest that afternoon to find a band to add to the bill, and a group from Fargo Central High called the Shadows won. Their lead singer, Robert Velline, chosen because he knew the words to all the hit songs, was catapulted into the spotlight, and soon found himself renamed Bobby Vee and being groomed for stardom. The next night, instead of Buddy Holly and Ritchie Valens, Frankie Avalon and Jimmy Clanton were on the tour.

In fact, the replacement of real rock and rollers by pretty faces after this incident was sort of a metaphor for what was happening to rock and roll itself. As it became more a part of the musical landscape, rock and roll was accepted not only by older listeners but by very young ones, too. They reacted to the simpler, more formulaic music that Tin Pan Alley and its imitators were making, as well as to the novelties, and they were also consuming more television than their older brothers and sisters. Even if Bobby Vee or Fabian or Bobby Rydell or Jimmy Clanton couldn't sing as well as some others could, they were cute, and they looked even cuter in closeup, say, when Dick Clark was pointing the microphone at them. Furthermore, these pretty faces weren't rebels in any meaningful way, and it wasn't hard to find defenders for teen idols who didn't cause trouble.

If they were a symptom of what was happening to teenage music, the other major group on the GAC "Winter Dance Party" represented a nice compromise. Dion and the Belmonts were Italians from the Bronx, and their first record, "I Wonder Why," clearly showed the influence of the black vocal groups, the Teenagers in particular. With its chanted nonsense syllables, close harmonies, and clear tenor lead by Dion DiMucci, it didn't sound like a rhythm-and-blues record although it had enough appeal to sell in rhythm-and-blues record shops, and the group performed for black audiences. Their next big record, "A Teenager in Love," refined the sound, putting it right in the middle, not the sugary pop of the Frankie Avalons of the world, but not so black that it would scare anybody, either. This was vocal group music that came from the black tradition that stretched back to the Orioles, that referred to it without actually being it.

This style was shaping up to be a trend. In 1958, three singers called the Teddy Bears, from Jerry Leiber's old Fairfax neighborhood in L.A., had released a song called "To Know Him Is To Love Him." It was quiet—in fact, it sounded like it had been recorded in a closet full of winter coats— Annette Bard's lead vocal was vulnerable and girlish, perfectly teenage. The backing, by Marshall Lieb and Phillip Spector, was very subdued, but it was hypnotic, and the song became a very big hit—even though Phillip, who had written and produced it, had taken the title from his father's tombstone. The Teddy Bears' record was followed by the Skyliners, three guys and a girl who took the old standard "Since I Don't Have You" and used a male singing falsetto instead of a female lead to achieve a sound that owed an equal debt to black vocal groups and to the McGuire Sisters.

Next came the Fleetwoods, two girls and a guy (in fact, when they started out they were known as Two Girls and a Guy), with the unforgettable "Come Softly To Me," another breathy, intimate, vulnerable song, with its equally unforgettable chant of *Be-doo-be-doo, dum-dum, dumby-doo-dum, be-doo-be-doo, dum-dum*, et cetera. Like the Skyliners, the Fleetwoods achieved a decent success with rhythm-and-blues audiences, too. And with a similar sound, although he was billed as a solo artist, there was Thomas Wayne, whose hit "Tragedy" sat uncomfortably on the airwaves during the weeks after (and, to be fair, since it wasn't intended as exploitation, before) the Iowa plane crash, telling of a guy whose girl had, inexplicably, been taken from him—by death? by fate?—causing him to moan, "Oh, oh, tragedy." Wayne, the fan press told all who were interested, was a student at Humes High in Memphis, Elvis Presley's alma mater.

Another trend that seemed to be shaping up at the start of 1959 was music from southern Louisiana. The Louisiana Cajuns spoke an odd variety of French, and they had an odd sort of soulfulness that transcended race and seemed neither white nor black. The first person from this area to try for a hit had been Bobby Charles, who had been annihilated by Bill Haley when he covered his song "See You Later, Alligator," but the modern swamp sound can be traced to Cookie and the Cupcakes, a Lake Charles-based black group, who released "Matilda" at the end of 1958. "Matilda" was the archetype, the basic song, and it introduced the lazy one, two-triplet, three, four-triplet bass line that is the hallmark of nearly all the music released on the Jin and Swallow labels, owned by Floyd Soileau in Ville Platte. Slightly faster than a slow dance, slower than a fast dance, this music was just right, and after "Matilda" made its mark, along came Rod Bernard, who was white, with "This Should Go On Forever," which Soileau leased to Chess's new pop line, Argo, and soon it charted, too.

The third big Cajun record actually came from Houston, where Jivin' Gene (Bourgeois, but they couldn't use a last name like that on a record) was singing in bars. Discovered by Huey P. Meaux, a Louisiana barber who was disc jockeying and cutting hair in Winnie, Texas (near Beaumont, where he had been friends with J. P. Richardson), Gene scored a good-size hit with "Breaking Up Is Hard To Do," which Meaux and Soileau cut in New Orleans at Cosimo's and leased to Mercury. It was enough of a hit that Meaux got in trouble when the first $25,000 check came from Mercury and he tried to deposit it in his Winnie bank. "They had the FBI, the narcotics, the IRS—everybody down on me," Meaux remembered. "They didn't think a little boy from Winnie would run into that kind of money except he stole it."

This string of hits established Meaux and Soileau, although they parted soon thereafter, founding separate regional pop music scenes in Houston and Ville Platte. Meaux produced Dale and Grace, Joe Barry, Barbara Lynn, and B. J. Thomas and the Triumphs in the next three years, enjoying at least regional success with each act; and Soileau was responsible for Clint West and the Boogie Kings, Cookie and the Cupcakes, Tommy McClain, and a whole raft of artists in the traditional Cajun style of the region. It could be said that, between Floyd Soileau and Eddie Shuler's Goldband Records (which also recorded blues by artists like Boozoo Chavis and Guitar Junior), these two men were responsible for the revival of Cajun culture that occurred in the late 1950s and early 1960s.

It is notable that these new musical empires that were beginning to spring up were recording pop—or what passed for pop locally—rather than rock and roll. Plenty of rock and roll was still being recorded, too, especially rockabilly, but few of these records achieved more than regional acceptance (indeed, few were ever heard even regionally) and they would go undiscovered until the 1970s, when rockabilly mania swept Europe and collectors resurrected them. Minor sensations like Ray Campi, Johnny Carroll, Charlie Feathers, Groovy Joe Poovey, Onie Wheeler, and Mac Curtis made some excellent (and some not so excellent) records for small labels (and in Carroll's and Curtis's cases, Decca and King), but none was very successful. Even Sun failed to launch any more rockabilly artists after Jerry Lee Lewis's career foundered, although it wasn't for lack of trying. Sonny Burgess, the "red clown" (so called because he and his band dyed their hair red and wore red suits), was every bit as intense a rockabilly wild man as Jerry Lee, but by the time his first records started coming out, nobody wanted to know about wild men anymore. It was a shame. Three years previously, a record like "Sadie's Back in Town," on which Burgess giggles, raves, and imitates Donald Duck, would probably have been at least a mild hit, but in late 1959, it was just another stiff piece of wax.

Even Sam Phillips was telling people that rock and roll was dead. Well, maybe not dead, but integrated into everything else. The "subdued" rock and roll beat was now part of the big picture, and the teens, "tired of the ruckus," were broadening their taste. A&R men would never again be so conservative. "They've been shook up," Sam told a reporter, "and they have learned. They were getting stereotyped in their old ways and couldn't catch on to the newer fellows who knew how to dig up a performer somewhere out in Cripple Creek. Now they're on. Meanwhile the new men stereotyped themselves by their own successes, thinking they could keep it up forever. It took artists like Perry Como to show how to marry the old and the new. Now a dj can pace a show with out-and-out rock and roll, the old standards, a lot of stuff in between, and still have a modern sound all the way through."

These days Sam was less directly involved in the Sun and Phillips International labels, and for the past few years had been leaving the work largely in the hands of his brother or Jack Clement, an eccentric performer and songwriter who himself cut some records for Sun. For insurance, he was investing in the Memphis-based Holiday Inn motel chain and owned a small chain of radio stations—on which rock and roll was prohibited—with the odd but seemingly effective gimmick of "femcees," an all-female lineup of air personalities. He owned a zinc mine in Yellville, Arkansas, and a few oil wells in Illinois, and was building a three-story studio complex in Memphis, which would do custom recording for other labels. Even rock and rollers were putting away money—Chuck Berry opened a nightclub in St. Louis in January and dubbed it Club Bandstand—and others were busy making it while they could.

Conway Twitty had a different view. "Playing with my band on dance dates as often as I do gives me a chance to know exactly what they want, just from their requests," he said. "I figured a ballad trend was getting very strong early last year, which is why we made 'It's Only Make Believe.' Right now, they seem to want a lot of cha-chas, but what they want at dances doesn't always reflect what they want on records. I think rock and roll is still very strong. The kids will want it for a long time. Some of the jockeys, I think, sometimes made a mistake in pushing the smoother stuff. They go too far in trying to get rid of the beat." And ever the modest country boy, he added, "But that's just my opinion."

To some extent, he was right. Alan Freed recorded yet another record gross at his holiday shows at the Loew's State Theater, and Irving Feld reported that advance sales on the "Biggest Show of Stars" for 1959 were the best since spring of 1957. The show, which was scheduled to go out at the end of March, was all rock and roll, with the Lloyd Price Orchestra, Clyde McPhatter, the Coasters, the Crests, Bo Diddley, Little Anthony and the Imperials, and more. On the other hand, the eight million "American Bandstand" viewers named Fabian the most promising vocalist of 1958; "Venus" by Frankie Avalon rode the top of the charts for months; and there was another Chipmunk record called "Alvin's Harmonica."

If there was a sign of life, it was in rhythm and blues. The Coasters–Leiber and Stoller marriage was still intact, and their first record of the year was a two-sided threat that managed to convey an aura of the old teenagerhood very nicely. "Three Cool Cats" was about hanging out, eating potato chips, and waiting for three cool chicks to come along, and it was nicely harmonized, finger-snappingly cool. But the other side was just as incendiary as "Yakety Yak" had been. "Charlie Brown" was the class cut-up, the guy who smoked in the auditorium, called the English teacher Daddy-O, and wondered, in the comic bass voice Will "Dub" Jones was so adept at using for punch lines, "Why's everybody always pickin' on me?" It was an immediate hit, of course, and even spurred a terrible answer record, "Charlie Brown Got Expelled," from a young artist who sounded like he'd rather preach than sing, Joe Tex, backed by his X-Class Mates.

Then, in a blast from the past, Hank Ballard and the Midnighters showed up on the charts again, first with "Teardrops on Your Letter," and then with a dance exploitation record, "The Twist," which described a dance— "round and round and up and down"—that black teens had been doing to medium up-tempo songs. The song surfaced only briefly on the rhythm-and-blues charts, but the dance was starting to become a big sensation, even if the Philly teens on "Bandstand" hadn't discovered it yet.

Another veteran, Lloyd Price, was enjoying success on ABC-Paramount with his big-band sound, which employed lots of female backup singers. It was a long way from his days at Specialty, perhaps, but Specialty could never have done justice to a song like "Personality," which required lots of brass swinging along behind Lloyd's assured vocal. And although vocal groups in the old streetcorner style were all but gone from the charts, Goldner had wooed the Flamingos away from Chess, where they had had a few minor hits, and come up with the radical idea of letting them do their own arrangements of standards. These he compiled into an album,

Flamingo Serenade, which was an audacious move all in itself, since none of the songs had been released on singles before. The cover showed the group in powder-blue dinner jackets with gold trim, with a bottle of champagne chilling in a silver ice bucket, signifying that such classics as "I'm In the Mood For Love," "Begin the Beguine," "As Time Goes By," and others could be found inside. For the first time in rhythm-and-blues history, a single was released at the same time as the album—"I Only Have Eyes For You," in a very avant-garde arrangement featuring an echo chamber, a strange falsetto soaring above parts of the song, and sophisticated vocal harmonies that would never be heard on any corner in the world, executed with breathtaking precision. It was the apotheosis of the doo-wop sound, and in its own way the end of an era.

It was Leiber and Stoller, still young and full of vigor, who were leading rhythm and blues into the future. First, though, they wrote an epitaph for the old days and released it on the B side of the follow-up to "Charlie Brown," which was a tribute to Western movies called "Along Came Jones." "Jones" was another good hit with its by-now-standard yakety King Curtis sax and its loving fun-poking at cliff-hanging movie situations (the bass warning, "If you don't give me the key to yo' ranch, I'm gonna blow you all to bits"). But the other side was a bit more esoteric, a sort of in-joke for the people who'd been along for the ride so far. Probably never intended for airplay, "That Is Rock and Roll" summed things up with fun and affection. First, the song wasn't really rock and roll, which may have been part of the joke: Its chord progression and plunky banjo were straight from commercial ragtime. It begins with the bass singer, "Dub" Jones, intoning, "In the beginning, there was nothing but rocks. Then, somebody invented the wheel, and things just began to roll." Then all hell breaks loose as they sing a nearly incomprehensible verse comparing rock-and-roll saxophone to a frog in a hollow log, another verse praising the guitar, move on to a bridge that declares, "That ain't no freight train that you hear / Rollin' down the railroad tracks / That's a country-born piano man / Playin' in between the cracks," before moving on to the last verse, the kicker, which one singer starts (intentionally) singing too soon: "You say the music's for the birds / And you can't understand the words / Well, honey if you did, you'd really blow your lid / Well, baby that is rock and roll."

But the next single recorded at Coastal Studio, on the afternoon of March 6, 1959, really pulled out all the stops. The Drifters had been a successful group for Atlantic with Clyde McPhatter, but after he left, the group floundered; finally, after an argument with their manager, George Treadwell, he fired them. Treadwell owned their name, so he just went out and found a good but unknown vocal group called the Five Crowns (or just the Crowns), whose lead singer, Benjamin Earl Soloman, who performed as Ben E. King, also wrote songs. Treadwell told Atlantic that the Drifters were back in business. Atlantic turned the project over to Leiber and Stoller, who found the song.

"There Goes My Baby" was a wistful, haunting tune set to a beat—*bom,*
ba-bom—called the baion that supposedly hailed from Brazil and was a
wonderful vehicle for a ballad. Still, as Jerry Leiber recalls, when they tried
to record it, "The session was falling apart, it was terrible. And for some
reason or another I vaguely remember we had a tympani that kept going out
of tune. We couldn't keep it in pitch. We were trying to create some kind of
collage. We were experimenting on a date because the things that were
planned for the date were falling apart. Nothing was really happening, so
we started to fool around, and I remember that Stan Applebaum was the
arranger on the date. Mike [Stoller] used to do all the skeleton charts: lay
out the bass line, the rhythm patterns, and those areas where different
colors would appear, but he would often not write the actual string line or
the reed line, though the main structure would be there. And Stanley wrote
something that sounded like some Caucasian takeoff and we had this Latin
beat going on this out-of-tune tympani and the Drifters were singing something in another key, but the total effect, there was something magnetic
about it. And the date was considered a total fiasco. I mean, everybody
thought it was just a waste, a terrible waste of time and money.

"We took the playbacks to Atlantic one afternoon to play them for Ahmet
and Jerry and we were playing the tapes back and we were all grieving and
we were saying, 'Oh, there's nothing salvageable about this,' and then we
played this one side and I said, and Mike said, 'There's something fascinating about it. You know, it's a fucking mess but there's something very
magnetic about it.' And Jerry Wexler was eating his lunch on his desk and
he said, 'Man, get out of here with that, I hate it. It's out of tune and it's
phony and it's shit and get it out of here!' But we kept on insisting that there
was something and Ahmet was listening, too, and he kept saying, 'You
know, I think . . . well, maybe we ought to, you know, try and put it out.'
And they put it out and it became number one in the country. And I'd be
listening to the radio sometimes and hear it and I was convinced it sounded
like two stations playing one thing."

The "two-stations-playing-one-thing" effect Leiber alludes to comes from
the instrumental break the strings play halfway through, a modal line
unrelated thematically or harmonically to the rest of the song. But the very
idea of using a lush string orchestra on a rhythm-and-blues date—even one
for a sophisticated rhythm-and-blues label like Atlantic—was unheard of.
Up to that point, for all their polish and pop moves, even people like Sam
Cooke and Jackie Wilson had never resorted to strings. Strings were for the
top rank, people like Sinatra, Peggy Lee. And as if the string orchestra
wasn't astonishing enough, the arrangement was way out of left field, and
the performance was electrifying, from Ben E. King's distraught, haunted
vocal to the Drifters chanting a *"Bom bom, duh duh duh duh dooo,* There
she goes" line in the background, swathed in echo, to that weird string
excursion. It was like no record ever made. Something new had been born.

Although "There Goes My Baby" reestablished the Drifters—didn't anybody notice that they didn't sound anything at all like the group that had had the name just a few years previously?—nobody rushed out to copy the record. The Coasters still sounded like the Coasters, Ray Charles still growled his gospel-tinged songs, and Chuck Berry still played his guitar like a-ringin' a bell. Ray Charles released one of his most famous records in mid-1959. "What'd I Say" was, in its own way, as revolutionary as "Save the Last Dance For Me." Five minutes of the simplest imaginable blues, issued on two sides of a single, it featured Charles playing a new Wurlitzer electric piano, which had a blunt, grunting sound. There really wasn't much to the song except split-second timing, the sort of call-and-response you found in the poorer black churches, and some back-and-forth moaning with his backup singers, the Raelettes—but it was a sound that pop music had never heard before. Naturally, it was a dance tune par excellence, and even though he made noises as much as he sang, Ray Charles was bringing a new earthiness, a new sensuality, to R&B.

As for Chuck Berry, he released another double-sided classic just as summer started. "Back in the U.S.A." was a heartwarming piece of wide-eyed patriotism about the singer's joy when he finally touches down at L.A. International Airport, because he is back in the U.S.A., "where hamburgers sizzle on an open grill night and day," which is as pure a Chuck Berry line as exists. It was so genuine that it was disarming. The other side, though, was even more heart-tugging. "Memphis," based on a very simple guitar riff, wasn't a rocker like most of Berry's best songs. It told of a lonely man trying to reestablish contact with a girl named Marie, who had, after a long time, tried to call him. A typical enough romantic situation, except that Berry twisted it at the end: it seems that Marie was the man's daughter, whom his wife had taken away, and now four-year-old Marie had somehow called him, and his uncle had taken the message and written it on the wall. He didn't have a name or an address, and all he knew was that they lived about a half-mile from the Mississippi bridge. He's still pleading as the song fades out. It's not teenage, not funny, not filled with tricky rhymes, but it is probably Berry's best-written song. Although "Back in the U.S.A." was a moderate hit, "Memphis" became one of those songs people learned because they liked it.

Still, songs like all these, by 1959, were very definitely becoming the exception rather than the rule. With Top Forty becoming more common throughout the nation, whether stations subscribed to Storz's system or some other, homogenization was taking place on a bigger scale than ever before. Top Forty playlists were usually based on trade-magazine charts and, therefore, tended to show national trends rather than regional ones. Furthermore, the trade magazine charts featured any record that sold well— be it pop, rock and roll, rhythm and blues, country and western, polka, Latin, or novelty. Thus records like Dave "Baby" Cortez's "The Happy Organ," Frank Pourcel's Orchestra's "Only You," Martin Denny's "Quiet

Village," and Santo & Johnny's steel-guitar instrumental "Sleep Walk" rode the Top Ten alongside Johnny Horton's historical songs "The Battle of New Orleans" and "Sink the Bismarck," the latter another epic and the longest Top Ten single yet; Marty Robbins's "El Paso"; Stonewall Jackson's "Waterloo"; and such oddities as jazz queen Dinah Washington's reading of "What a Diff'rence a Day Makes," the Browns' maudlin "The Three Bells," and Sammy Turner's weird version of the folk song "Lavender Blue."

Turner's song had a strange, indefinable sound, as if somebody was experimenting in the studio. It had been produced nominally by Leiber and Stoller, but actually by their friend Phil Spector, a young man who'd been sleeping on the floor of their office, who had been referred to them by Jerry Leiber's old mentor, Lester Sill. Phillip Spector had come from Los Angeles because his mother thought that with his talent in French, he should be a translator at the United Nations. But after a few months' stint as a court reporter, he grew determined to make it in music. He'd worked on producing some guitar instrumentals with Duane Eddy, and he'd done an over-dubbed record of his own singing in that same soft vocal-group style the Teddy Bears had pioneered and that had established the reputations of the Skyliners and the Fleetwoods. Atlantic's pop subsidiary, Trey, had released the record as being "The Spectors Three," which was true enough. He not only had musical talent, but he was brilliant in the recording studio, and Leiber and Stoller found that he was thinking along some of the same lines they were. They helped him make contacts around the Brill Building, the office building on Broadway that was the heart of Tin Pan Alley—A. J. Liebling immortalized it as the "Jollity Building" in his essay collection of the same name, published in the 1940s—and soon he'd be making some waves of his own.

Music was coming down with a case of the creeping blands. Elvis was in the army; George Goldner announced that Little Richard had changed his mind and would be recording again for him, but it never happened, and even though he was putting out wonderful records like "Let's Talk About Us," nobody would go near Jerry Lee Lewis. With the rise of the likes of Frankie Avalon and Fabian, the idea of finding a pretty face and seeing if it could sing had taken hold. Week after week, the fan and trade press was filled with smiling young men with perfect teeth, conservatively greased hair, and instantly forgettable names, served forth in hopes that the girls would swoon.* RCA, with another year to go before Elvis returned, signed somebody named Rod Laurin, who went out on a promotional tour for his first record and told the disc jockeys that Elvis would shift to non–rock and roll material once he was released. Colonel Parker blew up. "I don't

---

*One of these young men was Johnny Restivo, for instance, whose publicity noted that he had been chosen by "a health magazine" as "America's most perfectly-proportioned teenager," as if that were an excuse to give him a recording contract!

believe anybody connected with RCA Victor could make a comment like that!" And anyway, the Colonel was partially responsible for picking Elvis's material. The last anyone had heard, Rod Laurin was on a promotional tour of Australia. He may still be.

Even Elvis wasn't doing spectacularly with his only 1959 effort, "A Big Hunk o' Love" b/w "A Fool Such As I." He was driving jeeps and trucks and soldiering with the rest of the men, but still, it was hard to adjust to the hours soldiers worked after being an entertainer. Some kindly soul introduced Elvis to a drug called dextroamphetamine sulphate, or Dexedrine, to help him get through the day, and from then on, he made sure he had some handy. Otherwise he was living well, since his father and grandmother were along and he didn't have to bunk in the barracks, but he was plagued with tonsilitis and was hospitalized with it twice. In August, RCA released *A Date with Elvis*, which contained some miscellaneous cuts, the rest of the Sun sides, and was at first packaged with a 1960 calendar with his discharge date circled, four full-color pictures of Elvis in the army, a photo diary of his departure overseas, and a radiogram from Germany to his fans thanking them for their support.

Also in August, his next film, *G.I. Blues*, started shooting. They did all the parts Elvis wasn't in so that the film could be rush-released as soon as possible after his discharge in March. And to keep his fans loyal, RCA gave them a Christmas present in the form of a second greatest hits album entitled *50,000 Elvis Fans Can't Be Wrong*, offering retailers a special Christmas card from Elvis and the Colonel (in a Santa costume) that they could hand out to customers. Elvis himself, ever the good neighbor, donated a large check at Christmas to the Steinmuhle Orphanage in Freidberg. But even with these tokens, it was a long, cold winter.

And it was getting colder. The State Department was planning another tour to Moscow, this time to the American Fair, but once again, they announced well in advance that because of the desire to avoid controversy, no jazz or rock-and-roll acts would be booked. To ensure this, Ed Sullivan was hired to provide the entertainment, and he arranged a variety show that very much resembled his television program, including, for example, Marvin Roy, who performed the trick of removing lighted electric bulbs from his mouth.

Worse news from Washington came in November, when Federal Communications Commission (FCC) head Robert E. Lee mentioned in passing that radio stations taking payola might be jeopardizing their licenses. All of a sudden, the music business was sitting up, alert. Payola? Like what? A fifth of Scotch at Christmas? That hundred-dollar bill in the wastebasket? Malcolm Weldon, news director of WMCA in New York, voiced the opinion that "if payola exists, it is a form of commercial bribery, punishable by a fine of $500 or a year in jail or more." Murray Kaufman demanded an apology from Lee for his inferences, but an older, wiser jock, Bill Randle, had already warned jocks attending the Columbia Records Seminar that an investigation was coming. "At that time," he told reporters, "I commented, 'We haven't seen anything yet.' The statement still goes."

In Chicago, they were still shaking after the jukebox probe, so two disc jockeys decided to clear the air right away. Phil Lind of WAIT broadcast a taped discussion of payola in which he interviewed an anonymous small label owner from the West Coast who said that if he bowed to all the Chicago jockeys' demands when he was promoting a record, it would cost him $22,000 to get a record going. Lind immediately began getting phone calls threatening his life and had to be put under police protection. Show promoter Howard Miller was more philosophical about it: "I have no desire to name individuals," he told the press. "In most cases I couldn't prove what I know. I said in most cases. It would be unfair to name one or two and victimize a couple of guys for what is a much more widespread practice. Everybody in the industry knows payola is running rampant. I'm not speaking only of Chicago, because it's no more prevalent here than elsewhere. . . . Congress ought to devote its time to figuring out how to catch the Russians in the race to the moon. This is a job for policing by station management. . . . The main trouble with a long investigation is that a few get named, but the whole group gets hurt. It would be the same as all teenagers suffering today because of the delinquency of a few."

Still, payola wasn't specifically illegal, so the Harris subcommittee on Legislative Oversight decided to open an investigation to see if action was warranted. The first round of subpoenas brought some spectacular displays of breast-beating. Ed Cohn, of Philadelphia's Lesco Distributors, told the press that he gave cash, checks, household articles, and baby items to djs, but that the price of this payola got so high he wound up having to sell ten thousand copies of a record to break even. He also noted that when "Get a Job" went to Ember Records (and, as a result, got played on "Bandstand"), Wild Cat Music, a firm owned by Dick Clark's former producer, Tony Mammarella, was listed as co-publisher.

Syd Nathan, who hadn't produced a real hit in a while but who loved publicity, said that his payola budget was up to $2,000 a month, adding "I'm one of the small ones by comparison." He described payola as "plain blackmail and a dirty rotten mess that has gotten worse and worse." And over the lunch counters near the Brill Building, Alan Freed's name kept cropping up in connection with his publishing ventures. His producer at WNEW-TV, where his "Big Beat" show was now headquartered, said he wouldn't "pre-judge Freed. We are not concerned with interlocking activities unless unfair practices are involved." But over at WABC Radio, they were asking jocks to fill out a questionnaire—a very explicit one at that—detailing their outside interests.

What was the Harris subcommittee after? On November 14, it published a twenty-one-point memo on the practices under investigation.* Included

---

*Two points of this memo were not made public because they named specific companies.

were instances when networks favored records on labels they owned; when a radio or TV station employee received payments for playing records; when record hops were used to promote a jockey's outside interests; when payoffs were made to stations or employees in the form of false loans or mortgages; when such employees owned, partially or wholly, the music publishing company involved, the talent, the record companies, or the pressing plants; when there were false claims that records had hit the Top Forty or when ratings were rigged by paying off retailers to report which records were selling; when employees were given free records to sell to record stores; and when "key broadcast personnel" had "long criminal records."

These were heavy charges, but more important, they could be leveled at a substantial proportion of the industry, depending on how literally the Harris subcommittee intended them. Naturally, some were afraid. In Detroit alone, four major figures were immediately purged: Dale Young, host of WJBK's popular "Detroit Bandstand" show, quit, and management said they wouldn't replace him, while they fired Tom Clay, who admitted to taking $6,000 in payola over the past eighteen months, and Jack LeGoff, who defended payola in an editorial as "a part of American business"; Don McLeod quit and didn't say why. In Philadelphia, one of the city's biggest names, Joe Niagara, suddenly moved up the date of his resignation from WIBG; and in Boston, WILD fired three jockeys—Stan Richard, Bill Marlowe, and Joe Smith—presumably "to de-emphasize the role of the djs and emphasize the role of the station from now on." The firings looked so embarrassing that Smith contacted the press to explain that the dismissals had come with contract expirations, not because of payola, and that it was Mike Elliot and not himself who had been fired or quit.

Then, a week after the Harris memo was released, Alan Freed was fired from both his radio and television slots. He groused to New York Post columnist Earl Wilson that Dick Clark, not he, should be investigated because "he's on about three hundred TV stations. I'm on one." Wilson said Freed "had been talking to Washington investigators for the last forty-eight hours, and Clark had been one of the topics of discussion," but Freed dismissed the statement, saying he'd been misquoted. His last live show aired on Friday, November 27, 1959, and Freed made his defiant farewell speech, wearing the trademark plaid jacket he always wore for openings and closings. He mentioned that his first wife, Jackie, had given it to him in 1952. Then he said he was sorry to leave his fans, but "I know a bunch of ASCAP publishers who'll be glad I'm off the air."* And that was it—the old Moondog, Mr. Rock and Roll, the king of the Big Beat, was finished in New York and, by implication, the country.

The Harris hearings began on December 7, 1959, and suddenly every-

---

*Freed was referring to the ASCAP charges that BMI was using unfair business practices to get its songs played on the radio to the exclusion of ASCAP copyrights.

body in Washington wanted to climb on the bandwagon. It was a chance for the limelight, since 1960 was going to be an election year and show business was glamorous. There were many people surmising that the entire rock-and-roll phenomenon had been fueled by payola from the start. How else would you get people to listen to trash like that? So while the Harris subcommittee went into overtime, the Federal Trade Commission (FTC) announced a "massive investigation" of the record business and subpoenaed RCA Victor, London Records, and Bernard Lowe Enterprises of Philadelphia, along with five Philadelphia record distributors, to answer questions about deceptive trade practices. Not to be outdone, the Federal Communications Commission demanded that stations keep a detailed accounting of all programming for which payment had been received but not publicly acknowledged, as well as a comprehensive report on management plans and control payments to employees. As a coup de grace, the FCC also required that station personnel sign oaths that they had never accepted payola.

Now an atmosphere of panic began to set in at radio stations. At KDAY in Santa Monica, Califronia, the jocks took lie detector tests on television. In Detroit, disc jockey Mickey Shorr, who denied taking any payola, was told to quit or be fired nonetheless by the management at WXYZ. Bill Gavin, whose record-programming service was becoming more and more influential, warned that radio stations were sacrificing some of their biggest jockeys as scapegoats for their own ineptitude in neglecting to monitor payola all along, and that firing a few name personalities wouldn't solve anything. And in Albany, the New York District Attorney, Frank Hogan, announced his own payola probe, subpoenaing singers Bobby Darin, Eileen Rogers, Les Paul, and Mary Ford to testify about their experiences appearing on Alan Freed's television show.

As Washington scheduled hearings, the press geared up for what promised to be the biggest circus to hit town since the Army-McCarthy hearings. Jerry Blaine, head of Cosnat Distributors and Josie and Jubilee Records, said he'd loaned Alan Freed $11,000 in 1956 and had sold the loan to Morris Levy, head of Roulette Records. The *New York Post* then discovered that Roulette owned two mortages on Freed's Connecticut house, totaling $21,000, of which there was $16,493 still owing. As speculations grew, New York Attorney General Louis Lefkowitz hauled Freed in on December 10 to grill him about his relationship with Levy.

What a miserable Christmas 1959 seemed to be promising! Jockeys sat around morosely and told the joke of the record company guy who terrorized djs, saying, "If you don't play my record, I'll send you money!" That wasn't funny; Bill Randle had actually been called by a man who threatened to implicate him in payola if he didn't pay him off. Some department stores fretted briefly over whether they should continue to carry the Dick Clark clothing and accessory lines, then looked at the sales slips and reordered. Jockeys across the country went overboard on good deeds, collecting toys for needy children, putting on rock-and-roll spectaculars to benefit orphanages, living in department store windows until a certain amount of money was collected for charity, and otherwise trying to dispel the image of the disc jockey as a bribe-taking sleaze. *Billboard* followed the example of a lot of companies in the trade when it published a letter begging that Christmas gifts to its staff consist of nothing that could be regarded as exceeding the definition of "social amenities."

And still more bad news came rolling out of Washington. It was announced that activities at the Second Annual Deejay Convention, held at Miami's Americana Hotel the previous May, were under close scrutiny after stories surfaced about mass payoffs and orgies with prostitutes provided by record companies. Then, finally, an agenda was announced for the Harris subcommittee that said it would investigate findings gleaned from twenty-seven cities in which researchers had unearthed payola allegations. The FCC and the FTC both said they would be continuing with their examinations, and it looked like the whole shebang would get under way sometime in February 1960.

Could things possibly get any worse? Yes. Chuck Berry, the man who had just finished declaring how glad he was to be living in the U.S.A., was arrested in St. Louis and charged with a Mann Act violation, transporting a minor across state lines for immoral purposes. Even now the affair is clouded in mystery, but apparently Berry had hired a Spanish-speaking Apache girl to check hats in Club Bandstand, and when she didn't do her job well, he fired her. As it turned out, she was not only a prostitute with a record, but she was only fourteen years old, and she decided to get revenge on her boss by accusing him to the police. Racists were delighted. Here at long last was a reason to pillory that uppity Berry! Amid all the corruption investigations, nobody would want to touch a Chuck Berry record, so no doubt he would be effectively silenced until the case was resolved. (This was the second race–sex scandal of the year. On August 10, Tony Williams, David Lynch, Alex Hodge, and Paul Robi, the male members of the Platters, were arrested in a considerably more liberal city, Cincinnati, with four nineteen-year-old women, three white, one black. It was speculated that the disgrace would end the Platters' career—and it was too late to do anything about the title of Williams's forthcoming solo album, *A Girl Is a Girl Is a Girl*—but while there is no denying that it was bad publicity, the Platters weren't hard-core rock and roll enough to crucify. While they never regained the heights they had once known, they were not ruined by the scandal, and nobody went to jail.)

And just in case anybody was still feeling good, *Billboard's* December 14 issue had even more bad news: "The Chipmunk Song" had reentered the charts for the second year in a row, and was on the Hot 100 at number 89. Somebody call an exterminator!

13

THE DARK AGES

And so a new decade began. Remember the Fabulous Fifties? people asked each other. Remember Davy Crockett and Hula-Hoops? Remember rock and roll? Now the high school class of 1955 had graduated college and their entry into the world of careers, responsibilities, and mortgages brought on a nostalgia for what they perceived as simpler times, when the world had been fresh and young, when there were discoveries around every corner. Even Sputnik was nostalgia now, as the United States lobbed satellites into space fairly routinely and soon would send a man up there to circle the earth in a Sputnik of his own. In hindsight, the fifties seemed like better times, a veritable golden era. Who knew what kinds of evils lurked in a world where Chuck Berry could be busted on the Mann Act—an artist who wrote such sweet evocations of teenage innocence?

In the beginning, record companies disdained the nostalgia boom. It seemed that these young adults were just teenagers grown up, with teenagers' desires on grown-up budgets. True, they were buying stereo hi-fi rigs and albums, but not all the albums they bought were the stereo demonstration, *Ping-Pong Percussion* kind. So first a small California company, Original Sound, and then Roulette tried an experiment: the oldies-but-goodies album. It was easy enough to accomplish, for they simply leased songs from various indie labels, slapped them onto an album, and released it. There were no recording costs, probably no royalties to pay—the grateful groups would usually waive them, if they hadn't been cheated out of their rights—and there was no promotion to be done because the records had already been hits!

And the publishers were only too willing to lease them the sides, since indies were doing very poorly indeed. In 1959, for the first time, majors had outgrossed the indies and scored more chart positions; and worse, it was indies, more than anyone, who were targets of the forthcoming payola investigations. By now, for every success story like that of Chess or King or the Roulette/End/Gee miniconglomerate, there were a dozen dead or dying labels.

But oldies were a genuine trend. Disc jockeys—the ones who still controlled their own programming, anyway—quickly discovered that oldies helped them retain adult listeners, and as everybody knew, it was the adults who would buy the sponsors' products. And these days, adults and rock and roll weren't an incompatible combination. It might seem ludicrous to think of a twenty-four-year-old as an "oldie-but-goody" fan, but once again, old songs were in demand. Dootsie Williams reported that "Earth Angel" had never stopped selling, and as of the beginning of 1960, he was claiming to have released over four million records.* Then a four-year-old classic, "In The Still of the Nite," by the Five Satins, suddenly broke onto the pop charts at number ninety-three. The next week "Earth Angel" showed up on the "Bubbling Under" chart, and there were reports from retailers on the East and West coasts that the Mello Kings' "Tonight Tonight," a fairly obscure record in the same mold, was flying off the dusty shelves.

Was the trend just part of the inevitable retrospection that accompanies the changeover of a decade? Mitch Miller told a reporter that the 1960s would put more emphasis on what he saw as quality and professionalism, which in his case probably meant less wild rock and roll, but others saw a real gold mine. In January, Warner Bros. Records, which was a fairly new company committed mostly to releasing pop, pop jazz, and sound-track LPs, announced that it had signed Bill Haley—an amazing move for a fledgling label that had never even tried to have a hit single. A month later, Warners shocked the trade again by signing the Everly Brothers (who had just cut their last Cadence single in New York, a Gilbert Becaud ballad called "Let It Be Me," with a string orchestra conducted by Archie Bleyer) in a deal that would guarantee them nearly $750,000 over the next ten years. With many hit films under its corporate belt, there was no doubt that Warner Bros. had the money—but for the Everly Brothers? Nearly a million dollars? It almost dwarfed the $100,000 that Hugo and Luigi paid Sam Cooke, who still had plenty of material in the can over at Keen Records, to sign with RCA Victor; or the paltry sum with which ABC-Paramount had lured Ray Charles away from Atlantic. No, it was more than reliving the past. A realization was dawning that with Elvis Presley leading the way, Sam Cooke, the Everly Brothers, and the rest had become the Sinatras and Glenn Millers of a generation.

---

*Of course, he, like most indie record men, wasn't a member of the RIAA and thus wasn't subject to an audit, but the number doesn't seem too far off the mark.

And now Elvis, the king of them all, was coming home. His release from the army was set for March 3, and it had already been announced that he would be getting $125,000 for his first appearance—on Frank Sinatra's television show, of all places. On March 5, the press and a clutch of ultrafaithful fans braved an impending blizzard to get to Fort Dix, New Jersey, where nineteen-year-old Nancy Sinatra presented Elvis with a box of fancy shirts and apologized because her father couldn't make it. Various RCA people, Colonel Parker, and military personnel milled around and finally dispersed into the snow. It was a strangely anticlimactic finale, devoid of the expected hysteria. Was his calm reception a reflection of the times, of the assimilation of rock and roll, or was it a harbinger of things to come? Was it the end of an era? Had Elvis mania subsided? No, more likely it was the snow, which developed into a major winter storm.

Undaunted, RCA announced that they had a serial number and a promotion campaign set for his next record, although it hadn't even been recorded; and by March, the trade press was trumpeting, via a huge RCA ad, that the new single had advance orders of 1,275,077. At least Elvis's fans were faithful. Soon the single had a title too: "Stuck on You" b/w "Fame and Fortune."

With that question settled, Elvis relaxed a little more in Memphis, greeting his old friends, and then set about recording twelve more songs and heading out to Hollywood to do his scenes for *G.I. Blues*. Meanwhile, the recording session was packaged into an album called *Elvis Is Back*. This was a smart move, because the industry had discovered that it wasn't just young adults buying those albums; teenagers were too. More and more, singles were being pulled off albums, rather than vice versa, as in the past; and for the first time ever, singles occupied less than 20 percent of the market share of records. In fact, when all the figures for 1959 were in, it was discovered that six million albums had been sold, and fewer than five million singles.

The shift to albums was only one sign of the changed world that Elvis would find on his return. By now, the payola investigations were looming, although a survey taken in and around Chicago found that most teenagers had never heard the word *payola* and weren't familiar with the concept—not even in the suburbs, where, as the survey takers noted, they read newspapers in school. And a Roper poll taken at the end of 1959 showed that the public was profoundly apathetic about payola, ranking it way down on the list of its worries about crime; well below, say, juvenile delinquency.

Still, prudent industry people used the time before the hearings actually started to put their houses in order. In Philadelphia, Dick Clark offered his two music publishing companies, Sea Lark Music (BMI) and Arch (ASCAP), for sale, telling all parties that he'd welcome a buyer as soon as possible. The *New York Post* published a report alleging that Clark owned Mallard Pressing Corporation, giving credence to trade whispers that there were "hip" pressing plants where it behooved success-oriented small labels to do business if they wanted exposure for the records. An executive at Mallard retorted that Clark had sold Mallard,* but he wouldn't say to whom. The *Post* report also noted that Bernie Lowe, who had been summoned by the FTC in its first batch of subpoenas, was not only vice president of Mallard but also an executive of Cameo and Parkway Records, home of teen idol Bobby Rydell, among others; the distributor of Swan Records, the label in which Dick Clark had a one-third interest and on which teen idol Freddie Cannon recorded; and one of the heads of Mayland Music (BMI), which had three split copyrights with Sea Lark, Clark's BMI license.

Was this involvement unethical? Who could tell, in a mare's nest like that? Perhaps it was, though these were more implied than proved connections. But there is no doubt that Clark heaved a big sigh of relief when songwriter Aaron Schroeder, in partnership with Vera Hodes, who had managed the companies, took Sea Lark, Arch, and a smaller publisher, January, safely off his hands.

Some still believed that the payola scare would blow over or that the public would realize that it was just election-year showboating. True, Storz called off the National Disc Jockey Convention for 1960, but FCC Chairman John C. Doerfer told the press that he was discovering that payola was far less widespread than he'd originally thought. Stations seemed to be cooperating nicely, producing affidavits swearing they were monitoring the jockeys. But then, ironically, Doerfer himself became the first casualty of the payola hearings, as it was revealed that he had accepted "plane and yacht hospitality" from broadcasting mogul George Storer; and, embarrassed, he stepped down.

From there, the Harris subcommittee really swung into action and started its investigations in Cleveland, where an eternity ago Alan Freed had brought rock and roll to the Moondoggers. Two disc jockeys from KYW there, Joe Finan and Wesley Hopkins, were the first to be quizzed. They testified that Finan had received $15,000 a year in "consultant" fees from distributors, on top of his $40,000 a year salary; and that Hopkins had taken in $12,000 in undefined "listening fees" in excess of his $20,000 pay. Oren Harris told them they were pathetic young men, and the jocks countered that their services, listening to records for the labels, had saved the record companies thousands of dollars that might otherwise have been used to promote uncommercial records—particularly important, they said, because Cleveland was considered a crucial breakout market, and the rest of the country watched it for tomorrow's hits.

It was hard to tell what was more amusing, the names the djs gave the payments or the sanctimonious excuses they gave when asked if the money

*Later, Morris Ballen, the head of Diskmakers, Inc. (formerly Mallard), told the press that he'd bought the operation from Dick Clark and Bernie Lowe on December 14, 1959.

had influenced them. One jockey actually told the subcommittee, "It couldn't have been payola in my case, because I play generally good music and not the raucous rock and roll generally associated with payola." Wesley Hopkins denied knowing anything about money influencing his decision to play records, but when Representative Samuel Devine, Jr., of Ohio mentioned in passing that the third-floor men's room at KYW was known as the "payola booth," Hopkins broke out laughing.

Meanwhile, the press was having a field day with the Storz disc-jockey-convention corruption allegations, sometimes throwing reason to the winds. They seized on the fact that Dot Records had picked up the tab for Pat Boone's hotel room, but Boone was a Dot artist and was there promoting his records. The committee had confirmed that there were call girls at the convention, but if the legislators thought that made disc jockeys different from any other conventioneers, they were a lot more naive than they were letting on. Anyway, there was no concrete evidence presented that the prostitutes were provided by record companies or that they were anything other than free-lancers plying their trade among a receptive crowd.

Prostitution was illegal, of course, but the status of payola was still uncertain. To clarify the situation, Representative John Bennett (R., Michigan) introduced a bill making it—although the term *payola* was not clearly defined in the draft—punishable with a fine of up to $5,000 and up to two years in jail. Representative Emanuel Celler (D., New York) went a step further, with a bill making both giving and taking payola a crime, while announcing that payola was responsible for the "cacophonous music called rock and roll," which he believed would never have achieved fame, "especially among teenagers," if not for payola. It was the same old charge, and it echoed the sentiments of Thomas P. "Tip" O'Neill of Boston, who said that talking to delegates to a White House Youth Conference had convinced him that "the captive audience" of American youth must be safeguarded from the demoralizing effects of payola and "a type of sensuous music unfit for impressionable minds."

Armed with these definitions, the committee then, naturally, looked to Alan Freed. Freed hadn't let the lack of a job or the payola scandal worry him. He did one last show in New York at the Brooklyn Fox and the Apollo theaters with Bo Diddley, the Skyliners, Bobby Day, Jo Ann Campbell, and the Cadillacs; added Jackie Wilson and took it on the road one more time; and then delivered his star chamber testimony to the Harris probers. Once he'd been cleared, he announced that he'd been hired by KDAY in Los Angeles for $25,000 a year. It was a curious announcement, since the station had banned rock and roll, but Freed sloughed off that minor detail, saying he'd concentrate on rhythm and blues.

But they weren't through with him yet. In mid-May, New York District Attorney Frank Hogan arrested eight people on payola charges, including Freed, Mel Leeds, who had been a WINS jock and was about to start work on KDAY as program director, and veteran rhythm-and-blues jock Tommy

"Dr. Jive" Smalls. Freed and Leeds pleaded not guilty and, unlike Dr. Jive (who faded away soon after), were lucky enough to have their station behind them. KDAY's manager, Irv Phillips, said that he felt the two were "fall guys" and "we are pleased to have them on the staff. We are 100 percent behind both men. If Freed is free to do so, he'll definitely start his two-year contract with us this week." It was strong language in defense of somebody Hogan alleged had taken a total of $30,650 on twenty-six occasions from seven record companies over the course of a year—up to $7,000 a month. But it wouldn't help. Freed was to fight and fight this case, exhausting his financial and physical resources on appeals and legal maneuvers.

Then Bennett started howling for more blood: Dick Clark! Where was Dick Clark? Clark, after all, would "pinpoint the payola evil," Bennett said, more than the lesser djs they'd had on the stand so far. Calm down, his colleagues told him. There were over eighty business associates of Clark's under study, and if they didn't want to ruin that case completely, they had to be sure of the evidence before they started the hearing. Bennett was warned by Peter Mack (D., Illinois) and John Moss (D., California) not to stampede things or to "violate the American concept of decency and fair play." On the other hand, it was taking a long time.

Finally Clark was called for questioning, on April 26, and he very nearly blew it from the start. In his opening statement, he said he'd been "convicted and condemned" by the committee before he'd been allowed to testify. This did not sit well with the lawmakers, and they laid into Clark with a vengeance. After all, Clark had made a lot of money: He'd put $125 into Jamie Records in 1957, before it was a real record company, and that gave him a percentage of the firm. By the time he sold it in 1959, he'd made $31,575—an 11,900 percent return on his investment—in profits and in a salary that, he testified, was for "advice" he'd given the firm. But he specifically disavowed any relation to the payola that Jamie, through another partner, Harry Finfer (who was part-owner of Universal Record Distributing, a Philadelphia firm), had distributed to jocks. Even when payola was given to Tony Mammarella, who had produced "American Bandstand" from 1957 to 1959 and who had quit that job rather than divest himself of his own music-business enterprises, Clark denied any knowledge of it, although the two had shared a tiny, closet-size office with desks jammed together and only one telephone between them during much of the time that was under investigation.

The committee tried hard to get him, to pin him down, but Dick Clark just wouldn't let them do it. Wasn't it true, he was asked, that unlike any of the other ABC men, he was allowed to write his own antipayola affidavit with loopholes in the wording that would allow anybody who signed it to take payola and remain within the letter of what he had signed? And wasn't this because he had brought in $12 million for ABC, while another dj affiliated with the network (and it was clear that this was an allusion to the closed-door testimony Alan Freed had delivered) had only grossed the network $250,000? Clark snapped back that he was ready to sign "any affidavit."

But what about the half-ownership, with Bernie Lowe and Harry Chipetz, of another distributing company, Chips? A simple business deal, Clark retorted. He'd invested $10,000 and the company had made a profit. Fine; now what about Swan Records, another 50-percent ownership deal? What were these salaries about, $45,000 over two years? The company was run by Tony Mammarella and Bernie Binnick, Clark said, and all he did was advise them on the music to be released. And his ownership of Sea Lark and Arch, the music publishing companies? A standard practice in the industry. How about the 50 percent of the copyright on "At the Hop?" He'd actually done some lyric writing, he said, to make it more up to date, so teens would respond to it, and they had. Wasn't that worth something? Okay, and it was true that he'd accepted furs and jewelry for himself and his wife from Lou Bedell of Dore Records, but he'd thought they were personal gifts, had accepted them very reluctantly, and was upset to find out that Dore had written the gifts off as "promotion."

They let him go but called him in for a second day's worth of testimony, this time grilling ABC-network president Leonard Goldenson along with Clark. Goldenson stuck by Clark, calling him an "upright" young man whose "good character" led to his being retained on the air despite the controversy stirred up by his being called to testify at the payola hearings. Then Clark took the stand again, and while not backing off an inch, he didn't display any arrogance, either, as he patiently explained that his acquisition of copyrights, record companies, and shares in distributing companies and pressing plants were just opportunities to make money, and that he had "followed the rules of the game" by taking advantage of the opportunities offered him. He admitted that he knew payola existed, even within the companies he owned pieces of, but that he didn't consider handing out money—as opposed to taking it, which he had never done—to be payola. Then he discounted testimony Alan Freed had given that Freed had been asked, as a condition of being on ABC, to "lay heavily on Am-Par Records [a label owned by the network] and play nothing but Paramount theaters [also owned by the network] with your stage shows," saying nobody had ever made such a suggestion to him. Pressed further by Representative Moss, Clark said that he would only agree that he never passed up an opportunity to make money in the music business, because fame was fleeting and you had to make it while you could. Under oath, he swore that his divestiture was total, that he was no longer connected with any of the dozens of interests he'd had before signing the affidavit.

That looked like it. Clark bantered with Oren Harris about his ability to pick hits, and finally Harris told him, six hours after the grilling had started, that he was "an attractive and successful young man" who undoubtedly realized by now that the sort of network of corporations he'd been involved with was wrong. "You are a product of that system, not responsible for it," Harris said. "You took advantage of a unique opportunity to control too many elements in the popular music field through exposure of records to a vast teen-age audience." Clark, properly abashed, nodded, and the inquisition was over, at least for him.

A few more witnesses were called over the next couple of days, testimony by Bernie Lowe, George Goldner, and various other small label heads was scrutinized, and the Harris subcommittee, which had struck terror into the hearts of an entire industry, adjourned.

The new FCC chairman, Frederick W. Ford, epitomized the conciliatory feelings Washington had by replying to Tip O'Neill's blast at rock and roll, saying that it didn't seem, from any of his information, that payola had been responsible for rock and roll's rise. But then the FCC threw an unwitting monkey wrench in the works with Rule 317, a decision that ordered stations to either pay for the records they played or announce that they'd gotten them for free, as well as to specify which parts of a program consisted of material the station had been paid for, what promotional considerations had been given in respect to broadcast content, and so on. Rule 317 really drove people crazy, and some stations considered going to nonmusic formats just so they could avoid it. Ever afraid of more investigations, the radio industry played Caesar's wife and petitioned for a lightening up of 317, and eventually they would prevail.

While all this was going on, America's teenagers, blithely unaware that they were being manipulated by cynical payola-taking sleaze bags, continued to buy rock-and-roll records. If there was an overwhelming trend, it was, as Mitch Miller had noted, toward sophistication. It meant more care taken with arrangements, a turning away from traditional doo-wop and blues structures in rhythm and blues, and more of a mainstream pop sensibility coming forward in teen-oriented pop. One expression of mainstream pop tastes was the Philadelphia-machine output—the Fabians and various Bobbys—but another was a type of music that sat between pop, rock and roll, and country.

One of its chief practitioners was a farmer from Arkansas who saw himself as a sort of hillbilly beatnik. When he played bars, Charlie Rich would spend as much time picking out jazz on the piano as he did playing a rich chording style based on black gospel. His voice was pure blue-eyed soul, and he became Sam Phillips's last major discovery. His debut recording on Phillips International, "Lonely Weekends," got the full production, with a female chorus and big band, and you could almost hear Sam rubbing his hands together in the background, muttering "Okay, Elvis, we're raising the stakes."

Then there was the Sun grad who'd been miscast: Roy Orbison. Somehow Sam had never been able to exploit Orbison's plaintive high tenor, but up in

Nashville, Fred Foster had a good idea. Foster was involved with a new Nashville-based pop label, Monument, that Acuff-Rose had begun probably after seeing what Archie Bleyer had managed to do with the Everly Brothers, using Nashville musicians and Acuff-Rose songwriters. Foster was adept at big arrangements, and he realized that Orbison had not only range but an awesome amount of power. "Only the Lonely" was Orbison's first hit for Monument, and he wept, soared, and sang in such a striking and eccentric fashion that it hit the charts running. There was only one problem left to solve as Orbison's popularity grew—he wasn't very good-looking, and his eyes were set close together. So they found a pair of Ray-Ban Wayfarer sunglasses, pasted them on his face, and he looked fine.

And on the female side, Nashville also had Little Brenda Lee, although she was sixteen now, and not so little in some ways. At least she was old enough to put aside novelty material like her first record, "Rockin' Around the Christmas Tree," and start doing more mature, teen-oriented songs like "Sweet Nothin's" and "I'm Sorry," a painfully slow ballad that was a huge scrunch hit in the summer of 1960. All these performers had in common a rock-and-roll backbeat (or, on "I'm Sorry," piano triplets), but all were staking out stylistic territory they could occupy well into adulthood.

Rhythm and blues, too, was changing with the times. Billy Bland (no relation to the blues singer Bobby "Blue" Bland) established New York's Old Town label, which would become a haven for old-style rhythm and blues in the years to come, with a song called "Let the Little Girl Dance," an up-tempo workout in the style of Jackie Wilson and Sam Cooke. He was soon joined on the charts by Jimmy Jones, whose style was a little more raucous, but whose two hits, "Handy Man" and "Good Timin'," were definitely not reminiscent of anything that had come before. Sam Cooke scored his biggest hits since "You Send Me"—on Keen, not RCA, which hadn't found the right formula yet—with "Wonderful World," about a kid who wasn't doing so well in school but knew that if his girl said she loved him, it would be a wonderful world anyway. Simple, with a sweet melody and just enough rhythm to keep you dancing.

Some of these were still teen songs, addressed to teen concerns, though delivered in a smooth, contemporary style. But, because the rhythm-and-blues audience has a broader demographic—that is, it has many older people in it—than pop, some of the older and rougher styles kept showing up. James Brown now came into his own with "I'll Go Crazy," as rough and bizarre a record as he had ever released, and it inaugurated a string of hits that has continued almost unbroken to the present day. It showed that in his wild rhythmic variations and screeching vocal style, he had come upon something that was his own—not that, at this point, anybody else wanted to copy it. Yet he acknowledged its sources on his next single, "Think," a record that had been a mild hit for his label mates the "5" Royales, who themselves would continue to release records for a while, although they were more important for their songwriting and influence upon James Brown and other vocal groups than for the amount of money they were making for Syd Nathan.

But what of black rock and roll? Chuck Berry, his arrest notwithstanding, had managed to stay on the charts during the first half of the year with "Let It Rock," which, far from being an anthem, as its title promised, was a routine song about a train best described by the title it was recorded under, "Rockin' on the Railroad," and it featured more of Johnny Johnson's piano (which was more enthusiastic than skillful for a change) than it did of Chuck's guitar. He also resurfaced with a cha-cha, "Too Pooped to Pop," about a guy who was too old to dance. Neither were major efforts for someone like Chuck Berry.

For black rock and roll, it was time to look to New Orleans, where a new generation had arisen in the wake of Huey "Piano" Smith's success. Many of these artists were members of his band or belonged to the new crop just beginning to emerge on some poorly produced local records: pianist Allen Toussaint, who, as Tousan, had an Al Hirt–sponsored album deal with RCA cutting Muzak jazz; guitarist Mac Rebennack, a white artist with some exotic musical ideas (some of which he revealed on a strange, brooding instrumental called "Storm Warning"); and drummer Jessie Hill, who was the first of the new wave to have a hit. "Ooh Poo Pah Doo" was a novelty, but the serious rhythm Toussaint and drummer John Boudreaux pounded out was classic. It harked back to the second-line rhumbas that Professor Longhair had been playing since the late 1940s,* and this really was its first exposure on records. Along with Fats Domino's excursion into southern Louisiana–style swamp pop, "Before I Grow Too Old," which quickly became a standard with bands like the Boogie Kings, "Ooh Poo Pah Doo" signaled a renaissance in New Orleans that would really burst forth in the coming year.

Three other black rock-and-roll records emerged during the first part of 1960 that pointed the way. One was a one-shot, one was not, and one was the revival of a brilliant career. "Stay" by Maurice Williams and the Zodiacs was a stomper and a shouter—the sort of primitive R&B record that cooler heads might have thought was completely out of fashion. With the band shouting key words, Williams pleaded, whined, and shouted for his girl to stay. That was the whole song, but there was an impatience in the rhythm section that made it irresistible and, in its own way, modern.

Next came Gary "U.S." Bonds, who hailed from the Virginia coast, and he cashed in on the interest in New Orleans with a song of the same name,

---

*The term *second line* comes from the classic New Orleans jazz funeral, when a dirge was played going to the cemetery and a quick march coming back. The band's fans would line the street, waiting for its return, and, as it passed, would beat out a rhythm counter to the band's—hence the term *second line.* What the great New Orleans drummers and percussionists did was eliminate the first line from their playing, making the beat as much something that was inferred as played.

although he'd never been there. Like "Stay," "New Orleans" sounded like it had been recorded in the middle of a riot; and the style was so distinctive that Bonds used it to his advantage several times again. Djs, of course, loved to announce his records, since they were required to make public service announcements. Did "by U.S. Bonds" count? The FCC never said.

The third record was "Fool In Love," which began with three girls singing, "You're just a fool, you know you're in love" while an unearthly voice growled assent. Was it James Brown? No, it was actually a woman, and what a woman she was! And leave it to Ike Turner to have found her. Ike had kicked around since his glory days in Memphis, leading various Kings of Rhythm on Deep South tours, playing in dirt-floor dives, and occasionally signing on with an independent label to make some records with local talent, as he had in St. Louis for the Stevens label in 1959. What he'd always wanted to do was work with a woman, but the records he'd made with his wife Bonnie had stiffed as badly as the country-and-western records he'd made himself as Icky Renrut. Then, one day at yet another gig in Mississippi, a couple of sisters, the Bullock girls, had approached Ike about singing. It was shy Annie Mae who finally got up on stage, and Ike, ever the talent scout, heard a sound he liked. By the time Ike's band had finished the engagement and was ready to move on, he'd convinced Annie Mae that she should join him in the world of show business. Of course, her name wasn't suitable. First, Ike changed her last name the traditional way, somehow settling on Tina for a first name, and the Ike and Tina Turner Revue was born. The Revue was Ike's ticket out of the lower echelons; and when he approached Juggy Murray, a New York entrepreneur starting a slick record label called Sue, recording commercial, pop-oriented rhythm and blues, he found himself with a deal.

And now the wind of change was blowing from other directions, too. Earlier in the year, an indie label out of Detroit—Anna—had burst forth with an embarrassingly direct statement: "Money (That's What I Want)." It was as if the man behind the record, which was sung by Barrett Strong, was serving notice to the world—and, in fact, he was. Berry Gordy, Jr. had sold his jazz record store, pooled the money he'd made from his Jackie Wilson hits with some he borrowed from his sister, Anna (which is why her name was on the label), and threw together the session that produced this angry but funny number. It sounded like Ray Charles over a more aggressive rhythm section: Instead of laying behind the beat, jazz-style, or riding right on top of it, gospel-style, Berry's rhythm pushed impatiently, perfectly complementing the opening lines: "You say the best things in life are free / Well you can give them to the birds and bees / I want money."

He got it—and in mid-July, readers of trade magazines found a half-page ad with Gordy's face staring sternly out at them. "From out of the Midwest," the ad copy ran, "comes a new label destined to take its place among the leaders in the industry. TAMLA, prexied by one of the young, driving geniuses of the music business today: Berry Gordy, Jr., a man who has given you such great hits as 'You've Got What It Takes,' 'Money (That's What I Want),' 'I Love the Way You Love' and 'All the Love I've Got' and who now brings you a record soon to be numbered among his greatest successes, 'Way Over There' by the ('Bad Girl') Miracles."

The caption under the photo of Gordy introduced him as "Mr. Hitsville." Unfortunately, "Way Over There" went flopsville, and no doubt some of the older heads around were laughing at this brash young man who thought he could conquer the world—from Detroit, of all places. Not that Detroit was Nowheresville, but aside from Nolan Strong and the Diablos' eerie mid-1950s regional hit, "The Wind," and a strong showing by the Falcons' "You're So Fine" (which had been picked up by a major, Unart, and turned into a good-size hit in 1959), Detroit was hardly the place you'd expect to find Hitsville. It wasn't until the end of 1960 that Gordy found the one-two punch, with the Miracles' "Shop Around" on Tamla* and "Bye Bye Baby," by Mary Wells, on his new Motown label.

About an hour from Berry's Motown, down in Toledo, Ohio, there was a new instrumental style emerging that, after some hybridizations and graft-ings, would come to be identified as the sound of California. A young quintet, Johnny and the Hurricanes, achieved a small hit in 1959 with "Crossfire" and a bigger one later in the summer with "Red River Rock," a souped-up reading of the old cowboy song "Red River Valley." What was different about the Hurricanes was the way they pushed their sax and organ up front, with the organ tooting out the melody as the sax growled men-acingly in the background, and then the two instruments changed places. There was also a ferocious guitar break on "Red River Rock" that didn't go unnoticed, but it was the cheap, rinky-dink organ sound that was new, and that was undoubtedly what sold the record.

Another kind of instrumental was being pioneered by the Ventures, a combo from Seattle. The group was founded when Bob Bogle and Don Wilson met on a construction job and discovered that they both played guitar. Eventually they found a bass player, Nokie Edwards, and a drum-mer, Howie Johnston, and began to develop a sound inspired by James Burton, Ricky Nelson's guitarist, and various jazz artists of the day. Their first record, released on the local Blue Horizon label, was "Cookies and Coke"—a vocal, and a terrible mistake. But its flip side, "The Real McCoy," was an instrumental that set the band on its future course. Their next release, "Walk, Don't Run," was dominated by an infectious guitar interplay that made it infinitely replayable. Before long, there was always a Ventures record in release, and most of them were hits, either in the United States, in Japan, or in Europe.

*Berry wanted to name the label Tammie, but there already was a Tammy label.

The Ventures played solid-body instruments, totally electric—electronic—guitars, and in this, they were the wave of the future. With no resonating chamber to add natural sound to what the pickup was sending to the amplifier, electric guitars could be manipulated to create oddly distorted, distinctly unguitarlike sounds. And the younger teens paid heed: These guitars were fairly inexpensive, and the Ventures' songs were challenging but playable. Suddenly Ventures-style guitar combos were springing up everywhere. In the Northwest, Ventures territory, there was an epidemic of them: the Wailers, who would achieve fame with "Tall Cool One," and Paul Revere and the Raiders, who weren't entirely instrumental but who had an instrumental hit, "Like Long Hair," as their first release. And soon the guitar-combo sound would meld with the Hurricanes' cheap organ sound, and devotees of the surfing craze in southern California would adopt it in the form popularized by Dick Dale and the Deltones. Their 1961 hit "Let's Go Trippin'" had a title that was mysterious to all but the brotherhood of the surf, who would buy records by similar bands, with similar surf-oriented titles, by the hundreds of thousands in the next few years.

There was no doubt about it—all the traditional sounds were evolving. But amid all these changes, surprisingly enough, the next new craze came from an old-timer. Hank Ballard was suddenly on the charts again, first with "Finger Poppin' Time," a great teenage-flavored, clap-your-hands sort of record, and a song called "Let's Go, Let's Go, Let's Go," and finally a revival of "The Twist," which put Ballard on the charts three times by 1960. In fact, "The Twist" had never gone away, and by midsummer, the dance that went with it was approaching fad proportions. Then Cameo, a Philadelphia-based label, had Ernest Evans record it. Evans, a former chicken plucker, had had two unsuccessful singles with them ("The Class" and "Dancing Dinosaur") under the name Chubby Checker—Chubby Checker, Fats Domino, get it? Since Cameo was a Philly label, and since Dick Clark still maintained his identification with the City of Brotherly Love, suddenly the twist started showing up on "Bandstand."

The twist wasn't the first odd dance craze of 1960—Nat Kendrick and the Swans (actually James Brown in disguise) scored a hit with a record extolling the "Mashed Potato," a dance in which you seemed to be stomping spuds—but it turned out to be the most durable. After the push from "American Bandstand," Cameo claimed to have sold 200,000 copies of the record in its first week, and suddenly both it and Ballard's original (of which it was a nearly identical copy, right down to Ballard's signature cry of *eee-yah*, which had been around since the "Annie" records) started up the charts. Chubby claimed the top slot on the pop charts in short order, and Hank even managed to reach as high as number twenty-eight, although it's difficult to see what Syd Nathan could have done to improve Ballard's sales, short of moving "Bandstand" to Cincinnati.

Decidedly less danceable were the death songs that had begun to emerge and would continue as a trend through the decade. An early 1960 contribution was Mark Dinning's "Teen Angel," the story of a girl who died when she returned to a car stuck on a railroad track to retrieve her class ring, only to be obliterated by the oncoming train. It quickly became the number-one song in the country. Then in midsummer, somebody named Ray Peterson added to the canon a grisly ditty called "Tell Laura I Love Her," the saga of a boy who'd entered a stock-car race to win $1,000 to buy Laura an engagement ring. He'd been crunched, and his dying words formed the title of the song, which was soon firmly entrenched in the Top Ten.

The success prompted Peterson's label to license the song in England, and Decca UK pressed 25,000 copies of it without even bothering to listen to it (the title is innocuous enough, after all). But when the content was brought to Decca's attention, they scrapped the remaining stock of the record and apologized for releasing it, calling it "vulgar and tasteless."

EMI, a less genteel major, lost no time in putting the record out themselves, and in an unexpected display of indignation, the publisher, Marks Music, rose to the record's defense. One of the most distinguished firms of its sort in the United States, Marks demanded that Decca retract its "vulgar and tasteless" comment and threatened suit unless it did. Naturally the British government then stepped in, and the Public Prosecutor was asked to listen to the record to determine whether it violated the Obscene Publications Act. This action was instituted by Leonard D. Hodge, director of the British Safety Council, and undoubtedly was watched with mirth by teens on both sides of the Atlantic. It was much ado about nothing, and before long, there was a British version of the song trying to compete with the fading American original.

Anyway, the British wouldn't need us anymore: They were developing their own rock and roll and even offering to share it. Many of the artists under Larry Parnes's management, Billy Fury and the like, were releasing records stateside (although most bombed), and an actual good, American-sounding record was released at the end of 1960, one which was to inspire a generation of British rockers, "Shakin' All Over" by Johnny Kidd and the Pirates.

Although Europeans were now making their own rock and roll, they were also adopting older American artists whose careers were foundering at home, particularly rockabilly performers. Charlie Gracie and Sanford Clark, for example—two artists few Americans could identify—became fairly big stars in England. Gene Vincent, who had gotten off to such a promising start with "Be-Bop-A-Lula" but had never managed to establish himself in the United States, had a great British following, and they loved Eddie Cochran, who, not being a Southerner—or a poor white Southerner at any rate—was as close to acceptable as an American could be and still be a rock and roller. They admired the way he dressed (although there was also an element of British youth who went for Gene Vincent's black leather clothing) and copied it scrupulously, since British rock and rollers have always been even more fashion-conscious than their American counterparts.

So when a Vincent/Cochran tour of England was announced, the first tour of genuine American stars since Jerry Lee Lewis's fiasco, British rockers went wild. Their own emerging rock and roll stars, guys like Adam Faith and Cliff Richard, were all very nice, but Gene Vincent! Eddie Cochran! The performers would do week-long residencies, starting in Glasgow and working their way south, sharing the bill with such British acts as the Tony Sheridan Trio, Georgie Fame, Billy Fury, and Billy Raymond.

It was a great tour, and it probably lit the fuse of rock and roll in Britain like nothing ever had. Somewhere along the way Eddie's girlfriend (some said financée) Sharon Sheeley, a songwriter who had such credits as Ricky Nelson's hit "Poor Little Fool" to her name, joined them. Eddie was booked for ten more weeks, but he had some time off in between and he decided to fly back to the States to relax (and, it has been rumored, to marry Sharon). Gene Vincent was missing his wife Darlene, and decided to return as well. So they hired a limousine and headed off to Heathrow Airport to catch a flight home; but on their way through a small town called Chippenham in Wiltshire, driving seventy miles an hour, a tire blew, and the driver lost control of the car, skidding into a lamppost. Eddie suffered massive head injuries and never regained consciousness. Vincent broke some ribs, his collarbone, and his cursed leg. Sharon, too, was hospitalized. Vincent, who had looked up to Cochran as to an older brother, would never really recover from this incident, and he hit the skids, ruining his career. And even today, it is said, Eddie Cochran fans occasionally get together to hunt down the hapless driver, who was fined and lost his license for fifteen years, and beat the crap out of him.

By 1960, on both sides of the Atlantic, rock and roll had become an established fact—the official teenage music. Although it would still retain its power to raise conservative hackles—even today—the cries of outrage were growing fainter. Even within the industry, things were settling down. Dick Clark headed a group of Philadelphia disc jockeys dedicated to self-policing against payola; Mitch Miller was doing so well with the "Sing Along with Mitch" records he'd started making on a lark that Columbia relieved him of his A&R job (the label was well protected against rock and roll, in any event); and shortly after Christmas 1960, the Harris subcommittee released a 256-page report concluding that if payola ever saw a resurgence, the Justice Department, the FTC, and the FCC should clamp down hard. Not that it would ever be necessary, of course.

Murray Kaufman announced that he was going scientific, using a Univac computer to pick the hits on his New York radio show. Martin Block, who had the longest-running dj show of all time, retired in October. In Philadelphia, where minors' business affairs were administered by the forbiddingly titled Orphans' Court, Fabian Forte (he did have a last name!) asked permission to build a $7,000 studio in his parents' basement so he could rehearse (after a listen to his records, the judge undoubtedly agreed), while Bobby Rydell petitioned for permission to buy a 1961 Pontiac for $4,534, saying he needed it to get to appearances around the state. Once again, Elvis Presley was the year's biggest seller, although he shocked people with his first non–rock and roll effort, "It's Now or Never," a clever rewrite of "O Sole Mio" that apprised "serious" lovers of "good" music that he could too sing. And, just like clockwork, "The Chipmunk Song" entered the charts on December 12, 1960, at number sixty-six.

As America sailed into a new decade, rock and roll, the music of hooligans and streetcorner singers, the music of hillbillies who'd listened to too many R&B records, the music of misfits and oddballs, was dead. Just as teenagers, with their awesome purchasing power, were being courted by Hollywood and Madison Avenue, rock and roll had passed into the mainstream, fast becoming the province of established corporate interests rather than the renegade visionaries of the past. For a while, at least, the music would be in the hands of professionals, who knew what teens wanted and how to sell it to them. These developments might have outraged older rockers, who would hardly recognize the fruits of their creative vision. Still, as long as there were teenagers, those teenagers would want a special music that spoke to them. It's just that the language was going to change for a while.

14

THE NEW
TIN PAN ALLEY

Maybe the new music wasn't rock and roll, but then maybe it wasn't supposed to be rock and roll. What was emerging now was a brand-new kind of pop music, one that the old-time pop musicians, the Frank Sinatras and Patti Pages, might have derided, but one that everybody would have to agree was well crafted. Clearly the new pop had its roots in the old music, and that was one reason it was attracting a broader audience, in terms of age, than ever before. The new sound was emerging from the rebel forces who had conquered Tin Pan Alley, and although they were like the old-timers in many important ways, there was one difference: Like the people buying their records, they were younger.

In the vanguard was the hit-songwriting team Leiber and Stoller, who had decided that the strings in "There Goes My Baby" had given them a winning formula. The string section became part of the next few Drifters sessions, and somebody also had the great idea of doubling the tympani lines with orchestral bells, those metal tubes that hang from a frame and are struck with little metal mallets. Odd effects like that were creeping into a lot of sessions—even Etta James's "All I Could Do Was Cry" had a dainty flute offsetting her earthiness, a strange idea but an effective one.

Leiber and Stoller had virtually adopted the young Phil Spector, who hung around their offices offering his ideas. He may have attended the sessions for "Dance With Me," the Drifters' follow-up to "There Goes My Baby," and for their next big hit, another baion-inflected, string-lush number titled "This Magic Moment," brilliantly sung by Ben E. King. Spector was definitely there trying out his concepts on Ben E. King's last session with the group, "Save The Last Dance For Me." At the time, some

225

people commented that the song sounded like it had been recorded in a wind tunnel, an effect that probably came as much from Spector's feeling that such a muffled, echoey sound was atmospheric as from the primitive state of recording technology in those days, when overdubs, if there were enough of them, caused very noticeable tape hiss that could be obscured by adding echo. But Spector was after grand effects, there was no doubt about that, and Leiber and Stoller were glad to let him make them, even if it meant running the tape through the gate hundreds of times.

He got a real chance to experiment when Ben E. King went solo, with Atlantic's blessing, after "Save The Last Dance For Me." King's first release was a Leiber and Stoller composition, "Spanish Harlem," a lush production with a baion rhythm, a marimba answering each line, and a lavish swell of strings. Then to top things off, King, Leiber, and Stoller rearranged an old gospel standard, "Stand By Me," into yet another extravaganza. What a résumé Spector was developing, considering he was only twenty years old!

The trouble was, Spector wasn't credited on these records, so it was hard to prove conclusively that he did them or, if he was involved, just what he contributed. (Spector's own memory is no help here, either.) Hence, although he had an enviable niche, he was haunting the halls of the Brill Building and the Atlantic Building, making himself visible, looking for work. Naturally, as the protégé of Leiber and Stoller, with their string of hits, he was a very employable young producer, and before long, he found a slot he wanted.

Leiber and Stoller had been working with a label called Big Top, which needed producers for their subsidiary label, Dunes, and they recommended Spector. His first session was with Ray Peterson of "Tell Laura I Love Her" infamy, and Phil, conscious of the burgeoning folk revival, whipped up a version of the old folk song "Corinna, Corinna" for Peterson that went Top Ten. He had scored a hit on his very first try, and more important, one bearing the words "Produced by Phil Spector." Spector was fired up, and for his next record, he used a method that would become enshrined in the Spector legend: He took a singer with good looks but no voice in particular, Curtis Lee, and had him record a classic teen-style song, "Pretty Little Angel Eyes." It sounded like Dion and the Belmonts squared, with a yaketing sax, a bass voice chanting "yeah," and every other trick he could think of—and it was an even bigger hit.

It is said that back in the days of the Teddy Bears, Phil had created Spector's Four Commandments: (1) Music must be emotional and honest. (2) Create a sound on record that no one can copy or cover. (3) Make sure you get your money. (4) There's never a contract without a loophole. After his success with Curtis Lee, Spector decided to exercise number four. He walked into Leiber and Stoller's office, announced that they couldn't hold him to the contract he'd signed because he was a minor (he wouldn't turn twenty-one until December 26, 1961), and that he was quitting. As a chagrined Mike Stoller commented, "I don't think we were thrilled about it at the time, but people have to go the way they're happy."

Where Phil seemed to be happy next was over at Atlantic, producing a couple of flops with Bobby Darin,* but he soon left to go free-lance. He popped up next at the fledgling Musicor label, where songwriter-publisher Aaron Schroeder had scored a hit with another young songwriter, Gene Pitney (author of the Ricky Nelson hit "Hello Mary Lou"), early in 1961, "(I Wanna) Love My Life Away." Pitney had a nasal, reedy voice, but his delivery was powerful, and Spector decided to try for a follow-up hit. The resulting record, "Every Breath I Take," was the apogee of Spector's work to date, with a group chanting nonsense syllables, bombastic overdubbed drums,† tympani, strings, and Pitney wailing away in falsetto at the end of the song. Unfortunately it failed to chart, maybe because it was too avant-garde for the summer of 1961. So Phil moved on to the Gregmark label for a couple of sessions with the Paris Sisters, including the Teddy Bears-ish "I Love How You Love Me," and then to Garex, for a flop with Ray Sharpe, whose "Linda Lu," a regional Texas hit, had become a standard like "Louie Louie" for bands in the Lone Star State.

Completely undaunted by the losing streak, Spector was determined to get noticed. Now he began growing his hair until, as Tony Orlando, a Brill Building habitué and singer, recalled, "His hair was shoulder length, in what we call a page-boy, flipped up this way, both sides and the back . . . and when a guy walked into a room with long hair in '61, he was really a freak. You think there are freaks walking around now? Well, that was really being freaky. . . ." By then, Lester Sill had introduced him to Paul Case, general professional manager of Hill and Range Music, the company that administered Elvis Presley's copyrights. Case was one of the few Brill Building regulars who believed that if the old publishers were to survive, they had to find young songwriters who combined the professionalism of the old-timers with the feel teens wanted. He had encouraged Barry Mann, a young songwriter and performer whose novelty song about silly vocal-group syllables, "Who Put the Bomp (In the Bomp, Bomp, Bomp)," scored a hit in mid-1961. Now Case referred Spector to Johnny Mathis's manager, Helen Noga, who had some extra money to invest, and so Philles Records was born: Noga would provide the capital, Lester Sill would run the business, and Phil would create the hits.

Phil, meanwhile, had adopted a group of five girls, the Crystals, whom he saw as the perfect hit-making machine; and he had just the right song to start them off, "There's No Other (Like My Baby)," which he'd co-written with the mysterious L. Bates. By now, the super productions of the Drifters

---

*Possibly including a version of the old Nat "King" Cole hit, "Nature Boy."
† One hallmark of Spector's production style is to record the same notes over and over on overdubs, making the resultant sound "bigger."

had given outmoded vocal groups a new standard to aspire to, and new rhythm-and-blues song forms had superseded the old doo-wop street harmonies that had been part of the genre since the Orioles. Yet apart from a few quickly fading anomalies like the Chantels, these groups were still all male. Phil Spector strongly suspected that a female vocal group was just what the market needed, and his suspicions would soon be confirmed.

The spearhead of the female vocal group movement would not be the Crystals but the Shirelles, who had been singing together since 1953. They were four inseparable girlfriends who had been discovered in a junior high in Passaic, New Jersey, by Mary Jane Greenberg, a classmate of theirs whose mother, Florence, had a tiny indie called Tiara. The group had become so popular at talent shows and record hops that Florence had gambled on cutting them a single, "I Met Him on a Sunday," that became a local hit and was picked up by Decca. But Decca was never able to market the Shirelles properly, and so the group was kept out of circulation for years.

Finally, in 1959, Greenberg and the Shirelles won their freedom from Decca, and Greenberg set up her own Brill Building–based record company, Scepter. It was the right place and the right time. Not that they were overnight successes: Their first release, a version of what may be the "5" Royales' greatest song, "Dedicated to the One I Love," only reached number 89, and its follow-up, the charming "Please Be My Boyfriend," entirely missed the charts. But then Greenberg turned to Luther Dixon, a fine rhythm-and-blues songwriter, who gave her "Tonight's the Night." It was the quintessential teenage song, and it swept both the pop and the R&B charts in late 1960.

Now Greenberg sent Dixon prospecting for the follow-up. What he found, on an acetate demo that had been rejected by Columbia Records, was the start of a new era for the Brill Building and for teenage pop music in America. While the old-line music publishers like Marks ("Tell Laura I Love Her," written by Jeff Barry) and Hill and Range (Elvis's songs) struggled to keep up with changing times and changing tastes, younger firms were challenging them for chart supremacy. In the finest Brill Building tradition, many of these firms were nothing but an answering service and a cigar box for messages, but there were others, like Aldon Music, headed by Al Nevins and Don Kirshner, that had their ears to the street and were run by men young enough to remember teenage life in detail. Kirshner was a songwriter who had pitched his first tune to Frankie Laine while carrying the singer's bags at a resort, and with some tips from Laine, he established himself in Tin Pan Alley, where he hooked up with an older man, Al Nevins. Don convinced Nevins that with Nevins's connections and his own savvy, they could triumph in the burgeoning teenage market, so together they founded Aldon in May 1958.

Their first signings were the writers Neil Sedaka and Howard Greenfield, who had cut some songs for Atlantic Records. Sedaka had also made a few records himself, both solo and singing with a group, the Tokens. At first,

Sedaka and Greenfield were wary about making a long-term deal with Aldon,* although they'd been rejected by all the bigger labels, and instead they offered Aldon a few songs to push. Kirshner gave one Sedaka-Greenfield number called "Stupid Cupid" to his childhood friend, Concetta Franconero, now known as Connie Francis, an MGM Records artist with two hits to her credit. She recorded "Stupid Cupid" and it hit the charts, so Sedaka and Greenfield signed on as Aldon's first hit songwriting team.

They were the first of several: Kirschner and Nevins preferred writers to work in pairs, so they could bounce ideas off each other. Soon after Sedaka and Greenfield came Barry Mann, who was a real coup for Aldon, and shortly thereafter Cynthia Weil, an accomplished lyricist; later the two would marry. Gerry Goffin and Carole King were already married, two nineteen-year-olds from Long Island whose tales of teen romance were based on actual experience, part of the reason they rang so true. One Goffin-King production was a song nearly five minutes long, a real teenage epic with a country sound, that dealt with a tough issue nobody had ever written about before. After a little trimming, Kirshner shopped it to Mitch Miller, in hopes that Johnny Mathis would record it, but Mitch rejected it immediately. Then one day when Luther Dixon visited Kirshner, prospecting for Greenberg, he heard the demo and knew he'd struck gold.

Not only did "Will You Love Me Tomorrow" carry the story line of "Tonight's the Night" a little further, its lyrics were revolutionary. Forever, it seemed, the words of teen songs had been do-you-love-me or why-don't-you-love-me or gee-I-love-you, but there were some realities behind the coy lyrics that teenagers were living. This song laid it on the line: "Tonight you're mine, completely / You give your love so sweetly. / Tonight, the light of love is in your eyes, / But will you love me tomorrow."

Clearly the girl was going to give in, endangering her reputation, but she was willing to take the risk because she loved her boyfriend. Yet she couldn't help but wonder whether her love would be returned, the start of a lifetime romance, or whether he would vanish once he got what he wanted. The lyrics were as explicit as a record got in 1961—or even since, if it was going to hit the charts—and with Shirley Owens's vulnerable lead vocal, Goffin and King's hit melody, and a junior-Drifters-style string arrangement, it became not only a top hit in the United States, riding the charts for nearly four months and establishing the Shirelles and Spector as major forces, but it sold around the world. There were millions of teenage girls who wanted to hear that question asked, who wanted to ask it themselves, and they showed their gratitude to Shirley and the group wherever records were sold.

And the B side was just as good. It was called "Boys" and was such a frantic workout that the Beatles, then a young English band performing in

---

*Sedaka and Greenfield had only come to Aldon on a referral from kindly Doc Pomus, of Hill and Range, another of the era's great songwriters.

Hamburg, immediately adopted it for their set at the Star Club. The spectacular success even brought a revival of "Dedicated to the One I Love," the Shirelles' earlier failure, and now it, too, charted.

It also gave Phil Spector evidence that his instincts about the Crystals were correct. So he booked them into the Mirasound Recording Studios at 145 West Forty-seventh Street, where engineer Bill MacMeekan had a three-track machine that used half-inch tape.* Then, with a countoff on the piano, he and the group started work on "There's No Other (Like My Baby)." The girls sang like a choir, and Phil added echo, overdubbed and overdubbed—after all, three tracks were better than two—and released the final product as Philles 100 on October 30. Actually, Phil had secretly been holding out hope for the A side, "Oh Yeah Maybe Baby," a baion-flavored number with extremely tricky exotic percussion effects, but the more traditionally structured "There's No Other (Like My Baby)," with a more 1950s Chantels-style sound, was the one that hit—and hit big. It was emotional and honest, it had a sound that nobody could copy or cover, and when he began to get his money, he bought out Helen Noga, leaving just him and Lester Sill.

It was records like the Shirelles' and the Crystals' that made the trend watchers take notice. It seemed that in the era of the ready-made pop idol, teenagers were spurring a rhythm-and-blues revival. Not that rhythm and blues had gone away, or even that blues had gone away. Blues itself was becoming more spare and stripped down; and while Bobby "Blue" Bland, for instance, was continually on the charts with his big-band blues,† most of the music of that type was coming out of Chicago, where Chess was releasing influential music by Muddy Waters ("Got My Mojo Workin'"), Howlin' Wolf ("Spoonful"), and others; Vee-Jay was hot with Jimmy Reed, who was selling to college kids; and artists like Elmore James, Buddy Guy, Magic Sam, and Otis Rush kept up a steady stream of music that sold regionally and also to folk and jazz aficionados around the world. Rhythm and blues tended to hit the pop charts when it sold well, so R&B artists were becoming some of the biggest names of the day, including Sam Cooke, the Drifters, and Jerry Butler, a smooth-voiced crooner who had broken away from a vocal group called the Impressions and signed with Vee-Jay, where he had a million-seller in 1960 with "He Will Break Your Heart."

But where rock and roll butted up against rhythm and blues and made a very joyful noise was New Orleans. New Orleans is one of the areas in America (Texas is another) where music tends to be conservative in the most literal sense: Change comes slowly while artists digest the implications of every new stylistic nuance. Right to the end of the 1960s, it was possible to hear truly creative work being done there in forms of jazz that

---

*Spector, ever meticulous, made sure these details were included on the back of the Crystals' first album.
† In 1961, Bland was heading into his golden era with records like "Lead Me On," "I Pity the Fool," "Cry Cry Cry," "Turn On Your Love Light," and "Ain't That Loving You."

had passed into parody or museum-piece reverence elsewhere, since New Orleans jazz musicians never believed that just because newer styles had been developed, the older ideas were exhausted. For instance, they felt that just because Professor Longhair never achieved major success, that was no reason to accept that the raucous "second-line" rhythms of New Orleans were incompatible with rock and roll. Thus, when the new generation of studio musicians began making their new-sound R&B records at Cosimo's late in 1960, they preserved many older styles, although to their teenage audience, songs like Jessie Hill's "Ooh Poo Pah Doo" and Little Booker's "Gonzo" in 1960 (Little Booker was another Longhair disciple named James Booker) were simply good, modern, dance records.

These new-wave New Orleans records started hitting the market in force around the end of 1961, beginning with Lee Dorsey's silly song "Ya Ya." He had been preceded that spring by Ernie K-Doe (Ernest Kador, Jr.) and his inimitable "Mother-in-Law" and Clarence "Frog Man" Henry's two over-arranged singles, "I Don't Know Why, But I Do" and "You Always Hurt the One You Love," but it was Dorsey who really spurred the trend. Dorsey's earlier records had been unsuccessful, but they caught the attention of Bobby Robinson, owner of Fire and Fury Records in New York. Robinson was doing well with Elmore James, whose raw, emotional "The Sky Is Crying" inexplicably sold well in New York in 1960, and he decided to visit Dorsey on his way back from a convention in Florida. He found him way back in the funky Ninth Ward, in a shack with a group of children playing in the front yard, who were singing a game chant that went "Sittin' on the la la, yeah yeah," as Robinson and Dorsey conferred on material. As it turned out, Dorsey was dry, but the children's song stuck in Robinson's mind, so he called them in and asked them to sing it again. Robinson knew it had potential, and he and Dorsey jumped into his car and headed uptown, where they settled into a place called the Miller Bar to drink and work on the idea. Many beers later, they got it: "Sittin' in la la, waiting' for my ya ya"—as simple as a kids' song, not a bad thing in rock and roll. The next morning they called Allen Toussaint, the arranger on "Ooh Poo Pah Doo," and although he was contracted to Minit Records as an arranger, he agreed to play piano on the date. And so a hit was born.

Minit had been started in 1959 by Joe Banashak, who ran the major distributorship for indies in New Orleans. Banashak's first coup was hiring Allen Toussaint as his staff producer, arranger, songwriter, and piano player. Toussaint was the main exponent of what the locals called the carnival sound—a raucous, polyrhythmic beat that was solid but complex, like a rhythm-and-blues rhumba crossed with the second-line rhythms of Professor Longhair—and its expression in "Ooh Poo Pah Doo" and "Mother-in-Law" made Minit hotter than a two-dollar pistol on a Saturday night. Over the next two years, the label continued to produce such hits as Benny Spellman's "Lipstick Traces (on a Cigarette)" and the Showmen's "It Will Stand"—"it" being rock and roll, which for some reason wasn't deemed mentionable in the song's official title. But by far Minit's longest-lasting success, one who outlived the label,* was Irma Thomas, a singer whose songs of desolation and misery, like "It's Raining," "Ruler of My Heart," and "Wish Someone Would Care," were definitely in the new style, although shot through and through with blues.

New Orleans continued to interject conservative or off-the-wall sounds into the rhythm-and-blues mainstream throughout the end of the 1960s. The Dixie Cups were a girl group on the Red Bird label who hit the top with "Chapel of Love," but their true New Orleans colors showed in early 1965 with the weird, primitive "Iko Iko," a street chant taken from the New Orleans parade "Indians," black secret societies that march during Mardi Gras and on St. Joseph's Day. Lee Dorsey lay dormant until 1965, when Allen Toussaint came out of the army and joined forces with producer Marshall Sehorn. Then starting with "Ride Your Pony" and continuing through 1966 with "Get Out of My Life, Woman," "Working in the Coal Mine," and "Holy Cow," Dorsey and the Sansu house band produced a classic series of songs backed by Toussaint and a new band called the Meters, which included several members of a musical family, the Nevilles, some of whom had been making records in New Orleans since the mid-fifties. Always outside the mainstream, always with a fresh take on what may have seemed tired old material, the New Orleans musicians bridged the gap between rock and roll and rhythm and blues or soul longer than anybody else; and, in fact, although they are completely outside the marketplace at this point, they're still doing it to some extent today.

Philadelphia, too, was going strong. By 1962 Frankie and Fabian weren't its only offerings anymore. While a lot of what happened in Philadelphia wasn't nearly as creative as the music coming out of New York, it was no less commercial, and by defining the middle ground, it helped define the pop of this era. The indie record labels that grew up in Philadelphia in the early 1960s were largely the products of distributors turned record moguls, people like Bernie Lowe, Dick Clark's former henchman, whose Cameo-Parkway operation was virtually put into business by Chubby Checker and "The Twist."†

By 1961–1962, the twist had swept the nation because of the rise of the discotheque, a kind of nightclub (the prototype of which was Paris's Whisky au Go-Go, no relation to the Sunset Strip club of the same name) at which nothing but records was played. Discotheques produced other dance crazes, too, but it was the twist that brought them to public attention. Jackie Kennedy was twisting in the White House, Liz Taylor was twisting with Richard Burton, and despite the cries of the clergy and other watchdogs of public morality, the dance spread like wildfire across America because it

---

*The label fell into decline when Toussaint was drafted in 1963 and it was sold to Lew Chudd.

† At one point, Parkway had eight twist albums in print, six of which were by Checker and one of which was by the Meyer Davis Orchestra, Philadelphia's top society ork.

was so simple. And since it wasn't keyed to any particular rhythm or melody, any moderately vigorous song could be twisted to. Atlantic even resurrected some old sides and issued *Do the Twist with Ray Charles*, which was a very good album whether or not you were inclined to twist with it.

Soon variations appeared: the peppermint twist, which Joey Dee, who had been performing around New Jersey for some time without breaking through, made into a big hit in early 1962 (his band, the Starlighters, metamorphosed into the Young Rascals not long thereafter); and who could forget "Slow Twistin' "? Mount a board on a ball-bearing pivot and you had the Trim Twist, with which you could twist off those extra pounds in the privacy of your office.

But Bernie Lowe was smart enough to realize that there had to be life after the twist, and that his competitors who had missed out on the craze were developing other dances to make them rich. Cameo had helped pioneer the next dance fads with Dee Dee Sharp's "Mashed Potato Time" and "The Wah Watusi" by the Orlons, who followed up with the frantic "Don't Hang Up" and a true Philly anthem, "South Street," with its inimitable opening lines, "Where do all the hippies meet?* South Street, South Street!" The records were crudely produced, the instrumental work wasn't going to cause Phil Spector to lose any sleep, but they sold well and sounded not unlike some of the records coming out of Detroit. And while Cameo-Parkway dominated the dance scene (another big hit of theirs was the Dovells' "Bristol Stomp," one more declaration of fierce Philly pride that boasted that "The kids in Bristol are sharp as a pistol, when they do the Bristol Stomp"), most of the other Philly labels—Jamie-Guyden, Swan, Chancellor—were developing girl-group hits. Chancellor almost wound up atoning for Frankie Avalon, in fact, with Claudine Clark's stark evocation of teenage alienation, "Party Lights," in which a girl sits and stares at a party nearby—she can see its lights, they're red and gold, and green—to which she hasn't been invited. There's a quirky intensity to this song that makes the party seem the very center of the universe, and Clark's impassioned vocal makes it sound like she's been officially denied entrance to heaven. Not a bad metaphor for the dark side of the teenage experience.

The Philadelphia sound was partly a look back to the vocal-group era and partly an answer to Phil Spector's sound. It was New Jersey that bred the fusion of black vocal-group harmonies with the Philly teen-idol style. Frankie and the Four Lovers were a group discovered singing in a bowling alley cocktail lounge somewhere near Newark. They'd been recording with RCA since the late 1950s, and, in fact, had a small hit with "You're the

---

*In those days, the word *hippie* had a double meaning. To a jazz fan, it was a youngster who was trying desperately to be hip, to the point of ostentatious pseudo-bohemian behavior, but to teenagers, it meant a youngster in the know. Two sides of the same coin, perhaps, but not the same meaning as appeared a few years later in San Francisco and elsewhere.

Apple of My Eye," which veteran Otis Blackwell had written in exchange for their not recording "Don't Be Cruel" after his last-minute decision to send it to Elvis. Their main idiosyncrasy was lead singer Frankie Valli's stratospheric falsetto, which, though it got high, never got squeaky. In the early 1960s, Bob Gaudio, who had been in the Royal Teens ("Short Shorts") and had co-written some of the Teens' material, joined the group and they changed their name to the Four Seasons.

The Four Seasons became Vee-Jay's first whites, signing in 1962 under the production of Bob Crewe, a young man who had been wasting his talents on instrumentals and novelty discs. With "Sherry" and its follow-up, "Big Girls Don't Cry," they found the perfect middle ground between the old-style harmonies and pretty-boy pop, and their radical harmonies and Valli's astonishing range made them immediately identifiable on the radio. Crewe wisely kept their production simple, and although today many regard the Four Seasons' work as the most obvious schlock, it is well within, if a fairly decadent example of, the 1950s vocal-group tradition. And considering some of the other artists of the time, like Jay and the Americans, with their overblown bathetic numbers like "She Cried," the Four Seasons weren't so bad after all.

But the strongest sound of the future was being developed in Detroit, by "Mr. Hitsville," Berry Gordy, Jr. Building on the base that the Miracles gave him, he had his next success with Mary Wells's "Bye Bye Baby," and then he really consolidated this achievement by firing alternate shots from the Miracles on Tamla and Mary Wells on Motown. The Miracles' string of hits ("Everybody's Gotta Pay Some Dues," "What's So Good About Good-Bye," "I'll Try Something New") culminated with a masterpiece released late in 1962, "You've Really Got a Hold On Me." Mary Wells also fulfilled her early promise by charting "The One Who Really Loves You" and "You Beat Me to the Punch," and shooting the moon with the Smokey Robinson–written shocker "Two Lovers," in which a woman seems to be confessing to having two lovers, one good, one bad, but they turn out to be two aspects of the same man.

Talent seemed to grow on Detroit trees, and with the unique sound Gordy was getting with his musicians and the intense familial atmosphere in the company, making all of the artists and employees do their best at all times, Tamla, Motown, and their new cousin Gordy (on which the Contours recorded "Do You Love Me," the ultimate dance-craze record, in 1961) were making hits like there was no tomorrow. They were operating in a vacuum, copying nobody, although an argument might be made that the Marvelettes were a girl group, scoring hits during the girl-group era like "Please Mr. Postman," "Beechwood 4-5789," and "Playboy," then disappearing until 1965.

By 1962, Gordy was feeling confident enough to sneak a wonderful vocalist he'd heard singing with the Moonglows out of the still-successful group, and Marvin Gaye appeared on the scene, a tall, skinny singer with a background in the church and sex appeal that prostrated women wherever he sang. There was a churchiness to his early records that was pushed by that urgent Detroit rhythm section Gordy seemed to have a patent on: "Stubborn Kind of Fellow," "Hitch Hike," "Pride and Joy," and the most sanctified of all, "Can I Get a Witness."

Gaye's developing sound updated Jackie Wilson and Sam Cooke and buried Ray Charles's in the past—it was an urban style a thousand miles away from the Southern grit recorded on Atlantic. In an age when a youthful President was setting the style for the nation, Gordy, with typically justified arrogance, proclaimed the music on his records "The Sound of Young America," and judging from the numbers in which they sold, nobody was likely to contradict him. Still, he was just beginning, and it would take two groups—one, the Primes, a male group with an astonishing variety of talented singers in it, and the other, the Primettes, a trio of girls from the housing projects—to really push Motown/Tamla/Gordy to the heights. First, though, they had to change their names from the Primes to the Temptations; from the Primettes to the Supremes.

But even the older black sounds were evolving into something completely new. When Ray Charles left for ABC-Paramount late in 1959, wooed by a contract that guaranteed him $50,000 a year, it was a major loss for Atlantic. They were still scoring hits with the Drifters and Ben E. King, but they also knew that one of their strengths lay in the sort of artist Charles had been: one able to communicate to a wide variety of black (and white) people, from rural backwoods Southerners to urban sophisticates who were not above a little bacon in their greens to show people they remembered their roots. By now, with the burgeoning civil rights movement, the entire spectrum of black culture was coming to the attention of the nation at large, and Atlantic recognized that the smooth crooning of Sam Cooke, although it was wonderful, was only one small facet of black music. Surely there were other styles waiting to be tapped as well.

What Atlantic wanted was something grittier, and they found it first with Solomon Burke, a huge man with an incredible degree of personal magnetism gained from years of being a preacher, starting when he was a very young boy. Burke had begun making gospel records for Bess Berman at Apollo in the mid-1950s but had been overshadowed by Mahalia Jackson. Now he found a welcome home at Atlantic, where his first hit was a country song, "Just Out Of Reach Of My Two Open Arms," that dated from the 1930s. This late-1961 hit kicked off a string that remained unbroken through the 1960s, although unlike Ray Charles, Solomon Burke never crossed over onto the top of the pop charts, even with such masterpieces as "Cry To Me" and "If You Need Me," both of which most white youngsters had to wait for the Rolling Stones to hear.

The idea of recording a black man singing country music wasn't all that strange anymore, but it was really shocking when Ray Charles, after a few excellent singles in his old manner (a mellow reading of the Hoagy Carmichael classic "Georgia on My Mind," "Hit the Road, Jack," and "Unchain My Heart"), turned to country music for his next series of hits. Starting with Don Gibson's "I Can't Stop Loving You" in 1962, Charles scored with Jimmy Davis's "You Are My Sunshine," Hank Williams's "Your Cheatin' Heart," and finally released the epochal *Modern Sounds in Country and Western Music* album, all of which sold very well indeed, and all of which made the upper reaches of the pop charts.

These black music experiments, conducted all over the country, would usher in the future, but in the beginning of the 1960s, it was New York, and especially the Brill Building, that dominated. In 1962, Aldon Music had eighteen writers on its staff, all of whom were between nineteen and twenty-six years old, and it showed: That year Aldon swept the annual BMI awards banquet, where plaques were presented to the writers and publishers who had had the most airplay, sales, and recorded copyrights. They did it again in 1963, with Goffin and King picking up more gold for Aldon than their other writers, although Mann and Weil were coming into their own. It was Mann and Weil who noticed the trend that was developing in the wake of the ban-the-bomb and civil-rights movements and with young activist John F. Kennedy in the White House, and began writing socially conscious lyrics.

And it was to Mann and Weil that Phil Spector came when it was time to make another hit for the Crystals: "Uptown." It took a bit of quick talking (something Spector was very good at) to convince Barry Mann that this song of pride and love was suitable for his group, since Mann had intended it for Tony Orlando; but when Spector finally got it, he approached it with a reverence that made it far more than simply a follow-up to the Crystals' last record. With a mandolin strumming under the opening lines, the song expands into a full minisymphony, with clicking castanets, flamenco guitar, and both bowed and pizzicato strings. It was a simple enough story about a man who works downtown, where he's "a little man," but at night comes uptown to his girlfriend's tenement (rhymes with "Uptown where people don't have to pay much rent"), where she makes him feel important.

It was not a very typical teen topic, but with the tension between the minor-key "downtown" verses and the major-key "uptown" ones, and the drama of the whole thing, it caught teenage ears. Caught them so completely, in fact, that probably not 10 percent of the kids who bought the records noticed that there were no drums at all on it—just castanets, an insistent bass, and some sandpaper blocks rubbed together. Maybe it didn't sell quite as well as its predecessor, but it broke new ground both musically and lyrically. After all, as Barry Mann once commented, "When we were writing back then, we really did think we could change the world."

Spector then made one of the many bizarre moves that were beginning to characterize his career: With Philles going strong, he took an A&R job at Liberty Records. Day after day passed, and he sat at his desk playing with a toy hockey game instead of working. With his next Crystals record, it looked as if he were trying to commit commercial suicide: "He Hit Me (And It Felt Like a Kiss)" was a Goffin-King song with a weird downbeat melody and almost overtly masochistic lyrics. The Crystals themselves hated it, it was banned on radio, and still Phil sat at his desk. After five months, he turned in his resignation, along with a cockamamie story about going to Europe to rethink his career, but when somebody opined to Jerry Leiber that Phil had gone crazy, Jerry replied, "Yeah, Spector's crazy, all right: crazy like a fox." In fact, he was a flying fox, on his way to Los Angeles with a demo of "He's a Rebel," a Gene Pitney song that Liberty was planning to cut with Vikki Carr. Spector had heard a hit and sneaked it out of Liberty, planning to beat them to the record racks.

What happened next is very typical of Phil Spector, but no less typical of the entire pop music industry in those days. He was so excited by "He's a Rebel" that he had alerted Lester Sill to book time at Gold Star Studios in Hollywood, and to collect some of the best young players around and have them ready to record as soon as he deplaned. The saga of a guy who is lovable despite the fact that "he doesn't do what everybody else does" was another beam straight to the teenage psyche, and the fact that the Crystals couldn't make the session—some said they were afraid to fly, others said that Phil never intended to spend the money on airfare and hotels—meant that Phil called in a trio called the Blossoms, whose lead singer, Darlene Love, sounded very much like the Crystals' Barbara Alston anyway. He rushed the song into release—under the Crystals' name—and it entered the charts low but soon started somersaulting up them in fine fashion, dislodging Liberty's version with Vikki Carr.

In the meantime, Spector issued a letter to all the Philles distributors:

> I am pleased to advise that I have acquired complete and absolute control of Philles Records, Inc. I have purchased all other interests in this company. Lester Sill and Harry Finfer [a Philadelphia distributor who had consolidated the 25 percent Sill had let go] are no longer associated with Philles Records. I am assuming immediate direction of the entire company ... I will be devoting my full time to producing and recording for my company Philles Records ... I have the utmost confidence that I will continue in the hit making tradition ... I realize that certainly you, as my distributor, will play an important part in my success, and I implore your utmost cooperation in promoting my forthcoming releases. Thank you for all past and future considerations in my behalf. ...

And whammo! "He's a Rebel" was the number-one record in the country. Not a bad achievement for a twenty-one-year-old.

Soon Goffin and King, too, were coming into their own on Aldon's songwriters' label, Dimension. Its first record became its first hit, and its history is almost a fairy tale. One day Carole and Gerry were sitting at the piano writing, and, while their baby Sherry slept, their baby-sitter, seventeen-year-old Eva Narcissus Boyd, started dancing to the song they were playing. "What's that funny dance you're doing?" Gerry asked. "It looks like a locomotive train." In no time, they were in a studio cutting a demo, letting Eva sing the lyrics about the new dance craze "The Loco-Motion."

Aldon writers often felt that their promotional demos were better than the records made from them, but they had to pitch the songs to established artists to gain maximum sales. But when Cameo-Parkway turned the song down on behalf of Dee Dee Sharp and Chubby Checker,* Carole and Gerry begged Aldon to release it on Dimension, and in June 1962, it hit the charts. Little Eva, as she was now known, appeared on "American Bandstand" to demonstrate the dance, and in no time, the song went top five pop and to the pinnacle of the rhythm-and-blues charts. Spectorian in sound, with that pushing rhythm that not only fit the locomotive concept but also the rhythm of the times, it was a monster. Unfortunately, Little Eva's follow-ups didn't do much, although the album that was issued to capitalize on the hit was packed with great performances of Aldon and Goffin-King numbers like "Will You Love Me Tomorrow," "Breaking Up Is Hard to Do," "Some Kinda Wonderful," and "Run to Him."

Dimension was to have two more important artists, the Cookies and Carole King herself. The Cookies were a trio the Aldon group of writers often used on demo sessions. These sessions cost about a hundred dollars apiece, including the use of musicians and singers, and produced the song in a "demonstration" form that was then transferred to fragile "acetates"— aluminum discs sprayed with plastic on which the song was etched with a needle—that would last for about ten plays, long enough to see if the song would sell. Many demo musicians went on to greater success, often after demos that didn't sell got limited release by their authors.

The Cookies' first record was "Chains," perhaps better known in its cover version by the Beatles, but it got them a place on the pop charts. They followed up with "Don't Say Nothin' Bad About My Baby," which sold even better. As for Carole King herself, the records she cut for Dimension were just a continuation of the recording career she'd interrupted to work full-time as a writer. "It Might As Well Rain Until September" was a demo originally intended for Bobby Vee, who turned it down, and although it did only fairly in the States, it reached number three on the charts in Britain. King's follow-up efforts died, but they can be heard on an album called *Dimension Dolls* that the label rushed out late in 1962.

In April 1963, out of the blue, Nevins and Kirshner sold Aldon and its labels to Columbia Pictures–Screen Gems for $2 million cash, along with some stock. Fresh from sweeping the 1963 BMI Awards, the Aldon writers were shocked, although some continued to work for Kirshner, who had taken over Colpix Records. But the Aldon "family" was shattered and began

*Too bad, because Sharp was a very talented singer, and she could have used another hit. As it was, she wound up marrying Kenny Gamble, one of the young rhythm-and-blues producers emerging in Philadelphia at the time.

drifting apart by 1964, when the mantle of girl-group music would pass to Red Bird.

Red Bird was the brainchild of Jerry Leiber, Mike Stoller, and George Goldner. But it owed a great deal of what made it special to a remarkable woman named Ellie Greenwich, who, first with her partner, Tony Powers, and then later with her husband, Jeff Barry, was responsible for Phil Spector's next few hits. Greenwich was another young wonder from Long Island, a former schoolteacher who met her future husband at a family gathering shortly before "Tell Laura I Love Her" was cut and wound up singing on some of Jeff's demo sessions. But her big break was an accident. As she told Alan Betrock, "I just sat [in an office in the Brill Building] playing the piano, and in walks this guy and says, 'Hi, Carole'—he was expecting to see Carole King and listen to some of *her* material. When he saw I wasn't Carole, he asked who I was and I told him, and I played him some songs, and he said they were 'interesting,' and that I should come up and visit whenever I felt like it, to write or whatever. He said his name was Jerry Leiber and he introduced me to his partner Mike Stoller. I didn't know who they were, and then when I got home I saw their name on one of my records, and then another, and then another. All of these great records by the Coasters and the Drifters and Leiber and Stoller and Carole King. I couldn't believe it. I just started running around the house screaming."

Soon she'd signed on with their label, Trio Music, for $75 a week, despite an offer of $300 from Hill and Range. Her first record was the Exciters follow-up to their successful "Tell Him," but "He's Got the Power" didn't do nearly as well.* Still, she had a foot in the door. Then, as she told Betrock, "I was on a 'first refusal' basis with Leiber and Stoller at this point . . . I wrote '(Today I Met) The Boy I'm Gonna Marry' and Leiber and Stoller weren't too excited by it. I took it to Aaron Schroeder and he liked it and arranged for Phil Spector to hear that and some other songs. So in comes Phil and I'm sitting at the piano playing 'It Was Me Yesterday.' Phil was walking around the room fixing his clothes, looking in the mirror, and adjusting his hair—all the time making noises while I was playing my song. Finally I said, 'Either you want to hear my songs or you don't.' Phil exploded and stormed out of the room, and everyone in the office felt that Spector was gone for good." But he came back, and Greenwich later said, "I think he just liked the idea that I stood up to him, because we hit it off right away."

At this point, Spector was enjoying a fair success with the Crystals' next record—again, cut without the Crystals—a Mann-Weil tune titled "He's Sure the Boy I Love," and with a novelty revival of the Walt Disney tune "Zip-A-Dee-Doo-Dah," by Bob B. Soxx & the Blue Jeans, a trio he'd assembled around the Blossoms/Crystals lead singer, Darlene Love. However,

---

*The group later recorded "Do-Wah-Diddy," a Barry-Greenwich tune that did much better in a cover version by Manfred Mann.

neither of his next two records,* "Why Do Lovers Break Each Others' Hearts," by Bob B. Soxx, and "(Today I Met) The Boy I'm Gonna Marry," released as being by Darlene Love, managed to scale the heights, so he decided that he needed a blockbuster. And he got one from Greenwich and Barry. "Da Doo Ron Ron" was the apotheosis of the whole girl-group era.

The song would become Spector's most audacious production yet, the first of his famous "wall of sound" recordings in which seemingly thousands of instruments and singers labored together for the common good, all apparently placed inside a giant echoing cavern. To do it justice, he recorded most of the backing tracks in Los Angeles but then brought the tape to New York to have an actual Crystal, La La Brooks, sing the lead vocal. It was all done on three tracks and all mixed to mono (to the end of his career, Spector mistrusted stereo and even had some buttons saying "Back To Mono" printed up), and it seemed like the biggest sound in the world coming over the radio. "Da Doo Ron Ron" would become an immense hit not only in the United States but all over the globe, and it would launch Phil Spector on a spectacular new phase of his career.

His most creative period began when, early in 1963, he came across three Manhattan girls who had danced their way into the big time. Veronica Bennett, her sister Estelle, and their cousin Nedra Talley, who dressed alike and all had matching hairdos, first got admitted to the Peppermint Lounge when the doorman mistook them for the entertainment. Within weeks, they *were*, dancing at the club for ten dollars a night, and eventually they signed with Colpix first as Ronnie and the Relatives and then as the Ronettes. Spector was so sure this was the group that would consummate his success that he convinced them to quit Colpix and then visited Mrs. Bennett to swear that the Ronettes' first record would be a number-one hit. He promised, and he almost kept his word.

He dedicated all his considerable energies and talents to creating their first single. He began by taking two Barry-Greenwich songs, "Be My Baby" and "Baby I Love You," and repaired to Gold Star Studios to start the patient process of layering tracks on the songs. There was more than hit fever spurring him on: Although he was married to a woman named Annette Merar, Phil had fallen in love with Veronica Bennett and was determined to make her a star. That determination came through on "Be My Baby," and although he did not later consider it his masterpiece, it became the biggest hit Philles ever had, rising to number two on the pop charts. Even the follow-up, "Baby I Love You," while very nearly the earlier record's equal, was unable to surpass it.

The Ronettes were the rising stars of 1963, and Phil, full of joy at his success, blessed his audience with one of the strangest, but happiest, records of this whole period: *A Christmas Gift to You from Philles Records.*

---

*Phil also made a Crystals record, now "lost," to fulfill obligations to his former partners, a five-minute obscene opus called "Do the Screw," with his lawyer reciting the title at crucial points.

Featuring the entire Philles family singing traditional and Brill Building Christmas songs—Darlene Love's impassioned "White Christmas," the Ronettes' bouncy "Frosty the Snowman," a Spector-Greenwich-Barry number with Darlene pleading "Christmas (Baby Please Come Home)," and its last cut, with Phil giving his heartfelt thanks for everything while the orchestra plays "Silent Night"—this is an offbeat rock-and-roll classic that has withstood the test of time.

Yet despite the fact that the Ronettes spent the early months of 1964 touring with the Rolling Stones and being the toast of London—they would later (1966) tour with the Beatles in the United States—the buying public was proving fickle. Spector was so annoyed by the failure of "(The Best Part of) Breakin' Up" and "Do I Love You?" that he violated one of his firmest rules and hired a high-powered promo man, Danny Davis, to give his records a push. The next Ronettes release, "Walking in the Rain," managed to win a Grammy—for special effects of all things, but after all it *was* a rock and roll record—and to become enshrined as a classic Spector track without managing to rise any higher than number twenty-three on the charts. Still, he kept recording the Ronettes obsessively, even shelving the tracks when the ones he did release sold poorly.

Where he was succeeding in 1964 was with the Righteous Brothers—Bill Medley and Bobby Hatfield, two white R&B fans with perfectly meshed voices who had attracted a large black following in the two years they'd been together before Phil signed them in 1964. The first record they cut for him went straight to the top: "You've Lost That Lovin' Feeling" was a Mann-Weill-Spector number cut at just a hair more than dirge tempo, with all the drama and bombast people had come to expect from Spector's records. Three more hits followed in 1965: "Unchained Melody," "Ebb Tide," and "Just Once In My Life," and suddenly the two asked for a release from Philles, claiming that they needed more artistic control than Spector was giving them—easy enough to believe—and that they'd found it at Verve Records.

As quickly as it had risen, Spector's castle began to crumble. Although he was growing wealthy from his publishing deals, from working as a middleman for the Rolling Stones (and as an uncredited sideman and producer on some of their tracks), and from smart investments, all his artists began to leave except for the Ronettes. Soon, too, the musicians' union, deciding that Phil's multioverdubbing violated some statute, shut him down. He eventually got back in business, but his downward spiral had begun. He married Ronnie in the summer of 1966 and, in his growing paranoia, imprisoned her in his mansion. He became reclusive, apart from late-night confabs with Frank Zappa and Lenny Bruce, two of his best friends, at Canter's Deli on Lower Fairfax in Los Angeles. When Bruce overdosed on heroin in San Francisco, Phil's paranoia and seclusion only deepened. After Bruce's death, a police official visited Spector with some photos and negatives of Lenny's corpse sprawled near a toilet, with a hypodermic in his arm, and offered to sell them to Spector so that they wouldn't get printed. Spector forked over $5,000, but he felt an incredible amount of self-loathing for even being involved in such a transaction.

The legend of Phil Spector has it that he staked everything on one last record. Ike and Tina Turner had left Sue for Loma (a Warner Bros. rhythm-and-blues subsidiary), where they continued to make good records that didn't sell, so they looked to Phil Spector, who was known to be a magician who could appreciate a great female voice. Phil unearthed a song he'd written with Greenwich and Barry, "River Deep—Mountain High," which would become the most baroque and overstated Spector production yet. It was also a complete failure. Whether it was the changing times, the fact that distributors and other people in the industry were tired of dealing with this shrimpy egotist, or it just plain wasn't in the grooves, the record sank like a stone and dragged Philles Records to the bottom. Still, over the years, Spector would resurface from time to time, most notably with the Beatles, and Ronnie would, too (she cut a George Harrison–written song, "Try Some, Buy Some" in the early 1970s, but it, too, flopped), and although his influence would be heard for many years to come, his days as a boy genius were over for good.

Of course, while he was hot, Spector was the man to beat, so numerous other producers tried to replicate his production triumphs. Nobody ever really succeeded, but George "Shadow" Morton, working with Jeff Barry at Red Bird Records, came close. Red Bird had been doing well throughout 1964 with the Dixie Cups, the Jelly Beans, and, on their Blue Cat subsidiary, the Ad Libs, whose "The Boy from New York City" was the Blue Cat label's only real hit. Most of the songs were created by Jeff Barry and Ellie Greenwich in collaboration with various other Trio Music writers, and thanks to George Goldner's business expertise, the records were widely distributed and aired. But as good as these black pop acts were, Red Bird is probably best remembered today because of a group of tough white girls from a bad part of Queens, Mary and Betty Weiss (sisters) and Marge and Mary Ann Ganser (not only sisters but twins): the Shangri-Las. They dressed tough—they were tough—in black slacks and boots, and they had recorded one now-forgotten single with Kama-Sutra Productions in 1964. That same year George Morton, a high school friend of Ellie Greenwich, noticed that her name was on all the hit records he'd been studying while trying to break into the music business. He dropped in at her office, and Jeff Barry brushed him off with a promise to look at his material. But the problem was that at that point, Morton didn't have any.

In fact, he'd never even written a song, but that didn't stop him. He called up a friend with a basement studio, asking to borrow it, and another friend introduced him to the Shangri-Las. He got so involved in constructing the scam that he was already on his way to the studio before he realized that he didn't have a song to record. So he pulled over his car, and in twenty-two minutes, he claims, composed the song. Walking into the studio, he bluffed his way through the session, and then took his little reel of tape to show Jeff Barry what he could do.

As Ellie Greenwich remembers: "He came back and played us this weird little record. It was like seven minutes long with this long narration by George in the beginning. I knew there was no way we could put out anything like that, but I thought, 'Gee, that girl's voice is so strange, and the song is interesting.' So we played it for Leiber and Stoller and they said, 'Go cut it.'" She and Morton tightened it up, the girls went through it again, and suddenly it looked like they had a hit.

"Remember (Walkin' in the Sand)" was unlike anything teenagers had ever heard before. "Whatever will I do / With the night I gave to you?" asks the singer, as she laments the impersonal (by letter) way the boy she loves has ended their romance. She never comes to any conclusion, probably because she just can't stop remembering how they walked together in the sand on one magic night.

If Phil Spector was making "little symphonies for the kids," as somebody said, the Shangri-Las were making little soap operas; and their next record turned into one of the most controversial ever: "Leader of the Pack." It came out of a conversation between Barry and Morton about motorcycle gangs and the girls who fell in love with their leaders. But if "Remember" had been a soap opera, "Leader of the Pack" was a feature-length film crammed into two minutes and forty-eight seconds. "Is she really going out with him?" one girl asks. "I dunno, let's ask her," says the other. "Betty, is that Johnny's ring you're wearing?" they ask together. "Mm-hmmmm," she affirms. "Boy, it must really be fun riding with him." "Is he picking you up after school today?" Pause. "Mmm-Mmm," she denies. The girls realize their gaffe and quickly ask, "By the way, where'd you meet him?" They should have known better than to ask, because of the portentous piano note that is tolling like a death knell behind their initial questions. What Betty eventually tells them is that she met him at the candy store, but that when she tried to introduce him to her parents, they sent him away and forbade her ever to see him again. Tough though he was, he must have had tears in his eyes, because he drove crazily away from her house and ignored her cries of "Look out! Look out! Look out!" The motorcycle sounds merge with one of the world's longest skids and the sound of metal being bent and glass breaking. She swears eternal devotion, but, well, that's why he's not picking her up from school today.

"Leader of the Pack," with its sound effects, recitation, and drama and pathos, became a number-one hit almost overnight, and it caused one of the biggest furors of the time. Parents tried to ban it, editorialists railed against it, and the controversy drove it off a few radio stations. It was officially banned in England, where it nonetheless hit the higher reaches of the charts, and it even spawned a mocking novelty answer-record, "Leader of the Laundromat," by a group that called itself the Detergents.

Its success inspired George Morton to continue writing quintessentially teenage dramas for the Shangri-Las, songs like "Out in the Streets" and "Give Us Your Blessings," in which a young couple fail to gain approval from their parents and die in a horrible car accident. The group also recorded more conventional, less morbid material, like "Give Him a Great Big Kiss," a song about showing your boyfriend you appreciate him, but it is the soap operas for which they are best remembered. They capped their career—and the career of Red Bird Records—with "I Can Never Go Home Anymore," a psychodrama about an estranged mother and daughter, delivered by Mary in the thick Queens accent that marked all the group's records, with the chilling conclusion: "This girl got so lonely in the end / The angels took her for their friend / And I can never go home any more." But by the time 1966 rolled around, Mercury Records had taken the Shangri-Las, and Shadow Morton (George had earned the nickname for the way he sneaked around, showing up late for sessions, disappearing at crucial moments) went with them. Leiber and Stoller were tired of the label, and times were changing, so Red Bird flew off.

Even as 1963 dawned, American popular music had progressed radically from its character of only seven years earlier. By now, most of it was produced not by genius eccentrics who could spur record buyers and radio listeners to mass action, but by a group of undeniably talented (at best) or shrewdly calculating (at worst) professionals: songwriters, producers, music publishers, and engineers. The audience was fragmented, and the sort of national consensus that had established an artist like Elvis seemed an elusive ideal. Regionalism was back. In Fort Worth, Texas, for instance, a whole teen pop empire rose and toppled under the hand of Major Bill Smith, who may have outranked Colonel Tom Parker but whose ambitions were more squarely in line with those of Bob Marcucci of Philadelphia fame. Major Bill produced a number of local favorites but built his national reputation on one teen-death record, J. Frank Wilson's "Last Kiss"; one teen-love record, Paul and Paula's "Hey Paula"; and one light pop-rocker, Bruce Channel's "Hey! Baby," the song that made John Lennon want to learn harmonica. In Dallas and Fort Worth, Major Bill was a terror. To the rest of the country, he was just another record producer with some minor hits.

Teenagers were still buying records, and the record business was still a great place to make money—at least as great as it had been in Dick Clark's early days. One old genre that retained a fanatical following was black vocal-group music, and although new hits in the style kept arriving sporadically (the Jive Five's "My True Story" and the Marcells' "Blue Moon" in 1961, the Sensations' "Let Me In" in 1962, Ruby and the Romantics' "Our Day Will Come," the Drifters' haunting "Up on the Roof," and the Tymes' "So Much in Love" in 1963), a new group of fans, located mostly in New Jersey and Los Angeles, began to unearth and revivify vocal-group records of the past. On the West Coast, these cults were primarily devoted to forgotten old masters; but on the East Coast, their enthusiasms, expanded to include a cappella, spurred by the discovery of some rehearsal tapes of the Nutmegs singing without accompaniment, managed to sustain some new groups who adopted the old a cappella style, like the Camelots, the Zircons, and the Persuasions, who continue to perform today. But by 1963, there were surfers, folkies, teen idols, weird groups from Washington State that played guitar instrumentals and revived old records like "Louie Louie," twist maniacs, Brill Building popsters, girl groups, Motown musicians, and, from out of Belgium, the Singing Nun. Now, everybody was forced to choose a side.

And what of Elvis? With rock and roll so firmly a part of the scene, he wasn't as special as he had been, but he didn't let it bother him. He surrounded himself with an entourage that included his teenage wife-to-be, Patricia Beaulieu, and trusting the Colonel implicitly, let him make decisions about movies, and, unfortunately, the songs he recorded. The Colonel got a kickback from Hill and Range and so favored their songwriters, many of whom were mediocre or, worse, bland mainstream pop. It was symbolic that one of Elvis's first albums after his army tour was entitled *Something for Everybody*, which certainly wasn't what he'd started out to be. His shift toward pop was so pronounced that rumors circulated among unreconstructed rockers that he'd been fed chemicals or been replaced by a double while in Germany. He continued to release movies, but their quality never improved, so he never became a bankable film star, either.

Dick Clark stayed on television and never seemed to get any older; Chuck Berry finally went to jail on the Mann Act conviction (after the first verdict was overturned because his trial was overtly racist); and in September 1963, Jerry Lee Lewis's contract with Sun expired. Sam Phillips may not even have noticed.

And as for Alan Freed, "Mr. Rock and Roll," the man who had done so much to start it all, he finally stood trial in December 1962 and was fined $300 and given a six-month suspended sentence. Yet it didn't stop there. On March 16, 1964, by which time Freed was "retired" (in the show business sense: meaning he couldn't find work anywhere), he was indicted by the Internal Revenue Service on charges that he had failed to pay $47,920 on unreported income of $56,652 from 1957 to 1959. Freed was already a broken man, but this final assault did him in. His body fell apart, and he was hospitalized for uremia, and died, at the age of forty-three, on January 20, 1965. With Freed died a lot of the spirit that was rock and roll in its youth, the sense that there were amazing discoveries amid the static at the end of the radio dial, the possibility that there were adults who could help a teenager discover a new world, the sense of chaos and anarchy that was rock and roll's first contribution to teenage society.

Freed's death sounded the final requiem for an era that had been passing since the turning of the decade. Even in 1963, it looked as if there would never again be a time when the land was rocking in harmony, when teenagers communicated in a secret language and adults shook their heads in bewilderment. The high schoolers of Chuck Berry's "School Day" must have been certain that they'd seen something rare, a cosmic event like Halley's comet; a force that could bind together teenagers from all walks of life under the banner of rock and roll; a music that they could use to define themselves while they themselves were defining it; a thing of their very own. If they thought that, they were deluding themselves. Once lit, this fire could never be extinguished: That's how big an idea it was. Even when rock and roll seemed to be limping along in America, it was gathering force in a most unexpected place: England. Ring ring goes the bell. And hail hail rock and roll: Deliver us from the days of old.

THE
SIXTIES

by

GEOFFREY STOKES

15

ROLL OVER, FRANKIE AVALON

In 1973, years after the fact, critic Robert Christgau looked back a decade and drew a useful distinction between rock 'n' roll and the new form—rock—that superseded it. Rock, he wrote, "signifies something like 'all music deriving primarily from the energy and influence of the Beatles—and maybe Bob Dylan, and maybe you should stick pretensions in there someplace.'" The definition, as good a one as we have, is in some ways incomplete, however, for rock was more than just a *musical* development; it was a way of seeing the world, a way of life.

It was also an international business, eventually a very big business indeed, whose routine modes of operation were often in explicit conflict with the culture that supported it and even with the product that made it profitable.

Perhaps most important, it was *new*, less a gradually evolving development that the best business analysts of the late 1950s and early 1960s could have predicted and controlled than a mutant, the unanticipated offspring of Liverpool, Greenwich Village, and Memphis. Precisely because of this ambiguous relationship to its lineage, rock was almost immediately more diverse and eclectic than rock 'n' roll, yet the singular pronoun—it—isn't inaccurate. The music's audience, on both sides of the Atlantic, responded to quite different artistic approaches with the same openness and curiosity. Black, white, folkish, psychedelic, bluesy . . . it was *all* rock; and in a certain sense, the musical and social ways in which that paradox worked itself out in the 1960s is the story not only of a pop art form but of the generation that embraced it.

There were demographic and social factors opening the way for this new kind of pop, but there were musical reasons for its birth as well. Despite the high quality achieved by certain specific records in the prerock years, the 45s that marched in succession up the charts had about them the ineffable scent of *product*, as the industry's greater efficiency let imitation follow upon innovation with ever-increasing rapidity. Not even Elvis was immune. With each succeeding film, he seemed to lose more of the fire and energy that had made him a revelation, and by 1963, he was riding trends rather than setting them. In the fall of that year, he released the last Top Ten hit he would have for more than five years, a predictable and tepid novelty called "Bossa Nova Baby."

The comparatively few pockets of innovation within the American music industry's mainstream were geographical. Detroit, New Orleans, and Texas all had strong, idiosyncratic local scenes, but the most influential of these was based in Southern California, where a loose amalgam of studio musicians, writers, and producers made Sunset Boulevard a sometime rival to Times Square. Though the major L.A. figures—Lou Adler, Terry Melcher, Nick Venet, Phil Spector, Herb Alpert, P. F. Sloan, and Steve Barri among them—would eventually prove as protean as the Brill Building stars, the first California sound to hit big was surf music.

The original hits were instrumentals, dominated by a twanging, heavily reverbed guitar instead of the more usual sax. As such, surf music responded to a preference expressed by sunbronzed young men who lived for the next big wave—and in the process, developed a genuine subculture on the beaches around Malibu.* Surf music's first successful practitioner was journeyman Dick Dale, whose 1961 "Let's Go Trippin'" was a solid regional hit. Dale, who sometimes included vocal lines in his songs, was followed by a string of pure instrumentalists like the Chantays, Marketts, and Surfaris.

The surfers not only had their own music, they had their own language as well, and late in 1961, a couple of kids from Hawthorne, California, put the two together. Brian Wilson and Mike Love were cousins, and neither was an enthusiastic surfer; that role was played by Brian's brother Dennis. But through Dennis, the two had come to understand the surfers' mystique, and the song they wrote was "Surfin'." Along with a third brother, Carl, and neighborhood friend (and receiver for the Hawthorne High Cougars; Brian Wilson was their quarterback) Al Jardine, the still-nameless group booked time at a Beverly Hills recording studio and cut their first two songs. Murry Wilson, father of three-fifths of the band and himself a songwriter of the Lawrence Welk school, paid for the time, and one of his professional connections shipped the demo to local record labels. Herb Newman's indie

---

*Surfing was also a recognizable scene at Myrtle Beach and other southeast Atlantic beaches, but the Carolinas had no discernible music industry, so surf music was a California phenomenon.

company, Candix, picked up the record, and it was Newman, in consultation with Joe Saraceno of the Surfaris, who named the band. "We didn't even know we were the Beach Boys until the song came out," Mike Love would say later, but in the event, it was not a name they wanted to change, for the song became a regional hit, even reaching number seventy-five on the national charts. As Dennis Wilson recalled, "I remember when Carl, Brian, and I, and David Marks were driving in Brian's 1957 Ford down Hawthorne Boulevard and . . . the moment we heard that record on radio, that was the biggest high ever. Nothing will ever top the expression on Brian's face. Ever."

Working with local dj Roger Christian and a neighborhood friend, Gary Usher, Brian Wilson continued writing his paeans to girls, cars, and beaches. They returned to the studio to cut "Surfer Girl," "Surfin' Safari," and two other originals, but Newman didn't like them. Undaunted, Murry Wilson started carrying the tape, augmented by "409," to larger companies, finally reaching producer Nick Venet at Capitol. Venet, then too junior to sign the group on his own, asked Brian and Murry to come back in an hour. By the time they returned, he'd gotten permission to start the relationship that established the Beach Boys—and the white, bouncy, lighter-than-air sound of California pop—as a dominant sound of the early 1960s.

Among those who played follow the leader most successfully were Dean Torrance and Jan Berry. Jan and Dean were still in college when producer Lou Adler signed them. At the time, they had a vaguely black sound, working the interplay between falsetto and baritone that the Righteous Brothers were also exploring. They'd had a couple of respectable national hits before they found themselves headlining a show at which the pre-Capitol Beach Boys were opening, and the two groups wound up doing a few songs together onstage. The experience of working with two more harmony voices certainly broadened Brian's future vocal productions; the exposure to surf songs changed Jan and Dean's career completely. The two bands became friendly, often helping each other out in the studio, and because the Beach Boys were committed to "Surfin' U.S.A.," Brian gave the duo a shot at his unfinished "Surf City," for which Berry completed the lyrics. It became surf music's first number-one hit.

The lyrics, promising "two girls for every boy," were as typically air-headed as most of Wilson's work, but even early on, his skills as a producer and arranger were obvious. Though the Beach Boys' instrumental sound was often painfully thin, the floating vocals, with the Four Freshman-ish harmonies riding over a droned, propulsive burden ("inside outside, U.S.A." in "Surfin' U.S.A."; "rah, rah, rah, rah, sis boom bah" in "Be True to Your School") were rich, dense, and unquestionably special. Twenty years after the fact, they still sound fresh.

And, alas, fatuous. The world of affluent California high school kids was real, certainly, and Wilson tapped into it brilliantly, but it was also—in Wilson's work, but especially in the spate of surf and beach-party films churned out by Hollywood—mindless. To a certain degree, however, this mindless, chooga-chooga teen-dream hedonism was what made it so attractive to a nation of kids who never got any closer to the surf than the screen at a drive-in movie. That's not to say that there weren't full-time beach boys who partied on the sands all night to Dick Dale or the Ventures, but as the subsequent criminal adventures of Murf the Surf hint, even their lives weren't endless sunshine. In the Technicolor version, however, the one universal truth about the surfers' world was that they always had a good time. The boys and girls were blond and beautiful in their baggies and bikinis, and except for the occasional straw authority figure over whom they inevitably triumphed, the adult world didn't exist. They danced on the beaches, petted in the evening shadows, cruised the freeways, and rode endless waves without reference to any reality beyond their self-contained world. And while all this was, at least in its Hollywood manifestation, a manufactured artifact, the surfers' world was genuinely off-limits to most adults. Born of a leisure and an affluence that the surfers' parents, survivors of the Depression and a world war, were too old to enjoy in this particular way, California's beach culture was arguably the first genuine counter-culture.

But for all its undeniable attractiveness, it was a limited one. Precisely because it was such a calculatedly teen-pitched fantasy, many kids felt almost obligated to outgrow it. Since the saccharine Eisenhower world limned by the likes of Andy Williams and Dean Martin seemed, if possible, even less appealing, the college campuses looked elsewhere for their models. Faced with the choice between teen and treacle, a lot of young people turned to folk music.

By definition, folk music had always been there, but its validity as a real, popular alternative for educated, middle-class, urban/suburban types was first demonstrated by the Weavers in 1950, when their version of Leadbelly's "Goodnight Irene" was a number-one hit for thirteen weeks. The four (Ronnie Gilbert, Lee Hays, Fred Hellerman, and Pete Seeger) had a couple of respectable follow-ups, but their unabashedly left-wing politics didn't sit at all well during the McCarthy years, and their record company, Decca, abandoned them after the influential Walter Winchell took a couple of crude swipes at them in his widely syndicated column.

With that, the first folkies went underground—not by choice, but because they were driven there—and for the next several years, city folk was a coterie music more or less on the order of progressive jazz (though without jazz's ethnic base). It was played in a few clubs (some of them, like Max Gordon's famous Village Vanguard, jazz outposts as well) and released—as albums, never singles—on a handful of independent labels, of which Maynard Solomon's Vanguard, Moses Asch's Folkways, and Jac Holzman's Elektra were the most important. Pete Seeger, who recorded more than a score of albums for Folkways, was by far the most visible folksinger. Though he rarely worked in clubs, he toured widely, giving concerts at campuses, union halls, churches, and libraries. In his performances, two things were unalterably clear: The music was participatory, and it was political.

Less visibly, Folkways was releasing a steady stream of records based on the work of folklorists and collectors who were documenting American musical history. Some of these were field recordings; others were reissues of long-lost recordings. The most notable was Harry Smith's 1953 six-record *Anthology of American Folk Music*, which brought the music of the Carter Family, Mississippi John Hurt, Blind Lemon Jefferson, and the Memphis Jug Band to fledgling folkies. And because Folkways kept its catalog active for years, these rediscovered styles remained available as influences on an entire generation of musicians.

But eighty-year-old mountain dulcimer players don't make hit records. Folk's pop breakthrough, eight years after the Weavers, was fed by three kids who came on like surfers with brains. In 1958, when comedienne Phyllis Diller had to cancel an appearance at San Francisco's Purple Onion club, three Bay Area college students (Dave Guard, Bob Shane, and Nick Reynolds) who called themselves the Kingston Trio were booked as emergency fill-ins. Though they were not entirely new to the scene (they'd previously worked the hungry i, of "beatnik" fame), their shows at the somewhat straighter Purple Onion brought them a visit from Capitol Records' Voile Gilmore. Gilmore (the man whose approval Nick Venet would later need to sign the Beach Boys) signed them almost on the spot and produced their first album. Because the trio was essentially a folk act, no single was released, but after a Salt Lake City station put "Tom Dooley" into regular rotation, Capitol released the cut as a single. Six weeks after its chart debut, the song reached number one.

The song, a ballad about a convicted murderer actually called Tom Dula (his Carolina grave was found and cleaned up after the trio's hit), was about as traditional as you could get. And though the delivery was somewhat melodramatic, the song was not tricked up; the guitar and banjo accompaniment was basic in the extreme and the vocal harmonies were straightforward. At the same time, however, there was no attempt at "authenticity," no Southern accents or mountain nasality. It sounded like a bunch of clean-cut kids singing an old song at a fraternity party—which is very close to what it was, for the Kingston Trio was wholesome, wholesome, wholesome. Sure, they'd climbed up through San Francisco's coffeehouse scene, but they were collegiate rather than beatnik, amusing rather than ideological.* Naturally, hard-core folkies hated them.

The true-blue folkies were, once again, a distinct minority, for the trio not only went on to have a string of chart singles, but from the time of their debut until the arrival of the Beatles, they always had at least one entry among the top twenty in *Cashbox* magazine's annual compilation of best-selling albums. Prior to the Kingston Trio, mainstream performers as di-

---

*The one vaguely political cut from their debut album was taken from a Broadway review, and they didn't release a "protest" single until 1962's "Where Have All the Flowers Gone."

verse as Frankie Laine, Jo Stafford, Harry Belafonte, and Vaughn Monroe had scored occasional hits with folk (or folk-type) material, but these had been anomalies, demonstrating only that certain performers could sell a folk song. The long-running success of the Kingston Trio proved that folk songs as a class could sell, and the record industry reacted in time-honored fashion by spawning a host of largely forgettable imitators such as the Brothers Four, the Limeliters, the Gateway Trio, the Cumberland Three, and the Journeymen.

For every group the record companies either developed or signed, however, there were hundreds of kids—every campus in the country had a couple—slowly learning guitar chords as they worked their way through *The Burl Ives Songbook*. Suddenly every college town in America had a coffeehouse (in the basement of a Methodist church, like as not, but the waitresses wore black leotards anyway), and sales of acoustic guitars more than doubled in each of the three years following "Tom Dooley." Important scenes developed in Cambridge/Boston, and in Berkeley, where nearly all the major figures of the San Francisco rock explosion began as folkies. But in retrospect, perhaps the two most distinctive aspects of this post–Kingston Trio outburst were that it was democratic and participatory—everyone could play it, and a great many did—and that it *wasn't* rock 'n' roll. Instead, it was—rather too obviously in the smug attitudes many of its practitioners displayed—altogether higher, nobler, and more, you know, *serious*.

For *serious* serious, however, it was virtually necessary to go to Mecca: Greenwich Village, where black leotards were less a costume than a way of life. Going back to the late 1940s, Washington Square Park, in the center of the Village, had been the site of impromptu Sunday-afternoon song swaps that occasionally drew legends like Pete Seeger and Woody Guthrie. This was an activity for summer weekends, however; for the rest of the year, music moved indoors. The Village had had coffeehouses, mostly to serve its Italian population, long before it had bohemians, but by the late '50s, Mac Dougal Street and the other streets south of Washington Square were lined with them. Some offered poetry, others just a quiet place to sit with a book or newspaper, but a number featured folksingers. A lot of these places were traps for performers and tourists alike—the tourists overpaid for bitter coffee, and the performers earned only whatever extra change the audience could be induced to drop into a circulating basket—but even the worst of the basket houses gave young performers a chance to develop by working in front of live audiences. The best coffee houses offered a heady mix of first-class traditional and citybilly performers for demanding and knowledgeable local audiences. The Gaslight, down a few steps in a Mac Dougal Street basement, was the most important of these.

The Gaslight's bias was toward the traditional—when legendary Mississippi bluesman John Hurt was rediscovered, alive and still picking, in 1963, he played there—but it was open as well to a lively batch of eclectic locals: blues singer Dave "Snaker" Ray (who washed dishes at another coffeehouse), Peter Stampfel, Jim Kweskin and his jug band, instrumentalist Sandy Bull, and scores of others. On Tuesday nights—"hootenanny" nights—the microphones were open for brief sets by singers who, if they were unknown, would hurriedly audition backstage for the club's resident singer, Dave Van Ronk.

Van Ronk, Brooklyn-born and mostly Irish, despite the Dutch name, was and is a blues guitarist of awesome technical brilliance. As a teacher, arranger, and drinking buddy, he was perhaps the most influential of early 1960s Village folkies. Largely because of his sense of humor and genial, bearlike stage presence, he was also one of the few essentially traditional performers who regularly reached noncoterie audiences, and his comparative lack of commercial success has long been a puzzle to followers of the music scene. In her 1969 *Rock Encyclopedia*, critic Lillian Roxon (often given to enthusiastic overstatement but rarely to poor judgment) confidently predicted, "*his* time will come." But despite steady growth as a performer (the one-time blues shouter recorded the definitive readings of Joni Mitchell's "Both Sides Now" and of William Butler Yeats's "Song of Wandering Aengus"), it never has.

Around the corner from the Gaslight, a more high-rent, aboveground, and frankly commercial coffeehouse called the Bitter End was the scene for commercial folk's most important debut since the Kingston Trio. In 1961, manager Albert Grossman brought together two modestly established New York singers and a comedian who sang a little to form Peter, Paul and Mary. Peter Yarrow, Mary Travers, and Noel Paul Stookey didn't have the Kingston Trio's immediate success (their debut single, "Lemon Tree," went only to number 35), but as the most popular acoustic group of the 1960s, they had considerably greater longevity. As an indication of their success, their first album was number six on *Cashbox*'s annual list, and a year later, in 1963, they held the number-two and -three spots, beaten out only by the *West Side Story* sound track. From the outset, they were both more polished and more passionate than the Kingston Trio or any of its clones, and they were distinctly more political. In the fall of 1962, their version of Pete Seeger's "If I Had a Hammer" hit number two on the singles charts, bringing protest music firmly into the mainstream, and a year later, they did the same for unknown songwriter Bob Dylan, taking "Blowin' in the Wind" and "Don't Think Twice, It's All Right" into the Top Ten. More overtly activist than any group since the Weavers, they appeared regularly at civil rights and antiwar demonstrations—and unlike the Weavers, they had the enthusiastic support of their record company, Warner Bros.

At that time, Peter, Paul and Mary's only folkie rival in terms of album sales was the extremely unlikely Joan Baez. Baez, who'd been a Boston University student in the late 1950s and had become a favorite at Cambridge's Club 47, was unlikely for a couple of reasons. First, though her political commitments turned out to be at least as deep as Peter, Paul and Mary's, her performing repertoire was almost exclusively traditional; the most "modern" cut on her first album, which was dominated by narrative ballads, was "Wildwood Flower," first recorded by the Carter Family four decades earlier. Second, she recorded for the good-hearted but hitherto obscure New York independent, Vanguard.

Her first recorded effort, actually, had been a few cuts on *Folksingers Round Harvard Square*, released by the independent-shading-into-terminal Veritas label, but her first steps toward national prominence came during the 1959 Newport Folk Festival, when the well-established Chicago folkie Bob Gibson invited her onstage to share a couple of songs with him. Their "Jordan River" duet, recorded on Vanguard's *Newport '59* compilation, was one of the festival's highlights, and despite competition from several major labels, Vanguard, which had first dibs on the Newport tapes, actively and successfully pursued her. In performance, Baez was a startling contrast not only to the standard-model female pop singers (carefully coiffed, made up, calculatedly costumed, and perky) but to the other major female folkie icon, Mary Travers. Trained as an actress, Travers was high energy person-ified, dramatizing her songs and whipping her blond mane from side to side; Baez was self-contained, self-assured, seemed to wear little makeup, and performed in whatever comfortable clothes she'd worn during the day. Alone behind her guitar, she let her achingly pure soprano do the talking for her.

It did so with remarkable success. Her second album, 1961's *Joan Baez 2*, was certified gold, the first album from an independent label to reach that plateau. Its follow-up, *Joan Baez in Concert*, also went gold—both without benefit of a hit single or of discernible radio play. Clearly there was a new audience out there—one that had outgrown rock 'n' roll's teen dreams but was stubbornly refusing to grow into the mainstream "adult" pop of sound tracks, Broadway shows, and Frank Sinatra. Starting in 1963, when she began letting him appear unannounced at her concerts, much as Bob Gibson had introduced her at Newport, Baez began presenting Bob Dylan to that audience.

Dylan came to the Village from Minnesota in January 1961; though he'd sung in a high school rock 'n' roll band, he wanted to meet Woody Guthrie (and he did regularly visit Guthrie both in the New Jersey hospital to which disease had by then pretty much confined him and at weekend song swapping sessions held at a nearby private home). He began performing almost immediately at basket houses and hootenannies and, almost equally immediately, began to find admirers. The admiration was by no means universal, however, for even at that time, Dylan's trademark elusiveness made him hard to place. He wasn't traditional—though his repertoire was almost exclusively folk, he made no attempt at all to duplicate original folk styles. He certainly wasn't commercial—his voice was at once hoarse and nasal, his mumble sometimes impenetrable. He didn't even appear to be much of a songwriter—his original numbers tended to be comic excursions into Guthrie's "talking blues" form.

One thing he was for sure, however, was enormously energetic. Through that winter and spring, it seemed you could hardly go anywhere without Dylan—Huck Finn cap perched on his head, ratty corduroy sports jacket flying—popping up. He sang everywhere, tirelessly, at hoots and basket houses and parties, eventually becoming a regular at Gerdes' Folk City's Monday-night hoots. Of all the folk clubs in America, Gerdes' (by day, a workingman's bar) was probably the most important: it was roomy enough to hold almost three hundred people in comfort, and it had a liquor license, which made it so profitable that owner Mike Porco could afford to bring in major acts (and, occasionally, be shamed into getting the piano tuned or upgrading his sound equipment). Just about everybody worked there at one time or another—gospel, blues, Irish, bluegrass, commercial, Woody's children—and the Monday-night hoots were so well attended and important that when Peter, Paul and Mary were making their first "official" appearance at the Bitter End, they showed up at Gerdes' to do a set during one of their breaks.

In that luminous, if worn, setting, Dylan, touchingly eager to please at that point in his career, was something of a class clown. People tend to forget the comic underpinnings of his performances, but as Van Ronk has recalled, "He did all kinds of little Charlie Chaplin turns. His sense of timing was incredibly good, and he was hilariously funny. He was nervous, he was obviously quaking in his boots, but he used it. He had a kind of herky-jerky patter: a one-liner, long pause, another one-liner, a mutter, a mumble, a slam at the guitar. It was very effective." And all the time, Dylan was learning. He was a sponge, soaking up influences everywhere. He lived with the Van Ronks for a while—and used Van Ronk's arrangement of "House of the Rising Sun" on his first album—but Gerdes', with its parade of established performers, was his grad school.

It was also his placement office. After a successful New York stint as a soloist and in the folk/pop Songspinners (led by Kentucky-born Logan English, who ran Gerdes' Monday-night hoots), Carolyn Hester went to Boston for a long summer booking at Cambridge's Club 47 (her place in the Songspinners was taken by Judy Collins). When Dylan came up for a visit, she not only introduced him for guest sets but arranged for him to play harmonica on the album she was about to cut for Columbia Records. During rehearsals, he met, and intrigued, Columbia A&R man John Hammond, Sr.

Under the torpid leadership of Mitch ("Sing Along with Mitch") Miller, Columbia had been perhaps the stodgiest of major labels, and Hammond, who had produced some legendary Billie Holiday sides, had been brought back to the company specifically to develop performers who might appeal to a younger audience than its aging roster was reaching. His earliest signing, so politically controversial that it served as a ready symbol of the label's new openness, was Pete Seeger. Even before Hester cut her album, Hammond booked Dylan for a demo session.

When they returned to New York in the fall, Mike Porco (with some covert prompting from Albert Grossman, who was beginning to cast a managerial eye his way) booked Dylan for his second paying Gerdes' appearance, this time opening for the Greenbriar Boys. On the day of Hester's session, Dylan burst into the studio waving a copy of that morning's *New York Times*. In it, critic Robert Shelton had given him a rhapsodic review, saying that he was "bursting at the seams with talent," and concluding, "Mr. Dylan is vague about his antecedents and birthplace, but it matters less where he has been than where he is going, and that would appear to be straight up." Adding this imprimatur from the *Times* to his demo tape, Hammond promptly got Columbia to sign Dylan.

Even as these plans were going forward, however, Dylan fell under the spell of yet another member of Gerdes' faculty: Jack Elliott. The eldest son of an eminent Brooklyn physician, Elliott Charles Adnopoz turned himself into a cowboy by sheer force of will. And though Bob Dylan's (née Zimmerman) muttered hints about his travelin' days and ramblin' with Woody didn't ring true (he was barely out of grade school when Guthrie was hospitalized, and the soft, pudgy hands pictured on his first album cover had quite obviously never swung a hammer), Elliott was clearly the next best thing to Guthrie. In 1951, the twenty-year-old Elliott, his cowboy persona already established, had apprenticed himself to the thirty-year-old Guthrie. A year later, he moved with the Guthries to Topanga Canyon in California, where neighbors who dropped in to pick and sing included Frank Hamilton, who would start an influential Chicago music school; singer and collector Guy Carawan; and an Oregon banjo picker, Derroll Adams. After three years, Elliott had turned himself into a frighteningly reasonable facsimile of Guthrie, and in 1955, shortly after Guthrie was hospitalized, Elliott and Adams set out for Europe.

For most of the next six years, Elliott was based in England. There, away from the baleful influence of Joseph McCarthy, the folk revival was flourishing. During the 50s, Woody Guthrie even made the British charts a couple of times, courtesy of Lonnie Donegan, who added a simple shuffling rhythm section to his and other traditional songs in the skiffle music style then popular in England. Elliott, first as a living equivalent of Guthrie, later as a performer who'd found his own persona, established himself with Adams as a regular at London's Roundhouse. The small but influential Old Compton Street club was booked by Alexis Korner and Cyril Davies, godfathers of the British blues revival, but was open to every variety of folkie. Elliott, working with a flat pick and using a modified Carter Family lick, was a revelation to the strumming skifflers, and Scots traditional singer Alex Campbell has described him as "the biggest influence on guitar in this country." Though he charted no British singles, he recorded a half-dozen albums, most of which remained in print for more than ten years.

By the time he returned to New York in 1961, Elliott was a polished and seasoned performer who quickly moved to the top of the bill at Gerdes' and the Gaslight. His influence on Dylan was immediate and apparent (though

Dylan was sometimes at pain to deny it, he wound up tipping his hat to Elliott some fifteen years later, when Elliott was part of Dylan's Rolling Thunder tour). Israel Young, who ran the Folklore Center and produced Dylan's first uptown concert (the dismal, money-losing Carnegie Recital hall affair, held in November of 1961, drew fewer than sixty people; Young was always ahead of his time) described the show as Dylan doing "so many Jack Elliott things, even raising his leg the way Jack did, using those Elliott mannerisms, and using practically all Elliott material."

The Elliott phase, like the Van Ronk phase, and the Guthrie phase before it, eventually passed in the wake of yet another exciting import from England. Late in 1961, while his conviction on ten counts of contempt of Congress was still pending, Pete Seeger set off on a long English tour.* During the tour, he was struck by the number of folk songs (more precisely, folk-type songs) being written about contemporary events. A lot of these, developed along the famous Aldermaston peace marches, were ban the bomb–oriented; others focused on specific local events. Seeger returned to the States full of enthusiasm for a vehicle that would foster a similar American outpouring, and eventually he persuaded (and partly funded) Sis Cunningham, who'd worked with the Seeger-Guthrie Almanac Singers back in the pre-Weavers days, to start a mimeographed magazine of topical songs. It was called *Broadside*, and it was published biweekly; a year's subscription, twenty-two issues, cost five dollars.

Gil Turner, another Gerdes' regular, was named co-editor, and he tirelessly rounded up work from local singers, more often than not bringing the singers themselves uptown to the *Broadside* office near Columbia University, where they tried out their new songs on each other. Regulars included Phil Ochs, a recent escapee from the Ohio State journalism program who was doing a "singing newspaper" in a Village coffeehouse; Len Chandler, a classically trained oboist who'd played in the Akron Symphony and was the only black in the group; Peter La Farge, at thirty-one the old man, the adoptive son of Pulitzer Prize–winning novelist Oliver La Farge (*Laughing Boy*), who often drew on his Indian heritage; Tom Paxton, a middle-class Oklahoman who'd come to New York seeking an acting career; and Dylan. Spurred by the carrot of a regularly published forum and the stick of competition, songs—"Masters of War," "Blowin' in the Wind," "I Will Not Go Down Under the Ground," "Only A Hobo"—poured from Dylan; all but two cuts on his first album had been traditional, but his second contained only originals.

Seeger was, of course, delighted by *Broadside's* success, for virtually all the writers were as prolific, if not as skilled, as Dylan, and the result was a topical song explosion the likes of which hadn't been seen since the great union-organizing period three decades earlier. He characterized the writ-

---

*Seeger's conviction, later reversed, resulted from his 1955 refusal to cooperate with one of the various showy House Un-American Activities Committee hearings.

ers, fondly, as "Woody's children," and at least for a while, the left-wing populist streak in American music burst from the gray-flannel restraints of the Eisenhower years.

The politics was more than theoretical. The Village citybillies had been directly involved in protest actions as well as protest songs the previous summer, when a New York City parks commissioner, worried by the growing size of the crowds, tried to end the fifteen-year tradition of folk music in Washington Square. Singing picket lines had regularly surrounded his home and office until the antiguitar ruling was rescinded. More serious doings, however, were going on in the American South, as the civil rights movement continued to gather strength. Though music had not been a direct force in the original Montgomery, Alabama, bus boycott of 1955 and 1956 (the indirect importance of hymns and spirituals in the church-centered boycott was obvious), "freedom songs" began to come to the fore in the wake of 1960 lunch-counter sit-ins. At a sympathy demonstration, students from Fisk University turned the R&B tune "You Better Leave My Kitten Alone" into a mocking "You better leave desegregation alone."

The new wave of music differed from the old, lined-out, "long-meter" hymns, drawing instead on pop, blues, and modern gospel records. A surprisingly large number of songs were variations on white gospel tunes that had been used in union-organizing drives in the South during the 1930s. The main source for these seems to have been the Highlander Folk School, founded in Tennessee in 1932 as an offshoot of the Cumberland Presbyterian Church. Originally designed to teach local residents about agricultural co-ops, the school became heavily involved in the union movement; quite remarkably, for the time, all the programs it ran were integrated, and it was natural that the network of trained organizers who'd been at Highlander rapidly involved themselves in the burgeoning civil rights movement. In 1959, Highlander brought Woody Guthrie's Topanga Canyon neighbor Guy Carawan back to the South, sending out 6,000 letters to Highlander associates offering Carawan's services as a song leader to any organization that was working for integration. Laboring almost without pause over the next two years, Carawan carried songs like "Which Side Are You On," the Pete Seeger–Lee Hayes "Hammer Song," and the Almanac Singers' "I'm On My Way" with him.

Through his Guthrie-Seeger connections, Carawan also brought a trail of Northern singers into the South. Among the best known who sang at rallies and churches were Josh White, Jr.; actor Theodore Bikel; Dylan; Baez; Paxton; Chandler; Ochs; Peter, Paul and Mary; and, of course, Seeger himself. During the "freedom summers" (1964–65), when black and white college students from Northern campuses poured into the South to work as civil rights volunteers, these established singers were supplemented by hundreds of unknown amateurs. When Peter, Paul and Mary's 1963 recording of Dylan's "Blowin' in the Wind" broke through onto traditional Southern R&B stations and became an unofficial civil rights anthem, the identification of the folkies with the politics of progress was cemented. At that year's March on Washington, where Reverend Martin Luther King, Jr., gave his classic "I have a dream" speech, the musical performers included Dylan; Baez; Odetta; Peter, Paul and Mary; and Harry Belafonte.

Though the music industry continued trying to capitalize on the folk boom, the music's implicit and explicit politics made many major corporations nervous, and a lot of effort went into developing purveyors of impersonal, squeaky-clean folk pop like the Serendipity Singers and the New Christy Minstrels, whose commitment to the music as other than a paying proposition seemed minimal in the extreme.*

The sanitized performers were the major beneficiaries when folk music made its television debut in the summer of 1963, as ABC unveiled its weekly "Hootenanny" show. Televised from a different college campus each week, "Hootenanny" started strong (for a while, it was the network's second-rated program), but after the producers refused to let Pete Seeger appear because he wouldn't sign a "loyalty oath" to the American government, many major performers—Dylan, Baez, the Kingston Trio, and Peter, Paul and Mary among them—refused in principle to appear on the show, and it soon ran out of gas.

For a while, however, *hootenanny* was a magic word, and more than a hundred albums (thrown-together compilations, mostly) emblazoned with the term were released in less than a year. The silliest effort, perhaps, was a movie called *Hootenanny Hoot*, in which Johnny Cash, the Brothers Four, and the Gateway Trio labored through a saga about a brave director who comes up with the idea of putting hootenannies on television. ("I like it," says his assistant, "but will it sell soap?" To which Dylan, in an interview, responded, "We're not singing folk songs in order to sell soap. Hell, we don't even buy soap.")

Even without the benefits of television (and/or soap), the uneasy alliance of topical and traditional musicians continued to find large and receptive audiences. In the summer of 1963, major folk festivals were held in Mountain View, Arkansas; Brandeis University in Waltham, Massachusetts; Monterey, California; Covington, Kentucky; Asheville, North Carolina; Berkeley; Ontario and New Brunswick in Canada; Philadelphia; Pasadena; and, before fifty thousand fans on a July weekend, Newport, Rhode Island. Despite the bland blandishments of "Hootenanny," a large and restive audience was looking for something *real*.There were, however, a couple of aspects of this audience that troubled even those most sympathetic to its tastes. The first was its self-conscious sense of superiority to those (blacks and lower-class whites, to a large extent) who loved rock 'n' roll. The second was that the fondness for traditional music was an artificial, and to some extent unnatural, construction. No less committed a folkie than Sing

---

*The New Christy Minstrels first charted with Woody Guthrie's "This Land Is Your Land" in 1962; their final appearance, three years later, was with a song from Walt Disney's *Mary Poppins*.

Out! editor Irwin Silber addressed this in a prophetic 1964 article on the University of Chicago's tradition-centered folk festival:

Where an earlier generation marched for Spain or sang for the CIO, today's "protester" apparently believes that direct action is hopeless and foredoomed to frustrating failure. (Only the civil rights movement of recent years seems to have given rise to an activist protest on the campus.) Accordingly, a sizable body of nonconformist opinion which might once have found itself on the intellectual barricades is today finding its outlet in a highly-stylized, unlettered, individualistic folk music. . . . Perhaps this is both the strength and weakness of this devotion to traditional music. No art can truly flourish outside of its own time and place—and in the long run, college students (along with the rest of us) will have to find a means of expression which is uniquely of our own age.

In the extremely unlikely event that he read *Sing Out!* Brian Epstein would no doubt have agreed with Silber, for late in 1963, he was preparing to offer the youth of America a music for its own time. A scant couple of years earlier, in October 1961, he'd been sitting in his Nems Music Store in Liverpool when a local kid walked in and asked if he had a record called "My Bonnie" by a band called the Beatles. He'd almost certainly heard of the group, but he didn't have the record; since he prided himself on having an exhaustive stock, he tracked down the import disc and, according to all the official accounts, only then "discovered" that they, too, were from Liverpool. A couple of weeks later, when the band was booked for a lunchtime show at the Cavern Club, he went to see them.

At the time, Liverpool was a pop oasis in a sea of derivative sludge. If in America, at least for a while, the critical social divisions seemed to involve race (and perhaps age), in England, class was all. The viciously efficient winnowing system—some few went to public (i.e., private) school and Oxbridge; most went to state schools, where a national system of examinations (the 11-plus) further separated them into white collar and blue collar—virtually guaranteed that every English child would wind up doing pretty much what his or her parents had. And even those middle-class kids who struggled through the "red brick" provincial universities and got to go to work in the City, London's financial district, were forever distinguished from their betters by their accents. With very few exceptions indeed, the proper British accent was born, not made.

As Orwell had revealed in *Keep the Aspidistra Flying,* the strict hierarchy meant that working-class culture was painfully undervalued—by the working classes themselves. Not only success but even self-esteem depended on how close a family could come to a sort of thrice-removed gentility. And especially because that distant cultural model controlled the airwaves in the monopoly form of the BBC, there was little indigenous, celebratory music analogous to white America's rockabilly or country and western—and naturally, given the island's racial makeup, no blues or R&B worth mentioning.

Though there was, as Seeger had noticed, a lively topical song movement, this was largely supported by middle- and upper-class renegades, and despite some consciously political support from trade unions, its chief appeal was to bohemians and peace marchers. It was, however, specifically English (or, since Scots like Ewan MacColl and Alex Campbell were in its forefront, British), and it foreshadowed, in its harking back to English tradition, the Tolkienesque streak that would later distinguish British psychedelia from its American counterpart.

Translated, via skiffle, to the pop charts by Lonnie Donegan, the music showed considerable, if sexless, energy, and Donegan was one of the very few British chart makers to achieve any transatlantic success. Except for skiffle, however, the BBC's tasteful arbiters relentlessly filtered out anything resembling a rude, barbaric yawp, and pre-Beatles British rock 'n' roll was as pallid and derivative as the antimacassar-dotted middle-class parlor. Americans—Elvis, Del Shannon, the Everly Brothers—dominated the rock 'n' roll scene for the very sound reason that their British imitators (Cliff Richard, Adam Faith, the Shadows) were by any reasonable comparison bloodless and joyless.

"Proper" Liverpool, undistinguished and indistinguishable, fit the standard British mold. Gray, economically depressed, and provincial, the seaport city had a small upper class supporting a road-show culture that was a pale imitation of London's. But there was another Liverpool: working-class, Irish, Labour, scouse, chapel. Within it, a rock 'n' roll culture flourished, fed by the seaport city's cyclical inundation by American merchant seamen and their records. The Beatles (John Lennon, Paul McCartney, George Harrison, and, when Epstein first saw them, Pete Best on drums) combined the ebullient self-confidence of skiffle (which they'd started playing as the Quarrymen) with the raw energies of that imported culture and a club-steeped toughness developed during several tours in the even rougher German port city of Hamburg. Epstein (well known enough in local music circles that he got a hand when introduced after the Cavern show) thought they were "not very tidy and not very clean," but he arranged to meet with them.

They thought he was "posh," which by their council-house standard, he was. But the British establishment would hardly have agreed. He had gone to public school—the first in his family—but hadn't gone on to Oxford or Cambridge. Besides, he was a Jew and, though closeted, a homosexual; in ways that they couldn't at the time understand, he was as much an outsider as they. And if his attraction to the leather-jacketed boys was shaped by repressed sexuality, there is little doubt that he also saw them as an instrument that could smash through the barriers of British caste and class.

He was right. True, he booked them skillfully, engineered Best's departure in favor of Ringo Starr, and introduced them to the right record companies at the right time, but the throngs of screaming girls weren't cheering for the band's management. It was the force of their music and their personalities that created the unlikely phenomenon the newspapers, with some prompting from Epstein, began to call Beatlemania. The screaming, the fainting, the attempts to rip souvenirs from their idols' clothes were decidedly un-British—and unlikely for another reason as well. The *Observer*, that bellwether of proper sensibility, said it all when it quoted a fourteen-year-old London girl: "You usually think of film stars, pop singers, and so forth as living in glamorous places, Hollywood and so on. But the Beatles aren't like that. It's *Liverpool*—where *Z-cars* comes from."

If the trip from the Liverpool slums to London seemed difficult, the voyage from London to America was even harder, for transatlantic pop traffic was traditionally one-way. American rock 'n' rollers from Del Shannon on had regularly toured England and climbed onto the British charts, but British stars like Billy Fury tended to sound like pallid imitations of Elvis (or even Fabian) and almost universally flopped in the States. Indeed, it looked for a while as though this would be as true for the Beatles as it was for, say, Cliff Richard and the Shadows. Capitol, a major American record company that, as an EMI subsidiary, had first option on the Beatles' British releases, listened to "Please Please Me" and "From Me to You" and decided not to bother with the band. So the songs appeared, to virtually no attention at all, on a small Chicago indie, Vee-Jay records. After neither cracked the top 100, Vee-Jay lost interest as well, and "She Loves You"—up to that point, the largest-selling single record in British history—was released with similarly disappointing results on the even smaller and less powerful Swan label.

To all outward appearances, however, Epstein retained total confidence. When he came to New York to kick off the band's American campaign, he did it in style, taking a suite at the Regency and spending some two thousand pounds—at a time when the band was still filling old bookings at the decidedly pre-Beatlemania fees of fifty and sixty pounds a night. It was from that base that he struck a deal with Ed Sullivan.

The Sunday night "Ed Sullivan Show" was in many ways silly—lots of dog acts from European circuses—but it was phenomenally popular, and even a one-time appearance could confer or ratify stardom. Sullivan had done it for Elvis, and he could do it for the Beatles. And unlike most Americans, Sullivan had seen Beatlemania firsthand, when he happened to be at London airport as crowds nearly rioted to welcome the band back from a Stockholm trip. As he told the *New York Times*, "I made up my mind that this was the sort of mass hysteria that had characterized the Elvis Presley days," and he wasn't going to miss out on it. He booked them—with top billing—for three weeks in a row. He also did it for $2,400 a show, a little less than half his going rate for major attractions, a most persuasive indication of where—a scant two months before the Beatles were to capture America—the power lay in the Sullivan-Epstein negotiations.

Capitol Records, after some prompting from its parent company, began to take the band more seriously and agreed to release "I Want to Hold Your Hand." But Epstein, used to the BBC's total domination of the British airwaves, was leery of the sprawling U.S. market, so he began to woo the press on his own. Partly because of Epstein's charm, he did well indeed with the anglophiles, spreading the word of Beatlemania in the *New York Times Magazine* and the *New Yorker*, a publication that most emphatically did not pay much attention to rock 'n' roll. Britain had fallen to the Beatles in the traditional way—the band had scrabbled through hundreds of gigs in grimy venues and had won the loyalty of England's teens well before the Queen Mother noticed them, much less pronounced them "cute." If America—where class barriers, though not generation gaps, were less rigid—was going to go at all, it was going to go at once.

Capitol, in the way that giant record companies do when they smell tonnage, began to stir. When "I Want to Hold Your Hand" was released on January 13, Capitol got the djs to play it, but the kids who heard it and called up to ask for more were the final convincer. Suddenly realizing that these funny-looking kids might make it, the company came up with a $50,000 promotional budget—an unheard-of sum in those days—and hired a squad of Epstein-approved publicity men to drum up interest in the band's arrival. Djs in major markets got special promo kits, including a record that would allow each of them to conduct "exclusive" interviews with the lovable moptops, and New York City lamp posts suddenly began sporting "THE BEATLES ARE COMING" stickers.

Once the ice broke, the phenomenon began to gather speed. If the Beatles were indeed going to be the next big thing, no radio station wanted to be left out. They hyped the Beatles—and played "I Want to Hold Your Hand"— almost in self-defense. Four days after the record was released, it was number one on the *Cashbox* chart; it took two weeks longer for it to dislodge Bobby Vinton from atop the more conservative *Billboard* listings. And as the Beatles' plane neared New York on February 11, 1963, the area's fiercely competitive pop-music stations were vying to become *the* Beatle station. Not surprisingly, they filled the air with information about the band's incoming flight. And not surprisingly, kids began to gather at the airport.

Tom Wolfe, then a New York *Herald-Tribune* reporter, was at the airport as well. He estimated the crowd at four thousand; the *New York Times* said three. Whatever the size, it took more than a hundred of New York's Finest to keep the screaming girls from dismembering their idols on the spot. When the Beatles went inside a small waiting room to give what would become the standard Beatles-arrive-at-airport interviews, Wolfe noted that "some of the girls tried to throw themselves over a retaining wall."

At their initial airport press conference, the band lived up to Epstein's fondest hopes, delighting the American reporters. Asked to account for the group's success, John explained, "We have a press agent." And Wolfe quoted John (who was actually Ringo, but no matter, they all looked alike) in response to a question about what they thought of Beethoven, "He's crazy. Especially the poems. Lovely writer." All in all, most reporters agreed with the *New York Times*, which decided that "the Beatles wit was contagious," and there wasn't a negative story in the bunch.

Granted, the above examples of "Beatles wit" may seem modestly less scintillating twenty years on, but it's important to remember how much the Beatles, Dylan, and their sixties successors shaped our expectations of popular musicians. Bobby-soxers had screamed for Sinatra, and Elvis's hips had mesmerized a nation, but no one had taken their ideas seriously—or, for that matter, cared if they had any. Even when they were singing, and at their most intellectually persuasive (Sinatra's "House I Live In," for example, a film of which was used to cool high-school racial tensions), their words came from somewhere else. The Beatles sang their own songs, spoke their own thoughts. The folkies expected this as a matter of course from a Phil Ochs, but this was the first time that expectation had gone national. The resulting shock wasn't because the Beatles were always intelligent or witty, but that they ever were. Sure, they had to throw themselves over a retaining wall of media skepticism, but the wall was powerful low.

Buoyed by this flurry of favorable coverage, the band made their live American debut on Sullivan's February 9 show (*live* debut because NBC's Jack Paar, in a mini-coup, had aired a clip of a Bournemouth concert nine days earlier). There were more than 50,000 requests for the studio's 728 seats, and some 73 *million* Americans saw the show on television. Little wonder that the band's first American album, Capitol's *Meet the Beatles*, was at the top of *Billboard*'s February 15 album chart. Before the month was out, the Beatles, for the first time in the magazine's history, would have five singles simultaneously on the *Billboard* "Hot 100" charts, and the Lowell Toy Company, the Epstein-approved manufacturer of "official" Beatle wigs, was cranking out fifteen thousand a day.

Still, "grown-ups" took them more seriously as a sociological rather than as a musical phenomenon. The *New York Times* critic who reviewed their Lincoln's Birthday Carnegie Hall concert wrote almost exclusively about the shrieking audience, not even naming individual songs but referring to them as "the first," "the second," "the next," and so on. There were exceptions, however. In Anthony Scaduto's biography, *Dylan*, the singer describes a 1964 cross-country drive, with early Beatles all over the AM band: "They were doing things nobody else was doing. Their chords were outrageous, just outrageous, and their harmonies made it all valid. You could only do that with other musicians. Even if you're playing your own chords, you had to have other people playing with you. That was obvious. And it started me thinking about other people.

"But I just kept it to myself that I really dug them. Everybody else thought they were just for the teenyboppers, that they were gonna pass right away. But it was obvious to me that they had staying power. I knew they were pointing the direction where music had to go."

Before it got to where Dylan imagined it, however, pop music would make more than a few detours and retrogressions. Though the Beatles left America in late February and wouldn't return until August, they stayed on top of the singles chart until the second week in May. They were then knocked out of the box by Louis Armstrong's "Hello, Dolly" and Mary Wells's "My Guy," but they ended the month on top again with "Love Me Do." In the wake of their success, the American rock 'n' roll scene became an explosion of imported adventure. It all happened fast, too. A bare three days after the Beatles' Carnegie Hall appearance, a *Billboard* headline bannered, "U.S. ROCKS & REELS FROM BEATLES INVASION—BEATLES BEGIN NEW BRITISH ARTIST PUSH." With only modest exaggeration, the accompanying article proclaimed that "Great Britain hasn't been so influential on American affairs since 1775." Running desperately along behind the Beatles, every American company that could either signed or licensed performers who were (1) English, (2) male, (3) groups, and (4) long-haired. Among those already in the bag were Freddie and the Dreamers, Cliff Richard and the Shadows, Billy J. Kramer and the Dakotas, the Searchers, the Dave Clark Five, and Gerry and the Pacemakers. Still at large: the Hollies and the Rolling Stones.

Most of those scooped up in the initial burst of checkbook-waving could be categorized as beat groups. Despite the musical sophistication (and British commercial success) they'd achieved, they were, in the best sense of the phrase, "garage bands," enthusiastically imitative bashers whose dominant model was American pop. The Beatles themselves had discussed being influenced, vocally, by the Four Seasons' harmonies, and no one could fail to hear Buddy Holly, Chuck Berry, and Little Richard lurking in the background. In fact, one of the still charming features of records made by beat groups after the Beatles breakthrough is the sheer joy at being alive, being heard, being *rich* that fairly jumps off their grooves. That's probably why those who'd had the greatest pre-Beatle success in England—Cliff Richard and Billy J. Kramer—failed to make it big in America; they were too grown up, too *afraid*.

This is not a charge that could be levelled with any plausibility against the Dave Clark Five, whose "Glad All Over" signaled the British Invasion when it hit the American charts less than a week after the Beatles' initial Ed Sullivan appearance, eventually climbing to number six. Clark's band had formed in a London suburb, a couple of years earlier, when its members— members first of the Tottenham Hotspurs Supporters Club—were trying to raise money to follow the Spurs to Holland for a match. Though pianist Mike Smith, a year younger than Clark, was by most accounts the group's most sophisticated musician, Clark became leader by force of his personality. He became drummer because no one else was.

History thus confirms what internal evidence had amply suggested: Clark hadn't been behind a drum kit for very long when the band started recording. Indeed, if he hadn't been managing and producing the group himself, it's entirely possible that a studio musician would have taken over the percussion during recordings (as happened, for instance, to Ringo from time to time). This would have robbed the Dave Clark Five of its most—and maybe only—distinguishing feature, however, for Clark's chops were so rudimentary that he could do little more than keep the beat. And keep it he did, loudly. *Time* compared it to an air hammer, but it worked: "Bumpa-bumpa *wham-wham*, 'Glad all over'/bumpa-bumpa *wham-wham*, 'Glad all over.' " The sound hit, and it stuck. From 1964 to 1966, Dave Clark Five singles would crack the American charts eighteen times; seven of them—including a 1965 number one, "Over and Over"—would reach the Top Ten.

Initially the band's American label, Epic, had promoted them as "The Mersey Sound With the Liverpool Beat." This was, shall we say, misleading; the Dave Clark Five was London All Over, and the differences between the two cities were more than merely geographical. But Liverpool was hot, so no matter. Shortly before the Beatles left for America, however, the inevitable happened; "I Want to Hold Your Hand" finally fell from the number-one position on the U.K. singles charts. By then, it had set national sales records, and just about everyone who might conceivably have bought it had done so. It was succeeded, briefly but unquestionably, by "Glad All Over," and Epic found itself blessed with "the band that knocked the Beatles off the charts." Suddenly, prompted by alert publicists, "Glad All Over" migrated rapidly south and became "the Tottenham sound," which, according to one Epic press release, was "on its way towards overthrowing the reign of the Beatles in this country as well."

In the event, the spurious "Tottenham" sound didn't overthrow anything. The commodious American market had room for all comers, it seemed, and initially, non-London groups, especially those with imaginable links to Liverpool, dominated. At extreme ends of the spectrum, Liverpool produced both the Searchers and the Swingin' Blue Jeans. The Searchers formed in 1961, originally as a backup group for Johnny Sandon, a poppish, well-regarded local singer who never cracked the British top twenty. Soon they were on their own. Like most serious Liverpool beat groups, they worked the Hamburg scene; virtually alone among them, however, they resisted the rave-up urge, concentrating instead on gentle four-part vocal harmonies and chiming guitars. Both were prominent in their first British hit, a cover of the Drifters' "Sweets for My Sweet," that went to number one during the summer of 1963. The song didn't chart in the States, but in 1964, when they were genuine, certified Liverpudlians, the Searchers hit with "Needles and Pins."

Though it didn't go Top Ten in the States (peaking at number thirteen), it would become a major influence. The song was very much a pop artifact (written by Sonny Bono and Jack Nitzsche), but the overall sound of strummed guitars prefigures what was to become folk-rock; listen to the Searchers and you can almost hear the Byrds around the bend. Perhaps because their sound was more restrained than their Liverpudlian peers', the Searchers were either ahead of their time or behind it, and the group never really hit big in the States. ("Love Potion Number Nine," which became their only U.S. Top Ten record late in 1964, was a novelty number.) The fans who'd discovered—who worshipped—the Beatles wanted something more energetic than the Searchers. In the Swingin' Blue Jeans, they got everything they wanted.

Well, maybe *too* much. Though the Hamburg tapes proved that the Beatles could chug all night if they had to, their early recordings were relatively restrained: not so folkish as the Searchers, surely, but easy on the rave-ups. By contrast, the Swingin' Blue Jeans were *all* rave-up. Their high-energy "Hippie Hippie Shake," an overwhelm-the-drunken-sailors-in-Hamburg survival number if ever there was one, was a U.K. number two early in 1964, but it stalled at number twenty-four in America. Later that year, when "You're No Good" (U.K. number three) died at ninety-seven, it became clear that the Blue Jeans would be listed among the invaders' casualties.

The other successful acts emerging from Liverpool—Billy J. Kramer and Gerry and the Pacemakers—were notably more decorous than the Swingin' Blue Jeans. Kramer, indeed, was more crooner than rocker, and neither his Liverpool history nor the fact that he, like the Beatles, was managed by Brian Epstein could make him sound less old-fashioned; his first visit to the United States Top Ten, the double-sided "Little Children,"/"Bad to Me," was also his last. He was not without talent, but he'd spent too much time reining it in and making it acceptable to the BBC. The Liverpool connection gave him his one anachronistic hit; then the Liverpool energies displayed by other groups denied him any follow-ups.

Gerry and the Pacemakers, on the other hand, could hardly be more representative of the beat groups. Also managed by Epstein, they had once been genuine rivals of the Beatles, playing the Cavern and the Hamburg clubs and, at least initially, doing better on the charts. Their first three releases, also produced by George Martin, yielded three U.K. number-one hits during 1963; the Beatles hadn't gone number one until their third record. Live, the Pacemakers were somewhere between ingratiating and manic, dominated by lead singer Gerry Marsden's shameless eagerness to please. He cavorted and contorted like a Blackpool music hall compere, but jumped just a little higher, postured a bit more outrageously. Little of this came through on the group's records, however. These had, instead, a sound that was part Liverpool, part Martin: the guitars rang, the vocal harmonies were clean but conventional, and the energy levels were guaranteed not to frighten. If the Beatles hadn't been geniuses—or maybe just cantankerous and assertive—they could have been Gerry and the Pacemakers.

In which case the British invasion would have been only what it at first appeared to be: a fad—something of interest only to pubescent girls, and then not for long. Consider, for only a slightly briefer period than their original stardom, Freddie and the Dreamers, a Manchester group so evanescent as to make Gerry and the Pacemakers appear adamantine. Ex-milkman Freddie Garrity, who managed to look a little silly even when standing still, looked even sillier when he danced—which he did frequently—with the stiff-jointed semaphoring of a speed-crazed marionnette. Behind him, thuggish, balding, but gamely doing unison leg kicks, stood the Dreamers. The sound—"I'm Telling You Now" and the even more forgettable dance tune "Do the Freddie"—was bright and cheery, but it was also skiffle-cum-music-hall, rock only by courtesy. With the exception of the Hollies, who were such versatile, fashionable chameleons that they could almost be said to have had no individual style at all, the same music hall/skiffle history informed the other first-wave groups: the talented but aimless Wayne Fontana and the Mindbenders and the perpetually pubescent Herman's Hermits (of whom more later).

The one exception to this relentless sunniness—and a stunning exception it was, too—came out of Newcastle upon Tyne by way of Greenwich Village and the American South. In the summer of 1964, "House of the Rising Sun," recorded by the Animals, became the second post-Beatle British single to go number one in America. In doing so, it broke virtually every possible pop-music rule. To begin with, there was its subject matter: New Orleans whorehouses were not the stuff teen hits were made of. And then there was its length: at four and a half minutes, it challenged every radio playlist on both continents. Finally, there was its sound. The other first-wave bands, following in the Beatles' wake, were guitar-oriented and featured vocal harmonies whose ringing chords were—at the very least, though they could be more—unfailingly pretty. And unambiguously white. Instrumentally the Animals featured Alan Price's moody, threatening organ; vocally they were defined by Eric Burdon's full-bore moan: hoarse, gritty, impassioned, and in thrall to half-forgotten black styles.

Their history differed from the popcentric beat groups' as well; a full six years before "House of the Rising Sun" became a hit, sixteen-year-old Alan Price formed the first of many Alan Price Combos. He was eventually joined by bassist Chas Chandler (who would later "discover" and manage Jimi Hendrix) and by John Steel on drums. The three were working local clubs as a jazz trio when, in 1962, they added vocalist Eric Burdon and guitarist Hilton Valentine and metamorphosed into the Animals (actually they attempted to call themselves the Kansas City Five, but their commonsensical Geordie audiences knew a bunch of animals when they saw it). As the name change indicated, they were no longer purely Price's band but an R&B

collective. Partly because of Burdon's dominating personality and front-man role, they would never quite resolve the tensions resulting from the first change (Price himself left the band late in 1965, followed in short order by Steel, Valentine, and Chandler), but the band handled the second brilliantly: though they allowed Burdon's voice and self-created negritude full play, Price remained their internal A&R man. It was he who—long before most Britons had even heard the singer's name—lifted and reshaped both "Baby, Let Me Follow You Down" and "House of the Rising Sun" from Bob Dylan's first album. These were not only showstoppers in their club act but the first two songs they recorded.

A couple of years later, this sort of music would be called folk-rock, but neither the Animals nor manager-producer Mickie Most had a name for it at the time. Indeed, Mickie Most couldn't get "House" through the EMI bureaucracy until after the first Dylan borrowing had achieved some—though not top twenty—U.K. chart success. But the second release was a genuine monster—a transatlantic number one—and the Animals whisked to a weeklong gig at the Paramount Theater on Broadway in New York. There most of the things that would subsequently be said about the Rolling Stones were said about them: They were funny-looking, rude, and didn't quite look clean. But they knew how to put on a show; with the roly-poly Burdon posturing and screaming out front, they churned through the R&B repertoire they'd distilled in Manchester's clubs. Even then they were doing their wired version of John Lee Hooker's "Boom Boom," a song that by rights should have been their second giant hit when it was released later that year. It was, however, a little too bluesy for pop audiences (as well as a lot less ambiguous than "Rising Sun"), and it stalled at number forty-three.

Though the original lineup of Animals would never return to the United States Top Ten, they had two major influences on the pop scene that would follow them. The most obvious was that as a blues-based British band that was definitely not "cute," they opened the door the Stones and the other second-wave invaders would later waltz through. The second occurred in May of 1964, when Dylan was on tour in England. Not only did he meet the Beatles and turn them on to dope (not an insignificant moment in its own right), he heard the Animals' version of "Rising Sun." According to Anthony Scaduto's Dylan biography, he was floored by it, telling a friend on his return, "My God, ya oughtta hear what's going down over there. Eric Burdon, the Animals, ya know? Well, he's doing 'House of the Rising Sun' in rock. *Rock!* It's fuckin' *wild!* Blew my mind." Soon he would be bringin' it all back home.

While Burdon and others were bringing older black styles to the white, mainstream market, home-grown black music would suffer. Traditional R&B had drawn on a broader audience than most rock 'n' roll. Many black performers, particularly those depending on Brill Building material, sang occasional "teenage" songs, but the R&B market had never divided along the unbridgeable generational fissure Elvis and the early rock 'n' rollers had opened in the market. Most of its songs were ageless, and some, like Ben E. King's "Spanish Harlem," Sam Cooke's "Bring It on Home to Me," or the Miracles' "You've Really Got a Hold on Me," were timeless as well. In 1964, however, when pop sales depended on a Brit-crazed teenage audience, race became commercially critical.

Even before rock 'n' roll, there had been black singers who scored well with white audiences—Nat "King" Cole and the Mills Brothers, for example—but rock 'n' roll had opened white airwaves to black performers in an unprecedented way. Whether the reasons involved taste (Alan Freed), personal financial consideration (Freed again), or, once the ball had gotten rolling, a fear that listeners might defect to traditional R&B stations (Freed's frantically scrambling followers), mainstream radio djs began to pepper their playlists with black performers. And since record buyers bought what they heard on their radios, the number of black artists with Top Ten pop hits increased by more than 50 percent from 1955 to 1963. In that last pre-Beatles year, 37 of the 106 Top Ten records were by blacks, mostly performers such as the Miracles, Sam Cooke, the Marvelettes, Marvin Gaye, and the Impressions, who didn't, except in certain novelty tunes, condescend to "sing white." The British invasion threatened to wipe out that hard-won foothold, to remove the Copa-as-nirvana from well within the performers' grasps and substitute once again the chitlin-circuit grind.

The numbers were depressing. In 1964, only 21 of 101 Top Ten singles were by black artists, the lowest percentage since 1956. Most of this displacement—which began to chip away at certain styles of white pop as well, virtually eliminating country crossovers—was imported from across the Atlantic. In 1963, not a single British record had reached the U.S. Top Ten: a year later, nearly a third (31 of 101) belonged to the British. In that first year of the British invasion, only 2 records by black artists—Louis Armstrong's "Hello Dolly!" and "My Guy" by Motown's Mary Wells—made the Top Ten in *Cashbox*'s annual compilation of hit singles. Motown would recover—in a big way—a year later, but in 1964, for the first time in the company's history, its number of Top Ten singles declined from the year before. This was not a situation likely to sit well with Berry Gordy, Jr.

Pop had had its "geniuses" before Gordy—Colonel Tom Parker and Brian Epstein were promotional wonder workers—but none had his scope. A younger son in an extraordinarily close-knit Detroit family that had made the trek North from Georgia because they were *too* successful (and had, justifiably, grown fearful of the Klan), Gordy had entered the music business as a retailer, but he scored his first success as a songwriter, crafting "Reet Petite (The Finest Girl You Ever Want to Meet)" for Jackie Wilson. He became, however, far more than that. As the founder and hands-on leader of the Motown group of labels, Gordy was arranger, producer, A&R man, entrepreneur, and, eventually, America's foremost black capitalist.

He was also the leader of a corporate family every bit as close-knit as the Gordys, but for all that these ties were real—and testified to by the hundreds of blacks and whites who worked at the company during its early years—they didn't bind nearly as thoroughly as the contractual arrangements Gordy devised for his artists. Typically their royalty accounts were cross-collateralized—that is to say, Motown performers signed as songwriters on Gordy's Jobete publishing arm, so their recording costs were charged against their songwriting royalties—and salaries were routinely accounted as advances against subsequent royalties. And though personal managers or outside lawyers might have warned performers away from such contracts, Motown acts didn't *have* outside managers; their careers were directed by Gordy's International Talent Management, Inc.

The loss of freedom was real, but so were the services Gordy provided. He expected his artists to achieve (as he had), be loyal (as his family was), and crack the racial barriers that had also stood in his way. To an astonishing degree, they did. He also expected them to finish high school. Gordy himself had dropped out in the eleventh grade, later earning a high-school equivalency degree in the army.

All these expectations-cum-demands shaped the group that led the company's post-Beatles recovery—and the commercial resurgence of black pop. The Supremes (originally Florence Ballard, Mary Wilson, Barbara Martin, and Betty Travis) got their start in Detroit's Brewster-Douglass housing projects in 1959. Early on, Flo Ballard was their unquestioned leader; it was her big rich voice that attracted Eddie Kendricks and Paul Williams (of the then-Primes, soon to be Temptations), and they encouraged the girls, who started calling themselves the Primettes, to sing at their shows. When Travis's family felt all this activity was interfering with her schoolwork, she dropped out and Diana (then Diane) Ross took her place. Ross, who was sharing lead singing with Ballard, got them a Motown audition in 1960.

Typically (for Gordy, not the industry), he told them to finish high school and then come back, but they couldn't wait and signed instead with a local indie called Lupine. Their two records went nowhere, and soon—after Gordy had signed the Primes—the aspiring singers were hanging out at Motown almost every afternoon. They went for coffee, provided hand claps and background vocals, and soaked up a lot of professionalism. Early in 1961, Gordy finally offered them a contract. Ballard decided the group should be called the Supremes.

For the next three years, not much happened to them. Martin dropped out and Ross started singing lead on more and more of their records, but the records weren't selling. They toured hard, doing local promotional jaunts as well as the Motortown Revue, but the work didn't seem to pay off. In what must have been an act of sheerest desperation, Gordy even tried to have them cash in on the folk boom with an astonishingly awful song called "Rock and Roll Banjo Man." Finally, however, they were assigned to the Holland-Dozier-Holland production team, and their luck began to change. Their first H-D-H single, "When the Lovelight Starts Shining Through His Eyes," got to number twenty-three, a big jump for them, and in

July of 1964, they started on an incredible streak of five number-one hits in a row. Each set Ross's soft, breathy voice against the crackling Motown rhythms, forever establishing her voice as the Supremes sound. At the end of 1964, the only Motown record to outrank the Supremes on *Cashbox's* top singles compilation was Mary Wells's "My Guy."

Slightly above the Supreme's number-fifteen placement (for "Where Did Our Love Go?") on *Cashbox's* annual top singles compilation, the Top Ten included three figures making their last appearances. Dean Martin, wounded by rock 'n' roll, would be destroyed by rock (and deservedly so, too. During the Rolling Stones' ill-starred initial American tour, they appeared on "Hollywood Palace," only to endure Dean Martin's boozy, middle-brow attacks on their hair and their talent). Also departing, after a somewhat understated (by the rococo-country criteria that were his alone) "Oh, Pretty Woman," was first-generation rock 'n' roller Roy Orbison. Orbison's fading might have evoked a certain poignance—and Martin's a-job-well-done frisson—but the Kingsmen disappeared as they'd come; there had been no fanfare, and there would be no recessional.

Except, maybe, one more chorus (approximately the four billionth) of "Louie Louie." The song had originally been recorded in 1956 by its writer, Richard Berry. Berry had been around for a while even then, having scored a regional novelty hit with "The Big Break" and sung the part of "Henry" on Etta James's response to "Work with Me, Annie," but his original version dented neither the pop nor the R&B charts. It did, however, enter the teen subconscious, particularly (for reasons that remain obscure) in the Pacific Northwest. Gillett has cited a Seattle group, the Frantics (which would fragment and eventually become three-fifths of Moby Grape), as the first in the region to include it in their sets, but they never recorded it. That honor went to a mostly instrumental group, the Wailers, though their version went nowhere as well. But the song refused to go away, and late in 1963, two more Northwest groups took local-label shots at it: Paul Revere and the Raiders, and the Kingsmen.

Of the two, the Raiders' version was infinitely more polished, and it drew the attention of Columbia Records, which licensed it and released it nationally—to virtually no attention. In the summer of 1964, however, a Boston radio station began playing the Kingsmen's record. Murky, muddy, nearly unintelligible (probably due to the primitive mixing of Lynn Easton's vocal, but many listeners preferred to believe that the garble masked wonderfully unspeakable obscenities), and musically primitive—anyone could play those chords, which may be one reason so many Northwest bands had—it both worried American parents and defied the British, climbing all the way to number two on the pop charts. Though the Kingsmen would continue to record, and even scored a second Top Ten hit with the novelty "Jolly Green Giant" in 1965, the heavy-footed "Louie Louie" would be their first and last visit to such exalted heights. *Ave atque vale.*

It's almost embarrassing to speak of "significance" in any discussion of "Louie Louie," for the song surely resists learned exegesis. It did, however, illustrate a significant music industry trend that the coming rock hegemony would nearly erase: the discovery and national licensing of regional hits. It was by licensing arrangements with the original recording companies, for instance, that records by the Beatles and other first-wave British groups came to America, and most American companies exercised similar economic caution with home-grown groups. Let them record on a local label, and then if a record starts to move in their home region, buy the rights to it. This effectively transferred the costs of development to the people who could least afford it—at the then-acceptable risk that some other company would get to the band first. When the economic orientation of the industry subsequently changed from singles to albums—and when one group could mean tens of millions of dollars of income—the licensing system faded away, emerging again in modified form only in the early days of American punk.

But the Brill Building, that bastion of genuinely professional—and genuinely American—pop, wasn't going to yield to punks or the British without a fight. In the midst of Beatlemania, "Love Me Do" was pushed aside by the Dixie Cups' classic throwback, "Chapel of Love." The Dixie Cups, three teenagers who'd been singing together since grammar school, had formed a year earlier in New Orleans, but once they'd been put through their paces at Leiber and Stoller's newly formed Red Bird Records, all traces of their native city vanished; they came, by then, from the same never-never land that had produced the Shirelles, the Marvelettes, the Crystals, and the Chiffons ("Chapel of Love," their biggest—and only number one—hit, had actually been written for the Ronettes).

Unlike the Supremes, who also hit the charts for the first time that year, the Dixie Cups were a pure "girl group." There is never a hint that their minds and hearts are involved with anything (like, for instance, a profitable career in nightclubs) but The Boy. Their "Chapel of Love" is as fresh, innocent, and giddily appealing today as it was more than two decades ago, and it displaced the Beatles from the charts because it deserved to. Still, to some of their contemporaries, who can be forgiven their enthusiasms, and to some critics, who should surely have known better, the Dixie Cups and their (few) successors were simply an obstacle in the way of the Next Big Thing. In a 1973 book, for instance, New York Times rock critic Mike Jahn wrote: "The female vocal group of the early 1960s served to drive the concept of art completely away from rock 'n' roll. It served only to exploit the emotions of those who could identify with a song wherein a girl gloated about how her boyfriend was going to beat the crud out of someone who had been asking her out. I feel this genre represents the low point in the history of rock 'n' roll. . . ."

Well, not so fast. A little sorting out, here. True, the immediate pre-Beatle years weren't among the greatest in rock 'n' roll history, but neither were they undifferentiated pap. One only has to consider Fabian, Annette Funicello, Frankie Avalon, and Edd "Kookie" Byrnes to realize just how good the Dixie Cups and the Shangri-Las actually were. And among their comparative virtues, as it happens, was *precisely* that their performances linked "art"—or at least decent, respectable, Brill Building craft—to rock 'n' roll. In production (Spector, George "Shadow" Morton), composition (Goffin and King, Barry and Greenwich), *and* execution their work has proved considerably less ephemeral than much of that of the British invasion that shouldered them aside. The notion of "execution" is particularly important here, for though the various girl groups were hardly self-directed artifacts in the way later rockers would be, neither were they as faceless and interchangeable as their detractors would have it. "Leader of the Pack," for instance, a number-one record late in 1964, teeters constantly on the brink of ludicrousness. Shadow Morton's technically brilliant production—you want screeching tires, revving engines, melodrama aplenty? You got it—seems destined to push it over, but Mary Weiss's matter-of-fact lead vocal just barely hauls it back.

The Brill Building wasn't all sound effects, however. Taking a cue from Leiber and Stoller, producer Bert Berns kept the strings flowing in a major summertime hit, the Drifters' "Under the Boardwalk." If its chart rival "Louie Louie" was about sex, this—like the group's earlier Goffin-King "Up on the Roof"—was about romance. To be sure, the romance is urban and gritty, but Johnny Moore's fluid lead vocal keeps the song fresh during its welcome annual warm-weather reappearances. "Under the Boardwalk," however, was about teen romance. Spurred by the folkies' success, other parts of the industry were trying to follow the demographic bulge that supported the album market. With the confluence of Dylan and the Beatles, rock 'n' roll was about to grow up.

The Allman Brothers Band—Jaimoe Johanny Johanson, Duane Allman, Gregg Allman, Berry Oakley, Dickey Betts, Butch Trucks

The Animals—John Steel, Alan Price, Chas Chandler, Eric Burdon, Hilton Valentine

The Band—Garth Hudson, Levon Helm, Richard Manuel, Robbie Robertson, Rick Danko

Joan Baez

The Beach Boys—
Al Jardine, Dennis
Wilson, Brian
Wilson, Carl Wilson,
Mike Love

The Beatles—Paul McCartney, John Lennon,
George Harrison, Ringo Starr

**Big Brother and the Holding Company—David
Getz, Janis Joplin, Sam Andrews, James Gurley,
Peter Albin**

**James Brown—with the Famous Flames and the
James Brown Orchestra**

**The Paul Butterfield Blues Band—Paul Butterfield,
Jerome Arnold, Mike Bloomfield, Sam Lay, Mark
Naftalin, Elvin Bishop**

The Byrds—Roger McGuinn, Chris Hillman, Gene Clark, David Crosby, Michael Clarke

The Dave Clark Five

Cream—Jack Bruce, Ginger Baker, Eric Clapton

Creedence Clearwater Revival—Tom Fogerty, Doug Clifford, Stu Cook, John Fogerty

Crosby, Stills, Nash and Young—Neil Young, David Crosby, Stephen Stills, Graham Nash

The Doors—Jim Morrison, John Densmore, Ray Manzarek, Robby Krieger

Bob Dylan

Aretha Franklin

Marvin Gaye

The Faces—Ian McLagan, Kenney Jones, Ron
Wood, Rod Stewart, Ronnie Lane

The Fugs—Tuli Kupferberg, Ed Sanders, Ken Weaver

The Grateful Dead—Phil Lesh, Bill Kreutzmann, Jerry Garcia, Bob Weir, Pigpen

The Jimi Hendrix Experience—Mitch Mitchell, Jimi Hendrix, Noel Redding

The Jefferson Airplane—clockwise from top left: Marty Balin, Jack Casady, Grace Slick, Spencer Dryden, Jorma Kaukonen, Paul Kantner

Joni Mitchell

The Kinks—Peter Quaife, Mick Avory, Dave Davies, Ray Davies

The Monkees—David Jones, Peter Tork, Micky Dolenz, Mike Nesmith

Peter, Paul and Mary

Wilson Pickett

**The Righteous Brothers—
Bill Medley and Bobby Hatfield**

**Pink Floyd—Nick Mason, Rick Wright, Roger
Waters, Syd Barrett**

Otis Redding

The Miracles—Smokey Robinson, Claudette Rogers Robinson, Ronnie White, Pete Moore, Bobby Rogers

The Rolling Stones—Bill Wyman, Mick Jagger, Brian Jones, Charlie Watts, Keith Richards

Sam and Dave—Samuel Moore and Dave Prater

Simon and Garfunkel—Art Garfunkel and Paul Simon

The Supremes—Florence Ballard, Mary Wilson, Diana Ross

Sly Stone

Jackie Wilson

**The Temptations—David Ruffin, Melvin Franklin,
Otis Williams, Paul Williams, Eddie Kendricks**

**The Who—Pete Townshend, Keith Moon, Roger
Daltrey, John Entwistle**

Stevie Wonder

Frank Zappa and the Mothers of Invention

16

Brits Rule

Popular music was indeed undergoing a sea change—and rock would clearly supplant rock 'n' roll—but the process was hardly linear. A look at the number-one American singles during the first quarter of 1965, for instance, offers proto-rock (the Beatles' "I Feel Fine" and "Eight Days a Week"); Motown-toward-the-Copa twice (the Supremes' "Stop! In the Name of Love" and "Come See About Me") and toward-R&B once (the Temptations' Smokey Robinson–produced "My Girl"); stasis (Gary Lewis and the Playboys' derivative "This Diamond Ring"); conservatism ("Downtown," by—in *Variety*'s phrase—"Brit chirper" Petula Clark, whose ballad could have come straight from a slightly funky Tin Pan Alley, and whose preceding and subsequent hits contained nothing to equal it); and classicism (the Righteous Brothers' "You've Lost That Lovin' Feelin'").

This last *was* a Brill Building effort, at once a throwback to the heavily emotional ballads Roy Hamilton cut for Epic in the mid-fifties and a harbinger of soul. Blue-eyed soul, in this instance, but no matter; despite the Temptations and the Supremes, it went to number three on the R&B charts as well. Produced by Phil Spector and co-authored by Barry Mann and Cynthia Weil, it deserves attention not simply because it marked the last number-one record Spector would make during the 1960s, but for what it is.

Bill Medley and Bobby Hatfield had been kicking around the California club/session scene for a while before they got together in 1962, achieving modest success (number 49) early in 1963 with the forgettable novelty "Little Latin Lupe Lu." They came to Spector's attention a little over a year later, and he licensed them from Moonglow Records for his own Philles

277

label. When they arrived for their first Spector session, there was hardly room for them in the studio. Though the age of overdub was coming fast, Spector preferred to cut his records in a single take, not so much building his famous "wall of sound" brick by brick as pouring it in concrete. For this record, arranger Gene Page had brought together Spector's largest orchestra yet: strings, of course; a marimba; a melodic bass; and a persistent, sharp tambourine—and most of all, the Righteous Brothers' voices.

Medley's baritone—warm, sexy, almost relaxed—sang the opening verse; Hatfield's tenor—brassy, strangled, passionate—entered on the chorus. Its highly charged emotionalism seemed to prod Medley into passion of his own. Behind their inflamed call and response, the strings soared, dipped, and then, propelled by the tambourine back beat, nearly screamed. After the crescendo, the silence, broken only by single notes sustained on a lone bass, was as sudden as a plunge off of a cliff. But this wasn't the end, merely a gathering of strength so the whole process could be repeated—on, if possible, a level of even greater intensity. Whenever "Lovin' Feelin'" came on the radio, it reduced, for its three-minute span, the Supremes to little girls, the Beatles to fey pretenders.

Which they weren't, of course; but the Beatles were—and throughout their performing career forever would be—cast in the roles Brian Epstein had designed for them. In 1964, those roles would be codified in their first movie, Richard Lester's *A Hard Day's Night*. The film was originally conceived simply as a way to sell Beatles records (not to mention Beatles lunchboxes, pajamas, sweatshirts, and wigs), and unfortunately, the deal was struck before their phenomenal American triumphs. So it was shot cheaply, in black and white, over a tight six-week stretch between the Beatles' last Ed Sullivan appearance and a tour of Denmark and Holland, then edited and printed at breakneck speed. As Lester explained, "The idea was to make it as quickly as possible and get it out before their popularity faded."

Not surprisingly under the circumstances, *A Hard Day's Night* had the most rudimentary of plots. Written by their fellow Liverpudlian Alun Owen, it was a high-speed pseudodocumentary posing the (sole) question: will the lads make it through a "typical" day of press conferences, fan pursuit, encounters with disapproving elders, manic playfulness, and occasional self-doubt in time to play a concert for their adoring fans? Well, of course they will, but despite its threadbare and hackneyed story, the film was an unambiguous triumph of modernity—most obviously, of modern visual *style*. The camera, as it had been in French *nouvelle vague* films, was itself almost a character; restless, jumpy, it kept its audience constantly off-balance. Freed by the simpleminded plot from any obligation to linearity or even to character development, Lester was able to create a series of self-enclosed episodes that had the flash of—and required the attention span for—television commercials.

It was brilliant, but it wouldn't have worked without the Beatles (Lester's previous rock film, after all, had been 1961's dismal *It's Trad, Dad*, with Chubby Checker and Dusty Springfield). Playing a four-man picaro, they were cheeky, smart, innocent, ebullient, and—above all—themselves. As John later described Owen's screenwriting technique: "He stayed with us for two days and wrote the whole thing based on our characters then: me, witty; Ringo, dumb and cute; Paul, this; George, that." Owen almost certainly oversimplified, but at that point in the Beatles' career, those characters were unassumingly charming. Victims as well as beneficiaries of Epstein's genius, they *became* the characters from *A Hard Day's Night*.

Its London premiere on July 6 bewitched a vast audience of feverish fans, standing in block-long lines to see it five, ten, fifteen times. By the time it had reached New York in early August, Beatlemania had become a full-blown epidemic. Teenage girls jammed the theaters, singing along with the songs, shrieking and crying as each of the lovable moptops did his star turn. But even beyond the teen screamers, *A Hard Day's Night* reached out to a generation of Americans still recoiling from the shots that had killed John Kennedy less than a year before. More than their music, the characters the Beatles revealed in *A Hard Day's Night*—at once astonished, thrilled, and a little bit amused by their unbelievable success, revealing to a man, well, maybe to a *boy*, a sense of limitless, unbounded futurity—filled an aching void in the American soul.

It seems significant that among those leading critical cheers for the movie was former Kennedy aide Arthur Schlesinger, Jr. Writing in *Show* magazine, Schlesinger admitted he'd "approached the Beatles with apprehension, knowing only the idiotic hairdo and the melancholy wail. [But] . . . *A Hard Day's Night* is a smart and stylish film, exhilarating in its audacity and modernity." Leaving aside the question of how anyone could possibly have described the sound of the early Beatles records as "melancholy," Schlesinger's review is meaningful not merely for who he was but for its structure—the implication that all right-thinking people had already dismissed the Beatles as just another teenage fad, followed by astonishment at his own pleasure at their brash challenge to his assumptions. Consider Bosley Crowther in that organ of received opinion, the *New York Times*: "This is going to surprise you—it may knock you right out of your chair—but the new film with those incredible chaps, the Beatles, is a whale of a comedy. . . . I wouldn't have believed it either if I hadn't seen it with my own astonished eyes." Or *Newsweek's* anonymous critic: "With all the ill will in the world, one sits there, watching and listening—and feels one's intelligence dissolving in a pool of approbation."

This vaunted approbation did not prevent the reviewer from implying that appreciation of the Beatles must necessarily be unintelligent, but such quibbles were lost in the nearly universal acclaim from self-proclaimed skeptics. Cumulatively, they "koshered" *A Hard Day's Night* for the (equally self-proclaimed) intelligentsia. Once the kids who'd deserted

Buddy Holly for Brooks and Warren's *Well-Wrought Urn* got into the theaters, the film was perfectly capable of continuing the work on its own. Suddenly the Beatles were no longer the more or less exclusive property of their teenage fans; they belonged to everyone.

And virtually everyone belonged to them—including the album buyers who usually shunned rock 'n' roll (*A Hard Day's Night* topped the U.S. charts for fourteen weeks; its predecessor, *The Beatles' Second Album*, had been number one for only four). This sudden expansion of the rock audience to the nation's campuses—and beyond—would eventually remake the economics of the music industry and was probably responsible for the persistence of the self-justifying myth that the years 1959 to 1963 had been musically barren. In the short term, *A Hard Day's Night* produced the usual imitative responses (*Having a Wild Weekend*, starring the Dave Clark Five; *Ferry Cross the Mersey*, with Gerry and the Pacemakers), and the (if possible) even more ephemeral *Where the Boys Meet the Girls*, starring Herman's Hermits.

Unlikely as it seems in retrospect, Herman's Hermits, featuring the adenoidal voice of Peter Noone, was second only to the Beatles among first-wave British invaders. The ubiquitous Mickie Most discovered Noone in Manchester, and he both produced their records and managed their thoroughly successful, if brief, career. Noone and company, as air-headed as Freddie and the Dreamers—but much cuddlier—tore off a string of Top Ten hits during 1965 (seven in a row, including two number-ones: "Mrs. Brown You've Got a Lovely Daughter," and "I'm Henry the VIII I Am"), not quite equaling the Beatles but outstripping the Stones and all the other British bands. For a while, the segment of the music industry that measured quality in tonnage accounted them the Beatles' equal, and their *Best of* album stayed on the charts for a full 105 weeks.

But the Hermits' long-run appeal was limited by the conscious and craftsmanly decision to concentrate on the prepubescent market that had given the Beatles their first American audience. The Rolling Stones were after bigger game, and time, as they proclaimed, was on their side. Their triumph was a long way from obvious during the Hermits' heyday, however, for the second—and considerably tougher—wave of British bands hit the States to mixed and limited success. Indeed, when they and their records first arrived in America, the Stones were by no means the most successful among a wave that also included Manfred Mann, the Kinks, the Who, the Yardbirds, the Spencer Davis Group, and Them. Though these bands were not cut entirely from the same piece of cloth, they differed from the Beatles and the Merseybeat groups both musically and socially. First of all, even if their sound wasn't specifically blacker in the Stones/Stevie Winwood mode, they were more emotional, more open in a way their blues and R&B heroes had been. Second, like most American folkies, they were self-consciously bohemian; many of the leading figures were art school students who'd fallen in love with the blues at least partly to distance themselves from their comparatively middle-class backgrounds.

True, the operative word here is *comparative*. Among the Stones, for instance, only provincial Brian Jones had a background that could be called privileged, but none came from the council-house-and-dole grime that had spawned the Beatles. Their metier was the drab, lower-middle-class London suburban ring from which "making it" didn't imply some fantastic, undreamed-of break but only "application." That is, of course, if you wanted to make it on the limited terms England would allow. Mick Jagger did. He and Keith Richards had actually grown up together in Dartford but had gone in different directions after their eleven-plus exams, when in its infinite class-conscious wisdom, the British educational system had decided that grammar-school Mick was wheat, technical-school Keith, chaff. And thus, despite their shared fondness for the blues, they would almost certainly have remained but for a chance encounter on a London-bound train.

Jagger was commuting to the London School of Economics, where he was a student, and Richards to art school, where he was essentially marking time. As Richards recalled their meeting in a 1971 *Rolling Stone* interview: "It's really strange 'cause I knew Mick when I was really young . . . five, six, seven. We used to hang out together. Then I moved and didn't see him for a long time. I once met him selling ice cream outside the public library. I bought one. He was trying to make some extra money.

"So I got on this train one morning and there's Jagger and under his arm he has four or five albums. We recognized each other straight off. 'Hi man,' I say. 'Where ya going?' he says. And under his arm he's got Chuck Berry and Little Walter, Muddy Waters. 'You're into Chuck Berry, man, really? That's a coincidence.' He says, 'Yeah. I got a few more albums. Been writin' away to this Chess Records in Chicago and got a mailing list thing and . . . got it together, you know?'

"So I invited him up to my place for a cup of tea. He started playing me these records and I really turned on to it." In addition to a fondness for Richards's guitar-hero Chuck Berry, both shared an acquaintanceship with one of Richards's art-school pals, Dick Taylor, who would later go on to form the Pretty Things. It was under Taylor's auspices that the Jagger-Richards chance encounter flowered: "We'd all go to Dick Taylor's house, in his back room, some other cats would come along and play, and we'd try to play some of this Little Walter stuff and Chuck Berry stuff. No drummer or anything. Just two guitars and a little amplifier. Usual back room stuff. It fell into place very quickly."

There was more to the British blues scene than Dick Taylor's back room, of course, but not much more. What there was owed its existence chiefly to Cyril Davies and Alexis Korner. A musical generation older than Jagger and Richards (Korner was born in 1928, Davies in 1932), they had cofounded the first of many Blues Incorporateds in 1961. Before that, the two had been part of Chris Barber's Jazz Band, a "trad" group that had scored a freak Top Ten U.S. hit with "Petite Fleur" in 1959. Like most trad bands, Barber's played polite, ricky-ticky Dixieland, but they were fiercely proud of their seriousness, as white people who'd chosen to play black music for their livelihoods.

But what Korner and Davies wanted to play was R&B, not trad jazz, so they left Barber's group—an aesthetic split with economic consequences. There were a limited number of venues that would book *any* sort of black-white band, and at least apparently, a limited number of fans who'd pay to hear them. Caught in a squeeze between the trad bands and the Cliff Richard-ish rock scene, Korner was forced into entrepreneurship, establishing one-night-a-week blues "clubs" at any pub that would have him, first in Soho, then in Ealing, finally at the Marquee. Jagger and Richards caught up with him at Ealing, where they heard him introduce a special guest, "all the way up from Cheltenham."

As Richards recalled it, "Suddenly it's *Elmore James*, this cat, man. And it's *Brian*, man. . . . I said, what? What the fuck? Playing bar slide guitar!

"We get into Brian after he's finished 'Dust My Broom.' He's really fantastic and a gas. He's doin' the same as we'd been doin' . . . thinkin' he was the only cat in the world who was doin' it."

The original threesome, joined eventually by keyboardist Ian Stewart, bassist Bill Wyman (whose main attraction, since he was older and straighter, was his powerful amplifier), and drummer Charlie Watts (who'd long been their drummer of choice but who'd hesitated to give up his day job), began working regularly on the club scene, though not without difficulty that occasionally burst into violence. Keith, again: "Most of the clubs at that time were filled with dixieland bands, traditional jazz bands. . . . They had all the clubs under their control. [Then] R&B started to become the thing. And all these traddies, as they were called, started getting worried. So they started this very bitter opposition.

"Which is one reason I swung my guitar at Harold Pendleton's head . . . because he was the kingpin behind all that. He owned all these trad clubs and he got a cut from these trad bands, he couldn't bear to see them die. He couldn't afford it."

Still R&B was indeed becoming "the thing." Musicians who moved into Korner's orbit included not only the Stones but drummer Mick Avory (the Kinks), Ginger Baker, Jack Bruce, John Mayall, John Baldry, Eric Clapton, and Jimmy Page: a nascent pantheon of British rock. But bitter as it was, the blues-vs.-trad battle was taking place in an extremely small pond. Recording contracts were rare, and purism—as that purist Eric Clapton, who quit the Yardbirds to join John Mayall when they grew too poppish, recalled—was a badge of honor: "The blues musician is usually a fanatic; that's the common denominator among blues musicians, they're fanatics. In England, they're a lot more so 'cause they're divorced from the scene and don't really know where it's at. They don't know what it's like to be a blues musician in America like Mike Bloomfield does. They're all romantic about it and have a lot of ideals and notions. A lot of ego gets mixed into it and they think they're the only guys playing real music."

But then the Beatles came along and raised the stakes. All of a sudden, success didn't mean being able to give up your day job; it meant wealth and fame on an international scale. Amid charges of selling out and countercharges of old fartism prefiguring those that would split the American folkies, the young British blues bands confronted the lure of stardom. Most, quite reasonably, thought limousines preferable to the London underground.

The usual pattern—followed by the Stones, the Who, the Kinks, and the Yardbirds, among others—was to begin by recording blues and R&B numbers (usually to limited commercial enthusiasm) and, even while these traditional songs remained the mainstay of the groups' live shows, to gradually turn to contemporary, often self-composed songs. The Stones' early recordings are typical: Their first album, released in April 1964, featured songs from Slim Harpo, Rufus Thomas, Willie Dixon, Chuck Berry, and even Holland-Dozier-Holland. Stung by the charge that the Stones were ripping off black artists, Jagger wrote an impassioned letter to *Melody Maker* rebutting critics "who think we're just a beat group who came up overnight, knowing nothing about it, we invite them to examine our record collection, it contains things by Jimmy Reed, Elmore James, Hooker"; adding, with the calculation of a London School of Economics student, "These legendary characters wouldn't mean a light commercially today if groups were not going round Britain doing their numbers." (Nanker Phelge, though a presence on that debut album, didn't become central until later.*) But the Stones, romantics, attempted to remain truer to their American (non)roots than their contemporaries did. Their most artistically successful rivals tended to write about what they knew best—thus the Who's "My Generation" recapitulates a specific Mod-amphetamine style, and Ray Davies was almost obsessively English—while the Stones celebrated their own mythic America.

Among the high spots of their initial American tour, for instance, was a session cum genuflection at Marshall Chess's recording studios in Chicago, and early Jagger/Richards efforts like "Citadel" and "Under Assistant West Coast Promotion Man" reveal an absolute fascination with American personalities and artifacts. This love affair was not, however, entirely requited, for the scruffy, snaggle-toothed Stones were anything but cuddly. In addition to their grim "Hollywood Palace" appearance (at one point, the emcee introduced a trampolining tumbler with the remark: "This is the father of

---

*The pseudonym, eventually synonymous with Jagger-Richards, was early on given to the band's joint compositions. A 1964 *Rave* article citing Brian's explanation, "Nankies are little men who think they represent authority," also reported that "not all the Stones' friends are wealthy. Their oldest pal is Jimmy Phelge, a printer."

ɔlling Stones. He's been trying to kill himself ever since "), they drew
…, some six hundred people to an Omaha hall that could hold six
thousand. But despite their lack of a U.S. hit ("Tell Me [You're Coming
Back]" peaked at number 24, their cover of the Valentinos' "It's All Over
Now" at number 26), they not only sold out several shows but established
themselves as the tough alternative to the comparatively sweet and innocent Beatles. Since the Hamburg-hardened Beatles weren't half so sweet
and innocent as they appeared, this annoyed John Lennon for years, but it
was a natural consequence of Brian Epstein's manicuring of the Beatles'
image—and of Andrew Oldham busily stuffing dirt under the Stones'
fingernails.

Oldham—nineteen years old, mod, hip in a way that would never allow
him to confuse Billy J. Kramer with the Beatles—was an extremely minor
cog in Brian Epstein's organization when an April 1963 *Record Mirror*
review of a Stones show sent him to the Crawdaddy Club to see them. The
next day, in incongruous partnership with provincial music hall booker
Eric Easton, he was the band's co-manager. Easton had the capital and the
connections, but Oldham had the vision. In a 1972 *New Music Express*
interview, he recalled "seeing the Beatles when they were about eighth on
the bill to Helen Shapiro and Tommy Roe. I sat there with a lump in my
throat. In one night you knew they were going to be very big. It was just an
instinctive thing.

"From that night on, it registered subconsciously that when they made it,
another section of the public was gonna want an opposite." When he saw
the Stones, Oldham knew he'd found that counterweight. (Did this prevent
the Stones from using a Beatles' song, "I Wanna Be Your Man," as the
vehicle for their second U.K. chart appearance? Of course not. In the early
days, at least, the difference was image and contrivance.) So their hair was
longer than the Beatles', their physicality more aggressive, their records—
partly because neophyte producer Oldham couldn't have achieved the
clarity George Martin gave the Beatles even if he'd wanted to—murkier and
meaner. And except for Brian, they were a whole lot uglier.

Which didn't at all mean they weren't sexy, but that the sexuality they
projected was of a totally different order from the Beatles' innocent ebul-
lience. Marianne Faithfull, who experienced rather more of the Stones than
was healthy, captured their appeal when she talked, retrospectively, about
Keith: "He's the epitome of the Romantic Hero, and if you're a middle-class
girl and you've read your Byron, that's Keith Richards—even now. He's
turned into Count Dracula, but he's really an injured, tortured, damned
youth—which is really such fun, isn't it?"

Yet for all of Oldham's plotting, the Rolling Stones were slow in making a
transatlantic dent. If anything, Americans seemed to want more Beatles;
not only the Dave Clark Five, but even pallid Beatle clones like Herman's
Hermits and Gerry and the Pacemakers had greater initial U.S. success than

the Stones did. As late as May 1965, when the band played a week-long series at New York's Academy of Music (despite its name, an aging movie house), you could walk in off the street, no waiting, on an impulse. And their audience was much more like those who thronged Alan Freed's famous Brooklyn Paramount shows than the screaming girls who greeted the Beatles or Herman's Hermits—whiter than Freed's crowds by a large margin, of course, but nonetheless male, adolescent, and consciously rebellious against (at least) their parents. The Beatles were *too* popular—after *A Hard Day's Night* even adults liked them a little—while the scruffy Stones offered the same satisfactions a screaming Little Richard once had.

And the Stones, eventually cracking the U.S. Top Ten during their second American tour late in 1964 with "Time Is on My Side," didn't ease up on their evil-hearted image. Jagger snarled his way across America, emphasizing his lyrics' every sexual innuendo; Jones displayed an exhibitionistic pelvis thrust; and Richards appeared to be auditioning for a role as the Big Bad Wolf. During that tour, for instance, they made their Ed Sullivan show debut, promptly causing the host to issue a public apology: "I didn't see the group until the day before the broadcast. They were recommended by my scouts in England. I was shocked when I saw them. It took me seventeen years to build this show: I'm not going to have it destroyed in a matter of weeks." He promised—spuriously, in the event—that they would never again darken his stage.

The Stones survived Sullivan's discomfiture quite nicely indeed, but the Kinks—who'd achieved greater U.S. popularity than all the other second-wave toughs, including the Stones—never achieved the major American success that once seemed within their grasp. Their problem was less musical than social; the Stones were barred from a single television show, the Kinks from an entire country. To a great degree, they brought this on themselves, for the Kinks (Ray Davies, Dave Davies, Mick Avory, and Pete Quaife) were almost classically self-destructive.

Though they all grew up working-class around Muswell Hill in North London (Davies père was a gardener), and though Ray served the nearly obligatory apprenticeship in Alexis Korner's ambit, they were spared any Hamburg-like scuffling because their original lead singer (and subsequent co-manager), Robert Wace, was decidedly upper class and booked them regularly into deb parties when they were the Ravens. As manager—legend has it that Ray Davies instantly became their lead singer when Wace was driven from the stage one night by a cascade of upper-class boos and booze—he also financed the demo that landed them a recording contract.

Not that it seemed to do them a great deal of good. Their debut (produced by American Shel Talmy) was a cover of "Long Tall Sally" that the Beatles' version ate up, and the follow-up (a lame Ray Davies original, "You Still Want Me" b/w "I Took My Baby Home") sold less than five hundred copies—*considerably* less, by some reports. Around this time, however, according to a 1966 interview with *Melody Maker,* Dave Davies got frustrated by his cheapoid amplifier, "ripped up the speakers of this little amp," and hooked it directly into the regular Vox amplifier—essentially inventing an electronic version of the fuzz box that Link Wray had created mechanically. (Wray, however, had played crackling, buzzing melodies; Dave Davies was a flailer.) With brother Ray's words and melody and Dave's distorted, "Louie Louie" power chording, "You Really Got Me" went to number one in England and number seven in America.* Unlike the Kingsmen, however, the Kinks cloned their "Louie Louie," scoring a U.K. number two and another United States number seven with "All Day and All of the Night." When the spring of 1965 saw them doing even better with a down-tempoed "Tired of Waiting For You," it was time for them to undertake their debut United States tour.

The tour was unsuccessful in almost every respect, although the Kinks' first three U.S. singles had done much better than the Stones'. Audiences proved skeptical, and the band itself was—as its subsequent 1960s recordings demonstrated—somewhere between hostile and ambivalent about America. Typically, for Kinks of that vintage, the band began to take it out on one another, and a local steward from AFTRA (the American Federation of Television and Radio Artists) found himself in the middle of a classic punchup—as a result of which the union banned the Kinks from future U.S. tours for "unprofessional conduct."

Actually, and for similar reasons, the U.S. tour almost didn't happen. Three weeks before the band was due to arrive in New York, they were on a U.K. tour, playing in Cardiff, Wales, when Avory picked up a mike stand and smacked Dave Davies in the head, causing ten stitches and the sudden termination of the tour—and almost of the band as well. In the next day's London papers, however, all was sweetness and light, and Avory explained the melee as simply a bit of miscalculated stage business, part of a new routine for "You've Really Got Me." He explained the lacerations on his own face as having come from "a girl fan at Taunton."

Some years subsequently Ray Davies allowed that this tale was a trifle

---

*A word here about "You Really Got Me": There's been a running story that Jimmy Page, who was all over British sessions at the time, actually played the guitar lead on the record. This is plausible enough—nothing in Dave Davies's previous playing gave a hint of the song's distinctive sound—and Page was surely present during the sessions. He, however, has confirmed contributing only a little sweetening, and Ray Davies's version of the story, in a *Zigzag* interview, is that "the take of 'You Really Got Me' that was actually issued was the third . . . there was a demo thing with Dave playing lead, a second cut which may have had Jimmy Page (and which Pye still have), and a third which definitely had Dave on it. I know, I was standing right next to him when he played it—and that's the one which was released."

Almost ten years after the fact, however, the charge still rankled, and Ray Davies once responded to an interviewer's question about why the band had been "doing all these Led Zeppelin sendups" at a recent concert with, "Because Dave plays lead guitar on all their records."

disingenuous; "Well, you had to have something ready for the papers. In actual fact, Dave had got annoyed about something and went over and booted the drums about. Mick's drums, of course, were his treasured possession, so he retaliated by belting Dave . . . it was during 'Beautiful Delilah,' I remember. He was almost done for grievous bodily harm; the police down there wanted to charge him."

All in all, you would think, an unlikely wellspring for a series of songs limning the small triumphs and tragedies of Britain's proper white middle classes, but with the late-1965 American release of "A Well Respected Man," that was the direction the band took. Surprisingly, the song was never released as a British single but was a top-twenty American hit. Though Ray Davies's ballad of a suburban commuter, at once smug and frustrated in contemplating the often-adulterous "matrimonial stakes," is harsher and less compassionate than much of his later work, its telling eye for detail makes the Beatles' similarly conceived "Nowhere Man" seem both vague and supercilious; the Kinks' implied answer to their "Isn't he a lot like you and me?" was almost certainly, "Not on your life."

With the Kinks having both distanced themselves from rock's black roots and rendered themselves *hors de combat* in America, the only British group that could challenge the Beatles was the Rolling Stones. Their time arrived, with a vengeance, in the summer of 1965, with "I Can't Get No Satisfaction."

Perhaps for the first time in this new era, the song had its roots in technology. The Stones were on the Gulf Coast of Florida, in the midst of an American tour, when Keith Richards started to fool around with his brand new Gibson fuzz box. The device enabled him to tap into (and escape) the Avory/Davies sound with the touch of an electronic switch, and in the middle of the night, he began banging on Jagger's door, eager to show him a fuzz-tone guitar riff that he couldn't get out of his head. It stuck in Jagger's head, too, and the next day, sitting around the motel pool, he began work on the lyrics of "Satisfaction." Less than a week later, on May 12, the Stones laid down the song's basic tracks at Chess Studios in Chicago, finishing it up at an RCA studio in Los Angeles. The song was utterly unlike any previously released Jagger-Richards original, combining the urgency of their blues covers with the immediacy of a contemporary lyric. The soulish arrangement was new, too, giving the Stones their own built-in paradox by musically delivering what the lyrics insisted was unattainable.

Up until "Satisfaction," the Stones hadn't even been number two among the British invaders, and though Andrew Oldham's publicity machinations had served the band well in the press, it hadn't sold records. During the first year and a half of the British invasion, the Stones never cracked the U.S. top five (while number-one status went not only to the Beatles and Herman, but also to Peter and Gordon, the Animals, Manfred Mann, Freddie and the

Dreamers, and Wayne Fontana and the Mindbenders). But now "Satisfaction," its mumbled verses providing fodder for lubricious interpretation and its chorus an irresistible temptation to shout along, hit the charts in early May and took over the number-one slot within a month. When the follow-up, "Get Off My Cloud," also topped the U.S. charts, the Stones were firmly established as—at least—number two.

As Otis Redding's 1966 version established, "Satisfaction" was a perfectly credible soul song, and Richards has said it was inspired by Martha and the Vandellas' "Dancing in the Street." There seems no reason to dispute this—though "Satisfaction" is altogether darker and more ominous, the influence on the opening guitar figure (once you know about it, like an optical illusion in which a tree changes suddenly and unmistakably into a rabbit) is apparent. But other soul performers were also influencing the Stones. On their first trip to America, they'd gone uptown to the Apollo, where they saw Joe Tex, Wilson Pickett, and the James Brown Revue. Though the interest was less enduring than the fascination with the blues that had first brought them together, their midsummer album, *Out of Our Heads,* is virtually a soul echo of their earlier tributes to the blues, containing versions of Solomon Burke's "Cry to Me," Otis Redding's "That's How Strong My Love Is," Don Covay's "Mercy, Mercy," and Marvin Gaye's "Hitch Hike."

None of these songs, sincere though the homage undoubtedly was, is even close to the Stones' greatest work. Indeed, they're more like covers than reworkings, and none of them catches fire the way the Stones' earlier "Little Red Rooster" had. Interestingly, the Stones didn't even release their second U.K. number-one hit in America. "Little Red Rooster," dominated by Brian Jones on a biting slide guitar that would have sent Sullivan even further up the wall, topped the British charts between the Supremes' "Baby Love" and the Beatles' "I Feel Fine." Without being imitative in the Eric Burdon mode—even in 1964, Jagger was too much the ironist for that—it was clearly the "blackest" of the three, and the chance juxtaposition dramatized the black-into-white/white-into-black dichotomy that would play out over the next few years. The Beatles might have sailed above it all, but the Stones and the Supremes were pursuing opposing dreams. The former blues purists glamorized and mythologized black America, while the girls from the Detroit ghetto had their eyes firmly on that glittering, supper-club America where Fred Astaire and Ginger Rogers used to dance. Briefly, at least, America would be able to embrace both dreams.

Yet dreams and aspirations are powerful engines of change, and eventually—sooner rather than later—even rock's power to unite blacks and whites, poets and finger-poppers, would weaken. While it lasted, however, the alliances forged during the 1960s' first musical explosion were sometimes strange (1966's *The Big TNT Show* featured both Joan Baez and the Ronettes) but often magical. The historical moment is perhaps most gloriously captured in the 1965 film *The T.A.M.I. Show*, whose cast included the Beach Boys, Marvin Gaye, Jan and Dean, the Barbarians, Chuck Berry, the Supremes, Billy J. Kramer and the Dakotas, James Brown, Gerry and the Pacemakers, Smokey Robinson and the Miracles, and the Rolling Stones. Simply as a show—Brown blowing away Jagger, for instance—the film is marvelous, but the brilliant catholicity of its cast serves as a reminder of how narrow such subsequent pop icons as Monterey and Woodstock actually turned out to be.

17
RED CLAY VS. SEQUINS

During that week in December 1964 when the diverging dreams of the Stones and the Supremes were passing each other on the British charts, Sam Cooke, whose summertime Copa appearance had been celebrated with a seventy-foot Times Square billboard, checked into a Los Angeles motel with a young woman named Elisa Boyer. They registered, though Cooke was married to someone else, as Mr. and Mrs. Cooke, and went into a motel room where, Boyer would later testify, Cooke began to rip her clothes off. She escaped, carrying most of his clothes with her, and fled to call the police from a telephone booth. Cooke, dressed in a sport coat and shoes, chased her and began pounding at the motel manager's door, eventually breaking in on the 55-year-old manager, Bertha Franklin. She shot him three times with a .22 revolver, and when he kept coming at her, took up a heavy walking stick and began clubbing him. He was dead when the police arrived.

Cooke, an enormous influence on virtually every black musician of the 1960s—black/white as well as black/black—had his share of pop hits during his career, but he died too young to enjoy the kind of commercial success that would surely have come to him—in his own style—during 1965 and 1966, when white record buyers began to discover soul.

An attempt at a definition is in order here, but it should be prefaced with Louis Armstrong's response when pressed for a definition of jazz: "If you gotta ask what it is," Satchmo rasped, "you ain't never gonna know." Bearing that in mind, then, one of the bravest attempts at defining soul is this nondefinition from Lillian Roxon's eccentric 1969 classic, *Rock Encyclopedia*: "You have it—or you don't. Either way you can't define it. If you've lived through enough, if pain has been your constant companion and despair has seeped into your heart, lungs and guts so that no matter what good times come later they're always colored by that extra dimension of sorrow, it's so much a part of you that you can't sing or play without it coming through, then you may start to understand what goes into a performance by Aretha Franklin, B. B. King, or Otis Redding . . ." Fair enough—certainly no one would deny that B. B. King has soul—but neither he nor, for that matter, a number of Motown performers who'd surely paid at least their share of dues chose to make "soul music" of the sort that swept America and Europe beginning in 1965.

Its musical/technical definition is at once narrower and more inclusive, including church-derived vocal lines (especially call and response, spoken passages, and broken, repetitive phrases), secular (and for the male singers, often bragging, macho) lyrics, and a persistent, percussive rhythm section. The obvious pop progenitor of soul was Ray Charles, but even in such gospel-tinged secular hits as 1959's "Night Time Is the Right Time" and "What'd I Say?" the rhythm section plays a jazzier version of the R&B shuffle used earlier in Fats Domino's "I'm Walkin'" or Chuck Berry's "Maybellene"; there are more snares (and cymbals) than toms, and the rhythm guitar and bass notes ring rather than being choked off. At its 1965 extreme—in the work of James Brown's band, for instance—an isolated soul rhythm track would stand as a perfectly plausible predecessor to go-go music.

Though the soul that flowered in the mid-1960s embodied enough technical advances to consider it a separate genre, it was a continuation rather than an invention. Yet if the integrationist spirit had not been so widespread in the land (especially on those college campuses that had supplied so many recruits for the Southern "freedom summers" of 1964 and 1965), the developments that became soul might have continued to be shunted aside by the British, occurring only on the traditional race labels, measured only on the R&B charts. Still, the changing social situation was a necessary but not sufficient condition; the commercial triumph of soul required intelligent and well-timed marketing from R&B labels like Atlantic.

Pushed, then, by a triumvirate of musical, political, and commercial forces, it crossed over big in July of 1965, when within a week of each other Wilson Pickett's "In the Midnight Hour" and Brown's "Papa's Got a Brand New Bag (Part 1)" hit the pop charts.

Pickett, a veteran of the Detroit-based vocal group the Falcons, had actually come to the attention of Atlantic Records vice president Jerry Wexler in 1963, when he sang on a demo tape that included "If You Need Me." Wexler liked the song and gave it to Atlantic's Solomon Burke to record, but the company somehow neglected to purchase rights to the demo itself. Just as Atlantic had Burke's record ready for release, they discovered that Lloyd Price's Double-L Records had already obtained and released Pickett's demo. In an interview with Peter Guralnik, Wexler recalled trying to block the Double-L record legally because, "I would say that Pickett's record had the edge over ours," and when that failed, then throwing himself into the business of protecting his artist. "I went to work on that record. That record put me back into promotion, got me back into the studio, into the excitement of the record business, everything." Atlantic not only won the immediate battle (Burke's version was number 2 R&B, number 37 pop; Pickett's stalled at number 30 R&B, never reaching the pop top 50), it won Pickett's respect, and two years later, he signed with the company.

After a couple of singles that went nowhere, Wexler brought Pickett south to Memphis, to record at the Stax Records studio. Stax (formed in 1960 by Jim Stewart and Estellse Axton, originally as Satellite Records) was the Memphis label, and the unquestioned home of the "Memphis sound."

Memphis is, spiritually as well as geographically, midway between New Orleans and Detroit, and though east Tennessee had harbored abolitionist sympathies during the Civil War, Memphis was very much a Southern city. At the time of the civil rights struggle that was raging when Pickett and Wexler went to Memphis, some of the most violent antiblack activity in the South was taking place in Tennessee's Haywood and Fayette counties, just a few miles to the east. Yet Memphis itself, while it was no Atlanta, tolerated pockets of integration, and musically, at least, the city had been integrated with a vengeance when Elvis Presley came into Sam Phillip's Sun Records studio to sing Arthur Crudup's "That's All Right." And though Phillips had scored his greatest hits with rockabilly singers like Presley, Jerry Lee Lewis, and Carl Perkins, Sun both began and continued as a blues label, issuing records by, among others, Little Milton and Rufus Thomas.

Stax continued the tradition, scoring its first local hit with Rufus and Carla Thomas's "'Cause I Love You" and its first Top Ten record, "Last Night," with an all-white band, the Mar-Keys (featuring, not coincidentally, Estelle Axton's son Packy on sax). Partly because touring didn't suit some of its members, the Mar-Keys eventually split into the Memphis Horns and, when organist Booker T. Jones and drummer Al Jackson, Jr. (who had integrated the Mar-Keys on recording dates) joined with bassist Lewis Steinberg and guitarist Steve Cropper, Booker T. and the MGs. Eventually Steinberg was replaced by Donald "Duck" Dunn, whose looping, pulsing bass completed the MGs' sound. The band not only performed on its own but served as Stax's house band on early records by Otis Redding, Carla Thomas, Sam and Dave, Eddie Floyd, and Johnnie Taylor. Though the Motown house band, led by keyboardist Earl Van Dyke, was literally blacker, the Stax band was more Southern; and *Billboard* magazine once pointed out that "the emergence of the Memphis Sound, a much darker mixture than Motown or Atlantic, of Mississippi mud and country blues, suggested that white record buyers were ready for the real thing—not white kids singing or playing black, but black vocalists singing and playing black."

Partly because Wexler was himself an R&B producer of considerable note (Ray Charles's "I Got a Woman" and "What'd I Say?" among others), the relationship between Atlantic and Stax had gone beyond the distribution/accounting-ledger stage. Early in 1965, for instance, Atlantic sent nonpareil engineer Tom Dowd to Memphis for an Otis Redding session that would be issued on Stax's subsidiary label, Volt. Still, as Cropper recalled in a 1968 *Rolling Stone* interview, the arrival of Pickett and Wexler was big news: "At the time it was one of the first marriages between people from other parts of the country and our sound. Here came Wilson Pickett, who had been a soul singer for years. . . . He made the New York circuit clubs and stuff like that, which was good, and of course the things he did with the Falcons were good. He came down also with Jerry Wexler. It was kind of an experience for everybody, really, to work with somebody like that. At that time New York was far away."

In addition to playing with Pickett, the Stax team was supposed to write songs for him, too, but although Stax regular Eddie Floyd had sung with Pickett in the Falcons, none of the studio musicians had heard him. Cropper "grabbed the only album of his I could find in the studio, which was two or three cuts which he did at the Apollo, and at the end of each fadeout he'd say, 'Yeah, wait for the midnight hour, baby' and go into this thing. I thought that would be a heck of an idea for a tune, and when he came in I presented it to him, and he said, 'That's a good idea' and he said, 'I've got this little rhythm thing I've been working on for a good while.' It was really nothing to it, it was just a couple of changes, and we just started working with this. That was where it came from."

In New York, where session musicians charged by the hour rather than by the completed song, it's unlikely that Atlantic could have afforded such a developmental process for an as-yet-hitless performer (Dylan got away with it at CBS partly because the company was much better established, and partly because he was Dylan). But, as Wexler said in Gerri Hirshey's wonderful 1984 history of soul music, *Nowhere to Run*, the Memphis musicians were totally comfortable with improvisation. "It was different down there—a total departure from anything we'd known in New York, since it veered away from formal, written arrangements and back to head arrangements. By that I mean it put the creative burden back on the rhythm section, to a symbiosis between the producer and the rhythm section. It's instinctual. You don't know why you're doing it—maybe some of it comes from subconscious memory. But it's southern, very southern. Which is to say extremely ad-lib."

One of the most important of those ad-libs—one that helped define the soul sound for the next couple of years—was in effect *danced* by Wexler. They'd been doing a song for a while when suddenly, in the midst of the bridge, Wexler came bouncing out of the control booth and began to dance a version of the jerk. "Why don't you pick up on this thing here?" he asked.

Cropper again: "He said this was the way the kids were dancing; they were putting the accent on two. Basically, we'd been one-beat-accenters with an afterbeat, it was like 'boom dah,' but here this was a thing that went 'un-chaw,' just the reverse as far as the accent goes. The backbeat was somewhat delayed, and it just put it in that rhythm, and Al and I have been using that as a natural thing now, ever since we did it. We play a downbeat and then two is almost on but a little bit behind, only with a complete impact. It turned us on to a heck of a thing."

Al Jackson, still a little amazed three years after the fact, agreed. "It sounded really as though the two and four were late. It was so far behind that you wouldn't believe it, and how it came out like this, we don't know."

The effect, as all this "boom dah," "un-chaw" and "two and four" perhaps demonstrates, is difficult to verbalize, but among other things, the shift in accent gave Dunn more flexibility without at all sacrificing the beat. His individual bass lines grew a little more country, and the ensemble sound seemed not only to percolate but to lope. Motown's Detroit head-quarters proclaimed itself, immodestly but not inaccurately, "Hitsville, U.S.A.," and with equal justice, the sign in front of Stax read, "Soulsville, U.S.A."

The Stax claim is harder to quantify, but in the red clay–vs.–sequins debate, you can count up Motown's boast. If you danced during 1965, you danced to Motown, as the company charted ten Top Ten pop singles, double its 1964 total. Its giants were the Temptations, the Supremes, and the Four Tops. Of these, the Temptations were by far the most versatile.

They were an amalgam of a handful of different groups that had been singing around Detroit since the late 1950s. The Distants (Melvin Franklin, Otis Williams, Eldridge Bryant, Richard Street, and James Crawford) formed shortly after Otis Williams recruited bass Mel Franklin to fill a hole in Williams's group. In The Motown Story, Mel Franklin told Don Waller how it happened: He had recently come up to "the Big City" from Alabama, and "was always afraid of the guys that had processed hair and that other kind of look. You equated it with being in a gang." One day, as he was walking home from school, "I saw this tall, dark guy with a process coming, and he had on these shiny white shoes and this black leather jacket and stuff. I saw him coming and I crossed the street, because every time guys pass by they wanna put a stick on your shoulder and knock it off, make you fight with them, you know. And I got beat—I didn't have any big brothers, I'm the big brother.

"And so Otis crossed to the other side of the street where I was. That really made me afraid, so I crossed the street again. And he crossed the street again. By now, I'm trembling inside and my eyes are starting to water, 'cause I'm afraid, you know?"

Franklin fled, but when he got home a couple of hours later, "I saw Otis up at the door, so I hid behind a tree. I said, 'Oh, no. What in the hell is gonna happen to me?' Here he is talking to my mother.

"And my mother said, 'We can see you back there hidin' behind the tree. Come on out.'"

An hour later, Franklin was in the studio recording with the Distants. In 1960, the group left its label—and very nearly broke up as well—when Street and tenor James Crawford left the group. When they were replaced by Paul Williams and Eddie Kendricks from the Primes, however, the Temptations had four-fifths of what was to be their most successful lineup. Not only did Kendricks's falsetto leads help define the group's sound, but he and Williams brought in a lot of new material, supplementing the Distants' doo-wop with a more sophisticated style. As the Elgins, they were good enough, at least in Franklin's memory, that "whenever we'd be on a show that the Miracles were on, we made it plenty hot for them."

Berry Gordy, who was often around to watch his Miracles performing, apparently thought so, too, and one night, when he found himself standing next to Williams in the men's room, he recruited the group for Gordy Records. But after a half-dozen humdrum sides went nowhere (including one they recorded as the Pirates, a name they would have stuck with had the record clicked, for the Melody label), Bryant packed it in. He was replaced by David Ruffin.

Ruffin, a rural Mississippian, had been singing gospel since he was about six years old, and after finishing high school in Memphis, signed on for a hitch with the Dixie Nightingales. He came to Detroit, became friendly with one of Gordy's sisters, and was hired as a carpenter when Motown was expanding studio space. He was in the right place at the right time, and shared in the Tempts' first hit, 1964's "The Way You Do the Things You Do" (number 11). The lead on that song was taken by Eddie Kendricks, whose high-spirited falsetto ("If good looks was a minute, you know you could have been an hour") floated over the Tempts' ecstatic *whoo-hoos*. This was their second effort with Smokey Robinson as producer (Gordy himself had been behind the board on their earlier records), and they did two more singles behind Kendricks's lead before their fifth Robinson-produced record, which he also wrote, opened with Ruffin huskily exploring a typical Robinson paradox: "I've got sunshine on a cloudy day."

"My Girl," which reached number one in March, was indeed such a typical Robinson number that Smokey had planned to sing it himself, with the Miracles, but the Tempts—and the Motown system—persuaded him to give the song to them. Perhaps because he didn't want to have another falsetto singer taking lead on "his" song, Robinson put Ruffin out front, and when the song clicked, it not only gave Motown its first number one by a male group, it also gave the Tempts two lead singers. They were able to exploit this versatility brilliantly over the next few years, using Kendricks for happiness, Ruffin for heartbreak, and occasionally pulling out all the stops and letting them trade leads.

In addition, even among Motown's high-steppers, the Tempts had perhaps the most sizzling live show. They were athletic—Franklin had been an all-city basketball player in high school, and both Williams and Ruffin were capable of turning flips in the air—and even before they fell under the ministrations of Motown choreographer Cholly Atkins, Williams had been working them through precise, demanding routines. Given singers with such gymnastic skills, Atkins (who could also do more with less: he developed the stylized hand gestures that became the Supremes' trademark when he discovered that neither their talents nor their ankle-length sheath skirts allowed much dancing) challenged them with a flowing series of splits, flips, twirls, and microphone flings. If performing was schoolyard hoops, James Brown could probably take anybody one-on-one, but the Temptations were a team, and if they couldn't beat you with the break, they'd go backdoor to your heart.

In the physical sense, neither of the other huge Motown acts—the Supremes and the Four Tops—had the Temptations' moves. But in Holland-Dozier-Holland, they had perhaps even more impressive coaching. It's something of an oversimplification to speak of a "Motown sound"—Smokey Robinson's work, or Norman Whitfield's, is qualitatively different from H-D-H's—but so astonishing was the Holland-Dozier-Holland run of success that they came to define the company's style. From 1963 to 1966, the trio produced an astonishing twenty-eight top twenty hits, of which twelve went number one.

The three, Detroit born, had been around Motown in one capacity or another since the company's early days. Brian Holland, an engineer, had coproduced the Marvelettes' 1961 hit "Please Mr. Postman"; Lamont Dozier had recorded (as Lamont Anthony) for Berry Gordy's sister's company and joined the Motown performing roster (to no great success either time) in 1962; Eddie Holland, who joined his brother and Dozier as a producer in 1963, had scored an early Motown hit as a solo singer with 1962's "Jamie" (number 6 R&B, number 30 pop). This diversity of experience let them specialize: Brian worked the board and with keyboards and guitars on the basic track, Eddie focused on the lead vocal, and Lamont Dozier handled the background vocals and the rhythm section.

There was some overlap in the studio give-and-take, of course, but they were specialists in composing as well. Dozier and Brian Holland usually started out working together on the melody (Dozier), structure (Holland), and title (Dozier, again) of the song. After getting another Motown staffer to write out the chords in a key appropriate to the artist they were planning to use—none of the three wrote music—they would get the basic track laid down. Only then would it come to Eddie Holland, who was the team's lead lyricist. From there, once the composition and basic track had passed Motown's infamous quality control program, it was ready to go into the studio. It was this process that led serendipitously to the Supremes' first great success, "Where Did Our Love Go?"

H-D-H had originally planned the song for the Marvelettes, who were already established as hit makers. Of the Supremes' five previous releases, only two had climbed above the nineties and only one had cracked the top twenty-five. Gordy, however, assigned the song to the Supremes. "Of course," said Dozier, "we had already cut the track, and because of Gladys [Horton] singing it low like she does, the key was written real low. And it was actually too low for Diana.

"But this song that was in the wrong key is what gave Diana Ross her sound. 'Cause before then they always put Diana in the clouds and, to me, she sounded very thin up there. But because of the way the key was cut, she had to sing it low, and it came out very sentimental, very sexy."

The notion that you could take a song that was written and scored for one act and pass it on to another without any adjustment is, of course, typical Motown of the period. It was a producer's company, and three or four different acts might be given a shot working with a basic track (in sequence, with the currently hottest group given first crack) before a song was released. But whether working with the "very sentimental, very sexy" Supremes or the hoarse, impassioned shout of the Four Tops' Levi Stubbs, the H-D-H method remained constant.

To some extent, it was dictated by the limitations of Motown's recording facilities; even if the three had had Phil Spector–ish notions of grandiosity, they couldn't have fit all those musicians into the studio. As a result, overdubbing was standard, and the sequence went rhythm, vocal, percussion, horns, and strings. For the H-D-H sound, the third and fifth dubs were definitive.

Especially the third. Chuck Berry had long before described one of rock 'n' roll's definitive characteristics as "Got a backbeat, you can't lose it," but people did. For the folk-rockers, though they certainly had no objections if people wanted to dance to their music, the beat was an afterthought, almost a decoration. And for a lot of the new, "sophisticated" audience they brought to rock, the driving beat that had defined rock 'n' roll was an embarrassment, a reminder of acne and other high school agonies. H-D-H apparently figured that the non-R&B audience they were trying to reach had not only lost the backbeat but perhaps even the knack of finding it. So, on their third dubs, the trio drew an ineradicable road map. They used tambourines, hand claps, foot stomps, wood blocks, even cheap plastic ball points whacked together, all of them whanging down on that backbeat (on Martha and the Vandellas' "Dancing in the Streets," another Motown producer, Ivy Joe Hunter, wound up banging the floor with a set of automobile snow chains). Excessive this might have been, and formulaic for sure, but it worked. As Isaac Hayes, a Stax-Volt composer and producer before the days of *Hot Buttered Soul*, once put it: "What Motown did was very smart. They beat the kids over the head with it. That wasn't very soulful to us down at Stax, but baby, it *sold*."

Indeed it did, after the horns and strings (H-D-H's were usually arranged by one of the house horn players, Paul Riser), and perhaps some vocal sweetening to fatten the tracks, the songs were ready to go. Because Gordy liked his acts to be around the Motown headquarters anytime they weren't out on tour, there were always quality singers available, and it wasn't at all unusual to have, unacknowledged, Tops backing Tempts or the other way around. H-D-H were particularly partial to the Andantes (Marlene Barrow, Louvain Demps, and Jackie Hicks), a clear-voiced, poppish trio that recorded for Gordy's VIP label with little success, using them for high voices on Four Tops' cuts and to smooth out the Marvelettes' R&B edges.

Though H-D-H produced Top Ten singles for Martha and the Vandellas, Marvin Gaye, and even for Smokey and the Miracles (the untypical "Mickey's Monkey"), their greatest success came with the Supremes and the Four Tops. This quartet—Abdul "Duke" Fakir, Lawrence Payton, Renaldo "Obie" Benson, and lead singer Levi Stubbs—had been kicking around Detroit show business for a decade before coming to Motown. Originally as the Four Aims (a name changed because it was too similar to the Ames Brothers), they'd been supper-club regulars, alternating between a smooth Mills Brothers sound and their subsequent, harder-edged approach. They'd recorded with little discernible success for Chess, Red Top, and Columbia in the mid-1950s and early 1960s, but the professionalism of their club act had earned them a fan in Lamont Dozier, who finally lured them to Motown.

Initially Gordy concentrated on their supper-club side, and they recorded an album for his Workshop Jazz label as well as a couple of undistinguished singles. Mostly, however, they hung around the offices, playing a little cards, singing a considerable amount of backup, and waiting. But one night in 1964, while they were in the Twenty Grand watching the Temptations, Brian Holland came up to them and said, "I think I got a hit for you cats. Come back to the studio after the show is over and listen to it." At two or three in the morning, they not only listened to "Baby I Need Your Loving" but recorded it. Marked by the fire of Stubbs's attack—"*Got* to have all your loving"—it was the first in a chain of hits.

In 1965, they went number one with "I Can't Help Myself," also marked by Stubbs's trademark vocal stomp—"I can't *help* myself"—which replaced the Supremes' "Back in My Arms Again," giving the company its first back-to-back number ones.

One measure of how well the Tops and H-D-H worked together is a story that developed from their first number-one hit. In July of 1965, recognizing that it had a record by the country's top performers in its vaults, CBS decided to rerelease the Tops' 1960 Columbia effort, "Ain't That Love." Gordy got wind of it one morning and immediately set H-D-H to work on a rival single. It was written a little before noon, rehearsed with the band, and by the end of the day, the Tops had completed their vocals. Three days later, "It's the Same Old Song" was rush-released, entering the charts on the same day as CBS's effort. Columbia's "Ain't That Love" never rose any higher than number ninety-three, disappearing after a week, while "The Same Old Song" climbed to number five.

Though the Temptations and H-D-H's dynamic duo were the top Motown hitmakers of the period, they were hardly the only gold in Gordy's mine. The various Motown labels were loaded with acts whose commercial and artistic promise was still developing (Marvin Gaye, Stevie Wonder, Gladys Knight and the Pips), dependable R&B performers (Junior Walker, Kim Weston), as well as with "girl groups" (the classic Marvelettes, the eccentric Martha and the Vandellas) whose ability to climb the charts couldn't yet be discounted.

Each of these artists—and dozens of less well-known figures—received the Motown treatment. They got first-rate production (at least in a technical sense), brilliant promotion (Gordy, unlike traditional R&B company owners, had a sense about his acts' careers, not just their next records), and an education that included not only the infamous decorum training (in which women, for instance, learned to move gracefully and modestly in and out of cars), but money management and investment counseling. The artists, producers, promotion, and training added up to the Motown system, a system that might occasionally have held back performers who didn't fit into it smoothly but finally made the company the era's most dependable hit factory. It was the first, really, since the rock 'n' roll days when independent labels began challenging the majors' hegemony, and the last until relentless conglomeration and sheer weight led CBS and Warner Bros. to dominant positions almost a decade later.

Underneath it all, from ballad to novelty, was the label's one constant: Earl Van Dyke's studio band. Van Dyke actually replaced Ivy Joe Hunter at the keyboards when Hunter shifted to producing, but he, bassist James Jamerson, drummer Benny Benjamin and guitarists Robert White and Joe Messina (the sole white in the central group) were the core of a decade of Motown hits. When the band was at its best, Benjamin's kick and Jamerson's staccato bass actually functioned as a unit, establishing and then toying with the beat as one. Originally Benjamin was the group's leader (he was so prodigiously talented that whenever he missed a session, they called in two drummers to replace him), but his difficulties with drinking and drugs caused him to become more and more erratic in his scheduling—though not his work when he actually got behind his drum kit—and Van Dyke took over. Unlike the Stax house band, which was made up of kids (Booker T. joined up during a college vacation), the Motown house musicians were older, veterans of Detroit's funky jazz scene, and perhaps their greatest virtue is that they didn't have *a* sound but *all* the Motown sounds. And if they lacked the recognition that came to the Stax players, some of whom escaped anonymity when they toured as Booker T. and the MGs, that was more a product of the Motown system than of any limitation in their skills. As Van Dyke told Don Waller, "Berry Gordy was so tight on us, he never let us out of the country. Oh, Robert and I went over to England once on the Motortown Revue, but he kept Benny and James back in Detroit.

"He never let the four of us go out on the road at the same time. We did go out once, for a pair of weekend dates with Kim Weston. Berry heard about it and first thing Monday morning he called Mickey Stevenson into his office and chewed him out good. He told Mickey that was 'never ever to take place again. If they're not making enough here, pay 'em more.' " If someone wanted to cut a record at three in the morning, Gordy wanted his band around. And he did pay them well, too—at least $50,000 a year in uninflated mid-sixties' dollars—but that meant not only that they were always on call but that they were *his*. In 1965, after he'd discovered they'd woodshed-ded behind Edwin Starr's "Agent Double-O Soul," a hit for Eddie Wingate's rival Detroit label, Ric-Tic, Gordy fined them a thousand dollars each. According to Van Dyke, "When Wingate found out about it, he bogarted his way into the Motown Christmas party and paid our fines. He said he didn't care, he'd pay our fines and use us again. He gave us a bonus on the session, too."

Of the soul bands that did tour as backups, the prize for tightest probably belonged to James Brown's largely anonymous JBs (though Ike Turner's outfits would probably get a few votes, too). Brown had started his profes-sional career backed by the Famous Flames, formerly a gospel group called the Swans, and they remained, through various personnel shifts, part of the long-running James Brown Revue, but in the late 1950s, he added a stage band. His records, however, released by Federal, continued to feature the Flames because Federal wouldn't let him use the JBs in the studio. Brown cannily arranged for the JBs to record on the Dade label as Nat Kendrick and the Swans. After they scored a solid R&B and minor pop hit with "(Do the) Mashed Potato" early in 1960, Federal's parent company, King, wisely relented, and from that point on, Brown's records began taking on the syncopated staccato that would become his trademark.

He was still troubled by difficulties with his record company, however, which refused to bring out a live album because it thought people wouldn't buy live versions of music they already had. So using his own money— about five thousand dollars—Brown went ahead and cut *The James Brown Show Live at the Apollo* on his own. It was released in 1963, and although the fans who owned his singles were mostly black, *Live at the Apollo* crossed over and rode the pop charts for an astonishing sixty-six weeks. The label seemed unable to capitalize on Brown's approach to a white audience, however, and in 1964, he and his long-time booker, Universal Attractions' Ben Bart, formed Fair Deal Productions and released "Out of Sight" through a Mercury subsidiary. Not only was it a number-one R&B hit, but it spent weeks on the pop charts, peaking at number twenty-four. It also provoked a lengthy court battle (which would become moot when Polygram acquired both companies) that left Brown the instrumentalist free to continue recording for Mercury but Brown the vocalist obligated to King. King promptly renegotiated their contract to make Brown one of the very few performers, black or white, to have complete artistic control. In the summer of 1965, he used it to score his first Top Ten pop singles.

Brown's freedom to record his own chosen sounds led his music to its own logical—and unique—conclusion. For some time, the JBs had been growing gradually more percussive; the bass more staccato, the rhythm guitar damped and choked. By 1965, his band had reached a stage described by critic Robert Palmer in a passage that admits no improvement:

> Brown would sing a semi-improvised, loosely organized melody that wandered while the band riffed rhythmically on a single chord, the horns tersely punctuating Brown's declamatory phrases. With no chord changes and precious little melodic variety to sustain listener interest, rhythm became everything. Brown and his musicians and arrangers began to treat every instrument and voice in the group as if it were a drum. The horns played single-note bursts that were often sprung against the downbeats. The bass lines were broken up into choppy two- or three-note patterns, a procedure common in Latin music since the Forties but unusual in R&B. Brown's rhythm guitarist choked his guitar strings against the instrument's neck so hard that his playing began to sound like a jagged tin can being scraped with a pocket knife.

But for all the virtuosity of the band, in concert Brown was the show: He soared, he whirled, he flew through the air, then splayed on the floor in a contortionist's split; then, as if pulled by unseen strings, rose again, then slumped to his knees, begging for love; then swooped past the piano to pound out a few chords; then, in total exhaustion, sprawled on the floor again, helpless, at the foot of the mike stand.

As the band continued to play, the Famous Flames came forward, covered him with a cloak and led him, wobbly-kneed, toward the wings. But the music got to him. An arm shot out; he began to dance again; in a compacted drama more intense than before, he reprised the whole show—soaring, splitting, rising, falling, dying. Another colored cape this time, and this time it took three people to steer him offstage. But the music hit him *again*. Grabbed him, flung him around. His voice was reduced to a hoarse, sandpapery croak. But he sang anyway, *screamed* anyway. His electric-blue suit was drenched black with sweat. One of his knees was bleeding. The audience was screaming now, "James! *Jaaaaames!*"—either begging for more or pleading with him to stop while he was still alive. This time, when he was half-dragged, half-carried offstage, the show was over—but *no!* It *couldn't* be! He was fighting his way through the Flames, clawing and screaming. He'd risen! "James! *Jaaaames!*"

To be this free for 250 or 300 nights every year, Brown needed strict structure behind him, and JBs were whacked with heavy fines for fluffed notes or errant dance steps. Still, he seemed the wave of the future, and he was—relatively soon, too, with Sly and the Family Stone, and well into the eighties, with JB veterans Bootsy Collins and Bootsy's Rubber Band, and with Maceo Parker and Fred Wesley in George Clinton's extraterrestrial funk, as well as in virtually every Talking Heads rhythm line. But at the time, Brown was *sui generis*, and neither other musicians nor the mass audience could swallow him whole. Late in the summer of 1965, "Papa's Got a Brand New Bag" gave Brown his first Top Ten record on the pop charts, and its follow-up, "I Got You (I Feel Good)," went to number three, cracking the top five for the first time in Brown's career—and the last. Although he charted an astonishing thirty-one singles over the rest of the decade (the Beatles hit twenty-three times), only 1968's "I Got the Feelin' " reached as high as number six.

Not coincidentally, Brown would depart from the pop Top Ten for the rest of the decade immediately after 1968's "Say It Loud—I'm Black and Proud," a song that defined his separation from white mainstream pop even more clearly than his whirling-dervish performing style. By that time, the incipient split between black and white pop had widened into a chasm; yet though it was less visible during the civil rights years, it existed even then. Despite their firmly held integrationist ideology, the folkies and their followers were making and listening to a music that was essentially untouched by the innovations of Brown, Smokey Robinson, H-D-H, or the soul explosion.

18

AMERICAN MADE

In a simultaneous burst of innovation, entirely separate from the nation-wide explosion of soul, an entire new genre of white pop was gradually being created by a merger of the folkies' outsider intellectualism with the newly revivified energies of rock. At the center of this development—as writer, performer, arbiter of the *scene*—stood Bob Dylan.

Early on, however, the scene-making Dylan was too caustic, the perform-ing Dylan too eccentric, for even such tolerant enterprises as *The T.A.M.I. Show.* As he had when Peter, Paul and Mary eased his songs onto the pop charts in Milt Okun's acoustic arrangements, Dylan initially made himself felt in rock as a songwriter. This time the agents who smoothed his rough edges for the transition were the Byrds.

Cerebral, cool, withdrawn, the Byrds were Californians who drew their energy from neon lights rather than surf, and it's more than a little odd that this most cosmopolitan of groups found themselves cast as folkies. Actu-ally the Byrds didn't *want* to invent folk-rock; their ambition, at once simpler and more grandiose, was to be stars. As Roger (née Jim) McGuinn once told an interviewer, "Why did I decide to form the group? I saw the Beatles, that's why . . . bang, that's the answer, that's all. That was enough; it turned me on, you know. I wanted to get a four- or five-piece group together with electric instruments and try to do that because it looked like a lot of fun."

McGuinn, raised in Chicago and influenced by both Bob Gibson and the Old Town School of Folk Music's Frank Hamilton, had been a professional musician for about four years before the nucleus of the Byrds came to-gether. During a gig at the Troubadour in Los Angeles, he met Gene Clark, a

303

recent escapee from the New Christy Minstrels, and—almost immediately after the two had decided to form a group—David Crosby, who had toiled for a while with the middle-of-the-road Les Baxter Orchestra as one of Les Baxter's Balladeers. Crosby introduced them to Jim Dickson, an independent producer and an underground aesthetic force, who in turn hooked them up with Chris Hillman, a bluegrass artist–cum–folkie who was fluent on the mandolin. Then, in typical garage-band fashion, they began to settle on instruments. McGuinn played lead, Crosby moved from bass to rhythm guitar, Clark from rhythm guitar to vocals and tambourine, and Hillman to a new, bright-red Japanese bass. To finish off, they found a drummer, though cynics might suggest that Michael Clarke wasn't much of an addition. As McGuinn once said, "I knew he was a very good conga player, and David had known him in Big Sur—panhandling and painting. So, on the basis of his conga playing and his painting, we hired him as a rock drummer."

Among his other drawbacks, Clarke didn't have any drums, and in an interview with the irreplaceable British magazine *Zigzag*, Hillman recalled him showing up for rehearsals with drumsticks and cardboard boxes: "He knew a few basics, but he virtually learned from scratch . . . learned how to play enough to enable us to go out and perform. We were rehearsing eight hours a day for months and months in this old Hollywood studio and we just developed that sound and style . . . from nothing."

As the rehearsals ground on, Dickson, who would co-manage them with Eddie Tickner, negotiated a singles contract with Elektra, Jac Holzman's album-oriented folkie label. In rather too obvious homage to the Beatles and the other British invaders, they were billed as the Beefeaters, a name for which Holzman courageously accepts responsibility. When the record flopped—though its B side showed up as "It Won't Be Wrong" and as a single in 1966 on the *Turn! Turn! Turn!* album—Elektra dropped them, but Dickson was able to sign the band to Columbia Records. And so the Byrds were born.

Then Dickson found them a song, Dylan's "Mr. Tambourine Man," although, as Hillman recalled, "We didn't really like it or even understand it at the time, but he drove it down our throats until we realized what it was." During those rehearsals, the song began to take a new shape; when Dylan sang it, "Mr. Tambourine Man" was mysterious, private—and perhaps even a little threatening. In the Byrds' lush and soaring harmonies, it became an invitation. But when the time came to record it, Columbia thriftily limited the group's studio time, so producer Terry Melcher had them concentrate on those vocal lines, letting session men—Larry Knechtal on bass, Hal Blaine on drums, Leon Russell on guitar—handle all the instrumentals except McGuinn's twelve-string. Knechtal laid down perhaps the most famous opening bass line in rock, and when McGuinn's ringing twelve-string entered, the Byrds' sound informed Dylan's words, bringing together, for the first time, a purely American response to the British invasion.

"Mr. Tambourine Man" started slowly, not reaching the charts until the middle of May and not hitting number one until the last week in June. But when it did, the scuffling—Mike Clarke was *still* living in Jim Dickson's basement—had finally paid off. In that sense, of course, the Byrds were Everyband; the bowling alleys of Southern California were their Hamburg, their Marquee, their Motortown Revue. But because they'd gone number one by rocking a Dylan song, they were different. And so, even more important, was their audience. The purists among them were horrified, naturally, but "Mr. Tambourine Man" reached out and consolidated that postpubescent generation the Beatles had first attracted with *A Hard Day's Night.* The Byrds had flung open the door the British groups had pushed ajar, and through it came Donovan, Greenwich Village's Lovin' Spoonful, seasoned L.A. pros Sonny and Cher, surf music refugees the Turtles, the Mamas and the Papas, and Buffalo Springfield—not to mention Dylan himself.

Who had, in the way of chimerical geniuses, been on both sides of it all along. The 1963 Newport Folk Festival had seen him emerge as the champion of the folkies. His evening concert set, with Joan Baez's harmonics floating out, turned into a spontaneous singalong as Peter, Paul and Mary, the civil rights movement's Freedom Singers, and emcees Pete Seeger and Theodore Bikel joined him on "Blowin' in the Wind." It was a moment that brought together many disparate strands of the folk revival, and it is little wonder that Seeger and the other weary veterans of the McCarthy era saw Dylan as a vindication of their years of struggle.

At the same time, however, Dylan—and Columbia Records—was already reaching toward the pop market. Peter, Paul and Mary, taking two of his songs into the Top Ten before the year was out, established him as a songwriter to be reckoned with, and his own single of "Subterranean Homesick Blues" charted almost two months before the Byrds' version of "Mr. Tambourine Man." Though it barely dented the U.S. Top Forty (stopping at number 39), it went to number one in England. Certainly the Byrds, three thousand miles away in California, can't have been responsible for Dylan's embracing rock (though Anthony Scaduto reports that Dylan was sent an advance of their single). And neither—though as we've seen, he liked them early on—can the Beatles, or even the Animals. The British groups can perhaps be given indirect credit, however, for the way they'd opened Dylan's local influences. The pre–Al Kooper Blues Project was woodshedding around the Village, for instance, but perhaps no folkie was quite as catholic as Dylan's long-time accompanist, Bruce Langhorne.

Langhorne, though a black and therefore untypical, could hardly have been more a part of the folkie establishment. He'd played with Dylan on Carolyn Hester's album, and for a while during the early 60s, it seemed as though you couldn't pick up a made–in–New York folk album without seeing Langhorne's name in the musicians' credits. In his own performances, however, Langhorne had been playing occasional electrical guitar (in one case, on a duet of a Thelonius Monk tune with the equally eclectic

Sandy Bull) since at least 1960. By all accounts, the *Bringing It All Back Home* sessions were typical Dylan chaos, but to the extent that they can be said to have had an arranger other than Dylan himself, it was Langhorne.

But even before that album split the folkies down the middle, Dylan had taken a turn that disturbed his one-time mentors at *Sing Out!* and *Broadside* with 1964's aptly titled *Another Side of Bob Dylan.* Earlier in the year, Dylan had essentially retired the Protest Cup by outdistancing all contenders with *The Times They Are A-Changin'*, an album whose protest cuts included not only the title song but "The Lonesome Death of Hattie Carroll" and "When the Ship Comes In." That album, however, ended with "Restless Farewell," an intensely personal song, almost a closing note of dissatisfaction. *Another Side* took up that hint, explicitly rejecting "protest" in "My Back Pages" and turning instead to autobiographical introspection. "There aren't any finger pointing songs in here," Dylan told an interviewer at the time. "I don't want to write *for* people anymore—you know, be a spokesman. From now on I want to write from inside me. . . ."

This hardly seems an unreasonable or untypical desire—Dylan, like many of his contemporaries, was increasingly involved with drug-aided explorations of his own mind—but his performance of these songs at the 1964 Newport Folk Festival drew a cool response from much of the folkie establishment. In a famous and not entirely unsympathetic "Open Letter" published shortly thereafter, *Sing Out!*'s Silber wrote, "You said you weren't a writer of 'protest' songs—or any other category of songs for that matter—but you just wrote songs. Well, okay, call it anything you want. But any songwriter who tries to deal honestly with reality in this world is bound to write 'protest' songs. How can he help himself?

"Your new songs seem to be all inner-directed now, inner-probing, self-conscious—maybe even a little maudlin or a little cruel on occasion. . . ."

Though a number of Dylan's less sensitive detractors were quick to accuse him of selling out, *Another Side* actually sold less well than its two predecessors; a transition, it moved away from one audience without directly addressing a second. Yet if *Another Side* disappointed some of those who'd most admired Dylan, 1965's *Bringing It All Back Home* outraged them. Not only was this music not about Hattie Carroll, it was electric (and popular, too; *Bringing It All Back Home* went on to be Dylan's first gold album). This outrage finally boiled over during the 1965 Newport Folk Festival.

By the still-to-come standards of stadium rock, the Newport Folk Festivals were comparatively small potatoes, but as a gathering and validation of the folkie clan, their importance—especially the recordings that documented them—outstripped mere numbers. Freebody Park, where the nighttime concerts were staged, held only about 15,000 people, and though there might at any time be a few thousand non-ticketholders milling around outside, a total turnout of 25,000 for the three-day weekend would be a high estimate. Yet the lack of seating for the evening concerts didn't mean that the ticketless were denied a chance to hear music, and indeed many listeners felt that the festival's best music occurred during the afternoons, in "workshops"—sometimes mini-concerts, sometimes question-and-answer musical seminars—organized around specific themes like topical songs, Cajun fiddling, or folk dance.

It was at the blues workshop that a flareup violated the low-key Newport ethos, prefiguring Dylan's famous appearance and hinting that the "problem" might be less Dylan himself than the generational conflict that would be a hallmark of "the sixties."

The dispute involved the Paul Butterfield Blues Band. Chicago-based, Butterfield's band was *sui generis* in America. Though New York had certainly had its share of individual white folkie worshippers at the blues shrine—Dave Van Ronk was the most accomplished and inventive, John Hammond, Jr., the most painfully sincere—there was nothing in America that approximated the London blues scene that had spawned the Rolling Stones. What there was, however, was a living, continuing tradition of blues playing—alive, well, and electronically amplified—in those American cities that had substantial black populations. The tradition was probably most vital in Chicago, where at least a half-dozen thriving blues clubs competed, featuring such musicians as Muddy Waters, B. B. King, Junior Wells, and Hound Dog Taylor. Such clubs had perhaps always attracted a smattering of whites, rather in the way that Cole Porter's friends toured Harlem in the twenties, but in the early sixties, they began seeing a group of young men who came neither as slumming society folk nor as curators. These kids thought they could play the blues.

And eventually, some of them could. In what would have seemed bliss beyond belief to the romantic Brits, young musicians—some of them refugees from the university, others street-tough Chicago kids—like Paul Butterfield, Elvin Bishop, and Mike Bloomfield jammed regularly with genuwine black persons of the blues persuasion. This was often not a romantic experience. "You'd play a club," Bloomfield once recalled, "and there were a lot of pimps and bad guys, and if one of them had a gun, well, he'd be prepared to use it. I remember playing with Howlin' Wolf. He'd introduce us as, 'I got some white friends from the suboibs down here,' and I'd get up and be up there playing and some dude would pull a gun on another dude, and the whole band would just go hide.

"Oh, man, I remember a time I was standing at a bar and a guy walked in and he took a woman's head out of a paper bag and slammed it on the bar top. He said, 'Bartender, get this bitch a beer.' The guy had just sliced off his old lady's head in some horrible fight and took her head down to the bar to show the bartender." In scenes like this (though, fortunately, usually a good deal less dramatic), the musicians, black and white, who would eventually join the Paul Butterfield Blues Band paid their dues. And as musicians, if not as individuals, they were tight, disciplined, traditional, and almost explosive—surely not about to be concerned with some East Coast ideal of "authenticity."

Still, when Elektra Records, for which they were the first regularly signed electronic act, arranged for them to play at a Newport workshop, they were thrilled. They should have known better. A couple of years earlier, even Muddy Waters had been given a distant welcome by the Newport audience when he brought his band to the festival; the next year, Waters, who had as keen a sense of the dollar as most bar-weary veterans of the chitlin' circuit, came East as a solo—with an acoustic guitar. Despite this, there was a positive buzz about the Butterfield Band. They'd signed with Elektra, Albert Grossman was talking them up around the pool at the Viking, and besides, at least some of this year's Newport audience had liked *Bringing It All Back Home*. The turnout for the blues workshop was perhaps the heaviest of the festival.

Before Butterfield, however, there was a genuinely all-star parade of blues players, nearly all of whom fit neatly into the acceptable authentic mode, that is to say, old, black, and acoustic. The sets were short—two or three numbers seemed the rule—and the introductions, by famous folk song collector Alan Lomax, at once scholarly and warm. Naturally when a large electronic band succeeded these soloists, there was a delay for setting up the drums and amps, and for tuning together. Lomax, who had reportedly been annoyed that the band had been booked into "his" workshop at all, grew more and more upset, finally introducing them with, "Well, this afternoon you've heard some of the greatest blues musicians in America playing for you, and all they've had to do is come out and play. Now we've got some people who've spent fifteen minutes setting up, and now we'll see if they can play the blues at all."

Among those most upset by Lomax's condescension was Albert Grossman. Grossman, a founder of the festival who'd managed Chicago's Gate of Horn folk club before going on to more or less invent Peter, Paul and Mary and to manage a host of other acts, including Dylan, was an enormously loyal and intense advocate of the performers he handled and, it turned out, of those he was going to manage. He headed straight for Lomax, and as Bloomfield recalled it, said, " 'How can you give these guys this type of introduction? This is really out of line. You're a real prick to do this.' They got into a fistfight—these two elderly guys—right there in front of the stage, rolling in the dirt while we were playing, and I was screaming 'Kick his ass, Albert! Stomp 'im!' There was bad blood rising, you could tell."

The bad blood came to a boil halfway through the final night's concert, when Dylan made his long-awaited appearance. This was emphatically a new Dylan. Gone was the Huck Finn cap (he was modishly attired in an outrageous polka-dot Carnaby Street shirt), and gone, too, the pudginess (mostly as a result of drugs, it subsequently developed), replaced by a lean figure in shades—and the fans were not at all sure they liked it.

And when he launched into "Maggie's Farm"—straight-ahead, crunching rock—the folkie establishment was so certain they didn't that reliable reports have Pete Seeger attempting to yank the plug on his one-time protégé. The audience began shouting during the opening number (whether because they hated the music or because the pickup band's sound mix was so murky it buried Dylan's voice is still a matter of debate), and after his third song, Dylan quit the stage. Peter Yarrow attempted to talk him into coming back and doing an acoustic number to calm the audience down so the show could go on, and Dylan, by then a professional, complied. What he played was an entirely accurate statement of his relationship with the more doctrinaire folkies, "It's All Over Now, Baby Blue."

A month later, at the tennis stadium in Forest Hills, there was no ambiguity about what was causing screams of outrage from the crowd. Dylan had done an acoustic set for the first half of the show, for which he earned a standing ovation, and then returned with his then band (Al Kooper, Harvey Brooks, Levon Helm, and Robbie Robertson) after intermission. As Kooper recalled: "Harvey and I had lived in Forest Hills, so it was our old stomping ground and we thought it would be all right. Then we got ready to go out and do the second part as an electric band. Then Bob took us to one side. 'It's gonna be very weird out there,' he said, '. . . anything could happen . . . I just want you to know that.' So we went out, and boy, was it fucking weird. It was the end of August, but as soon as we got onstage, the wind came up . . . it was like a hurricane. It blew all the mike stands over, the temperature dropped right down, and the wind was just howling and whistling around that bowl . . . God must have been watching.

"Well, we played the first thirty seconds, and the audience just started booing. I could hardly believe it, because we were really good. Then people started rushing the stage to grab him, and I got knocked over, right on my ass out there on stage, and it was incredible . . . he just stood there, with the wind blowing his hair out sideways . . . and the booing went on . . . I'll never forget it."

Kooper has described himself as amazed by Dylan's reaction at the postconcert party—he "walked right over and hugged me. 'Wasn't it fantastic?' he said. He was really happy about it"—but he shouldn't have been. It was characteristic Dylan; even in his early Folk City days, he'd radiated an absolute self-confidence that was, in retrospect, far more typical of rock 'n' roll performers than of folkies.

It was that edge, that *sureness*, that characterized the album he recorded between Newport and Forest Hills—*Highway 61 Revisited*, unquestionably one of the decade's greatest records.

Though it was recorded at CBS's New York studio and featured New York's top session men, most of it was produced by Nashville's Bob Johnston (the most notable exception was the album's giant hit, "Like a Rolling Stone," for which Tom Wilson was in the chair). But the producer really didn't matter; as Mike Bloomfield told Ed Ward, it was very much

Dylan's album: "Bob would start singing the songs, and we'd start fitting the music in around him. The producer, the arranger, they had no function, and terrible things were happening, like Dylan was singing songs that were ten minutes long eight times. How could anybody be expected to sing 'Desolation Row' eight times? That's a long fucking song, man! And we were trying to figure out some grooves that fit, some concept. . . . There was no game plan! The day before, he was still writing the songs! . . . If anybody had an idea for a sound, it was Al Kooper, and he and I were the low men on the rung."

Kooper, who hadn't been in on any of the Woodstock rehearsal sessions, arrived at Tom Wilson's invitation, but he almost didn't play. He recalls sitting there with his guitar plugged in, feeling confident among other New York session players, when "this Bloomfield walked in, Stratocaster not even in a case, winter outside. The guitar was wet; he wipes it off with a pillowcase or something, plugs it in, and starts to play. I said, 'Well, I'm not playing any guitar on *this* session,' and I packed my guitar up."

Resigned to a spectator's role, he sat in the booth, but after a few takes, Paul Griffen was shifted from organ to piano, "so I grabbed Tom Wilson and said, 'Hey, let me play the organ.'"

" 'But you can't even play organ,' he said.

" 'Come on, Tom, just give me a try. If you don't like it, just tell me through the mike. I've got something good.' Of course, I didn't, and I was sitting there with no idea of what I was going to play—I knew the theory of keyboards, but I didn't play too well. Well, the song was very complicated; it wasn't written down, and the structure was very difficult to comprehend there and then . . . and I didn't even know how to work the organ. Then Tom shouted, 'Okay, let's roll it.'

"Well, Jesus! Those cats were playing so loud that I couldn't even hear what I was playing . . . so I was just going by the knowledge that if you play C, it goes okay with an F chord, and so on. Well, I had no idea what was coming out of that organ, but we did the whole take there and then— straight through without stopping. Then we went back to listen, and about a quarter of the way through the playback, Dylan said to Tom Wilson, 'Turn up the organ track.' Tom said, 'Oh, man, that cat's not an organ player.'

" 'Don't tell me who's an organ player and who's not,' Dylan said. 'Turn up the organ.' Well, that track was 'Like a Rolling Stone,' and that take was the one they used on the record."

That song, which concluded the Forest Hills concert, had been among the most lustily booed, but something in its snarling, impassioned viciousness (*not*, obviously, the usual stuff of pop hits) reached an audience larger than Dylan had ever before approached. Sparked by a West Coast concert tour, on which he was greeted enthusiastically by people who'd been indifferent to the old, Woody Guthrie–esque Dylan, it climbed to number two on the charts. In addition to cracking the content conventions of the day, its 6:07 length shattered the 3-minute barrier beloved by radio programmers. Perhaps most important, though, it opened the range of "natural voice" possibilities that would be available to subsequent performers. Though there had always been a place for weird or unbeautiful voices in pop, that place was the "novelty" ghetto, and as "Positively 4th Street" proved later in the year, Dylan was no novelty.

But even though CBS, and Hammond in particular, must have understood this, neither did the company treat Dylan like an "ordinary" pop act. The difference between the way the company's West Coast operation treated the Byrds and the extraordinary degree of freedom Dylan received in the studio had something to do with the differences between Los Angeles and New York, of course, but more with Dylan's place in the folkie continuum. For the performers who recorded on Folkways, Elektra, Vanguard, Riverside, Prestige, and other independent folkie labels, "artist's control" wasn't something they needed to struggle to attain but a matter of routine.

And why not? Studio and distribution costs were low, promotion consisted mostly of the performers themselves trying to scratch out livings by touring (and selling their albums out of cardboard boxes after their shows), session musicians were virtually nonexistent, the repertoire was endless and mostly in public domain, and, except for Elektra and Vanguard, production values were relatively unimportant. Given all that, who was going to bother telling Dave Van Ronk which blues to sing or Jack Elliott which Woody Guthrie song to choose? There was certainly no need to look for a hit single—or, indeed, for any singles at all. Folkies recorded, and bought, albums, and even folk-influenced acts with straightforwardly commercial aspirations (Peter, Paul and Mary, for example) had the bulk of their sales in the album market.

Initially, at least, this was the pattern both Dylan and CBS had expected, and their expectations had been fulfilled by the way Dylan's initial recordings sold. When he "went electric," he simply carried the homemade aspects of folkie recording along with him, and none of his records ever achieved—or even aimed for—the standard industry level of studio gloss. Since this didn't prevent *Bringing It All Back Home* from selling a million copies, it hardly seemed worth correcting.

But even after that album was in the can, Dylan was still performing on the folkie circuit. In March of 1965, he and Joan Baez, then lovers, did a national tour together as co-billed headliners. They had performed together frequently during the previous year, sometimes when she showed up unannounced at one of his shows, more often when she introduced him to the larger crowds she was then drawing. Their relationship was growing troubled, however (less from any folkie-rocker split than from Dylan's increasingly apolitical stance and his equally increasing use of speed), and it finally fell apart later that year during the English tour captured in D. A. Pennebaker's film *Don't Look Back*. Though she was a major character in the film, Baez didn't perform with Dylan in England. Commercially, he didn't need her; emotionally, he didn't want her. Two weeks into his triumphant capture of England, Baez jumped off the merry-go-round and went to France to stay with her family. The romance of the peace queen and the rock 'n' roll king was over.

Pennebaker's gritty, telling documentary of that tour wasn't released until 1967, but the Dylan it captured—sneering at a *Time* reporter; crushing a worshipful student; taunting a party guest; putting on, and putting down, anyone who wasn't fully as hip as he—was widely reported in the world press. The bohemian/beatnik culture that had once sustained him had always been quietly contemptuous of the bourgeoisie, but Dylan, a one-man generation gap, was openly derisive even of "good elders" like those clustered around *Broadside.*

Except, perhaps, for the early, pre-tamed Elvis, there really wasn't a musical antecedent. The Beatles, at least in their Epstein-manicured *personae*, were cheeky, but Dylan was brutal. And the classic teenage pose of the fifties song (of which the "Wouldn't It Be Nice" Beach Boys were the logical extension) involved wanting to be grown-up so that either (a) the enduring teenage love would prove that the parents were wrong all along, or (b) they could enter the presumably attractive world of adult pleasure and privilege. The theme was, "They don't understand, but somehow we'll *make* them"; to find an equivalent of Dylan's "They don't understand, so fuck 'em," you have to look toward Marlon Brando and James Dean in their motorcycle jackets.

After he returned from England to find himself emerging as a certified pop star on this side of the Atlantic as well, Dylan took that attitude *everywhere.* It was with him in the Kettle of Fish on MacDougal Street, where he could still, just barely, sit and have a drink with Phil Ochs, Eric Andersen, Dave Van Ronk, David Blue, or Bobby Neuwirth without being bothered by fans, and it was with him onstage during the grinding national tours Grossman organized for him. For all that he had effectively renounced conventional politics, the notion that he embodied—that what he and his expanding coterie believed, what they did, what they *were*, was immeasurably superior to the orthodox culture surrounding them—was a profoundly political and prescient idea. It didn't translate immediately to his contemporaries, though you could hear it in some of Phil Ochs's work (and Lennon's "Happy Xmas War Is Over" would pick up on Ochs's "I Believe the War is Over"), but it informed Buffalo Springfield's seminal "For What It's Worth (Stop, Hey, What's That Sound)" and would be at the core of virtually all the important San Francisco music.

For a different set of reasons, Dylan's attitude was even slower to be felt among—or at least voiced by—black musicians. At a time when the entire political thrust of the black community was geared to the struggle for integration, announcements that mainstream white society wasn't worth getting into were at least irrelevant and perhaps even incomprehensible. Though Dick Gregory might joke about finally getting served at a Woolworth's lunch counter only to find out the food was lousy, the subversive sentiment underlying the joke would remain buried until the twin notions of black pride and black power caught fire among the younger generation of blacks.

Indeed, to be anything more than sour grapes, the Dylanesque snarl *had* to spring from a position of comparative privilege: you can't reject what people aren't willing to give you in the first place. It came naturally to the middle-class Stones, for instance, but considerably more slowly to the genuinely working-class Beatles. Even as Dylan was captivating British audiences during the *Don't Look Back* European tour, the Beatles were getting to enjoy the first fruits of privilege.

In June 1965, they found their names on Queen Elizabeth II's birthday honors list as Members of the Order of the British Empire. This was more than just a social gesture, for in a large and growing international industry, the Beatles had almost singlehandedly reversed the balance of trade (as the year opened, more than a quarter of the singles on *Billboard's* "Hot 100" list were by British artists). Some of the Queen's previous honorees didn't see things in this straightforward way, however, and a few—including a member of the Canadian Parliament who wrote that he didn't want to be placed "on the same level as vulgar nincompoops"—returned their MBEs; later, for quite different reasons, John would echo their gesture.

Before they received their royal honors, however, the band was off to America: ten cities, ten giant outdoor arenas, ten woefully inadequate sound systems, four visually distant and aurally garbled dots banging through a half-hour's worth of singles, several hundred thousand teenage girls ululating, and a million or so dollars in the bank.

Their record sales continued undiminished as well, so the tour (which might have counted as the birth of stadium rock if the sound system had let their appearances be concerts rather than *events*) was just one more piece of evidence that they'd conquered America. Or, more accurately, part of America: the screaming crowds they drew remained overwhelmingly white, predominantly female, and young enough to wear, with all apparent seriousness, buttons reading "I Love . . . [with the name of the adored object]."

And objects is what they were, which was getting to be not enough for the developing rock audience. If you wanted to see—and hear—the Beatles, however, there was always *Help!*, but that, too, proved inadequate. Released on July 29, 1965, to coincide with their American tour—and shot *almost* as quickly as *A Hard Day's Night, Help!* has suffered the usual fate of sequels and been dismissed as at once more expensive and less inventive than its predecessor. It was indeed more expensive—Technicolor and on-location shooting ranging from the Alps to the Bahamas saw to that—but it is less disappointing now, on videotape, than it was then. Sure, the film was gimmicky—George called it a "fast-moving comic strip"—but it had the comics' two-dimensional charm. Its problem was us; we wanted three. The boys were, in fact, no more cartoonish than they'd been in *A Hard Day's*

Night—each was still basically a one-trick pony—but fans hoped the new movie would answer their increasingly passionate question: What is (select one: George, Paul, John, Ringo) *really* like? As a quasidocumentary, *A Hard Day's Night* gave the illusion that it might answer such a question; *Help!'s* loonily improbable plot held its audience at a distance, offering entertainment instead of intimacy.

Why wasn't entertainment enough? After all, nobody complained that Bing and Bob didn't bare their souls during *Road to Morocco*. Partly, the answer was blowin' in the technology; television had made a generation used to celebrities who were "at home" to us. And partly, too, it was that the Beatles' comparative exoticism—their Liverpudlian Englishness—made them a mystery that needed to be solved. But it was Dylan, too. "Mr. Tambourine Man" was evocative and mystifying, but the elfin figure in the Huck Finn cap was just a memory by now; "Like a Rolling Stone" and "Positively 4th Street" were scarifyingly intimate trips into the maelstrom of a complex soul. Once Dylan's folkie audience began to merge with the Beatles', it started asking "Why can't *they* do that? Are they (dread word) *superficial?*"

The question—and the expectation behind it—hinted at the inevitable dissolution of the temporarily united rock audience. To the very real differences of age, class, and race that euphoria and musical wonderment had momentarily masked, Dylan and the other folkies making their ways into the rock mainstream had created a revolution of rising expectations. The Beatles' charm, their cheek, even their musical brilliance, wasn't going to be enough for long.

19

DOPE AND ITS DISCONTENTS

By now, the Beatles, who were fans long before they were musicians, were listening to Dylan and those he'd inspired. Lennon, whose *In His Own Write* and *A Spaniard in the Works* had marked him as the Fab Four's most (only?) "literary" member, was especially stimulated. As he told *Rolling Stone*, "I used to write a book or stories on one hand and write songs on the other. And I'd be writing completely free form in the book and just on a bit of paper, but when I'd start to write a song I'd be thinking dee duh dee duh do dooo do de do de doo. And it took Dylan and all that was going on then to say, Oh, come on now, that's the same bit, I'm just singing the words." With *Rubber Soul*, released at the end of 1965, Lennon discovered how to bring poet and rocker into comfortable coexistence on vinyl. From its ever-so-slightly-psychedelic cover (the rippling faces; the bulging and distorted letters that would become, heightened, the trademark of San Francisco poster art) to its mystifying, secret-password language, the album was not only the Beatles' next giant step but rock's as well.

To begin with, it had been recorded—and was marketed—as an album. The American version (less chopped up than usual, though Capitol held back "Nowhere Man" in order to release it as a single) soared to the top of the charts without the spur of advance single hits. But even more important, the album represented a major shift away from the group's consuming focus on romantic love. It was hardly an abandonment of the theme—the album led off with the thoroughly winning "I've Just Seen a Face," in which only the chord changes were startling—but when they announced that the Word was Love, their aim was more grandiose. "Nowhere Man" was completely without redeeming romantic importance (even Ray Davies had

315

given his well-respected man a girl next door), and "In My Life," though it had the sound of a romantic ballad, was about friendship. And who could tell what "Norwegian Wood" was about?

That cut was the Beatles' watershed. Earlier, in "Help!" they'd begun to expand the pop vernacular with words like "self-assured" and lines like "My independence seems to vanish in the haze," yet for all that Lennon once described that song as a genuine cry for help, it was finally "about" their old favorite: boy-meets-girl. Though boy surely met girl in "Norwegian Wood"—and though it had a strong narrative structure—it's impossible to describe the song as "about" anything. The vocabulary wasn't so much expanded as obscure, or perhaps private. Indeed, *attempting* to interpret it marked you as a member of a somewhat self-satisfied coterie just as surely as knowing the words to "Get a Job" had a decade earlier.

But there was a crucial difference. For that first, 1950s generation of teenagers, the assumption was that once you got a job/got married/graduated from high school, you would leave Little Richard behind and embrace Perry Como. Together, the Beatles and Dylan pushed that *terminus ad quem* so far into adulthood that it became meaningless. The rock audience was growing, not only thanks to the baby boom, but because comparatively fewer teenagers were dropping out of it in their twenties. The net effect was that the age at which the generation gap (measured by someone's shouting, or even wishing to shout, "Turn that radio down!") clicked in was being pushed upward, and the number of people on the rock 'n' roll side of it was further swollen as the baby boomers hit adolescence. Especially because it was by the Beatles, "Norwegian Wood," which captivated and mystified the young Beatle fans as fully as it fascinated and held the old, validated the notion that rock lyrics could—indeed, should—be about something other than holding hands at the sock hop.

Unfortunately, even as it helped forge unity across a generation that defined itself culturally rather than chronologically, the Dylan/*Rubber Soul* parlay also planted the seeds of discord by promoting the confusion of rock lyrics and poetry.

The first number-one single of 1966, Simon and Garfunkel's "The Sounds of Silence," provides an example that's more than merely convenient. "Hello, darkness, my old friend . . . A figure softly creeping . . . The words of the prophet are written on the subway walls . . . The vision that was chanting in my brain . . ." What *is* this?

Not, it would seem, popular music—not according to the standards established in the Brill Building, Motown, and Memphis. On the other hand, a number-one record is popular by definition, and despite being even murkier than "Norwegian Wood" (which, for all its ambiguity, had a story-line), the record not only held the number-one spot for a week before being dislodged by the Beatles' "We Can Work It Out," it hung on and made a return to the top three weeks later. It's got a good beat and you can think to it?

Actually—and leaving aside for the moment the question of whether you could think to it only if you were not in the habit of thinking very hard—when the song was first released, it didn't even have a good beat. Paul Simon had written the song in 1963, during his hard-core folkie days, and it was originally released in 1964 as one of the few originals on an all-acoustic album, *Wednesday Morning, Three a.m.*, that also included Dylan's "The Times They Are A-Changin'" and a handful of folkie chestnuts. It stiffed.

The experience was not unfamiliar to Simon and Garfunkel. Friends since sixth grade, when they appeared in a school production of *Alice in Wonderland* (Simon played the white rabbit; Garfunkel, the Cheshire cat), they'd recorded an Everly Brothers–ish single, "Hey, Schoolgirl," as Tom and Jerry in 1957. It made a respectable (number 49) showing on the charts, and the two got to appear on Dick Clark's "American Bandstand." But subsequent Tom and Jerry singles died, and they abandoned Tom and Jerry and went, like all good boys from Forest Hills, to college.

They kept their hands in, however. Garfunkel recorded as Artie Garr; Simon nibbled at the bottom of the charts as a member of Tico and the Triumphs ("Motorcycle," number 99, 1962) and as Jerry Landis ("The Lone Teen Ranger," number 97, 1963); and when they got out of college, they reunited as a folk duo, working the Village coffeehouses and Folk City. From this came the contract that yielded *Wednesday Morning, Three a.m.*, and from this also came, apparently, oblivion. The two broke up, and Simon went to England—where American folkies could still scratch out an existence—and recorded a solo album of original songs while working as a fledgling producer.

In that summer, however, as folk-rock began to catch on, a couple of New England radio stations began giving airtime to "The Sounds of Silence," and Columbia's Tom Wilson—who'd signed and produced the first album—pricked up his ears. In June, after Dylan's "Like a Rolling Stone" session, he asked some of the New York studio players to stay around and dub a rhythm track, including electric guitar, onto the original version. The rest, as they say, is history—or at least a pleasant Cinderella story.

Hearing the news that he had a number-one record, Simon promptly returned from England, and the two rejoined for a promotional tour and to cut their second album—this time mostly songs from Simon's English record. Over the rest of the year, they charted four more singles: "Homeward Bound" (number 5), "I Am a Rock" (number 3), "The Dangling Conversation" (number 25), and "A Hazy Shade of Winter" (number 13). The third of these showed Simon's songwriting at its most precious extreme ("You read your Emily Dickinson, and I my Robert Frost," indeed), but except for an uncharacteristic mismatch of word and rhythm (who pronounced it "bookmarkers"?), Simon showed considerable mastery of his craft. And the two unquestionably sang like angels—or at least like Everly Brothers, which is close enough to rock 'n' roll heaven.

As lyricist, Simon was working the same well-worn ground of teenage isolation and anxiety that had been the staple of pre-Beatles rock 'n' rollers like Paul Anka ("Puppy Love") and Dickie Lee ("Patches"), but with an older, more explicitly personal, and at least potentially bohemian sense of displacement—and found he was speaking to a growing community of the disaffected.

Just a couple of years earlier, the talented but unglamorous Simon would have had only two musical careers open to him: the Brill Building and the folkie circuit. He'd actually done a bit of each when circumstance offered him a considerably more attractive deal; he could be a rock star. Not surprisingly, he took it.

Also unsurprisingly, a lot of people thought the touring travails of "a poet and a one-man band" didn't sound half-bad and tried to follow him. The singer-songwriter style, as it developed over the years, was marked by three characteristics: inflated, though not necessarily "poetic," language (see Simon and Dylan); an obsessive concern with self (ditto); and a half-hearted approach to rock (*not* ditto). This second characteristic tended to rule out most of the Dylan-generation folkies (though Ochs's *Pleasures of the Harbor* comes close), for they were more comfortable with irony than emotionalism.

Simon's disaffection, however, was wafer thin. The freak nature of their success meant that he and Garfunkel never had to grind their work through the club scene; on their first national tour, mostly of college campuses, they were already headliners. Conversely, the Velvet Underground, the most disaffected of the disaffected, never cracked the top 100 and even achieved most of their critical success after they'd broken up.

On the one hand, this is not so odd—their subject matter (heroin, sadomasochism, homosexuality, violence) was a little off-putting—yet if the public was willing to accept a self-proclaimed poet as an authentic voice of alienation, it seems strange that they should reject a journalist. And it was as a journalist, despite the time he'd spent studying and writing poetry as an undergraduate at Syracuse University, that the Velvet Underground's lyricist and lead singer, Lou Reed, was most effective. With a broad definition of what counted as "news," Reed took as his beat the seamier sides of New York's underground street life and told the uncompromising truth about it. Songs like "Heroin," "I'm Waiting for My Man," and "Venus in Furs" weren't the sort of thing that moved over the AP wires, but they were as authentically New Journalism as anything Tom Wolfe ever wrote. Reed rarely sentimentalized and almost never prettified, and even as *Time* and *Life* were discovering how cute and colorful the hippies were, Reed was walking around counting the scabs and sores, listening to the grinding teeth and empty promises of a thousand junkies.

The music—mostly inspired by John Cale, though Reed was a trained pianist—was as uncompromisingly straightforward as Reed's vision. Indeed, it was if anything too brutal in its simplicity. Cale, perhaps from his association with avant-garde composer La Monte Young, was exploring the uses of the drone, and for beat, the band depended on a shifting series of drummers who (just) managed to keep accurate time but played with equally clocklike fire. It was punk two musical generations ahead of itself; nothing quite so defiantly rock 'n' roll simple would capture the attention of the culturati again until the Ramones, the Clash, and the other new wave bands—all of whom acknowledged some debt to the Velvet Underground— appeared in the mid-1970s.

Meanwhile, while Reed and the Velvet Underground were gigging at the Café Bizarre in Greenwich Village and still waiting for Andy Warhol to discover them and canonize them as superstars, Dylan, the original angst-meister, whose influence Reed has often acknowledged, was bringing out *Blonde on Blonde*. Writing of the album, which contained the haunting "Visions of Johanna," the epic "Sad-Eyed Lady of the Lowlands," put-downs like "Just Like a Woman" and the mock-gleeful "Rainy Day Women #12 & 35," critic Paul Nelson suggested that for Dylan, "physical objects are no longer merely physical objects but moral and intellectual properties as well; the whole world is flattened into a plasticity that is cerebral, not physical, and we are free to float with the images in all their kinetic brilliance."

Nelson is certainly right about the kinetic brilliance of the individual images—the *Blonde on Blonde* Dylan is an erupting volcano of words and pictures—and probably right about the essentially solipsistic nature of Dylan's imagination. The world exists within, and for, him, and he takes the pathetic fallacy one better. Indeed, the compassion in some of the album's songs, something many critics have noted, may well exist mostly because Dylan knows he's almost always talking about himself.

For a quick counterargument, however, consider Dylan's biographer Anthony Scaduto: "With *Blonde on Blonde* . . . Dylan reflects on Zen. Man intrinsically lacks nothing; man is whole, a perfect circle which cannot be subtracted from or added to. But man is conned into believing that his body and his mind are separate from that of other beings, and he becomes increasingly obsessed by the idea of 'I' or ego. This disorder leads to such ideas as 'this is mine and that is yours.' But man cannot know the meaning of life. . . ."

Scaduto's musing stands as an unmistakable artifact of its time—of the fact that willy-nilly, rock was being dragged toward high-cultural legitimacy. English teachers (only the "with-it" junior faculty, to be sure) were assigning rock lyrics to their poetry classes, fanning the fires of "relevance" that had first sparked into life in the aftermath of Berkeley's free-speech movement; and Leonard Bernstein, that most unimpeachable cultural guru, did a CBS-TV special on rock during which he anointed fifteen-year-old Janis Ian and made her song about an interracial high school romance, "Society's Child (Baby I've Been Thinking)," a startling nationwide hit. Popular music had come a long—and not entirely good—way from the times when Steve Allen could score easy laughs by treating his television audience to a dramatic "poetic" reading from Gene Vincent's 1956 hit, "Be-Bop-A-Lula."

Not everyone was thrilled by this development. Within the music industry, all this poetry business was a problem for radio. If you couldn't even tell what a song meant, who could predict the kind of trouble the FCC might give you for playing it? Besides, a lot of the cuts were too long for the standard pop format, and they were hard to sell ads against. Not only were they depressing, but with the audience stretching out in all directions, it was hard to know whether you should be pitching Clearasil or Tide—or maybe *Les Fleurs du Mal*. In some ways, the market was just too big; it *ought* to be segmented again.

For a very different set of reasons, some of pop's traditional listeners agreed, for within a few weeks of Simon and Garfunkel's trip to the top with "Sounds of Silence," the number-one slot was captured by Tommy James and the Shondells' "Hanky Panky." (That song, as it happened, narrowly beat out another Paul Simon composition, the Cyrcle's "Red Rubber Ball," which he'd written wearing his Brill Building hat as "Jerry Landis.") The success of "Hanky Panky" meant more than just that there was always room for a lucky novelty song to score; it meant that a significant proportion of the record-buying audience was rejecting rock's hifalutin' claims to culture. Like the Four Seasons' hits, "Hanky Panky" was supported mostly by blue-collar white ethnics—the kids who wouldn't go to college, and who would (the boys, at least) go off to Vietnam. In a sense, the charts were more diverse than they'd been at any time since the young Elvis had chased Perry Como, but this time the internal split that supported the different kinds of music wasn't drawn so much along generational lines as along class divisions. Soon the subtly elitist nature of so much theoretically universal rock would foster a reaction of *ressentiment*, reflected indirectly by Sergent Barry Sadler's "The Ballad of the Green Berets" and more directly in Merle Haggard's later "Okie from Muskogee."

In more benign cases, however, the elitism simply fostered boredom. If it had a good beat, a lot of kids didn't *want* to think about it, thank you, and listening to "Eve of Destruction" (which, not coincidentally, was succeeded at the top of the charts by the McCoys' "Hang On Sloopy"), who's to say they were wrong?

This gap would grow more apparent as the first flush of Beatlemania faded and the major labels began trying to reassert their control of the market. In 1966, their initial vehicle for these attempts was television: the early prime-time "Shindig" and "Hullabaloo," along with Dick Clark's late-afternoon "Where the Action Is." Though "Shindig" started off with an adventurous and catholic booking policy, these shows were almost indistinguishable in format. There was a clean-cut house band (Clark made stars of Paul Revere and the Raiders), clean-cut dancers (including go-go girls in sequined but modest leotards), lip-synching guest stars (usually clean-cut, but exceptions were made for established English acts), flashing spotlights (no strobes yet), and an atmosphere so unshakably upbeat that if Reverend Billy Graham had happened to tune in, he would have found little to displease him.

For a while, at least with younger teens, the shows seemed to work. Because they were pitched so directly at rock's youngest fans, they couldn't resuscitate old rock 'n' rollers (only the original wild men, like Jerry Lee Lewis and, for one brief shining moment in 1968, Elvis, made it through the sixties with much in the way of dignity or cachet), and except for Motown's most tightly choreographed performers, black acts were somewhat under-represented. Still, if you really wanted to see Frankie Avalon-esque "teen idols" like regulars Steve Alaimo, Tommy Roe, or Gary Lewis and the Playboys, you could.

But the shows needed both parts of rock's divided audience—Dylan's fans along with the Four Seasons'—to survive, and they fell between two stools. When they laundered rock as "Hootenanny" had laundered folk, they lost half the equation; when they waxed poetic, they lost the other. Clark's afternoon show—the most conservative of the three—survived, but by late spring of 1966, though they were still capable of selling records, the prime-time efforts had disappeared from the screen. Their demographic place was taken by something even more cynical and market effective, albeit harmless in the event: a weekly sitcom called "The Monkees."

The idea was simplicity itself: to rip off Richard Lester and the Hard Day's Night Beatles for a weekly television series. The process began late in 1965, with an ad in Daily Variety announcing a casting call for "Folk and Rock Musicians-Singers for Acting Roles in a New TV Series. Running parts for four insane boys, age 17–24." Some four or five hundred "insane boys" answered the ad (among the more famous rejects: Danny Hutton, later of Three Dog Night; and Stephen Stills, passed over because of imperfect teeth and incipient baldness). The chosen four turned out to be English actor and ex-jockey David Jones, former child actor Mickey Dolenz, modestly successful folkie Michael Nesmith, and less successful folkie Peter Tork (who'd been referred by his friend, imperfect Stephen Stills).

Whatever they were or had been in real life, the four were innocent, cuddly, lovable moptops on television, and the show, which started its run in the fall, went straight to teenage America's hearts. And Monkees' records, starting with their first release, "Last Train to Clarksville," fairly leapt off the shelves. Forget Tork's and Nesmith's years scuffling around the fringes of the music business; the Monkees appeared to be an instant, overnight, and totally synthetic success. Serious rock fans hated them.

Partly this was because they were innocent, cuddly, and lovable at a time when the original fab four was leaving cuddliness behind with a ven-geance; partly it was the manufactured aura surrounding the whole project. "They don't even play their own instruments," was the standard put-down, and you can be sure the Byrds were keeping quiet about who played what on "Mr. Tambourine Man." Dolenz and Jones, the Monkees who'd been theater trained, didn't seem particularly uncomfortable being television stars who played the role of musicians, but Tork and Nesmith had a tougher time of it. They wanted to be musicians, not merely actors playing a part. And as children of their ever-so-authentic times, they were pained by the ambivalence. As Peter Tork put it in an early eighties interview with Bruce Pollock: "The thing about the Monkees operation is that it wasn't just the four guys. It was the producers, Burt Schneider and Bob Rafelson, Don Kirshner, who oversaw the music, Tommy Boyce and Bobby Hart, the songwriters—the whole crew. The four of us were just the front. I mean, I've heard that Mickey said later we weren't the Monkees any more than Lorne Greene was a Cartwright, which is true. At the same time, we were the Monkees. If we'd been a group, we would have fought to be a group or we would have broken up as a group. But we were a project, a TV show, a record-making machine."

And as such machines go, they were well oiled and finely tuned. Using not only Boyce and Hart but Neil Diamond ("I'm a Believer") and their other contacts from Svengali Kirshner's Brill Building days, the Monkees were blessed with singable songs, and they sang them creditably. The productions were clean, the studio musicians impeccable, and if the whole thing seemed passionless, even the Monkees' biggest detractors would have to admit that their albums have worn considerably better than some contemporaneous offerings from "serious" groups.

They certainly got more airplay, and it had long been a music business truism that airplay—particularly on AM "Top Forty" stations—was the single most important component in selling records. Despite the Monkees' success, television's ability to boost record sales was limited—at least until the days of MTV—by its need for broad-based demographics. To the record companies, it appeared that Top Forty radio remained their only dependable marketing tool, even if it was painfully ill adapted to the new forms of rock that were developing around the country.

Ostensibly, at least, the issue that united radio programmers and record companies—what amounted to a conspiracy—was drugs. In these (mostly) prepsychedelic days, drugs were a middle-class bogeyman, and even the hint that a song had "drug lyrics" was enough to get it banned from the AM airwaves. Since those most likely to perform such songs were "hippies"— likely to resist record company control—radio's timidity became a vehicle for sanitizing and conventionalizing not only lyrics but behavior.

As they had been with folk-rock, the Byrds were pioneers, this time with considerably less happy results. Gene Clark wrote the lyrics to "Eight Miles High" in the wake of the Byrds' disastrous tour of England the previous summer, and it was released as a single in April of 1966. Instrumentally, fired by McGuinn's John Coltrane–influenced lead guitar and Crosby's (or someone's) pounding, accelerating rhythm, it was a daring pop song: lyrically, it turned out to be even more so. Though McGuinn insists to this day—and will give you a line-by-line explication if you press insistently enough—that the song was about their flight to London and its aftermath, it certainly sounded trippy enough to anybody who *wanted* to hear it as a dope song. Despite (or maybe because of) these drug overtones, the single began its run toward the top twenty. Five weeks out of the box, however, Bill Gavin's tip sheet—an independent publication with great influence on radio programming—reported that the song was running into difficulties at some stations because of its druggie lyrics. Always aware that "immoral" broadcasting could jeopardize their licenses, a number of other radio stations immediately dropped it from their playlists. Despite this, the song managed one last lurch up the charts (peaking at number 14, the last time the Byrds would get even that high), then dropped rapidly into oblivion. The two follow-up singles from the *Fifth Dimension* album did notably less well, and McGuinn has often described the band as "blacklisted."

That probably exaggerates the case (for one thing, "Mr. Spaceman" simply wasn't as good as "Eight Miles High"), but the business—radio and records—was undoubtedly running scared. And not just of drugs, either. Shortly after the "Eight Miles High" debacle, the last gasp of white Philadelphia/Frankie Avalon rock, clean-cut Lou Christie, got himself in trouble with "Rhapsody in the Rain." This follow-up to his number-one "Lightnin' Strikes" was released in March, and though it received some initial airplay, several radio chains refused to add it because the song contained the following lines: "On our first date, we were making out in the rain; And in this car, our love went much too far." Faced with resistance, Christie raced back into the studio and overdubbed a more acceptable version: "On our first date, we fell in love in the rain; And in this car, love came like a shooting star." The revised version was a top-twenty hit.

There was, however, no surgical way of censoring songs like "Eight Miles High" or "White Rabbit," which the Great Society was regularly performing in San Francisco. The problem wasn't a specific line or two but an entire, more or less subversive ethos. For most adults, the line was clear: The very first, er, reefer meant addiction, followed, in no particular order, by heroin, white slavery, running away from home, jail, and not getting into Harvard. Had they known what was going on at Harvard, where Tim Leary and Richard Alpert were conducting their early clinical LSD experiments with the eager cooperation of many Cambridge undergraduates, parents might not have been so worried.

But they were, and given the quality of information they had to work with, not without cause. For something was indeed happening here, and if Mr. Jones didn't know precisely what it was, he had a pretty keen idea that it involved dope. All over America, in ever-increasing numbers, kids were slowly waving their fingers in the air and asking each other, "Have you ever looked at your hands, man? I mean *really* looked at your hands. They're *beautiful*, man. Wow." If there had been a secret teenage language in the fifties, the sixties were about to produce an entire separate culture. Fueled, in part, by drugs, the counterculture's rapid growth turned the nay-sayers into King Canutes—who would continue, many of them, to fight a rear-guard action because they misperceived the nature of the threat. From the outside, the counterculture probably looked like simple hedonism, but its aesthetic hallmark was a patient, tolerant curiosity. This had a lot to do with drugs, of course. After all, if a tiny pill and a green house plant could put you in the middle of a steaming jungle, you tended to take new experiences with a certain equanimity. Beyond this, the routine discovery of beauty or terror in everyday objects naturally led to skepticism about the allegedly special values of "high culture." In that sense, the rise of pop art (and its more obviously psychedelic successor, op art) was related to the then-stunning notion that Chuck Berry and Alessandro Scarlatti were peers. Given the ability of the drug-altered consciousness to transform experiences, beauty lay in the mind of the beholder.

But if everything was potentially equal, then everything—music, under-ground comics, high-volume guitar assaults, delicate raga, anonymous sex, emotional commitment—deserved to be sampled, savored, given a chance to develop. This was, understandably, a little hard for parents to take; and the resulting generation gap, the first that didn't axiomatically appear to be "just a phase," was especially deep because on some level, the kids be-lieved at least a little bit of the message their panicky parents were emanat-ing. Combined with the headiness of dope itself, it was easy for kids to think they *would* change, be completely and irrevocably different from their parents' generation. This wasn't Peter Pan revisited, either; no nannies need apply. They would grow older, but *better*. Good-bye suburbs, good-bye barbecue, good-bye accountants and loopholes, good-bye beauty salons, good-bye M-1 rifles . . . Hello peace, love, and understanding.

The script for *Wild in the Streets* (eventually released in 1968) was already making its way around Hollywood: The kids would force a reduc-tion of the voting age to fourteen, see, and then they'd elect this rock star president and ship everyone over the age of thirty to concentration camps where they'd make all the adults eat acid. . . .

To a degree that now seems ludicrous, people on both sides of the dope barrier actually *believed* some version of this crap. And as their children were drifting smilingly away, a lot of adults, who really should have known better, panicked. In order to protect home, family, and the American way (not to mention their own privileges and power), they decided to eradicate the Dope Menace while there was still time—starting with all those drug songs on the radio.

"Rainy Day Women #12 & 35," Dylan's let's-go-get-stoned exhortation, which reached number two on the charts, had survived because its lyrics were so typically obscure that they could plausibly be about alcohol (as Ray Charles's "Let's Go Get Stoned" claimed to be). But even Dylan didn't escape unscathed, as *Variety* gloatingly reported that one radio station in Cleveland—Cleveland! Home of Alan Freed! The city that gave the then-unknown Rolling Stones their warmest American welcome!—actually asked the local police narcotics bureau to examine "Rainy Day Women" and "Eight Miles High" for "suitability": "When the language—narcotics style—was explained, the shellacs were dumped."

Censorship was everywhere, and in "sophisticated" New York—which was (and is) actually one of the most conservative radio markets in the country—the battle came to a head not over Dylan or the Byrds but over "They're Coming to Take Me Away, Ha-Haaa!" a trivial, albeit offensive, novelty about "funny farms" by one "Napoleon XIV." Late in July, as the song was still climbing the charts, radio station WMCA, New York's second-largest Top Forty station, suddenly pulled it off; a week later, the largest, WABC, also dropped it from the playlist. Deprived of significant radio play in the nation's largest market, the song stalled at number three. Though "They're Coming to Take Me Away" had few defenders in and of itself, its sudden disappearance, coupled with the difficulties faced by Dylan and the Byrds and the complete radio blackout of local favorites the Fugs, caused *Village Voice* rock critic (and virtual inventor of the field) Richard Goldstein to devote a column to WMCA's "Good-Guy Censors." Among other things, Goldstein quoted a "Good Guy" dj as saying, "I hate those grubby singers who complain about the bomb hanging over our heads and our society being a mess," and another, Jack Spector, as refusing to play releases by the Fugs because "I don't like what their name implies."

In truth, it would have been asking a lot to expect any Top Forty station to give a great deal of airplay to a band whose "hits" included both the salacious "Coca-Cola Douche" and a gentle version of William Blake's nineteenth-century poem "Ah, Sunflower [Weary of Time]," but Goldstein's column sparked a letter-writing campaign to the station. Among the correspondents was poet Allen Ginsberg, who weighed in with the advice:

> We are perhaps in an impasse of racial history and spiritual evolution wherein, with electronic networks linking consciousness together, divine lyric statements do emerge from individual souls that move youthful hearts to an understanding deeper than hysteria. It is inhuman and unworthy of record broadcasters to ignore this noble democratic impulse and shy away from moments when the art approaches its archetypal heart and serves as a medium for moral statement. . . .
>
> Miraculously, intentions and lyrics of popular music have evolved to include true Poetics. At such a stage, business as usual against so-called "controversial" works of Poetry are not "neutral" acts, they are aggressive and vile attacks on human liberty and beauty. . . .

At one point in his lengthy letter, Ginsberg even invokes Plato: "When the mode of music changes, the walls of the city shake," a prophecy, however hypothetical, that would reassure neither the FCC nor the average station owner.

Still, even Goldstein admitted that WMCA was "the most progressive and most perceptive local pop station on the AM band." In the clash between Ginsberg's "true poetics" and philistinism, there were stations far worse, and because of Bill Drake, there would be more, far more of them.

Drake, who'd gotten into radio a number of years earlier as a country dj in his home state of Georgia, had migrated to California, where he served as program director for a couple of independent Top Forty stations in Fresno and San Diego. He made each of them number one in its market. This did not escape the notice of the RKO General chain, whose Los Angeles station, KHJ, had been fighting a losing battle against KFWB for close to ten years. None of the half-dozen format changes they'd tried had made much of a dent, so in 1965, they hired Drake to design and implement a version of his successful formula.

This involved, compared to the speed-crazed screaming common to AM radio at the time, a noticeably cleaner sound. Drake shortened the station jingle so it could be played more often, ideally in front of every record; shifted the time of the newscast to twenty minutes before the hour (so that if listeners fled to a rival during the news, they'd be back when that station broadcast its top-of-the-hour news, giving Drake's station forty minutes of the hour); ran nonstop (but very simple) contests; and cut the djs' between-songs raps to the barest minimum. All this enabled his stations to play—as they tirelessly proclaimed—"Much More Music."

On a simple minutes-per-hour basis, the claim was true. But, in fact, they were playing "much more" of much *less* music, for Drake relentlessly tightened his stations' playlists. The old Top Forty format, with a handful of permissible album cuts and oldies tossed in as extras, was jettisoned, and KHJ's playlist shrank from about fifty songs to thirty-five. And those thirty-five were to be played in strict rotation, with the top three appearing most often, then the remainder of the top ten, which were to be played more than the mid- and bottom-chart records in a corporately predetermined ratio. Drake's rationale came from a survey he conducted of some six thousand Los Angeles teenagers. Its aim was to find out what would make them do the worst thing a station owner could imagine—lean forward in the car and push a button to change from his station to another. By far the biggest reason for changing stations, mentioned by 47 percent of the kids, was that they heard a record they didn't like. By cutting down on the number of records his stations could play, Drake minimized the chance that a listener would hear something he didn't like. After all, as he once told an interviewer, "It stands to reason. If you're playing the thirty-fifth worst record in town and somebody else is playing the eighty-seventh worst record in town, you're better off than they are."

Like many extremely simple ideas, Drake's worked. KHJ rapidly became the number-one station in its market, and RKO assigned Drake to its San Francisco outlet as well. Eventually he would take control of the chain nationally and serve as consultant to dozens of other stations as well, but even those owners and programmers who had no contractual ties with him took his lesson to heart: Tight playlists boost audiences. More listeners meant higher advertising rates, which meant you could increase profits even while you were reducing the number of ads and playing "Much More [Less] Music." Together with the antidrug, antisex backlash, the nationally shrinking playlist dramatically reduced the opportunities for experimentation or eccentricity.

There were albums, of course, but if you couldn't hear them, how would you know which ones to buy? Without airplay, bands that weren't part of one or another corporate juggernaut were reduced to relying on print for publicity. But of the traditional fanzines, only *Hit Parader* was adventurous enough to range regularly beyond acts that teenagers were already hearing on their Drake-influenced radios, and the first "serious" American rock publication, *Crawdaddy*, was only in its infancy.

Help came from an extremely unlikely source—the United States government—when the FCC announced that in the interests of diversity, it would bar licensees at FM stations from simply duplicating the AM stations' programming. In April 1965 New York City radio station WOR decided that its FM outlet, which had been duplicating AM's talk shows, would switch to a "contemporary music" format. Recorded music was the cheapest way to follow the law, and the station certainly didn't anticipate a revolution, for as its new program director, WOR hired Murray "the K" Kaufman (erstwhile "Fifth Beatle" and well-known dj screamer). But depite his days of ranting about submarine races into AM mikes, Kaufman was no fool. He saw a developing market for postpubescent rock, and in FM stereo, he saw a medium that could exploit that market. When the new WOR-FM went on the air that summer, its mix of album cuts, lengthy sets, and soft-spoken djs made it the first "progressive rock" station in the country—the first, it turned out, of many.

The rise of these stations meant that for the first time, rock's most ambitious and adventurous performers had access to enough megawatts that record companies could sell their work in a more-or-less familiar way. The existence of this alternative route to sales sharply altered the industry balance between the poets and the teenyboppers in favor of the poets, but its effects were felt outside the industry as well, especially in San Francisco. There, unlike New York, where restrictive cabaret laws sharply limited the playing of amplified instruments in clubs, progressive radio would form a symbiotic partnership with a thriving local music scene. Even more important, it would become the communications medium for the burgeoning underground culture.

20

THE PROS
TURN WEIRD

W hy San Francisco? A number of theories have been tried out over the years, but the best guess involves a mixture of demographics and history. For openers, besides the national population bulge in young people, San Francisco had an additional influx of students who'd been drawn by Berkeley (and, to a lesser extent, by other Bay Area colleges) and decided to stay. Others had come to San Francisco precisely because it *was* San Francisco: It had the mountains, the beaches and the bay, nightlife, a literary tradition—the West Coast cradle of the beats, it was the long-time center of literary bohemia and radical politics—and lots of cheap housing in comparatively safe neighborhoods. Also—and this mattered a great deal to the influx of East Coast expatriates—it wasn't high-pressure New York or Brahmin Boston, but a frontier town that had kept a little of its "anything goes" ethic.

These strains had come together in the early 1960s in a confrontation that many white college students found to be a symbolic equivalent of the civil rights movement. The Free Speech Movement, with Joan Baez as an "outside agitator," had revivified a dormant radical political tradition and brought it together with the established bohemian/artistic community, giving birth to radical theater groups like the San Francisco Mime Troupe. Finally, and significantly, "Owsley"—Augustus Owsley Stanley III—a well-born amateur chemist, set up his laboratory in the Bay Area, manufacturing a literally dizzying variety of high-quality hallucinogens that he often gave away for free.

So the recipe went something like: take one lively tradition of cultural and political radicalism, add several thousand kids, one heady victory in the Free Speech Movement, considerable affluence (and considerable disgust with the suburban and governmental uses of that affluence), and a large quantity of dope. Stir well and let explode.

The key to San Francisco—the way in which bohemianism shaped radicalism rather than the other way around—was an overriding belief in the value of spontaneity. New York had had "happenings" long before San Francisco had its first "be-in," but even when the audiences became part of the action, happenings were *performances*. Whatever the room for improvisation, there was an organizing intelligence, an avant-pop theatricalism that was reflected, years later, in the art/rock performances that emerged from the Kitchen, a performance space in New York's SoHo. By contrast, the be-ins and the acid tests were *events* that reflected the tolerant, open, "let's see what happens" San Francisco formula.

Having once seen the acid-induced light at such events, it was inevitable that delighted discoverers of beauty would try to carry it with them beyond the boundaries of a particular park or hall. And so the streets in certain neighborhoods, most notably Haight-Ashbury, became events as well, featuring incense, beads, flowers, long hair, free schools, relaxed sex, and the sweet and pervasive smell of marijuana. The same drives were obviously stirring on college campuses all across the country, but the San Francisco *style* eventually supplanted the more directed forms of protest that had been modeled on the civil rights experience in the South. Partly that was because the causes of protest—indeed, of unrest—on campuses were less sharply defined, the villains less readily identifiable, but it was also because the San Francisco model seemed like so much more fun. "We Shall Overcome" and the other freedom songs had a certain dignity and emotional appeal, but it was San Francisco that gave birth to the undeniably attractive idea that you could boogie your way to revolution.

There have been various starting dates advanced for the genesis of the "San Francisco sound." Some hold for May 30, 1965, when a band known as the Terrazzo Brothers (later to be the Mystery Trend) played for a mostly-artists dance at a defunct skating rink called the Primalon; others say it didn't properly begin in San Francisco at all but across the border in Nevada, at the faded mining boomtown of Virginia City.

Like the Byrds, the Charlatans came together in the wake of *A Hard Day's Night*. Artist George Hunter, who'd been staging happenings at San Francisco State, got together with SF State music student Richard Olson and ex-LA folkie Mike Wilhelm to start doing electrified versions of Wilhelm's traditional repertoire. In the fall, they were joined by antique-store owner Michael Ferguson, who played keyboards and provided them with trademark turn-of-the-century cowboy costumes from his Magic Theater For Madmen Only shop. By the end of the year, when their original drummer hadn't worked out, they'd recruited folkie Dan Hicks to teach himself drums. Mostly they rehearsed, because there wasn't yet anywhere much to play, but in June of 1965, the owner of a shoot- 'em-up Virginia City bar decided to dress his place up a little and sent bartender Chan Laughlin off to hire the Byrds.

Somehow Laughlin wound up in San Francisco, eight hundred miles north of the Byrds (who were at any rate unlikely to abandon their recording career to work as a bar band), where he spotted two long-haired guys on the streets of North Beach. "Are you the Byrds?" he asked.

"No," said Olson and Wilhelm, but they were a rock band. Was he looking for one? He was, and after a meeting with Hunter, Laughlin invited them to Virginia City for the summer. As Olson later told *Zigzag,* "When we first got there, all the local people really flashed on us . . . but as time passed, they realized where we were really at and began to hate us. You see, we were acting as a magnet to the whole of the emerging hippie scene which was just beginning to flourish up and down the coast—and longhairs started coming in not only from Reno and San Francisco, but even from as far away as Seattle and Portland. The place was swarming with heads, because this was months before the Family Dog or Avalon scenes and it was one of the few places you could go and hear turned-on music."

At least as played by the Charlatans, turned-on music seemed to be defined as "old-timey stretched-out blues songs performed by people who were themselves stoned for the dancing and tribe-gathering pleasure of an audience that was likewise." Fundamentally good-time dance music, it lacked the aural distortions and lyrical "profundity" of full-fledged psyche-delic efforts. As Olson's mention of "heads" implies, it was cheerful music for dope smokers, while acid rock aimed less to enhance reality than to replace it with some more colorful and sensual alternative.

Early on, for instance, the Jefferson Airplane were practitioners of head music rather than acid rock. Their starting point came as word of the Charlatans' success was first filtering back to San Francisco, when banjo/guitar picker Paul Kantner came offstage from a "hoot" at the Drinking Gourd to be greeted by Marty Balin's invitation to start a group. Balin was running the Matrix, a mostly folkie club on Fillmore Street, and was looking to build a house band. Initially it, too, was to be folk-oriented, and the next two recruits were blues guitarist Jorma Kaukonen and Baez-ish vocalist Signe Toly Anderson. A few weeks later, they added stand-up bassist Bob Harvey and drummer Skip Spence. (Actually, like Hicks with the Charlatans, Michael Clarke with the Byrds, and far too many first-generation folk-rock "drummers," Spence wasn't a drummer at all but had played guitar.) Unlike the eclectic Charlatans, the band was folk-rock in the mode of the Bay Area's We Five. Hollow-bodied guitars lightly amplified, sweet vocal harmonies, and a ragbag of contemporary songs by Dylan and folkies like Gordon Lightfoot and Fred Neil were the order of the day. They first performed at the Matrix in mid-August, taking their name from a dog

Kaukonen had christened "Blind Thomas Jefferson Airplane" in honor of a nonexistent blues singer.

Almost immediately, they had a manager (Matthew Katz) and a burgeoning coterie of fans that included a semislumming Palo Alto couple who had moved to the city and were into the film scene at SF State; on the night they fiirst saw the Airplane, Grace and Jerry Slick decided to form their own band. Which, together with Jerry's brother Darby (lead guitar), David Minor (rhythm guitar), and, eventually, Peter Vandergelder (bass), they did. Unlike most of the fledgling bands, the Great Society (tip of the ironic hat both to LBJ and to Grace's Palo Alto past) preferred to work with their original songs rather than covers, mostly because, as Darby Slick says in Gene Sculatti and Davin Seay's *San Francisco Nights*, "We figured if we did only our own material, audiences wouldn't know when we were screwing up." They rocked a lot less ambivalently than the Airplane's folkies-manqué, however, and among their compositions was Grace's, Darby's, and Jerry's "Somebody to Love" and Darby's "White Rabbit." They played their first local show, at the Coffee Gallery, barely a month after the Airplane's debut, and were also, with the Airplane, performers at the Family Dog's first concert in October.

Like Bill Drake's "Much More Music," the Family Dog's idea was absolutely simple: to present rock music in a place where you could dance and didn't have to booze but could turn on. They rented Longshoremen's Hall, a self-consciously modern building near Fishermen's Wharf, hired the Great Society and Jefferson Airplane (which by then included Kaukonen's friend Jack Casady on electric bass), got before and after publicity from the San Francisco *Chronicle's* Ralph J. Gleason, sold tickets, and had a dance. Hundreds of hallucinations—by definition private—went public, and if it turned out your dance partner suddenly developed five heads, you naturally understood that it wasn't his or her fault. Every freak in town was there, and a good time was had by all. Among the dancers at the Family Dog's first gathering was Chet Helms, who would eventually take over their production. A transplanted Texan, Helms was running a series of Wednesday-night jams in the basement of an about-to-be-demolished mansion on Page Street in Haight-Ashbury. From these sessions, a house band that Helms would manage gradually emerged. Originally a Rolling Stones-ish effort, the lineup came to include Sam Andrews (guitar), Peter Albin (bass), Dave Getz (drums), and Jim Gurley (lead guitar). They called themselves Big Brother and the Holding Company.

Before the Family Dog collective decided producing the dances seemed too much like work, however, they hosted two more shows: at the first, the Charlatans opened for the Lovin' Spoonful; at the second, for Frank Zappa's Mothers. On the same night that the Charlatans and the Mothers were at Longshoremen's Hall, the radical San Francisco Mime Troupe was having the first of many benefits it would need to keep alive and out of jail. The show was opened by the Mystery Trend (ex-Terrazzo Brothers), and included the Airplane, jazzman John Handy, and the Fugs. (Undaunted by lack of airplay, the furry Fugs had gone on a cross-country tour, and their boho-political style made San Francisco a natural stop for them. Solely as a result of their personal appearances, their album, *The Virgin Fugs*, had sold a remarkable 40,000 copies). The show raised close to $5,000 toward the agitprop Mime Troupe's bail and legal expenses, and in the process demonstrated that there were more freaks in San Francisco than anyone had realized—enough of them to fill two halls simultaneously. Perhaps most important in the long run, the show marked the production debut of the Mime Troupe's manager, Bill Graham.

There were some differences between the Family Dog and Mime Troupe shows—acid at the Family Dog, booze at the Mime Troupe; light shows starting at the second Family Dog, local poets at the Mime Troupe—but it was Graham who was brought in to produce the famous Trips Festival at the Longshoremen's Hall in January of 1966. It was a three-day event, fomented mostly by Ken Kesey's Merry Pranksters and their "acid test" house band, the Warlocks, formerly (mostly) Mother McCree's Uptown Jug Champions and soon to be the Grateful Dead. The Warlocks/Dead had perhaps the most musicianly background of the early SF bands. Jerry Garcia, a banjo picker and guitarist, was accomplished enough that he could scratch out a living giving lessons, and bass player Phil Lesh had actually been trained as a classical composer at Oakland's Mills College. The original lineup was rounded out by "Pigpen" (Ron McKernan), a long-time blues buff, suburban folkie Bob Weir, and a drummer, Bill Kreutzmann, who was actually a drummer. During the Trips Festival, ten thousand people turned out to dance to the Dead and virtually every other San Francisco band, hear poetry, watch films, see slide shows, and congratulate themselves on being there. It was, given the debt to "happenings," avant-garde art as mass culture, but at the end of those three days, it was clear to Graham that what people enjoyed most was the music. Shortly afterward, he rented the Fillmore, and the logo on his psychedelic posters soon carried no mention of the Mime Troupe, reading only "Bill Graham Presents."

For the first few months of the year, Helms (as the Family Dog) and Graham actually alternated weekends at the Fillmore, but their fragile detente split apart in April and Helms took a lease on the Avalon Ballroom, a late-Victorian structure that still had velvet-flocked wallpaper. It was there Helms presented a concert billed as "The Quick and the Dead," bringing together what had become the Bay Area's two top bands.

Certainly if Garcia had a rival on guitar, it was Quicksilver Messenger Service's John Cipollina. Though he'd done some time on Marin County's folkie scene, Cipollina, unlike Garcia, was always a rock 'n' roller, always an electric instrumentalist. Even in junior high school, he once told an interviewer, "While most kids were drawing '49 Fords or '50 Mercs on their binders, I was drawing chopped and channeled Telecasters. It just wasn't socially acceptable. I mean, I was ostracized from the local folk scene, completely blackballed. Barbara Dane was the only folkie who would let me play with her. All-acoustic Martins were the mainstay; folk music was an attempt to do something 'refined.' Playing electric guitar was just another way of saying *fuck*. It was an unwritten law: It's okay to play rock 'n' roll until you were eighteen; after that it was folk."

Late in 1964, when the recently graduated Cipollina was living on a Sausalito houseboat, he began playing with harp player Jim Murray, and the two were soon recruited to form a band by singer Dino Valenti. Although he'd hung out on MacDougal Street, New York's folk bastion, with Fred Neil and Vince Martin, Valenti was no refined folkie but a tough street kid who even then regularly carried a knife strapped to his ankle. Still, he had energy, intensity, original material (he wrote "Get Together"), a manager (dj Tom Donahue), and a vision. Unfortunately, he also had a habit or three, and before the band could play its first gig at Donahue's club, he got busted for marijuana possession. Cipollina and Murray plugged along, however, recruiting hard-core folkie David Freiberg as bassist and (eventually, after Skip Spence, among others) two other garage band vets: rhythm guitarist Gary Duncan and drummer Greg Elmore. With them on board, San Francisco had its first rock 'n' roll rock band.

And by the beginning of 1966, Quicksilver was the tightest band around; unlike most other local bands, they had a rhythm section that kept actual, propulsive time. They even had a manager, Ron Polte, who found them an eighty-eight-acre ranch north of the city where they could rehearse unbothered and unbothering—and where they could play out the same sort of cowboy fantasies the Charlatans had introduced. In a 1976 essay in *The Rolling Stone Illustrated History of Rock & Roll*, Charles Perry described Quicksilver as "the drugstore cowboy band" and the Dead as "psychedelic Indians, prophets of retribalism," and the two played out these roles in a number of ways. One night at Quicksilver's ranch, as Cipollina recalled in a Zigzag interview, he and his friends were toking up in the bunkhouse when the Dead clan, in warpaint and feathers, burst in. "They were all over us before we knew what happened, carrying tomahawks and firing arrows into the walls." The bushwhacked cowboys plotted their revenge. "Two weeks later, the Dead were due to play the Fillmore with the Airplane. . . . Our plan was to wear all our cowboy gear, masks and guns, and take over the stage. We practiced a fifteen-minute version of 'Kawliga Was a Wooden Indian,' which we were going to play on their instruments to humiliate them." Unfortunately, the avenging cowboys arrived at the Fillmore to find it swarming with police who feared that tensions over a recent police shooting might erupt into a full-fledged ghetto riot. Quicksilver, masked and carrying guns, was surely not welcome. As Cipollina recalled, "We tried to explain, but they wouldn't believe we were anything less than hippie revolutionaries bent on exploiting the indignation of the blacks," and Freiberg and Murray were briefly jailed.

Despite the stain on their honor, the cowboys were able to give the Indians a run for it onstage, and the two bands appeared secure atop the San Francisco music community, with Big Brother, the Airplane, the Great Society, and the feckless Charlatans right behind them. That picture changed rapidly, however, when Helms's old Texas buddy Janis Joplin came back to California to join Big Brother, and when Signe Toly Anderson, who decided that her new baby made it impossible for her to stay with the Airplane, was replaced by the Great Society's Grace Slick. Without Slick, the Great Society rapidly folded, but the Airplane and Big Brother were firmly in San Francisco's front rank. Still, though the Airplane issued a record in 1966, the San Francisco scene remained largely unrecorded and local.

And, to some degree, deliberately amateurish, rejecting slick professionalism as an article of hippie faith. As a result, nationally, the sound of California meant the sound of Los Angeles. The West Coast industry had always been centered there, and for a while, at least, the music industry would still feed on itself. New performers came to L.A. because they wanted to get into the recording mainstream, and the lucky ones got contracts either through their session work or through appearances in the lively club scene the industry's presence helped support.

With the advent of rock, this club scene became particularly important to L.A., for New York's cabaret laws virtually eliminated places where new acts could be discovered. Inevitably, and with quite dramatic suddenness, rock made Los Angeles and environs the center of the American music industry. Historian Charlie Gillett discovered "a crude index" of the shift by looking at where chart-topping singles were produced during the years 1963 to 1965. In the first year, made-in-New York records held the number-one position for twenty-six weeks, Los Angeles for only three (Texas-made records held the position for ten). A year later, London dominated (up to twenty-three from zero in 1963), but New York, with twelve, still had four times as many as Los Angeles's three. In 1965, however, though London still accounted for twenty-three weeks, Los Angeles had jumped to twenty as New York plummeted to one. Naturally enough, a number of New York musicians migrated west as well, among them three of the four Mamas and Papas, whose initial single, "California Dreamin'," hit the charts in January, eventually becoming a number-four hit.

The group's history was wittily reprised in their self-referential 1967 hit, "Creeque Alley"; in brief, it involved a variety of failed folk-pop groups including the Journeymen (John Phillips), the Halifax Three (Denny Doherty), the Big Three (Cass Elliot), the Mugwumps (Elliot and Doherty, with Zal Yanovsky and John Sebastian), and the New Journeymen (Phillips, Doherty, and Phillips's California wife, Michelle Gilliam Phillips). Eventually the New Journeymen hooked up with Elliot, and in 1965, the group found themselves living in Los Angeles with a friend, ex–New Christy Minstrel Barry McGuire, whose slickly manufactured "protest" song, "Eve of Destruction," was a number-one hit that year for Lou Adler's independent Dunhill label.

Adler, a consummate pop pro, had been around the music business for years, writing and producing hits for (among others) Jan and Dean and Johnny Rivers before starting his own company. McGuire was one of his first signings, and as Adler recalled in a 1968 *Rolling Stone* interview, "Barry told me some friends of his were in town and that they could sing. I told him to have them come to a session . . . John Phillips did the talking for the group."

As Phillips remembered it, "We hung around and hung around, waiting to sing. Lou was slumped over the board—big hat, three days' growth of beard—he kept saying, 'I'll get to you, I'll get to you.'" When he did, they sang five songs in a row: "Monday, Monday," "I've Got a Feeling," "Once Was a Time," "Go Where You Wanna Go," and "California Dreamin'." When they finished, according to Adler, "I couldn't talk." He could, however, produce a check for $1,500 signing the group to both a recording and a personal management contract. And while they were there, they backed McGuire on a few songs for his second album, including "California Dreamin'," as well as recording their own single "Go Where You Wanna Go"/"Somebody Groovy." Dunhill had actually pressed and shipped the record, but three days after it was officially released, Adler had a dream and recalled it. His subconscious had somehow told him that "California Dreamin'" was too strong a song to be buried on McGuire's album. So, largely as a money-saving measure, the Mamas and the Papas simply edited McGuire's voice from the tapes and added more of their own vocals.

"California Dreamin'," the first of eight top-thirty singles for the Mamas and the Papas, might have been a hit no matter what it was about, for the group's hallmark harmonies—controlled, elaborate, cool—were an extraordinarily beautiful pop sound. But it also offered a vision of California that was as romantic as the Beach Boys' 1965 "California Girls," without any of that song's holdover teenage ethos. Perhaps because the harmonies were so haunting, Phillips's skepticism about such literally sacred cows as religion escaped censorship, but even while Phillips tantalized Easterners with a California that was enigmatically magical, the Mamas and the Papas implicitly rejected the free-form looseness of San Francisco. Probably because they were vocally oriented, they were song oriented as well, creating a lushness that turned even their cover version of the Shirelles' 1959 "Dedicated to the One I Love" into a three-minute chorale.

To some extent, the vocal emphasis was a reflection of the folk-pop past, closer in spirit to their old running mates in New York's Lovin' Spoonful (or even to Peter, Paul and Mary, who would do a creditable Mamas and Papas imitation on "I Dig Rock and Roll Music" in 1967) than to big-beat rockers, but by this time, Los Angeles was also home to a harder-edged music that found its inspiration in blues, jazz, and R&B. On the basis of its first album, Love appeared to be in the folk-rock bag, but Memphis-born Arthur Lee had started the decade playing in Arthur Lee and the LAGs, a group modeled on Stax-Volt's Booker T. and the MGs, and Love was to develop into an eccentrically eclectic band, with notable AM hits (1966's "My Little Red Book," a David-Bacharach song), and FM explorations (the 18:57 "Revelation," which took up an entire side of the album the group recorded later in the year). If there hadn't been a San Francisco, Love might have invented it, but despite a loyal cult following (especially in England), the band never fared as well in the marketplace as its fans hoped, possibly because Lee strongly resisted touring.

However, Lee's rejection of the usual commercial path seemed more rooted in personality than theory; though they had a notably more professional attitude toward performance than Lee's, other Los Angeles performers of the period like Captain Beefheart (Don Van Vliet) and Frank Zappa treated the traditional paths to commercial success with almost theological disdain. Zappa and Van Vliet had formed their tastes as high school friends in the Mojave Desert town of Lancaster, California. R&B freaks early on—Van Vliet was especially influenced by the blues of Howlin' Wolf—they played together briefly in a number of unrecorded bands. Zappa escaped Lancaster fairly early and came to L.A.; in 1964, he met a five-piece R&B band called the Soul Giants playing at a nondescript bar in Pomona. When the guitarist and vocalist had a falling out, the guitarist split and Zappa was invited to join. Soon the Soul Giants became his band, the Mothers of Invention. As he said in a 1968 interview, "So I began working with them at the Broadside—playing stuff like 'Gloria' and 'Louie Louie'—and I thought they sounded pretty good . . . too good for bars. They had been gigging in terrible places—Orange County, for instance, which is a bad place to be unless you belong to the John Birch Society—so I said, 'Okay, you guys . . . I've got this plan. We are going to get rich. You probably won't believe it now, but if you just bear with me, we'll go out and do it.'" One of the musicians demurred: "Dave Coronado said, 'No . . . I don't want to do it. We'd never be able to get any work playing that kind of music. I've got a job in a bowling alley and I'm going to split.' So he did just that. We decided we didn't need a sax player anyway."

The dismissive attitude was one Zappa would often show toward musicians who worked with him—both he and Vliet regarded them as vehicles for attaining a sound—but one can hardly blame Coronado for being a little skeptical about Zappa's vision. Consider Zappa's description of one 1966 song from an interview in *Jazz & Pop* magazine: "The time, the time—it's fantastic. It's four bars of 4/4, one bar 8/8, one bar of 9/8—okay? And then it goes 8/8, 9/8, 8/8, 9/8, 8/8, 9/8, and then it goes 8/8, 4/8, 5/8, 6/8, and back to 4/4 again." That is to say, it didn't have a good beat, but maybe you could dance to it anyway.

And if you couldn't, the Mothers were a *listening* band. Though they were often lumped together with the Fugs (both played the San Francisco ballrooms early on; they had long-run competing bookings within a few blocks of each other in Greenwich Village; both were older and self-consciously uglier than the run-of-the-mill—even the psychedelic mill—rock group; and though both sported plenty of fashionably long hair, its fashion seemed more of the Bowery than of Carnaby Street), the groups were at bottom dissimilar. The Fugs (Ed Sanders, Tuli Kupferberg, and Ken Weaver, with various instrumental backups) were musically primitive garage band poets who'd been bemused by the erotic and playful possibilities of rock; Zappa was an inventive musician and compulsive parodist whose high school–deviant sensibility was perfect for puncturing varieties of "hip" (and much less effective when it came to clobbering squares in songs like his early "Plastic People").

Both, however, delighted in shock-rock, and the Fugs' tributes to sex—group, solo, and serial—were the lyric equivalent of Zappa's daunting time changes. As a result, neither seemed to have much in the way of commercial potential, and the Fugs achieved major-label distribution only in decline. Polite only by comparison, Zappa's band—which not only survived but had a few top-thirty albums—can at least partly trace its success to some chance-taking by the same man who electrified Dylan and Simon and Garfunkel: producer Tom Wilson.

Wilson had been lured to MGM/Verve by Jerry Schoenbaum early in the year, and the two built an outstanding roster, signing singer-songwriter Tim Hardin, Laura Nyro, Janis Ian, the Velvet Underground, and the Mothers. It was Wilson who went for the Mothers; immediately after he'd caught the end of a set (including "The Watts Riot Song") at the Whisky-a-Go-Go, he came backstage and announced he wanted to make a record with them. "I didn't see him again for four months," according to Zappa. "I imagine he went back to New York and told them he'd signed another R&B band from the Coast."

However Wilson had described the signing in New York, when he returned to the Coast for the Mothers' first recording session, "that's when he discovered we weren't just another R&B band." Wilson promptly booked additional studio time and scrapped plans to do a single, deciding to go for an album instead. "At the time," according to Zappa, "the average cost of a typical rock album was around $5,000. The start-to-finish cost of *Freak Out!* was around $21,000. MGM wasn't too happy to learn that." Though the costs did run higher than anticipated, this was partly Wilson's—and hence MGM's—doing. Zappa again: "The first track we cut was 'Any Way the Wind Blows,' and then 'Who Are the Brain Police?'—and when Wilson heard those he was so impressed that he got on the phone to New York. As a result, I got a more or less unlimited budget to complete this monstrosity. The next day, I had whipped up all the arrangements for a twenty-two piece orchestra . . . the Mothers plus seventeen pieces."

Not surprisingly, mixing and editing took a long time, adding significantly to the session expenses, and Zappa felt that "Wilson was really sticking his neck out . . . he laid his job on the line by producing a double album." Indeed, the decision to release a debut double album of poly-rhythmic, apparently improvised, and lyrically obscure music by a band few people had ever heard of was in its own way as eccentric as Zappa's music, and initially the company got a little panicky. "When it was finally released, MGM already felt they'd spent too much for it and weren't about to spend any more promoting it—but then it started selling all over the place . . . like it would sell forty copies in a town the size of a pumpkin seed in the middle of Wyoming! So they began promoting it in major markets and ended up with fair sales."

In addition to initial "fair sales," the company wound up with a catalog item that would stay lively for a decade or more. But the Mothers were lucky as well as good; Zappa's old running mate from Lancaster, Don Van Vliet, had considerably more trouble getting started. His career had begun a couple of years earlier with a version of "Diddy Wah Diddy" that was a modest local hit for A&M Records. But the company rejected a follow-up album, mostly Van Vliet's original music, as "too negative," and the band broke up. Eventually Van Vliet put together another aggregation and redid the material for Buddah Records; the debut album, *Safe As Milk*, remained bluesy, and the band, with Beefheart in Howlin' Wolf mode, toured extensively to promote it. But almost in mid-tour, Beefheart's music took a radical swerve to the irregular polyrhythms and quirky vocal harmonies (including Van Vliet taking advantage of a singing range spanning more than seven octaves) that it would stay with, through thin and thin, for the rest of the decade. Audiences were fascinated, and the revamped band toured heavily enough to build an enthusiastic cult following. However, despite the Captain's obsessive care (not only did he rename each of his musicians, he taught them his arrangements note-for-note), his sound—Elmore James meets Archie Shepp somewhere on the road to Oz—re-mained influential (even into the eighties, where it can be heard on records by Devo, the Contortions, and others) rather than popular.

By comparison, the Los Angeles records that were big hits during the year were considerably more conventional. These included Nancy Sinatra's "These Boots Are Made for Walkin'" (white-bread sado-masochism written for her by producer Lee Hazelwood, who, according to *Time* magazine, urged her on by saying "You're not a sweet young thing. You're not the virgin next door. You've been married and divorced. You're a grown woman. I know there's garbage in there somewhere"), and an untoward interruption of the rock era by her father. Frank Sinatra's "Strangers in the Night," an unsurpassably straight ballad, was not only his first number-one hit ever but his first Top Ten record since 1956. A follow-up, "That's Life," also went Top Ten that year and subsequent albums sold well, but except for 1967's duet with daughter Nancy on "Somethin' Stupid," which Hazel-wood co-produced, he wouldn't crack the top twenty for the rest of the decade.

The year's final two L.A. number-one records featured Johnny Rivers (his own "Poor Side of Town," produced by Lou Adler), who'd been a major draw at the Whisky ever since he came across town as its first performer when it opened in 1964, and the Beach Boys' "Good Vibrations."

Perhaps it was that they'd been stung by the way "serious" rock fans were dismissing them (surf music, after all, had died even before the Beatles, and teen music was something of an endangered species), or perhaps it was just that Brian Wilson was getting older, quirkier, druggier, and more depressed, but 1966's traditional Beach Boys summer album, *Pet Sounds*, signaled a new direction for the group. Some of this was apparent in the lyrics— though it opened with the upbeat and uptempo "Wouldn't It Be Nice," it wound down into the bittersweet "Where did your long hair go?/Where is the little girl I used to know?" of "Caroline, No"—but it was most marked in the orchestration. Most tracks were heavily sweetened with strings, added percussion, and layer upon layer of overdubbed vocals, giving the group a heavier, almost viscous sound—but one that maintained its clarity through Brian's obsessively careful production. Though it didn't fare quite as well as the immediately preceding albums, *Pet Sounds* reached the Top Ten and yielded hit singles in "Sloop John B" (number 3) and "Wouldn't It Be Nice" (number 8). Immediately after *Pet Sounds* was finished, Brian started work on "Good Vibrations."

The song opens quietly, organ triplets and flutes leading into Carl Wilson's initially understated vocal. Gradually the instruments build behind him: a stand-up bass, a theremin, still undefinable varieties of percussion; and the vocal line—doubled, redoubled, overdubbed, harmonized— achieves the richness of a choir without losing any of its breathy intimacy. It took Brian more than six months, $16,000 (at a time when MGM thought $21,000 was too much for an entire double album), and some seventeen recording sessions to get the song right, but he finally did, coming as close as he would get to his symphony.

Despite the obvious differences between them, Zappa and Wilson were similar in a critically important way: They were creatures of the recording studio, and they were perfectionists. The San Francisco bands, by contrast, were creatures of the dance hall, believers in inspiration. For all that the Mothers sounded free and freaky compared to the scrubbed-up Beach Boys, they were every bit as tightly disciplined, and both groups raised the level of polish and sheen rock fans were growing to expect from the records they bought.

For at least a while, however, the raw energy that had characterized the great rock 'n' roll of the 1950s would coexist with studio polish. Late in 1966, a band called ? and the Mysterians had the year's out-of-left-field hit with "96 Tears." The band was made up of Mexican-Americans who'd been brought up in Michigan's Saginaw Valley, where they played dances as XYZ. The record, with its Freddie Fender-style vocal and punctuating organ sustain, would be worth a mention in any case, but it deserves special notice as the last of a garage-rock tradition that had brought hits to bands like the Kingsmen, the Standells, and the Texas-based Sam the Sham and the Pharaohs (whose independent local hit, "Haunted House," led them to MGM and to national promotion for 1965's "Wooly Bully").

Noticing that "96 Tears," an original composition by ? himself (Rudy Martinez), was going over big, their manager formed a record label, Pa-Go-Go, and recorded a single in her living room. When it broke on a major Detroit station, Neil Bogart, who'd been the key promotional force behind "Wooly Bully," licensed it for his Cameo label. For one week in late October, it held the number-one spot on the charts, giving hope to garage bands all over America. But the hope was illusory—or at least would be postponed until the Akron/Atlanta (and maybe Ramones) outburst led by musicians who were barely out of grade school when ?'s home recording was a hit.

The growing demand for professional product was linked, of course, to the increasing sophistication of the rock audience. But perhaps even more important, rock had quickly become the province of the majors, not the indie labels that had nurtured rock 'n' roll. The majors had learned their lesson—they wouldn't be left behind this time—and they cultivated the new music in a way few independents could hope to match. One advantage the majors provided was substantial studio budgets (or, as with the early Byrds, top-of-the-line studio musicians). As the decade went on, any record that didn't have a professional gloss began to sound out of place, and radio programmers, who didn't want anyone touching the dial, wouldn't give such records airtime. Though the occasional novelty record might sneak through, the minimum production standard rose steadily throughout the 1960s, finally leading audiences to demand elaborate technical efforts and to develop a worshipful attitude toward instrumental prowess. Put together with the continuing star mystique, these trends would eventually enshrine a phalanx of "guitar heroes."

At the immediate moment, however, professionalism was virtually synonymous with studio musicianship, and the industry's genuine guitar heroes were anonymous; thus the greatest challenge to L.A.'s industrial dominance was the lower-keyed Nashville sound that Bob Dylan captured on *Blonde on Blonde*, with the help of Nashville-based producer Bob Johnston and country-session stalwart Charlie McCoy. Robbie Robertson and Al Kooper had come down from New York (and Joe South over from Atlanta), but the bulk of the musicians were the "Nashville Cats" eulogized by the Lovin' Spoonful a few months after *Blonde on Blonde* appeared. Though these country musicians were surely bluesy, and maybe stoned, the grooves they settled into were a little less frenetic than those of the New York session men who'd backed Dylan's previous rock forays; their sound, in this respect, was remarkably like that displayed by Dylan's touring band—which would subsequently surface on its own as the Band.

Partly as a result of *Blonde on Blonde*'s commercial and musical success—and partly, too, because Dylan was Dylan and by definition a trendsetter—it suddenly seemed that *everyone* was going to Nashville to record. In the short run, not much came of this but steady paychecks for the Area Code 615 musicians, but over time, the cross-fertilization of rock and country helped counter the Billy Sherrill–sweetened sound then dominating the country charts and also provided an entree for the seventies wave of songwriters and singers who would be collectively lumped together as "outlaws." It's possible that Dylan himself might have made more of the Nashville connection, but on July 29, 1966, as he was riding his Triumph 500 motorcycle to a Woodstock repair shop, its back wheel locked. Dylan was flung to the pavement, suffering a near-fatal broken neck and a number of dangerous internal injuries. For the next eighteen months, he would be effectively *hors de combat*, and Nashville's rise made little dent on the state's other locus of recording professionalism.

Also, with one or two exceptions (mostly older ballad singers like Brook Benton and Clyde McPhatter, who remained under contract to crossover-oriented Mercury Records), the rise of Nashville was a primarily white affair; Memphis's recording industry was integrated. During 1966, the Stax-Volt session men turned out R&B hits for Carla Thomas, Sam and Dave, and Johnnie Taylor as well as crossovers for Thomas ("B-A-B-Y," number 14), Eddie Floyd ("Knock on Wood," number 28), and Sam and Dave. One measure of the pop world's breadth at the time is that the duo's classic "Hold On! I'm A-Comin'" (number 21) had its genesis when the songwriting team of David Porter and Isaac Hayes was in the studio working on a new song. Porter excused himself, and when he didn't come back after a few minutes, Hayes went all around the building shouting his name. Finally, from the other side of the bathroom door, came Porter's voice: "Hold on. I'm a-comin'." Even in the headiest days of psychedelia, "Take me for a trip aboard your magic swirling ship" was not the sort of line that would arise in ordinary conversation.

But such occurrences were s.o.p. in Memphis. Otis Redding's hit, "Respect," evolved from a conversation between Redding and drummer Al Jackson. "We were speaking about life in general, the ups and downs and what have you," Jackson said in a *Rolling Stone* interview. "I said, 'What are you griping about, you're on the road all the time, all you can look for is a little respect when you come home.' He wrote the tune from our conversation. We laughed about it quite a few times. In fact, Otis laughed about it all the way to the bank."

But "Respect" broke biggest, more than a year later, for Aretha Franklin; Redding's 1965 original was a number four R&B hit but stalled at number thirty-five on the pop charts. At the time, and for most of his life, Redding's brand of earthy Memphis soul wasn't crossing over with any regularity. It had taken him a while to find that style; unlike most of the great Memphis soul singers, he'd begun not on the gospel circuit but as a screaming rock 'n' roller in the mode of a slightly older Macon, Georgia, singer, Little Richard. Gradually this influence—more than an influence, really; Redding's early "Shout Bamalama" is a virtual copy of Little Richard—gave way to the balladic intensity of Sam Cooke, whose classic "Shake" was a regular high spot of Redding's stage show. Cooke was, however, more truly an influence than a model, and even as Redding's singing became more melodic and openly emotional, his voice kept a hint of grit and a palimpsest of potential explosiveness.

He came to Stax in 1962. By then he was singing with Johnny Jenkins and the Pinetoppers, and though he wasn't scheduled to record, he agreed to drive Jenkins to a solo session Atlantic had set up at Stax. When Jenkins's session ended with forty minutes of studio time still available, Redding talked his way into cutting two sides with the Stax house band. Jim Stewart hated the first, a Little Richard-style number, but after one listen to the second, Redding's own "These Arms of Mine," signed the singer to a contract. The song was a hit (number 20 R&B; number 85 pop) and began Redding's long and fruitful association with the Memphis musicians.

Within a couple of years, Redding had become a major star on the chitlin' circuit, earning the name "Mr. Pitiful" not only for his late 1965 hit but for performing the persona he developed. In songs like "Pain in My Heart" and "That's How Strong My Love Is," Redding tempered his imposing physical and vocal force with an aura of sweet, wounded vulnerability. With these songs, he escaped his musical influences and became himself—and the combination of power and pain was irresistible. Even though he was stubborn about sticking to the kind of material he knew he did best—at a time when up-tempo soul provided the most obvious entree to the pop charts— it seemed only a matter of time until white America would discover him.

For all that Stax gave Redding, a band, a sound, a start—and even, in some ways, a home—the label might inadvertently have delayed that moment by an unfortunate business decision limiting the label's abilities to interact with outside artists. Early in 1966, in a misguided attempt to establish a monopoly on the Memphis sound, the studio closed its doors to performers who weren't under contract to the company. This led Atlantic's Jerry Wexler to Rick Hall's Fame studio and the Muscle Shoals sound in Alabama, where the year saw Atlantic getting quite satisfactory results with Wilson Pickett's chugging "Land of 1000 Dances" (number 6) and "Mustang Sally" (number 23), and with the label's third number-one single, Percy Sledge's "When a Man Loves a Woman."

In *Nowhere to Run*, Sledge told Gerri Hirshey that he hadn't so much composed the song as had it torn from him. He was singing at a dance in Sheffield, Alabama, moonlighting from his job as a hospital orderly, when he realized love troubles had brought him so low he couldn't work through his standard repertoire of Top Forty and R&B covers. As his bass and organ player improvised a melody behind him, Sledge poured out a song-sermon on the travails of love. "Wasn't no heavy thought to it," he told her. "I was just so damned *sad*."

Eventually Sledge formalized the song and auditioned it for local producer/dj/record retailer/studio owner Quinn Ivy, who recorded it using Rick Hall's musicians. It was Sledge's first record, but the song was his and the style was his own. He also found an enormous reservoir of support in the local musicians, and has said that Muscle Shoals players felt "like family" to him (which in a sense, they were; his cousin was among the Fame regulars). Even more than the musicians, however, he told Hirshey that Muscle Shoals had a special secret ingredient: "It sits right at the bottom of the mountains. Mountains all the way around us, and we have the best bass sound in the *world*. When you've got mountains standing that high up over you, all the way around for like fifty, sixty miles, *then* you've got a bass track."

Still, the flatness of the Midwest wasn't hurting Berry Gordy, who, in 1966, had another strong year. Although the Supremes didn't quite match their astonishing 1964–65 stretch (when six out of seven releases went to number one), two of their four 1966 releases shot to the top ("You Can't Hurry Love" and "You Keep Me Hangin' On"); and "My World is Empty Without You" and "Love Is Like an Itching in My Heart" were both Top Ten. Perhaps the last of these, "You Keep Me Hangin' On," which hit the charts the last week of October, is the most interesting, for its shifting tempos showed Holland-Dozier-Holland exploring the musical vocabulary of rock rather than ringing changes off R&B. Though it was a number-one R&B hit as well,* it highlighted the long-standing "whitening" trend at Motown. The company's charm school had always explicitly stated it was training its pupils to play "at the White House and Buckingham Palace"—and over the next few years, the music of the Supremes, especially, would do more than nod toward white purchasing, if not political, power.

H-D-H also scored significantly with the Four Tops this year. The quartet had done well indeed with the hastily produced "It's the Same Old Song" in 1965, but neither of its follow-ups cracked the Top Ten, and their May 1966 release, "Loving You Is Sweeter Than Ever," stalled at number forty-five, the worst the Four Tops had fared on Motown. Clearly a change was needed, and H-D-H found it with "Reach Out and I'll Be There," with its anthemic bridge. Though this would be the Tops' last number one, H-D-H followed it up with their own (and Motown's) typical reworkings, and two soundalikes, "Standing in the Shadows of Love" and 1967's "Bernadette," also went Top Ten. Unhappily, by the time this string ran out and the group once again needed revitalization, H-D-H and Motown were embroiled in a royalties dispute that preoccupied the producers.

*The Supremes, unlike most Motown artists, had always tended to do better on the pop charts than on the R&B compilations.

In addition, there was a storm brewing in the highly directive company over the issue of artists' control. The first chink in the company's armor was discovered almost by accident, and though other Motown artists eventually followed, the biblical prophecy proved true: A little (albeit noticeably taller) child would lead them.

In the two and a half years since *Little Stevie Wonder, The 12-Year-Old Genius* (who was thirteen when the song was released) had scored a number-one hit with "Fingertips—Part 2," Motown seemed to have little idea what to do with him. The company didn't want him pegged as strictly a novelty act, so it tried a number of different approaches, hoping that one or another would click.* The first attempted follow-up was an album called *With a Song in My Heart*, which sounds exactly like what it was—a typical Motown attempt to "upscale" one of their artists by dosing him with standards and strings. This album, which includes "When You Wish Upon a Star" and "Put On a Happy Face," is perhaps the only record Wonder ever made on which he sounds acutely uncomfortable. When the album stiffed, as well it should have, the company took the even more unlikely step of casting the blind black city kid as a surfer in the shameless *Stevie at the Beach*. Subsequent cameos in *Muscle Beach Party* and *Bikini Beach* helped neither his career nor his artistry.

Most of his singles fared no better; the novelty-ish "Hey Harmonica Man" barely cracked the top thirty (number 29) late in 1964, but none of the others did even that well, and three failed to chart entirely. Live, however, Wonder unfailingly got audiences going at the Motortown Revues (because of his age, he usually opened), where he'd begun to add one of his own compositions, "Uptight (Everything's Allright)" to his set. He long pressed to record the song, but Motown continued to dictate his material, using the rationale that Wonder was still a child. By 1965, though the diminutive had dropped from his billing, he was on a child's allowance of $2.50 a week during Motown's annual European tour. Understandably resentful, Wonder would insist on guarantees of financial and artistic freedom when he renegotiated his contract at age twenty-one, and years later, he did a riff on his "career crisis" on the "Saturday Night Live" television show. In the skit, Wonder approached a record executive and said, "People are always trying to tell me what to play, what kind of music I should be doing. I'd like to do some songs that are more meaningful to me."

The executive responded, "Don't get artsy on me, Stevie. Boy geniuses are a dime a dozen. I love you, so don't push me." In real life, he did push, however, and when Motown finally released "Uptight (Everything's All-

---

*In fact, Stevie had always been hard to place. When he first came to Motown, the label tried to bill him as a soulful singer, in a Ray Charles homage called *Tribute to Uncle Ray*. But even though the liner notes stressed that he was a singer, playing no instruments, the company simultaneously issued *The Jazz Soul of Little Stevie*, on which he did no singing whatsoever and played harp, percussion, and keyboards. After "Fingertips," the confusion grew worse.

right)" (with co-writing credits to Hank Cosby and Sylvia Moy), it reached number 3 on the charts in early 1966. The song established Wonder both as a writer (the subsequent *Up Tight* album included four of his songs) and as a solid recording act (his three subsequent 1966 singles released all were top twenty, and two were Top Ten). Still, it would take a while for Wonder's one-man youth rebellion to loosen the buttons of America's most conservative record company.

Other labels were finding themselves forced to adjust more rapidly to the changing definitions and expectations of pop, as artists began to experiment with new techniques, ideas, and poses. The challenge of maintaining radio-acceptable polish while giving performers room to grow was real. The Stones, for example, were beginning to move away from their Chuck Berry base. Though they continued to run second to the Beatles during 1966, they had Top Ten U.S. singles with a straight ballad ("As Tears Go By," number 6), a frenetic teen psychorocker ("19th Nervous Breakdown," number 2), a psychedelic raga-rock venture ("Paint It Black," number 1), an antisuburban put-down ("Mother's Little Helper," number 8, backed with a pseudo-Elizabethan drug song, "Lady Jane," number 24), and a low-rent Freudian rocker ("Have You Seen Your Mother, Baby, Standing in the Shadow?" number 9), which came in a remarkably outré picture sleeve featuring the Stones in full drag.

By contrast, the Beatles were still performing in matching outfits and being marketed as cute, but their mid-1966 single, "Paperback Writer" b/w "Rain," neatly illustrates the twin thrusts of lyrical innovation and studio perfection. "Paperback Writer," a McCartney effort, took the form of a letter from a struggling writer to a publisher—a subject at the time so unusual for a pop single that it understandably seemed to fall easily under the "disaffected" or "alienated" rubric. Compared to what even the Beatles had done before, it did; but again, its slyly subversive notions about the nature of art are in retrospect less important than the June/moon teen love it *doesn't* contain.

Like virtually all McCartney's work, however, "Paperback Writer" was musically brilliant pop, picking up on the slashing power chords that were beginning to be heard in British clubs and transforming them into ringing melodies. But if this showed the Beatles at their evolutionary best, the B side, Lennon's "Rain," launched them headfirst into the psychedelic revolution. As Lennon recalled in a 1968 *Rolling Stone* interview, "I got home about five in the morning, stoned out of me head, I staggered up to the tape recorder and I put it on, but it came out backwards, and I was in a trance in the earphones, what *is* it?—what *is* it? It's too *much*, you know, and I really wanted the whole song backwards, almost, and that was it. So we tagged it on the end. I just happened to have the tape the wrong way round, it just came out backwards, it just blew me mind. The voice sounds like an old Indian."

This single, which pushed well beyond the bounds of anything on *Rubber Soul* (which had itself been a breakthrough a mere six months earlier), whetted their adult fans' appetites for the new album, and *Revolver* did not disappoint fanciers of the psychedelic. Even Ringo's token novelty number, the irresistibly catchy "Yellow Submarine," yielded a trip metaphor, and George, in addition to the impassioned affluence-protest of "Taxman," contributed "Love to You," which not only used the sitar but tried to combine Indian patterns and sequences with Western pop. Paul came up with a solid romantic ballad, of course, in "Here, There, and Everywhere," but pushed along the album's theme of dislocation and disturbance most tellingly with the enigmatic "Eleanor Rigby." Though the tune was not McCartney's strongest, Martin's string arrangement (no Beatle actually played on the cut) embellished and propelled it without at all obscuring the words. In this case, McCartney's words were more important than usual, and the ambiguities in the narrative (what did it mean that "no one would hear" Father McKenzie's sermon? what was the McKenzie/McCartney relationship? why was nobody saved?) would have kept Beatleologists occupied quite nicely even if Lennon hadn't weighed in with some songs that weren't so much enigmatic as impenetrable.

Even though Capitol had pinched the drug-drenched "Dr. Robert" and the hauntingly mysterious "And Your Bird Can Sing" for the ragbag *Yesterday . . . and Today*, the American *Revolver* contained "She Said She Said," Lennon's account of an acid encounter with Peter Fonda, and the band's most "psychedelic" effort yet, when Martin took the tape loops of "Rain" a step further on "Tomorrow Never Knows." Lennon had wanted a chorus of Tibetan monks to chant in the background over "Turn off your mind, relax, and float downstream," but a more modest solution was found when each of the Beatles created a tape loop on his home recorder and Martin fed them into the mix at different speeds and in different directions. With Lennon's voice filtered through a rotating Leslie speaker, the sound was properly unearthly; the Beatles were no longer teen angels but electronic Pied Pipers of psychedelicism.

These magical sounds were also unreproducible outside the studio, so many of *Revolver*'s cuts could not be performed on the Beatles' subsequent concert tour of Europe, Japan, and the Far East. In the Philippines, where they broke their previous record by playing to almost 100,000 fans at an outdoor date in Manila, they faced mobs considerably more threatening than the girls who still beseiged their hotels. Through some still-mysterious glitch in communications, the Beatles failed to attend (or never got an invitation to) a state dinner hosted by the Philippine dictator's wife, Imelda Marcos. Since all the national media had been alerted that they were coming, all of them ran features focusing on the disappointment of the guests and the insult to the Marcoses and, indeed, to the entire people of the Philippines. Seeing these news stories, Brian Epstein ordered the sleepy Beatles directly to the airport, where their dash to a plane was interrupted by attacks from a hostile crowd policed with notably half-hearted enthusiasm by Marcos's security forces.

Though it was less dramatically physical, the Beatles for the first time faced significant hostility in America as well. It began with the infamous "butcher-boy" cover they did to protest *Yesterday . . . and Today*, a bastard U.S. compilation album (some oldies and three tracks lifted from the British *Revolver*) put out by Capitol just two months before *Revolver* was due. Responding to protests from distributors and from the media, Capitol pulled back 750,000 jackets showing the lads in butcher's aprons surrounded by chunks of meat and dismembered baby dolls, substituting an innocuous photo of them gathered around a steamer trunk. This quarter-million-dollar investment in keeping the moptops lovable was then threatened when the magazine *Datebook* got hold of an interview Lennon had done with the *Evening Standard's* Maureen Cleave a few months earlier and printed the most controversial passages out of context. Even in context, Lennon's original remarks might have been found upsetting. "Christianity will go. It will vanish and shrink. I needn't argue about that; I'm right and will be proved right. We're more popular than Jesus right now. I don't know which will go first, rock 'n' roll or Christianity. Jesus was all right, but his disciples were thick and ordinary. It's them twisting it that ruins it for me." Blown up in tabloid headlines—"LENNON: BEATLES "MORE POPULAR THAN JESUS"—they were inflammatory.

Across the South, which had never taken to the Beatles with the enthusiasm of the rest of the country, public burnings of Beatles records were organized both by fundamentalist ministers and by radio stations. The people who had earlier made Staff Sergeant Barry Sadler's "The Ballad of the Green Berets" a number-one hit seemed ready to nuke the Fab Four, and on the London stock exchange, shares in the Beatles' publishing firm, Northern Songs Ltd., reacted negatively. Brian Epstein reacted as well, flying to America to say that Lennon's remarks had been misunderstood and making a public offer to release any promoter who wished from his contract for the band's upcoming tour.

Not surprisingly, no one took him up, and after a more or less contrite Lennon delivered a sort of apology at their first-day press conference ("I was not saying we were greater or better"), the tour went on its uneventful way. Onstage, they went through the dutiful motions, not even trying any songs from *Revolver* but cranking out versions of their old songs that neither they nor their audiences could hear. The illusion of a straight-line connection between the 1963–64 model Fab Four and what the band had actually become was perhaps satisfying to fans so young they'd been introduced to the Beatles via the Monkees, but it neither fooled—nor even concerned—the millions of American kids who were getting stoned and trying to puzzle out the meanings of "Norwegian Wood" or "Eleanor

Rigby." Initially the Beatles' importance had been the revivifying and unifying energy they brought to pop, but the times—that is to say, a set of inclinations and expectations that they, as aging pop fans, shared with much of their audience—had made them generational spokesmen.

The impact they had in this role both drew on their unique legacy and depended, at least to some extent, on their continuing to be the Beatles. The need for unity was both functional (as it turned out, John needed Paul's melodic sense; Paul needed John's skepticism; George needed their sense of pop; and because he kept his feet so unhesitatingly on the ground, they all needed Ringo, who cherished them like a fan) and mythic, for the Beatles, as the Fab Four growing up together *on behalf* of their fans, were irreplaceable.

But of course it's not easy for four adults to agree how—or even if—the world should be saved, and the unity that gave them their power was constantly jeopardized by it. Thus, despite all its strengths, it was significant that *Revolver* contained little that could be defined as the—or even *a*— Beatles sound but was a collection of quite diverse sounds and approaches. And after the American tour that was timed to the album's release, the band, for the first significant time, diverged as well.

During their post-tour break, George, already quite serious about Indian music and growing more so about Indian religious belief, went with his wife to India in order to study with sitar master Ravi Shankar. Paul, still dating Jane Asher, cut a wide and visible swath through London's pop/ society/art scene before going on an African trip with road manager Mal Evans (never entirely happy when not working, he also tossed off some music for a light film called *The Family Way*). And John, with Ringo as sidekick, went on location to Germany and Spain to play the part of the hapless Tommy in Richard Lester's grim comedy, *How I Won the War.*

It was during this break that they stunned many of their fans—not to mention the music business—by announcing that the world's premier pop group would no longer perform live. With the others out of the country, the job of explanation fell to Paul, who told *New Musical Express:* "One reason we don't want to tour anymore is that when we're onstage nobody can hear us or listen to us. Another is that our onstage act hasn't improved one bit since we started touring four years ago.

"Most of our tracks nowadays have big orchestras. We couldn't produce the sound onstage without an orchestra. . . . We feel that only through recordings do people listen to us, so that's our most important form of communication."

For the Beatles, of course, Beatlemania made touring and live performance more of an unrelenting hassle than for any other group, but the impulse to see the locus of their work as the studio, not the stage, was a logical outgrowth of the drive toward professionalism that touched every segment of the industry. The odd thing, in retrospect, is that more groups didn't follow their example.

To some degree, bands continued to perform live for economic reasons; not only were tours directly profitable, they sold records. But there was also something of a mystique about touring, as the plethora of "live" albums demonstrates, about establishing face-to-face contact with an audience. Finally, perhaps more important to the fans than to the musicians, live appearances formed the signal for a gathering of the tribes, and even as the Beatles were saying good-bye to all that, such ritual gatherings were beginning to achieve a cultural resonance of their own.

21

BOOGIE AND BACKLASH

*B*illboard's charts contain a category of near-misses, of records showing significant sales and airplay action that haven't quite yet made it to the charts, that the magazine calls "bubbling under." This is not a bad way to describe the counterculture in 1966 and 1967. Still in some ways secret—because of narcotics' laws, the potent unifying/defining force of marijuana was necessarily shared clandestinely—it was beginning to become more public. Most notably, a self-consciously underground press—the *East Village Other* (EVO), the *Berkeley Barb,* the *Los Angeles Free Press*—was beginning to serve those local hippie communities that had achieved critical mass. A grab bag of comic strips, poetry, local news, rock criticism, and ambivalent politics,* these publications served at once to define and energize local countercultural scenes and to make the entire phenomenon more visible to the straight world.

As time went on, however, external circumstances—nationally, the escalation of the war in Vietnam and the expansion of the military draft; locally, aggressive drug busts and antiloitering sweeps—forced the papers and their readers to become more political. Given an activist bent and a faith in demonstrations inherited from the civil rights movement, the hippie communities thus differed both in substance and style from their bohemian-beat predecessors, and even more important, they differed in *size.*

Some of this growth, as we've seen, was demographic, but the unifying

---

*In 1966, after EVO gave its front page and editorial to a candidate for the New York State Constitutional Convention who supported legalizing marijuana and abortion, the paper was inundated with letters accusing it of selling out.

effect of rock was also critical. For all that they'd done their best to fracture the academic hold on the language of poetry, the beats who'd read their poems to the accompaniment of jazz musicians were practicing an elite art. Ginsberg, Corso, Ferlinghetti, and the others were infinitely more accessible than T. S. Eliot, but they were a long way from mass culture. By definition, pop music is popular, and the first dramatic public demonstration of the counterculture's growing size and strength responded to rock's siren call.

It happened, inevitably, in San Francisco. On January 14, 1967, some twenty thousand people turned up in Golden Gate Park for the first Human Be-In. As the title for the event implies, this was neither rally nor demo but a simple showing of the colors. The mass nature of the turnout sent political signals, however, for in addition to the usual San Francisco suspects—the Quick, the Dead, and the Airplane—and a nod to the Bay Area's jazz scene from Dizzy Gillespie, the major musical attraction was Berkeley's Country Joe and the Fish.

Like the Grateful Dead, the Fish had folkie–jug band roots; lead singer Joe McDonald had been loosely associated with *Rag Baby*, an East Bay *Broadside*-like magazine of topical political songs, and played in the Instant Action Jug Band with Barry Melton and Bruce Barthol. Although they, too, went electric early in 1966, metamorphosing with the addition of an organist and a drummer into Country Joe and the Fish, they remained uncompromisingly political; this may, indeed, have been in their genes, for McDonald's parents were well-known old lefties and Melton grew up in Woody Guthrie's old Brooklyn apartment building.

Perhaps because "protest songs" were a commercially recognizable genre, Country Joe and the Fish were among the first San Francisco bands to get picked up by a record label. In late 1966, producer Sam Charters signed them to a $35,000 contract (with only a $5,000 advance) with New York's Vanguard Records, an independent label known primarily for a roster of folkie acts dating back to the Weavers. Although independent, Vanguard was hardly struggling—Joan Baez had seen to that—and had a respect for its artists that was much more typical of folk than of pop labels. The Fish was given time to record properly, and in Charters, they had a sympathetic producer. Their best-known song, "I-Feel-Like-I'm-Fixin'-to-Die Rag," was a wonderful mixture of happy, ricky-ticky melody and grimly mordant lyrics, and its catchy chorus "1-2-3, What're we fightin' for/Don't ask me, I don't give a damn/Next stop is Vietnam/And it's 5-6-7, open up the pearly gates/Ain't no time to wonder why/(Whoopee!) We're all bound to die"— made it a national anthem for the antiwar movement. Despite limited radio play, both albums the band released during 1967 charted quite respectably.

Charters and Vanguard were good for and to Country Joe and the Fish (the only discernible censorship was the FCC-oriented decision that led to the transparent alteration of their trademark, "Gimme an F!" cheer from F-U-C-K to F-I-S-H, a ruse so deliberately undeceptive it amused rather than annoyed).

The other early San Francisco signings were less fortunate, however, especially for Big Brother and the Holding Company. Early in the summer of 1966, their managerial relationship with Chet Helms had been allowed to evaporate—no hard feelings, apparently, but Helms couldn't handle both a band and the Avalon—but before the final dissolution, Helms had arranged for them to audition with Mainstream Records, a Chicago-based company whose resources were even less impressive than Vanguard's, and whose track record (outside the jazz field) was close to nonexistent. The band wanted to record, though—partly because Elektra's Paul Rothschild had already been nosing around Janis Joplin, trying to convince her to leave Big Brother and sign with Elektra as a single—but they decided to hold out for a better deal than Mainstream could—or would—offer. They did, however, accept Mainstream president Bob Shad's offer to set them up with some Chicago bookings. Without a record company advance to keep them going, they could use the money, so in August of 1966, they established the San Francisco sound's easternmost beachhead.

Not surprisingly, the Hog Butcher of the World found them a little weird. In Myra Friedman's biography of Joplin, white blues boy Nick Gravenites recalled their engagement: "They were just too freaky! This chick had this hair hanging down and she was dressed in this *bedspread!* And the jewelry! Chicken bones! Voodoo shit! And this patchouli perfume, *reeking!* Her complexion was a wipe-out. She had this sore throat and she was screeching like a wounded owl! I didn't really like the sound, but I was impressed. They were aliens and they were sticking it out!" Other Chicagoans were even less impressed, and as their month-long engagement entered its final week, the club owner approached them with the unhappy news that they weren't going to get paid.

Broke and desperate, without even enough money to return to San Francisco, the band suddenly found Shad's Mainstream contract turning into an offer they couldn't refuse. The advance was low and the royalty rate even lower, but who complains about the paint job on a life raft? If nothing else, a signed contract would put an end to Joplin's flirtation with Elektra. Unfortunately, the recording sessions were low budget in the extreme; Peter Albin, their leader, recalled, "The whole thing was cut in two evenings in Chicago and two day sessions in L.A. Shad produced. We weren't allowed into the mixing booth, and he never let us do more than thirteen takes. He said it was unlucky to go past thirteen." Despite this, the record isn't entirely disastrous, but it was of little immediate fiscal or promotional benefit to the band (though it would eventually prove a gold mine for Mainstream). For whatever reasons, mostly that Mainstream, like many jazz labels, was itself scratching, the record sat in the can for months, and wasn't released until late in the year.

What all this meant was that at the time of the Be-In, only the Airplane had released an album (which, despite some real effort from RCA, hadn't even cracked the top-hundred list), and except for occasional appearances on nonprofit (and low-audience) Pacifica Radio, none of them had received any regular airplay. Yet they drew twenty thousand beaded, fringed incense-carriers to Golden Gate Park—and when twenty thousand people talk, money walks. Since there was no licensing of British hits here, and with the then-unimportant exception of Fantasy Records, no local independent companies of note, the majors—RCA, Columbia, MGM, Capitol, et al.—and the attractively understated Warner Bros. waged checkbook warfare. By the end of the year, every major San Francisco band (and a score or so of minor ones) had signed a recording contract. And most of them, drawing on the melancholy experience of Big Brother, had signed for serious advances with major companies. Within a year, American capitalism would be protecting its investment by spending a lot of money spreading San Francisco's anarcho-pacifistic hedonism around the world.

At least until their records hit and they began spawning imitators, however, the San Francisco bands—and their scene—were unique, for the few packets of attempted psychedelic ecstasy in Los Angeles and New York essayed a different, harder sound. The Bronx-based Blues Magoos, the first professedly psychedelic band to crack the top-twenty album list in late 1966 with *Psychedelic Lollipop*, started as a softish blues-rock band and ended as a loud one. Except for the title of their album, little about them recapitulated the psychedelic experience, and when the band broke up in 1969, lead singer/guitarist Peppy Castro returned to the soft-rock sound in a group called Barnaby Bye.

A more lasting impression was made by Vanilla Fudge. Though it contained some talented players (Tim Bogert on bass, Carmine Appice on drums), this offshoot of a pair of Long Island bar bands was almost indistinguishable from a hundred other such groups, except for one thing. Not only did they play loud (which everybody did), they played slow. V-e-e-e-r-r-ry sl-l-l-l-o-o-o-o-w-w. Whatever else can be said about this gimmick, it was at least marginally psychedelic—as anyone who's waited, stoned, for the spaghetti water to boil can tell you, marijuana and acid both play games with your mental time clock. With tempos slowed down drastically, Vanilla Fudge drill-pressed their way through molasses-paced versions of the Supremes' "You Keep Me Hangin' On" and Cher's "Bang Bang." This was not a bad trick (during the summer of 1967, George Harrison delighted in playing Vanilla Fudge's version of "Eleanor Rigby" for his guests), and their eponymous debut album went gold. It was, however, virtually their only trick, and especially in live performance, the novelty wore off fairly quickly, revealing, behind all that incense, just another ponderous, ham-handed bar band from Long Island.

Oddly, the closest equivalent to a San Francisco scene emerged in London. As in San Francisco, alternative radio was critical. In pre-Beatles England, except for Radio Luxembourg's evening English-language broadcasts, the only radio outlet for popular music was the BBC's Light Programme, which—only partly because of Grundyism; its absurd mandate was to satisfy *all* tastes in pop—was notoriously inhospitable to rock. The picture began to change quite radically on Easter Sunday, 1964, when the public-school voice of Simon Dee was heard to say, "Good morning, ladies and gentlemen. This is Radio Caroline broadcasting 199, your all-day music station."

Radio Caroline was the first of the ship-based "pirate" radio stations and was so hugely successful that by the time *Revolver* was released, nine other offshore broadcasters were challenging Auntie Beeb's monopoly and speaking to ever-larger numbers of young listeners. Unlike the Mods and Rockers, however, London's "underground" didn't spring unbidden from English soil. The scene and style were frankly imitative of the exotic wonders young Englishmen were beginning to hear of from across the waters, but the high cost of transatlantic/transcontinental travel (even with student discounts) and the absence of San Francisco recordings meant that the London underground was *musically* original. And perhaps its most original figure of all was Syd Barrett.

Barrett had grown up thoroughly middle-class in Cambridge, where his father was a well-known doctor, but the family fortunes took a downswing on his father's death when Barrett was fourteen years old. Barrett was playing guitar by then, but his most marked talent seemed to be in painting, and in 1965, he accepted a scholarship to the Camberwell School of Art in London. There he discovered acid and an older Cambridge friend named Roger Waters, who was playing bass in a vaguely jazz oriented rock group called the Architectural Abdabs. When Barrett joined the group, it included Waters's fellow architecture student Nick Mason on drums, Rick Wright on keyboards, and guitarist Bob Close. Soon Close would depart, for Barrett, at nineteen already a dominant personality, was beginning to experiment with feedback. As the new de facto leader, Barrett rechristened the band, in honor of Georgia bluesmen Pink Anderson and Floyd Council, the Pink Floyd Sound. And before long, despite this nominal fealty to the blues and R&B—and a repertoire that remained "other people's greatest hits"—the Pink Floyd Sound was distinguished from its contemporaries (and maybe from conventional ideas of music as well) by Barrett's lengthy, distorted improvisations.

As Peter Jenner recalled one Marquee gig, they "were playing a mixture of R&B and electronic noises . . . and I was really intrigued because in between the routine stuff like 'Louie Louie' and 'Roadrunner,' they were playing these very weird breaks—so weird that I couldn't even work out which instrument the sound was coming from. It was all very bizarre and just what I was looking for—a far-out, electronic, freaky pop group."

Jenner, though solidly established as a London School of Economics lecturer, had indeed been looking for something. With John "Hoppy" Hopkins, a one-man hippie clearinghouse and switchboard, he'd produced an avant-garde jazz record by AMM, which English Elektra under the aegis of Joe Boyd had released, but it didn't take a university economist to figure out that electronic jazz wasn't the pathway to riches. Jenner, inspired by a long friendship with Eric Clapton, began searching for a pop group to manage. So he tracked Waters and Mason down to their Highgate flat, and as Waters later recalled in a Zigzag interview, said, "You lads could be bigger than the Beatles."

The band was dubious, but Jenner began pushing them to abandon R&B and play more of Barrett's original compositions, outfitting them with a thousand pounds' worth of new equipment, with capital secured from an old friend, Andrew King. Jenner and King also managed to construct a primitive light show machine that depended heavily on colored cellophane for its effects. This was a long way from the liquid lights of San Francisco's ballrooms, but the music Barrett was writing was equally distant from America. Barrett was touched with that peculiarly English middle-class fondness for fantasy that affected bands as different as Traffic and the Incredible String Band, and he composed hypnotic drones informed equally by Tolkien, Lewis Carroll, Arthurian legends, music-hall drag humor, and LSD, which the band could stretch into half-hour aural backdrops for hallucinogenized dancers. Yet, for all his fantastical explorations, Barrett showed an entirely unexpected gift for melody and for conciseness that hinted at singles' success—if they could find someone to record them.

Their break came in the spring of 1967, when Hopkins, then operating UFO, London's first psychedelic club, held a benefit to raise funds for the fledgling underground paper *International Times* (later *IT*), which had been busted for obscenity.

Held at Alexandra Palace, itself a bit of Victorian fantasy, the benefit was as important in its way as San Francisco's first Human Be-In and drew an astonishing five thousand longhairs. Inside the cavernous structure, there were bands (often two at once, playing at full volume from opposite ends of the hall), an unending display of film and lights, and Hopkins himself, gleefully dispensing bananas (on the optimistic but unfounded rumor that you could somehow smoke the skins and get high). About dawn, as the glass walls of Ally Pally began to turn pink, Pink Floyd finally came on. "It was a perfect setting," Jenner told *Zigzag*. "Everyone had been waiting for them and everybody was on acid; that event was the peak of acid use in England. . . . Everybody was on it—the bands, the organizers, the audience—and I certainly was." The band, celebrating the appearance of their first single, the Joy Boyd–produced "Arnold Layne," on the British charts, blew the crowd away, becoming everybody's psychedelic darlings.

Sadly, "Arnold Layne," a catchy ditty about a transvestite's evening raids on neighborhood laundry lines, peaked and died at number twenty. England's pirate stations were beginning to feel Parliamentary heat from the threatened Marine Offenses Act, and though Radio Caroline gave the song airplay, Radio London refused on grounds of taste. Undaunted, Jenner and King promptly booked the group into London's Queen Elizabeth Hall for an unprecedented solo concert. In those days, no top British group played much longer than a half hour, and the Beatles were zipping through their road shows in twenty-eight minutes, so three- and four-act shows were the rule. Here was Pink Floyd, with only an initial single under their belts, going it alone with what the music-press advertisements called "Games for May: Space-age relaxation for the climax of spring—electronic compositions, color and image projections, girls, and The Pink Floyd."

Amazingly, the hall sold out, and, at least as Jenner described it, the crowd got more than its money's worth: "We got this guy from EMI to erect speakers at the back of the hall, too, which was like the predecessor of the Asimuth Co-ordinator [later a staple of arena rock sound systems]. We had an incredible light show by then as well, and the concert, which was the first pop show ever held in the hall, was just unbelievable. At one stage, one of the roadies came on dressed in admiral's gear and tossed armfuls of daffodils up in the air . . . it was just amazing, and everybody went berserk." Including, in the aftermath of the event, the hall's management, which was mightily displeased to find daffodils ground into its carpets and soap rings, from the bubbles that had filled the place, staining its leather-cushioned seats.

The large turnout and enthusiastic reception convinced EMI that Pink Floyd was going to be a giant group, but the company was more than a little nervous about the band's weirdness, so despite Boyd's success with "Arnold Layne," they shunted him aside in favor of an in-house producer, Norman "Hurricane" Smith. With Smith in the booth, their second record, "See Emily Play," which Barrett had written as "Games of May" for their Queen Elizabeth Hall concert, immediately became the most-played record on Radio London, eventually reaching number six on the nationwide charts.

By now, as mid-level superstars, they were hooked into one of the typical British touring shows: Headliner Jimi Hendrix at forty minutes; the Move had thirty; Pink Floyd had seventeen; Andy Fairweather-Low's mod band, Amen Corner, fifteen; the heavy-organ Nice, twelve; and local opening acts, progressively diminishing amounts. The audiences, prepped by "Arnold Layne" and "See Emily Play," expected the band's seventeen minutes to follow the appropriate formula: here a song, there a song, but everywhere their two hits. This was not what a self-consciously experimental band was about to do, and if the provinces didn't like it, too bad.

The provinces didn't like it, actually, and as Waters told *Zigzag*, "They were pouring pints of beer onto us from the balcony. That was most unpleasant, and very dangerous too. . . . The worst thing that ever happened to me was a penny which made a great cut in the middle of my forehead. . . ." Soon Barrett rebelled, refusing to do promotional gigs, and the band had to cancel four thousand pounds' worth of bookings. Still, they were able to hold their act together in the studio and released their first album, *The Piper at the Gates of Dawn* (U.S., *Pink Floyd*), in time for an autumn U.S. tour that began at Fillmore West.

It was a good spot for them to start, but the initial enthusiastic welcome didn't sustain itself in the Midwest, and Barrett once again began to show signs of fraying at the edges. Despite the lack of movement on the band's single, Capitol Records had maneuvered them onto Dick Clark's "American Bandstand" where they could lip-synch "See Emily Play" and maybe sell a few copies of it. Barrett was having none of this, however, and whenever the camera zoomed in on him, his lips stayed resolutely closed.

This tour, too, was cut short, and on a subsequent English tour, Barrett often refused even to come onstage, leaving the rest of the band to scrabble among lower-billed acts to find substitutes who could approximate Barrett's guitar lines. Clearly the situation couldn't last—and didn't. In March of 1968, less than a year after their debut single, Barrett was replaced by an old school friend, Dave Gilmour. Five years later, when *The Dark Side of the Moon* began an unprecedented ten-year run on the U.S. charts, the band managed to pull off the difficult trick of combining huge commercial success with a sort of Grateful Dead belovedness. This incarnation of Pink Floyd, with Rick Wright's keyboard variations and inventively repetitious structures was by no means an uninteresting band, but many early fans feel Barrett's departure cost them much of their genius and all their sense of humor.

The London psychedelic scene dried up at about the same time Barrett left Pink Floyd. Harassed almost from its inception by London police, the underground lost its cohesive center when Hopkins was arrested and sentenced to nine months for cannabis possession. UFO staggered on for a while but became less a gathering of friends than a weekend tourist stop; on the way down, however, it provided a venue not only for Pink Floyd but for experimental artistes like Soft Machine and Procol Harum, as well as for rockers like Savoy Brown and the Social Deviants. When it finally folded, some of the slack was picked up by Middle Earth, a Covent Garden club that also featured visiting Americans like Beefheart and the Byrds, but Middle Earth was itself a target for police seeking drug-crazed hippies— one raid, in March of 1968, involved 150 cops, who searched the patrons for over five hours, coming up with only eleven arrests.

Now eleven arrests for all this police time isn't particularly efficient; what it proves, probably, is that in any crowd of 750 flamboyant, anarchistic, international freaks, you'll find eleven who are too stoned to dump their pockets when the cops bust down the doors. What it strongly suggests is that London's police were less interested in drugs than in the particular, high-profile variety of drug users who were writing naughty things about the police and every other conceivable target in *IT* and *Oz*.

Less visible and, for the most part, less troublesome, the mods were outwardly conventional. As Peter Townshend of the Who recalled in a 1968 *Rolling Stone* interview, "It was acceptable, this was important. You could be a bank clerk, man, it was acceptable. To be a mod, you had to have short hair, money enough to buy a real smart suit, good shoes, good shirts, you had to be able to dance like a madman. You had to be in possession of plenty of pills all the time and always be pilled up. You had to have a scooter covered in lamps. You had to have like an army anorak to wear on the scooter. And that was being a mod and that was the end of the story."

In that interview, Townshend consistently referred to himself as having been, more of less always, a mod—and indeed, with his background, he could have been. But the actual crafter of the Who's mod image seems to have been their original "discoverer" and manager, the unquestionably mod Peter Meaden.

At the time Meaden first saw the Who, they were the Detours, an R&B band made up of Townshend, Roger Daltrey, bassist John Entwistle, and drummer Doug Sanden. Townshend, Daltrey, and Entwistle had grown up together in the working-class propriety of Shepherd's Bush, a west London neighborhood that was a few tube stops—and a few light-years—from the hippie ghetto of Notting Hill Gate. Townshend and Entwistle had played dixieland in a trad band together (Entwistle played trumpet; Townshend, whose father was a dance-band saxophonist, played banjo), but it broke apart on graduation. Entwistle got a lower-level job in the local tax collection bureau, and Townshend, like so many other British rock 'n' rollers, went on to art college. Daltrey, a sheet-metal worker, was moonlighting as lead guitarist and vocalist in a blues band for which he recruited Entwistle as bassist. When the rhythm guitarist departed, it was Entwistle who talked Townshend into joining the group. Shortly afterward, Daltrey—who was as energetic as Entwistle was stolid, as handsome as Townshend was funny-looking—moved out front as vocalist, leaving the self-taught Townshend to play lead, which he did in rhythm guitarist's fashion, rolling and crashing chords rather than picking sustained melodies. Their repertoire was still pretty much Beatles and blues, but the defining elements of their musical style were already in place when Meaden saw them.

Meaden had some money—from doorknob manufacturer Helmut Gordon—and he had his vision. Before he could implement it, however, he told the band they'd have to change drummers: Sanden was too old. His career with the band ended abruptly one night during a suburban gig when Keith Moon, a surf-crazed drummer who was playing in a band called (of course) the Beach Combers, asked if he could sit in with them. As Moon recalled in a 1972 *Rolling Stone* interview, "They said go ahead and I got behind this other guy's drums and did one song—'Road Runner.' I'd had several drinks to get me courage up and when I got onstage I went arrrgg-*Ghhhhh* on the drums, broke the bass drum pedal and two skins and got off. I figured that was it. I was scared to death.

"Afterwards I was sitting at the bar and Pete came over. He said: 'You . . . come 'ere.' I said, mild as you please: 'Yeryes?' And Roger, who was the spokesman then, said: 'What are you doing next Monday?' I said: 'Nothing.' I was working during the day, selling plaster. He said: 'You'll have to give up work . . . there's this gig on Monday. If you want to come, we'll pick you up in the van.' I said: 'Right.' . . . And that was it. Nobody ever said: 'You're in.' They just said: 'What are you doing Monday?' "

There had been, and would be, a parade of "guitar geniuses" in rock's first era, but Moon, with Ginger Baker a distant second, was virtually alone among its drummers. Working on an oversize, tom-laden kit, he was relentless, energetic, and melodic. Together with Townshend's power chording and Entwistle's spare, impeccable bass patterns, the full-volume fury of Moon's barrage gave the group an extraordinary density. Utterly without self-indulgence (no "Toad" drum solos for the Who), Moon redefined the rock drummer's art; after him, keeping time would be necessary but not sufficient.

With Moon having transformed the band's sound, Meaden set about transforming their image. The experience, for Townshend, was magical. "I know the feeling of what it's like to be a mod among two million mods and it's incredible," he told *Rolling Stone*. "It's like being, it's like being— suddenly you're the only white man at the Apollo. Someone comes up and touches you and you become black." At this time, the band changed its name to the High Numbers (*numbers*, in mod parlance, were perhaps even more in-crowdy than *faces*, and *high* referred at once to eminence and chemical ingestion), and set about writing suitably mod songs in order to challenge the Small Faces. Their debut record, "I'm the Face," and an instructions-to-the-tailor number called "Zoot Suit," was so drenched in mod language and mod concerns that *Record Mirror* greeted it as "the first authentic mod record." This echoed, rather too closely, a Fontana Records press release, but it's true that the Who's esoteric focus made them difficult to export. They lacked souvenir quality, for one thing, and the sound on their singles—harsh, distorted, angular—was too much for AM radio to bear. Though they had half a dozen U.K. Top Ten singles in 1965 and 1966, they hit the U.S. charts only twice, and then only the bottom reaches ("I Can't Explain," number 93, 1965; "My Generation," number 74, 1966).

Not surprisingly, their American debut tour was decidedly low key—so understated, in fact, that *tour* doesn't quite apply. In March of 1967, the band appeared for one week as part of New York dj Murray the K's annual Easter show. Kaufman had been running these things for years as an AM Top Forty jock, and despite having assembled the beginnings of an FM progressive audience and a remarkable series of acts (in addition to the Who, performers included Albert Grossman's the Paupers, local favorites Jim & Jean, and the Blues Project, Wilson Pickett, Mitch Ryder, and, also in their U.S. debut, Cream), Kaufman stuck with the traditional format, jerking bands off the stage after two or three numbers. In his *The British Invasion*, Nicholas Schaffner describes the Who's segment as "for this particular fan . . . the most thrilling ten minutes in rock and roll memory."

The reason was an explosive closing ritual Townshend had discovered, he has said, by accident: "We were just kicking around in a club which we played in every Tuesday and I was playing the guitar and it hit the ceiling. It broke and it kind of shocked me 'cause I wasn't ready for it to go. I didn't particularly want it to go, but it went.

"And it was an incredible thing, it being so precious to me, and I was expecting everybody to go, 'Wow he's broken his guitar,' but nobody did anything which made me kind of angry in a way, and, determined to get this precious event noticed by the audience, I proceeded to make a big thing of breaking the guitar. I pounded all over the stage with it and I threw the bits on the stage and I picked up my spare guitar and carried on as though I really meant to do it." By the time the Who finally reached America, the accident had become an integral part of their act. Townshend tortured his guitar, windmilling his arm, swooping down on the strings and punishing them; Daltrey twirled his hand mike like a lariat; Moon pounded his drums remorselessly. Finally, smashing his instrument against the stacked amplifiers, Townshend began to put it out of its misery, Moon began flinging his drums across the stage as Daltrey pounded his mike onto the floor, stepping on it, grinding it as it screamed in feedback agony. In their twenty-one segments of Murray the K's Easter show, according to Schaffner, the Who destroyed five guitars, four speaker cabinets, twenty-two microphones, and sixteen percussion instruments—but all to little avail. Boosted by added airplay from Kaufman, "Happy Jack" only managed to struggle up the chart to number twenty-four.

The band returned to England, where their next single, "Pictures of Lilly," was a respectable number-four hit, but at least partly because the lyrics frightened American radio stations—which rarely played songs un-ambiguously about masturbation to a pin-up picture—it failed to crack the American top fifty. "Lilly" was still on the British charts when the band hurriedly returned to the studio to record two Jagger-Richards songs made famous by the Stones: "The Last Time"/"Under My Thumb." Although it was never released in the States, the record was an important gesture supporting Mick Jagger and Keith Richards, who'd just received extraor-dinarily heavy sentences stemming from their arrests on drug possession charges. The rush-released single reached only number forty-four on the British charts, but because it crossed the nearly unbridgeable English class lines—mods reaching out to middle classes, London to the suburbs—it stood as a symbol of the generational, us-against-them unity that was emerging on both sides of the Atlantic.

The Stones needed all the help they could get, for they'd been certifying their outlaw status by tromping pretty heavily on Establishment toes. Now, however, they weren't confining themselves to saying "No, we don't want any of that," but started denouncing "that"—the British way of life—as more immoral than the path they'd chosen. In one famous interview, Brian Jones attacked "the basic immoralities which are tolerated in present-day society—the war in Vietnam, persecution of homosexuals, illegality of abortion and drug taking," and announced that the world was "soon to enter the age of Aquarius. . . . There is a young revolution in thought and manner about to take place."

These provocative—and agenda-setting—words and gestures made the Stones the most obvious targets of the mounting backlash even as the counterculture movement was growing. The first blow was struck on a Sunday morning in February 1967, when the *News of the World*, a hugely popular British scandal sheet, published the second of its "investigations into Pop Stars and Drugs." The allegations about Jagger were veiled but were clear enough so that when Jagger was interviewed that afternoon in a previously scheduled television appearance, he was asked about them. He announced that a libel action had already been undertaken.

This was, in the manner of Oscar Wilde's famous backfiring libel suit, a serious miscalculation. At 7:55 P.M. exactly a week later, police—acting, as it subsequently developed, on a tip received from *News of the World*— knocked on the door of Richards's thatched-roof country home, Redlands. Inside were Jagger, coming down after twelve hours of his first acid trip; Richards; singer Marianne Faithfull, who, contemplating a soothing bath, was naked except for a fur rug wrapped around her; artist Robert Fraser; and a mysterious and unidentified "Mr. X."

After a thorough search, the police came up with some residues of hashish in a pipe and traces of it in a metal container, four amphetamines in a pharmaceutical package in Jagger's jacket pocket, and a substantial packet of hashish in Mr. X's possession. Mr. X, however, was allowed to leave the country for Canada, fueling speculation that he'd been *News of the World's*—and hence the police's—informer. Though his departure made it clear the police were after the Stones and would probably not under any circumstances have been inclined to shrug off even the pitiful evidence of drug use they did manage to find, Jagger and Richards, full of themselves as well as of acid, surely didn't do their cause any good by their behavior. As Richards recalled in 1971, "We were just gliding off from a twelve-hour trip. You know how that freaks people out when they walk in on you. The vibes were so funny for them. I told one of the women they'd brought with them to search the ladies, 'Would you mind stepping off that Moroccan cushion. Because you're ruining the tapestries.' We were playing it like that. They tried to get us to turn the record player off and we said, 'No, we won't turn it off, but we'll turn it down.' As they went, as they started going out the door, somebody put on 'Rainy Day Women, Everybody must get stoned.'"

Somewhat surprisingly, news of the bust was slow leaking out (Richards has alleged that the police were waiting for a payoff), but *News of the World*, of course, eventually broke the story. It wasn't until later, in mid-March, that summonses against Richards and Jagger were officially announced; they appeared for a pretrial hearing in the West Sussex court that had jurisdiction over Richards's home on May 10. On that very day, in what can hardly have been a coincidence, a dozen police appeared at Brian Jones's London flat, where they found, without much difficulty, a quantity of cannabis. The next day's papers announced Jones's arrest alongside word that Jagger and Richards would have to stand trial in late June.

Jagger's case came first, and despite testimony from his physician that his pills, which he'd bought over the counter in Italy, were pharmacologically similar to those the doctor had frequently prescribed for him, he was found guilty. As a convicted criminal awaiting sentence, he was jailed overnight and returned to court in shackles for Richards's trial the following morning. The charge against Richards was ostensibly more mild—allowing dangerous drugs to be used in his home—but was also less straightforward. Much circumstantial evidence was introduced and a great deal of attention was paid to Faithfull's behavior (as part of the jolly trippers' attempts to *épater* the police, she had occasionally let her fur rug slip). Apparently in an attempt to argue that she must have been drug-addled, Richards was asked if he wouldn't "in ordinary circumstances" expect a young woman to behave differently. His answer, "I'm not concerned with your petty morals which are illegitimate," did not play well in the provinces, and he, too, was found guilty.

The sensational press had a field day with "the lady in the rug," and the *Sunday Times* soberly observed that the proceedings became "a show trial, in which the prurient press coverage played an essential and predictable role. Because of the publicity, the decision on their sentences grew into a critical expression of public policy." Brian Jones's thoughts about a youth revolution notwithstanding, public policy in West Sussex clearly disapproved of drugs, nudity, arrogance, and the Stones. Jagger was sentenced to three months and Richards to an entire year. "When he gave me the year's sentence," Richards said, "he called me 'scum' and 'filth' and 'People like this shouldn't be . . .'"

Though their attorneys promptly filed an appeal, Jagger and Richards spent three days in prison waiting for it to be approved. The severity of the sentences brought forth a spontaneous storm of protest: The Who rush-released their Jagger-Richards single, advertisements protesting the drug laws themselves began appearing in the papers, and even Paul McCartney, bemused though he might have been by his exploration of Eastern thought, made a statement that could have been construed as supportive. "God is the space between us," he explained. "God is the table in front of you. It just happened I realize all this through weed." The most important action outside the judicial system itself, however, came from a two-thousand-word editorial in the *Times*. Its mere existence was a surprise—British law sharply limits newspapers' ability to comment on *sub judice* events—but editor William Rees-Mogg's tone was devastating: "It would be wrong to speculate on the Judge's reasons, which we do not know. It is, however, possible to consider the public reaction. There are many who take a primitive view of the matter. They consider that Mr. Jagger has 'got what was coming to him.' They resent the arrogant quality of the Rolling Stones' performances, dislike their songs, dislike their influence on teenagers and broadly suspect them of decadence. . . ." After noting that Jagger's was "about as mild a case as can ever have been brought before the courts," Rees-Moggs concluded, "If we are going to make any case a symbol of the conflict between the sound traditional values of Britain and the new hedonism, then we must be sure that the sound traditional virtues include those of tolerance and equity." On July 31, the Court of Criminal Appeal, perhaps bulwarked by the knowledge that the *Times* would approve, released the two.

This was, however, merely a temporary truce. Jagger and Richards weathered their experience pretty well, and the Stones certainly reaped a bumper crop of publicity, but even though he faced a less savage judge, the drug busts wounded Brian Jones badly. His initial arrest resulted in a sentence of nine months for possession of "Indian hemp," and though the sentence was eventually changed to probation, he was promptly rearrested in another raid. In the months that followed, he was twice hospitalized for nervous breakdowns, and his personality, which had once been strong enough to make him a leader of the fledgling Stones, began to fragment. Though still active and inventive in the recording studio, he also suffered long spells of inattention and prolonged silences. Keith, at least, blamed the changes directly on the police and prison authorities: "They really roughed him up, man. He wasn't a cat that could stand that kind of shit and they really went for him like when hound dogs smell blood. 'There's one that'll break if we keep on.' And they busted him and busted him. That cat got so paranoid at the end like they did to Lenny Bruce, the same tactics. Break him down. Maybe with Mick and me they felt, well, they're just old lags."

Another damaging consequence of the raids was that now the band, with its three convicted criminals, was barred from touring in America. Prior to this—and after, in countries that would admit them—the Stones had always thrived on live performance, and the emphasis now thrown on their recorded output was doubly unfortunate because their legal distractions and Brian's difficulties limited their time in the studio. Americans got *Flowers*, a pastiche Oldham had cobbled together from some unreleased British album cuts and padded with songs already released in the States. Their new summertime single, "We Love You," died at number fifty on the U.S. charts, though its B side, the previously recorded "Dandelion," made it to number fourteen.

Backlash was building in the States as well, and the 1967 "riots" on Sunset Strip in Los Angeles were a harbinger of things to come. The Strip, a major commercial street, had been something of a youth mecca ever since the late 1950s, when Edd Byrnes had been parking cars on television's "77 Sunset Strip." By 1967, kids—mostly white, middle-class kids—had cruised, strolled, hung out, flirted, drank, fought, and generally carried on along it for close to a decade, establishing claim to the turf by a sort of sequential squatters' rights.

For most of this period, the kids had coexisted reasonably well with the Strip's adult businesses and clubs; the kids weren't out in force until after nine-to-five operations had closed and were on their way back to their suburban beds by the time the nightclub business got serious. As the 1960s ripened, however, the pattern began to change: Demographics, relaxed post-Eisenhower parenting, and the emergence of rock clubs that drew a young audience combined to bring more kids to the Strip and to keep them there longer. The Strip's businessmen began to complain.

The city responded, initially, with stepped-up police patrols, then with strict enforcement of new antiloitering laws, but to little avail. The kids responded by staying where they were. At this point, a number of Strip businesses banded together to stop serving "hippie" customers; the kids answered with a goofily innocent "strike," clogging the sidewalks in front of the bigots' establishments. When the order went out to clear the streets, truncheon-wielding police waded into the singing crowds, and what had been a demonstration rapidly became a riot.

To a great extent, it was a police riot. The original impetus to remove the kids had come from the business establishment, but the task of doing it fell on an ill-supervised police force that was, it developed, seething with resentment against the rich demi-hippies and all they stood for. The conflict was brutal—and largely one-sided—and as Monkees-reject Stephen Stills watched the drama unfold on television news, he began writing a song for his new band, Buffalo Springfield: "There's something happening here/What it is ain't exactly clear/There's a man with a gun over there/Telling me, I've got to beware/I think it's time we stopped, children/What's that sound?/Everybody look what's going down."

Generational conflict had been a standard pop theme since the days of Nat King Cole's sweet lament "Too Young" and the Coasters' petulant "Yakety Yak," and in the Silhouettes' 1958 hit "Get a Job," mom and girlfriend united to tame the adolescent male. Behind these songs lurked a sense of inevitability that had faded with Dylan's announcement that the times were a-changin' and that was directly challenged by the Who's "My Generation." But Buffalo Springfield's "For What It's Worth (Stop, Hey What's That Sound)," as the first explicit document of an unbridgeable generational chasm, helped consolidate the youth movement. Released in 1966, it reached the charts the following January, going as high as number seven.

It was the band's fourth, and most powerful, single. Musically, its minor chords and unresolved chorus, singed by Neil Young's guitar, were insinuatingly eerie, and Richie Furay's vocal interpretation of trenchant images balanced the songwriter's husky whisper to give the verses a counterpoised, clean innocence. Strong as it was, however, their first hit wasn't a "typical"

Buffalo Springfield song. Nothing was. In Young, Stills, Furay, and (occasionally) Jim Messina, the band had four lead vocalists and three quite different songwriters, allowing Buffalo Springfield to range easily from Furay's classic country-rockers through Stills's blues-tinged compositions to Neil Young's plaintive and mysterious narrative ballads.

The Texas-born Stills had played for a while in a rock 'n' roll band while he was a student at the University of Florida, but had moved on to the New York folk scene, where he was mightily influenced by Fred Neil, a MacDougal Street regular whose singer-songwriter sets were often backed by the Lovin' Spoonful's John Sebastian and Cream's producer, Felix Pappalardi. Working the basket houses for a while, Stills finally found a steady gig as a member and arranger of the Au Go Go Singers, an East Coast version of the New Christy Minstrels. There he met Richie Furay. Like Stills, who arrived in New York in 1964, Furay came to the Village too late to enjoy the folkies' most spontaneously creative period, and after *A Hard Day's Night* hit the screens, both decided that rock was a more interesting avenue than the slickly commercial "folk" the Au Go Gos purveyed. Stills left for Los Angeles to explore the prospect (where in addition to his abortive Monkees tryout, he worked briefly and unfruitfully with the enigmatic Van Dyke Parks), and soon called Furay—who was only too delighted to come. The two began to work out a few songs together, including "Nowadays Clancy Can't Even Sing," which Furay had learned from Neil Young when their paths intersected on the folkie circuit.

Young, a Canadian, had been a rock 'n' roller during his high school days in Winnipeg, fronting Neil Young and the Squires. This effort lasted until the beginning of the rock era—long enough for the band to add a few Beatles covers to its act—but when graduation freed Young to escape to Toronto, he became a fixture on its lively folk club scene. He continued to toy with rock, however, and when a subsequent band called the Mynah Birds (which included future punk funkster Rick James) packed it in, he and bassist Bruce Palmer loaded themselves and their gear into Young's Pontiac hearse and headed for Los Angeles. There, in March of 1966, as Furay told *Zigzag*, a freak of L.A. traffic gave birth to Buffalo Springfield: "Stephen and I were driving down Sunset Boulevard when we got caught up in a traffic jam. As we sat there, we noticed that the car in front was a hearse with Ontario plates—and Stephen, knowing that Neil used to drive around in an old hearse, shouted, 'That's just got to be Neil!'

"Well, we rushed out and sure enough, there sat Neil and Bruce Palmer. Neil had come out to Los Angeles looking for us and, being unable to find us, was just about to go to San Francisco." The four went back to Stills and Furay's apartment, where the two showed Young their arrangement of "Clancy." "He liked it," Furay recalled, "and that was it! We started a rock 'n' roll band."

Given the level of talent in the band—enough to provide the nuclei for both Poco and Crosby, Stills, Nash and Young—it's perhaps not surprising that their gigs at the Whisky rapidly led to a recording contract and to national tours with the Byrds and the Beach Boys. Vocalist/drummer Dewey Martin, whom Young recruited from the Dillards (over objections from Stills, who favored Billy Mundi), completed the original lineup, all of whom played on the debut album. But almost as soon as it was released— and well before they'd had a chance to establish their identity with any firmness—the band began to fly apart. Stills and Young, particularly, were often at each other's throats, and Palmer kept on running into trouble with the immigration authorities. Beginning in May of 1967, Palmer was replaced, sequentially, by ex-Squire Ken Koblun, Jim Fielder, and, finally, Jim Messina—and Doug Hastings often filled in for Young during those increasingly frequent periods when he decided he'd quit the band. By the time they entered the studio late in the year to record their second album, they were relying to a great degree on session musicians as Band-Aids to hold a fragmenting act together.

They managed to get *Buffalo Springfield Again* out in time for the Christmas season, but its follow-up, 1968's *Last Time Around*, was an assemblage of tapes somehow crunched together by Jim Messina. By May of 1968, three months before the record was released, the band had shattered, its promise unfulfilled.

Although "For What It's Worth" was their sole Top Ten—or even Top Forty—record, Buffalo Springfield was anything but a one-hit wonder. Hugely influential even after their demise, they were probably the first band to burst from "folk-rock" to "country-rock," paving the way for the Byrds' *Sweetheart of the Rodeo* and for the Flying Burrito Brothers, and their trademark sound—strummed acoustics under searing electric solos—anticipated the Eagles by years. But it was perhaps the *attitude*, the drawing of the line in "For What It's Worth," that was the band's immediately evident legacy. Once they'd announced that it was time to choose, they opened the doors for the manifesto writers.

For a while, the preeminent voice of warlike youth—"We want the world and we want it now"—belonged to the Doors. From the time they first broke on the scene in 1967, the Doors were mature, fully formed, and dominated by the vision of Jim Morrison. However theatrical his poses appear in retrospect, Morrison's vision seemed genuinely tormented—aggressively fascinated with death, reptiles, and forbidden varieties of sex. This facile decadence proved easier to imitate than the Doors' organ-rich music, and most of the records by Doors-influenced bands like Alice Cooper haven't worn well. But to a number of listeners, they seemed effective blows against the backlash, a necessary escalation in our domestic generational warfare.

The band, as a notion, had perhaps even a more romantically California beginning than Buffalo Springfield. Morrison had come west to study at UCLA's film school but was soon spending most of his time hanging around the beaches of Venice, eating acid and writing free-form "poetry." One night he ran into keyboardist Ray Manzarek, whom he'd known at the film school, and began reciting "Moonlight Drive" to him. Shortly after hearing, "Let's swim through the ocean/Let's climb through the tide/Penetrate the evening/That the city sleeps to hide," Manzarek, who was gigging with his brothers in a rock 'n' roll band called Rick and the Ravens, suggested they form a band. As he told an interviewer, "We decided to get a group together and make a million dollars."

As a first step, Manzarek recruited drummer John Densmore from his transcendental meditation class, and they began rehearsing. As Morrison recalled in a 1969 *Rolling Stone* interview, Rick and the Ravens "had a contract with World Pacific. They'd tried to get a couple singles out and nothing happened. Well, they still had their contract to do a few more sides and we'd gotten together by then, and so we went in and cut six sides in about three hours." At that time, Ray Manzarek was playing piano, his brothers played harp and guitar, and along with a woman whom Morrison recalled only as "a girl bass player," they made a demo.

After a long string of rejections, Columbia A&R man Billy James heard something promising and signed the group to a six-month contract, during which the company would produce a given number of sides. Nothing came of the deal in the long run, but it did get the band some first-class equipment. Among the booty was a Vox organ that Manzarek began playing in place of the piano.

Shortly after this, Densmore recruited guitarist Robby Krieger (also in the TM class) from their former band, the Psychedelic Rangers, and the four began working obscure L.A. clubs like the London Fog, a forty-by-fifteen room that held perhaps seventy-five people. "I'll tell you how we booked into that place," Densmore told *Zigzag*. "We went down there on audition night with about fifty of our friends in the audience. They applauded frantically, of course, and the manager thought, 'My God, they must be good.' He hired us, and then couldn't understand why the club was so empty every night afterwards."

At the time, they were doing their share of "Louie Louie" and "In the Midnight Hour" for potential dancers, but they were also dropping in some of their original material. On their last night at the London Fog, Ronnie Haran came by and arranged for them to be booked at the Whisky, where they became house band for some six months, playing as opening act for locals like Buffalo Springfield and the Turtles and for touring acts like Them.

By then, the deal with Columbia had lapsed, and the Doors' sound had evolved. Morrison's vision had grown darker and more convoluted, and Manzarek and Krieger had perfected a boiling organ-guitar interplay that extended the electric blues vocabulary. It was an essentially new band that Elektra's Jac Holzman saw when he visited the Whisky. He wasn't quite sure about them and came back a couple more times before he offered them a contract. Unlike the Columbia deal, this involved a real-dollar advance, but the band was nonetheless hesitant. Elektra was a folkie label, and except for

Krieger's brief undergraduate stint in a jug band, they were rockers. The deciding factor—in addition, of course, to the fact that no one else was offering them any money—was that Elektra also had a contract with local heroes Love, and, as Densmore recalled, "We felt that if Elektra could make us as big as Love, that'd be fine."

Elektra did better. Holzman put them together with producer Paul Rothschild, and within two weeks, they'd completed their initial album, which was released in January 1967. At that point in its history, Elektra hadn't had much experience in the singles market, and though they pulled a single— the aggressively hard-driving "Break on Through"—they didn't panic or retreat from their commitment to the band when it stiffed. Instead, they promoted the album, arranging bookings for the band in all the proper "underground" stops, among them the WOR-FM first anniversary concert at what would eventually become the Fillmore East. In smaller New York clubs, like Steve Paul's low-ceilinged and overheated Scene, where intimacy was virtually enforced by the surroundings, the Doors were mesmeric. When Manzarek's inescapable organ continuo interwove with Krieger's take-no-prisoners guitar in the orgasmic bridge to "Light My Fire," the Doors *owned* their audience.

Yet for all the power of the band, Morrison dominated. Almost eerily detached, he sang to the microphone, turning his audience into eavesdroppers, voyeurs on his private world of incest and violence. His eleven- or twelve-minute voyage down the corridors of darkness in "The End" left the audience exhausted and exhilarated—and perhaps even a little frightened. Heard on record now, the song seems almost ludicrously exaggerated and Morrison a 1960s version of the Fat Boy in *Pickwick Papers* ("I wants to make yer flesh creep"), but at the time, he was a revelation—not a breath of fresh air, surely, but a chilling gust from the Kansas of *In Cold Blood*.

Given the themes that initial album reprised, that it achieved any success at all is a tribute both to the band's originality and Elektra's ability to persuade radio programmers to gamble. Those that did were mostly with the so-called progressive stations, and the album had achieved modest chart success when the company began to notice something of a pattern. A few stations were on the band's version of Bertolt Brecht's "Alabama Song," but by far the greatest number were playing "Light My Fire." At 6:50, however, the song was far too long for any but the most adventurous stations to program, so Elektra called the band back to the studio to shorten it. The effort was unsuccessful—perhaps because the Doors were pressing to have the original version released—so Rothschild did an edit, snipping the instrumental bridge to bring it down to an AM-size bite. It took off, going all the way to number one and staying there for three weeks.

Once "Light My Fire" established itself as a solid hit, the same Top Forty stations that wouldn't have touched the long version if Elektra had released it originally began to *choose* the full-length album cut. This was entirely consistent with the tight playlist philosophy—why have a hit hold your listeners for three minutes when it can hold them for seven?—but the fact that AM radio stations were giving top-three rotation to a song that was available only on an album had a huge marketing effect. The demonstration that with radio play an unknown band could sell albums rather than just singles wasn't lost on the record industry—especially because albums were so much more profitable. Companies that had been hesitant about shipping albums to the developing FM progressives quickly adjusted as they watched *The Doors* climb all the way to number two before getting stuck behind the Beatles' unbudgeable *Sgt. Pepper's Lonely Hearts Club Band.*

Indeed, *Sgt. Pepper* seemed so definitive in the summer of 1967 that listeners not unreasonably believed it would become the standard by which every rock record in the immediate future would be measured. And for all that parts of the album now sound trite or empty, there can be no doubt that it was both a cultural milestone and a breakthrough as an artifact.

One has to remember—and one measure of the Beatles' achievement is that it is an effort to do so—that even in 1967, it was still almost inconceivable that a group could make an album that claimed, *as an album, an entity,* to be a work of art. Thus as late as November 1966, when word that the Beatles would no longer perform live began to spread, the London *Sunday Times,* announcing that "last week, it emerged that the Beatle phenomenon was ending," presented a long and generally sympathetic obituary bidding them farewell. "In a sense," the article continued, "the very best of the Beatles' music was an expression of sheer delight at being a tightly-knit group of attractive young up-and-comers. Maturity, the waning of their collective narcissism, and the development of separate interests was bound to kill this phenomenon."

Eventually, perhaps, this article would turn out to be not so far off the mark, but six weeks after it appeared, the Beatles were in the studio beginning work on *Sgt. Pepper.* "Beginning" because this was to be a new kind of album. Up until now, the Beatles had released albums on the standard pop timetable: one for the summer and one at Christmas. Indeed, aided by bits-and-snippets albums pieced together from British releases, they'd exceeded the usual schedule, issuing thirteen albums in the two and a half years between their first U.S. album and *Revolver.* Except, perhaps, for some of *Revolver,* these albums had been conventional in structure as well as schedule; they were made of actual or imaginable singles assembled in a sequence that seemed largely arbitrary. Thus the Beatles' first album had been recorded in a single day at a cost of about $2,000. *Sgt. Pepper* would take four months and cost a totally unprecedented $100,000. As word of what was going on gradually leaked out—and as the length between albums gradually stretched to ten months, a silence broken only by the tantalizing and somewhat enigmatic double-sided single "Strawberry

Fields Forever"/"Penny Lane"—Beatles fans (that is to say, everyone from prepubes wearing I Love John buttons to Ned Rorem and Arthur Schlesinger, Jr.) were anticipating something very special indeed.

And it was. On June 2, 1967, after a couple of weeks of teases from favored radio stations, *Sgt. Pepper* was released in America. As critic and fan Langdon Winner recalled that moment less than a year later (that is to say, before nostalgia had hopelessly romanticized it), "I happened to be driving across the country on Interstate 80. In each city where I stopped for gas or food—Laramie, Ogalala, Moline, South Bend—the melodies wafted in from some far-off transistor radio or portable hi-fi. It was the most amazing thing I've ever heard. For a brief while, the irreparably fragmented consciousness of the West was unified, at least in the minds of the young."

The fans were, in a sense, more united than the album. An almost astonishingly eclectic grab bag of musical and lyrical approaches ranging from English music hall to Indian monastery, it was a cornucopia, a kaleidoscope whose patterns altered sharply from one cut to another, or even, as in the title cut—which boldly asserted the links between vaudeville, rock, and 1940s crooning—within the same song. Unity across the entire album, however, depended in part on George Martin's production (the bandless segues from one song to the next, the overall consistency of timbre and balance), and in part on ingenious exigeses from those who *wanted* it to be unified. That said, however, there were enough common elements among the songs to lend credence to those who've praised *Sgt. Pepper* as a conceptual whole.

Chief among these, implied in the transition from the album cover to the title cut, is an assertion about the shaping power of imagination. That is to say, no matter what costumes they don, these four people are the Beatles, and not Sgt. Pepper's Lonely Hearts Club Band. But when the thoroughly modern Beatles announce that they are vaudevillians and sing as if they were, the intensity of the performance—as sentimental, glitzy, show-biz sorts—gives them credibility. Once established, that deliberately paradoxical credibility carries all the way through to the album's darkest cut, the closing "A Day in the Life," with its painfully drawn-out final chord. Even the weakest songs—McCartney's "She's Leaving Home" is a tepid recapitulation of "Eleanor Rigby"—are beautifully performed, and even they have lines—"Fun is the one thing that money can't buy"—that rang true for large portions of the Beatles' audience.

If anything, the problem with that line is that it rang *too* true, confirming rather than extending the cultural perceptions of the young. The Beatles, for once, weren't ahead of their audience, and *Sgt. Pepper* can be seen as a summing up of what that audience believed rather than as an expansion of it. "Within You Without You" offered five-and-dime mysticism; "With a Little Help from My Friends" affirmed the values of communalism; "Lucy in the Sky with Diamonds" purveyed poster-art fantasy. The vocabulary, too, was the established counterculture vernacular, and lines like "Blew his mind" or "I'd Love to turn you on" created a field day for the *ressentiment* of antidrug—and probably just antiyoung—forces on both sides of the Atlantic.

In England, for instance, the BBC refused even to play "A Day in the Life," the first time a Beatles song would be banned, apparently finding it full of subversive drug references. This seems a ludicrously simple misreading of the song, but the Beeb was a veritable Roland Barthes compared to the likes of American Vice-President Spiro Agnew, who later tried to stop American radio stations from playing "With a Little Help from My Friends" on the basis that these "friends" were chemical. The debate divided mainstream America: *McCall's* magazine said rock, "music to make the mind and/or body dance," was "the new language of the contemporary state of mind. It contains freedom, participation, energy, love, sexuality, honesty and rebellion. It scorns convention, pretense, sentimentality and false patriotism," while *Holiday* complained of producers that "in songs meant for children of twelve or even younger they proclaim that it is wise and hip and inside to dissolve your responsibilities and problems of a difficult world into mists of marijuana, LSD or heroin."

No such divisions were found on the right, however, and at least some of their "analysis" made its way into the nation's police departments. *Insurgent* magazine ran a workshop in Chicago that led to a Chicago detective's filing a departmental memo reporting that "the reason the Beatles and other folk-rock groups received such success in the music field was because they were backed by the Entertainment Section of the Communist Party, and that music was a weapon used to win children and young adults to Marxism. It was also stated that Paul McCartney of the Beatles was a member of the Young Communist League." Others didn't even believe McCartney had it in him. One Dr. Joseph Crow, a sociologist and jeweler described in the John Birch Society's magazine as "possibly the country's Number One expert on musical subversion," listened to *Sgt. Pepper* and decided that "some of the newer Beatles songs are the same simple types they were doing four years ago, but other songs are of a very high quality and show an acute awareness of the principles of rhythm and brainwashing. Neither Lennon nor McCartney were world-beaters in school, nor have they had technical training in music. For them to have written some of their songs is like someone who has not had physics or math inventing the A-bomb. Because of its technical excellence it is possible that this music is put together by behavioral scientists in some 'think tank.' . . .

"I have no idea whether The Beatles know what they are doing or whether they are being used by some enormously sophisticated people, but it really doesn't make any difference. It's results that count, and The Beatles are the leading pied-pipers creating promiscuity, an epidemic of drugs, youth class-consciousness, and an atmosphere for social revolution."

22

LOVE FOR SALE

Though Dr. Crow's imagination was more active (and his politics more paranoid) than the average adult's, he was well within a tradition of "experts" making fools of themselves over rock 'n' roll. After a disturbance outside a 1957 Alan Freed show, the *New York Times* quoted a Columbia University professor drawing a parallel between rock 'n' roll and the fourteenth-century "contagious epidemic of dance fury" known as St. Vitus' dance. He also connected teen dancing with fascist rallies and warned, "If we cannot stem the tide with its waves of rhythmic narcosis and of future waves of vicarious craze, we are preparing our own downfall in the midst of pandemic funeral dances."

Even a broken clock is right twice a day, however, and Crow's formulation—"promiscuity, an epidemic of drugs, youth class-consciousness, and an atmosphere for social revolution"—wasn't an entirely inaccurate sketch of 1967's "summer of love." Though the signs were everywhere, they were most marked in the summer-long party held in San Francisco.

Not without a certain cynicism, the invitations had been minted in Los Angeles by a couple of transplanted New York folkies and a music-biz mogul. John Phillips wrote the words, Scott McKenzie sang them in an achingly pure tenor, and Lou Adler sold them by the ton. "If you're going to San Francisco," McKenzie warbled, "Be sure to wear, some flowers in your hair . . . All across the nation . . . A new generation . . . people in motion . . ."

Not only in motion, but in *costume*. Everywhere you looked, on certain streets of certain towns, and most assuredly in Haight-Ashbury, colors exploded. Striped kaftans met Afghani drawstrings met circus-clown polka

372

dots met paisley shawls met finger bells met peacock feathers met dashikis met body paint met bare feet met chiming bangles met Burmese robes met hair: long hair, longer than the Beatles' hair. And your name, before you changed it to Craze, used to be Arthur.

The hair and the costumes led inevitably to gawkers and finger-pointers (and hence to the self-mocking "Are You a Boy or Are You a Girl" by the Boston-based Barbarians), but in hundreds of crash pads in the Haight, Dinkytown, the East Village, Cambridge, Old Town, and Coconut Grove, the boys and girls—the air thick with marijuana, incense, and insouciance—seemed to have no trouble at all sorting one another out. America had come a long way from *The Man in the Gray Flannel Suit*, an icon barely a decade old.

The speed and breadth of the change was unprecedented. Even as the brightly colored citizens of the counterculture were gearing up for the cataclysm over Vietnam, a Harvard professor was looking back over the turmoil of the thirties and blithely announcing The End of Ideology. There would be differences between the two major parties, of course, but these would be at the margins; secure at the center was a shared consensus about what America was. The last great social problem—racial injustice—had been settled when Eisenhower sent the troops into Little Rock, and all that was left now was a little fine tuning.

Actually, had the forces of the established state been able to stand back from the counterculture and let its growing citizenry alone, the professor's vision might not have been so quickly and thoroughly disproved. But that would have been impossible, for there were mini–Haight-Ashbury's sprouting on every college campus in the country, and in quite a few high schools as well. Every draft notice and every dope bust virtually forced these young people to see the state as an enemy.

In 1967, the counterculture even sprouted its own national newspaper, when *Rolling Stone* was born in San Francisco. For a while—it would be an influence for more than a decade—it was virtually the sole means of communication among certifiably hip big-city centers and the fledgling doubters scattered all across the country. One reason for the magazine's success, certainly, was its focus on rock—the *lingua franca* of the counterculture.

There is, of course, more than faint irony in the notion of the capitalist engine gearing up to carry the counterculture's skeptical messages, but if music was going to be the medium, the major record companies wanted their piece of the action. During that summer of love, the critical intersection in the ambivalent relationship between the record industry and the counterculture was the Monterey International Pop Festival. Though this first of rock festivals not unjustifiably came to be regarded as a hippie-made celebration of peace, love, and understanding, its roots were unquestionably commercial. In March 1967, inspired by the remarkable turnout for the first Human Be-In up the coast, a young Los Angeles booker named Ben

Shapiro came up with the idea for a "music mart," a showcase for serious and/or experimental rock groups. He and partner Alan Pariser tried to get record company backing for the event, but the companies seemed notably uninterested in investing large sums in an ephemeral enterprise over which they would have no control. Undaunted, Shapiro and Pariser raised some $50,000 on their own, booked the Monterey County Fairgrounds for the June 16 weekend, and signed Ravi Shankar, an old Shapiro client, as the first act in their very much for-profit festival. They also retained Derek Taylor, formerly with the Beatles and now lending a touch of hip class to Los Angeles, as their publicist.

So far, so good. But by this time in 1967, even $50,000 wasn't going to hire three days' worth of major acts. The Mamas and the Papas, offered $5,000, turned Shapiro down, but John Phillips was intrigued by the idea of a musically adventurous festival. Together with Paul Simon, whom Shapiro had also approached, Phillips urged Shapiro and Pariser to scrap their notions of profit in favor of an artist-run nonprofit festival loosely modeled on the Newport Folk Festival, which Phillips and Simon remembered fondly from their folkie days. When Taylor, considerably closer to the center of the Los Angeles scene than either Shapiro or Pariser, agreed, the two went along with the idea. They quickly put together an all-star musicians' board, including Paul McCartney, Brian Wilson, and Smokey Robinson, and began asking performers to work for expenses only in a charitable cause.

A lot of the recruiting was done—and an increasing share of the power taken—by Phillips's manager, Lou Adler. Adler had put up $10,000 toward buying out Shapiro and Pariser (as had Phillips, Simon and Garfunkel, and L.A. producer Terry Melcher), and it soon became so apparent he was running the show that Shapiro, claiming that Adler was perverting the original notion of the festival by turning it into a parade of established acts, dropped out of the event entirely. "The whole thing was put together in six weeks," Adler later recalled. "If we had known how big it was going to be, we might not have jumped in. Of course," he added, "if Monterey had known how big it was going to be, it might not have happened anyway." During those frantic six weeks, Adler was everywhere: booking artists; getting the stage and sound systems built; arranging for an ABC-TV film crew to cover the event (for a $400,000 fee); hiring ushers; arranging for flights, food, and lodging for the performers; and negotiating with an increasingly skittish Monterey police force as well as with San Francisco acts skeptical about the Los Angeles power base and agents skeptical about letting their acts work for expenses-only—when Adler already had $400,000 in the bank from film rights.

Amazingly, the event was an almost unqualified success. But although it's a tribute to Adler that things went as well as they did, there were problems. Despite Brian Wilson's presence on the board, the Beach Boys, beset by problems with Carl Wilson's draft status and the delivery of their much-awaited magnum opus, *Smile*, to Capitol Records (and by doubts about where all the profits from this nonprofit festival were going to go), withdrew at the last minute. This was, it turned out, a decision that wound up hurting the band, which passed up the chance to headline before the new, "hip" audience and shake their teenybopper image, more than it hurt the festival.

Though the Beach Boys were unquestionably big, they were also just another white band from L.A., of which the festival had plenty, including the Byrds, the Mamas and the Papas, and Buffalo Springfield. The paucity of black artists of similar stature was a real problem, however. Otis Redding, whose appearance established him as an FM staple, was the festival's sole soul. The Impressions were advertised as performing but canceled in a dispute, and Dionne Warwick, really a supper club singer by now, was refused permission to appear when the San Francisco hotel that had already signed her to an exclusive contract decided Monterey was too close for comfort. Most disappointingly, Smokey Robinson's presence on the board didn't produce a single Motown act—not even his own group, the Miracles.

Yet on almost every level, the festival worked: for the fans (as *Newsweek* rhapsodized, "They landed at Monterey last week and built a city of sound, a hippie heaven of soul and rock blues and funk"); for the media (there were lots of good visuals, and the irresistible air of an *event*); and finally, perhaps, for the mostly unrecorded San Francisco bands (who proved they could hold the stage as equals with the festival's certified stars). Absent credible black rivalry, Janis Joplin walked away with an afternoon blues show, earning Big Brother and the Holding Company both an unanticipated appearance in the closing night's concert and the attention of megamanager Albert Grossman (there to watch over the debut of his latest acquisition, the Mike Bloomfield–Buddy Miles Electric Flag) and CBS Records president Clive Davis. This twin killing subsequently earned them Grossman as manager, and Grossman persuaded Davis to pony up a quarter-million dollars to buy the band out of its desperation-inspired Mainstream contract. Also signed in the wake of the festival—to Capitol, for six-figure advances—Quicksilver Messenger Service and the Steve Miller Band.

Indeed, about the only acts for whom a Monterey appearance didn't pay dividends were Laura Nyro (the New York singer-songwriter seemed to try too hard for the laid-back audience) and the Byrds. David Crosby had used the occasion to issue a rap about JFK's assassination and the wonderfulness of acid that an infuriated McGuinn felt kept the band out of the subsequent film, and before the year was out, he fired Crosby. (Crosby himself, however, improved the occasion by sitting in with Buffalo Springfield, thus sowing the seeds for Crosby, Stills and Nash).

Aside from Redding, whose performance promised him a major entree into the mainstream pop market, the festival's big winners among the musicians were the Who and Jimi Hendrix. Though the audience was rife with Beatle rumors (*Sgt. Pepper* played as intermission music) and though Brian Jones, pale and ethereal, was present as a spectator, neither of the British giants performed, and England's honor was placed in the Who's extremely capable hands. Also, it is true, somewhat violent hands. They were nearly unknown at the time, and the audience's initial reaction was one of polite curiosity. But applause built, and when the band launched into "My Generation" at Sunday night's closing concert, they blissfully shattered the "good-vibes, mellow" ambience that had surrounded them, working the crowd into a frenzy (and Lou Adler, who protected one bank of amplifiers with his own body, into a panic) with their patented smash-em-up finale. As a reward, or perhaps a punishment, the Who were signed to do their first cross-country tour—opening for Herman's Hermits.

The near-impossible task of following them fell to the Grateful Dead, who earned Adler's respect, a Warner Bros. contract, and the undying love of the fans outside the gate whom they invited in, by restoring the crowd's sunny mood with their stretched-out boogies and gently pulsing dance music.

After them came Hendrix. He saw the Who's bet and raised it. Even in the film, Hendrix's literally pyrotechnic performance was a flamboyant challenge to all that had come before it. Hendrix, it seemed, had decided to offer more of everything—more volume, more distortion, more grimacing, more erotic gymnastics, more I-am-a-star-and-you'll-never-forget-it strutting. It was grotesque but also fascinating, in the way nature films of scorpions stinging themselves to death are. The critics were unimpressed: San Francisco patron saint Ralph J. Gleason reported that he yawned, and Robert Christgau, writing for *Esquire*, dismissed him as "a psychedelic Uncle Tom." But the audience, as Christgau also reported, loved it.

There was, it turned out, much to love—almost none of it in Hendrix's carefully calculated performing persona. Hendrix, despite his exhausting English exoticism, was born middle-class in Seattle in 1942. He started fooling around with the guitar before he hit his teens. "The first guitarist I was aware of," he once said, "was Muddy Waters. I heard one of his old records when I was a little boy and it scared me to death, because I heard all of those sounds." After a stint in the army—he enlisted at seventeen and was medically discharged two years later after a parachuting accident—he began working, "patent leather shoes and hairdo combined," as a backup musician on the chitlin circuit. Calling himself Jimmy James, he moved to New York late in 1964; by which time he'd played behind Sam Cooke, the Isley Brothers, Ike and Tina Turner, and Jackie Wilson. During all that time on the road, he'd been learning his craft (he once recalled slipping away from a Memphis gig with the Top Forty R&B Soul Hit Parade to jam with Steve Cropper), but when he hit New York, he found himself on the folkie circuit, typecast as a blues guitarist. Even honoring the conventions of the twelve-bar form, however, he was inventive, sometimes fooling around with fuzz tone and feedback. He had yet to develop a vocal style, though, and spent as much time backing white blues singer John Hammond, Jr., as performing on his own.

Nevertheless, he was beginning to attract some serious attention from musicians who were into electric guitar. Mike Bloomfield, introduced at Monterey as "one of the two or three best guitarists in the world," later recalled his first experience with Hendrix in a *Guitar Player* interview: "I was performing with Paul Butterfield, and I was the hot-shot guitarist on the block—I thought I was *it*. I went right across the street to see him. Hendrix knew who I was, and that day, in front of my eyes, he burned me to death. I didn't even get my guitar out. H-bombs were going off, guided missiles were flying—I can't tell you the sounds he was getting out of his instrument. He was getting every sound I was ever to hear him make right there in that room with a Stratocaster, a Twin [amplifier], a Maestro fuzz tone, and that was all—he was doing it mainly through extreme volume. How he did this, I wish I understood. He just got right up in my face with that axe, and I didn't even want to pick up a guitar for the next year."

Chas Chandler, the Animals' former bassist, was impressed along more practical lines. In the fall of 1966, he promised Hendrix that if he came to England, he'd be a star. And very quickly indeed, Hendrix was—his first single, "Hey Joe," hit the British charts in January 1967. ("Chas knows a lot of phone numbers," he once explained.) By then, Chandler had partnered him with Noel Redding and Mitch Mitchell to form the Jimi Hendrix Experience, dressed the three like Carnaby Street gypsies, and generally encouraged Hendrix to flaunt his outrageousness. Again, musicians were among Hendrix's biggest fans, and it was Monterey director Paul McCartney who insisted that Hendrix be offered a spot on the festival bill.

It is not too much to say that Hendrix genuinely revolutionized the way other musicians looked at the electric guitar. True, he could always sit down and spin out an improvised blues line, but what set him apart from his contemporaries was his mastery of the instrument's—and the studio's—electronic (im)possibilities. Certainly there'd been other guitarists who had incorporated feedback in their solos, but Hendrix was the first—and of his generation, probably the only—to tame it, to make it fluid, flexible, and even melodic. All these qualities, and all that Bloomfield had heard, were present on Hendrix's incredibly adventurous first album, *Are You Experienced?* Fascinating though that album was, and still is, as a listening experience, industry observers were stunned by its sales figures: Though neither of the two singles from it ("Purple Haze" and "Foxey Lady") even cracked the top sixty, the album sold a half-million copies, reaching number five on the *Billboard* charts.

This success was coming to an unconventional, often unmelodic black musician whose singles AM radio stations had avoided like the plague. Hendrix's breakthrough was in some respects the equivalent of the first four-minute mile, and he opened the industry doors to a wide range of musical, intellectual, psychedelic, and role-playing experiments. Finally, however, because the poet/sex object was above all a musician, he opened the imaginations of guitarists all over the world, forever raising the stakes in the guitar-hero game.

At this initial period in his brief stardom, however, Hendrix was an anomaly. Onstage at Monterey, and certainly in England, he had achieved his success almost totally among whites—and within a white audience; for large numbers of black Americans, the notion of a summer of love was a cruel joke. Particularly for big-city blacks outside the South, the summers following the civil rights movement's greatest successes were the summers of riots. Detroit, Harlem, Watts—one after another, usually but not always following an incident of perceived police brutality, the ghettos exploded into flames and violence. Up against the Northern reality of continuing black unemployment—the joblessness soaring most spectacularly among young black males—the hopes engendered by Dr. King's victories turned to ashes. As the Kerner commission, the panel appointed by President Johnson to study the riots and their implications, reported, America was in a very real sense two nations.

This gap was reflected in the music scene. Most black pop musicians (as distinct from jazz performers) continued to work within AM's traditional expectations; this was especially true at Motown, which had no reason to abandon its successful formulas. Initially the policy served the company well, for as AM stations found themselves confronted with a wave of unconventional new sounds, they increasingly relied on Motown's tried-and-true product as the backbone of their playlists. As a result, however, the emerging FM progressives looked elsewhere for their black artists. As Rachel Donahue, an original KMPX dj and the wife of its founder, put it, "Tom's feeling was you had to let people distinguish us from the AM stations in town and they were playing lots of pop Motown. So we didn't."

This policy meant, in essence, that the bulk of the music that was most popular with black listeners (and to some degree with younger teens of all races) wasn't played on the stations that were drawing an ever-increasing white youth audience. Many FM progressives cheerfully played "psyche-delicized" black performers—Hendrix, Arthur Lee, Richie Havens, the Chambers Brothers—and at least some of their playlists included blues performers who seldom if ever appeared on Top Forty radio, but they overwhelmingly featured album cuts by white performers. Since both AM pop and the dwindling number of R&B stations focused on singles—and since albums, with their potential catalog value, were notably more profit-able—this split placed developing black performers at a further economic disadvantage. Motown's already established performers continued to thrive, but the new black artists who crossed over in the late 1960s (with the possible exception of Stevie Wonder, who was a self-made exception to Motown's usual patterns) emerged less from Gordy's AM pipeline than from the FM progressives. Chief among these was Aretha Franklin.

Not that she was an overnight success; born in Memphis in 1942, Franklin had also been born into music. Her father, Reverend C. L. Franklin, who came north to Detroit to serve as pastor of the 4,500-member New Bethel Baptist Church, was not only an important and militant black political voice but a nationally known figure whose recorded sermons and songs on the Chess label commanded a following. Her mother, who separated from Rev. Franklin when Aretha was six and died four years later, was a gospel singer as well, and all three Franklin sisters—Aretha, Carolyn, and Erma—were singing in their father's church when they were still children. Aretha was only fourteen when she made her first records, recorded at the New Bethel Church, and was soon traveling on the gospel circuit with her father. There she performed with virtually every major gospel singer in the country, including the young Sam Cooke, with whom she became friendly, and was particularly influenced, she has said, by Clara Ward, James Cleveland, and Mahalia Jackson.

By the end of the 1950s, though she still retained much gospel inflection, she'd turned to pop, and a demo record she'd cut for songwriter Curtis Lewis caught the attention of Columbia A&R man John Hammond. He was most interested in the singer, whom he described as "the best voice I've heard since Billie Holiday," but he took the song as well, and Lewis's "Today I Sing the Blues" became her first Columbia record.

The song was a solid R&B hit, reaching number ten on the charts, and in another time—or on another label—Franklin's career would have been off to a running start. But this was 1960, when crossovers didn't come as easily as they would later in the decade, and at any rate, Columbia didn't have a particularly strong or active "race music" division (its one major black artist, Johnny Mathis, was marketed white, hitting the pop charts twenty times from 1957 to 1960 while scoring only three R&B hits). Indeed, the company's strength didn't lie in singles at all; under the calculating leadership of A&R chief Mitch Miller, it took singles hits where it could find them but concentrated on the "adult" album market. At Columbia, a Top Ten R&B single didn't count for much.

And so the company went to work on Franklin, turning her into a marketable product in its mold, not hers. For a while, she was very happy indeed. She had seen the gospel circuit firsthand, after all, and knew enough of the chitlin circuit to know she wanted more (at her very first Columbia recording session, she had startled producer John Hammond by insisting that "Over the Rainbow" be added to the blues-oriented songs he'd prepared for her). So she was a willing accomplice as the company began assigning her to producers who were less attuned than Hammond to blues and jazz, sweetening her records with syrupy swoops of strings, taking her away from the piano and setting session musicians in her place, and selecting her material—not only the predictable show tunes and politely subdued jazz standards, but Al Jolson songs; in 1961, "Rock-a-Bye Your Baby with a Dixie Melody" scratched into the pop Top Forty. But this reverse minstrel show was her only pop success, and at the age of nineteen, with a decade of performing among the brightest gospel stars in the nation behind her, she even took singing lessons—with a teacher Columbia chose for her.

None of it worked. She lost her R&B audience, never again hitting the Top Ten on Columbia after 1961, without generating sufficient numbers of white fans, so when her contract expired late in 1966, the company chose not to pick up her option. By then, of course, the business had undergone its post-Beatles/post-Dylan transformations. But even if someone at Columbia had had the wit to look at the then all-male soul explosion and see that Franklin might be part of it, Columbia was in hot pursuit of the singer-songwriter/rock market—and quite successfully, too. Franklin and her then husband and manager, Ted White, went home to Detroit.

For a while, she thought about quitting the business entirely; she'd sold her soul, and hadn't gotten even a mess of pottage for it. But at Atlantic, the company that had achieved such great crossover success with performers like Wilson Pickett, Percy Sledge, and Solomon Burke, Jerry Wexler had an idea about selling Aretha's soul in an entirely different way. He talked to White, negotiated a deal, and in late January of 1967, Franklin and White were on their way to Muscle Shoals, Alabama.

Wexler, who was there with crack engineer Tom Dowd, has described White as being a little nervous when he reached the studios. Even the tiny airport that served Muscle Shoals was a reminder of how far they'd fallen since the days when Columbia was promising to make Franklin a star. But Alabama had changed, too; the band was integrated, and Franklin, buoyed by the friendly presence of New York session man King Curtis on sax, sat right down at the piano and got comfortable. Wexler, deliberately self-effacing, stayed out of the way as she and the band began working their way through some new songs; he was the producer, but for the first time in a half-dozen years, Franklin's ideas were taken at least as seriously as anyone else's. It was she who roughed out the arrangements, determining what her vocal line would be, and the band worked its way into a groove behind her.

With Wexler and Dowd channeling the discovery onto tape, the moment was captured. Less than two weeks after it was recorded, Atlantic released the single "I Never Loved a Man (The Way I Love You)," and two weeks after that, the song had sold close to a quarter-million copies. Eventually it would sell a million—the first of many gold records for Franklin—but a scant four days after it was released, before she or Atlantic would really have had a sense of what was to happen, she was back in the studio again. This time, it was in New York; with King Curtis in the lead, Wexler had assembled a group of New York session players he thought might be able to capture the Muscle Shoals–Memphis groove Atlantic had been working for the past couple of years. The songs out of that session—"Baby, Baby, Baby," "A Change Is Gonna Come," "Soul Serenade," and, most of all, Otis Redding's "Respect"—proved that the magic wasn't in the mountains.

"Respect" soared to the top of the pop and R&B charts; early in the summer of 1967, it was number one with *everyone*, and the album, *I Never Loved a Man*, also went gold, winding up number thirteen on *Cashbox's* annual compilation of top albums. The bestselling single, and most of the album, were secular R&B in content, but their feel was straight out of Rev. C. L. Franklin's church. The singer's emotions—grief, delight, pride, sorrow-beyond-measure yoked inextricably with ecstasy—were palpable in a way that made the also-rans on the charts seem pallid and attenuated—including the offerings from the label that had conclusively proved that black crossover was possible.

Still, Motown was having a most successful year. In addition to setting their record for Top Ten singles, Berry Gordy's labels hit the *Cashbox* annual top albums list six times, with two entries from Diana Ross and the Supremes, three from the Four Tops, and one from the Temptations. In addition, 1967 saw the debut, as a duo, of Marvin Gaye and Tammi Terrell, who cracked the top twenty with a smoldering version of "Ain't No Mountain High Enough." Gaye, whom Gordy had spotted singing as one of Harvey Fuqua's Moonglows in 1961, had been among Motown's first signings. In the days when nearly everyone did everything, he'd worked as a session drummer, playing on all Smokey Robinson and the Miracles' early hits, and cracking the charts himself with his fourth release, "Stubborn Kind of Fellow," assisted by the Vandellas, in 1962. By then, in an act that enabled the company's press releases to refer to him as "The Prince of Motown," Gaye married Berry Gordy's sister Anna, seventeen years his senior. Working with virtually every producer in the Motown stable—but playing, unacknowledged, many of the instruments in arrangements of his own—he'd scored a respectable string of mid-sixties hits (most notably, "How Sweet It Is to Be Loved by You," number 6, 1964, and "Ain't That Peculiar," number 8, 1965) before joining forces with Terrell. He had worked with female partners before, notably Mary Wells and Kim Weston, but with Terrell, he achieved a new, sensuous flexibility.

They were an odd pair—he a sanctified Southerner steeped in gospel, she a city-bred former college student who'd toured with James Brown—but their voices blended magically. Like all Motown's records, theirs were manufactured artifacts, but in their first hit and its follow-up ("Your Precious Love," a number 5 hit produced by Ashford and Simpson), the communication between the two seemed so direct and emotional that romantic listeners felt like eavesdroppers on an intensely passionate private moment. In point of fact, Gaye always insisted that the two were never lovers (and she spent a lot of time with David Ruffin), but it was the illusion that mattered—an illusion that made Terrell's onstage collapse in his arms during a 1967 string of one-nighters seem a tragedy of life as well as of art.

They were singing at Hampden-Sydney, a college in Virginia, and had just finished "Your Precious Love" when she crumpled. At first, they thought that the crippling headaches she confessed to when she was revived reflected emotional strain, but they soon learned she had a brain tumor. Surgery, the first of eight operations, temporarily relieved the pain but left her debilitated, slurring her words and unable to recall lyrics that had once seemed part of her. Though live performance was clearly impossible, she struggled to continue recording—and Gaye labored tirelessly with her in the studio—but soon even this was beyond her. Terrell died in 1970, and her last chart appearance, a duet including overdubs from Valerie Simpson with Gaye on "The Onion Song," was posthumous.

Her death hit Gaye hard and was perhaps the major reason that he stopped touring, unable to perform in public, for nearly four years, but even during her illness, he had begun to grow estranged from Motown. Later, he would come to see her death as symbolizing the death of all innocent romantics, himself included, but initially he blamed the company for what happened to her, adding a layer of emotional bitterness to the restiveness many of the company's most versatile performers were beginning to express during the late 1960s. Partly because Gaye was older and a practiced hand in the studio—and partly, too, because he was "the Prince of Motown"—he made some dents in the company's lock-step rigidities, paving the way for the emancipation of Stevie Wonder. As Gaye told his biographer, David Ritz, "When I was fighting for the right of the Motown artist to express himself, Stevie knew I was also fighting for him. He gained from that fight, and the world gains from his genius."

That genius was growing more apparent as Wonder himself was growing, and 1967's "I Was Made to Love Her" (number 1 R&B, number 2 pop) was his most ambitious and accomplished record yet. The guitar rhythms, especially, were off-center and cranky, and the vocal an astonishing tour de force of sustained sound. It was also perhaps the most gospel-inflected of the company's hits in a year when Aretha Franklin was taking the Detroit gospel sound to the top of the charts.

At Motown, though, the major thrust was still toward "sophistication"—which made it a major blow when, late in the year, the Holland-Dozier-Holland royalty dispute escalated out of control. Motown hit the three with a $4 million suit, claiming that they had failed to deliver material and had thus breached their Motown contract. The allegation was true, to a degree, for the three had indeed been withholding services pending satisfaction of their financial questions, but the countersuit so thoroughly alienated them that any possibility of a rapprochement was destroyed.

Several artists—the Four Tops were the most visible—became casualties of the battle that raged on the corporate levels above them. Motown had many other talented producers on staff, but only H-D-H had the chemistry to work with certain artists; as the Tops' Larry Payton told Gerri Hirshey, "They were really the whole thing for us. I mean, they had us *down*. . . . When they left, it devastated us. Without them, we couldn't get a hit record. Nobody else could do it for us. Besides, we weren't getting much action anymore as an act. As Motown grew—and I think even Berry would agree with this—they couldn't concentrate on everybody."

In the long run, Motown would survive the loss of Holland-Dozier-Holland better than the producers would survive their departure from the company, but for the moment, even the Supremes wavered. The act—which, in a signal of things to come, Gordy had renamed Diana Ross and the Supremes, officially turning Ross's erstwhile partners into her backup singers—closed out 1967 in the Top Ten with an H-D-H leftover, "In and Out of Love," but neither of their next two releases reached even the top twenty-five. For a group that had scored fourteen Top Tens, including ten number ones, in its previous fifteen releases (the only exception, "Nothing but Heartaches," stalled at number eleven), the comedown was dramatic.

The Supremes had other problems as well. Even before the name change, founding member Florence Ballard was becoming increasingly restive in her backup role. In the group's early days, she had often served as lead singer (Ross sang lead on their first recording, Ballard on their second), and in their heyday, her voice remained so much the group's strongest that Lamont Dozier regularly positioned her farther away from the mike than the others during recording sessions. Early in 1967, shortly after her one solo, "People," was dropped from their nightclub act, Ballard was ready to quit the group. And though she didn't quite cut the cord, she did start missing occasional shows, leaving Ross and Mary Wilson to improvise their way through performances alone. In a company as disciplined as Motown, this would not do, and Cindy Birdsong was recruited from Philadelphia's Patti LaBelle and the Bluebelles—then a conventional "girl group"—to audition as a stand-in (à la Glen Campbell for Brian Wilson in the Beach Boys) for Ballard. She debuted with them, onstage at the Hollywood Bowl, in late April.

Ballard remained with the group, however, singing on their next number one, "The Happening," and performing with them at the Copa and the Coconut Grove. She was increasingly erratic, however, and Birdsong was more or less constantly on call. At this point, it began to become obvious that however specific Ballard's original complaints about being relegated to the second-banana position had been, the malaise that continued to grip her went beyond mere grievance. There was talk that she was drinking too much, and it certainly appeared that she was gaining a lot of weight, but the day after Gordy finally fired her in the middle of a Las Vegas engagement, she was admitted to Ford Hospital in Detroit for acute exhaustion. The illness remained unspecified, however, and though she made sporadic and occasionally striking attempts at a solo comeback, her life turned increasingly sour. After a long legal battle, she got a generous settlement from Motown, but she was bilked of nearly all her money, was separated from her husband, and, in a plunge back to the life the Supremes seemed to have forever escaped, was finally reduced to receiving welfare in order to support her children. In February 1976, she died, only thirty-two, of a heart attack.

These bitter fissures within the Motown "family" prefigured a break between the company and the city that had nurtured it. His eye on a film career for Ross, Gordy was looking west toward Hollywood, and though the company would continue to thrive economically after the move, its distance from the Detroit sound that Gordy had brought to teenagers all over the country would become more than merely geographical. Without H-D-H—and without Earl Van Dyke's Funk Brothers, who chose to stay behind—the company's output would become less formulaic and predictable in its own Motown vein but would move ever closer to the conventions of the pop/supper club mainstream.

Though Gordy's attention might be wandering, Motown would remain, for at least the rest of the decade, both the country's major black-owned business and the music industry's major developer of black crossover hits. For a brief while in the mid-1960s, however, Chicago enjoyed a renaissance sparked by Curtis Mayfield and Carl Davis. Mayfield had, of course, been a figure on the national and local music scenes since 1958, when his Impressions (then with Jerry Butler on lead vocal) scored with "For Your Precious Love." Even more significant, when Mayfield re-formed the group in the early 1960s, they had several crossover hits that combined Mayfield's bass-heavy, reverbed guitar (descended, at least in part, from "Pop" Staples of the Staples Singers) and equally gospelish vocal lines with lyrics strongly influenced by the language of the civil rights movement. In 1964 and 1965, songs like "Keep on Pushing," "Amen," and "People Get Ready" had shared a vocabulary with folk-rock's white-oriented protest songs, but as the focus of the civil rights struggle shifted north, the corresponding changes in the rhetoric of black empowerment proved too much for even the FM progressives. Though the Impressions never faded from the scene completely, there was a decade-long stretch between 1964's "Amen" and their next visit to the pop Top Ten.

Up until 1966, Mayfield had also been working as a producer and staff writer with Carl Davis at Okeh Records, a CBS R&B subsidiary. In that year, however, he founded his own Windy C Records, which produced a number of mid-chart hits for the Five Stairsteps (a teen group whose 1967 "Oooh, Baby Baby" anticipated the Jackson 5's sound) before foundering in a welter of business miscalculations. Soon Davis left, too, to form an independent production company that rapidly yielded two major hits, "Whispers (Gettin' Louder)" and "(Your Love Keeps Lifting Me) Higher and Higher," for Jackie Wilson. These two cuts, released on the Brunswick label, which Davis eventually joined, showcased Wilson as a soul singer and stand as among the best attempts to capture his elusive style on record.

Like Mayfield, Wilson had been around since the late 1950s, first charting in 1957 with "Reet Petite," a song written by his good friend Berry Gordy, Jr. Boyishly handsome, athletic (a former Golden Gloves champion), and gifted with an extraordinary range that rivaled Sam Cooke's, Wilson was a charismatic live performer who made some of the 1960s' best records—as well as some of its worst. Indeed, sometimes Wilson managed to sound like two entirely different people on a single release. His biggest pop hit, 1960's "Night," had him belting in the big-voiced "Cara Mia" mode, while its flip side, "Doggin' Around," was down-home and bluesy. His record company, Brunswick, seemed to have little idea of what to do with him. Too often it simply imprisoned him in sugary string arrangements, and while Wilson's talent was almost always obvious (even his 1965 "Danny Boy" contains some astonishing singing), it was almost always wasted on inferior material. Given what he accomplished during a career that was directionless and meandering, he might well have been the sort of protean artist who could really have benefited from the management styles of Motown.

At Brunswick, Davis went on to create a brass-oriented, punchy style that produced hits for Tyrone Davis and Barbara Acklin, but no follow-up hits for Jackie Wilson. This sound, an updated version of the irregular rhythms Mayfield had pioneered with the Impressions and with Major Lance, came close to defining a "Chicago style," but Brunswick was a remarkably erratic record company in its promotion and distribution efforts, and the sound failed to find a permanent niche in the market. With the 1968 death of Leonard Chess, whose Chess and Checker labels had provided an honest home for Chicago performers since 1947, Chicago's run at Motown faded as well.

By then, however, attention was beginning to shift toward Philadelphia, where Kenny Gamble and Leon Huff were developing their own distinctive soul sound. In the early 1970s, when producer Thom Bell began to hit his stride, Gamble and Huff would develop an empire along with a style, but their first Top Ten hit came in 1967, with the Soul Survivors' "Expressway to Your Heart." For the Survivors (who were, in a way that soon would no longer typify Philadelphia, as Italian as Frankie Avalon or Fabian), their heady success was a one-shot; for Gamble and Huff, it was only a beginning.

Well, maybe a middle. By 1967, the two had been kicking around Philadelphia's quirky music scene ever since "American Bandstand" had been riding high. Gamble, Thom Bell, and, for a while, Huff had been part of a band called the Romeos, and though they never caught on as performers, the Romeos developed a fluid instrumental style hallmarked by guitarist Roland Chambers (later equally important in MFSB, a band that would be to Philadelphia what Booker T. and the MGs were to Memphis). But Gamble and Huff were producers and writers as well as performers, and working behind the likes of Len Barry and Danny and the Juniors, they developed the Motown knack of giving their music a backbeat so strong even white folks couldn't lose it.

"Expressway to Your Heart" clearly fell in this tradition. The beat was so heavy it threatened to become turgid, but it was lightened, in a strange way, by a running sound track of blaring auto horns and racing engines. These special effects made the song something of a novelty hit, and for a while, that had seemed to be the producers' direction, as Gamble and Huff turned out a succession of endearingly dumb hits like "Cowboys to Girls" and "(Love Is Like a) Baseball Game" ("Love is like a baseball game/Three strikes you're out") for the Intruders. But late in 1967, when Jerry Butler carried his sagging career east to Philadelphia to work with them, it turned out that "Baseball Game" had been strictly minor league.

Butler, like his childhood friend Curtis Mayfield, had been a gospel singer before he got seduced by rock 'n' roll, but though he'd been Mississippi-born, he was Chicago-bred, and his most successful records were always more informed by the moaning eroticism of South Side blues than by sanctified shouts. A writer—he'd composed "For Your Precious Love" as an exercise in a high school English class—as well as a singer, he'd left the Impressions shortly after it became a hit and scored impressive early success with Mayfield's "He Will Break Your Heart" (number 7 pop, number 1 R&B) in 1960. But rather like Jackie Wilson's, Butler's career seemed aimless; he appeared occasionally on the pop charts with odd choices like "Moon River" and even "Theme from Taras Bulba (The Wishing Star)." Obviously these were a long way from the blues, and unlike virtually every major black performer of the era except the Supremes, Butler actually did better on the pop charts than he did with the R&B audience. In 1967, shortly after he'd been reduced to issuing an inferior remake of "For Your Precious Love," he left Vee-Jay for Mercury, who suggested he get together with Gamble and Huff.

By then, as comparison of the two versions of "For Your Precious Love" amply demonstrates, Butler's natural vocal range had shifted considerably south; the distinctive R&B tenor had matured, or maybe decayed, to a light baritone. Gamble and Huff started Butler singing higher than he had in years, and the rough edges and breaks the effort gave his voice seemed to add emotion and even passion to his singing. The voice, almost torn asunder by the pains of lost love, was supported by a rhythm section that had all the punch of Motown's but was comparatively subdued, using a lot of vibes, marimbas, and even harpsichords. Above all, there were melodic guitar fills, flowing single lines influenced by Wes Montgomery's jazz fluidity rather than Motown's staccato chords. The sound was creamy (and not at all Creamy), and it was eminently salable. Using his own songs and those written with or by Gamble and Huff, Butler not only found the charts again but began to carve out a new persona as "The Ice Man," the apotheosis of pained and almost painful cool.

The unfolding of a personality, over time, through a performer's songs was a dramatic break from the assembly-line approach still in force at Motown. It was, in fact, very much more along the lines demonstrated by

Dylan, Joplin, or the Stones, and one suspects that if Butler and Mayfield had been white, they could have ridden to considerable popularity classified as singer-songwriters. In that sense, their comparative (though hardly absolute) failures illustrate the growing divergence between the consciously experimental white pop that was on its way to becoming the musical mainstream and the Apollonian formalism of Motown. That Mayfield, especially, who by any reasonable aesthetic criteria *should* have crossed over, found himself "too black" for the mainstream audience is a damning statement about that audience's shrinking openness—as well, perhaps, as about rock's increasing "high art" pretensions. While there was no doubt that the established media were infinitely more receptive both to rock and to certain countercultural values than they had ever been before, that acceptance—which threatened to resegregate the music—had exacted a terrible price.

23

THE COUNTER-COUNTERCULTURE

By 1968, with the *New York Review of Books* reviewing *Sgt. Pepper*, high school teachers explicating the "poetry" of Bob Dylan to their classes, and "psychedelic" artists like Peter Max doing corporate advertising campaigns, it was clear that the *artistic* manifestations of the counterculture had entered the realm of the received culture. Yet while the greater part of a generation may have accepted casual sex, available dope, and anarcho-pacifist politics as a great leap forward, the majority of America emphatically rejected these values. Particularly when politics were involved, the ideological fissures were deepening not only along generational lines but class lines as well. As the children of blue-collar parents trooped off to the war in ever greater numbers—and as the number of corpses coming home in body bags grew proportionally—words like *traitor* became an operative part of the American political vocabulary for the first time since Senator Joe McCarthy was running wild. In the face of this split, rock's hegemony was all the more remarkable.

While individual artists had always radiated a cocky confidence, somewhere along the line, the music had become, as a whole, more sure of itself, of its claim to the charts. Indeed, for a while, the audience seemed not only limitless but omnivorous, and there was no *type* of rock that didn't attract buyers in large, satisfying numbers. Although specific albums or specific artists would from time to time disappoint, overall sales of rock albums were soaring. In 1963, the last pre-Beatles year, *Cashbox's* annual list of the top fifty albums contained eleven that had been certified "gold" (more than a million dollars in sales); three years later, it held thirty-two.

Given the seemingly boundless market, it became easy for record companies to grant performers artistic freedom. So, for a couple of years, it seemed that nothing human was alien to rock. Raga, blues, jazz, classics . . . everything was grist for the mill. The one exception, perhaps, was Nashville-style, mainstream country music, which combined stylistic stodginess with stubbornly traditional values that could not have been more at odds with the counterculture's musical and social experimentation—which is what made Bob Dylan's next move such a shock.

When Dylan went down in his 1966 motorcycle accident, he was perhaps at the peak of his oracular influence. *Blonde on Blonde*, then on the charts, was an obscure, involuted, jigsaw puzzle. At the time, he stood unquestionably in the Beatles-Stones-Dylan triad at the apex of the rock world, but during his period of enforced silence, that world changed around him. The Beatles had issued not only *Revolver* but *Sgt. Pepper*, and the Stones had (not quite successfully) riposted with *Their Satanic Majesties Request*. In addition, pretenders fully as gnomic as Dylan at his most obscure had appeared; the Doors and Hendrix are only the most obvious examples among many. Columbia had, of course, done its best to fill the Dylanless void with a *Greatest Hits* package, and though there's no disputing the album's excellence, one reason for its remarkable success—it became a million-seller, pulling two earlier releases along with it—was the audience's hunger for some word—*any* word—from Dylan. Thus when news began to spread during the end of 1967 that there would finally be a new album, the expectant question wasn't merely What would he *say*? but What would he *do*?

The answer, *John Wesley Harding*, pulled the rug from under the questioners completely. Recorded in Nashville in the late fall of 1967, the record opened with the title song—and *it* opened with a few acoustic guitar chords, then, along with a huskier and deeper voice than Dylan had used before, a bass (Charlie McCoy) and drum (Kenny Buttrey). And that was all. A few cuts were ornamented by Pete Drake's restrained steel, but the album would have been understated even by the standards of 1964. In January 1968, it was as though Dylan had flung open the window of an overheated room and let a blast of pure air carve a path through the mingled smoke of hash and incense. Everything about the album was clean. The songs were short—of the dozen cuts, only one clocked over five minutes—and many of them ("All Along the Watchtower," "Wicked Messenger") were freighted with religious imagery. Otherwise they were as sparse and down-home as the "big brass bed" in "Lay Lady Lay." It seemed that Dylan, who'd always been prolix, creating a wall of words to stand between himself and his listeners, had decided to stand naked. After *Sgt. Pepper's* doublefold cast of thousands and *Satanic Majesties'* three-dimensional color, even the album's cover—a small snapshot of Dylan and a few friends in the woods tacked up on a gray background—carved out new ground that might, if you stopped to think about it, be old. Taken purely as strategy, *John Wesley Harding* was brilliant.

But it was a record as well as a ploy, and the more one listened to it, the more illusory its simplicity became. Though the songs seemed, for Dylan, oddly impersonal, he was still a riddler exploring riddles—the same ones he'd been chasing ever since he'd abandoned the more obvious simplicities of his *Broadside* days. As critic Ellen Willis described it, "It is as if Jean-Paul Sartre were playing the five-string banjo and confining himself to stating all of his theories in words of under four letters." It was at once comforting and off-putting, meaningless and magical—and, as always with Dylan, trendsetting.

All of a sudden, the country sound was hot, as dozens of noncountry performers (especially folkies in eclipse like Joan Baez, Ian and Sylvia, and Buffy Sainte-Marie, whose adverb in "I'm Gonna Be a Country Girl Again" seemed wishful thinking) dutifully trooped south to record ostentatiously country-style music. This was handy for the studio musicians, who (like Booker T. and MFSB) got themselves a recording contract as Area Code 615, but additional work for Nashville Cats wasn't what *John Wesley Harding* was about. It had to do with God (J-W-H) of course, but also with America. Dylan was surely too sophisticated to believe what Pete Seeger said at the end of the Carnegie Hall tribute to Woody Guthrie at which Dylan made his first live appearance since the accident—"Woody wants to say to you to take this music to the world, because if you do, maybe we won't have any more fascists"—but Dylan was also smart enough to know that Seeger wasn't stupid. While the rest of America and England was off touching the sky on a head trip, Dylan, reclaiming America for the counterculture, was aimed at the heart—and the heartland. His faith/belief/guess/hope was later repaid in a way Seeger would have understood at Chicago, and at peace marches for some time to come. Dylan had liberated an American vernacular, and when the cops charged, demonstrators—Dylan fans—were sustained by the belief that *we* knew America, *we* were the patriots.

It would have seemed unlikely that this vision would be translated by a group that was 80 percent Canadian, but the Band had an edge. Levon Helm, born in Arkansas in 1942, was its oldest member in both chronology and seniority. In the late 1950s, he'd gone north to Canada as part of rockabilly singer Ronnie Hawkins's backup band, the Hawks. Hawkins had tapped into the rockabilly boom a little late, scoring two minor U.S. hits in 1959 but correctly figured he could carve out a living performing in the muscular mining towns to the north. "Those places were so tough," he said in a later *Rolling Stone* interview, "you had to show your razor and puke twice before they'd let you in. Dress for the occasion was brass knucks and combat boots." The work was hard, at least partly because Hawkins was as obsessive rehearsing his Hawks as James Brown was with his Flames, and not entirely remunerative. "We used to have to carry the Arkansas credit card—a siphon hose and a five-gallon can," Hawkins remembered. "I was the only rock 'n' roll singer that performed every night with chafed lips." It was also cold, and one by one, all Hawkins's Arkansas Hawks but Helm flew south. Robbie Robertson, whom Dylan once described as "the only mathematical guitar genius I've ever run into who doesn't offend my intestinal nervousness with his rearguard sound" (whatever *that* means), was hired as a road manager/quippie when he was only fifteen, and he segued soon thereafter into a guitarist's role. Though he'd been born and raised in Toronto, Canada's folkie central, Robertson was always a rock 'n' roller, leaving school in his early teens to front his own band. Organist Garth Hudson was country, and had planned to attend agricultural college until he started playing horn and wound up in what he described as "a vaudeville band." Rick Danko, country-plus, was raised in Canada's tobacco belt, where he used to listen to the "Grand Ole Opry" on a battery radio because there was no electricity in his home until he was ten years old. Rich Manuel, also a "Grand Ole Opry" listener, joined Hawkins when he was seventeen. "From Molasses, Texas, to Timmins, Canada, which is a mining town about a hundred miles from the tree line," in Robertson's words, they paid heavy dues. And driven by Hawkins's perfectionism and the discipline of the road, they matured. "They were boys when they started," said Hawkins, "but they were men when they finished. They'd seen damn near everything there is to see. They'd practiced, played, and fucked in every town you care to name."

They also became former students passed master. Restless, they migrated to New York and rapidly attracted the attention of Village musicians. With John Hammond, Jr., as intermediary, Robertson began jamming with Dylan at his MacDougal Street home. And then, one night when they were playing on the Jersey shore, they got a call from Dylan. "We'd never heard of Dylan," Helm said, which, given that he has made a point of not listening to anyone, may have been true for him if not for Robertson, "but he'd heard of us. He said, 'You wanna play the Hollywood Bowl?' So we asked him who else was gonna be on the show. 'Just us,' he said."

And just them—allowing for Helm's departure and return—they were, until Dylan's motorcycle accident. Back again to being Levon and the Hawks, they gigged for a while, but got another call from Dylan: He was feeling ready to play a little; could they come to Woodstock? For a princely $125 a month, they rented a furnished house they promptly named Big Pink. Having spent their entire adult lives in motels (if they were lucky; their cars if they weren't), they had a home. Naturally enough, they almost immediately built a recording studio in the basement, and when Dylan started feeling well enough to play, they started spending evenings there. Some, at least, of the results surfaced first as the bootlegged "Basement Tapes" (some of which were officially released nine years after the fact in 1975), a free-flowing mix of rock oldies, folk songs, Band originals, Dylan songs, and collaborations they developed as they played. Dylan went one way with what they did, the Band another: "There is the music from Bob's house," Robertson once tried to explain, "and there is the music from our house. *John Wesley Harding* comes from Bob's house. The two sure are different."

Well, yes and no. The lyrics were often as elusive as *John Wesley Harding's*—"We can talk about it now/It's the same old riddle, only start in the middle/I'd fix it but I don't know how/We could try and reason, but you might think it's treason/One voice for all/Echoing around the hall. . . ."— but the Band's songs' narrative structure and matter-of-fact tone gave them an implied clarity. And though the rhythms were unfamiliar and canted off-center in service to the lyrics, the tightness of the ensemble playing provided an ostensive definition of the "come on, people, get together" ethic that most San Francisco bands could only sing about. And it was *ensemble* playing, too: dense and precise, with no extraneous solos, absolutely without self-indulgence, the singers and players rotating leads and instruments (and the spotlight) in pursuit of a collective end. In a period rife with grandiose experiments, the record was as startlingly spare as Dylan's, but its sound was altogether richer, satisfying the emotions as well as the mind. Dizzy Gillespie once said, "It took me twenty years to learn what to leave out." With *Big Pink*, the Band announced they'd figured it out too.

The strengths of *John Wesley Harding* and *Big Pink* weren't necessarily linked to their countryish sound—the Rascals reached a peak of pruned emotionalism with "People Got to Be Free," the highly charged response to the assassinations of Dr. King and Robert Kennedy that was a number-one single during the summer—but even before Dylan did a duet with the host on Johnny Cash's TV show, many musicians had begun exploring country's sense of rootedness. In commercial terms, country was—like R&B—minority music, and as Ray Charles's *Modern Sounds in Country and Western Music* had so successfully demonstrated six years earlier, there were emotional links between the two. Both were affirmations of minority values in the midst of a changing and sometimes threatening world; though their writers and performers didn't always avail themselves of the opportunity, both were marked by a direct and honest emotionalism that set them apart from the theatrics employed by the Eddie Fishers of the 1950s or by the manipulated teen idols in the prerock years. No one ever cut through the crap cleaner than Hank Williams. Williams, of course, had sung about booze, women, dissipation—subjects with which rockers were not unfamiliar—but at least some of the more obvious values reflected by mid-1960s country music—word-is-bond dealings, family loyalty, clean air and clear skies—were attractive to counterculturists as well. Responding at once to an antiurban utopianism dating back at least to Thomas Jefferson and to the endless hassles of apartment burglaries and muggings in the East Village and the Fillmore district, growing numbers of young people went— or at least talked about going—"back to the land."

Yet even the most attractive values are susceptible to *schlockmeisters,* and at the time rockers were discovering C&W's virtues, Nashville was dominated by "modern country" like Bobby Goldsboro's "Honey" (the year's only number-one crossover). Large parts of what was once rural America were suburbanizing, and "modern country" wrapped a blanket of propriety around Hank Williams's rough and rowdy legacy. Producers like Billy Sherrill, a dominant Nashville figure, even swamped country's traditional instruments, with the single exception of the pedal steel guitar, in a swirl of strings. What marked Sherrill's productions as "country," finally, was a certain ineradicable vocal timbre and a rock-hard commitment to "old-fashioned" values like fidelity, fistfighting, and patriotism. Though Sherrill produced a number of mid-chart crossovers like Tammy Wynette's "D-I-V-O-R-C-E" and "Stand by Your Man," these were almost always socially regressive.

But for one too brief moment late in 1968, country came fully alive and knocked the rock audience off its feet. At Christmastime of that year, Elvis made a TV special that took him straight back to the roots of his first Sun records. (Much has been made of his first single's homage to Arthur Crudup, but the flipside of "That's All Right" was a passionate reworking of bluegrass picker Bill Monroe's "Blue Moon of Kentucky.") Spinning off from his spectacular televised success, Presley returned to Memphis to record for the first time in fourteen years. That session's "Suspicious Minds" gave him his first number-one hit since 1962, and the album, *From Elvis to Memphis*, stands as the emotional and musical high spot of his post-Beatles career.

Neither the passion nor the chart success endured long, however, and within a couple of years, he was back to earning easy money on the Vegas circuit and making ever more forgettable movies. Country, however, continued to flower, taking the direction Presley had pointed in his earliest Memphis days. Thus it was performers like Johnny Cash, whose stripped-down arrangements the Nashville establishment condemned as hopelessly out of date, who proved to be far more in tune with the times. Cash, who had released a version of Dylan's "It Ain't Me, Babe" in 1964, was particularly receptive to the handful of C&W writers who were willing to express counterculture skepticism in country's language and metaphors. Among the writers who came to modest prominence in the wake of the Dylan/Cash team-up were Tony Joe White (whose own "Polk Salad Annie," produced with a rocking edge by Billy Swan, became a Top Ten pop hit in 1969) and Kris Kristofferson. This former Rhodes scholar who began by cleaning ashtrays in a Nashville studio wrote much-covered country hits for Roger Miller ("Me and Bobby McGee"), for Cash and Ray Stevens ("Sunday Morning Coming Down"), and for Sammi Smith ("Help Me Make It Through the Night").

The rock-into-country effect would finally break through in a major way in the early 1970s, when Willie Nelson returned from Texas and Waylon Jennings from the excesses of his 1969 hit version of "MacArthur Park." By comparison, the expanding effect country had on the traditional rock vocabulary was much more quickly visible.

Mostly this countrification took place in Los Angeles; except perhaps for Moby Grape and, later, Creedence Clearwater Revival, San Francisco bands were committed to the blues and were at any rate increasingly self-referential. Buffalo Springfield—most obviously in Richie Furay's songs, most tellingly in Neil Young's—was perhaps the first committed rock band to essay a country sound, but it fell to the Byrds, once again, to amplify Dylan successfully. After a series of fiery personnel changes in late 1967 and early 1968, McGuinn reorganized his band, bringing in Gram Parsons, a (briefly) Harvard-educated singer and songwriter who'd already demonstrated an ability to blend urban grit and country keening with the International Submarine Band, and bringing out the Byrds' last perfect album, *Sweetheart of the Rodeo.* There were Dylan songs, a Woody Guthrie tune, a Louvin Brothers classic, and a handful of originals, all delivered with such heartbreaking sincerity that a casual listener might be unaware of the careful distance at which the band held the music. This wasn't the "let's go back to the land and get our heads together" stuff it later degenerated into; the Byrds were too much children of their times to believe that the songs they were singing held any answers that could work for *them,* but they were honest enough to admit a degree of envy for those who really could "like the Christian life." It's that envy, together with affection, that kept the Byrds' versions of these songs free from condescension and that provided the vocals with a skewed passion as genuine as that of the originals.

This was obviously a difficult tightrope to walk, and the Byrds fell off it when Parsons quit rather than tour segregated South Africa. Though Parsons's subsequent band, the Flying Burrito Brothers, did it even better on their first album, *The Gilded Palace of Sin,* most imitators fell short. In their different ways, Poco, Linda Ronstadt's various bands (including, eventually, the Eagles), Swampwater, Shiloh, the Stone Canyon Band, J. D. Souther, Firefall, and dozens of others all took a shot. They captured the sound of country fairly well, but rarely plumbed its red-dirt soul.

A similar archivalist's interest—and shortcomings—can be seen in the white blues bands that blossomed at this time. Perhaps because the truths of country music were too close for the comfort of suburban whites, blues were the dominant rock idiom favored by most of the musicians who consciously took inspiration from the past; and then, too, the Rolling Stones had effectively "koshered" rock for a generation of British blues purists. Unfortunately, for every Eric Clapton or Keith Richards, who so assimilated the blues' form and emotional content that they breathed life into the twelve-bar structure, there were dozens who merely played the standard riffs louder than they'd ever been played before. It would be possible, I suppose, for a devotee to make qualitative distinctions among such British bands as Savoy Brown, Foghat, Ten Years After (despite Alvin Lee's undoubted chops, ultimately soulless), Climax Blues Band, John Mayall's various Bluesbreakers, and the others that regularly plodded through the Fillmores, but what distinguished them was less important than what they had in common. Mostly they shared pedestrian vocals, a sodden beat, and interminable fleet-fingered guitar solos—and, live, alas, drum solos as well. Mostly, too, they would inadvertently demonstrate how good Cream was.

All three members of Cream—Jack Bruce, Ginger Baker, and Eric Clapton—had served time in the English R&B movement. From about 1963 until late 1965, Baker and Bruce had played in the Graham Bond Organization, a Blues Incorporated spinoff that had steady work and critical respect but little recording success. Clapton (like Lennon and Richards, an art school dropout) had begun playing in the Roosters, an R&B band whose founders, departed by the time he joined up, included Brian Jones and Manfred Mann vocalist Paul Jones. After a brief and doomed stint with Casey Jones and the Engineers ("Casey" had been Cass of Liverpool's Cass and the Casanovas, and was trying retroactively to climb on the cart behind the Beatles), Clapton joined up with some other Stones-inspired Crawdaddy Club regulars a few months after they'd formed the Yardbirds. Astutely managed by Georgio Gomelsky, who gave Clapton the ironic "Slowhand" tag, the Yardbirds succeeded the Stones to a Crawdaddy residency. Despite several obstacles (Clapton, broke, was playing an old Kay guitar whose fingerboard was so warped he had to capo it halfway up the neck), the group began to catch on. "At first," Clapton has said, "I played exactly like Chuck Berry for six or seven months. You couldn't have told the difference when I was with the Yardbirds. Then I got into older bluesmen. Because he was so readily available, I dug Big Bill Broonzy; then I heard a lot of cats I had never heard before: Robert Johnson and Skip James and Blind Boy Fuller. I just finally got completely overwhelmed in this brand-new world. I studied it and listened to it and went right down in it and came back up in it."

By then, the band had graduated to a Friday-night residency at the Marquee, but its other members were, unlike Clapton, growing away from the strict blues form. Urged on by Gomelsky, they were developing a poppier, even prepsychedelic sound, and though Clapton held center stage during their signature raveups, he and the rest of the band were headed apart. Steeped-in-blues Clapton found the slick "For Your Love" the last straw; even as the record began its climb up the British charts (it would peak at number 2), Clapton quit and got a job working in construction. Later that year, the single reached number six in America, and the Yardbirds— now with Jeff Beck on lead guitar—went on to a respectable international career.

Clapton, caked with cement from his day job, found himself raised to heroic status for his integrity, and when he joined one of the various lineups of John Mayall's Bluesbreakers and began delving even more deeply into Chicago style, graffiti reading "Clapton Is God" started to appear around London. Though he took off to spend the summer of 1965 in Greece, Clapton found a Bluesbreakers' slot still waiting on his return. By then, Jack Bruce had replaced Mayall's bassist John McVie.

As Bruce recalled in a Zigzag interview, "When Eric started to play . . . whew, I'd never heard anything like it before. He'd seen and heard me with

Graham, but I'd never seen him before—but when we played together, we had an instant rapport, which led to us having long chats together about what our aims and hopes were. I thought that although the blues were great, there was more than that . . . it was the beginning rather than the end."

Mayall's band wasn't the place for any such experimentation, however, and besides, Bruce was soon to leave it. "He was paying terrible money and we had this gig wagon which was the most undemocratic thing you've ever seen. It was a Thames van with a bed built into the back for Mayall to occupy on the way back from gigs. The rest of the band had to squash into the front. . . ." When he got a chance to join the more popular, if less "authentic," Manfred Mann band, Bruce was ready. "I hadn't been married long and I was trying to pay the rent and eat, and I'd had enough of scuffling. I mean, I didn't mind scuffling on my own, but with a chick that I'd just taken away from her school and her family . . . I wanted us to have a place to live."

McVie returned, and the Bruce-less Bluesbreakers landed a recording contract. Though they didn't reach the U.K. singles charts, their July 1966 album, featuring Clapton, was a British number six. At this point, Clapton had scored a Yardbirds hit playing stretched-out raveups and a Blues-breaker hit playing "authentic"—that is to say, derivative—Chicago blues. As Clapton recalled, however, neither was enough. "I decided I wanted to go further than that band was going. They were stuck to their thing, which was playing Chicago blues. I wanted to go somewhere else and put my kind of guitar playing in a different context, in a new kind of pop music context. I thought that music was more valid than Chicago blues for me, 'cause rock 'n' roll is more like folk music contemporary."

Cream, that new context, initially developed during a midsummer Oxford gig, when jazz-influenced drummer Ginger Baker sat in with the band. He and Clapton hit it off almost immediately, and when Baker suggested starting a band, Clapton agreed, suggesting that they try to recruit Bruce as well. As Bruce put it, "Well, I was still taking the bus and was obviously pissed off at playing 'Pretty Flamingo,' so we went round to Neasden, where Ginger lives, set up in his front room, played, and it was fine. So Cream started."

Unlike Mayall's operation, Cream was a genuine band, and despite Clapton's comparative fame, it functioned financially and artistically as a unit. No one was a sideman; everyone took solos. Though Clapton's licks remained bluesy, Cream allowed him much more room to stretch out than Mayall had. All three stretched out, in fact, and especially live, the most striking result of their improvisatory collaboration was volume. Cream could create a wall of noise that was physically palpable, and when all three musicians coalesced and caught fire, they almost literally bowled audiences over. On record, they were more problematic—Bruce, a merely adequate vocalist, was overstrained, and some of the solos slipped from inspiration to indulgence—but all their U.K. albums (and all but their first

U.S. release) went Top Ten. When 1968's *Wheels of Fire* climbed all the way to the top of the American charts, Cream became the inspiration for an entire wave of British blues bands—and godfather, certainly, to the coming heavy metal explosion. By then, however, Clapton was once again growing dissatisfied. At the peak of their popularity, he walked away.

Not all of the British blues bands who came in the wake of Cream followed the usual humdrum pattern. Two notable exceptions were the Jeff Beck Group, with Rod Stewart on vocals, and Traffic, which began as a blues band. Stewart, a banjo-picking folkie, first slid over into rock in 1964 as a blues harp player with a band called Jimmy Powell and the 5 Dimensions. He was not very good: "I couldn't play the harp at all—I used to blow it, and wondered why I kept running out of breath," he told *Zigzag*. Then, after a turn with Long John Baldry, during which he flowered into Rod the Mod ("I used to be more worried about what I looked like than the music"), Stewart joined Brian Auger's Steampacket, but left it before the band ever recorded. Finally, in 1967, he hooked up with Beck, Ron Wood, and Micky Waller in Beck's new group. They were immediately distinctive, not just because of Stewart's gritty vocals but because the Wood/Waller rhythm section left air for Beck's guitar. They were bluesy, certainly, and Wood and Waller could play with real punch, but the overall sound was lighter and more fluid than any of the other British blues bands.

Except, of course, for Traffic, which moved away from the strictures of the blues form fairly quickly in order to explore fantasies grounded more closely in the English countryside than in Chicago or New Orleans. Certainly in its blues phase, and probably thereafter, Traffic's most obvious strength lay in Stevie Winwood's vocals. Winwood had burst onto the scene late in 1966, when the first of the Spencer Davis Group's two Top Ten hits, "Gimme Some Lovin'" and "I'm a Man," hit the American charts. Davis, a university-trained blues fanatic, was the group's well-organized leader, but Winwood was its soul. Eighteen when "Gimme Some Lovin'" was released, Winwood—"the finest white blues singer I have ever heard regardless of age or environment," in Al Kooper's words—was unreal. But he wanted to do more than sing (and play; he was an expressive organist as well) the blues, and in 1967, he got together with Dave Mason (guitar), Chris Wood (sax, flutes), and Jim Capaldi (drums) to form a more adventurous band. For some six months, Traffic lived and wrote and tripped and practiced in a Berkshire cottage that eventually loomed large in their mythology, and then came out with a stunning first album that included the singles "Paper Sun" and "Hole in My Shoe."

But by the time the album was released in America, Mason had quit, and when Traffic came to the States, it was as a trio. On that tour, without Mason's craftsmanly sense of pop to restrain his desire to explore, Winwood sometimes seemed out of control, and Traffic meandered rather than punched. But on the way back to England, the trio ran across Mason in New York City and a reconciliation was accomplished. It was back to the cottage again, which may have been somewhat less idyllic than romanticists have pictured it. Writer David Dalton, visiting the cottage in 1969, reported the following conversation with Winwood:

"As we come down the dirt road up to the cottage, we see a beekeeper disappear into some bushes. Stevie says, 'I heard him talking to his bees the other day.'

" 'That must have been interesting.'

" 'Not really. It was more like, "Git in thar yer bastards." ' "

From this stay emerged their second album, *Traffic*, a U.S. top twenty. Almost as soon as it was released, they broke up again, this time with Wood, Mason, and Capaldi going off to form a group with organist Mick Weaver. This was a remarkably ill timed decision commercially, for they were unable to tour behind the album. It was a wonderful mix of blues-inflected vocals, elfin narrative, and free-flowing instrumentals that might otherwise have established them as major international stars. But instead of promoting *Traffic*, Mason and company were woodshedding in a Worcestershire cottage, and Winwood was jamming with Eric Clapton on their way to forming the somewhat more blues-oriented supergroup, Blind Faith. Too bad, especially because, as subsequent events were to demonstrate, Winwood and Mason needed each other.

Among blues-influenced American bands, there was none with Traffic's versatility. Electric Flag was full of promise—*any* blues band that contained Mike Bloomfield was full of promise—but managed to record only two albums before it dissolved in a smack-*vs.*-acid split. Yet despite its Chicago roots, Electric Flag was, during its brief incarnation, considerably more than just a blues band. Buddy Miles was an uncompromising and dominating rock drummer, and the horns were jazz derived. The mix was sometimes strikingly innovative, sometimes merely chaotic, but in its very makeup, the band implied that for creative musicians, the blues had become a dry hole. Though the original Blood, Sweat and Tears usually delivered on some of the Blues Project's promise before Al Kooper and Randy Brecker split (Brecker for the Thad Jones-Mel Lewis Band, Kooper to supersession-hood), it, too, suffered similar musical tensions.

The band had developed out of a Café au Go Go benefit Kooper had thrown for himself, and their first album, *Child Is Father to the Man*, was sensitively produced by John Simon. Song oriented, with seven Kooper originals, one by fellow Blues Project vet Steve Katz, and nifty covers of Harry Nilsson, Randy Newman, and Goffin/King, it reached a respectable if not spectacular number forty-seven on the album charts. Though the horn punctuations were more Maynard Ferguson than Memphis, there was a touch of soul to songs like "I Can't Quit Her," and the jazz-rock synthesis definitely favored the second syllable. This suited Kooper well, but many of the other musicians grew restive, and when he reminded them that BS and T was *his* band, it didn't wash. Hostilities grew so intense that Kooper quit, and when Columbia president Clive Davis asked him to stay until a replacement came on, Kooper said, "I can't. They're gonna punch the shit out of me if I do." Without Kooper and Brecker—and with James William Guercio's heavy hand replacing John Simon's—the band, though popular, turned ponderous, entirely leaving its blues roots.

Virtually alone among American groups, the J. Geils Band, from Boston, demonstrated continuing fealty to traditional blues, with former WBCN disc jockey Peter Wolf as a credible if erratic vocalist. But most of the American blues bands, unlike the dogged British boogiers, were looking for new directions. Most, inspired by Cream and Hendrix, turned up their amplifiers and went in a heavier direction.

The first of these to score nationally was Blue Cheer, a power trio from, of all places, San Francisco. The band, led by midwesterner Dickie Peterson, had formed near the end of 1966, and shortly afterward—during a time when chemist Owsley and the Grateful Dead were feuding—hooked up with Owsley, who named one of his more popular products after them. Peterson, who played bass, was actually a fairly gifted vocalist, but under the twin influences of Owsley and Cream, the band came to be better known for its instrumental performances. Above all, these were loud— louder than Cream, louder than Hendrix, louder, perhaps, than the threshold of pain. "They play so hot and heavy they make cottage cheese out of the air," their ex-Hells Angel manager said. But since guitarist Leigh Stephens was neither Clapton nor Hendrix, they were also pretty boring. Forced by studio discipline and their record company's expectations to turn out a single, they obliged with a credible version of "Summertime Blues." Though it equaled neither Eddie Cochran's original nor the Who's brilliant cover, it was a top-twenty summertime hit.

There was still no name for what Blue Cheer did (unless you count playing-repetitive-chords-as-loud-as-you-can-on-acid-which-makes-almost-anything-sound-interesting), but Steppenwolf, which had been a flash in the pan as a Toronto-based blues group called Sparrow, remedied that when they moved to Los Angeles, accepted a name change, and released "Born to Be Wild." Though considerably more inventive than Blue Cheer, Steppenwolf, too, featured power chords, and a line from the number-two single, "heavy metal thunder" (which they'd lifted from William Burroughs's *Naked Lunch*), became an abbreviated term for the music. Its main Los Angeles practitioner wasn't Steppenwolf, however, but Iron Butterfly, an aggregate for which the term *heavy* seems inadequate. To the basic power trio format, Iron Butterfly added lead Doug Ingle's organ, enabling them—with the electric guitar's sustain—to create a wall of sound so nearly impenetrable that the moment during their seventeen-minute "In-A-Gadda-Da-Vida" when the band retired for a drum solo came almost as a relief. Since the drum solo went on for close to three minutes, it was also a relief when the band returned.

Despite the extremely ambiguous nature of this success, Iron Butterfly was a giant commercial group. Supported by tours with the Doors and the

Airplane, their first album rode the charts for almost a year, and their second—*In-A-Gadda-Da-Vida*—was on the charts for 140 weeks, more than half of them in the Top Ten, making it the largest-selling record in Atlantic's history up to that time. Their success was comparatively short-lived, however. The follow-up album went to number three, but the group faded rapidly thereafter. Except for Blue Cheer's initial hit, neither they nor Iron Butterfly ever cracked the top twenty with a single (which shows that singles buyers weren't as dumb as FM fans thought), but they did give birth to a genre.

As the style spread east (critic Lillian Roxon once suggested it began on the West Coast because bands out there had to play that loud to be heard by East Coast critic/aesthetes), it began to fragment in ways that reflected Steppenwolf's nonaesthetic differences from the other West Coast heavy metal pioneers.

The late Lester Bangs once made an international taxonomy of heavy metal groups, dividing the British into Working Class and Aristocrats, Americans (all of whom he regarded as Industrial Working Class) into American Revolutionary and Boogie bands. (Both Blue Cheer and Iron Butterfly, e.g., were almost deliberately mindless—if you could boogie to a march, they were Boogie bands—but Steppenwolf was so deeply political that founder John Kay's electoral run for the Los Angeles City Council seemed almost preordained.) Though the Revolutionary wing, animated by the belief that rock was an anticapitalist as well as an anti(high)culture weapon, was very much a creature of its times, its musicians (maybe because they were smarter to begin with) showed somewhat more staying power. Steppenwolf, despite a tendency to repeat itself, was on the charts until leader John Kay left in 1972, and MC5, out of the Detroit/Ann Arbor radical scene, buffeted by in-and-out record company support and considerably more consistent police attention, was both a popular success, with a top thirty album, and a critical favorite. The initial album from MC5, a live and typically superheated effort, ran into trouble with Elektra Records over the spoken intro, "Kick out the jams, motherfuckers." After some stores refused to stock the album, Elektra asked for an overdub, but the band's initial response was to cover a recalcitrant store's windows with Elektra stationery bearing a "Fuck You" legend. After that, MC5 ran ads in underground papers complaining that their company was chickenshit,* and their relationship with Elektra soon short-circuited.

Their troubles escalated during the subsequent between-label limbo when their manager, political theorist and activist John Sinclair, was jailed on a marijuana charge. Though they eventually hooked up with Atlantic, where critic Jon Landau produced their *Back in the USA* album, they'd lost momentum as well as a manager, and despite the album's passionate cult

---

*MC5 did, however, cut a GP version of "Kick Out the Jams" in which "brothers and sisters" substituted for the no-radio-play phrase.

and critical success, cults and critics don't pay the bills. Atlantic abandoned them, and fairly soon afterward, this best of the American Revolutionary heavy metal bands broke up, its potential sadly unrealized. Despite their lack of immediate success, however, their albums made them an important influence on a subsequent generation of bands, and as new wave/punk bands began to develop on both sides of the Atlantic, their albums were reissued in England in 1977, and the first was restored to Elektra's catalog a few years later.

Though he, too, had only marginal commercial success, the other major Michigan influence—neither a boogie artist nor a revolutionary but a weirdo—was Iggy Stooge (or sometimes Iggy Pop) of Iggy and the Stooges. Iggy (born James Osterberg) was a rock 'n' roll drummer turned blues drummer turned rock superstar; that he lacked, at the time, anything resembling a superstar's audience meant little to Iggy. He always performed—diving into the crowd, cutting himself with shards of glass, throwing up, rubbing himself with chunks of raw beef—as though the fans were present for *his* entertainment. By the time such performances were over, many of them—Michigan frat boys and their dates—no longer were present at all; Iggy probably achieved the highest walk-out ratio ever reached by a rock performer of talent. And the talent was real; at their raw and overpowering best, the Stooges were much more than a geek show (after you've bitten the heads off thirty chickens, the thirty-first becomes a less impressive statement), and through the unpredictable agency of David Bowie, Iggy eventually became an icon for the early British punk bands.

Like him, such bands brought a dangerous flash of unpredictability to the stage with them. The most impressive thing about the Stooges, something their records could never capture, was that even Iggy's most legendary excesses never seemed contrived. When he cut himself, he bled real blood, and if some inner demon was pushing him to die for his art—in your lap—he would.

With Iggy, MC5, and Steppenwolf, rock had obviously come a long way from flower power. This was angry music for angry times. Curiously, the agent by which much of this anger would burst on the consciousness of the American people was a scholarly, poetry-loving senator from Minnesota, Eugene McCarthy. In 1968, McCarthy agreed to carry the antiwar banner into the Democratic presidential race, challenging Lyndon Johnson. When the New Hampshire primary found him shorthanded, longtime activist Allard Lowenstein took to the "Dump Johnson" road visiting campuses throughout the Northeast, urging students to come to New Hampshire and give some time to the McCarthy campaign.

As it had been in 1964, when Lowenstein was recruiting for the first "freedom summer," the response was enthusiastic, and thousands of students cut their hair and beards, donning "proper" clothing to come to New Hampshire as "Clean for Gene" volunteers. Virtually overnight, they changed the tenor of the campaign, turning it into a high-spirited youth crusade. Hundreds of New Hampshire residents, from tech-belt Boston expatriates to taciturn Yankees in the northern mill towns, gave the volunteers beds (or at least sleeping-bag space), and tens of thousands opened their doors to hear earnest campaign pitches. Aided both by the shock of the Tet offensive and undue complacency from the local Johnson forces, McCarthy and his army of kids embarrassed the President and demonstrated his vulnerability. Shortly after the New Hampshire primary, Lyndon Johnson announced that he would not seek a second term in office.

But after that victory, things began to go sour. Robert Kennedy finally declared his candidacy, splitting the antiwar vote, and once-liberal Vice President Hubert Humphrey, wrapping himself in Johnson's tattered banner, rallied the Cro Magnon Democrats around his candidacy. The three-way battle ended suddenly in California, when an assassin's bullets struck down Kennedy on the night of his most important victory.

Gradually, stupidly, tragically, many elected Kennedy delegates began to drift toward Humphrey. A holding action by Senator George McGovern slowed the tide, but as the Chicago convention neared, it began to look more and more as though the party leadership would simply roll on over the antiwar voters who'd refused to support Humphrey. Spontaneously in some cases, in response to organizing efforts by East Coast radicals in others, a lot of young Americans headed for Chicago to protest.

Though most had been asked to come, the San Francisco bands were notably absent, and *Rolling Stone* expressed skepticism about the whole notion. Chicago cops were tough, and Mayor Richard Daley had made it quite clear that *he* wasn't going to stand for any of this "protest" nonsense. Most of the protesters were aware of this; they were not some group of innocents lured by the promise of music (indeed, among prominent American bands, only MC5 played for the demonstrators). They practiced anti-teargas techniques, and the experienced wore padded clothing and hard hats. None of it mattered. The Humphrey forces were brutally efficient inside the hall; the cops and the National Guard simply brutal outside it. A lot of idealists lost their innocence along with their teeth.

Millions of Americans watched the brutality unfold on their television screens, millions heard a United States senator denounce the "security forces" for gestapo tactics (and those who could read lips saw Richard Daley shouting "Go fuck yourself, Jew bastard" at him). When it turned out that the majority of Americans *approved* of what they'd seen on television, the organizers—too late for their bruised and bloody followers—lost their innocence as well. A large part of a generation that had put its trust in the American political system was changed forever. Some of those who'd rung doorbells in the dozens of primary states retreated into cynicism and, in Voltaire's phrase, to "cultivating their own gardens." Others were radicalized. All, however, were for at least a time estranged, internal exiles within their own country.

24

TROUBLES IN PEPPERLAND

After Chicago, and by no means entirely by coincidence, the Rolling Stones, an ocean away, moved from the wilted "Dandelion" to the strutting, convention-echoing "Street Fighting Man"—and to something darker as well. "Please allow me to introduce myself," sang Jagger on *Beggar's Banquet*. "I'm a man of wealth and taste." This was surely not art rock, but it was certainly artful, and on this album, the Stones demonstrated their taste (and solidified their wealth) by turning away from the psychedelic "importance" of *Their Satanic Majesties Request* to produce their hardest-rocking album since 1966's *Aftermath*. In turning metaphorically from San Francisco to Chicago, they were returning, albeit in a much more sophisticated way, to Chicago's music as well.

To a certain extent, despite Nicky Hopkins's piano coming to the forefront and Brian Jones's beautiful slide guitar and tamboura, *Beggar's Banquet* was Richards's album, with his notions driving the band. As Richards later told a British interviewer, disappointment with *Satanic Majesties* had sent him back to his beloved blues records (a collection he modestly described as "over a thousand records") and set him to begin reinventing the Stones' sound: "It involved literally learning the guitar all over again. You had to apply yourself in almost the same way as when you started. I really enjoyed it."

Jones was the only Rolling Stone who didn't. At various times, Richards, Jagger, and Bill Wyman all described *Beggar's Banquet* as their favorite Stones' album, but Jones, who had a tough time keeping organized and functional in the studio, was disappointed that the stripped-down album had no room for his experiments in electronic music, telling an interviewer that as a result, "I might like to do something separately." In his desire to do more than "just" rock, Jones was hardly alone. Especially in England, the drive to stretch rock's boundaries was strong. But perhaps because he was genuinely middle class and less subject to cultural intimidation than the working-class kids who dominated British pop, Jones's electronic notions were more promising than those of the classical-pomp school (from which even the Who, with Townshend's increasing talk of a rock opera to be called *Deaf, Dumb, and Blind Boy*, weren't immune). To that extent, Jones's estrangement from the other Stones reflected splits within rock culture itself.

The conflicting impulses between high and popular art were perhaps more visible in England than in America because the class system, which put such a premium on "high" art, was more painfully in operation in England. Consider, for instance, the Moody Blues, who were once a second-level Birmingham beat group assembled from the remains of bands like the Avengers, the Rebels, and the Diplomats. In 1965, they had the great good luck to tour America as the Beatles' opening act, earning a U.S. number ten (U.K. number 1) with "Go Now." After that, however, the hits dried up for them, and when the band's most obvious asset, lead singer Denny Laine, left them, it seemed reasonable to suppose that their career was over. When Justin Hayward and ex-Rebel John Lodge joined them to replace Laine and departed bassist Clint Warwick, Lodge had to sell his personal amps and other equipment to finance a three-month go-to-Belgium-and-get-it-together tour. When the ex-beatsters returned with the idea of attempting a classics/rock fusion, they were a trifle ahead of their time (as flutist Ray Thomas put it, "Everyone thought we were crazy") and wound up gigging ceaselessly just to keep themselves alive. But after *Sgt. Pepper* showed the way, Decca Records, in an uncharacteristic burst of U.K. commercial flower power, underwrote a studio effort aimed at the album rather than the singles market. Accompanied by members of the London Festival Orchestra, the band came up with *Days of Future Passed*. Fueled by the British success of "Nights in White Satin" as a single, the album scored well there and eventually crossed the ocean and climbed to number three on the U.S. charts. Even more than Procul Harum (whose nod toward Bach in "A Whiter Shade of Pale" was untypical of the group), the Moody Blues established a particularly British version of art rock.

Unlike American art rockers, whose high-culture heroes (if any) were Kerouac, Ginsberg, and the other anti–high culture beats, the British art bands acted as though rock were something that needed to be gussied up with a little bit of "good music"—by which they did not, alas, mean Chuck Berry. Now there are many good things to be said about Beethoven, but as Berry had earlier pointed out with considerable persuasiveness, he didn't rock. The attempt to make him do so led to emphasizing the beat in order to create a repetitive and sometimes compelling rhythm into which medicinal doses of art could be inserted. Though the resulting sound was occasionally similar, the *intent* was different from that of those blues-derived bands like Led Zeppelin that veered toward heavy metal.

The audiences were different as well. While rock listeners on both sides of the Atlantic were in general growing older, the music was growing less class bound as well. The British art rockers were consciously aiming at their "betters," the people in suits and bowlers. Unconsciously they were laying the ground for the explosion of punk rock a decade or more down the road.

Though many of the mods had effortlessly become hippies as flower power went international a year earlier, the British class system and economy allowed less stylistic freedom than America's, and a substantial portion were left behind. In an important 1972 essay, British critic Pete Fowler quoted a twenty-year-old Birmingham apprentice: "I was fifteen in 1967, and all I remember is what a drag it was. One minute we had the Spencer Davis Group playing here, and the Stones played here a lot, and the Yardbirds and the Animals. Then suddenly—nothing. Nothing at all. I hated fucking *Sgt. Pepper* and that thing the Stones did with 'She's a Rainbow' on it. Me and my mates spent most of the time in the pub after that. I mean, you could hardly dance to the Pink Floyd, could you?"

No, you couldn't, and *of course* art wasn't everything. One might have expected this to be understood almost intuitively in San Francisco, but it was for reasons of art—as well as for money and fame—that Janis Joplin was leaving Big Brother and the Holding Company. She'd resisted Paul Rothschild's earlier attempts to pull her away to Elektra as a single act, but when the band recorded its first Columbia album, producer John Simon was so unhappy with the inability of the band to reach what he considered minimal professional standards that he pulled his name from the credits. Prompted by Grossman and CBS, Joplin agreed to go with a new band.

The parting was officially amicable—Sam Andrews would go with her—but amicability was much strained by the reality that Big Brother and the Holding Company *including* Janis Joplin had several months of bookings they were obliged to work through. They ground through those dates like a divorcing couple grimly occupying the same house until the kids went back to school. In Minneapolis, as an exhausted Joplin panted into the mike, Peter Albin filled the time until she was ready to sing by announcing, "Now we're doing our imitation of Lassie." During the intermission, she launched an attack on him, "Man, he called me a dog! On stage, in front of everybody. I don't have to take that shit!" There were more words, and as the *Rolling Stone* reporter who was present put it, "Vibrations are what they call bad."

On one level, the breakup of Big Brother was just a reprise of Grace Slick's jump from the Great Society to the Jefferson Airplane, or of founding member Jim Murray being forced from Quicksilver Messenger Service. Talented musicians *always* want to work at their best and with the best; for the near-best, the process is cruel, and San Francisco's rhetoric of love couldn't change that. It could, however, raise musicians' expectations, and the cruelty involved in breaking up Big Brother *after* the band had made it seemed gratuitous.

Grossman took the heat for it—as he would have even if the split had been Joplin's idea exclusively; part of a manager's job is to protect his stars—but the forces impelling the split were larger than any single manager or any single record company. Producer John Simon hinted at them in Myra Friedman's Joplin biography: "I always thought they were a great *performance* band, but I *didn't* think they made it as a recording band. I *liked* seeing them; I *liked* the excitement in the audience, but there was a time when what was music and what the public *thought* was music were very far apart. . . . Look, they made a lot of people happy. That's *important* and it *counts* and it shouldn't be held against them that they couldn't make music! They had a cult and a following and as a San Francisco phenomenon, they were in their element and then . . . well . . . for some probably psychological reason, Clive Davis forced them to make a record! I'm *serious.* You know, there's studied music and there's tribal music and their stuff leaned more toward tribal music. What they *should* have had was an Alan Lomax field recording from San Francisco. I mean, *that's* justice."

The obvious solution—using session musicians—ran up against the entire notion of equal-membership groups that was at the heart of the San Francisco explosion. And no matter how bizarre it seems that a band that could make a lot of people happy couldn't make music, Simon was serious. The folkies, in their way, had been on to something, but what made the explosion of rock so thrilling wasn't just the music but the explosion itself: the sudden and successful onslaught on the mainstream that made it just barely plausible when the Doors sang "We want the world and we want it . . . *Now!*" The Fillmores were a lot bigger than Folk City, but you couldn't fit the world into them. You got to the world on records. Grossman was a major manager, Bill Graham a major impresario, Big Brother a major act, but by 1968, rock was a billion-dollar business driven not by managers, impresarios, or even musicians but by record companies. As rock became the received music, their demand for product—professionally competent product for the burgeoning FM progressives—was insatiable.

After Monterey showed that the product was there—and that the audience was potentially vast—the industry was determined to get back in the saddle. Joplin's yielding to her record company is a mini-example, and at least some industry figures had bigger ideas. Why, they asked, had San Francisco happened? And why *only* San Francisco? Couldn't there be an East Coast equivalent that would make just as much money? A smaller coastal city with a lot of college kids in it, say? Seemed like a swell idea to independent producer Alan Lorber. Armed with a working arrangement with MGM Records, he began signing Boston groups late in 1967. He would record them and license the tapes to MGM; the company would promote and distribute the records. In September of that year, Record World reported that "Lorber feels that Boston will be more successful as a talent center than San Francisco had been. He feels that there was only a moderate talent situation in San Francisco which was backed and forced by strong commercial interests." In their East Coast company town, Lorber and MGM would provide the backing and forcing. And so the Boss-town sound was born.

As it happened, there was a genuine Boston sound—that of an acoustic guitar in the hands of someone like Joan Baez or Tom Rush or any of the musicians who moved in and out of Club 47. Though this turned out to include some genuine blues-oriented rockers like Peter Wolf, Al Wilson, and, by adoption, the Chambers Brothers, coffeehouses were not ballrooms; Boston's nearest equivalent to the Fillmore, the Boston Tea Party, booked imported bands for the most part. Since folk wasn't commercial, however, Lorber set out to find East Coast psychedelia, signing fledgling bands of promising, if derivative and undeveloped, talent. MGM's launch—for the Ultimate Spinach, Orpheus, and Wes Farrell's Beacon Street Union—was set for January. MGM had arranged a series of press parties for the three groups. Ultimate Spinach got cross-country treatment; Beacon Street Union and Orpheus were feted in New York. Trade paper ads, promising "the sound heard round the world," ran in all the major outlets, and Ultimate Spinach was booked for a company-supported West Coast tour.

All this, from the original signings to food and drink for the press, cost money—money that by the curious logic then prevailing, MGM virtually had to spend. Though the company had signed first-wave rock performers brilliantly (its Verve subsidiary had the Mothers, the Blues Project, the Velvet Underground, Tim Hardin, Richie Havens, Laura Nyro, and Janis Ian), it hadn't marketed them successfully. Of its major British groups, the Animals had broken up and Herman's Hermits had faded badly. Plus, caught up in a transition between the people who'd put together the early rock signings and new leadership the company hoped might generate profits as well as prestige, MGM had missed out on San Francisco. With its overhead high (you think Herman's Hermits were a drag on the bottom line? MGM was still paying Connie Francis), it desperately needed new product. Investing a few hundred thousand dollars in the Boston sound could hardly be worse than spending promo money on Herman's Hermits—and might be many, many millions of times better.

And so, with Ultimate Spinach getting a good reception on its West Coast tour, MGM's execs must have been dancing in the suites when the January 28 Newsweek went for the okey-doke and published a loving puff piece on the virtually nonexistent "Boss-town Sound." If the bands had been better and/or more mature, the newsmag might have been prescient. Indeed, the story was almost a self-fulfilling prophecy. The album by Ultimate Spinach, an inoffensive aggregate ultimately victimized by all this, was selling 25,000 copies a week out of the box, and the band was inundated with more bookings than it could handle.

In more ways than one. It simply wasn't good enough to live up to the unreal expectations the company's efforts had built—especially when an anti-Boston critical backlash (led by San Francisco's *Rolling Stone*) made it considerably hipper to put down Ultimate Spinach and the other Boston bands than it had ever been to like them. And because they lacked the years of gigging that give a band tightness and resilience, their live shows disappointed rather than built their audiences. By summer, even as MGM exec Mort Nasatir was telling *The Wall Street Journal* (in a statement that must have been rehearsed, but was dumb anyway), "Some of this music is so intellectual that it is a little like the poems of T. S. Eliot with his seven layers of ambiguity in each line," the band was in trouble. A year later, despite, or maybe because of, selling more than a million dollars' worth of albums—it was out of business.

Between the backlash and Ultimate Spinach's breakup the elaborate hype wound up losing MGM some money—at least a hundred thousand 1968 dollars, and perhaps as much as five times that. Given the possibility of enormous gain, the one-time loss was bearable, but in addition, the company became comparatively unattractive to new performers and to established artists seeking to change labels, weakening it for several years down the road. This unanticipated consequence retrospectively raised the risks of the entire promotion, but even if the company had had foreknowledge, it's important to remember that in 1968, other manipulations at least as cynical could—and did—succeed. Chief among these was "bubblegum music."

In its apparent lack of sophistication, bubblegum music seemed a cross between ? and the Mysterians and Tommy James and the Shondells, but regardless of their faults or virtues, American garage bands were spontaneous self-creations. By contrast, the new crop of bubblegum bands— Ohio Express, the 1910 Fruitgum Company, and Crazy Elephant (all of whom played Carnegie Hall, yet)—were studio musicians gathered together by producers Jerry Kasenetz and Jeff Katz, who provided raw material for promo man Neil Bogart's year-old Buddah label. Bogart, correctly sensing that preteens were being left behind by the artification of rock, marketed singles like "Simon Says," "Yummy Yummy Yummy," and "1, 2, 3, Red Light" directly for the eleven-year-old market. Just as the national affluence had let their big brothers and sisters start buying albums, it let the microboppers buy singles—which they did in very great numbers indeed. Ohio Express and 1910 Fruitgum Company (who shared, such were the economic advantages of the Kasenetz-Katz system, the same lead singer) both had gold singles. Their success caused the predictable outbursts of scorn from the old folks who listened to the Jefferson Airplane, but as singles heard occasionally on AM radio, most of the songs were eminently singable and hook-laden, and lead singer Joey Levine, whether whining for the Fruitgum Company or droning for Ohio Express, had a genuine if annoying style.

The charm wore extremely thin in album-size doses, however, and taken simply as music, the bubblegum efforts of the Archies were probably better. This isn't all that surprising, for most were written by Jeff Barry, who had earlier demonstrated a delightful way with nonsense in hits like "Da Doo Ron Ron" and "Do Wah Diddy Diddy." As a commercial proposition, however, the Archies were even more cynically conceived than the Kasenetz-Katz groups. When the Monkees began to fade—partly because that's what most TV shows do—their inventor, Don Kirshner, came up with a brilliant idea. Working with the Monkees had been profitable but also a pain in the neck because the band members like Mike Nesmith began to get ideas that Kirshner felt were above their station. He would do the same thing he did with the Monkees, but would target the TV show for a slightly younger audience. That way he could use conveniently two-dimensional cartoon figures and let interchangeable session musicians do the singing for them. No more complaints that this or that Monkee wanted to play his own instruments or write his own songs, no scenes in which group members offered to punch record company executives in the face—*he would never have to deal with real people at all.*

It worked. Though the Archies didn't sell as many records as the Monkees, probably because eleven-year-olds didn't have as much money as older teens, they charted six records during their brief TV career, including a 1969 number one, "Sugar, Sugar."

Now attempts to manipulate the record-buying audience were hardly new; on a somewhat cruder level, that's what the payola scandals had been about. But that such efforts could even be tried, much less succeed, at this time was a reflection of conditions specific to 1968. The year before—with Monterey, Aretha Franklin, *Sgt. Pepper*—had been rock's year of triumph. With the occasional exception, nonrock performers had been driven from the charts, and the major figures of rock were not only selling albums by the ton but were accepted as "serious" cultural figures by such guardians of the conventions as the *New York Times* and Britain's *Observer.* In political terms, rock had won a landslide as great as Lyndon Johnson's in 1964 or Ronald Reagan's twenty years later. And as the political analogy suggests, what happened next was inevitable.

As the aftermath of those elections demonstrates, when you win by *too much*, your coalition breaks up. The rock audience had grown so large that it was possible for industry figures to turn a tidy profit not by swallowing the whole apple but by targeting segments of it. Thus, spurred by the spread of FM rock stations and record companies' search for the higher profits associated with album sales, the singles and album markets began once again to diverge. Though Motown, for instance, broke its old record with fourteen Top Ten singles, only two albums—a Supremes' *Greatest Hits* collection and the Tempts' *I Wish It Would Rain*—made *Cashbox's* annual top fifty list, and then ony at numbers twenty-nine and thirty. Bubblegum occupied four of the magazine's top-fifty singles slots but was unrepresented among albums. Also missing were some white singles artists of genuine skill, like the Box Tops and John Fred and His Playboy Band. Though Fred's *Agnes English* did scrabble onto the lower reaches of the album charts, it received little FM play and was apparently propelled by AM listeners who'd heard the single. The comparative failure of subsequent albums that were, if anything, even better at least implied that an AM hit somehow tarnished a band's reputation for "seriousness."

Radio was influential in a similar divergence between British and American hits as well. After the pirate stations were finally outlawed, the BBC made a gesture toward younger listeners by inaugurating its pop service, Radio One. Perhaps because of its quasigovernmental status, Radio One understandably emphasized home-grown performers, and black Americans were particularly underrepresented. This was reflected on the charts, and in 1968, the only black American performer to score a U.K. number one was Louis Armstrong. In 1972, when the Beeb did a compilation of the previous decade's greatest hits, Armstrong and (with the prerock era, "I Can't Stop Loving You," from 1962) Ray Charles were the only American blacks on the list. But a look at 1968's charts indicates that the transatlantic split involved more than just blacks and whites. Of the year's fifteen American number-one records, more than half failed even to reach the British top twenty; of the twenty-one singles that topped the British charts, nine failed to reach the U.S. top twenty and five never reached the charts at all. Of all thirty-six number ones, only the Beatles' "Hey Jude" was tops in both countries (Marvin Gaye's "I Heard It Through the Grapevine," however, eventually scored in England a year later).

In the United States, black acts were still a staple of AM programming, and for Memphis soul, 1968 was the year of Sam and Dave. Some years earlier, Sam Moore, the pair's high-voiced lead, had unknowingly given Johnnie Taylor's career a boost. Moore, a preacher's grandson steeped in gospel, was approached in his native Miami by the Soul Stirrers' manager: Sam Cooke was leaving the group; would he like to join? Moore said yes, but on the weekend before he was to leave town, he went to a Jackie Wilson show. He was floored. *This* was what he wanted to do, and gospel lost Moore before it ever got him. Taylor took Cooke's place instead, and Moore stayed in Miami, working local clubs. One night, when he was running an amateur show, a man in a short-order cook's greasy whites joined him. It was Dave Prater, come from red-clay Georgia to the big city to sing, and whose day job was a night job working a grill. He was only on a break that first night, but it was the beginning of a long-running show.

They tried New York first, cutting a few sides with Roulette, but none dented either the pop or R&B charts, and they were back in Miami when Jerry Wexler found them, signed them, and sent them to Memphis. In 1966, they had their first R&B number one with "Hold On! I'm A-Comin'," and as

1968 began, their first visit to the pop Top Ten (an R&B number 1), "Soul Man," was still riding the charts. The follow-up, "I Thank You" (number 9 pop; number 4 R&B) was also a major success, and in 1968, the thirty-five musicians, quippies, and money-watchers who made up the Sam and Dave Revue were all over the country. It was a wonderful show; Sam and Dave were *tight*. They were masters of the rapid-fire interchange; sometimes it almost seemed to be a conversation between Moore's hard-edged questions and Prater's rock-bottom answers; sometimes one voice echoed the other, and sometimes pulsing horn riffs triangulated the ongoing dialog. Finally, at the moments that counted—on the bridges and the sweat-soaked windup—they were together in pure gospel harmonies.

They were, it seemed, together everywhere. The jackets came off simultaneously, tossed in opposite directions to waiting hands, then the vests. But by the time the year was out, they were no longer speaking. This wasn't a matter of who got to lie down on the big tour bus and who had to sit upright, but was an unbridgeable chasm. During the year, in what police characterize as a "domestic dispute," Prater shot his wife. In the face. She lived, but at least some of Sam and Dave died. As Moore told Hirshey more than a decade after the fact, "I told him I'd work and travel with him, but that I would never speak or look at him." And for thirteen more years of occasionally interrupted touring—tossing microphones back and forth, doing spins, singing harmonies that lifted audiences from their seats—he didn't.

Yet there was never a hint of any estrangement onstage, and indeed, those shows might have been richer and more emotionally direct because they were the only way the two former friends communicated. Neither was there any evidence of Moore's secret battle with heroin, a struggle he neither escaped nor acknowledged until after the team had finally—or, given their on-and-off history, apparently finally—broken up in the early 1980s.

Death is final, and in the year of Sam and Dave, Memphis suffered the tragic loss of its greatest talent. Otis Redding's European tours had made him a transatlantic giant (toward the end of 1967, *Melody Maker's* readers voted him the world's best male vocalist, the first time during the 1960s they'd chosen anyone but Elvis), but his Monterey triumph established him as a major figure in his native land. On December 7 of that year, he'd gone into the Stax studio to record a song he'd written shortly after Monterey, when he was relaxing on a Sausalito houseboat. Three days later, he was dead, the victim of a Wisconsin plane crash that claimed four members of the Bar-Kays, his touring band, as well. "(Sittin' On) The Dock of the Bay," which Stax released early in 1968, became Redding's first and last number-one single, as well as the first posthumous number one.

The death was a blow to Redding's fans, but it was potentially devastating to Stax. As Steve Cropper put it, Redding had been "King of Soul, King of Stax, King of Everything that evolved around us," feelings captured by "Tribute to a King [Otis Redding]" the song Booker T. wrote for William

Bell. The mourning was real, but two days after Redding's death, company president Jim Stewart called the still-grieving Stax family together and said, as Cropper recalled, "one simple thing, 'Man, we've got to keep going.'" Though this was, of course, precisely the sort of thing a cynic might imagine a record company president saying, the Stax musicians discovered that work was therapeutic: "The next day, we went into a session, not to try to prove anything or to try to forget what was going on but just to try to find out ourselves and find out where we were." And Memphis artists went on to have a year that rivaled 1967. Booker T. and the MGs had a solid hit with "Soul Limbo"; and Johnnie Taylor, who'd replaced Sam Cooke as lead singer in the Soul Stirrers when Cooke went secular but had been kicking around Stax for years without much success, hooked up with producer Don Davis for "Who's Making Love," (number 5 pop, number 1 R&B), earning the label its first gold record.

Though these records found substantial white audiences, they didn't compromise their soul in order to do so, and as the 1960s drew to a close, the question of black identity was being felt as keenly by musicians as it was by blacks in other areas of society. It had, after all, been little more than a decade since the ethos prevailing at the industry's major record companies ran toward separate and unequal treatment. The Chords and Little Richard were allowed their successes in the relatively unremunerative R&B field, but pop breakthroughs were reserved as much as possible (you couldn't control the kids all the time, and djs like Alan Freed, who kept on playing black records even when "nicer" covers were available, sometimes made life difficult) for the Crew Cuts or Pat Boone. Partly as a result of the civil rights movement, black labels like Motown had grown and found enormous mainstream success, as had Stax and Atlantic, working with black performers. But now, with the shift from singles to ever-more-elaborate albums raising costs to an all-time high, the message to assimilate was stronger than at any time since the first rock 'n' roll era.

This, of course, was not the message in a large part of the black community, particularly among young people who were influenced by the black-power notions of Stokely Carmichael and H. Rap Brown. Even before the April 1968 assassination of Martin Luther King, Jr., his integrationist message had begun to lose ground to the more radical rhetoric of the Student Nonviolent Coordinating Committee (SNCC) and Malcolm X. King's death, and its aftermath, drew a line between the races that even innocently sincere performers like Eric Burdon could no longer aim to cross. And it also cut out whites who saw the civil rights movement, antiwar activity, and rock as a single politico-cultural continuum, for it soon became clear that black power advocates weren't kidding.

Even Motown would feel beleaguered by black-power pressures on one hand and its loss of the white FM audience on the other. And at the beginning of 1968, Motown was torn by further internal dissension as well. For one thing, David Ruffin had left the Temptations. He has since described it as being fired, and Motown historian Don Waller has ascribed it to Ruffin's wanting a billing change—to "David Ruffin and the Temptations"—that would give greater recognition to his role as lead singer. But the black-white aesthetic and marketing split were involved as well, for Ruffin has at other times made it clear that his idea of success didn't at all involve singing some equivalent of "Impossible Dream" in Vegas. But whatever the cause, Ruffin's departure from the Tempts seemed irreparable. He sued Motown for release from his contract; Motown in turn sued him for breaching it.

At least in terms of the numbers of lawyers involved, this was a reprise of the Holland-Dozier-Holland departure, but in Detroit's best industrial tradition, Gordy had built an engine with replaceable parts. Responding to the Supremes' slide, he got some of Motown's top writers together and, as writer Deke Richards told Randy Torraborrelli, Ross's biographer, "put together some very strong forces [and] locked us up in the Ponchartrain Hotel in Detroit until we came up with a hit song. He would check with us every now and then, asking 'Did you get it? Did you get it?' Eventually, we got it." After that, Gordy put together a five-man production team (listed as "The Clan" on the label) and used all of them for "Love Child." Although the music had the Supremes' typical upbeat sweetness, the lyrics told the story of an illegitimate daughter's escape from the real Brewster Projects world outside Motown's magical studio. This nod to the sociopolitical agenda of rock was a seminal break from Motown's long-standing preoccupation with romantic love. When the Supremes abandoned sequins for sweatshirts to present the song on the Ed Sullivan show, the gesture was complete.

This uncharacteristic consideration of quotidian black reality took the Supremes back to the upper reaches of the charts, reaching number one at the end of November. After two weeks in that spot, they were replaced by yet another nonformula Motown record, Marvin Gaye's sinuous "I Heard It Through the Grapevine." Like Sam and Dave's "Soul Man," this began with a tambourine riff, but it was a sustained, threatening, moody shake. In typical Motown manner, the song had been recorded by a fistful of performers (including the Miracles and the Isley Brothers) and had been a 1967 number-two hit for Gladys Knight and the Pips. Gaye's version earned release as a single only after In the Groove's first single stiffed, and radio stations began to pull "Grapevine" from the album. Not only did the quickly released single top the charts, it held the number-one slot for a full seven weeks.

The same week Gaye hit number one, Motown's remarkable resurgence was sealed when Stevie Wonder's "For Once in My Life" jumped up and gave the company the top three positions on the pop charts. But perhaps the most impressive comeback belonged to the Ruffin-less Temptations. With Dennis Edwards replacing Ruffin and Norman Whitfield taking over for Smokey Robinson in the booth, their new "five lead" format let Melvin

Franklin's extraordinary bass come forward for the first time in the group's long history—and gave Motown its first Grammy Award with "Cloud Nine." The psychedelicized sound, with its call-and-response consideration of an earthly Nirvana, which the group showed here and over the next couple of years, was revolutionary for Motown, but as Franklin later said, "We kinda stole it from Sly."

Sylvester Stewart was still in grammar school in Vallejo, California— "like Watts, but with more whites"—when a schoolmate gave him his nickname by inadvertently writing "Slyvester" on a class list. Even before that, as a four-year-old member of the Stewart Family, he'd cut his first record, "On the Battlefield for My Lord." By the time he reached adolescence, Stewart had kept the nickname but abandoned gospel for rock 'n' roll and a group called Joey Piazza and the Continentals. Though he was an indifferent student—"High school was terrible. It was boring for me 'cause either I was too smart, or too dumb to realize what I could learn"—Stewart went on to Vallejo Junior College, where he studied music theory. He also went to something called the Chris Borden School of Modern Broadcasting, where he learned to manipulate turntables and slug in recorded commercials. Armed with these tools of the dj's trade, Stewart (who then became Stone) got a slot at a second-level East Bay black station, where he astonished by adding Dylan, the scatological and hip comedy of Lord Buckley, and the Beatles to the playlist—and *gaining* listeners.

It was at about the time of his minor-league radio debut that Stone hooked up with Tom Donahue. Donahue had just leapt away from being KYA's "Big Daddy" to work at starting Autumn Records. Stone, who could by then play virtually any instrument known to Western culture, became staff producer. He turned out to be a good one, scoring hits with the Beau Brummels and cutting the first, Great Society, version of "Somebody to Love." This wasn't exactly a cross-cultural success—Stone, who not incorrectly thought the band was instrumentally on the lame side, attempted to sit in and do better, but this both bruised egos and violated the San Francisco underground's communal ethic. However, even though he lacked the necessary bedside manner, Stone was a better producer than Donahue was a bookkeeper. The hits went out, but the money didn't come in, and when Autumn went bankrupt, Stone was back to being a full-time dj.

Except that he was by then already fooling around with a prototype Family Stone called the Stoners, doing weekend suburban gigs with a band he wanted to incorporate *all* music—and maybe a bit of Lord Buckley as well. It was promising. He left KSOL. The promise didn't work out. He went back to being a dj—this time on the Bay Area's major black station, KDIA, which his tastes similarly astonished. He was there when high school rock 'n' roll buddy Jerry Martini dropped by for a visit. Stone drew him into the family as a saxophonist, but he also doubled on keyboards and brass. At the time, Martini's cousin, Greg Errico (we are talking the *family* Stone, here) was in a band called the VIPs with Stone's younger brother Freddie. When the Stoners turned into the Family Stone a few months down the road, both jumped to join. Cynthia Robinson, who'd played sax in Sly's high school marching band, his piano-playing sister Rosie (born between Sly and Freddie), and cousin Larry Graham, Jr. (whose snapped-string bass bottomed the band and whose singing liberated Mel Franklin) completed the lineup.

Though they came to be as tight as any of James Brown's aggregates, Brown's bands were his servants; the Family Stone was democratic to a fare-thee-well. And the act, if that's the right word for something that seemed so free, had its equivalent of a Berkshire cottage in a blue-collar Redwood City club called, with a nod to the British, Winchester Cathedral. It didn't observe London closing hours, though; on weekends, the club ran all night, and the Family Stone worked from two to five A.M.

Redwood City, in 1967, was distant from the San Francisco music scene in ways that mileage couldn't measure, but they had dancing in common, and the Family Stone's reputation gradually spread north. One record, two, a Fillmore gig, an album . . . Soul had its conventions, rock—maybe, arty San Francisco, especially—its own. The Family Stone took everything as it came, rolling expectations into a ball they dribbled a few times, then shaked and baked into a back-door jam. "Everyday People" shouldered Tommy James and the Shondells aside to spend a month of 1968 at the top of the singles chart.

Sly's achievement was real, but it had been made *commercially* possible by Jimi Hendrix, who'd at once invented and legitimized black psychedelia. In 1968, Hendrix was off the ground more often than not, solidifying the Monterey splash by a round of cross-country touring that must sometimes have made him feel he was back doing steps behind Ike and Tina Turner. One important effect of this grind was that as the dates piled up, Hendrix gradually began to trim the lighter-fluid aspects of his performance, letting his remarkable musicianship come to the fore. This was fully apparent on the remarkable *Electric Ladyland*, a chart-topping double album he somehow found time to record and release during the year. There, as he did on those nights when he sensed the audience was into music rather than flash, he both found structure in a series of jams and reached back to the Muddy Waters sound that had so impressed him in his youth. Especially in "Voodoo Chile," Hendrix assimilated the blues, then took them and twirled them around his head like a lariat. The sound, and the emotional pitch, was blacker than anything he'd recorded before, earning the right not only to claim "soul" but to proclaim that it had been psyche-delicized.

This heady combination caused Hendrix some problems at the hands of the mass media. Early in 1969, *Look* magazine did a feature on him titled "Jimi Hendrix Socks It to the White Cats." Coupled with the illustration—Hendrix at a swimming pool, with white women in bikinis dancing attendance on him—the opening page seemed almost calculated both to annoy black separatists and inflame the growing white backlash. And the overheated prose—"For the volatile hard-core—the fourteen-to-nineteen bag—Jimi is not so much the Experience as a menace to public health. Plugged in and zonked, he has only to step across the stage (which he does like a high-strutting chicken going after a kernel of corn) to turn on their high-pitched passion"—surely didn't help.

Shortly after this, Hendrix began to come under increasing pressure from politically active black friends to move away from the psychedelia that had launched him and to assert his blackness in his music. The blues guitarist in him surely responded, and late in June, he announced that he was breaking up the Experience to perform with Billy Cox and Buddy Miles. The breakup wasn't absolute; though Noel Redding involved himself in Fat Mattress, his own band, Mitch Mitchell was among the regulars who gathered at the Liberty, New York, home Hendrix rented through most of the summer and fall. Though there were all kinds of music coming out of the house (avant-garde pianist Michael Ephron was occasionally present), Juma Lewis, who headed the Aboriginal Music Society in Woodstock, was a continuing and major influence.

Despite the reality of the external pressures on him, a good part of the changes Hendrix's music was undergoing during his retreat—most notably the shift to more structured compositions—was internally generated. He'd taken psychedelia about as far as it could go (*Rolling Stone* had dubbed him 1968's top touring performer), and without at all limiting his flashy, trademark effects, he was beginning to get away from ever-expanding whorls and pare his digressions to the minimum. For all its astonishing technical fireworks, for instance, his Woodstock "Star Spangled Banner" is much more concise than his Monterey playing had been.

To a certain extent, psychedelia—the music as pure experience—was giving way all over the map. Narrative structures, especially in the fantasy genre, emerged as one way forward, but this folkloric sci-fi approach seemed particularly British. By this time, the Beatles were international citizens of the world, but the path for the great popularizers of psychedelia was by no means clear.

The year had started badly for them, with the near-universal panning of their *Magical Mystery Tour* TV special, an unintended demonstration of the perils of formlessness—and of life without Brian Epstein. Yes, he'd been a bit of a mother hen, but he'd more than earned his management fees by serving as a willing focus for their various discontents. At a minimum, he thus kept them from taking out their occasional frustrations on each other; at best, because they knew from experience that even when they disagreed with him, they could trust him to have their best interests uppermost, his having the final say freed them to be individually and collectively creative. After Epstein's sudden and unexpected death, Paul had taken the responsibility for the *Magical Mystery* film, but those well-intentioned efforts had sown seeds of resentment.

One thing they all agreed on after Epstein's death, however, was that no one could replace him and they would now run their various business operations by themselves. Having so announced, they went off to India to continue studies with the Maharishi Mahesh Yogi, but this group effort failed as well. Ringo, complaining of spicy food, left after ten days, and Paul shortly thereafter. George and John stayed longest, but by the time they left, both had become disillusioned with the guru, and John wrote "Sexy Sadie" to denounce him. George's disillusionment was only with the man not the method, and on returning to London, he enrolled in a more rigorous program of Krishna Consciousness. For the first time, one of the Beatles was signifying that something was more important to him than the institution of Beatleness. Meanwhile, Paul and John went to New York to announce their new corporate vehicle, Apple Corps. Without Epstein, this turned out to be a management disaster of such remarkable proportions that when the first-year results for Apple Corps, Ltd., were finally audited in 1970, the book-keepers had to write off no fewer than three cars because they'd disappeared entirely.

Artistically, however, the year was much more successful. *Yellow Submarine,* a cartoon supplied to United Artists in fulfillment of contract options, was charming (and it provoked what was surely a first: a suggestion from the *New York Times*'s film critic that viewers might benefit if they toked up first, for the film's particular virtues were "certainly accessible to people who are not high, but in an overstimulated urban environment, probably rarely"). The storyline of *Yellow Submarine* had been put together largely without the Beatles, however, and in the recording studio, they began to retreat from psychedelia with "Lady Madonna," a rollicking single that prompted Ringo to say, "It sounds just like Elvis, doesn't it?" The follow-up, the 7:11 "Hey Jude," was not only the longest number-one single ever but the Beatles' biggest hit, entering the American charts at number ten and staying on them for seventeen weeks.

"Jude" was a McCartney song, written partly in response to his painful breakup with Jane Asher and partly to young Julian Lennon in the wake of John's breakup with his Liverpool-bred wife, Cynthia. It was these difficulties rather than musical differences that made recording a follow-up album to *Sgt. Pepper* so trying. In fact, the sessions for their first Apple album (officially called *The Beatles* but universally known as *The White Album*) produced the first Beatles breakup. In the studio, John had his thing, Paul his, and George—though he was increasingly unhappy that the compositions then starting to pour out of him weren't getting recorded as fast as the Lennon-McCartney efforts—always had at least *some* songs to supervise. But the fourth Beatle was a fifth wheel, and when Paul suggested that he should play drums on one of his own songs, Ringo walked out. When he walked back in a week later, telling reporters that Paul was "very determined; he goes on and on to see if he can get his own way," Ringo found that a repentant McCartney had garlanded his drum kit with flowers.

He also found a bed, occupied by Yoko Ono, who couldn't bear to have a touch of the flu separate her from John. John had first met her at her one-woman London art show in 1966, and "just realized that she knew everything I knew—and more, probably—and that it was coming out of a woman's head, it just bowled me over. It was like finding gold or something." At the time, Ono was an established figure in the avant-garde art community, as much a celebrity in that rarefied world as the Beatles were in their larger one. She was by no means indifferent to rock, however, for her works, like that of many other performance artists, gleefully integrated pop culture.

This didn't mean that her work was aimed at a mass audience, however, and like many artists who chose to work for an elite, she was often accused of pretentiousness. Yet the content of her shows was anything but pretentious, for with a lively sense of humor and some Rube Goldberg whimsy, she attacked the very notion of "high art."

In short, she was independent, ambitious, talented, and tough. Totally unlike the proper bourgeois Cynthia, she personified the women's movement for John, and over the course of a chaste two-year courtship, he fell profoundly in love. By then, the Lennons' marriage was badly frayed, and one night, when Cynthia was visiting Spain, the two went back to John's house, where they made a record together. "It was midnight when we started *Two Virgins*," he later told *Rolling Stone*, and "it was dawn when we finished, and then we made love at dawn. It was very beautiful." They shared this beauty with the world in November, by releasing *Two Virgins* as an album with that typical bit of Ono visual shockery, the notorious full-frontal-nudity cover.

Lovable moptops did not show their cocks in public, and despite the addition of a plain brown wrapper, thousands of copies were confiscated. A rush-released American single by one Rainbo, "John, You Went Too Far This Time," didn't chart, though it probably reflected the Beatles' younger fans' feelings pretty well. But John and Yoko's album troubled the other Beatles far less than the relationship itself; as Paul put it, "John's in love with Yoko, and he's no longer in love with the three of us."

And they were not in love with her. Her behavior—assertive, independent, and intellectually arrogant—shocked their essentially provincial sensibilities. She was at best an annoyance and at worst—when she started making musical suggestions—a threat. Without especially intending to demonstrate what a wrong sort of woman Ono was, Paul, on the rebound from Jane *and* from John, rather rapidly settled down with Linda Eastman, a sometime photographer better known as a prominent New York groupie. In that latter role, she had chosen subservience as a way of life, and she was unchallenging, loyal, self-effacing, pretty-shading-into-beautiful, bourgeois . . . in short, everything Ono wasn't; and Paul loved her.

Each in his own way, Paul and John were affirming a continuing belief in an ideal that had animated them when they wrote and recorded their earliest songs: the primacy of romantic love. Set against this, however, was another ideal, one that had achieved almost mythic proportions for a generation of fans, and perhaps for John and Paul themselves: the primacy of the Beatles. One or another would have to be bruised.

Under the circumstances, *The White Album* understandably broke no new ground. Perhaps because they were unconsciously trying to recapture their rock 'n' roll pasts, it breezed from Fats Domino through their own history, and whatever tensions had scarred them in the studio weren't audible on the joyful romp. Riding the wave of generous rediscovery that had seen Dylan return to simplicity and Elvis return to the number-one singles slot, it sped to the top of the charts. But at least one Beatle felt it was deeply flawed; as John later said, "There isn't any Beatle music on it. . . . It was John and the band, Paul and the band, George and the band, like that."

25

WOODSTOCK...
AND ALTAMONT

The Beatles were on the way to becoming the rock era's most famous breakup, but they had plenty of less illustrious company. There were probably as many reasons for breakups as there were bands—certainly personality clashes can never be discounted—but by this point in the 1960s, "musical differences" had become more than a press agent's cover-up, for just as the rock market had become enormous, so had the scope of the music. Since virtually anything sung or played by someone who regarded him or herself as a rock musician counted as rock, the wide-open nature of the field was bound to beckon musicians in different directions.

At least some musicians argued that the whole *idea* of fixed, self-contained groups had become hopelessly out of date. Frank Zappa did a lot of talking about a "rock pool." In a *Rolling Stone* interview, he broached the idea of musicians getting together one show at a time. There would be no rehearsals (no touring! no managers!!), just spontaneous, one-time-only-buy-your-tickets-now jamming. When *Super Session* with Al Kooper (Blood Sweat and Tears), Mike Bloomfield (Electric Flag), and Steve Stills (Buffalo Springfield) became a bestseller, Zappa's idea took on some momentary plausibility. That it happened only sporadically (*Grape Jam*, Willie Nelson's Fourth of July picnics, the Concert for Bangladesh) had something to do with musicians' egos and a great deal to do with the economics of supporting a band until it became well-enough established to sell records. This bottom-line imperative meant that "supergroups" (like the Clapton/Winwood Blind Faith, in which the musicians' fame was enough to guarantee significant sales for a debut album) were as close as the industry came to

Zappa's notion. Still, that the rock pool failed to develop was less important than that people genuinely believed it *could.*

The sense of limitless possibility it implied was shared, in a somewhat different way, by the counterculture. In fact, it was probably inaccurate to speak any longer of *the* counterculture. Politically it ranged from the Weather Underground to libertarian communes, from Jane Fonda to Dick Gregory, from Eldridge Cleaver to Jesse Jackson. It included radical feminists, feminist liberals, men who regarded "women's position in the movement" as prone, and Hell's Angels. It embraced Waylon and Willie, Delaney and Bonnie, and the early, tentative gay activists. Some things remained beyond the pale, of course—once again, there was Richard Nixon to kick around—but if the American counterculture could be imagined as speaking with one voice, that voice would have been saying something like "You are what you think you are."

Rock, like the counterculture, was a state of mind, an act of will. If Dylan, or CBS, wanted to call *Nashville Skyline* rock, even though it was about as straightforwardly country as music could get, so be it. Indeed, inspired in part by Dylan and the Byrds, in part by the need to cool out after Chicago, there was a lot of countryish activity among rockers, some of it from quite surprising sources. Dylan had given a hint of his direction with *John Wesley Harding*, after all, but for the Grateful Dead, the quintessential San Francisco blues and boogie band, to come out with albums as old-timey as *Workingman's Dead* and *American Beauty* was a genuine surprise. It's a credit to the band's often maligned musicianship that this music isn't quite so simple as it seemed (the "Sugar Magnolia" shift from A/C#m/F#m/E to E/B/F#/E is a subtle piece of work), but it's significant that a band renowned for orchestralizing acid trips did two straight albums of mellowing-out music.

And despite the distant rumble of heavy metal, there was on one wing of the rock continuum a flowering of softer, lyrical sounds whose foremost exponents were probably Crosby, Stills, Nash, and (sometimes) Young, a group that almost met Zappa's criterion of just happening to come together. After *Super Session*, Stills spent the next few months "taking lessons" by hanging out and jamming with Jimi Hendrix ("I followed him around so much that people thought we were fags, and others thought I was some kind of groupie"). Back home in California, he began spending time with David Crosby, who'd jammed with Buffalo Springfield at Monterey when he was still a Byrd. As Crosby recalled, one night when the Hollies were in town, "We were at Joni Mitchell's . . . Cass was there, Stephen was there, me, and Willie [Graham Nash], just us five hangin' out. You know how it is this time of night, so we were singin' as you might imagine. We sang a lot. What happened was we started singing a country song of Stephen's called 'Helplessly Hoping.' And I had already worked out the third harmony. Stephen and I just started singin' it, Willie looked at the rafters for about ten seconds, listened, and started singin' the other part like he'd been singin' it all his life."

As Stills recalled, "Crosby and me just looked at each other—it was one of those moments, you know?" On the way home, believing they'd discovered a magic combination, they talked about it. Crosby "was saying 'no he'd never do it . . . those guys have been together forever. But, boy, what a sound!' We were really full of it, but didn't dare approach him, so we came to the conclusion that we'd get Cass to ask him—we were just too afraid."

They needn't have been. The Hollies were indeed successful, but not in the way Nash wanted. The Manchester-based Hollies had largely missed out on the first wave of the British invasion. A beat group, they'd been neither as frenetic as the Dave Clark Five nor as gimmicky as Herman's Hermits, and despite their soaring vocal harmonies, their string of English hits didn't translate to America until 1966's "Bus Stop." Though other hits followed, a 1964-style success wasn't what Nash wanted in 1969, and as the group's chief writer, he'd been trying to orient it toward a more personal sort of music. To no avail, however, so he was displeased not only by the potential lack of royalties when guitarist Tony Hicks pushed for them to make their next album all Dylan songs.

Under the circumstances, Nash was entirely ready to leave, but there was a problem. Though Crosby was under no obligation to any record company, Nash was signed to EMI in England and Epic, a CBS subsidiary, in America. Stills went to Atlantic Records president Ahmet Ertegun, with whom he was under contract. As Stills remembered it, Ertegun's reaction was, "Ah, man, why do you make me go through all this trouble with Sir Joseph and Clive Davis just because you want harmony?" but he agreed to deal with Sir Joseph Lockwood at EMI. Meanwhile, Stills agreed to approach his ex–band mate Richie Furay, who had by then formed Poco. Like Stills, he and his new band were still under contract to Atlantic, but they hadn't yet made a record. "I said, 'Hey, Richie, you've got a country group, right . . . but what's a country group going to do on Atlantic, which, after all, is an R&B label. How would you like to be on Columbia?'"

As it happened, Columbia president Clive Davis owed Ertegun and Stills something of a favor. Though Stills hadn't notified Atlantic before he played on the Al Kooper *Super Session* album for Columbia, Ertegun had given CBS a release without holding them up. And so, in best baseball tradition, the labels worked a Nash-for-Poco trade. Equally in the tradition, it helped both clubs: Atlantic got a certified supergroup, though it, too, broke up; CBS both kept the Hollies, who fared perfectly well without Nash, and got nearly a decade of mid-chart hits from Poco. Still, Poco was pleasant at best; the *writers* were in CS and N—and, eventually, CSN and Y.

Despite their much-publicized differences in Buffalo Springfield, it was Stills who recruited Young—though only at Ahmet Ertegun's suggestion. CS and N were about to go out on tour, and while Nash and Crosby "were in favor of us going out as a sort of augmented Simon and Garfunkel," Stills had different ideas. Harmonies were nice enough in their place, but that place was generally in a rock 'n' roll band, and the three eventually compromised on a half-acoustic/half-electric show. In May, when Ertegun, who'd also had Young under contract during Buffalo Springfield days, learned that Stills was auditioning New York keyboardists for the band, he suggested taking Young on instead; that way Stills could shift to keyboards himself. Young had been to one of their rehearsals and liked their sound, and though he wasn't as fascinated by vocal harmonies as Crosby and Nash, he was intrigued by the four-part possibilities.

By that time, however, after a solid solo album that had failed to chart, Young had started to work with three musicians from the Rockets, recording "Cinnamon Girl" and the harder-edged "Down by the River" and "Cowgirl in the Sand," for the *Everybody Knows This Is Nowhere* album. Originally they were to get together only in the studio, but it went so well— Young: "To me, these guys were the American Rolling Stones . . . there has never been a bad night with them"—that they decided to go on the road as Neil Young and Crazy Horse. Though he was strongly tempted by Stills's offer, Young was both obligated to and drawn by Crazy Horse, so rather than choosing between the two prospects, he decided he could do both.

For a while, he could. As part of CSN and Y, he recorded *Déjà Vu*. The album's sweet and complex harmonies, a product of hundreds of hours in the studio, were close to perfect—if anything, the album was perfect to a fault. For three months, however, the band couldn't tour to promote it because Young was recording *After the Gold Rush* with Crazy Horse and gigging with them. There's no need to feel sorry for Young's partners in CSN and Y; when they finally took to the road for a series of stadium tours during the summer of 1970, they did so as the highest-paid American group in history. But it's true that Young's commitment to them was tenuous—he once described it as, "I play lead guitar, and occasionally I'll sing a song"— and after the tour, they, too, broke up for a few years, leaving Poco and the other soft-rockers to attempt, generally with less success, their marriage of shimmering country-choir vocals with guitar-driven hard rock.

Few split-and-merge dramas were as spectacularly successful as the Springfield into Poco and CSN and Y sequence, but two British combinations are worth mentioning. In 1969, shortly after Fairport Convention's second album—in a tradition-conscious version of the American "mellowing out" trend—had signaled the band's turn toward England's folk heritage, singer Ian Matthews left the group to form Matthews' Southern Comfort and score a U.K. number one by beating out CSN and Y's version of "Woodstock." Even without Matthews, however, the Fairport vocal lineup of Sandy Denny and guitarists Simon Nicol and Richard Thompson remained strong, and when session fiddler Dave Swarbrick formally joined the group, its four-part harmonies were gloriously restored for the landmark *Liege and Lief* album. But shortly after its release established the commercial and artistic viability of rocking genuine folk material in a way that had largely eluded American folk-rockers of both the folk and rock variety, founding member Ashley Hutchings left to form the band that would eventually become Steeleye Span, Fairport's only real rival among a host of imitators. The development of three successful bands from the original Fairport was gradual (Fairport, indeed, continued shooting off sparks for another decade), and in that sense was more unusual in the quality of results than as a process.

The merger that shook the London pop world during the summer of 1969 was considerably more seismic. It involved the Herd, which, because lead singer Peter Frampton was so aggressively cute, didn't get much critical respect but had charted two Top Ten singles; the Jeff Beck Group; and the Small Faces. "Faces" they were, in the mod sense, and physically diminutive as well, but as long ago as the summer of 1965, Steve Marriott, Ian McLagan, Kenney Jones, and Ronnie Lane had been the mod band. Next to them, the Who were parvenus, and in 1966 and 1967, they hit the British Top Ten six times. Initially this was a rocking vehicle for Marriott's blues-shouter voice, but with 1967's "Itchycoo Park" (at number 16, their only U.S. top twenty single), they showed clear signs of being psychedelicized. The element of complete unpredictability in their subsequent music was even more radical than the adjustments in their mod clothing, and both the follow-up, the powerful raveup "Tin Soldier" (U.K., number 9; U.S., number 73) and 1968's "Lazy Sunday" (U.K. number 2), with its kazoos and Marriott's solicitous "How's your bird's lumbago?" signaled significant, if weird, growth, and they managed the difficult feat of attracting the English underground without entirely losing their young mod followers.

"Lazy Sunday" was part of *Ogden's Nut Gone Flake*, the 1968 album that consolidated that growth—and unhappily demonstrated that the Small Faces' cockney lunacy was as esoteric an English pleasure as Fairport's Arthurian excursions. It included other music-hall madness as well as trademark rockers and inspired if sometimes unintelligible verbal links between them. Unhappily, the album drew more American attention for its round packaging than for its contents, and though it topped the British charts, it died at number 159 in the U.S. The band remained popular in Britain, particularly because the Beatles' decision to stop touring, the Stones' disruption by drug busts and Brian's troubles, and the Who's preoccupation with *Tommy* made it the country's major live attraction.

But something Marriott once said about those shows indicated implicit dissatisfaction with the direction the band was taking: "On records, we always had a manager and producer who wanted hits, so they were usually gimmicky and contrived. On stage, we were raw rockers." Marriott was far happier as a rocker than in psychedelic mode, and when the American failure of *Ogden's Nut Gone Flake* convinced him that the economic rewards for doing what he didn't like were insufficient, he joined the Herd's Peter Frampton (mod London's "Face of the Year") to form Humble Pie. With drummer Jerry Shirley and ex–Spooky Tooth bassist Greg Ridley, this was a teenybopper supergroup. There were now, for the first time, enough young teenagers who had grown up on rock to support a band of their own, and Humble Pie was the first to successfully jump down a rung on the generational ladder. Big brother and big sister might have wanted Nut Gone's exoticism, but the microboppers were delighted to have big, recognizable stars doing straight-ahead dance music, and Humble Pie's first British single, "Natural Born Boogie," was a number-four hit. But the comparative failure of the interesting and largely acoustic album, *Town and Country*, convinced them that beat bettered bucolic, and from then until they dissolved in 1975 (especially after Frampton left late in 1971), they were your basic clog-the-Fillmore British boogie band.

The remaining Small Faces promptly hooked up with Rod Stewart and Ron Wood from the Jeff Beck Group, becoming, in deference to Wood's and Stewart's height, the plain ol' Faces. After a comparatively slow start, the loose and boozy Faces had five successful years in parallel with Stewart's somewhat more disciplined solo career. Though they weren't a particularly inventive group, their sprightly rhythm section kept their good-time boogies from plodding. Like Humble Pie, they managed a U.S. Top Ten album and some stray singles hits; unlike them, they were always fun to see.

Different as they were, both groups typified the mid-level bands that survived largely by touring; the money they actually lived on depended on concert earnings. In the case of genuine bands (as distinct from the James Brown–style leader and hired hands), it took a heap of touring for a one-sixth share (minus agents' and managers' fees) to cover the mortgage. (In addition to the influence of Cream, this may be one reason for the plethora of power trios.) Though the British blues bands were almost legendarily indefatigable, every sort of sound was to be found in this stratum. The New Riders of the Purple Sage and the Flying Burrito Brothers offered druggy country-rock; Grand Funk Railroad and Black Oak Arkansas provided heavy metal; Spirit and Larry Coryell rocked jazz; Asleep at the Wheel and ZZ Top showed just how big Texas was, and Bob Seger sang the heart out of his own straight-ahead rock songs. All of them, however, even those bands for whose existence William of Occam would have been hard pressed to find a reason, performed one critically important function: In hundreds of different cities across the country, they brought like-minded audiences together to share joints and music—and to remind each other that they were, after all, a community.

Though these mid-level bands were, in essence, the cement of the counterculture, their schedules were often set by their record companies. Particularly when an act released a new album, record companies tended to pick up some of the costs for its touring. Their outlay was relatively small, and the payback—for tours sold records—immediate. Besides, the money the bands earned from touring let the major companies have their recording services essentially for free. In the typical contract, studio costs were treated as an advance against royalties, and until a band's sales moved into tonnage—by which time their record company was hip-deep in earnings—it usually earned no cash royalties at all. For those few that did make it, however, the economic rewards of stardom, in publishing royalties alone, were enormous (and the subsequent touring schedule a *lot* easier). Small wonder that lots of folks were chasing stardom in an unseemly hurry. Jeff Beck, for instance, had precipitated Wood's and Stewart's departure by his inadequately disguised intention to be rid of them so he could form a power trio with ex–Vanilla Fudgies Tim Bogert and Carmine Appice.

The artistic rewards could be even more limitless than the financial. With one notable exception, the album-buying public was *extremely* catholic, and very solid hits were achieved by a remarkable range of performers, from Dylan to Grand Funk, Simon and Garfunkel to Alice Cooper, the Dead to the Velvet Underground, Johnny Cash to the Stones . . . The list, which could be expanded almost indefinitely, encouraged performers to go for it; since almost anything could become a hit, why not give your own vision a chance?

Consider, as a model of eccentricity rewarded, Arlo Guthrie. Literally one of Woody's children, Guthrie began working East Coast folkie coffeehouses in the mid-1960s. Among his songs was a fifteen-minute talking/singing blues saga of Thanksgiving garbage and the antiwar movement. It was called "Alice's Restaurant," and a tape of it became a midnight staple on New York's Pacifica radio station, WBAI. It became a hit of sorts (during fund-raising marathons, competing listeners pledged money to have it either played or silenced), and the quiet furor eventually led to a recording contract and, soon after, a movie.

As the movie *Alice's Restaurant* showed the entire country, the quasi-fictional Arlo was an archetypal counterculture hero, but one-of-a-kind performers with quite different credentials flourished as well. Ravi Shankar, George Harrison's erstwhile sitar teacher, toured college towns quite successfully, and former folkie Judy Collins emerged as perhaps the generation's only singer of art songs. The most remarkable anomaly of all, perhaps, was one of those rarities, a black folkie: Richie Havens. Havens brought his trademark open-tuning guitar strum and distinctive vocal stylings to many of the late-sixties' major festivals. Though his vocal inflections were unquestionably black—as a teenager, he'd been a gospel singer in his native Bedford-Stuyvesant section of Brooklyn—his repertoire was straight out of the white rock mainstream.

But for the more common run of black performers, 1969 was a tough year. Solomon Burke didn't make the pop Top Forty; Wilson Pickett got to number twenty-three, but only by covering the Beatles' "Hey Jude"; Joe Tex's "Buying a Book" stalled at number forty-seven; Clarence Carter's "Snatching It Back" at number thirty-one; Percy Sledge barely cracked the top one hundred, and though Joe Simon reached the top twenty with "The Chokin' Kind" (number 13), his follow-up died at number seventy-two.

From Memphis, only Booker T. and the MGs reached the Top Ten; the next-best effort was Isaac Hayes's "Walk On By." Even Aretha Franklin fell on comparatively hard times; despite covers of "Eleanor Rigby" and "The Weight" with a soaring guitar from studio whiz Duane Allman, she failed to have a Top Ten single, and after a year in which she had number-two and number-three albums, her 1969 efforts stalled in the mid-teens. In the singles market, only Motown emerged unbruised, but their dedication to that market in the face of consumers' shift to albums made them nearly unique.

The only black artists gathering real attention were the handful who assimilated white counterculture *values*. The Chambers Brothers, Mississippi-via-Los Angeles-via-Boston folkie gospel singers, were a very big act (their 1968 gospel/psychedelic single, "Time Has Come Today," was a number 11 pop hit), and Sly Stone continued his rise. His number-one single, "Everyday People," was an eloquent plea for tolerance, but though the band itself was integrated, it was the Family Stone's music that best practiced what Sly preached. Jerry Butler, who'd been through it *all* by then, captured that music in a 1970 interview: "Sly has taken black music and integrated it more than anybody else. To me, 'Hot Fun in the Summertime' is like an ice cream song but when he shouts 'oh yeah,' he goes right to church. But all those things in there—he's made them all lay, and fit, and not be offensive and not be overbearing, and it becomes Sly. That's him. He's all of those things: he's black, white, electric, unamplified, all of that. . . . Sly has opened up black kids' eyes to the other acid groups. Because they were hip to Sly and wanted to go with Sly, they started to see this other stuff. Hendrix hasn't touched the black market. Black people don't know who Jimi Hendrix is until they see him on TV or something. But Sly is such a great talent, man. You know he's definitely an innovator but you really don't know which way he's taking it."

Not surprisingly, in that 1969 summer of festivals, Hendrix and the Family Stone were the premier black attractions. The festivals were all in some way children of Monterey. Though there were only 7,100 ticket holders, and perhaps four or five times that many who'd dropped by because the weekend sounded like fun (and maybe they could get in for free), the influence of the 1968 film *Monterey Pop* was as great on the rock audience as the festival itself had been on the industry. Monterey looked wonderful. Peace, love, flowers, great music, the strong hint of sex and dope . . . how could it be bad?

Partly it could be because promoters had also learned some lessons from Monterey—though not, in too many cases, enough of them. The central lesson was economic: Monterey was profitable. Largely because the artists had performed for expenses only, the festival cleared close to a quarter-million dollars despite relatively small ticket sales. That meant if you put together a bill that would draw enough people into a larger area, you could pay plenty for the acts and still turn a profit. There were a couple of practical problems with this theory, however; chief among them that there were few promoters who had the experience to handle the logistics—sanitation, security, food, water, medical backup—involved in bringing together crowds of the necessary size. Add, as Bill Graham had remarked at his Fillmores, the fact that grass was no longer the sole drug of choice and was often being replaced by the incendiary combination of Ripple 'n' reds, and the possibilities for disaster were obvious.

That possibility existed even if a festival promoter was both honest and well capitalized. Those who were neither—or even only one—ran into real trouble. They might have enough money to make an initial payment to a roster of acts and then begin advertising them in order to sell tickets. If ticket sales came in, fine, but if not, then the promoters would have to decide which acts would get their next payment and be locked into appearing. Sometimes they reported the results of this triage in subsequent advertising, sometimes, either over-optimistically or dishonestly, not. A lot of festivals never happened at all, burning ticket buyers; and others were marred by last-minute scrimping on sound systems and other overhead. Put together inaudible or garbled performances by bands that weren't the ones crowds had paid to hear, add inadequate (which often translated into brutal) security, hunger, thirst, heat, and barbiturates, and people were bound to be hurt.

Even under relatively benign circumstances, there were often problems. During Easter week, some 25,000 people came to Palm Springs, California, in the annual spring break migration. Largely because many of the state's beaches were closed by an oil spill, this number was considerably larger than expected—and well over the 15,000 capacity of the two festival sites. On the first night, when John Mayall, the Butterfield Blues Band, and Procol Harum were performing at a drive-in theater, several thousand gate crashers came in over and through (one of them opening a hole for others with his car) the fence. This brought in the police, though in a relatively understated fashion, and caused the town to promulgate a series of emergency parking and camping regulations designed to empty the town as much as possible. To little avail, however, and on the festival's second and final night, as Ike and Tina Turner were performing in a more secure minor-league baseball stadium, some 5,000 beered-up kids milled around outside.

They mustered a few rushes toward the stadium, but the police, growing a little less restrained each time, kept them back. Soon the cops activated the underground sprinkler system on the lawn where many of the students were gathered and added to the discomfort by focusing a blinding sixty-inch spotlight on them. There were skirmishes at the edges of the crowd, and then, as the police began an advance, the crowd started to move. Some raced through a nearby shopping center, breaking a few windows and harassing, though not injuring, shoppers. Several hundred found themselves at an adjacent Shell station, flinging stones, bottles, and sand-filled beer cans in the general direction of the police. Within a few moments, all the station's front and side windows were shattered, and gasoline was spewing from its hoses. Inside, owner Harlan Moore reached for his .22 rifle and fired into the crowd, seriously wounding a sixteen-year-old boy and hitting a twenty-year-old woman in the breast. After that, the cops started using tear gas.

Only a couple of blocks away, inside the stadium, the show went on, with most of the audience enjoying the music and cooled by announcements from L.A. dj B. Mitchell Reed, apparently unaware of what was happening outside. But when the news reports appeared—146 hospitalized, 2 shot, 250 arrested—the distinction between the people who were listening to the music and those who weren't was blurred; it was "Riot *at* rock festival," not "Riot *near* . . ."

As a result, the music itself emerged with a black eye. But rock 'n' roll will stand, and Palm Springs's more important immediate effect was on communities that had already signed on as festival sites for the coming summer. Statutes against unlawful assembly were trotted out, special ordinances against mass gatherings passed, and expensive security deposits demanded from already overstretched promoters. In cases in which the promoters were competent and honest, such civic outbursts were panicky and paranoid; in other cases—especially because events have a way of snowballing and at least some increasingly militant (or simply anomic) fans thought riots sounded like a swell idea—they might have been prudent.

In either case, they fed an antirock—more specifically, an antirock *fan* (read "radical, long-haired, dope-smoking, promiscuous hippie")—backlash that right-wing politicians gleefully exploited. Some of the pols were small-time (Philadelphia police chief Frank Rizzo, running for mayor, stood outside a popular rock ballroom called the Electric Factory and pledged to "turn this joint into a parking lot"), but bigger fish were involved as well. In the wake of a fading Jim Morrison's Miami cock-flash during a tepidly received Doors' concert (an act apparently stirred more by desperation and flop-sweat than by revolutionary ideology), thirty thousand people turned out to hear the Lettermen and Anita Bryant at a compensatory "Rally for Decency." The event's organizers were congratulated by none other than the President of the United States (so far as is known, however, Nixon did not send the same crew his congratulations when the Baltimore event they staged a month later degenerated into a riot, pretty much along racial lines, when the advertised promise of a James Brown show wasn't fulfilled).

Though the Baltimore eruption could presumably have fostered an argument that a *lack* of music caused rioting, the rock-equals-riots configuration began to take hold and, given the nervousness of many cops at the "off the pigs" rhetoric that was among Chicago's legacies, it turned out to be something of a self-fulfilling prophecy. Two weekends after Palm Springs, at the L.A. Free Festival in Venice, the crowd's protests when a kid was handcuffed generated 116 more arrests before a note was played; in May, the Mounties had to be called in to the Aldergrove Beach Rock Festival in British Columbia after a gang of bikers raided the show. The Newport 1969 Festival near Los Angeles in June was more successful musically—150,000 fans heard three days' worth of acts, including Hendrix, Creedence, Steppenwolf, Jethro Tull, and Booker T. and the MGs—but it closed its books with 75 arrests, 300 injuries, and over $50,000 in damage to nearby properties; a week later, a similar lineup played before 50,000 fans at the Denver Pop Festival, but when the police moved into the crowd to break up some fighting, they wound up using billy clubs and tear gas.

Still, when the festivals worked, they were marvelous. Toronto, with the Band and Procol Harum, drew 50,000 without incident, and the Atlanta Pop Festival, where 140,000 turned out for—and got—peace, love, Joe Cocker, Creedence Clearwater Revival, Johnny Winter, Paul Butterfield, Led Zeppelin, and Janis Joplin, successfully planted freak culture's flag in the hitherto solid South. But neither of these, and nothing since, rivaled Woodstock.

It didn't happen in Woodstock (it was supposed to happen in nearby Wallkill, which didn't sound nearly as hip, but the townsfolk got nervous and barred the festival less than a month before it was scheduled), and almost didn't happen at all. But other communities were less worried—or perhaps hungrier—than relatively affluent Wallkill, and from a half-dozen offers, the promoters paid farmer Max Yasgur $50,000 for the use of his six-hundred-acre farm in Bethel. There was a flurry of local opposition there, too, but Bethel, New York, was light-years from Palm Springs, California, and the logic expressed in one letter to the local paper—"The results will bring an economic boost to the County, without it costing the taxpayers a cent"—carried the day. All through the summer, it was clear that Woodstock was going to be *the* festival; there was real money behind it, and the promoters had signed a dazzling collection of performers.

They'd done more than that, however. Arranging to fly members of Wavy Gravy's Hog Farm commune in from New Mexico to provide low-key agents of order and well-seasoned calming influences for bad trips turned out to be perhaps the most important $16,000 they spent, and they'd hired three hundred specially screened off-duty New York City cops to provide more traditional security if it was needed. With the Hog Farm's supply of whole grains, a medical tent, portosans, water, they seemed easily able to accommodate the 150,000 expected arrivals; indeed, they were so confident that they arranged with local authorities that no "real" police would be present.

Two things went (apparently, at least) radically wrong. First, as a result of NYPD pressure, the New York cops canceled at the last minute, and the promoters had to improvise a substitute force in a hurry. There were enough of them, easily recognizable in Day-Glo red T-shirts, but they were essentially untrained. Second, some 400,000 people showed up.

Roads were jammed for miles, and by Friday morning, state police were urging motorists to avoid the area entirely. No one paid any attention, however, and as all attempts to collect tickets were abandoned, the tent city spread beyond the now-trampled fences toward the field's far corners. It was on its way to becoming the state's third largest city—with no police, inadequate food and water, unlimited dope, and portable toilets that were already foul. And then it started to rain.

Almost everything that could possibly have gone wrong did, and none of it mattered. The music—what could be heard of it on the edges of the crowd where even the first-rate sound system was spotty—was all that anyone could have hoped—but the crowd itself was miraculous. Max Yasgur, who got what sounded like the weekend's largest ovation when he came onstage Sunday afternoon, put it best: "You are the largest group of people ever assembled in one place at one time . . . and you have proven something to the world . . . that half a million kids can get together for fun and music and have nothing but fun and music."

There were problems—bad trips, cut feet, dehydration, drug busts outside the festival grounds, even three deaths (two drug overdoses, a ruptured appendix, and a tractor accident)—but these were balanced symbolically by three births and practically by something that was more than the avoidance of disaster: the creation of a spontaneously functioning community. On Monday, the *New York Times* editorial page thundered that Woodstock was "an outrageous event" and asked, "What kind of culture is it that can produce so colossal a mess?" But just one day later, in a stunning reversal, the newspaper of record decided it had been "a phenomenon of innocence. . . . They came, it seems, to enjoy their own society, to exult in a life style that is its own declaration of independence . . . with Henry the Fifth, they could say at Bethel, 'He that outlives this day, and comes safe home, will stand a-tiptoe when this day is nam'd.'" And for a while, at least, the "Woodstock nation" was real.

As the record albums and film from Woodstock made clear, the music was real, too, but it was in some ways dwarfed by the near-miracle surrounding it. Among the promoters, however, the spirit of Woodstock faded with remarkable rapidity, and the partnership that had brought together the greatest participatory show on earth was sundered in a rain of threats, recriminations, and lawsuits. One fortuitous result of the dispute about just how much money had been made (or lost) for whom is that *Variety* was able to obtain and print a roster of all the performers and what they were paid. It ranges upward from the union-scale $375 paid to a band called Quill, and its higher reaches provide a bottom-line ranking of the Woodstock nation's most popular performers.

$18,000	The Jimi Hendrix Experience [actually Hendrix and some of his Woodstock jammers]
$15,000	Blood, Sweat and Tears
$10,000	Joan Baez, Creedence Clearwater Revival

$7,500	The Jefferson Airplane, the Band, Janis Joplin
$7,000	Sly and the Family Stone
$6,500	Canned Heat
$6,250	The Who
$6,000	Richie Havens
$5,000	Crosby, Stills, Nash and Young; Arlo Guthrie
$4,500	Ravi Shankar
$3,750	Johnny Winter
$3,250	Ten Years After
$2,500	Country Joe and the Fish, Grateful Dead

There are a number of surprises on (and off) this list. Some of them reflect accidents of timing; early in the year, when commitments for the festival were first being lined up, blues-rockers Canned Heat, veterans of Monterey, had their second straight top-twenty single on the charts, while Crosby, Stills, and Nash had yet to release any records at all.* It also contains only two women (two and a fraction if you count Grace Slick of the Airplane), and only three blacks, none of them soul performers (indeed, of the three, only Sly and the Family Stone ever appeared on the R&B charts). At that, the ratio of blacks among the performers was notably greater than that of the blacks among the audience.

Among those who earned less than $2,500 from their Woodstock appearances but went on to considerably greater success—largely because of Woodstock—the most musically important were Santana and Joe Cocker. The Latin-influenced Santana, the last major group to emerge from San Francisco during the decade, had come together in 1967 as the Santana Blues Band. The band had evolved during jam sessions, and Carlos Santana became its official leader primarily because the local musicians' union required one. As the opening act at several Fillmore West bills, they built a local following that earned them a Woodstock shot, where their "Soul Sacrifice" grabbed the attention of the fans, the filmmakers, and Columbia Records, which promptly signed them. Their debut album, *Santana*, was released later in the year and eventually went to number one.

Joe Cocker's success was a longer time coming. Back in Sheffield, England, when he was only four years old, he accidentally came upon a copy of Ray Charles's classic *Yes Indeed!* ("It was a cosmic buzz," he told *Rolling Stone*, but "I thought it was another Little Richard at first"). Always influenced by Charles, he worked with a number of forgotten local bands, and in 1964, Decca offered him a contract. Wisely, he didn't give up his day job but took a six-month leave, and after his version of the Beatles' "I'll Cry Instead" stiffed, he was back to working as a pipe fitter for the East Midland Gas Board. But the single earned attention from Jimmy Page, then Britain's number-one session musician, and from Stevie Winwood. Three years later,

*Five years later, Crosby, Stills, Nash and Young would gross $9.4 million, of which their net was usually 80 percent, on a tour of just twenty-four cities.

when Cocker and the Grease Band were ready to record again, Page, Winwood, and Procol Harum organist Matthew Fisher sat in. The title single from the album *With a Little Help from My Friends* was a U.K. number one and led to an American tour and contract with A&M. The single, a tortured, bluesy rendition of what had been a cheery song in the hands of the Fab Four, went only to number sixty-eight on the U.S. charts, and Cocker wound up at Woodstock because it was a convenient stop on his American promotional tour.

There the Ray Charles influence remained so strong in his voice that he was the closest the festival came to a soul singer, but his performing style—a spastic, herky-jerky, impassioned combat with himself—was *sui generis* and especially impressive on film. That tour brought him an American audience and, even more important, linked him with Leon Russell. Cocker, who rarely wrote his own material, had been running short of songs that turned him on ("About the only people who are still buzzing me are Dylan and the Beatles") but was excited when his manager played him a tape of Russell's "Delta Lady." They wound up recording it in Russell's home studio, and Russell signed on with Cocker, helping to produce the second album and pulling together the Mad Dogs and Englishmen, an amorphous (though professional) assemblage of instrumentalists, vocalists, animals, children, and tinker lads who performed with and around Cocker on a famously chaotic post-Woodstock tour.

Like Santana to the West, Sha Na Na came to Woodstock through bookings at Fillmore East. A group of Columbia University students who offered campy versions of doo-wop hits, they were fun live at Woodstock and good-natured stars on film. Their success was real, but—especially after Henry Gross's departure for a solo career in 1970—nonmusical. Theirs was, deliberately, music of nonsignificance, a break from the moral and political freight that rock was bearing. Though it took nearly a decade after Woodstock for them to translate their live popularity to the real stardom that came when they began a syndicated TV show, they planted the seeds of rock's rejection at the site of its greatest triumph.

Though two British acts appeared on the list of Woodstock's highest-paid performers, English acts were somewhat underrepresented given the American popularity of second-wave British blues. Because of Alvin Lee's extraordinarily fast and even crowded guitar lines, Ten Years After was a better-than-average representative of the genre, but at $6,250, the Who, perched on the edge of joining the Beatles and the Stones in the pantheon of British rock, might have been the promoters' greatest bargain.

The time leading up to Woodstock had been comparatively fallow for the Who. The year 1967 had ended with a one-two punch: "I Can See for Miles," their first—and only—American Top Ten single, and, in the spirit of *Sgt. Pepper* and *Satanic Majesties*, their first "concept" album, *The Who Sell Out*. But theirs was a concept with a difference. Without at all abandoning (or, at any rate, misplacing) rock as the Stones had, *Sell Out* lovingly placed rock in its perfect context: pop radio. There were commercials, jingles (some of them actually taken from Radio London), and dj patter linking the songs, which included not only "I Can See for Miles" but the airy "Rael" and needle-sharp "Tattoo" as well. The songs and performance were the band's most consistent yet (Sell Out was always Keith Moon's favorite Who allbum) and, in England, added up to a potent political statement. The pirate radio stations had finally been shut down, leaving only the BBC's cautious please-the-old-folks-too Radio One as an outlet for pop; the Who's affectionate farewell to the pirates was a pointed reminder of what had been lost.

In America, however, where AM pop was disdained by the hipper-than-thou, Sell Out had the context of no context. As a result, it was just car-radio stuff, not the progressive sound beloved of album buyers. Even with a hit single and a heavy promotional tour behind it, Sell Out just barely scraped into the Top Fifty. On the other hand, number forty-eight on the album charts was better than the Who had ever done before, and MCA wanted new product.

As a populist lover of pop, Townshend actually approved of this: "Compositions come out so fast in rock because there's a demand created and contracts have to be fulfilled," he told Rolling Stone. "I mean, who ever put Beethoven under contract. Prince Charming may have asked him to do this and that, but there was none of this six records a year. The pressures of the pop industry are part and parcel of it all." But for all the music business's problems, these pressures were "about the only fucking healthy thing about it! It's like . . . teenagers getting screwed up because their parents won't change for them. The commercial market refuses to change at the speed musicians and composers might wish. It has its own pace, adjusted by the mass, which is to me absolutely the most important thing on earth."

So Townshend understood when MCA, after tapes of the band's spring Fillmore East shows didn't work out and its "opera" was still in the hazy future, simply pulled a batch of songs out of previous albums and re-packaged them for the American market as Magic Bus: The Who on Tour. But he didn't approve. Yes, the band had failed to meet the demands Townshend recognized as central, but by offering recycled stuff and pretending it was live, the company was making the band accomplices in a more serious betrayal of its audience. "They have lived to regret it," he said four years later, "but not to delete it."

Purely as a commercial proposition, however, the opera Tommy proved worth the wait. Not only did it go all the way to number four on the U.S. charts, it (and the Who's longevity as a hardworking touring band) so thoroughly established the Who as major figures that every new album for the next decade also went Top Ten. Artistically, it was iffier. There were dead spots on the double album (most of which, like "Cousin Kevin" and "Christmas," the band simply dropped from their live performances), and Daltry's interpretations were by no means as strong as they would become after he'd performed the songs live for a couple of years (compare them, for instance, with his more expressive vocals on the 1972 orchestral version). These faults combined to expose a third: Essentially an internal psychological drama, the story lacked dramatic action. Live, the band more than made up for this (and even the recorded version worked very well indeed as the score for a balletic adaptation when The Royal Canadian Ballet took it on the road), and their performances of it at Woodstock, at the Fillmore East, and finally at the Metropolitan Opera House itself significantly stretched the spatial limitations of rock.

Somewhat surprisingly, the Kinks were among the beneficiaries. Early in the year, their most perfect album, (The Kings Are) the Village Green Preservation Society, a modest English success late in 1968, had stiffed entirely in America, failing to make the charts altogether. It was, in fact, a modest record, the first produced by Ray Davies, and the largely acoustic arrangements were as pastoral as the sensibility behind lines like "God save little shops, china cups, and virginity." Despite some brilliant songs—most notably "The Last of the Steam-Powered Trains" and "People Take Pictures of Each Other"—the concepts behind this concept album failed to travel well. For the band, however, it was an easy step from its loose unities to the narrative structure of Arthur (or the Decline and Fall of the British Empire).

Less grandiose, and therefore tighter, than Tommy, the Kinks' album continued Davies's straitlaced Village Green themes. But, as almost always in rock, melody and performance overwhelmed "content," and difficult as Davies's vision might have been to swallow in the year of Woodstock, the bouncily regressive "Victoria" ("Long ago, life was clean/Sex was bad and obscene") gave the group its first U.S. chart appearance since 1966.

With a major push from Warners, the "rock opera" album climbed to number 105 on the charts. This, too, was the band's highest showing since 1966, but it almost certainly could have been better if they'd taken advantage of their U.S. tour. Over the summer, Warners achieved peace with the musicians' union, and the Kinks were once again allowed to perform in America. But their performances were aimless, pointless, and often tuneless, adding another painful chapter to their self-destructive history.

Though the Kinks appeared (wrongly, as it turned out) to be well on the downward road, 1969 saw England present the world with two quite different but equally interesting guitar-hero bands: Led Zeppelin and King Crimson. Both were led by a "guitar genius," by then almost traditional for British bands, but Led Zep started with its resident guitarist's credentials solidly established. For as long as there had been a British rock scene, Jimmy Page was its preeminent session man, having worked with the Who, Them, the Kinks, Tom Jones, Herman's Hermits, and virtually everyone else. In 1966, "the session world started to get very dreary," and he opted to join the Yardbirds when Paul Samwell-Smith left them to become a producer. Initially he played bass, but he switched to lead guitar when Beck, sick ("I had this throat thing come on—inflamed tonsils—and what with inflamed tonsils, an inflamed brain, and an inflamed cock . . .") dropped out in the midst of a Dick Clark "Caravan of Stars" tour of America. The Beck-less Yardbirds carried on as a quartet for close to two years, during which they never hit the top forty, and when they finally packed it in in July 1968, Page was left with the Yardbirds' name and some unfulfilled Scandinavian gigs (for which the advance money had long ago been spent). He had to pull a band together in a hurry, and turned to fellow session man John Paul Jones, with whom he'd worked on Donovan's *Hurdy Gurdy Man* album as bassist. The two then tried unsuccessfully to recruit vocalist Terry Reid and drummer R. J. Wilson; when Reid recommended the comparatively unknown vocalist Robert Plant, Page journeyed to Birmingham.

"I went up to see him sing," he told *Zigzag*. "He was in a group called Obstweedle or Hobbstweedle, something like that, who were playing at a teachers' training college outside of Birmingham—to an audience of about twelve." Page didn't like the repertoire ("He was a Moby Grape fanatic and they were doing all those kinds of numbers—semi-obscure West Coast stuff"), but thought Plant was "fantastic"—especially since he was gigging to virtually no one in the Midlands. "What amazed me more than anything else, especially after the first LP was finished, was that nothing significant had happened to him before. . . . You'd have thought he'd have been *noticed* at least, especially when they tried to exploit the Birmingham group scene as the successor to the Liverpool thing, but no." Under the circumstances, Plant was delighted to join; it was he who recommended old friend John Bonham (who'd also done some work on *Hurdy Gurdy Man*), but the band was very much Page's, and Plant sacrificed his own singing preferences. "He suppressed his personal tastes to a degree, I suppose. . . . he was very keen on Moby Grape and even more so on the Buffalo Springfield."

"Suppressed his tastes to a degree" has to stand as one of the great examples of British understatement, for it's difficult to imagine a band less like Buffalo Springfield than Led Zeppelin. The sound on their debut album was almost completely stripped of lyricism. Page's guitar was probably more like Hendrix's than anyone else's, but he played with the session man's spare precision. Analyzed note for note, there seems nothing extra, nothing gratuitous, in Page's fingering, but all his restraint goes by the boards when it comes to distortion. Everything is filtered, bent, fuzzed, reverbed, echoed—including Plant's voice and Jones's heavy-bottomed bass. Against this, Bonham's drums are left flat; though he is busy, the technical trick keeps him light. As producer and arranger (Glyn Johns was engineer), Page invented a hard-rock style that would still be influencing bands fifteen years later.

Though less influential, probably because more eccentric, King Crimson's Robert Fripp was an even more inventive guitarist than Page, but he was never to master Page's ability to shape a group and, having done so, to keep it together. In King Crimson's initial five-year span (Fripp revived the name with yet another band in 1981), it recorded with five different lineups and was unable to tour at all from the end of 1969 until April of 1971 because no one lineup was ever around long enough. As Fripp, the only constant through this chaos, said during the course of the band's fifth lineup, "It's a prima facie case of instability. The next question is 'Why should Crimson be unstable?' One could infer that I am an unstable personality, but I think most people tend to disagree with that."

Onstage, Fripp didn't seem so much unstable as private. Acutely private. Even Jimmy Page allowed himself a modest amount of physical flash during Led Zep's tours, but Fripp usually performed sitting on a stool, embracing his guitar as though neither his band nor the audience was present. Even before he began to work with "Frippertronics" in the late 1970s, it seemed that Fripp could make his guitar do *anything*. Including, though this was not among his more obvious skills, play superb and subtle backup; led on by Fripp's promptings and supported by his fills, Greg Lake actually *sang*; a year later, with Emerson, Lake and Palmer, he merely declaimed. If Fripp specialized in anything, it was surprise: an altered rhythm, a jarring dissonance in the midst of a melody (and vice versa), sudden dips and swoops when one would expect a sustained note, followed by notes sustained almost beyond the listeners' endurance. It was for these qualities that he was most valued in New York's avant-garde music scene in the early and mid-1980s, and even at Crimson's most portentous, Fripp always kept their audiences pleasantly off-balance.

But Fripp, for all the impish humor that kept peeking through his solos, was like Page in one crucial way: Each successive album revealed that its predecessor had actually been restrained. Fripp constantly pushed his art of surprise to the very edge; one step further and surprise would have been impossible, because nothing, or everything, could have been anticipated. Neither the heavy metal bands following Led Zeppelin nor the post-Crimson art rockers ever managed with any consistency to situate their restraint with the precision of Page or Fripp. Given the year, they went, it appears even more clearly in retrospect, as far as you could go.

In one direction, that is; Dylan, with *John Wesley Harding* and *Nashville Skyline*, had gone about as far as you could go in the other. This push to opposite extremes—to quiet country and heavy metal—might seem to imply that the conventions of rock were growing stale. But the middle ground was hardly barren; it merely took genius to bring it to life, and the Beatles and the Stones, geniuses both, were surely the year's most inspired middle-of-the-roaders. *Abbey Road*, the B side especially, may be a little bloodless and overprofessional, but it was certainly the band's best album since *Sgt. Pepper* and arguably the best since *Rubber Soul*. Without the professionalism, it wouldn't have been made at all.

The year had started with the band's decision, sparked by Paul, but unanimously accepted, to take the *White Album*'s rock 'n' roll historicity a step further and make an album of Dylanesque simplicity. Starting on

.uary 2, as a documentary film crew recorded their recording, the band
orked on a "roots" album to be called *Get Back*. While they were in the
studio, *Disc* printed an interview with John during which he discussed the
chaotic state of affairs at Apple, saying, "If it carries on like this we'll be
broke in six months." Among the readers was fiery New York manager
Allen Klein, whose impressive client roster included the Stones. He called
Lennon to express his interest in coming over to straighten things out, and
John promptly invited him to England.

The trouble with this was that Paul, at dinner with his future father-in-
law, copyright lawyer Lee Eastman, had told his version of the sad Apple
story, and Eastman had volunteered to help by sending his son and law
partner John to London. John Eastman knew little about music or the music
industry, but he knew that Brian Epstein's old management firm was still
taking 25 percent off the top of the Beatles' earnings, and that Apple was
about to be clobbered by the estate taxes from Brian's death. He came up
with a solution to which they all agreed and had already started negotiations when Klein arrived in London to meet with John and Yoko at the
Dorchester Hotel. John and Yoko were impressed, but when Linda Eastman
heard the news, her first reaction was, "Oh, shit."

Hers was a prescient comment, but even Paul was impressed by the
problems Klein discovered in John Eastman's scheme, and he agreed that
the band needed more information from their record company before
pushing on with it. Klein negotiated a three-week waiting period with
Epstein's brother Clive, but in only two weeks, Clive Epstein sold the
management company, with its 25 percent of the Beatles' earnings, to an
investment trust. He'd done so, he said, because of a letter he'd received
from John Eastman (who was, he added, "a little too young to be negotiating
at that level").

Further problems were developing at the recording/filming of *Get Back*.
This time it was George who felt Paul was overreaching. George had returned to the studios, confident and with a lot of new songs to share, from a
short American tour with Eric Clapton, only to discover that he was to be
held to his usual two songs per album. "I quickly discovered I was up
against the same old Paul," he testified during the suit Paul later brought
against Allen Klein. "In front of the cameras, as we were actually being
filmed, Paul started to get at me about the way I was playing. I had always
let him have his own way, even when this meant the songs which I had
composed were not being recorded. At the same time I was helping to
record his songs and into the bargain I was having to put up with him
telling me how to play my own musical instrument." As a result, George
became—also like Ringo, for a brief time—the second Beatle to leave the
band.

George's feelings about Paul were probably accurate, but Paul wasn't an
entirely unsympathetic figure. When the others had lost interest in Apple
Corps, it was Paul who accepted the responsibility they'd shrugged off. Or,

to be more accurate, *tried* to accept it; repairing the mess at Apple was as much beyond his abilities as it would have been for any of the others, and though there's something touching about the image of him wandering around the building to make sure there was enough toilet paper in the lavatories, such gestures were more symbolic than substantive. But Apple's problems were of the sort that *some* skilled outsider, whether Klein, Eastman, or a third figure the four could somehow agree on, could fix. Except, perhaps, for Brian Epstein, no outsider could hold the Beatles together; his death meant that the strength would have to come from themselves, and with John preoccupied by Yoko, and George and Ringo disaffected, the burden fell on Paul. In the event, this was beyond him, but a tape-recorded exchange from the filming process indicates both that he tried and that he failed:

Paul: I mean we've been very negative since Mr. Epstein passed away. . . . That's why all of us in turn have been sick of the group. It is a bit of a drag. It's like when you're growing up—your daddy goes away at a certain point in your life and then you stand on your own feet. Daddy has gone away now, you know. I think we either go home, or we do it.

It's discipline we need. Mr. Epstein, he said, "Get suits on," and we did. And so we were always fighting that discipline a bit. But now it's silly to fight that discipline if it's our own. It's self-imposed these days, so we do as little as possible. But I think we need a bit more if we are going to get on with it.

George: Well, if that's what "doing it" is, I don't want to do anything.

That being the case, they abandoned the project and went home, leaving, perhaps, the Beatles behind them. On March 12, Paul married Linda. There were crowds of photographers and fans outside the Marylebone Registry Office, but the newlyweds quickly escaped them, retiring for a protracted period of seclusion to McCartney's new Scottish farm near Mull of Kintyre. Eight days later, John and Yoko wed at a private ceremony on the Rock of Gibraltar. "It was perfect," John said. "Quiet, quick, and British." They did not go into seclusion.

Instead, the honeymooners went promptly to the Amsterdam Hilton, where they invited fifty reporters to a bedside "happening." The term, and to some degree the event itself, was probably an Ono borrowing from the early 1960s New York downtown art scene in which she'd begun to shape her own works. But the Amsterdam police could hardly have been expected to know that, and fearing the obvious, they issued a statement sternly warning that "If people are invited to such a 'happening,' the police will certainly act." John and Yoko spared them, if not the rest of us, by appearing in pajamas, each holding a single tulip, and announcing that they were going to stay in bed for a week as "a protest against all the suffering and violence in the world." From there, it was on to Vienna for "bagism" (as a protest against prejudgment by appearances, they conducted this press conference from within a large sack set on a table), then back to London to plant fifty acorns (also for peace), and finally to Montreal for another week-long nap. In what turned out to be a grimly ironic comment, Lennon later said of these episodes, "Our policy is not to be taken seriously. All the serious people like Martin Luther King and Kennedy got shot. We're willing to be the world's clowns."

While he was in London, John wanted to record his newly written "The Ballad of John and Yoko" as a Beatles single, and though Ringo and George were unavailable, Paul (how could he not? he loved Linda *and* John) obligingly sat in on drums. Despite a "Christ, you know it ain't easy" chorus that effectively barred it from most American radio stations and stiff competition from the Beatles own "Get Back," the impassioned rocker got to number eight on the U.S. charts (John returned the favor a few weeks later when he credited "Give Peace a Chance," which he recorded with the Plastic Ono Band, to Lennon/McCartney).

Both honeymoons were cut short, however, when Dick James, publisher of the entire Lennon/McCartney catalog, announced he was selling the copyrights to Sir Lew Grade's entertainment conglomerate. John went back to London, but before he left, he abandoned talk of peace to dig in his Scouse heels: "I won't sell," he told a reporter. "They are my shares and my songs and I want to keep a bit of the end product. I don't have to ring Paul; I know damn well he feels the same as I do."

Paul did, and the four began a proxy fight. And though he continued to express his doubts about Klein's wisdom, he was pleased when Klein both negotiated a recording contract with EMI that would pay the band the highest royalties in industry history and arranged a settlement with Epstein's old company that returned control over their own earnings to the Beatles. As they signed the two agreements—and waited to see how the battle for their songs would go—the four were so united they willingly accepted Paul's suggestion that they return to the studio and try for another album.

Abbey Road took less time to record than any album since *Help!* and had more genuine Beatles' songs, in the sense of three-part harmonies rather than individual overdubs, than anything since *Rubber Soul*. Especially when one of George's two allotted cuts was for the first time released as the A side of a single (a decision vindicated when "Something" became a monster transatlantic hit), the band seemed more together than it had in years. And then John announced that he wanted to leave. "I want a divorce," he said.

The remark accurately captured the nature of what the Beatles had been, but it didn't leave much room for argument. Ringo and George had had grievances; John had a dream, and the rest of the band wisely said about the only thing that can be said under such circumstances: "Let's wait and see, maybe things will work out." With that hope, however dim, of a reconciliation, the four (with Paul in an odd alliance with Allen Klein) agreed to keep this most serious threat to their continued existence secret until they were sure, at which time they would make a joint announcement.

At this point, with the Beatles dying, their fans suddenly became concerned that Paul was dead. The rumor (too mild a word for it, actually; *mass delusion* might be better) began when a Detroit FM dj, Russ Gibb of WKNR, acting on a listener's tip, began playing parts of certain Beatles' records backward. And especially if you were primed for it, it did sound as though the "number nines" on the *White Album* were "Turn me on, dead man," reversed, and that the nonsense syllables between "I'm So Tired," and "Blackbird" were "Paul is dead, miss him, miss him." With this as a start, it took a million or so English-major fans not long at all to find more. The student newspaper at the University of Michigan picked up the ball, and from there, word of Paul's death raced east and west. For many, *Abbey Road's* cover was the clincher: not only was Paul barefoot while the others were shod, the license plate visible on a Volkswagen parked in the background read 28 IF—precisely the age Paul would have been, *if* he had lived. Paul, it seemed, had died in a car crash on November 9, 1966 (which of course explained why the band had stopped touring while they recruited someone who could substitute, disguised and enhanced by electronic trickery, in the studio).

Initially Paul—alive, well, and, as it happened, twenty-seven years old— was amused, and the Beatles' labels weren't about to go out of their way to quash the rumor, for clue hunters pulled not only *Sgt. Pepper* but even *Magical Mystery Tour* back onto the charts. As the story grew more and more elaborate, Paul let it be while he worked on the debut solo album that would prove he was alive. Meanwhile, George and John were busily demonstrating that they, at least, were still among the living.

George would eventually play with Eric Clapton on a Delaney and Bonnie tour that afforded him, as one of the duo's many "friends," the chance to go onstage in relative anonymity. John, typically, took a more visible role. In September, the promoters of a Toronto rock 'n' roll revival finally got through to Apple on the phone and invited him and Yoko to the show. Lennon's reaction was negative; it would be too much like the king and queen sitting in the royal box at the opera. But even while he was talking to them, the idea of performing some oldies hit him, and he put them on hold while he called George about getting a band together. When George said yes, so did John. He was so pleased by the notion that immediately after he hung up, he burst into an impromptu rendition of "Blue Suede Shoes" that set the half-dozen people in the office cheering.

Clapton was the key, however, and when it appeared that Harrison couldn't track him down, the idea was scrapped. But when Harrison finally found him in Europe less than a day before they'd have to depart, the show was on again. In addition to Clapton, this first live version of the Plastic Ono Band included old Hamburg pal Klaus Voormann on bass and young drummer (soon to be a member of Yes) Alan White. John was nervous, throwing up during airborne rehearsals on the flight over, and his introduction was mumbled and apologetic. But with "Blue Suede Shoes," "Money," "Dizzy," "Yer Blues," and—"this is what we came for, really"—"Give Peace a Chance," he convinced himself, and the crowd, that he could still play, still rock. Even Yoko's tough reception during her harsh and willfully atonal vocal solos soured the experience hardly at all, and the Plastic Ono Band (John and Yoko, backed by Clapton, Voormann, and Ringo) promptly recorded "Cold Turkey." This stripped-down scream about the pains of kicking wasn't the stuff hits are made of (though it reached number 30 in the United States and number 14 in the United Kingdom), but John was so disappointed he listed its comparatively poor chart showing along with England's support for the Vietnam War and for the Nigerians in Biafra when he returned his BME to the queen as a gesture of protest. He was, however, disappointed rather than discouraged, and the Plastic Ono Band (this time with Harrison and Keith Moon) performed at a London Christmas benefit concern for UNICEF.

Except for the abbreviated rooftop scene in Let It Be, the film the Beatles salvaged from the making of their "roots" album, this was the first time any of the Beatles had performed live in England in almost four years, but it was neither the largest nor the most important English concert of the year. That dual honor went to the Rolling Stones' free Hyde Park appearance on July 5, 1969. The lowest crowd estimate was 300,000, the highest 650,000; taking into account the relative populations of England and America, this was, at minimum, an event ten times the magnitude of Woodstock. It took place because Jagger was unhappy with a television show.

In December of 1968, the Stones were looking for a way to promote Beggar's Banquet, and with their ability to tour sharply circumscribed by Brian's legal, chemical, and psychological situation, they hit on the idea of a TV special. It was pulled together very quickly, and on the morning of December 10, an invitation-only audience filed into a cavernous North London studio to attend the Rolling Stones Circus. The canvas of a semicircular circus tent filled one end of the studio; there was a ring and sawdust on the floor, aerial apparatus overhead. The audience, dressed for the cameras in a rainbow of specially issued ponchos, was, like the half-tent, part of the set. After considerable fussing with technical equipment, Jagger, dressed as a ringmaster, introduced the performers. It was literally a circus: fire-eaters, acrobats, clowns, musicians, horses. Naturally the thing was a nightmare to light and film, and there were interminable delays between acts, but those who were there—the film has never been released—describe it as magical nonetheless.

At eight o'clock, all hands finally broke for dinner while a stage was set up for a genuine English supersession featuring Lennon, Clapton, Keith Richards on bass, and Hendrix's drummer Mitch Mitchell. After several takes of warm-ups on oldies, they launched into "Yer Blues" from the White

Album. Then Yoko and classical violinist Ivry Gitlis came out and joined them for a set of her songs. Then another break. Then the Who doing their first "opera," "A Quick One While He's Away." And a break. Then Gitlis playing Paganini's First Violin Concerto—twice. Then another break, and finally, seventeen hours after the first fans arrived, the Stones. Five more hours, at six in the morning, and director Michael Lindsay-Hogg finally declared a wrap.

Perhaps it was just that the whole thing went on too long for musicians and fans alike, but whatever the cause, Jagger was dissatisfied with the Stones' sequences and, except for a Who segment subsequently cannibalized for *The Kids Are Alright*, none of the film was ever released.

Their promotion problem still unsolved, the Stones returned from a vacation to begin studio work on their next album, *Let It Bleed*. There, when Brian seemed either unwilling or unable to participate, they finally confronted his problems. As Jagger later said, "We felt like we had a wooden leg. We wanted to go out and play, but Brian couldn't." Once charismatic enough to rival Jagger's leadership, at least with the fans—and always, even before the Stones existed, the offstage embodiment of the band's onstage persona—Jones had, by 1969, in critic Robert Christgau's telling phrase, "fucked and doped himself beyond usefulness." So he was fired. He left the band quietly, with a professionalism that seemed to have long escaped him; on June 8, sped on his way by a golden handshake of 100,000 pounds per annum, he announced that he had quit.

By then, though most of *Let It Bleed* was played by a quartet, ex-Blues-breaker Mick Taylor had done some sessions with the band, and he was Jones's obvious replacement. This meant that not only the album but the "new" Stones required promotion. Now, however, though Taylor then and always would lack Jones's stage presence, a live concert was possible, so they set up the Hyde Park appearance as Taylor's public debut. Two days before the event, despite the presence of a live-in nurse, Jones was dead, drowned in his own swimming pool during the course of a party. The coroner's verdict was "death by misadventure," and the show went on.

Despite or because of security from London Hell's Angels, gentleness was the afternoon rule. The good opening acts—King Crimson, Family—were received enthusiastically; the less good—the Screw, Battered Ornaments—were allowed to escape without humiliation. Then, after stage manager Sam Cutler had asked the audience to remain silent in memory of Brian Jones, the Stones themselves appeared. Jagger, resplendent in white, was greeted with applause, which he quieted with an anguished "No-o-o-o-o," and the audience hushed. He allowed that a good time would be coming, but first, "I would really like to say something about Brian." Then the strutting, street-fighting midnight rambler did something that few rock performers would have dared—or, having dared, gotten away with—he began reciting from Shelley's "Adonais." Had that vast crowd been truly listening, they would have found the first stanza he chose as chilling as anything the Stones would sing that afternoon:

> Peace, peace! he is not dead, he doth not sleep—
> He hath awakened from the dream of life—
> 'Tis we, who, lost in stormy visions, keep
> With phantoms an unprofitable strife,
> And in mad trance strike with our spirit's knife
> Invulnerable nothings. We decay
> Like corpses in a charnel; fear and grief
> Convulse us and consume us day by day,
> And cold hopes swarm like worms within our living clay.

But after that, somehow, just as Jagger had promised, a good time was had by all, and the Hyde Park concert was by every measure a triumph. Among other things, tales of the day spread across the Atlantic, whetting appetites for a Stones tour. Which, now that Taylor had replaced Jones, they were able to undertake. In November, timed to coincide with the American release of *Let It Bleed*, they arrived in California to begin a thirteen-city, eighteen-show tour, their first American appearances since 1966. This time, everything was different. The music was tighter, the performance more theatrical, and even the audience had changed, for the tour was such a success that by the time they reached Madison Square Garden, the Stones were not only popular but fashionable. Though some fans came to hear the music, a disquietingly large portion of the audience was there merely because it was the place to be. Even at precedent-setting prices, tickets were so hot an extra show was added, and probably half the crowd that finally got into see them was nearing the age over which they could no longer be trusted, and many had quite obviously passed it.

In New York, at least, ticket prices didn't seem to matter, but earlier in the tour, when the $5.50 to $8.50 range for the Oakland show was announced, *San Francisco Chronicle* columnist Ralph J. Gleason weighed in with a column denouncing the band as ripoff artists. One reason tickets were expensive is that the Stones demanded audio and video systems that would make arena rock work, and even in hard-core consumer terms, they were by a large margin a better dollar-for-dollar value than either Blind Faith or the Doors. But the criticism stung. Jagger was asked whether, in light of the high ticket-prices, the band would consider doing a free concert somewhere along the way. "There has been talk of that," he said. "I should think toward the end. We'll have to see how things go."

The schedule didn't leave much time for thinking, however. And after two hours plus on the stage every night, Jagger in his Uncle Sam hat and flowing scarf, leaping, dancing, shouting, moaning, the band driving relentlessly behind him, not much energy was left for long-range planning. But as the tour went on and the audiences seemed more and more excited, the idea of a climactic free concert grew on the band. Road manager Sam

Cutler spent increasing amounts of time on the phone with Rock Scully, manager of the Grateful Dead. Long distance, the Stones reached a site agreement with the Sears Point Raceway. It seemed like a most generous offer: no charge, but the Stones would be responsible for obtaining local and state health and safety clearances, provide at least a hundred experienced security officers, reimburse the raceway for preparation and restoration of the grounds, and donate any profits to a fund for Vietnamese orphans.

At the last minute, however, the offer became a lot less generous. The Raceway's parent corporation, Filmways, was also owner of a subsidiary called Concert Associates, through which it had promoted the Stones' concerts at the Inglewood Forum outside Los Angeles. Concert Associates believed it had a promise of an added date after the Stones returned from their East Coast swing, and when that unwritten promise went unfulfilled, Filmways suddenly upped the ante for the Raceway. If the concert was filmed, which they knew it would be, Filmways would have exclusive U.S. distribution rights; if these were not available, they would take $100,000 cash instead. In either case, the Stones would have to put an additional $100,000 in escrow as a damage fund.

Less than twenty-four hours before the concert was set to start, the Stones retained prominent San Francisco attorney Melvin Belli to negotiate a path through the thicket. When Filmways proved immovable, it was Belli who arranged the contract with the Altamont Speedway. Given the haste with which the contract was arranged, even the best efforts of Chip Monck and his construction crew—the people who'd designed and built the stage at Woodstock—could produce only a low stage. With anything like a decent running start, fans could hurdle it. This put a premium on security, and acting both on the advice of Rock Scully and the memory of Hyde Park, Cutler hired the local Hell's Angels for $500 worth of beer.

Even if the anticipated maximum of 100,00 fans had come out, there would have been problems; prior to the concert, the largest crowd ever to attend Altamont Speedway had been the 6,500 fans drawn by a demolition derby. As the time for the concert neared, however, some 300,000 fans were either there or on the way. They weren't even close to enough toilets, and the sound system, which would have been strained to reach 100,000 fans, was totally inadequate. By the time the first notes were played, a Woodstock-size crowd was spilling over the borders of a site only 15 percent as big as Yasgur's farm. Things would get worse as the day wore on.

The Angels were everybody's favorite scapegoats, and they probably deserved everything negative that was said about them. What positive acts there were—and some were reported—were drowned in a flood of violence. During the Airplane's set, for instance, Marty Balin tried to interfere with the methodical beating being administered to a black man near the foot of the stage, and the band wound up finishing the last half of "Somebody to Love" with Balin, offhandedly punched out by an Angel, stretched unconscious on the stage. At scattered points in the audience, the violence was, if anything, worse. Many of the Angels were carrying loaded pool cues, and though they confiscated a lot of film, there remain innumerable photographs of Angels wielding them to near-lethal effect. Back in London, Mick Taylor said, "The people that were working with us getting the concert together [that is, the Dead] thought it would be a good idea to have them as a security force. But . . . they were using it as an excuse. They're just very, very violent people.

"I think we expected probably something like the Hell's Angels that were our security force at Hyde Park, but of course they're not the real Hell's Angels, they're completely phony. These guys in California are the real thing—they're very violent."

Though the Stones made marvelous music, nothing they could have done would have saved the day. And only their refusing to appear, which would almost surely have caused greater havoc, might have saved Meredith Hunter from death at the Angels' hands. Still, as David Crosby pointed out, the Angels weren't entirely to blame: "Remember, the Angels were asked to be there. . . . They've always showed up at gatherings, but they were not asked to guard a stage. This time they were and they did it. In their mind, guard a stage means guard it. That means if anyone comes near it, you do them in, and in the Angels' style if you do them in, you do them in. Blame is the dumbest trip there is; there isn't any blame."

Okay, no blame. Naïveté? Over-optimism? Too much faith in the Woodstock nation? Too much trust in the Grateful Dead as guides to the local scene? Failure, as many local residents suggested, to realize the moon was in Scorpio? Retribution for the Stones' cultivated lawless image? For their constant toying with violence in their stage act? Blame may be the dumbest trip there is, but blame it on the Rolling Stones.

Even before the horror passed, the symbol makers took over. And Altamont, as Robert Christgau suggested, was made to order for them: "Time: The final month of the decade that spawned that unprecedented and probably insupportable contradiction in terms, mass bohemia, popularly known as the counterculture. Occasion: On America's ultimate frontier some three hundred thousand bohemians come together with their chosen images, five formerly lower- to middle-class Englishmen who fuse Afro-American music with European sensibility. Denouement: An Afro-American bohemian is murdered by a lower-class white Hell's Angel while the Englishmen do a song called 'Sympathy for the Devil.'"

And yes, the symbolism *was* too easy, but it was a way of making sense out of chaos. And especially given the role in which the Stones had cast themselves, seeing Altamont as the *terminus ad quem* was irresistible. If it had just been the other acts—the Airplane, the Dead, CSN and Y—at Altamont, the day's melancholy events might have been a blip on the radar screen, but willy-nilly, the Stones made it stand for more. Meredith Hunter died at Altamont, but a generation's faith in itself was mortally wounded.

26

TRIMMING THE SAILS

T hough Altamont might indeed have borne too much symbolic, end-of-an-era freight, there's no question it was followed, in both the singles and the album markets, by a retreat from the hard-driving macho rock the Stones exemplified. The one exception, churning out seven Top Ten singles, from "Proud Mary" to "Lookin' Out My Back Door," during 1969 and 1970, was Creedence Clearwater Revival. But Creedence (John and Tom Fogerty, Stu Cook, and Doug Clifford) had *always* been an exception. At a time when the other Bay Area bands were exploring the universe by means of elaborated psychedelic blues, Creedence was tight, terse, and committed to the singles form. Always intelligent, and emotional in a (usually) understated way, Creedence's closest analog, perhaps, was that other rock 'n' roll throwback, the Band. Like them, Creedence was workmanlike and consciously unflashy, but the Californians also made nearly irresistible dance music.

They had, however, virtually no imitators, and bodies, as well as shell-shocked souls, seemed in retreat. This was not without its positive aspects (the flowering of some singer-songwriters who'd been quietly exploring psychological and personal crannies amid the excitement of the past few years), but often the retreat was less a planned withdrawal than a rout. This was particularly obvious in the AM-dominated singles market, where Altamont's bad vibes combined with Vice President Spiro Agnew's increasingly strident attacks on rock culture to make already timid AM stations even more cautious, or perhaps cowardly.

Thus in the last full week of 1969, Peter, Paul, and Mary, who, since the civil rights era, had worked free at almost every demonstration worth the name, finally achieved their first number-one hit ever, with John Denver's "Leaving on a Jet Plane," an entirely innocuous ditty guaranteed to offend no one. Then B. J. Thomas checked in with Burt Bacharach and Hal David's mechanically sprightly "Raindrops Keep Fallin' on My Head." With an enormous boost from the hit movie *Butch Cassidy and the Sundance Kid*, "Raindrops" remained the number-one song for a month. It was a harmless enough record—adult bubblegum—but very much in the Brill Building tradition; the song was written, arranged, and shopped around to various singers, including Ray Stevens and Bob Dylan (?!), before Bacharach gave it to journeyman B. J. Thomas (whom, also in best Brill Building tradition, he prudently signed to a management contract).

Adult bubblegum was immediately followed by soul bubblegum when Motown brought forth the Jackson 5. There are many versions floating around about the Jacksons' "discovery." For years, the official Motown line credited Diana Ross, but it's likely that Bobby Taylor (of the markedly less glamorous and successful Vancouvers) was actually the first Motown performer to recommend the group to Gordy. By that time, however, the Gary, Indiana, band had already recorded three singles and was a regular supporting act at Chicago's Regal Club, opening for the Tempts and Gladys Knight, among other Motown performers. It was there, in fact, that Freddie Perren, who (as part of "The Corporation," with Fonce Mizell, Deke Richards, and an ex *officio* Gordy) wrote and produced the group's first three Motown singles, first saw them. He was playing piano with Jerry Butler, and the Jackson 5 was opening: "Michael was tiny," he has remembered, "and I felt so sorry for him, because it was a nightclub. I said this little kid's gonna go out there and they're gonna murder him. Michael went out there and brought the house down. I wish we had gone on first."

By then the Jackson 5 had been performing for almost three years. Five of nine children belonging to Joe and Katherine Jackson, they'd gotten their start when the second oldest son, Tito, began fooling around after school with his father's discarded guitar. Joe Jackson had been in an R&B group called the Falcons (a Gary band, not the Detroit aggregation that featured Wilson Pickett and Eddie Floyd), but as his family began to grow, the Falcons weren't bringing in enough money, and he took a job in one of Gary's steel mills. His old guitar meant a lot to him, though, so Tito's first reward for playing it was corporal punishment. Only after that did his father say, "Now, let's see how well you're playing that thing."

Well enough, it turned out, that when brothers Jackie and Jermaine joined on vocals, it appeared that Joe Jackson's sons might be able to take up the family trade he'd been forced to abandon. When Marlon and five-year-old Michael joined in, and a couple of cousins signed on to play piano and drums, the Jackson 5 went pro. Almost immediately it became clear that Michael was their main attraction. They could all sing pretty well, and all of them danced, but Michael was a diminutive dervish, a portable James Brown. Best of all, from a practical point of view, he was almost irresistibly cute, and for a long time, the band made more money from the spontaneous outpouring of bills and coins from their audiences than they did from club owners.

Even with Gordy's famous "allowance" system in force, this would all change when the Jacksons reached Motown. But not in a hurry. First Gordy sent them to the label's headquarters in Los Angeles, where Motown's West Coast manager, producer Hal Davis, started them on intense prerecording rehearsals. After they'd been out there for a while, studying deportment, Perren, Mizell, and Richards came into the studio with a song they'd written with Gordy for Gladys Knight and the Pips. When they got the rhythm track down, however, the three thought the sound on "I Wanna Be Free" was good enough that Gordy might give it to Diana Ross. When they played it for Gordy, however, he announced it was indeed just right—but for the Jackson 5, and so could they rewrite the lyrics. They did, and soon set about teaching what was now called "I Want You Back" to the Jacksons. Former schoolteacher Freddie Perren was the professor: "To produce the way I produce," he has said, "there is an element of teaching, because you have to teach them the song the way you want it sung, so they know it before they begin to express it themselves."

Though older artists might have been allowed room to "express" a song themselves, the emphasis for the Jackson 5's debut was on getting it right. "I remember us working on 'I Want You Back' for three weeks," Jermaine recalled. "Just rehearsing it and rehearsing it. The Corporation—Berry Gordy, Fonce Mizell, Deke Richards, and Freddie Perren—wrote it and they wanted the song a certain way. When we got it right, then we recorded it." The effort was amply repaid; "I Want You Back" was—is—a great record. The Sly-ified rhythm track, with its pronounced popping bass lines, cut right through anything else that was playing on the radio, and Michael Jackson's lead vocal had all the boundless energy you would expect from a ten-year-old, but the high voltage was channeled by the sort of control that comes only with years of practice—which, of course, Michael had. Finally, the hook was unforgettable. Everything about the record (except, perhaps, for Michael Jackson's genes) was contrived and manipulated, and it thoroughly deserved to be number one.

Apparently included among the millions of Americans who couldn't get "I Want You Back" out of their heads was Freddie Perren. In line with Motown's "if you've got a hit, do it again" philosophy, he and his co-workers set out to craft the follow-up: "The music of 'ABC' is the chorus of 'I Want You Back,'" he told Fred Bronson. "All we did was take that music and keep playing it, adding a couple of steps to it. We cut the track for 'ABC' before 'I Want You Back' was really a big hit." Lightning struck twice with "ABC," then a third time with "The Love You Save," making the Jackson 5 the first rock performers to have their first three singles top the charts.

After that, Gordy struck. With brilliant timing and typical keep-'em-humble logic, he removed the Jackson 5 from their original producers and shifted them to Hal Davis. As perhaps an even greater gamble, Gordy wanted to break the up-tempo pattern of their hits and, if such a thing could be possible after three consecutive number ones, broaden their appeal even further by giving them a ballad to sing. Gordy's gamble paid off handsomely when "I'll Be There" not only reached number one but became Motown's largest selling record yet.

Without taking anything away from the admittedly special talents of the Jackson 5, their unprecedented—and unsucceeded—feat of four number ones in four tries implied a considerable amount of room at the top of the singles charts (although the album market remained somewhat more adventurous). Retreating from Altamont, the Rolling Stones went through the entire year without charting a single, and though the Beatles had two number ones (and George Harrison a solo third), all were gentle; none rocked with any authority. The gap was filled, for a time, by bands whose confident strut marked them as obvious heirs of the 1960s—Sly's "Thank You (Falettinme Be Mice Elf Again)," the Guess Who's "American Woman," and Three Dog Night's "Mama Told Me (Not to Come)"—but for two of the three bands, that well was running dry.

Because he was by far the most talented and inventive of the three, Sly's dry spell (it would be almost two years before he again returned to the Top Ten) was the most painful. Especially after the integrationism of "Everyday People," a number of the black political and social leaders he admired began to urge Sly to be more black-centered in his writing and performing. This was, on another level, similar to the pressure Jimi Hendrix had felt, and Sly's manager, David Kapralik, later told *Rolling Stone* that "Sylvester Stewart had enormous pressures on him to align himself with the voices of despair and nihilism. . . . The poor kid was torn apart." In retrospect, "Thank You (Falettinme . . .)" certainly doesn't sound all that frightening, but in its wake, Sly lost a good part of his white audience. Still, it is emphatically not necessary to accept Kapralik's judgment that those black voices close to Sly were expressing "despair and nihilism" to realize that Sly was caught between a rock and a hard place—and to regret that he chose the (Peruvian) rock, heavy consumption of which caused his appearances to become more and more erratic. In Washington, an audience waited some five hours for Sly to show up (doing several thousand dollars' worth of damage to the theater in the restive interim), and other audiences waited in perpetuity.

By the time of their greatest hit, the Guess Who was also troubled, though in a more workaday way. The band had been together for almost seven years by the time "American Woman" hit, but had been through a number of personnel changes during those years. Founding member and lead vocalist Chad Allan left during the group's first U.S. tour in 1965 and was replaced by another Canadian, Burton Cummings. Cummings and another founding member, guitarist Randy Bachman, were the core of the group for the next five years. Though they had several Canadian hits, largely because they were regulars on the CBC's weekly "Where It's At" show, they didn't break through in the States until 1969, with "These Eyes" (number 6) and "Laughing" (number 10). By the time "American Woman" charted, however, Cummings and Bachman had already fallen out. Some of their disagreements were artistic, but most had to do with life on the road. During the year, Bachman converted to Mormonism and, as a result, grew increasingly uncomfortable with the band's life on the road. Before the year was out, he quit (eventually to form Bachman-Turner Overdrive).

Three Dog Night, which had a considerably longer and more successful career ("Mama Told Me [Not to Come]" was only the first of three number-one singles), was an uninspiring but solidly professional seven-member aggregate featuring three lead vocalists—Cory Wells, Chuck Negron, and Monkee-reject Danny Hutton. Though they wrote little of their own material, they were tasteful and catholic in their selections from other writers. Not only did "Mama Told Me" bring a Randy Newman song to the top of the charts for the first time, but in 1972, they rescued Earl Robinson's and David Arkin's integrationist anthem, "Black and White," from nearly twenty years of neglect and carried it, too (in a fairly honorable arrangement), to the number-one position. As a singles-oriented band with soul echoes, successful enough to score eighteen consecutive top-twenty hits, they were considerably kinder to songwriters than critics who admired those songwriters were to them; if the passage of time hasn't made them any better than professional, their craftsmanship has spared them the embarrassment time has visited on a number of more ambitious bands.

Still, among the year's top singles, the cutting edge came from a most unlikely source: Motown. After the success of "Love Child" and "Cloud Nine," Gordy had given Norman Whitfield and Barrett Strong a green light to psychedelicize—and politicize—the Temptations. Among the songs they wrote as part of this effort was "War," included on the Tempts' *Psychedelic Shack*. The album included other songs dealing with social issues, but "War" received an attention-getting amount of play on college radio stations, and there was some thought of releasing the album cut as a single. But in order not to compete with the Tempts' already scheduled "Ball of Confusion (That's What the World Is Today)," the song, with an extremely similar rhythm track, was ceded to Edwin Starr and gave him his first and only number-one hit (Motown's next 1970 number one, Diana Ross's remake of the 1967 Marvin Gaye–Tammi Terrell hit, "Ain't No Mountain High Enough," was startling in its six-minute album version, but most of the tension and interest was edited out of the hit single).

Though 1970 surely produced more than its share of weak chart-toppers (other artists who either reached or started toward number one during the year included the Carpenters, the Partridge Family, Bread, Dawn, and the Osmonds), the year's number-one number one would have been among the great songs of any year. Paul Simon's writing had begun a noticeable move away from English-major "sensitivity" and toward a more universal variety with the 1968 hit *Bookends*. Though a follow-up was much awaited, it was delayed partly because Simon was a slow worker, partly because Garfunkel was filming *Catch-22*. Because of the film, Simon told *Rolling Stone*, many of the cuts are essentially solos, and the occasions when the two did manage to get together were marred by moments of tension that endured long after the album was winging up the charts. Ironically, one of these struck the two old high-school buddies during the recording of Simon's soaring hymn to the value and pleasures of enduring friendship, "Bridge Over Troubled Water." For whatever reasons, Garfunkel "didn't want to sing it himself. . . . He felt I should have done it. And many times I think I'm sorry I didn't do it. . . . when I'd be sitting off to the side . . . and Artie would be singing 'Bridge,' people would stomp and cheer when it was over, and I would think, 'That's my song, man. Thank you very much, I wrote that song.' . . . It's not a very generous thing to think, but I did think that."

By the time Simon wrote "Bridge" in 1969, he'd already been a rock 'n' roller, a folkie, a Brill Building popster, and an international rock star; despite the richness of this background, however, he was often regarded as just one more among the group that was beginning to be called the singer-songwriters. The term is something of a catch-all, designed to include anyone who in another era would likely have been called a folkie, wasn't in a band, wrote his or her own songs, and performed them in a way that implied the lyrics were more important than (certainly) the beat and (maybe) the melody. Though the imprecise inclusiveness hints that the descriptive phrase might have been coined by a promo man trying to piggyback a record onto the air ("They're very hot now, singer-songwriters, very hot"), the phenomenon, at least on the major-stardom level, was comparatively new. One of the many reasons that Dylan stood out so was that in the post-Beatles era, rock was essentially music made by *groups*. Even by the loosest interpretation, the last singer-songwriter to top the singles charts had been Johnny Rivers, with his co-written "Poor Side of Town," in 1966. Socially, too, the era had been one of communalism, a coming together that reached its spiritual apex at Woodstock, its nadir at Altamont. It is perhaps not entirely coincidental that 1971 saw an outburst of solo performers as a generation suffered an Altamont-induced hangover; over the period of a few months, even though singer-songwriters scored their greatest successes in the album market, singles by Carole King, James Taylor, Melanie, and Don McLean went to number one.

Of these, only King was a songwriter in the classic mode. Though she'd played in a high school rock 'n' roll band, the bulk of her professional career had been spent in the Brill Building, providing music for classics like "Up on the Roof" and "The Loco-Motion." In 1968, however, she began gigging with a couple of Village musicians, releasing an album, *Now That Everything's Been Said*, as the City. Though the album included "You've Got a Friend," it went nowhere. Encouraged by James Taylor (who obviously liked the song very much), King continued to perform sporadically as a single. In a guitar era, she was something of an anomaly, for she almost hid behind her piano, allowing the audience only fleeting glimpses of her. Her finely crafted lyrics worked in much the same way: introspective and self-referential, they appeared revelatory, but she held them, like precious artifacts, at a little distance.

By contrast, Melanie Safka had always wanted to be a performer and had studied acting at the American Academy of Dramatic Arts. She was writing songs even then, however, and in the late 1960s became a regular on the shrinking New York folk club circuit. Her 1969 "What Have They Done to My Song," was a top-twenty U.S. hit for the New Seekers, and she performed (as one of the folkie fill-ins when rain made using electronic instruments risky) at Woodstock. She delivered her always childlike and sometimes childish lyrics in a vulnerable, appealingly cracked voice, and though she sometimes essayed the grand scope ("Beautiful People," and the Woodstock-inspired "Lay Down [Candles in the Rain]"), her greatest commercial success came when she exploited her childlike vocal qualities in the sexual innuendo of "Brand New Key." Though the song was a number-one hit, it pinioned her image so firmly that she wound up withdrawing from performance until the whole thing blew over.

Don McLean was also a folkie, certified by no less than Pete Seeger, who chose him to perform at Hudson River Sloop benefits. This led to a year-long state-sponsored gig as 1968's "Hudson River Troubador," singing songs of ecological purity and American history up and down the Hudson. This sense of historicity went into McLean's "American Pie," an eight-minute chronicle of American pop inspired by the airplane deaths of Ritchie Valens, the Big Bopper, and Buddy Holly. It wasn't quite a one-shot, but its effect was as stifling on McLean's career as "Brand New Key" had been on Melanie's, and for a number of years, he simply refused to play it at all, avoiding pop stardom to perform, with obvious pleasure and satisfaction, on the folkie circuit.

Though she would never achieve equal ranking as a singles artist, one of the most important of the first-wave singer-songwriters was Joni Mitchell, who wrote tough, unsparing first-person songs about herself, her friends, and her lovers (and sometimes about the, you know, meaning of life) and delivered them in a voice that sounded as though she'd swallowed a mouse. Initally this was not a winning combination. Her 1967 debut album missed the charts entirely, and 1968's *Joni Mitchell* scraped onto the charts at number 189. Like Randy Newman, Joni Mitchell enjoyed her early success from other people's covers: Judy Collins did "Michael from Mountains" and "Both Sides Now" (U.S. number 8, 1968), and Tom Rush's 1968 tape of "The Circle Game" was for a while the most requested song on Boston radio. But unlike him, she was a self-taught musician who'd moved from ukelele to guitar with the aid of a Pete Seeger instruction record she came across while she was a commercial art student at the Alberta College of Art in Calgary, Canada.

But, as she told *Rolling Stone*, "I didn't have the patience to copy a style that was already known," and after she left art school and moved to Toronto, she began to refine a percussive open-tuning strum as she performed in the city's coffeehouses. By the time she and her then-husband moved to Detroit in 1966, Mitchell had become a polished performer and almost immediately established herself—in a low-key folkie way—as a local star. Word of mouth then led to a couple of New York bookings and, as a result, a record contract with Warner Bros. But it wasn't until after she'd recorded a first album in her thin soprano that a change opened the way toward a career as more than a writer of other people's hits: "I used to be a breathy little soprano, then one day I found I could sing low. At first I thought I'd lost my voice forever. I could sing either a breathy high part or a raspy low part. Then the two came together by themselves. It was uncomfortable for a while, but I worked on it, and now I've got this voice."

She had a lower register now and swooped in and out of it with obvious delight, beginning to exhibit complete control of her mature style with 1970's *Ladies of the Canyon* (U.S. number 27), an album that also saw her shift away from self-conscious poetics and flash a wry sense of humor. When she applied it to herself, as she would in the next year's winning *Blue*, her sophisticated self-deprecation set her apart from near-rivals like Laura Nyro and Melanie. More significant than the differences among them, however, is the fact that the arrival of the singer-songwriter boomlet moved women into the pop forefront for the first time since the Beatles precipitated the decline of the girl groups. Laura Nyro recovered from her Monterey debacle and whiled her way through unexpected rhythms and soulish phrasing to achieve a solid cult following; Judy Collins moved from protest and art song to autobiographical reminiscence; Dory Previn pitilessly (except for a soupçon of self-pity) dissected her ex-husband, and old folkie Joan Baez emerged as a surprisingly effective memoirist. Still, the year's biggest splash was made by the middle-class male blues of James Taylor.

Taylor grew up in an atmosphere of privilege; his father was dean of a North Carolina medical school, and the family regularly summered on the island of Martha's Vineyard. There, during his early teens, Taylor began playing local hoots, but winters found him back in boarding school, where he grew so depressed he wound up spending nearly a year as a patient at the McLean Psychiatric Hospital in Massachusetts. Discharged from the hospital, Taylor headed for Greenwich Village, where he (1) joined old Vineyard friend Danny Kortchmar in a band called the Flying Machine, and (2) began to shoot smack. As a result of (2), (1) didn't last very long, and partly in an attempt to kick, Taylor fled New York for London. There, armed with an introduction from Kortchmar, he auditioned for Peter Asher, who was then heading Apple Records' A and R operation, and became the label's first non-Beatle signing.

Despite the presence of "Carolina in My Mind," which later developed into a standard, Taylor's Apple album did not go far. It did, however, lend him some of the Beatles' cachet, and when he returned to America and (after yet another hospital stay, this one to treat his addiction) started performing again, people were eager to hear him. At a Gaslight gig early in 1970, more than 2,000 people showed up at the 150-seat club, and the long lines and traffic tie-ups along Greenwich Village's MacDougal Street led to a spate of newspaper coverage that brought attention to his just-released second record. When a single shipped, later in the summer (on Warner Bros., where Asher had gone from Apple), "Fire and Rain" took off, climbing to number three, the same slot reached by *Sweet Baby James*. Though the album was altogether less threatening than efforts by Mitchell or Leonard Cohen, its success wasn't undeserved, for Taylor was a first-rate acoustic guitarist and subtly fluid singer. Despite these virtues, however, his work even then seemed to be less a push *beyond* rock's conventions in the way that Cohen and Mitchell's more challenging compositions were than a retreat to safer ground. The ironic distance Taylor took from his own life in songs like "Knocking 'Round the Zoo" (a cheery ditty about his time in the bin) was itself perhaps a risk of sorts, but such cool detachment was a major step back from the freely embraced emotions—love, fear, envy, even the slightly simpleminded joy at just being there in front of the microphone in a recording studio—that had distinguished rock 'n' roll from Tin Pan Alley pop and, with a couple more turns of the screw, rock from rock 'n' roll.

The retreat wasn't musical; Taylor wrote melodies and arrangements of considerable complexity. The guitar chords on the verse of the deceptively simple "Anywhere Like Heaven" were G, G/F#, Em, G⁷, Am⁷, D, C, Bm, A, Am, G, G/F#, Em, G⁷, C, Am, F, C (whew). If not a long way from anywhere, this is surely a long way from the three-chord children of Woody. The retreat was spiritual—to a place where when joy knocked on the door, the peephole stayed open for an inordinately long time, and if the door finally opened a crack, the visitor had to go through a body search of soul-shriveling thoroughness.

Compared to Leonard Cohen, however, Taylor was Mr. Sunshine. Cohen, like Joni Mitchell a Canadian, was an established poet and novelist long before he became a performer, and he had a poet's practiced eye for unobtrusive metaphor (a lover's hair spread "across the pillow like a sleepy summer storm") and detail (Suzanne's "tea from China"). "Suzanne" originally appeared in a 1966 collection of Cohen's verse, and after he'd set some of the poems to old-folkie guitar chords, Judy Collins discovered both the song and the songwriter, helping his performing career by bringing him onstage during her concerts and arranging a Newport Folk Festival appearance for him. For all their moments of beauty, however, Cohen's songs project a vision of almost unrelieved bleakness. Indeed, there was a certain amount of sexual role reversal between the two Canadians: Mitchell came on as tough, adventurous, a devil-may-care romancer, and Cohen as a vulnerable, wounded victim. Only an extremely inattentive listener would willingly follow Suzanne to her place by the river after hearing Cohen's song.

Van Morrison, sometimes bruised, sometimes bruising, was perhaps the most protean of the group. He was essentially a beneficiary of the singer-songwriter vogue, for he had never been cut out to be a conventional pop star. Back in 1967, when he'd gone Top Ten with "Brown Eyed Girl," he said, "I'm sick of hearing 'what's your favorite color,' or 'what kind of girls do you like.' There was one point where these people I was with just thought that all there was in the world was interviews like that. I did about four a day, and I just got so pissed off I was ready to . . . Like all these teeny-bopper magazines. Everybody just asked me dumb questions and they had dumb faces. Bang Records was a mistake for me, it was the wrong label. That just wasn't my market."

There was at the time some question whether Morrison had *any* market. After his post-Them solo career crashed, he was reduced to working as a solo acoustic opening act for lesser musicians—and to doing so with such little success that a penny-throwing audience once chased him from the stage of New York's Café au Go Go. After too many nights like that one, he withdrew not only from performing but from America. Though all the evidence suggested Morrison was by then just another burnt-out pop case, he began writing again during his retreat to Belfast and returned to his Woodstock home with the music for his astonishing *Astral Weeks* in hand. Though his lyrics remained elusive, their spirit was more generous and open than his earlier work, and he was this time blessed with a record company, Warner Bros., that had shown itself willing to give audiences time to come to terms with uningratiating performers like Randy Newman and Joni Mitchell.

Warner Bros. assigned producer Lew Merenstein to the record, and he showed no signs of being frightened or put off by the complexities of Morrison's work. Merenstein assembled a great session cast (including Richard Davis on bass and Connie Kay, of the Modern Jazz Quartet, on drums), and put together outstanding string charts. The jazz-oriented rhythm section, Morrison's R&B voice, and the brassy strings combined with his writing to make a record about which critic Greil Marcus wrote, "With *Astral Weeks*, Morrison opened the way to a new career, and established himself as a performer who deserved to be ranked with the creators of the very best rock and roll music."

The record stiffed. It generated no singles and failed to reach the top two hundred albums. But it did generate some critical attention, as well as some FM play, and Warner Bros.' next move was something of a measure of the growing power of rock critics: a year later, the company brought Morrison back to the studio as his own producer. "It was the first time I'd ever done it," he said, "and I had to tax my imagination for all sorts of stuff," but the mutual gamble paid off. *Moondance* reached number twenty-nine on the albums chart, and the single, "Domino," went Top Ten. As a producer, Morrison demonstrated perhaps the best touch with horns north of Memphis; as a performer, though he would still have to wrestle with his private devils onstage, 1970 set him firmly on his way.

Meanwhile, Bob Dylan—who'd been a singer-songwriter before the term existed and would remain one after the vogue evaporated—was largely marking time. *New Morning* returned to the rhythms of rock after his country excursion, but the passionate edge that had made his early rock efforts so distinctive was largely missing. *Self-Portrait*, which as a portrait of the artist based on the songs by other people that had shaped him, was interesting as an intellectual concept, but Dylan's interpretations added nothing to the originals Elvis, Jerry Lee Lewis, Hank Williams, the Everly Brothers, and even Paul Simon had recorded. Perhaps the best indication of a failure of imagination that his fans hoped was only temporary was his decision to publish his long-delayed novel, *Tarantula*. He'd known it was a wreck—he'd refused to publish it during the earlier period when his musical creativity was strong—and his earlier judgment was confirmed by the critical disapprobation (or, worse yet, yawns) it received.

Whether for good or evil, however, there were signs that he was coming out of his reclusive shell. He moved back to Greenwich Village from Woodstock and began to be seen occasionally in local watering holes. More oddly, he gave his hat a second tip to high culture by appearing at Princeton University's graduation to accept an honorary degree.

This decision to honor Princeton by letting it honor him did not sit well with many of his admirers, for further escalation of the Vietnam War had plunged many of the nation's campuses into enraged and frustrated demonstrations. With the Nixon Administration leading cheers for the "silent majority's" backlash, a number of local officials overreacted. At Kent State University in Ohio, a largely peaceful demonstration ended in tragedy when panicky national guardsmen fired into the crowd, killing four people, and all across the country, student strikes shut down campuses in memorium.

The event was memorialized as well by Crosby, Stills, Nash, and Young, whose angry and pessimistic "Ohio" (number 14) showed that topical songs still retained some vitality—more vitality than the foursome that made it, actually, for after one more chart record, the back-to-the land "Our House," the group broke up. Though Stills subsequently recorded some pleasant enough country-rock as a solo and with the group Manassas, only Young retained much individual importance over the next years.

Among other Woodstock veterans, Joe Cocker criss-crossed the United States in 1970 with what seemed like a cast of thousands but was only Leon Russell and forty-two of his closest human and canine friends. Somewhere along the line, the entourage (and the album and film that followed) began to be called Mad Dogs and Englishmen, and except for the fact that it was midnight rather than the noonday sun that they basked in, the description was apt. It was, at any rate, an astonishing . . . *show* isn't quite the right word for it, actually; it implies a bit too much organization. *Event* is probably best. Leon Russell, racing from piano to organ, from stage right to stage left, retains Mephistophelian vividness, as does an infant in a basket downstage left and a trio of back-up singers (Rita Coolidge, for sure, Merry Clayton maybe, and someone else). Cocker, the ostensible star, was Trilby to Russell's Svengali, and it's no accident that when the carnival finally folded its tents, it was Russell, not Cocker, who emerged as its major figure. After years of session work, Mad Dogs and Englishmen was his ticket to stardom. It came perilously close, however, to being Cocker's ticket to the farm. He staggered away from it, exhausted and (given the size of his supporting cast) nearly broke, and returned to England, where he made only three public appearances—and no records—over the next year and a half.

While Cocker was exhausting himself, the Who were regrouping. Though *Tommy* had rocketed them to the critics' pantheon—and had been the band's largest-selling album by far—it had been a couple of years in the making, and even leaving aside the market imperatives that called for a quick successor, the elaborate opera was a tough act to follow. They responded to their own challenge the way Dylan had responded to *Sgt. Pepper:* They simplified. First, they bought time with a concert album, *Live at Leeds,* consisting primarily of pre-*Tommy* material (U.S. number 4), then went into the studio to begin recording what is probably their best album, *Who's Next.* Like the live album, *Who's Next* would be straight-ahead rock 'n' roll, but with the key difference that it gave play to Townshend's work on the synthesizer—and to the sound that would be theirs over the next several years.

With the single and highly important exception of Creedence Clearwater Revival, a band that continued to crunch out wonderful singles despite their straight-ahead, East Bay rock having for years seemed too simple to satisfy San Francisco's flowery aspirations, San Francisco was in disarray. The Dead, still exploring their country vein, were a visible and audible presence, but Big Brother was rudderless and the Airplane, with Jorma Kaukonen and Jack Casady devoting their energies to their new band, Hot Tuna, in limbo. To the extent that there was a future implied (rather than Creedence's recapitulations of the past, however brilliant), it seemed to be in the Afro-Cuban synthesis of Santana and the funk of Oakland's Tower of Power.

Honorary San Franciscans Ten Years After rode the Woodstock wave to hit the U.S. top fifteen with the unlikely *Cricklewood Green,* but the British blues boom appeared to have played itself out (by this time, Alvin Lee and Co. were such regulars on the New York and San Francisco scenes that they hardly counted any longer as British). Traffic, for instance, moved well away from its blues beginnings to record the folk-influenced *John Barleycorn Must Die,* earning its first gold record. Among younger British bands, the heavier sound inspired by Led Zep was dominant. Free, which had been gigging for a couple of years, hit with "All Right Now" (U.S., number 4; U.K., number 2) and a U.S. top twenty album. Less melodic and lots louder, Birmingham's Black Sabbath also had a hit single, "Paranoid" (U.S., number 61; U.K., number 4), which brought their earlier album, *Black Sabbath*, to number 23 in America. Deep Purple did a mid-year metamorphosis from enlightened psychedelia *(Deep Purple For Group and Orchestra)* to hard rock *(Deep Purple in Rock)*; and Mott the Hoople offered pared-down rock with its debut album, *Mott the Hoople* (U.S. number 185).

Led Zeppelin, by far the dominant British band, continued on a roll, scoring its second straight U.S. number-one album *(Led Zeppelin III)*, and its first and only Top Ten single, "Whole Lotta Love" (U.S. number 4). Increasingly, the band would add explorations of Celtic myth to its work, and though this seems yet another reprise of a British preoccupation with legend and fantasy, Led Zep's instrumental experimentation kept the band anything but anachronistic. At about this time, indeed, Page began working with strummed acoustic tracks under his electric solos, establishing a style that a number of U.S. bands (Heart, for example, and Boston) would still be echoing almost a decade later.

The premier British blues guitarist, Eric Clapton, was also moving away from the form. He opened 1970 in the studio with some veterans of the Delaney and Bonnie tour, and the album that resulted yielded his first top-twenty hit, J. J. Cale's country-tinged shuffle, "After Midnight" (number 18). That studio experience convinced him that he could organize a non-supergroup band, and even before the solo album was released, Clapton had begun Derek and the Dominos with Carl Radle, Bobby Whitlock, and Jim Gordon. Together they produced what was unquestionably the year's outstanding song, "Layla." This melting, multilayered monument, from the double album *Layla*, would have been among the great records of any year, raised to the pantheon by the Anglo-American twin lead guitars of Clapton and Duane Allman.

Allman eventually got to be known as part of the Allman Brothers band, but his first success came as a studio musician for Rick Hall at Muscle Shoals. This brought him to the attention of Atlantic's Jerry Wexler, who eventually signed him to a solo contract. They'd actually begun to work under the Allman Brothers name when Clapton and company came down to Criterion Studios in Miami to record *Layla*. Allman had once driven all the way from Los Angeles to San Francisco to hear Clapton play, so when he learned that the band was coming into town, he called Atlantic's super-engineer Tom Dowd to make sure he could come over and watch: "So I went down to listen, and Eric knew me, man, greeted me like an old friend! The cat is really a prince—he said, 'Come on, you got to play on this record'—and so I did. We'd sit down and plan it out, work out our different parts and try it one time. Then we'd say, 'Well, let's try some more of this in here, and some of that in there,' everybody contributed, just sorting it out, Memphis-style. Most of it was cut live, not much overdubbing—and it was all done in ten days." The title song, largely because a mental subtraction of Allman's high slide leaves what feels like a complete track, certainly sounds overdubbed—and perfectly so. The effect is of Allman finding, or somehow inventing, holes in its solid structure and filling them with a lachrymose intensity that raises the song's already high emotional stakes another notch or two.

By then, the band that Allman had assembled (a partial reunion of the old Allman Joys/Hourglass pulled together from shards of two Jacksonville groups called the 31st of February and the Second Coming) was at work on its second album, *Idlewild South*. The first, *The Allman Brothers Band* (U.S. number 188) had been a regional hit in the South, where one or another version of the band had been gigging for close to ten years, and when the band began to tour nationally, nearly everyone who heard them wanted something to remember them by; *Idlewild South* was a solid success, reaching number thirty-eight on the album charts. Though the band's trademark sound—Gregg Allman's laconic, contorted blues vocals and percussive keyboards, Duane Allman's and Dickey Betts's twinned and twined lead guitars, the double drums of Jai Johanny Johanson and Butch Trucks, Berry Oakley's understated, unflappable bass—was already there on the first album, it was as a live act that they reached their highest levels. Stretching out a blues, like a (much) more disciplined Grateful Dead, the band offered an unequaled combination of fire and precision. Betts wasn't an Eric Clapton (indeed, after Duane's death, there were too many occasions when he wasn't even Dickey Betts), but there were nights when Allman's guitar struck something in him and the two equaled anything *Layla* had to offer. As the year ended, some argued persuasively that the Allmans were already America's best rock group, and it seemed they would only grow better.

On October 29, 1971, however, Duane Allman was killed in a motorcycle accident, and though the band soldiered on gamely, death cut short the possibilities of greatness. It is perhaps a measure of Altamont's symbolic power that despite the quantity of brilliant music produced in its wake by Altamont performers, the year seemed at the time to be dominated by death. Within a few autumn weeks of each other, three performers who'd contributed to both the myth and the reality of Monterey and Woodstock were dead.

Canned Heat's Al Wilson was first. Nearly blind, Wilson had for a long time been subject to fits of depression, which he had increasingly been holding at bay with heroin. Over the summer, the band had launched a small blues counterinvasion of England, performing at the Isle of Wight Festival and earning an international hit with Wilbert Harrison's "Let's Work Together." By the time it peaked on the charts, however, Wilson was dead of a drug overdose, in Torrance, California, September 3, 1970.

Jimi Hendrix was next, two weeks later, in London. He, too, had performed at the Isle of Wight in August, with bassist Billy Cox and original

Experience member Mitch Mitchell on drums. It had been a mixed year for Hendrix; its early hours found him onstage at Fillmore East, headlining a New Year's Eve concert with his new Band of Gypsies (Cox and drummer Buddy Miles). The recordings of that performance, the only record released by the band, is better than the show seemed at the time, but compared to its stunning predecessors, the live album is pretty lackluster. Hendrix himself seemed troubled by the direction the band was taking, and during an antiwar benefit concert held that spring in Madison Square Garden, he suddenly stopped playing and walked offstage in the middle of the band's set. Soon, however, his Electric Ladyland studio in Greenwich Village was finished, and Hendrix spent most of the summer working out in it, sometimes alone, sometimes with a shifting cast of friends, often with Cox and Mitchell, with whom he recorded the last album he authorized, *Cry of Love*.

It was a creditable album, but not, by Hendrix's standards, a breakthrough. Talking to *Rolling Stone* after Hendrix's death, the studio's supervising engineer, Eddie Kramer, gave some idea of those standards: "He had to have everything just perfect . . . and he never did the same thing twice. He'd lay down tracks, and every time he put his guitar over it and played it different. Sometimes he'd take tapes home and listen to them all night, and the next day he'd come in and do it entirely different. You should have seen him—he'd be down there grimacing and straining, trying to get it to come out of the guitar the way he heard it in his head. If you could ever transcribe the sound in a man's head directly onto the tape . . . Whew!" Kramer also expressed the fear—justifiable, as events proved—that Hendrix's high standards would be posthumously trashed by the release of uncompleted work.

Hendrix had, indeed, hardly died when the spiritual warfare for his corpse and legacy began. Death came to him mid-morning on September 18. At about 10:20 that morning, Monika Danneman, in whose London flat he'd spent the night, woke up to find him sleeping normally. She needed cigarettes, and as she told a Coroner's Court, "just before I was about to go out, I looked at him again and there was sick on his nose and mouth. I tried to wake him up but couldn't. I then saw that he had taken some of my sleeping pills. They are German and are called Vesperax. They are in packets of ten and I thought he had taken the lot, but a policeman found one on the floor. He must have taken them shortly after I started to go to sleep [at about 7 A.M.]. He would have had to get out of bed and go to a cupboard to get the tablets." Danneman phoned a friend for advice, then called an ambulance. Though he was still alive when it arrived, Hendrix died en route to the hospital.

The coroner, unable to find evidence arguing persuasively for either accident or suicide, reported an open verdict, but Eric Burdon caused a momentary stir when he announced that he had a copy of a five-page poem Hendrix wrote to Danneman shortly before his death. It was, he said, a "suicide note." On BBC television, Burdon claimed that Hendrix "made his exit when he wanted to," and further announced Hendrix was ". . . handing me a legacy to continue the work of bringing the audio-visual medium together." This last seems to have been a plug for a never-released film Burdon was working on called *The Truth About Jimi Hendrix.*

There were films about Janis Joplin, too. Unlike Hendrix, who seemed directionless in his final months, she'd appeared to have a good year, musically. The Kozmic Blues Band, her first post–Big Brother band, made its final appearance with her at a Madison Square Garden concert in December of 1969. It had not lived up either to her hopes or to Grossman's, and after their first San Francisco appearance, Ralph J. Gleason had written in the *San Francisco Chronicle* that "the new band is a drag. They can play OK but they are a pale version of the Memphis-Detroit bands from the rhythm & blues shows and Janis, though in good voice, seems bent on becoming Aretha Franklin. . . . The best thing that could be done would be for her to scrap this band and go right back to being a member of Big Brother . . . (if they'll have her)." She didn't do that; though she jammed with the re-formed Big Brother at Winterland in April of 1970. Full Tilt Boogie Band was coming together, and she debuted with them in Lexington, Kentucky, on June 12. They gigged throughout the summer, closing before forty thousand fans at Harvard Stadium in August, then headed west to Los Angeles to begin recording their first album together. By all accounts, including the finished evidence of *Pearl,* the sessions were going well, and late on the afternoon of October 4, Joplin was to pick up her fiancée, Seth Morgan, at the Burbank Airport. She didn't show, and when road manager John Cooke saw her car still in the lot at the Landmark Motor Hotel, he went up to her room to look for her. He found her, dead, facedown on the carpet a few steps inside her room. The Los Angeles coroner later determined she'd died from an overdose of heroin, a drug she'd had an on-and-off affair with for most of her performing life. On March 20, 1971, she achieved her first and only number-one single with the posthumously released "Me and Bobby McGee."

The deaths of Hendrix and Joplin within a three-week period hit the music and its fans hard, making the final breakup of the Beatles seem almost an anticlimax. In a sense, though autopsies for the group still go on, it was, for the signs had been obvious for more than a year. On April 9, 1970, Paul finally pulled the plug. On that date, he released advance copies of the solo album he'd quietly recorded at his Scottish farm. Ringo had gone to Scotland to ask McCartney to hold it so as not to interfere with *Let It Be,* but as Ringo later testified in a court action, "To my dismay, he went completely out of control, shouting at me, prodding his fingers toward my face and saying 'I'll finish you now' and 'You'll pay.'" After that, it came as small surprise when advance copies of the solo album carried with it a self-conducted "interview" in which McCartney announced that the Beatles were finished, because of "personal differences, business differences, musical differences—but most of all because I have a better time with my family."

There were hopes that this might be yet another false alarm—Apple, indeed, put out a press release hinting cautious optimism—but McCartney didn't relent. In London, on December 31, 1970, he brought suit in High Court to dissolve the Beatles' partnership officially. Except for the squabbling over money, the year, the Beatles, and an era had ended.

THE
SEVENTIES
AND BEYOND

by
KEN TUCKER

THE EARLY 1970s

On December 31, 1970, Paul McCartney filed a legal motion in London High Court against "The Beatles Company," the first step to dissolve legally the most popular rock band in the history of the music. "The Long and Winding Road," the Beatles hit single released earlier that year, might have been used as evidence of why the breakup was appropriate or, indeed, necessary. Maudlin, turgid, and maddeningly self-indulgent, produced by Phil Spector as a Wall of Sludge, "The Long and Winding Road" was not the way to remember the band that had changed the face of popular music.

Indeed, even at the dawn of the 1970s, it was clear that the Beatles and the important bands that followed in their wake had dramatically expanded the entire idea of what constituted rock and roll. The Beatles had shown that virtually anything, from Indian raga to your last acid flashback, could inspire the composition of a rock song. Artists felt increasingly free to pursue their own interests. If you liked soft melodies and precise word play, you didn't have to worry about being scorned as a throwback to Steve & Eydie—there was a whole group of adult postfolkies exploring this sort of thing: singer-songwriters. If, on the other hand, you were a classically trained pianist who liked to dabble in metaphysics in your spare time, well, so were a healthy percentage of your rock music colleagues, and thus was born art rock. In this sense, the growing size of the rock audience and the industry that had grown up to accommodate it encouraged fragmentation by encouraging musicians' ambitions. For a while there it was possible to create whatever you wanted, because chances were there was a market for it, and certainly there was an increasingly sophisticated business surrounding it to make your experiment known to a mass audience.

467

And the size of the rock audience was growing. The teens who had screamed at John-Paul-George-Ringo were now in their twenties; the bemused Chuck Berry fans were now in their thirties—but the audience was also expanding with the constant additions of new, young fans as well. Whereas in the previous two decades, a record was a hit if it sold half a million copies, by the middle of the seventies, a big hit was expected to "go multiplatinum"—to sell in multiples of a million copies. Major acts found themselves obliged to perform before larger numbers of people. Very quickly, the concept of spontaneous mass events like Woodstock metamorphosed into an efficiently organized business of stadium concerts— major acts now filled arenas that had previously been reserved for sporting events.

In the previous decade, rock was the stuff of the counterculture; in the 1970s and on into the 1980s, this music *was* the culture. In the 1960s, the music's authenticity was measured by the distance it placed between its rebellious, unkempt, adversarial point of view and the acquiescent, mannerly, tame world of professional entertainment. In the 1970s, this notion gradually came to be viewed as unrealistic and immature. For some long-time rock fans, this was proof positive that rock was no longer any good, that it had sold out and become family entertainment only slightly more daring than Buddy Hackett's nightclub act. For others, though, it suggested the enormous outreach and ambition of the music. For the first time in its history, large numbers of people began to think that maybe rock and roll really *was* here to stay; that it could grow and become an artistic medium that could adapt to its aging audience as well as continue to attract the young fans who would remain the lifeblood of the music. What some saw as the death of rock as a challenging, creative medium, others recognized as an opportunity to spread the music's diverse messages to an unprecedented number of people. And, in some cases, to get rich while doing it.

Let's not underestimate that last part. The first half of the 1970s enjoyed an economy that could support an industry growing at the steady rate of 25 percent each year. The economic drain of the Vietnam War hadn't hit the average music consumer, and with the fall of Saigon in 1975, it was assumed that more able-bodied citizens would be out there roaming the shopping malls with ready discretionary income. Which is to say, the audience for rock was exploding, fueled by enough money to transform the music into big business.

It's significant that at the start of the decade, the cant term for music within the industry was *product:* The music had become merchandise to be packaged and sold. Following good capitalist theory, the music industry began to approach its product as a series of alternatives, of choices for the consumer. This was the neatest way to package the growing sprawl of 1970s popular music, and thus the profusion of products lining the record store shelves arranged by neat labels: *singer-songwriters, heavy metal, soft rock, art rock, country rock, disco, reggae,* and *punk.*

Radio, too, was discovering what television had already learned: demographics. The 1960s radio revolution—free-form programming, in which a rock record was followed by jazz followed by a cut from Joan Baez's latest—became passé. The notion of *formating*, of programming a certain kind of music for a certain segment of the audience to sell a certain kind of product, became the prevailing practice. By the end of the decade, the result would be the rise of AOR—"album-oriented rock." Radio stations that chose this format offered listeners a strict diet of white hard rock artists, from Led Zeppelin to name-this-week's-heavy-metal-rage. The idea was to attract the ideal demographic group for advertisers—white teenagers with discretionary income to burn. As a business move, it worked. Similar formats included soft rock (pass the James Taylor, please) and urban contemporary (biz code for black music).

Does this suggest a conservative turn in the history of rock? Sure, even as it mirrors that same turn in the world in which this music existed. The crucial American political event in 1970 was the killing of four students by the National Guard during a Vietnam War protest at Ohio's Kent State University. The crucial American political event in 1980 was the election of President Ronald Reagan, he of the conservative "mandate." In between, we lived through what Tom Wolfe indelibly christened the "Me Decade." At its baldest, this meant "me first," a notion confirmed in the autobiographical musings of the singer-songwriters and by the bold self-assertiveness of much black pop music as well as the look-at-me tantrums of the punks.

At its subtlest, however, it meant a reexamination of what rock music was and of what it could be. The music, its audience, and its industry would spend the seventies tussling with such self-consciousness; it would emerge from its tumultuous contemplation in the eighties a reinvigorated art form, still able to excite, to shock, to comfort, and to inspire.

27

THE INVASION OF THE SINGER-SONGWRITERS

Singer-songwriters were the first notable rock movement to emerge in the 1970s. The music being produced by such artists as James Taylor, Joni Mitchell, and Carole King was intimate, confessional, and "personal" music, with precise, semiautobiographical lyrics and moderate amplification—at a time when rock could make your ears ring. As such, it was highly appealing to one of the audience's largest segments: young urban collegiates—proto-yuppies—people old enough to remember the folk-music boom of the sixties but who first got really excited about popular music with the Beatles.

Indeed, upon the breakup of the Beatles, it looked as if the now-dispersed members of the ultimate rock band were going to become singer-songwriters themselves. Each of the four left that group with the urge to establish his individuality, to explain to the huge audience the Beatles had created what he thought of that experience, and to introduce ideas and musical styles that the built-in democracy of a group did not permit. John Lennon commenced 1970 by completing "Instant Karma!" in one day January 26. "I wrote it for breakfast, recorded it for lunch, and we're putting it out for dinner," he remarked. On April 10, Paul McCartney released his first solo album, *McCartney*, a homemade affair of tuneful, whimsical pop songs. On May 13, the now-ironical, dully literal-minded Beatles film *Let It Be* opened. On December 11, *John Lennon/Plastic Ono Band* was released, along with its first single, "Mother," the artistic fruit of four months of Lennon/Ono therapy with primal-scream therapist Arthur Janov. A year in the life . . .

471

The careers of all four of the post-Beatles describe details of death and rebirth, anger and release, revenge and reclusiveness. But while John Lennon and Paul McCartney embarked on work that challenged their previous group's music, George Harrison and Ringo Starr led far more uneven, equivocal careers.

Harrison had started off the 1970s with a bang, releasing *All Things Must Pass* (1970), a rock album whose lyrics evinced the dreamy spirituality to which Harrison was then devoted but whose music glowed with the pop-symphonic style of producer Phil Spector. (In 1976, the biggest hit from *All Things Must Pass*, "My Sweet Lord," would be the subject of a plagiarism suit brought by the authors of the 1960s Chiffons hit "He's So Fine," with the judge finding that Harrison had "unknowingly plagiarized" the tune. But in the early 1970s Harrison was riding high.)

In 1971, Harrison organized and hosted two concerts in New York's Madison Square Garden to benefit the starving people of Bangladesh. His guests included Ringo, Bob Dylan, and Eric Clapton, and the bestselling three-record set that resulted from these shows, *Concert for Bangladesh*, won a Grammy award. Harrison's Bangladesh effort can be viewed as a paradigm—and a cautionary tale—for the rock charity events that proliferated in the early 1980s: He devoted himself to a cause for which he felt passionately; the music that resulted was roundly enjoyed by millions; but the profits from the concerts became the object of considerable controversy. During an audit of the Beatle-founded Apple Records that lasted nine years, the Bangladesh concert profits were impounded; only $2 million, of profits, estimated to total at least five times that sum, had been sent to the needy in Africa through UNICEF. It was not until 1981 that UNICEF received a check for $8.8 million from Harrison and his colleagues. As well intentioned as Harrison had been, it became clear that rock's move into the area of charity needed more sophisticated business skills than Harrison and his organization could then muster.

As the seventies progressed, both he and Ringo Starr would all but pass from rock history. Harrison would form his own record label, Dark Horse, in 1974, but except for his tribute to John Lennon, "All Those Years Ago," a number-two chart success in 1981, he did not achieve commercial recognition after 1974.

He led such an increasingly reclusive life that in 1985, rock pioneer Carl Perkins spoke to an interviewer about a cable TV special in which he had appeared with Harrison and noted, "Before we went on, George was real nervous and I felt him freezin' right up on me. But then I pitched him a guitar break that he wasn't expecting. . . . I could tell by the grin on his face that his fears were leaving. His wife Olivia was just so happy; she told me after the taping, 'Carl, I don't know what to say to you, because I saw my old George so happy tonight. . . . I saw something there that I hadn't seen in a long time.' "

Ringo, by contrast, proceeded to lead a more public life in the 1970s and

1980s; with his wife, actress Barbara Bach, he would float through a succession of TV shows and movies. Starr's recording career began promisingly at the start of the 1970s with the heartfelt cover tunes that dominated *Sentimental Journey* and *Beaucoups of Blues* (both 1970), and with the hit singles "It Don't Come Easy," "Back Off Boogaloo," "You're Sixteen," "Oh My My," "Only You," "Photograph," and "No No Song," all early- to mid-1970s successes. In some ways, Starr's post-Beatles life is even more aimless and sad than Harrison's—always a limited singer with an adorable personality, Starr increasingly traded on his Beatles fame to prop up a half-hearted career.

John Lennon's post-Beatles life was the most complicated; at its deepest level, it was unknowable. *John Lennon/Plastic Ono Band* represented his cry of freedom from the rock band he'd come to hate as well as a demonstration of the power of his new partnership with Yoko Ono. With its release, Lennon was to spend the 1970s engaged in furious, often drastic political gestures, from the recording of rock-and-roll screeds to the example he set as a retired self-described "househusband."

In 1971, Lennon issued *Imagine*, an album of mostly carefully crafted material that proved John could match Paul as a pop tunesmith. By late December 1971, *Imagine* would become the number one record in the United States, and it was nothing less than a personal tour of the ironic Beatle's mental mansion. The song titles suggest the areas of revelation: "Jealous Guy," "Gimme Some Truth," "Oh Yoko!" "I Don't Want to Be a Soldier," "It's So Hard," "Crippled Inside." Fortunately, its confessional impulse was bolstered by extraordinary, rip-out-the-lungs vocals and beautifully unironic pop and rock melodies. During this time, too, Lennon and Ono cozied up to pop radicals such as Abbie Hoffman and Jerry Rubin, creating political rock music like the single "Power to the People" (1971) and the album *Some Time in New York City* (1972), the latter recorded with the New York band Elephant's Memory.

The man of whom Lennon asked, "How Do You Sleep?", the winsome Beatle, Paul, was trying to become a politically responsible singer-songwriter with the earnest-but-no-cigar "Give Ireland Back to the Irish," which was a bit too have-another-pint nostalgic to be effective, even if the BBC did grant it the honor of being banned. Yet Paul's life after the breakup is most easily understood: McCartney's best instincts were those of the businessman and the family man; he knew what he wanted and he went after it. McCartney rebuilt his musical career more completely than any of the other three—he had the most commercial success, with his band Wings, and he dealt with the burden of being an ex-Beatle with an offhand grace that is becoming of the man who wrote careful pop songs like "Michelle" and "The Long and Winding Road."

It was the Beatles' own company, Apple, that would help spur the singer-songwriter trend by debuting its archetypal artist, James Taylor, in 1968. But it was Taylor's second album, *Sweet Baby James*, released by Warner

Bros. in 1970, that virtually defined the genre. It was a collection of pretty melodies, romantic navel-gazing, and the dreamiest set of death wishes since Ray Peterson's "Tell Laura I Love Her" a decade earlier. Unlike that innocent bit of melodrama, however, Taylor's work was characterized by a confessional impulse tempered by a musical reserve that is anathema to the best rock and roll. He also possessed an ever-rare skill at extending a metaphor throughout the length of a song. It was primarily due to Taylor—a measure of the way he imposed his Sylvia Plath-in-a-denim-shirt sensibility on the rock world—that people began using the term *singer-songwriter* to describe the scribes who came in his wake.

And, boy, did they come—from Joni Mitchell to Crosby, Stills, and Nash, from Carole King to Jackson Browne. Just one thing, though: Was this music rock? Not according to Lester Bangs, to cite just one—though probably the most eloquent—demurrer. In 1971, Bangs, writing for a mimeographed rock magazine called *Who Put the Bomp?*, paused in the middle of a ten-thousand-word appreciation of the Troggs' "Wild Thing" to describe a dream he'd had about running a thin red line across Taylor's neck with a broken wine bottle. "That's how deep the feeling goes," wrote fellow critic Robert Christgau.

But love him or hate him, Taylor expanded the idea of what rock and roll was all about. For Taylor, it was, first and foremost, a vehicle for autobiography of the baldest sort. This is what distinguished him from his folkie forebearers even more than his use of rock instrumentation—that he conveyed almost no sense that there was a big world out there, that there were social issues and problems bigger than his own private obsessions.

Joni Mitchell would become Taylor's main competition, or parallel narcissist, although she expressed her self-absorption in more artful terms, yielding the high-water mark of the genre in 1971; *Blue*, a song cycle about being hypnotized by love and then breaking its trance that is unmatched for the power of its conversational details and beautifully complex melodies. By the time *Blue* reaches its conclusion with "The Last Time I Saw Richard," Mitchell sounds world weary and quietly angry, disgusted with her own commitment to romanticism. She had burrowed so far into herself that she transcended singer-songwriterly self-pity, to emerge a sharp, savvy artist. After *Blue*, Mitchell would continue to synthesize poetic precision, folk sensitivity, and rock rhythms on through the massively popular albums *For the Roses* (1972) and *Court and Spark*, before beginning a wayward affair with jazz. By 1979, she would be saying things like, "There is great rock and roll. But great rock and roll within the context of music, historically, is slight."

Along with *Blue*, Neil Young's *Harvest*, the February 1972 release that would become the most commercially successful album of his career, stands as a definitive 1970s singer-songwriter document. Quirky and personal, but not so much so that it could not yield a big hit single ("Heart of Gold"), *Harvest* was a model of the form: It alluded regularly to pastoral pleasures while deriding—and in the case of "The Needle and the Damage Done," confronting with some bravery—urban temptations. Although Young was allergic to needles himself, his bedraggled, perennially stoned-out look was nonetheless his badge of authenticity for an audience enthralled by anyone who looked as if he was in dire straits for chemical reasons. With his whiny voice and perpetual pout, Young could have been insufferable; instead, he backed up his pose with a gift for "poetic" lyrics sustaining metaphors and melodies that actually rocked hard instead of merely alluding to it—unlike, say, Don McLean's "American Pie," which by January 1972 was becoming the most popular song in the country. Another product of the now-entrenched singer-songwriter ethos, "American Pie" recast rock-and-roll history as a jaunty tune with tricky rhythms: bargain basement James Taylor.

Equalling McLean's commercial success—indeed, surpassing it—was Carole King and her megahit album *Tapestry*. Almost thirty by 1971, Carole King was more than an industry pro; she was an industry pro able to switch genres (from girl-group rock to singer-songwriter pop) without undue cynicism. When King sang "You've Got a Friend" in a warm, appealingly worn alto voice, she wasn't (merely) cashing in on a trend—she was apotheosizing it. With *Tapestry*, she came to embody the singer-songwriter movement that yielded James Taylor and Joni Mitchell and Neil Young—and, for that matter, Brewer and Shipley, whose "One Toke Over the Line" was banned by Manhattan's WNBC-AM on March 27, 1971, for the supposedly druggy implications of its title.

Within the first year of its release, *Tapestry* sold over five million copies. At the time, this was an unprecedented number for a pop album by an artist who, although she had helped create such early 1960s classics as Little Eva's "The Loco-Motion," was relatively unknown. The success moved Robert Christgau, writing in Long Island's *Newsday*, to exult, "*Tapestry* is a triumph of mass culture . . . [an] ineluctable cultural presence." Why? Because it had become one of the bestselling albums of all time while also being a first-rate rock album, one that offered proto-feminist notions within a pop context.

Tapestry was only the first of a series of 1970s blockbuster albums—records that sold so many copies that the sales figures pushed the music, good or not, into the realm of ineluctable cultural presences. The Woodstock generation, with its vast purchasing power, had become a community that could exert an influence on the rock industry. Translated into everyday terms, this most often meant no more than the fact that *Tapestry* became a de rigueur addition to every thoughtful young white person's record collection.

Soon, singer-songwriters were emerging in all shapes and sizes: Norman Greenbaum, the Tom Robbins of 1970, began what sounded like a highly promising career with the eccentric single "Spirit in the Sky," only to retire soon after to lead the life of a farmer. Rick Nelson—once Ricky Nelson, maker of excellent Hollywood rockabilly singles and teen-idol star of the TV show *The Adventures of Ozzie and Harriet*—was booed off the stage of Madison Square Garden on October 15, 1971, for not adhering to the oldies-only policy of the Richard Nader–produced nostalgia show at which he appeared. This experience inspired Nelson to write the very singer-song-writerly "Garden Party," self-conscious, soft, and catchy, and the result was a Top Ten hit in 1972.

The beginning of the 1970s was also rather kind to a true veteran singer-songwriter: Chuck Berry, who scored a surprise number-one hit single in 1972 with "My Ding-a-Ling." The song, his first certified million-seller and his first number one song on the pop charts, was taken from *The London Chuck Berry Sessions*, a lackluster collection of greatest hits plus this oddity. Some thought it pathetic that the great Berry should regain the spotlight on the strength of what was little more than a shouted bathroom joke, but the success had its own kind of justice: Its very immaturity introduced Chuck Berry to a whole new generation of kids who had no idea who he was.

That same year millions of people would spend the summer trying to guess who Carly Simon was talking to when she demurely sneered, "You probably think this song is about you." Warren Beatty (with whom Simon was said to be dallying)? Mick Jagger (who sang backup vocals on the record)? The critic Ellen Willis would remark that the success of "You're So Vain" proved that rock and roll is so democratic that even a rich person can make a great single, a bon mot that sums up one perfectly sensible response to this record. After all, the most Carly Simon (daughter of Richard Simon, half of publishing's Simon and Schuster) had contributed to rock before this was the insufferably self-pitying "That's the Way I've Always Heard It Should Be," a more modest hit the year before. And all Simon would go on to do would be to release a series of ever-more-shallow pop-rock albums, marry James Taylor, and have photographer Norman Seeff shoot her in a series of skimpy-clothed album-cover pinups. But at least once, on "You're So Vain," Simon transcended the assiduous pettiness of her career to give a great performance on a miraculously unknowable, beguiling song.

In 1972, Paul Simon would also enter the solo stakes after leaving Simon and Garfunkel, the most popular folk-pop duo of the era. His first solo release would be *Paul Simon*, a collection of sharply observed, deliberately small-scale pop songs that stood in luminous contrast to the bombastic, solemn "Bridge over Troubled Water." *Paul Simon* did not overreach for any grand metaphors; instead it homed in on quotidian specifics and ended up yielding a couple of hit singles: the reggae-inflected "Mother and Child Reunion" that went top five, intricate time changes and all, and the salsa-flavored "Me and Julio Down by the Schoolyard."

Some 1970s stars built their entire careers on hit singles, never managing (or bothering) to create albums that sustained the success they achieved through singles. For example, the Carpenters, despised by rock fans but beloved by the same people who adored the winsome, Paul McCartney side of the Beatles, began a long string of hit singles in 1970 with "(They Long to Be) Close to You," a wispy Burt Bacharach tune sung with pristine breathiness by siblings Karen and Richard Carpenter. The Carpenters' gentle, keyboard-dominated sound was Richard's doing; he arranged and produced most of the pair's hits, which were constant for the first half of the decade: "We've Only Just Begun," "For All We Know," "Rainy Days and Monday," "Superstar," "Sing," "Yesterday Once More," and a flaccid cover of the Marvelettes' "Please Mr. Postman" sold millions and won the duo the raft of Grammy awards that the music industry, conservative to the core, was only too eager to press upon them. The only album that can be said to equal the sheer hit power of their singles was, logically enough, *Singles 1969–1973*.

A quintessential 1970s singles artist was Harry Chapin, who managed to combine sentimental folk-based narratives with rock instrumentation and a declamatory singing style to yield many a talky, earnest hit, the first of which was "Taxi" (1972). At the time, Chapin's chatty, intimate style was heard as something of an AM-radio breakthrough—"Taxi" lasted longer than four minutes, mighty long for the average AM hit it became—but actually he was just a throwback to the sort of folkie ironies that boiled down to "I'm a star singing about the days when I was a working-class stiff like you stiffs." Chapin's subsequent hit singles included the I'm-selfish-but-beautiful "Cat's in the Cradle," and "W.O.L.D.," the latter an exceptionally cagey idea—a song about a self-pitying disc jockey that, of course, disc jockeys loved to play.

An even more wildly popular singles artist of the early 1970s was John Denver, a singer-songwriter born in New Mexico, whose big break came in the 1960s when he was invited to join folkie superstar act the Chad Mitchell Trio. Denver left the trio in 1969 and immediately wrote a hit for Peter, Paul, and Mary, "Leaving on a Jet Plane." Denver's own recording career took off in 1971 with the gold single "Take Me Home, Country Roads," a song that typified his style: warm, reedy vocals that regularly cracked with sincerity, comfy country-pop melodics, and lyrics that stressed the virtues of rural living with the wide-eyed conviction of a former architecture major.

With his moon face, round glasses, and wide smile, Denver became a post/hippie sex symbol with the singles to back it up: "Rocky Mountain High," "Thank God I'm a Country Boy," and "Annie's Song," among others, continued his success, as did a mid-1970s television-variety series and film acting jobs that included *Oh, God!* with George Burns.

But the term *singer-songwriter* had been coined to describe the likes of James Taylor and Joni Mitchell, pop musicians aspiring to be poets. By this definition, Jim Morrison of the Doors was a singer-songwriter, and in some ways, he was a more authentic pop poet than either Taylor or Mitchell. Morrison had spent the last half of the previous decade writing his version of vers libre, shocking people by using blunt words as incantations of creativity, and emulating the example of a poet maudit like Rimbaud—that is, live hard, die young (or at least *write* young), and leave a beautiful corpse.

This is precisely what Jim Morrison did in Paris on July 3, 1971, although his corpse is said to have been less beautiful than bloated from whatever excesses you believe singer-songwriters favor. The words on Morrison's death certificate said simply "heart attack."

Like Jim Morrison, singer-songwriter Gram Parsons would die before fulfilling his promise, on September 19, 1973, in a motel in the Mojave desert outside Los Angeles. Parsons had spent the 1960s refining country rock with the Byrds and then the Flying Burrito Brothers, as well as releasing a pair of starkly beautiful solo albums. Less than a week after his death, his body was stolen and burned at the Joshua Tree National Monument by his long-time friend Phil Kaufman, who claimed that this was the way Parsons had told him he wanted to shuffle off the mortal coil.

A day after Parsons died, Jim Croce was killed in a plane crash over Louisiana. Croce was on the verge of pop stardom with such pleasant folk-pop ditties as "You Don't Mess Around with Jim," "Operator," and "Bad, Bad Leroy Brown," a song later recorded by Frank Sinatra, of all people.

In a business move that received absolutely no attention at the time, veteran talent scout–producer John Hammond signed Bruce Springsteen to Columbia Records on June 9, 1972.

And what of that ultimate singer-songwriter, a model for James Taylor, Joni Mitchell, and Bruce Springsteen alike—Bob Dylan? As usual, he was unfathomable but fascinating. In 1971, he released "George Jackson," a single about the assassination of the jailed black militant leader and theorist, and five days later followed up with the standard-product *Greatest Hits Volume II* album. (The song was, in a sense, the returning of a favor, since Jackson's colleagues Huey Newton and Bobby Seale had hatched the idea of the Black Panthers while listening to "Ballad of a Thin Man.") *Rolling Stone* magazine wrote at the time that "the song immediately divided Dylan speculators into two camps: those who see it as the poet's return to social relevance and those who felt that it's a cheap way for Dylan to get a lot of people off his back." But Dylan had never been anything less than socially relevant; even the jus'-folks simplicity of *New Morning* a year before had been a clear message to his followers that their Bob was aligning himself with the democratic working class, not the upscale music business types. And there is no denying Dylan's impact and the uses to which he put his influence: A hell of a lot of people who had no idea who George Jackson was became aware of his murder primarily because Bob Dylan's "George Jackson" became a Top Forty single, and this despite the fact that the song was heavily censored around the country—most of the time, simply pulled from the radio playlist—because it contained the word *shit*.

Having put himself on the line to this extent, it made a certain amount of sense that Dylan's next response would be to hide himself away for a while. He made a movie with *Wild Bunch* director Sam Peckinpah, and when *Pat Garrett and Billy the Kid* was released in 1973, there was Dylan as Alias, an enigmatic, mostly mute character who did little more than sit around and gaze with clouded blue eyes two feet over the head of songwriter-turned-actor Kris Kristofferson.

It is this posture—a highly ambivalent one of wary watchfulness, intense self-consciousness, and blithe self-absorption—that can stand as an apt symbol for all the early 1970s singer-songwriters. Soon enough, like any pop trend, the genre would exhaust itself—there were only so many stories one could tell about oneself, after all. After the fragmentation of the first half of the decade, the best of the singer-songwriters would become part of rock's reunification as a mass music: James Taylor would find a way to use synthesizers that did not seem antithetical to his simple purposes, for example; Joni Mitchell would find new musical formats in jazz. But at the start of the decade, the singer-songwriters brought a new emotional directness and musical subtlety that would come to represent one end of the fractionating spectrum of rock.

The other white rock styles of the early seventies owed little to folk music; hard rock, art rock, and heavy metal drew upon the blues and, in some cases, even classical and avant-garde music to form the basis for popular success.

28

HARD ROCK ON THE RISE

Where the singer-songwriters took great care to maintain the illusion of intimacy with their audience, the louder, more aggressive forms of early 1970s rock broke decisively with this tendency—saw it, in fact, as of little importance. Hard rock, art rock (also known as progressive rock), and heavy metal were the flip side of singer-songwriter mannerliness. This more dramatic music was designed to be played in the increasingly large arenas that rock's burgeoning audience could fill; this was music that took full advantage of the steady advances in technology that enabled rock musicians to offer their fans a more elaborate performance.

The distinctions between these subgenres are slight but telling. Hard rock was rock's blues base electrified and upped in volume; art rock added a layer of aesthetic pretension and an ambition to be taken seriously in classical or avant-garde musical circles; heavy metal wanted to be the rock music equivalent of a horror movie—loud, exaggerated, rude, out for thrills only.

The art rock bands presumed to take for granted the cultural equality of rock and all other forms of music. This was, after all, the first generation of musicians who could be both formally trained (i.e., aware of the classical music tradition) and immersed in pop (i.e., the Beatles had penetrated everywhere, even to concert piano students). A new generation of well-educated middle-class people thought it important to connect this music to an established cultural tradition (nineteenth century Romantic and early twentieth century avant-garde were the preferred eras). Thus the cliché of a formally trained, university-educated student who throws it all away for the joy of primitive rock and roll gave way to a new cliché: the musical prodigy hunched over his guitar/piano/synthesizer, feverishly composing the most elaborate variations imaginable on . . . rock and roll.

In August 1970, at Plymouth Guild Hall in England, keyboardist Keith Emerson, guitarist Greg Lake, and drummer Carl Palmer made their debut appearance as Emerson, Lake, and Palmer, makers of an art rock form that eschewed pop catchiness in favor of an unholy mating of classical music complexity played with hard rock fervor. Less than a year later, Emerson, Lake, and Palmer would become major stars in America and England with their bastardized, rococco interpretation of Mussorgsky's *Pictures at an Exhibition*. Say what you will about their pretensions, attending an Emerson, Lake, and Palmer concert was, among other things, a demonstration in state-of-the-art concertgoing, from the use of banks of synthesizers to reproduce the sounds of an orchestra to the most elaborate and precise amplification for the aural pleasure of the now arena-size audiences to which major acts routinely played.

The art rock crew also found a willing home for their work on the radio, since their long, discursive compositions fit right in with FM radio's expansive format and shameless pandering to the "sophisticated" listener. Just a few years earlier, it would have been impossible for Emerson, Lake, and Palmer's "Pictures at an Exhibition" to become anything resembling a hit in the three-minute-single world of AM Top Forty radio; now "Pictures" was just the sort of thing a weary college student wanted to hear after a hard day out on the barricades protesting the Vietnam War.

This was also true of Jethro Tull, an English act that became more popular in America than in its homeland. Formed by flutist Ian Anderson in the late 1960s, Jethro Tull made its American breakthrough with 1970's *Benefit* and, more especially, the tour the band made to promote it. For it was as a live act that Jethro Tull came fully into its own: Onstage, Ian Anderson played the florid eccentric, letting his long, ratty hair sweep over his face as he huffed and puffed over his flute, glaring malevolently at the audience and abruptly whipping the flute behind his back to sing in a reedy, sarcastic tone.

Tull's music was often typical progressive rock, with its extended verses, multiple choruses, stabs at structural complexity, and ostentatious borrowings from the Romantic classical composers. What distinguished Anderson from his colleagues, however, was that he was a showman with a sense of misanthropic humor and an urge to tell stories—he came across as a first-rate Fagin who wrote like a third-rate Dickens. Tull's greatest commercial successes, *Aqualung* (1971), *Thick As a Brick* (1972), and *A Passion Play* (1973), described loose, garrulous tales; they were concept albums that mocked organized religion and business world conformity. These themes were certainly nothing new as rock music targets, but during this peak period, Anderson sang passionately and therefore well, and he wrote himself a few catchy choruses that undercut all the balderdash.

Most of the other popular art rock bands were similarly longwinded, with intermittent bursts of pop accessibility. Yes, kindred spirits with Emerson, Lake, and Palmer in the matters of classical music echoes and earnest sobersidedness, created its best work in *The Yes Album* (1971). There, "I've Seen All Good People" stood out as a small triumph of pretensions enlivened by a powerful, unifying guitar riff and atypically rough, lusty harmonies.

In fact, while the band's supporters revered them for their album-length concepts, Yes at its best pulled off one good song per release: "Roundabout" on *Fragile* (1971) and the title track on *Close to the Edge* (1972) are pertinent examples. On *Tales from Topographic Oceans* (1973), they just went over the edge.

Acts like Yes and ELP, as well as Rush, Uriah Heep, and Genesis (which would later yield more conventional pop stars in the solo careers of members Phil Collins and Peter Gabriel) appealed to that segment of the rock audience that yearned to have its music taken seriously by the middlebrow cultural establishment that detested rock on principle. Art rock fans had the satisfaction of being able to pick out the high-culture references ostentatiously sprinkled through the music and lyrics, while the musicians themselves had the opportunity to display their formal training in elaborate showcases. One important exception was Pink Floyd.

In 1973, Pink Floyd released *Dark Side of the Moon*, the album that was to establish this art rock band's name in the rock-and-roll history books. The album was a typically dense, knotty collection of stentorian pop hymns to paranoia and schizophrenia that even yielded the group's first rock-radio hit, the mordant "Money." *Dark Side of the Moon* entered the *Billboard* album chart soon after its release—and stayed there; as of this writing, *Dark Side of the Moon* has been on the charts for more than thirteen years, evincing the longest shelf life of any rock album in history.

By the seventies, Pink Floyd had survived the departure of Syd Barrett and had fully integrated his replacement, guitarist-singer David Gilmour, into the group. Roger Waters came to dominate the songwriting of the band, and it was his vision—cynical, misanthropic, fatalistic—that permeated the band's increasingly ambitious music.

This style peaked in 1979 with the release of *The Wall*, a two-record meditation on the evils of enforced education, the perils of rock stardom, and the inhumanity of all bureaucracies. To promote *The Wall*, the band created a stage show so elaborate that they decided to present it in only three places: London, Manhattan, and Los Angeles. Its central prop was a massive white wall that was erected slowly, brick by brick, as the music was being played; the building of the wall served as the climax of the show, and when it was done, it completely obscured Pink Floyd from the audience. Then the wall came tumbling down, and the band emerged from the rubble, tootling on acoustic instruments.

But Pink Floyd was a winning, regularly deflating influence on the puffed-up self-importance of most art rock, which was easily as interested in its status as art as it was with its position in the rock world. Its air of exclusivity gave off the whiff of a private club. By contrast, hard rock had an air of genial welcome—it never set itself above its audience. In matters of unpretentiousness, power, and invention, the best such hard rock band in America during the first half of the 1970s may well have been Lynyrd Skynyrd, a Jacksonville, Florida, group led by singer Ronnie Van Zant. Working with the same blues/country/rock-and-roll roots as the Allman Brothers Band, Skynyrd added an appreciation for nascent hard rock, and benefitted from Van Zant's talent for writing terse, pointed lyrics. Thus it was that in 1973, the band was ideally suited for its first big break— Skynyrd served as the opening act for the Who, then embarked on an American tour to promote *Quadrophenia*. Skynyrd's blunt boogie was well accepted by the stadium crowds the Who was courting, and a year later, Skynyrd scored its first radio hit, "Sweet Home Alabama." This song staked out Ronnie Van Zant's proudly working class stance, taking Neil Young's song "Southern Man" to task by name for its Southern stereotypes.

In his far-from-reactionary pro-America, pro-family stance, Ronnie Van Zant was a genuinely prescient figure in early-1970s rock. His songs prefigured much of the sentiment of rock in the early 1980s from bands such as R.E.M., the Long Ryders, and the dBs. Like virtually all the popular hard rock acts of this era, however, Lynyrd Skynyrd found a large, adoring audience long before it reaped critical praise, and—again like virtually all hard rock bands—it never received any extensive mass media coverage. Bands like Lynyrd Skynyrd were much too vulgar—too loud, too blunt, sartorially unkempt or eccentric as a matter of style—for the curious mass audience attracted to rock by the Beatles and the Stones; for the readership of, say, *Life* magazine. The mass audience accepted the Beatles because they were articulate, witty, and, various haircuts aside, cute; the Stones, with their ostentatious rudeness, were pushing mass taste's limit. Skynyrd and their contemporaries—bands such as Grand Funk Railroad, the J. Geils Band, Aerosmith, the James Gang—became rock stars of varying degree without ever penetrating mainstream culture. The rock audience had become so big that it could now nurture and enclose entire careers without having to exploit other mass culture media such as television and the movies. In his 1981 book *Sound Effects: Youth, Leisure, and the Politics of Rock and Roll*, British critic Simon Frith observed that

> rock forms of production and consumption were perfected between 1967 and 1971, as an increasing number of bands and performers aimed their music at an album-buying market of hip, mostly male music freaks. This was the period in which Jethro Tull, Emerson, Lake, and Palmer, Pink Floyd, Yes, and the rest of the rock super-groups established their popularity; it was the time when Led Zeppelin became the world's number-one

live attraction and album band without releasing a single. Rock music meant lengthy studio work-outs, rich and elaborate sounds; it was music made for expensive stereos and FM radio and campus concerts.

Maximizing the profits from this situation meant, at its baldest, clamping down: the "free form" FM radio station of the late 1960s and early 1970s became a thing of the past, as station owners instituted various formats designed by "radio consultants" to increase audience numbers and, by extension, their profits. The most notorious—commercially successful, aesthetically disastrous—of these radio formats was AOR, which aimed its programming at an extremely specific, limited listenership: white males between the ages of thirteen and twenty-five.

To do this, AOR stations offered the kind of music that their surveys told them appealed most to these ideal listeners—the kind of aggressive hard rock made primarily if not exclusively by white musicians, emphasizing prominent guitar hooks and a matter-of-fact sexism: dominance (emotional, sexual, aesthetic, marketplace) was all. These stations narrowed the very definition of rock and roll: by AOR guidelines, black artists didn't play it, and neither did women. This represented an institutionalized racism and sexism that would later be blithely adopted by the most successful purveyor of rock videos, cable television's MTV, in the early 1980s.

The success of AOR would give rise to a generation of bands whose music fit AOR specifications impeccably—that is, to the point of anonymity. Journey, Styx, REO Speedwagon, Rush, Kansas, Supertramp, as well as lesser-knowns like Ambrosia, Gentle Giant, and Nazareth were all prime examples of bands that made impersonal radio fodder with considerable commercial success. Dubbed *faceless bands* by critics, they were groups whose appeal had nothing to do with their personalities—indeed, many of their most ardent fans were hard pressed to name the individual members of their favorite groups. Still, throughout the first half of the 1970s, most radio stations adopting the AOR format saw their ratings rise, and even soar.

The absolute pillar of AOR programming was the prototypical heavy metal band Led Zeppelin, who on September 16, 1970, were voted England's most popular group in the *Melody Maker* annual opinion poll; it was the first time in eight years that the Beatles hadn't won this honor. This represents a significant shift in taste that undoubtedly hastened the breakup of the Beatles and that embodied a new, rabid interest in loud but intricate rock music that was echoed on the other side of the pond.

Steeped in the blues, mindful of the mournful romantic passion of Eric Clapton's 1960s guitar work, wholly in thrall to Jimi Hendrix's Wall of Feedback pyrotechnics, Zeppelin forged the most audacious version of loud rock and roll in the 1970s. Although their overpowering volume and truculent demeanor helped consign them most conveniently to the heavy metal

29

WHAM, GLAM, THANK YOU, MA'AM

The artistic pretensions of art rock and the philistine forthrightness of heavy metal found a meeting place in glam-rock. "Glam"— a blunt truncation of *glamorous*—emphasized outrageously flamboyant fashions: platform shoes, glittery costumes, garish make-up plastered on the faces of its primarily male performers. These shock tactics were in part smart stagecraft: Rock's growing audience was piling into huge arenas to see their faves, and the performers sought ways to be noticed by the back rows. Glam-rock style also tweaked the public's curiosity about rock stars by reducing such questions to the very crudest one—were all these guys fags, or what?

The most important trendsetter in this area was David Bowie, whose pose on the cover of the 1971 album *The Man Who Sold the World*—David in a flowing gown, his cheeks and lips rouged, his hair swept back in a butch pageboy cut—was at least as important to many fans as the music itself.

Bowie, however, maintained a certain distance from his glamorous image; even then it seemed to be just a phase he was going through, a costume he would drop as soon as something more provocative struck him. A far more satisfying exemplar of the glam-rock impulse was Marc Bolan, leader and visual symbol of the band Tyrannosaurus Rex. Bolan, born Mark Feld in London in 1978, was a prescient trendsetter. By the time he was fifteen, he was known as a particularly stylish mod, and in fact he had a brief career as a model. With his big, soulful eyes, bee-stung lips, and long, curly hair, Bolan was an ideal example of the sort of androgyny that fascinated the pop scene in England and, to a lesser extent, America. In Bolan, glam-rock

487

found an adroit scene-maker who was well aware of the British precedents for his aesthetic sensibility: In interviews, he frequently invoked the examples of such artists of decadence as Aubrey Beardsley and Oscar Wilde.

It took a while for Bolan to hit his stride. The first version of Tyrannosaurus Rex was an equal partnership with singer-songwriter Steve Peregrine Took, and in the late sixties the band made soggy folk-rock weighed down with rococco hymns to nymphs, unicorns, and wood fairies: the band's albums barely supported titles such as *My People Were Fair and Had Sky in Their Hair but Now They're Content to Wear Stars on Their Brow* (1968) and *Prophets, Seers and Sages* (1969).

When Took quit in 1970, Bolan took up the electric guitar with a vengeance and shortened the band's name to T. Rex. While continuing to exaggerate his fey, sensitive persona, Bolan made the crucial, cagey decision to pick up the tempo of the music and emphasize an increasingly "heavy," razor-edged guitar style. After a number two British hit with the soft-rock tune "Ride a White Swan," Bolan sharpened his attack and released the series of singles that made him a star: "Hot Love," "Bang a Gong," "Get It On", and "Jeepster," all released in England in 1971, each featuring a single, crunching guitar riff and Bolan's urgent murmur of a voice: Bo Diddley meets Dorian Gray. All three songs became Top Five hits.

Bolan's ascent to glam-rock deification was swift and brief. He had a reputation for being temperamental, high-strung, and sometimes just plain high. A diminutive man, he toured in glittery platform boots and frequently wore a tall black stovepipe hat on stage. His string of hit singles continued in 1972—"Telegram Sam," "Metal Guru," "Children of the Revolution" (in which his hippie sappiness persisted: the chorus was "Oh, you won't fool the children of the revolution")—as did his fame, but glam-rock was a cruelly fickle trend. T. Rex was the subject of a documentary called *Born to Boogie*, directed by fan Ringo Starr, but by the time the movie hit the theaters in late 1973, T. Rex had peaked, and the film flopped. A hefty segment of Bolan's audience was a teenybopper contingent that began favoring pure teenybop acts like the Osmonds and David Cassidy. Another chunk of T. Rex fans soon converted to heavier glam-rockers like the bubblegum-with-teeth act Sweet, masterminded by the songwriting-production team of Mike Chapman and Nicky Chinn.

The result was that by 1973, Bolan found himself a washed-up teen idol. Over the next few years, he divorced his wife (it was always an irony that the androgynous teen hero was a rather conventional family man), gained an amount of weight unbecoming to any glam-rocker this side of Gary Glitter, and broke up his band. In 1975, Bolan would forge a new version of T. Rex and try to associate himself with the then-nascent punk-rock movement, with scant success. On September 16, 1977, Bolan was killed when a car driven by his girlfriend Gloria Jones skidded off the road; he was thirty years old.

If Marc Bolan was the bad-news Tinkerbell of glam-rock, Gary Glitter was its portly Peter Pan. Glitter was in his thirties before he scored his biggest hits, the thumping, primal rock anthems "Rock and Roll Parts 1 and 2," "Didn't Know I Loved You (Till I Saw You Rock and Roll)," and "Do You Wanna Touch Me," all top five hits in Britain in 1972 and 1973. Although he never became a star in America—his only number one U.S. hit was "Rock and Roll (Part 2)"—he was a beloved joke in England. Propped up in enormous platform boots, his sequined jumpsuits bulging from the girth of the Glitter gut, Gary was nonetheless a British pop star in the Elvis Presley tradition: He excited teens and middle-aged women and was considered by the public to be a decent, humble fellow, no matter how outrageously he decked himself out.

Ultimately, however, the one glam-rocker to sustain a career was Bowie. As a pop-culture changeling flitting from pose to pose, David Bowie has been overrated. At base, there isn't much difference between Ziggy Stardust (Bowie's first successful "character" in 1972) and the Elephant Man (whom Bowie embodied on Broadway in 1980); they're both ugly misfits who want to control their worlds.

But there were an awful lot of misfits on both sides of the Atlantic—indeed, throughout the world—who seemed to think David Bowie was an apt role model. In any case, by the mid-1970s, Bowie had become the biggest English sensation since Beatlemania. David Jones—middle-class art student, adept of Marcel Marceau's mime, Bob Dylan disciple—had gradually transformed himself into David Bowie, for whom gimmick and art were inseparable.

Born in 1947, Bowie's first successful band was a late-sixties folk-rock group called David Jones and the Lower Third. The group offered a cross between Dylan's self-conscious literariness and the Beatles' *Sgt. Pepper* psychedelia. From the start, Bowie's most significant contribution to rock was his vocal style: Singing through a clenched jaw, emitting languid upper-class British pronunciations in a haughty croon, Bowie was at once a throwback to English theatricalism and the originator of a method that has been relentlessly aped ever since. Try to imagine Oscar Wilde as a rock star and you've got David Bowie's voice floating through your skull.

Like so many other fledgling stars, Bowie needed a high-powered manager to get his music to the masses. Bowie's Svengali was Tony DeFries, who went so far as to call himself the Col. Tom Parker of the Seventies. DeFries would also preside over the careers of Mott the Hoople and Iggy Stooge/Pop; the latter was once inspired to remark, "Tony is a great artist. His art is in handling money, in maneuvering it so that it builds up. He doesn't do it just for the money; it's an artistic gesture." Be that as it may, there is no denying DeFries's hard-nosed calculation. Before DeFries, David Jones/David Bowie was a moony crooner in search of a beat. After DeFries's aggressive promotion, he was David Bowie/Ziggy Stardust, and a star.

If Marc Bolan was the bad-news Tinkerbell of glam-rock, Gary Glitter was its portly Peter Pan. Glitter was in his thirties before he scored his biggest hits, the thumping, primal rock anthems "Rock and Roll Parts 1 and 2," "Didn't Know I Loved You (Till I Saw You Rock and Roll)," and "Do You Wanna Touch Me," all top five hits in Britain in 1972 and 1973. Although he never became a star in America—his only number one U.S. hit was "Rock and Roll (Part 2)"—he was a beloved joke in England. Propped up in enormous platform boots, his sequined jumpsuits bulging from the girth of the Glitter gut, Gary was nonetheless a British pop star in the Elvis Presley tradition: He excited teens and middle-aged women and was considered by the public to be a decent, humble fellow, no matter how outrageously he decked himself out.

Ultimately, however, the one glam-rocker to sustain a career was Bowie. As a pop-culture changeling flitting from pose to pose, David Bowie has been overrated. At base, there isn't much difference between Ziggy Stardust (Bowie's first successful "character" in 1972) and the Elephant Man (whom Bowie embodied on Broadway in 1980); they're both ugly misfits who want to control their worlds.

But there were an awful lot of misfits on both sides of the Atlantic—indeed, throughout the world—who seemed to think David Bowie was an apt role model. In any case, by the mid-1970s, Bowie had become the biggest English sensation since Beatlemania. David Jones—middle-class art student, adept of Marcel Marceau's mime, Bob Dylan disciple—had gradually transformed himself into David Bowie, for whom gimmick and art were inseparable.

Born in 1947, Bowie's first successful band was a late-sixties folk-rock group called David Jones and the Lower Third. The group offered a cross between Dylan's self-conscious literariness and the Beatles' *Sgt. Pepper* psychedelia. From the start, Bowie's most significant contribution to rock was his vocal style: Singing through a clenched jaw, emitting languid upper-class British pronunciations in a haughty croon, Bowie was at once a throwback to English theatricalism and the originator of a method that has been relentlessly aped ever since. Try to imagine Oscar Wilde as a rock star and you've got David Bowie's voice floating through your skull.

Like so many other fledgling stars, Bowie needed a high-powered manager to get his music to the masses. Bowie's Svengali was Tony DeFries, who went so far as to call himself the Col. Tom Parker of the Seventies. DeFries would also preside over the careers of Mott the Hoople and Iggy Stooge/Pop; the latter was once inspired to remark, "Tony is a great artist. His art is in handling money, in maneuvering it so that it builds up. He doesn't do it just for the money; it's an artistic gesture." Be that as it may, there is no denying DeFries's hard-nosed calculation. Before DeFries, David Jones/David Bowie was a moony crooner in search of a beat. After DeFries's aggressive promotion, he was David Bowie/Ziggy Stardust, and a star.

Hunky Dory, in 1972, was Bowie's first clear explanation of himself. In the face of the hippie era's sincerity, intimacy, and generosity, Bowie presented irony, distance, and self-absorption. *Hunky Dory* yielded Bowie's first and finest anthem, "Changes," a song that announced the arrival of a new counterculture—a young generation of overdressed pessimists, androgynous nay-sayers who sneered and batted their eyelashes as a matter of cultural prerogative. Bowie courted camp with some subtlety: *Hunky Dory's* "Oh! You Pretty Things" may have been oh-so-arch, but it was also aggressive rock and roll. In fact, the secret of Bowie's musical appeal may be that he was a strong traditional rock songwriter, mindful of verse, book, and chorus, who knew how to overlay his material with fashionable ideas and poses.

After *Hunky Dory* caused a stir, *The Rise and Fall of Ziggy Stardust and the Spiders from Mars* (1972) caused a sensation. Bowie, drenched in elaborate makeup (equal parts kabuki and kookie), his face a mask of druggy insouciance, was an even cannier commercial calculation. Ziggy was a satisfying teen idol—a rock star who craved anonymity; an alien who craved love just like most Earth-bound adolescents—and the Spiders from Mars were a satisfying rock band. Led by guitarist Mick Ronson punching out tough, catchy songs like "Suffragette City," Bowie's music was fast and terse: In his own words, "Wham, bam, thank you, ma'am."

Bowie continued and elaborated upon this aural punch on *Aladdin Sane* (1973) and *Diamond Dogs* (1974). At the same time, his example was proving enormously influential. Among those listening was Bryan Ferry, still another art student who, along with bassist Graham Simpson, in 1971 formed Roxy Music, certainly the artiest of the bands associated in its initial stages with Bowie and the glam-rock trend and probably the driest, most reserved band in the history of rock.

Ferry and Simpson were joined by three other musicians, the most significant of whom was Brian Eno, an experimenter in the new technology of computerized keyboards, tape machines, and synthesizers. Ferry envisioned Roxy Music as a vehicle for his own archly romantic songwriting and bored-aristocrat crooning style, but this was a notion disputed early on by Eno, who had ideas of his own about how to best express Ferry's dream of bringing a world-weary sophistication to rock.

With Eno and Ferry battling for control, Roxy Music's first two albums, *Roxy Music* (1972) and *For Your Pleasure* (1973), are a hodgepodge of styles, from yearning pop ballads to lengthy synthesizer improvisations. As a result of the intramural friction, Eno left after the second album to pursue a career as a solo artist and producer. Years later, Ferry would say with a polite sniff, "You see, Eno is a very clever fellow, but he's not really a musician. He doesn't know how to play anything. All he can do is manipulate those machines of his. What he does he does very well, but it's necessarily limited music, I think."

Eno was replaced by violinist-keyboardist Eddie Jobson, and in 1973, the band released *Stranded,* an album that summed up Ferry's concerns. Propelled by the ferocious guitar work of Phil Manzanera and the drumming of Paul Thompson, *Stranded* began with Ferry moaning, "Wish everybody would leave me alone" and ended with him very alone indeed, gazing forlornly at a "Sunset" and bewailing his fate as a lonely guy. *Stranded* crystallized Ferry's meticulously cultivated image. He sang in a bored drawl that regularly cracked or became ragged around the edges due to cries of love and protestations of romance—Ferry was the suave king of unrequited love, left immobile with passion. Or, as he sang at the climax of "Street Life," his voice ascending to a girlish falsetto on the last word: "Loving you is all I can dooooo."

Ferry acted as if he could afford to do nothing but love you—his favorite stage costumes included impeccable black tuxedos and crisp white dinner jackets. At the height of his post-glam fop period, he took to wearing stylized bullfighter's outfits. Naive fans claimed he brought classiness to rock; smarter ones knew he was bringing class (upper-upper) and camp.

Roxy Music was an immediate success in England, where Ferry's accent and visual symbols were understood and appreciated as the wry jokes they were. In America, the band attracted a cult following of Anglophiles and art rock sympathizers who grooved on Manzanera's more wild flights of guitar complexity, notably "The Bogus Man" on *For Your Pleasure* and the overheated solo in the center of "Amazona" on *Stranded.*

In 1973, Ferry released his first solo album. *These Foolish Things* was both an instant camp classic and something better than that: a joke so good it became a statement of philosophy. The album consisted entirely of Ferry's fey interpretations of other people's hits from many periods of pop music. Thus his fruity baritone wept during Lesley Gore's "It's My Party"; he declaimed Bob Dylan's "A Hard Rain's A-Gonna Fall" as if he were intoning admonitions from the King James Old Testament. Ferry had the gall to tackle Lennon-McCartney's "You Won't See Me" and make it over into a fervent admission of guilt and adoration. *These Foolish Things* remains a fascinating instance of a quirky artist appropriating other artists' work to fashion a highly personal, revealing document.

Undaunted by their lack of American success (in fact, rarely failing to mention just this fact in every interview they gave), Roxy Music continued to release albums to wild acclaim in England from both critics and the public. *Country Life* (1974) caused a stir in the United States mainly because of its cover—two slinky models in see-through underwear. To placate American record store owners, the cover was hastily modified, but inside, Ferry was pursuing his demons unfettered: The haughty grandeur of "The Thrill of It All," "All I Want Is You," and the anthemic "Casanova" developed fresh variations on his playboy-stunned-by love persona.

A band in a similar commercial position—adored in England, cultivated in America—was Mott the Hoople. The feistiest English act to follow in David Bowie's wake, Mott the Hoople was a highly idiosyncratic hard rock band whose allure was enhanced by the very fact that it seemed doomed to failure right from the start.

Mott the Hoople (the band's name is taken from the 1849 Willard Manus novel) began its recording career around the same time as Bowie. *Mott*, the band's debut album, was released in 1969, and by then, the band's members were old pros led by a former newspaperman and bricklayer named Ian Hunter. He was willful, intelligent, corrosively sarcastic, and profoundly influenced by the garrulous poesy of Bob Dylan. He even sang like Dylan: "I had never sung before in my life," Hunter later said, "and I figured I'd do like him . . . because he nearly talks, and I thought that's how you learn to sing."

Hunter's hoarse croak and his wittily misanthropic lyrics combined with guitarist Mick Ralphs's heavy yet rhythmic lead guitar style to create a sound that was at once artily ironic and crudely straightforward. Hunter and Ralphs maintained a fierce competition, challenging each other in writing songs and arguing constantly over who would sing lead on what track (even though Ralphs's grainy alto voice was a far less distinctive instrument than Hunter's). It was a band that, even onstage, always seemed on the verge of breaking up. The result was an exciting, if highly uneven, stage show.

Mott the Hoople became a popular British act with the release, in 1971, of *Brain Capers*. This was due not only to the general excellence of the album's material (the eerie "Death May Be Your Santa Claus" and Hunter's lovely "Sweet Angeline") but also to the fact that Bowie's glam-rock style— platform boots, androgynous hairstyles, and glittery costumes—had taken hold on the band: Overseen by high-powered manager Guy Stevens, they'd become fashion-conscious.

Soon enough David Bowie let it be known that he was interested in producing Mott the Hoople. He offered them the choice of his own "Suffragette City" or a new song he'd written, "All the Young Dudes"; they chose the latter. It's lucky they did: "All the Young Dudes" was poignant and stirring, a foppish anthem with grandeur. So was the album of the same title that they recorded with Bowie and released in late 1972. *All the Young Dudes* included what was certainly Hunter and Ralphs's finest collaboration, the raunchy, funny "One of the Boys," as well as a genially sloppy version of Lou Reed's "Sweet Jane" (remarked Hunter, "I couldn't understand what the song was about, not being a New York fag").

The influence of Bowie, particularly on Hunter, was profound. "I never realized you had to concentrate so much," said Hunter years later. "I mean, I was pretty lazy . . . right up through the *Mott* album [released in 1973]. Before all that, we'd spent a year with Bowie; I'd seen a concentration. Like with his lyrics—he'd tear them to pieces after he'd done them, which is something I never did."

Then, too, Bowie had done Hunter a big favor—he made Hunter the central star of Mott the Hoople, giving him virtually all the lead vocals and making sure he was the group's visual focal point on the band's tour to promote *All the Young Dudes*. The Bowie connection had its disadvantages though; for one thing, the media assumed that Mott the Hoople was as interested in sexual adventurism as old Ziggy Stardust seemed to be. Or, as Hunter put it in *Reflections of a Rock Star*, his journal of the band's November-December 1972 U.S. tour, "We became instant queers. Of course we weren't. It was all very funny."

Mott the Hoople then went on to prove that the band wasn't merely David Bowie's puppet. Bowie moved on to other projects, and the band followed *Dudes* with the almost equally excellent *Mott* (1973), arranged and almost entirely written by Hunter. *Mott* contained "All the Way from Memphis," a great rhythm-and-blues rocker that was as much of a concert-audience favorite as "All the Young Dudes." Shortly before entering the recording studio to record *The Hoople* (1976), however, Mick Ralphs left the band to start the hard rock band he'd always wanted; with former Free lead singer Paul Rodgers, Free drummer Simon Kirke, and King Crimson bassist Boz Burrell, Ralphs formed Bad Company, which immediately enjoyed greater British and American commercial success than Mott the Hoople had ever achieved, if never approaching Mott in musical quality.

In 1975, Hunter was admitted to a New Jersey hospital, suffering from exhaustion, and soon after resigned from the band. Mott the Hoople limped along for a few more albums before disbanding. Hunter would pursue an erratic solo career into the 1980s—his 1979 album *You're Never Alone with a Schizophrenic* yielded critical praise and the minor hit "Just Another Night"—and the always promising, always thwarted career of Mott the Hoople slipped into history.

Amid the glitter rock and the imposition of David Bowie's would-be Brechtian-alienation effect upon the rock audience, there were still any number of English warhorses who were doing quite well, thank you. Rod Stewart, himself misperceived by the English music press as a would-be glam-rocker with his glittery scarves and platform boots, decided to record one solo album for every record he made with his band the Faces, and he demonstrated the various, glorious ways a British-born Scotsman can sing rhythm and blues on his early-seventies solo albums *Gasoline Alley*, *Every Picture Tells a Story*, and *Never a Dull Moment*.

These albums were marvels of rough passion, prickly sensitivity, and raucous humor. They told stories: While rock critics were busy averring that Randy Newman was the only singer-songwriter around who assiduously avoided the use of pseudo-autobiography in his work, Rod Stewart was busy inhabiting the mind of a teenage boy primping in front of a mirror before a big date, or impersonating an elderly gentleman worrying over the wild life his granddaughter is leading. Stewart, always proud, even boastful, of his working-class heritage, was determined to express that birthright in the most precisely detailed yet loosely executed music he could manage.

Stewart developed his American audience by playing his exemplary songs with the Faces on a series of tours beginning in 1970. Although he was beginning to record with different musicians, he toured with the Faces because, he said at the time, "If I chose a band, I'd choose the same guys I got in that band anyway." The Faces—lead guitarist Ron Wood, keyboardist Ian McLagan, bassist Ronnie Lane, and drummer Kenny Jones—certainly matched Stewart's own image of rock-and-roll unpretentiousness; indeed, the primary criticism everybody had of the band was that they were immensely likeable and deplorably sloppy. Stewart, who liked pubs almost as much as he liked soccer and rock (and probably in that order), used the Faces' looseness to his own purposes—as a dramatic contrast to the sharp realism of his lyrics, and as a musical complement to his own raspy vocalizing. The emphasis that Stewart achieved on his solo albums—a loopy but commanding front man plus rag-tag but passionate back-up band—was a chemistry that the Faces never produced on their own albums.

Which is not to say that the Faces weren't one of the most viscerally pleasurable bands that ever bashed away at electric instruments. In the privacy of your own home, it was sheer ecstasy to ponder Stewart's lyrical details and the scratchy expressiveness of his voice; in concert, the fun lay in watching Kenny Jones slam away at the drums as if to pull every song along all by himself, while Ronnie Lane and Ron Wood laid out loud funky variations on the most elementary Chuck Berry riffs. Stewart once explained that in the beginning of the Faces, "nobody wanted to listen to us and nobody was taking us very seriously, and we decided to go 'round to the pub beforehand. Call it Dutch courage if you want, but that's what it was down to. We were just lacking confidence, and I think all the boys enjoyed a drink more than anything else. It wasn't a conscious thing that we wanted to be different from any other band."

Nevertheless, they were. Fans of Stewart and the Faces—Rod dubbed them the Tartan Horde—were zealous in their protective feelings toward these amiable, skilled drunks, and the fact that Stewart just happened to make emotionally mature, moving music simply enhanced the miracle of this bunch of determinedly dissolute rockers. Soon enough, Rod Stewart would slip into a superstardom of exceptionally public decadence; when punk rockers wanted to justify their contempt for the established rock order, they would sneer most eloquently at Stewart's Spandex tights, his dalliances with fourth-rate Hollywood sex bombs, his debasement of talent to become the insecurely arrogant Rod "Da Ya Think I'm Sexy" Stewart. But at the start of the seventies, Rod the Mod was a proto-punk himself, leader of a band that despised the truisms and verities of the increasingly entrenched rock industry as much as the Sex Pistols or the Clash ever would.

The even more famous naughty boys of this era, the Rolling Stones, weren't feeling particularly chipper at the dawn of 1970. In San Francisco on January 8 of that year, a Hell's Angel named Alan Passaro went on trial for the murder of Meredith Hunter, a deed committed at the Altamont rock festival headlined by the Stones on the preceding December 6 (he was later found not guilty). One of the primary pieces of evidence employed by the prosecution was the climactic footage of a documentary film then playing all across the country: the Maysles Brothers' *Gimme Shelter*, a film about the Stones' 1969 U. S. tour that culminated with footage of Hunter's death.

A few months later, in July, Stones lead singer Mick Jagger could be seen once again in the movies, as the star of the Tony Richardson mess *Ned Kelly*. Soon after, director Jean-Luc Godard's documentary screed about the Stones versus dialectical communism, *Sympathy for the Devil (One Plus One)*, opened to unstifled yawns—except in Paris, where New Jersey expatriate Patti Smith was busy leading a life of bohemian destitution. For her and her sister Linda, the film's glimpse of the Stones confirmed the band's ultimate coolness: "Oh God, we were there [in the movie house] night and day. We'd come in the morning and watch it over and over and over again, for five days running." Soon after, Smith began performing rock songs herself, copping no small aspect of her pose from Brian Jones.

Close on the heels of *One Plus One* was *Performance*, the Nicolas Roeg film that flopped at the box office but immediately attracted a cult audience for the way it offered up its star, Mick Jagger, as a perfect icon of decadence, cruelty, and nihilism.

Oh, yes: the Rolling Stones were also releasing music at the start of the decade. *Get Yer Ya-Yas Out!*, in 1970, was an agreeably rough-and-tumble live album documenting that 1969 tour, with particularly sharp, stinging guitar work on "Love in Vain" by then-Stone Mick Taylor. The next year would see the release of *Sticky Fingers*, featuring a controversial cover designed by Andy Warhol—a close-up of a man's crotch in jeans, with a real zipper you could pull down if you dared. Inside—on the album that is—the Stones simultaneously played up to their increasingly contrived "evil" image with songs like "Bitch" and "Sister Morphine" while transcending that posturing with great dark rock like "Moonlight Mile" and the my-aren't-we-racist? my aren't-we-sexist? hit single "Brown Sugar."

These were good albums, but 1972 yielded a masterpiece: *Exile on Main Street*, two records of thick, remorseless rock and roll. The sound of Keith Richards's guitar has the implacable force of a monster on a rampage; Jagger's furry, slurry voice sounds drugged out and utterly without hope. *Exile on Main Street* (its original title was to be *Tropical Disease*) offered the Rolling Stones without romanticism; for anyone with ears and brains, it said more about the dead end of the Rolling Stones' expensive-drug, cheap-sex image than all the sermons that would ever be delivered to denounce it. Or perhaps, even more unsettlingly—we are talking about the Rolling Stones, after all—*Exile* represents the creativity that drugs can inspire. Either way, Keith summed it up years later when he remarked, "While I was a junkie, I learned to ski and I made *Exile on Main Street*."

In a year that saw George Wallace shot and crippled in a Maryland shopping center and most of the Israeli weight-lifting team murdered at the Munich Olympics, *Exile on Main Street* fit right into the world culture. Never had an album so willfully crude, so difficult to comprehend (what were they talking about in these lyrics that couldn't be heard?), been such a hit.

Exile was also the climax of the Stones' long romance with black music. It was an album as profoundly influenced by Robert Johnson's blues as it was by Sly Stone's increasingly cynical, jagged-edged version of modern soul.

At its best this music made the connection that Jagger and Richards had always stressed—that rock derived from black blues, and there was no reason that, if Muddy Waters was playing the blues into his sixties, the Stones might not rock into their sixties as well. As the decade proceeded, it seemed as if, once more, the music wanted it all: to live fast but die old, to endure as a cheerful rebuke to the Who's Pete Townshend's line, "Hope I die before I get old." The singer-songwriters had suggested that the way to endure was to slow it down a little, to grow up, to mature; the glam-rockers decided to dress up and emulate Dorian Gray while invoking art with a capital A; the hardest rockers' implicit retort was that only by harking back to the crudest, roughest, toughest aspects of the first generation of rock music could you hope to carry on the tradition in an honest, and profitable, way.

30

B<small>LACK</small> R<small>OCK</small> <small>IN</small>
<small>THE</small> 1970<small>S</small>

T<small>HE</small> early 1970s in rock can be defined in terms of fragmentation, a word that carries the connotations of confusion and scatteration. And indeed, just as much as white rock, the records being made by black musicians during this period lacked a sense of unity, an implicit common purpose, that had existed a decade earlier. Jimi Hendrix had held within himself a unified image of what the future of black rock could be—his synthesis of black blues and white hard rock was a sure, confident, exciting one. With his death in 1970, black rock lost its center, and the ensuing confusion was echoed in Motown's sputtering decline as the primary production line for black stars.

In the midst of this, however, there were hopeful signs and exhilarating music. In Philadelphia, producers-songwriters Kenneth Gamble and Leon Huff would invent their own version of Detroit's Motown—Philadelphia International Records—with a string of hit singles and new acts that offered a sleek, urbane, fresh version of rhythm and blues. Quirky but original acts like Barry White and Isaac Hayes would gain entrance to the mainstream. And pushing his talent to the limit was Sly Stone, the only black artist aside from Hendrix who seemed capable of putting all the fragments together: a black/white audience coalition, a black/white musical synthesis, and a sense of black/white politics that gave his best compositions a polemicized edge no musician, black or white, could match.

Without succumbing to the facile, hack's temptation to equate his life as a star with his brothers' lives as political pawns, Stone nonetheless fused these matters into the thick, moody music of *There's a Riot Goin' On* (1971), one of the most bleak, despairing, yet emotionally charged albums any pop artist has ever recorded. Unlike earlier Family Stone albums, there was no sense of celebration or joyousness on *Riot*. Stone turned his music—and himself—inside out: His earlier hit "Thank You Fallettinme Be Mice Elf Again" became, on *Riot*, "Thank You for Talkin' to Me Africa," a slowed, malevolent version of the pop hit made deadly, flat, and cynical. It was a song difficult to listen to but impossible to dismiss. What Stone's music suggested was that soul music, in its most chipper, choreographed, commercial form, was an increasingly outdated concept. The ominous bass guitar lines and intricate, implacable rhythms that Stone brought into the mainstream of popular music would resurface later in the decade in the funk of artists such as George Clinton and Rick James.

At the start of the decade, however, there was an explosion of ambition in black popular music. From Curtis Mayfield's "Superfly" and "Freddie's Dead" to the Staples Singers' "Respect Yourself" and "I'll Take You There," with the O'Jays' "Back Stabbers" and War's "The World Is a Ghetto" in between, pop musicians had never been more successful in expressing intensely personal, frequently angry emotions in music that reached out to a large and varied audience. Rather than register dismay or hostility in the face of this deluge of prickly hits, the white rock audience listened and learned. In turn, black artists seized the opportunity to expand the idea of black pop music.

The slit-eyed pessimism of Sly and the Family Stone's *There's a Riot Goin' On* was succeeded by the bristling irony of *Fresh* (1973), in which Stone took simple catch phrases—"babies makin' babies," "thankful 'n' thoughtful"—and turned them into back-to-Africa chants that reverberated with delicate, complex rhythms. That the album climaxed with a slow, muzzy-voiced version of the Doris Day hit "Que Sera, Sera" only intensified Sly Stone's complicated achievement: While addressing a funny rumor of the time (it was said that Stone and Day, certainly the most unlikely media couple ever, were having an affair), Stone managed to turn his joke into a veiled threat at, and finally a dismissal of, white America.

Stevie Wonder was making his own jokes, attacks, and escapes. As early as 1971's *Where I'm Coming From*, he had broken from Berry Gordy's imposed production supervisors to create his own albums. His leverage? He'd threatened to take his genius and leave Motown when his contract expired, something Gordy knew his wobbly company could not endure. But it wasn't until 1972's *Talking Book*—complete with a title reproduced in braille, as if to claim this work for his own in the most personal terms— that Wonder fully succeeded in writing and producing an entire album's worth of first-rate, innovative songs. A single from the album, the driving, jiving "Superstition," became Wonder's first number one pop hit in ten years; indeed, *Talking Book* reintroduced Stevie Wonder to a white rock audience that still thought of him as "Little" Stevie Wonder.

Wonder topped himself with 1973's *Innervisions*, a multilayered album of inner-city lamentations that climaxed with "Living in the City," the extraordinarily cinematic set piece that followed a young black man from his country home in "Hard Times, Mississippi" to his illegal arrest in New York City. While frequently a sentimentalist of awesome proportions, Wonder was also capable of redeeming that sentimentalism with the terse beauty of his melodies and the gritty melismatics of his vocals. Thus it's no surprise that "You Are the Sunshine of My Life" has become a middle-of-the-road standard; what's amazing is that Wonder's version of it remains charming and even moving after its hundreds of drippy cover versions.

Wonder and Sly Stone vied in an unofficial contest for the title of White America's Most Admired Black Musician. Over the next few years, Wonder would seem to win, primarily because Stone gave up. In 1974, *Small Talk* was a commercial bomb; at the same time, Stone began missing concert dates, and rumors of drug use became rampant. So pervasive had been Sly Stone's presence in the early 1970s and so thorough was his disappearance from the rock scene in the mid-1970s, that he was able to call his 1976 release *Heard Ya Missed Me, Well I'm Back*, and the joke was only half-hearted. So was the music. For the rest of the decade Stone failed to record music of any consequence.

Stevie Wonder, by contrast, continued to release ambitious, increasingly sprawling albums—*Fulfillingness' First Finale* in 1974 and *Songs in the Key of Life* in 1976—that, while frequently uneven, nevertheless testified to his ability to make discursive, even self-indulgent compositions take on the strength and focus of major pop statements. He had proved to Motown that his idiosyncratic, fiercely independent form of recording—he regularly played all the instrumental parts himself, for example—could be commercially successful. Indeed, Wonder was Motown's only consistently popular act, with the exception of Marvin Gaye's albums and occasional smash singles from the Temptations, Diana Ross, and the Jackson 5.

In 1974, the Jackson 5 had a big disco hit with "Dancing Machine," an insinuating riff that, in concert, astutely exploited the stunningly smooth robotlike moves Michael Jackson could execute with apparent ease. "Dancing Machine" came along just in time, rescuing the brothers from a recent string of singles and albums whose prickly soul harmonies flew in the face of disco smoothness.

"Dancing Machine," however, was a fluke, only the beginning of the slow, steady unraveling of the Jackson 5. "Being at a record company is like being at school," Michael Jackson would say. "If you're not happy with the principal or the school, you go to another. . . . For the *Dancing Machine* album, we were forced to use several producers when we only wanted one producer for the entire album, so it would have one sound. Instead, we had a bunch of different sounds and it wasn't as good as it could have been."

By 1975, the group had become antsy; their career was in commercial limbo. Motown Records did not seem to know what sort of material suited a former-kid-singer-plus-siblings group whose kid singer had gone through an adolescent change of voice. Nonetheless, Berry Gordy and his minions weren't willing to let the Jackson brothers do anything so radical as write or produce their own material. Gordy ended up alienating talented artists by denying them the chance to flex their creative muscles.

Meanwhile, the group was being courted by Epic Records, and with the aggressive presence of their manager-father, Joe Jackson, behind them, they moved to leave Motown. The rift finally came in 1976, complicated by the fact that one Jackson, Jermaine, had married his soon-to-be-former boss's daughter, Hazel Gordy. As a result of this tug of allegiances, Jermaine would stay on as a Motown artist until the end of the decade and was replaced in the lineup by his brother Randy.

The separation from Motown would have other costs as well: Among various concessions, the group agreed to give Motown all rights to their act's name. Thus it was that the Jackson 5 became "the Jacksons." And thus it was that Motown vice-chairman Michael Roshkind was quoted as saying, "We own the name 'The Jackson 5'; we can put together another Jackson 5 any time we want." As of this writing, Motown hasn't made good on Roshkind's threat.

Among Gordy's other losses in this era was Gladys Knight and the Pips, who would hit their stride only after they left Motown Records in 1973. Knight had always been a much more willful and independent singer than most vocalists in the Motown stable; while she was not a songwriter herself, she had firm ideas about what songs she should be covering. She and her Pips—two cousins and her older brother Merald "Bubba" Knight—recorded a string of hit singles for Buddah Records in the mid-seventies, including "Midnight Train to Georgia," "Best Thing That Ever Happened to Me," and "I've Got to Use My Imagination." A warm, intelligent woman who sang in a gritty but supple gospelish tenor with sharp, often ironic phrasing, Gladys Knight was always denied the across-the-board superstardom she seemed to deserve: While at the height of their fame, she and the Pips were consigned to hosting a mediocre television variety show (sort of "The Sonny and Cher Comedy Hour" crossed with "The Flip Wilson Show") and her one foray into movie acting was the disastrous *Pipe Dreams*, a romance set on the Alaskan pipeline, of all places.

Clearly, Motown Records was at a loss to compete with a rock and roll industry that esteemed the experimentation of Sly Stone as well as the outer limits of white rock (what, for example, must Berry Gordy have made of David Bowie?). Motown's traditionally paternalistic, hands-on career guidance was frustrating many of its most ambitious artists, and its entrenched corporate-think wasn't making the transition into the 1970s—too much of Motown's run-of-the-mill product was rehashed, dissipirited sixties soul that never came close to achieving the popularity of its groundbreaking work of that earlier decade.

Another record company suggested that the way to thrive was to offer a dramatic alternative. Philadelphia International Records, founded by producers-songwriters Kenneth Gamble and Leon Huff, was the 1970s soul Cinderella story, rising to the top of the charts in a very short period and heralding a genre that would in a very short time become one of the most controversial pop offshoots ever: disco.

Like all black pop music of this era, though, Philadelphia International had ties to Motown. Gamble, Huff, and their future partner, Thom Bell, along with a crew of Philadelphia musicians, played behind the Supremes on their 1968 hit "I'm Gonna Make You Love Me." Working out of Sigma Sound recording studio on Philadelphia's North Twelfth Street, this same set of increasingly in-demand musicians provided the velvet hammer of power behind such late sixties/early seventies successes as Dusty Springfield's "Brand New Me," the Delfonics' "La-La Means I Love You," Joe Simon's "Drowning in the Sea of Love," and Jerry Butler's string of "Ice Man"–era hits.

Clive Davis, president of Columbia Records in the late sixties and early seventies, noticed the way Gamble and Huff were taking down-on-their-luck artists and helping them rebuild their careers with songs full of sharp lyrics and lush orchestration. He agreed to distribute the records produced by Gamble and Huff's fledgling company, and in 1972, Philadelphia International Records had its first major hit, the O'Jays' "Back Stabbers."

With its cool, sinuous background music, its hard, harsh vocals, and its potent political message, "Back Stabbers" was an immediately riveting hit, one that rapidly crossed over from the rhythm-and-blues charts to the pop market. In the first nine months of its operation, Philadelphia International sold ten million singles and two million albums; it was an unprecedented phenomenon. Out of its headquarters at 309 South Broad Street, Gamble and Huff oversaw more than fifteen acts, and were personally involved in the songwriting, production, and business aspects of each act's career. Some were one-shot wonders, such as Billy Paul, whose jazzily sung ballad "Me and Mrs. Jones" was a smash in 1972 that Paul would never repeat. Other acts built a succession of hits; the best known of these groups were the O'Jays ("Love Train," "For the Love of Money," "Back Stabbers") and Harold Melvin and the Blue Notes, featuring drummer-turned-singer Teddy Pendergrass ("If You Don't Know Me By Now," "The Love I Lost," "Wake Up, Everybody").

All Gamble and Huff's acts used the body of Philly studio musicians who became known as MFSB (which stood for "Mother, Father, Sister, Brother") and who were a hit-making act in their own right, with instrumentals such as "Sexy" and "TSOP (The Sound of Philadelphia)." The latter became the theme song for the most popular black-music dance television show of the era, "Soul Train." By 1975, with grosses of $25 million to $30 million a year, Philadelphia International Records was the second-largest black-owned company in America (Motown was the largest).

By the middle of the decade, however, Philadelphia International was headed for a fall. In 1975, Gamble and Huff were indicted for payola. Eventually the charges against Huff were dropped and Gamble paid a $2,500 fine, but the legal tangles interfered crucially with the team's creative work. They left the songwriting to others, with near-disastrous results. Then, too, Kenny Gamble had developed something of a messianic streak; he became involved with local politics, squaring off against Mayor Frank Rizzo on social issues, but also indulging himself in a kind of self-invented mysticism-cum-self-help philosophy. On the back of the O'Jays' 1976 *Message in Our Music* record, for example, he wrote: "Understand while you dance. The word with music is one of the strongest, if not the strongest, means of communication on the planet Earth. It is the only natural science known to man. The word with music can do its part to calm the savage beast that lives in every man. The message is Unity."

Increasingly, though, unity was the one thing Philadelphia International lacked. Gamble's wife, Dee Dee Sharp (singer of the immortal sixties hit "Mashed Potato Time"), divorced him in 1976; some say the split drove Gamble close to a breakdown. Some key staff members, such as songwriters Gene McFadden and John Whitehead, left the organization (they would score one huge hit as a performing act in 1979 with "Ain't No Stoppin' Us Now"). Teddy Pendergrass left Harold Melvin and the Blue Notes in 1976 but remained with Philadelphia International to launch a highly successful solo career that was cut short when he was paralyzed from the neck down in a March 1982 auto accident.

Producer-songwriter Thom Bell, the third member of Gamble and Huff's Mighty Three music publishing company, allied himself with Atlantic Records and began to produce hits for the Spinners such as "The Rubberband Man," "I'll Be Around," and "Could It Be I'm Falling in Love," all of them powered by the high, sharp voice of lead singer Phillipe Wynne.

Out on the West Coast, someone who had been listening closely to Gamble and Huff's romantic "Philly Sound" was veteran producer-arranger Barry White. In the early 1970s, White organized a female singing group, Love Unlimited, and a large band, the Love Unlimited Orchestra. Playing thick, string-soaked music decorated with atmospheric sound effects, the aggregation hit it big with the 1972 single "Walking in the Rain with the One I Love." Installing himself as a grunting, groaning lead singer, White floated into the mid-seventies with such singles as "Never, Never Gonna Give You Up," "You're the First, the Last, My Everything," and "Let the Music Play." Pretty soon White lapsed into self-parody: He covered his immense frame in furs and gold jewelry, looking like a cross between Liberace and Jackie Gleason; his concerts became gaudy displays in which the band repeated White's disco-pulsed makeout music for hours at a time with only minor variations.

White's model had been the self-proclaimed Black Moses, Isaac Hayes, the veteran Stax Records songwriter who, as 1969 shaded into 1970, seemed to be black pop's most notable innovator. His *Hot Buttered Soul*, released in 1969 and one of the dominant pop albums of the following year, was probably the most aesthetically influential makeout record ever recorded. Hayes's lugubrious vocals, his murmured protestations of love, and his music's ceaseless undulations extended and exaggerated traditional soul balladry to a dramatic degree. And as if the music wasn't enough, Hayes had *image* coming out of his ears: In place of a shirt, he preferred chains looped across his burly chest; in place of hair, he preferred a gleaming bald pate. Perhaps because the glare of this trademark was too bright, his face was frequently shrouded in large sunglasses. All in all, Hayes offered pop ideas that other artists spent the decade borrowing: Barry White took his voice, Teddy Pendergrass his bare chest.

Hayes's career had begun calmly and admirably enough. With David Porter, Hayes had co-written Sam and Dave's most popular hits, "Hold On, I'm A-Comin'" and "Soul Man," as well as producing and playing keyboards behind many Stax Records acts of the sixties. By 1967, he was ready to begin recording himself as a solo artist, and using the Bar-Kays' rhythm section, he released two forgettable albums before *Hot Buttered Soul* changed the direction of 1970s soul.

The essence of Hayes's success on this album was that he decided to make soul music as a jazz artist might, lengthening and improvising on a single idea. Like a jazz player, he seized on corny pop tunes and made them his own, the most famous example on this album being Hayes's eighteen-minute interpretation of Jimmy Webb's "By the Time I Get to Phoenix."

Hayes became a romantic idol not merely because love was his obsessive subject matter but because he used lovemaking as the elaborate, grandly overstated organizing principle of his music. His gentle, rambling spoken introductions to many songs were the foreplay, while the repetition of the simple melodies and the damp layers of orchestral strings delayed the climax of any given song until almost past endurance.

Having secured the number one position on both the soul and jazz charts in 1970, Hayes was not about to relinquish his winning formula. In fact, he quickly ran it into the ground over the next year, on *The Isaac Hayes Movement*. Then, in late 1971, he redeemed himself by adapting his style to a different but highly complementary medium by writing the score for the ultimate blaxploitation film, *Shaft*.

For *Shaft*, Hayes used the dense textures of his music to suggest the thick intrigues of the movie's hero, detective John Shaft (Richard Roundtree). Hayes reached back in black music history to update the call-and-response ("Who's the man all the women want to love?" rumbled Hayes; "Shaft!" yelped the female chorus); he parodied the hep-cat coolness of Henry Mancini in conveying movie action tension by scraping a single electric guitar string over and over until your nerves were popping. Along with Curtis Mayfield's work on *Superfly*, Hayes's *Shaft* score changed Hollywood's idea of the use of rock music in movie sound tracks.

Meanwhile, Hayes continued to grow ever more full of himself. With his next release, a double album called *Black Moses*, he took to traveling the country with a twenty-piece orchestra—they wore tuxedos, he wore gold chains. The height of his black-stud image was achieved on the 1973 double album *Live at the Sahara Tahoe*, and he repeated himself on the subsequent film scores for *Tough Guys* and *Truck Turner* (in which he also played the title role). By the time disco hit, Hayes was little better than a joke. He would go on to presage rap music with his 1979 album collaboration with Millie Jackson, *Royal Rappin's*, and he persisted in acting, out-woodening Kurt Russell in John Carpenter's *Escape from New York* (1980). He also declared bankruptcy in 1976. But before all these embarrassments, Isaac Hayes began the decade of the 1970s by enlarging our notions of what black pop musicians were "supposed" to do.

As the arc of Isaac Hayes's career suggests, the early 1970s was a time of restless ambition for black rock musicians—from knotty "concept" albums to film sound track hack work, it looked as if these innovators might participate as acknowledged equals in the burgeoning rock industry. This meant not only the idea that blacks might become superstars whose audiences knew no racial boundaries; it also meant the opportunity for blacks to sell out to the entertainment establishment as frequently as white rockers did.

But the increasing racial segregation of radio formats, the rise of controversial disco, and the unevenness or increasingly sporadic appearance of new music by some of the biggest black stars (Sly, Stevie Wonder, Marvin Gaye) all combined to limit the exposure black rock music might have had in mainstream popular culture. Thrown back on itself, black music returned to its roots, and in the latter half of the 1970s it re-emerged with funk (an artful updating of rhythm and blues) as well as rap music, a genre that was the exact opposite of polished soul music and that presented a new set of challenges to the rock audience.

To the ultimate detriment of rock in the early 1970s, however, the superstar acts that came to dominate the first half of the decade were white, not black, rockers.

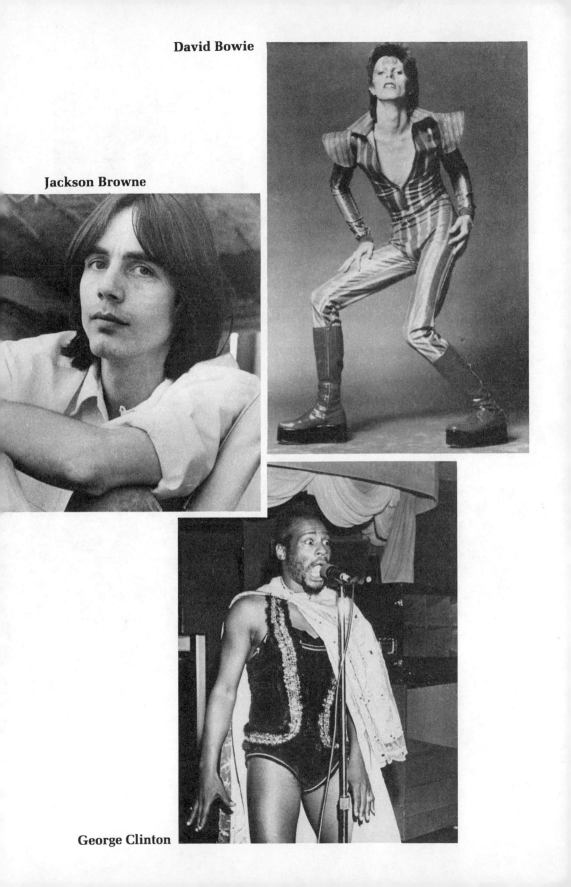

David Bowie

Jackson Browne

George Clinton

Elvis Costello

Bryan Ferry

Al Green

Jethro Tull's Ian Anderson

Bob Marley

Randy Newman

The New York Dolls

The Police—Sting, Andy Summers, Stewart Copeland

Prince

Lou Reed

The Sex Pistols—Paul Cook, Sid Vicious, Johnny Rotten, Steve Jones

Donna Summer

The Ramones—Johnny Ramone, Marky Ramone,
Joey Ramone, Dee Dee Ramone

Bruce Springsteen

The Talking Heads—Tina Weymouth, Jerry Harrison, David Byrne, Chris Frantz

James Taylor

Van Halen—Alex Van Halen, David Lee Roth, Eddie Van Halen, Michael Anthony

Neil Young

31

THE "NEW BEATLES"

Even as rock fragmented, there was nostalgia for the recent past, for the unity that the Beatles had seemed to provide for the rock audience. During the first half of the 1970s, a number of acts came along that tempted pundits to employ the phrase "logical successors to the Beatles"—Elton John, Fleetwood Mac, Peter Frampton, or name-your-fave-rave. What these acts had in common was that their appeal transcended the rapidly hardening genre classifications—they made hits that were both soft and hard, ballads and rockers, hits that borrowed from different genres (reggae, disco, country) while retaining the pop melodicism that pleased a huge mass audience.

"My success was a freak," said Elton John in 1979. "I was just the right person in the right place at the right time." But John's ascendancy from earnest young singer-songwriter to flamboyant rock idol wasn't a fluke—he met the needs of his era. John's lyrics, initially written entirely by chum Bernie Taupin, were the sort of bonehead poesy that begged to be slurred by a rock singer, not enunciated by a sensitive postfolkie.

The twenty-year-old Reginald Dwight changed his name to Elton John in 1967 around the time he met Taupin. John had already endured a short stint as a member of Bluesology, a rhythm-and-blues band whose primary distinction was that it backed English blues blusterer Long John Baldry for a short time.

In 1969, John released his debut album, _Empty Sky_; a year later, _Elton John_ was issued and became John's first American release. _Elton John_ concluded with "Your Song," a pretty ballad with a weepy lyric that became John's first American Top Ten hit. However, it took John's stage performances—his pianohopping antics and garish costumes—to establish him as a media star in America; his new fans seemed especially taken with the way his onstage demeanor contrasted with the brooding introspectiveness of the music he and Taupin were creating.

John's piano style owed a lot to Jerry Lee Lewis—not in the manner in which he played the instrument (in fact, he was a well-trained, mannerly player on all but the crudest rockers, to which he self-consciously adjusted his style accordingly) but rather in the way he attacked it: kicking over the piano stool, executing handstands on the keyboard, leaping on top of the instrument and jumping up and down like a fey gorilla. When John deployed these tactics at Los Angeles's Troubadour nightclub in August 1970, Los Angeles *Times* rock critic Robert Hilburn came away raving: "One of the most important new acts of this new decade." To receive such a notice from the newspaper most esteemed by the West Coast music industry gave this, John's first American tour, a tremendous boost. It is one of the most clear-cut examples of the increasing influence a critic could occasionally wield in helping a new act gain attention from the public and support from his record company.

While John was in America, "Your Song" climbed into the Top Ten, and his record label, MCA, began an Elton deluge: *Tumbleweed Connection* was released while *Elton John* was still ascending the charts, an unusual and risky commercial move that paid off when the latter album immediately began to sell as quickly as *Elton John*. By early 1971, MCA had also released *11-17-70* a live album taken from the radio broadcast of a wild New York City club performance. Meanwhile, Paramount Records issued the John-Taupin sound track for the mediocre movie *Friends*; it is an album John has repudiated as having been poorly recorded and lacking in quality material, and he is correct. As quickly as October 1971, MCA released still another new John album, *Madman Across the Water*, but by now, John was an even bigger star in America than he was in England, and its popularity was virtually assured.

Until this point, Elton John's success was based primarily on lustily sung sentimentalisms like "Your Song" and "Levon." With 1972's *Honky Chateau*, however, John established his credentials as an interesting rock-and-roller, as opposed to being merely an ostentatious pop star. Working with his best—his most terse, self-effacing yet forceful—band, which consisted of guitarist Davey Johnstone, drummer Nigel Olsson, and bassist Dee Murray, John demonstrated a willingness to go beyond well-crafted pop to achieve a surprisingly rough rock studio style. This extends even to "Rocket Man," a ballad saved from bathos by the awkward, swift swelling of its chorus, as well as "And I Think I'm Gonna Kill Myself," a bit of adolescent self-pity redeemed by the rock-and-roll crudity of the melody and the bluntness of the lyric. It helped that John had parted from arranger Paul Buckmaster, who had drenched most of John's earlier work in soggy string sections; it helped, too, that Taupin's lyrics were being swallowed whole by John, thus freeing John's excellent melodies from their greatest liability.

By the mid-1970s, Elton John was a garishly dressed rock star on his way to becoming a show-biz celebrity. Now his stage dress became even more outlandish—spangled drum major's outfits, oversize neon-lit glasses that spelled out *ELTON*—and his shows became displays of multiple costume changes and fast, furious recitations of a growing body of hits. *Honky Chateau* was the first of seven consecutive number-one albums in the United States, and John racked up a prodigious list of top-five singles: "Crocodile Rock," "Daniel," "Goodbye Yellow Brick Road," "Bennie and the Jets," "Don't Let the Sun Go Down on Me," "The Bitch Is Back," a lugubrious cover of the Beatles' "Lucy in the Sky with Diamonds," "Philadelphia Freedom," "Someone Saved My Life Tonight," and "Island Girl."

During this period, John established himself as a pop-cultural presence in a variety of ways. He purchased a soccer team, the Watford Football Club, soccer being his primary passion after music. In 1973, he formed his own record label, Rocket Records, distributed by MCA; this was a typical vanity prize bestowed upon bestselling rock stars of the era (the Rolling Stones and Led Zeppelin were similarly indulged, for example). John's label yielded some non-John successes: Neil Sedaka's 1975–1976 pair of comeback hits, "Laughter in the Rain" and "Bad Blood," as well as Elton's 1976 duet with Kiki Dee, "Don't Go Breakin' My Heart." In 1975, the singer cheerfully admitted to *Rolling Stone* that he was bisexual, but his honesty backfired on him. Perhaps because he hadn't realized the basically conservative nature of his predominantly young American fans, John was greeted with a hailstorm of abuse in many parts of this great land. "I really didn't think people would care," he said later. "Especially in Britain, where people are much more broadminded. In America, it's slightly different. I've had more people insult me in the streets of America; you know, call me a faggot. And yet America's supposed to be the great liberated free-minded society—which of course it isn't. It's just fucked up. I couldn't ever live there. It would drive me crazy." In response to this controversy and to his own waning enthusiasm ("I'd burnt out all my ambition; I'd seemed to have done just about everything in five years and I couldn't do any more—sell any more records, play to any bigger audiences"), he grew increasingly reclusive, which combined with the relative failure of his 1976 double-album sulk *Blue Moves* (it only made it to number 3 and yielded only one Top Ten single, "Sorry Seems to Be the Hardest Word") to give Elton John the look of a loser, a budding has-been.

John's decline coincided with the rise of punk/new wave rock, a genre that found in old Elton a particularly ripe symbol of rock's big-business fatuousness. To his credit, John remained open-minded about the new music of the period and even shared many of the same feelings the punks held about the rock business. "I feel the rock industry has become just that—an industry," he told British journalist Roy Carr. "And I abhor it, especially as one of those who started it: becoming the first million-dollar-plus signing to an American record company, complete with full-page ads in the *New York Times* and whatever." And in 1978, when England's Capitol Radio gave him an award as Best Male Singer of the Year, in his acceptance speech, John said that Elvis Costello should have been given the prize. "I honestly felt that of all the people who had emerged, Elvis Costello was the most important—by far the best songwriter and the best record-maker," he told Carr in a 1978 *New Musical Express* interview. He prided himself on being "the ultimate rock fan," an ordinary, nearsighted fellow who by dint of hard work and love of music became a superstar, in his glory days regarded as the only performer who could assume the Beatles' mantle, both in terms of records sold and screams inspired.

In fact, it was during John's 1974 Thanksgiving show at Madison Square Garden that John Lennon would make his final public appearance, hopping onstage to accompany John on his own "Whatever Gets You Thru the Night," "Lucy in the Sky with Diamonds," and "I Saw Her Standing There." As the decade progressed, Lennon was becoming increasingly withdrawn from the rock audience he had done so much to consolidate. *Mind Games* and *Walls and Bridges* represented his artistic output in 1973 and 1974 respectively, but their comparatively weak music was overshadowed by Lennon/Ono's increasingly public life: Yoko Ono's battle to regain custody of her daughter Kyoko from her former husband Tony Cox (a fight won in March 1973), and Lennon's tussle with U.S. immigration, eager to have him deported and using his 1968 drug bust as a legal excuse. Shortly after recording *Mind Games*, Yoko banished John from her presence, and he moved to Los Angeles, where he led a generally dissolute life with chums such as Harry Nilsson, with whom he recorded the album *Pussy Cats*. John and Yoko finally reconciled in late 1974. In October 1975, the U.S. Court of Appeals overturned his deportation order, and two days later, on October 9 (John's thirty-fifth birthday), Yoko gave birth to Sean Ono Lennon.

For the next five years, Lennon dropped out from the music world, releasing no new music, tending to baby Sean, puttering around Manhattan. In this way, Lennon rejected the commercial rat race the rock industry had become in the mid-1970s and made way for other star acts that pursued their own eccentricities, such as, most dramatically, Fleetwood Mac. Fleetwood Mac must be considered the ultimate journeymen, excellent musicians who, through intelligent persistence, became one of the oddest superstar acts to go multiplatinum.

Formed in 1967 as a blues-rock band led by former John Mayall's Blues-breakers guitarist Peter Green, Fleetwood Mac's two constant members have been its rhythm section: drummer Mick Fleetwood and Bassist John McVie. Both men had been Bluesbreakers, and it was Fleetwood Mac's triumphant debut at the 1967 British Jazz and Blues Festival that secured the fledgling band a record contract. Green, Fleetwood, McVie, and guitarist Jeremy

Spenser were instant hits in England, where the band's debut album, *Fleetwood Mac*, remained in the Top Ten for thirteen months. American acceptance was slow in coming; on their first American tour, for example, they were third-billed to Jethro Tull and Joe Cocker. This resistance is understandable: In England, the blues is a popular genre; in America, the blues is a cult music.

The band shifted its personnel with every album. In 1970, Green left the band, unsettled by a profound spiritual crisis. As he recalled at the time, "I woke up one night, sweating heavily and feeling like I couldn't move. . . . That night I wrote 'Green Manalishi,' a song that was written out of fear, really. I think I realized at the time that it was very powerful stuff." "Green Manalishi," with its dark-toned, riven guitar lines, certainly suggested the roiling emotions Green was experiencing, but the song—an immediate smash in England when it was released a few months after its composition—didn't convey the repulsion Green had begun to feel toward his stardom.

"In May 1970, Peter told me privately that he felt it was wrong that a group of entertainers such as Fleetwood Mac should earn such vast sums of money when, in fact, other people in the world didn't have enough to eat," the band's then-manager Clifford Davis told journalist Sam Sutherland in 1978. "He put to the band the following proposition: That all profits other than running costs earned by the band be given to needy people by way of donating to various trust funds, etc. Fleetwood and McVie did not wish to go along with this line of thought, and although Peter respected their decision, he felt he could no longer be associated with the band merely for his own financial ends."

The result was that Green left the band and subsequently gave away virtually all of his small fortune to various charities. "I thought I had too much money to be happy and normal, and I got sort of panicky, I guess," Green said to Sutherland. "Thousands of pounds is just too much for a working person to handle all of a sudden and I felt I didn't deserve it. I didn't want it anymore." Guilt-ridden and depressed, Green made a brief retirement from the music business but reemerged to record two solo albums featuring hauntingly beautiful—if obscure and rather aimless— guitar compositions.

After numerous other personnel changes, stability of a very quirky sort was achieved in 1974 when guitarist Lindsey Buckingham and singer Stevie Nicks (who had recorded a spacey-folkie album called *Buckingham-Nicks* in 1973) joined the group. This lineup—Buckingham, Nicks, Fleetwood, McVie, and Keyboardist-singer Christine McVie—inaugurated Fleetwood Mac's commencement as a pop-rock band, a different entity from the blues group the band had once been. The band got a new producer, Keith Olsen (indeed, it was Olsen who had introduced Fleetwood Mac to Buckingham and Nicks), and on 1975's *Fleetwood Mac*, Olsen brightened and clarified what had been the group's increasingly murky sound. Buoyed by the pop sensibility of Buckingham, anchored by the Fleetwood-McVie rhythm section, given emotional maturity by Christine McVie's warm, grainy alto, and commercialized by Stevie Nicks's space cadet/sexpot stage persona, *Fleetwood Mac* was a slow starter that eventually sold over four million copies, making it one of the bestselling albums in rock history.

The most unexpected superstar of the 1970s was Peter Frampton, an amiable baby-face from England who in 1976 just happened to sell ten million copies of a collection of old nonhits called *Frampton Comes Alive!* Frampton's early career as part of the Herd (and later Humble Pie) had established him as a late-1960s teenybopper/pinup boy; but like all teen sensations, he had a necessarily limited lifespan—the girls outgrew him by the end of the decade. But Frampton's ambitions didn't die when Humble Pie broke up. He immediately set about recording a series of solo albums whose backup musicians suggest the respect he had from his colleagues: Ringo Starr, Billy Preston, Klaus Voormann, and ex-Herd chum Andy Bown all played on one or another of the four studio albums Frampton released before *Frampton Comes Alive! Frampton Comes Alive!* was another slow starter, receiving in the United States, for example, the minimal sort of radio play that such an obscure English musician would merit. But constant touring here and in England was paying off: Frampton had a solid cult of fans in the United States by the time of *Comes Alive!* and something about that album's combination of catchy pop-rock and enthusiastic crowd noise captured the ears of America.

Frampton Comes Alive! yielded a series of hit singles—"Show Me the Way," "Baby I Love Your Way," "Do You Feel Like We Do"—and once again (but for the first time in America), Frampton ascended to the peak of teen idolatry, his long, curly blond hair and quavery tenor voice suggesting to female fans that here was a cuddlesome new dreamboat who could also be justified for his considerable musicianship.

For over a year, *Frampton Comes Alive!* dominated the record charts and the radio in a way no other album of the period had; it didn't matter that the album had been met with a shrug by the critics, it didn't matter that this music had nothing to do with the upcoming trends of the time—disco in America and pub-rock in England. *Frampton Comes Alive!* was a throwback to an earlier era of rock and roll: pretty boy with a hook makes it. It just so happened that Peter Frampton came along with his hooks at a time when the rock audience was willing to pay for its pleasure in unprecedented numbers.

Frampton never equaled the success of *Comes Alive!* In fact, his career went into a singularly abrupt tailspin. He surfaced very briefly in 1978 to enact the role of the one and only Billy Shears in Robert Stigwood's film version of *Sgt. Pepper's Lonely Hearts Club Band*. Frampton was forgettable, as was the movie, except for one anecdote: Years after its release, the film's screenwriter, former *New York Times* pop pundit Henry Edwards, received a check for a considerable sum—royalties from the sales of the (get this) novelization of his script for *Sgt. Pepper*. Edwards, as intelligent and genial a hack as anyone could imagine, observed, "Who could possibly have bought that paperback? What a wonderful country."

Yet, for all the superstar excesses of the era, the vast new rock audience did allow room for all sorts of extremes in popular music. At one end of the spectrum, there was now a huge market for the treacle of a singer-songwriter like Barry Manilow, a former pianist and arranger for Bette Midler whose schlock balladry became Arista Records' biggest seller. On the other end, heavy metal and art rock would continue to fill arenas while hard rock dominated the radio airwaves. And in between, there lay a smattering of quirky, genre-busting artists who would flourish throughout the mid-1970s.

Some of them, like Neil Young, Al Green, and Steely Dan, deployed their eccentricities to create, for a period, highly commercial music. Others, like Randy Newman, Van Dyke Parks, and Harry Nilsson, were perceived as having a certain amount of commercial potential, and their record companies made investments in sustaining recording careers that might otherwise have been denied such stubborn, individual artists. A few of them would attract enough of a cult following to carry on for years, hovering at the edges of the industry.

In particular, Randy Newman's ascension to (critical) fame and (relative) fortune offers a paradigm for cult stardom in the 1970s. Newman was the scion of a musical Hollywood dynasty—his uncles Alfred and Lionel Newman composed movie scores for numerous films. Randy's father, a doctor, made sure that his son was receiving classical music lessons by the time Randy was seven years old. Randy eventually graduated from UCLA with a degree in music composition, even though he was later to lament, "I was so lazy. I wish I could go back; I didn't pay attention and I didn't learn enough. I'm still always intimidated when I have to work with 'real musicians.'"

What does all this have to do with rock and roll? As it turned out, a fair amount. Newman may have been studying (and for that matter loving) Mozart, but he also developed a furtive love for New Orleans rock and roll—Fats Domino, Professor Longhair, Huey "Piano" Smith—all the most eccentric keyboard stylists of their day. He began to write rock and pop songs, and his pedigree and his technical prowess landed him a job as a staff songwriter in New York. He wrote the B sides for a number of rock hits, and hit it relatively big when then-superstar Judy Collins recorded his "I Think It's Going to Rain Today" on her *In My Life* album in 1966. In England, ex-Animal Alan Price became entranced with Newman's compositions and recorded a few of them, scoring a British hit with "Simon Smith and the Amazing Dancing Bear."

All this led to Newman's signing to Warner Bros. Records as a continuation of that label's interest in singer-songwriters. (Warners' most valuable player in this department was, of course, Sweet Baby James Taylor.) It didn't seem to matter that Newman's voice was little more than a froggy mumble; it was his point of view that Warner Bros. prized. Still, his debut album, *Randy Newman Creates Something New Under the Sun* (1968), sold so poorly that Warner Bros. at one point offered its few brave purchasers the opportunity to trade in their copies for some other, undoubtedly more popular, piece of Warners product—surely one of the more unusual bits of promotion for a company known for its unusual promotion strategies. Nonetheless, the album contained a remarkably vivid display of the sort of oddness and beauty that would characterize much of Newman's music. Newman's lyrics specialized in barbed clichés: "Love Story" follows a perfect relationship to its logical conclusion—the lovers become a helpless doddering couple in an old-folks' home. "Davy the Fat Boy" tells of a fellow so obese his parents commit him to a circus freak show; the song's chorus: "Isn't he, isn't he . . . round."

To some of the few people who listened, it seemed as if Newman might actually be making fun of his variously peculiar protagonists, a truly scandalous notion in this era of sensitive, oh-so-understanding singer-songwriters. Newman's next album, *12 Songs* (1970), only confirmed this suspicion. Not so coincidentally, the album is his masterpiece: *12 Songs*, produced by his boyhood friend and rising Warners exec Lenny Waronker, brought together all of Newman's influences, from raunchy rock ("Let's Burn Down the Cornfield," and "Have You Seen My Baby?") to pop so elegant it bordered on classical complexity ("Suzanne"). That the lyrics to the ineffably beautiful, lulling "Suzanne" told the story of a rapist stalking his victim from the rapist's point of view only made Newman more fascinating—and more unlikely to sell in Sweet Baby James–style numbers.

But the early 1970s was a time when critical acclaim was considered sufficient to keep an artist assured of a record contract; record companies were eager for respect, desperate to be seen by the public as hip, and they had the money to finance such vanities. This was lucky for Newman, who had raves coming out of his ears. Paul McCartney even called to say how much he liked *12 Songs*.

This is not to say that Warner Bros. didn't try to make their Randy a star: Newman's next release, *Live* (1971), was intended to prove to a much wider audience what a droll fellow Newman was in performance. It was also obvious that Warners wanted to defuse the disturbing ambiguity of most of Newman's material—by releasing a record on which a live audience chuckled and guffawed through the cruelties so matter-of-factly catalogued on "Davy the Fat Boy" and "Yellow Man" ("Got to have a yellow woman when you're a yellow man," sang Newman), the record company hoped to convince everyone that, hey, these were just jokes, folks.

Warners' ploy failed—*Live* didn't sell particularly well, although it was picked up by hip disc jockeys and received more airplay than Newman's earlier albums—but even more important, it became very clear that there was a level on which Randy Newman wasn't joking at all. His next release,

Sail Away (1972), used as its title song a jaunty ditty sung by an American sailor hoping to lure Africans onto his slave ship: "Climb aboard, little wog, sail away with me."

The rest of *Sail Away* demonstrated Newman's ever-widening command of orchestral arrangements in the service of his quirky pop compositions while broadening his irony so that even the dimwitted might catch on: "God's Song (That's Why I Love Mankind)" is the sort of sacrilegious josh that would shock only pious children or the then-nascent Moral Majority, while "Political Science," otherwise known as "Let's Drop the Big One and See What Happens," immediately became Newman's most-requested concert number and the most tiresome millstone around his neck.

Or so it was until "Short People," the 1977 novelty hit from the otherwise self-parodic *Little Criminals* that got Newman into the Top Ten and into hot water with people who took his gibes against diminutiveness literally. Between *Sail Away* and *Little Criminals*, however, Newman released a truly subtle beauty, *Good Old Boys* (1974), a song cycle about Louisiana governor Huey P. Long and inspired by T. Harry Williams's biography of the Kingfish. *Good Old Boys* consisted of a series of beautiful lamentations phrased in the harshest, most straightforward language, a sustained excoriation of racism and the exploitation of the working class.

Hurt by the public's rejection of such brave work, made wary by the success-through-misunderstanding of "Short People," Newman was inspired to release his most misanthropic, convoluted work in *Born Again* (1979), a remarkably prescient, underrated album right down to its then-unusual title. *Born Again* tried to embody greed with a straight face ("It's Money That I Love"); parody the swinging-singles life-style ("The Girls in My Life Part 1"); and offer a defense of disco in the guise of a virulently antidisco song ("Pretty Boy"). It also contained a small masterpiece, "The Story of a Rock and Roll Band," an obsessive, remarkably detailed decimation of, of all things, the mediocre pop-rock band the Electric Light Orchestra. As far as Newman himself was concerned, though, the high point of *Born Again* was a song that was the most maligned on a most-maligned album: "Mr. Sheep," a song whose narrator is a tough young punk who mercilessly taunts a middle-aged businessman. Most critics perceived the song as the tamest sort of satire—what could be more clichéd than to make fun of middle-class values? "The critics were so stupid about that song," fumed Newman in 1983. "It was a parody of the sort of person who would make fun of a middle-class businessman—the critics missed one whole level of that song. Plus, that song has the best vocal I've ever sung. It was really difficult to do: I wanted to sound really mean, really vicious, and I think I did it. Tore my vocal cords doing it, too—that's the main reason I can't sing 'Mr. Sheep' in concert; it would ruin my voice for the rest of the night. But the critics, who are supposed to have been my greatest supporters, the reason I can keep recording, because I get such great reviews—they were way off on that one. They didn't get it." Newman went on to do more excellent work—he composed lovely scores for the movies *Ragtime* and *The Natural*, and his 1983 album *Trouble in Paradise* brought him success on his own terms, with the surprise cult hit "I Love L.A."

Newman's ambivalence about "the critics" remained a recurring theme among other eccentric or cult-audience artists in the 1970s. Neil Young, for example, was just as querulous, and perhaps even more puzzled, by the critical acclaim he amassed. Young is a most quixotic figure: a rock superstar who in mid-career rejected fame to pursue a highly eccentric, eclectic path. Or, as he put it himself in the liner notes of his triple-album retrospective, *Decade* (1976): "'Heart of Gold' put me in the middle of the road. Traveling there soon became a bore so I headed for the ditch. A rougher ride but I saw some more interesting people there."

After the success of *Harvest* in 1972, Young did indeed find himself in the middle of the road. He had commenced in the 1970s with what would prove one of that decade's strongest albums, *After the Gold Rush*, a bristlingly intelligent, ferociously rough-edged collection of songs whose lyrics would have been unbearably despairing had the music not been such exhilarating rock and roll. Coming after *Gold Rush*, *Harvest* seemed like a tame disappointment, but in retrospect, *Harvest's* musical gentility—the characteristic that made "Heart of Gold" such an immediate middle-of-the-road hit single—is of a piece with Young's thrashing rock-outs. Both modes are governed by his voice, a reedy trill that has proved an exceptionally expressive instrument over the years, and his guitar sound, a folk-based style that regularly erupts in gushes of feedback that only seem shapeless. When he's working at the height of his powers, Young's voice, lead guitar, and lyrics combine to make music in which the most private and ephemeral emotions are represented in the rock-song format.

For Young, the height of his powers included such commercial disasters as *On the Beach* (1974), a rambling but compelling series of songs climaxing with "Ambulance Blues," whose pivotal line is "It's hard to know the meaning of this song"; *Tonight's the Night* (1975), a corrosive, unsparing song cycle about the death-by-heroin-overdose of Young's friend and roadie Bruce Berry; *Zuma* (1975), which climaxes with the sprawling, mesmerizing epics "Danger Bird" and "Cortez the Killer"; and *Comes a Time* (1978), Young's surprise return to *Harvest's* folkie pastoral, strengthened and made witty from his years in the commercial wilderness. Although he never again approached his early 1970s success, for a while there, Neil Young was that very rare bird: a rock-and-roll eccentric who made money for his record company.

Al Green, too, would enjoy a period of commercial renown as a major black pop-music sex symbol of the 1970s, and he would prove to be one of the decade's most quixotic stars as well. Born in Forrest City, Arkansas, in 1946, Green began singing at the age of nine in his family's own gospel group, the Green Brothers; he was kicked out of that group in his early teens, he later recalled, when he "heard some Jackie Wilson and Sam Cooke records—it was all over then; that's what I knew I had to do." He then sang with a few other vocal groups and had even recorded a few albums by the time Willie Mitchell, a rhythm-and-blues veteran talent-scouting for Hi Records, discovered Green singing in a bar in Texas.

Mitchell dragged Green back to Memphis with him, where the pair recorded a series of songs Mitchell had either written or bought from other songwriters. But it wasn't until Green convinced the very reluctant Mitchell to record some of his own compositions that Green emerged as a startlingly original artist. His first album produced by Mitchell, *Al Green Gets Next to You*, established him as a quirky combination of Sam Cooke and Otis Redding, with a voice that was both sensuous and coy, passionate and quiet. The highlight of the album was Green's own song, "Tired of Being Alone," that climaxed with a high keening moan that immediately became his trademark.

With "Tired of Being Alone," Green's career really took off. A smooth, up-tempo ballad with a gently coursing beat, "Tired" was unlike anything else on the radio—funkier than the increasingly slick and poppish Motown product of the period, yet far more slinky and accessible than the increasingly complex, rough music of Sly Stone.

Green followed this up with "Let's Stay Together," a plea for fidelity and enduring romantic relationships that stood in dramatic contrast to the posthippie anything-goes rhetoric of the day. Hit followed hit—"Look What You Done for Me," "I'm Still in Love with You," "You Ought to Be with Me"—each of them characterized by Green's guttural whisper-to-a-scream crooning and Mitchell's thumping, horn-punctuated production style.

For all the success of the songs he wrote or co-wrote (with Mitchell or drummer Al Jackson), Green's albums were additionally fascinating for his choice of cover material and the highly idiosyncratic interpretations he gave well-known songs. These ranged from a whispered, heart-stopping version of the Bee Gees' "How Can You Mend a Broken Heart?" to an interpretation of country performer Buck Owens's "Together Again" that reminded the few listeners who knew of the song's author that Green's vision of music was shaped by the sound of country as much as it was by the blues and soul.

The album that summons up the full force of Green's artistry is 1973's *Call Me*, featuring the soaring, searching title hit single and a few country songs whose interpretive vocals rival both Ray Charles and Willie Nelson, as well as some of the gospel music that would presage his future.

On his album jackets, Green liked to present himself as a doe-eyed innocent, his collar turned up against a cold, harsh wind, his sad little mouth twisted into a hopeful grin. In concert, however, Green gave full play to his contradictions. Onstage, he teased lines along until the audience screamed for him to finish a verse; he would sing so passionately that he would forget (or is that "forget"?) to use his microphone. He stretched a song such as "Love and Happiness" to unbelievable—and sometimes unendurable—lengths. He invariably concluded each show by running offstage to gather up a massive bouquet of roses, which he would then fling out into the front rows of female admirers.

In October 1974, one of those female admirers came close to ruining her hero's career when she threw a pot of steaming-hot grits at him and soon after killed herself. Her motives were vague in the manner of virtually all rock-star tragedies—the story Green tells is that she could not accept that he wasn't as much in love with her as she was with him, as likely a tale as any—but the event took Green out of action. And after what became known as the grits incident, Green's albums became more uneven—he seemed less confident, and in many of his recorded and public performances, he seemed to be holding back, as if to avoid revealing too much of himself. Nonetheless, Green recorded some rich music during this period, some of it from very unlikely sources, such as his delicate, witty reinventions of "To Sir with Love," the syrupy hit for Lulu in the 1960s, and Burt Bachrach/Hal David's "I Say a Little Prayer." Green's uneven albums were, increasingly, paralleled by uneven sales figures.

In 1977, Green took hold of his career for one magnificent moment when he broke with Willie Mitchell and produced *The Belle Album* himself. At the height of disco, in the midst of Peter Frampton and Fleetwood Mac, Green recorded an album dominated by acoustic instrumentation and intimations of religiosity. "It's you that I want, but it's Him that I need," he murmured on "Belle," and this song proved to be a turning point in Green's life. Released to ecstatic reviews and the worst sales figures of his career, *The Belle Album* was Al Green's last album of secular pop music. By the end of the decade, he was pursuing gospel music as a full-time career, refusing to perform his earlier pop hits.

But for much of the 1970s, Al Green stood as one of the most remarkable—and remarkably consistent—of commercial hit makers. Scoring most of his major hits before the rise of disco, Green was able to extend the influence of his own stylistic models—not just Sam Cooke and Jackie Wilson, but also Wilson Pickett, Curtis Mayfield, Smokey Robinson, the Four Tops' Levi Stubbs, and gospel singers such as Shirley Ceasar and the Five Blind Boys—and, indeed, as the decade wore on, only Elton John would rival him as a hit-singles king. Yet by virtue of his being black and a highly unpredictable artist, Green was largely ignored by the American mass media—no television network was going to give airtime to an oddball who, as he did one night at Broadway's Uris Theater, gave away his shoes to a pair of women after he'd run out of roses. Green was at once something new and the end of a line—a willful eccentric and the last of the great soul men.

It wasn't only solo artists who were pursuing these offbeat visions. One of the oddest acts of the 1970s, Steely Dan, not only wasn't a conventional rock band, it wasn't really even a band at all. Steely Dan was bassist Walter

Becker and singer-keyboardist Donald Fagen, two Bard College protoyuppies who thought it would be a lark to build a group around William Burroughs's nickname for a dildo. (Their drummer in an early Bard band was fellow classmate, later comedian-actor, Chevy Chase.) Teaming up in 1967, Becker and Fagen worked briefly in the Brill Building, where their eccentric ideas about pop-song construction rewarded them with respect from their peers but very few purchases from artists eager to turn their prolix ditties into hits.

From Brill the two traveled to ABC Records to labor as song-rewrite men (they coud get in less trouble if they tinkered with other hacks' songs rather than their own quirky originals); in 1970 and 1971, they even toured as backup musicians for an ABC act, Jay and the Americans, an experience that convinced them that touring was a chore to be avoided at all costs. As a result, Steely Dan became the best-known American band never to tour America (although they did occasional one-shot concerts). Finally, working with anonymous session men in 1972, Becker and Fagen recorded and released "Do It Again," a moody, ominous rock tune spiced with samba rhythms. It became a Top Ten hit single, and Steely Dan was born.

It's hard to say why "Do It Again" or its follow-up success from the band's debut album *Can't Buy a Thrill* (1972), "Reeling in the Years," hit pop pay dirt. For one thing, the songs sounded as if they came from completely different bands—the sensuous Latin tinge of "Do It Again" is replaced on "Reeling in the Years," by a bright pop chorus and a skittering guitar solo by Elliot Randall. Clearly, this was a band with an image problem. For another, the lyrics devised by Becker and Fagen were impenetrable little puzzles that yielded none of the usual pop sentiments. Instead of exulting in a love affair or bemoaning a fractured romance, Steely Dan songs said, "I'm a fool to do your dirty work," and "Only a fool would say that" and "Brooklyn owes the charmer under me" (huh?).

Nonetheless, this complicated, obsessively self-absorbed music appealed not only to AM radio listeners but to a burgeoning audience of rock fans who prided themselves on their appreciation of ironic distance and technical expertise. Steely Dan's second album, *Countdown to Ecstasy* (1973), didn't fare nearly as well on the charts—it peaked at number thirty-five— but it confirmed this antiband's sizable cult, for whom the hard-edged, bitter pleasures of songs like "Bodhissattva," "Your Gold Teeth," and "My Old School" were manna from pop heaven.

In keeping with Steely Dan's persistent commercial perversity, the group's most abstruse album, *Pretzel Logic* (1974), yielded its biggest AM hit, "Rikki Don't Lose That Number," a number-four smash. The album also included a beautiful, larky version of Duke Ellington's "East St. Louis Toodle-Oo," not exactly standard rock album fare, and neither was a remark Fagen made to a reporter around this time: "I think one of the best things about rock and roll as opposed to jazz is precision and a professional sound. That's what I like about popular music. We strive for that sort of slick sound." This, at a time when right-thinking people were decrying slickness and punk-rock was aborning. But by Steely Dan's pretzeled logic, it fit right in.

Steely Dan would continue to pursue complexity-through-slickness on *Katy Lied* (1975), the lugubrious *The Royal Scam* (1976), and the excessively slick *Aja* (1977)—all, especially the last album, considerable commercial successes. By the end of the decade, Becker and Fagen had gone their separate ways—Becker surfaced briefly as a producer in 1985 for China Crisis, an English band that sounded a lot like . . . Steely Dan, while Donald Fagen won acclaim for a solo album, *The Nightfly*, in 1982.

One thing all these commercially dicey, willfully eccentric artists had in common was the support of the rock critics, who championed the musicians' originality and kept their names before that portion of the rock audience that read newspaper and magazine coverage of rock music.

Rock criticism, nurtured in the late 1960s by devoted fans who wanted to discuss the music in serious terms, flourished in the pages not only of *Rolling Stone* magazine but also in *Crawdaddy*, the Detroit-based *Creem*, and a slew of ostensible fan mags that, in various periods of their publishing history, permitted sober discussion of albums and artists to interrupt the color spreads and breathless gossip.

The history as well as the problems of rock criticism in the 1970s were definitively summarized by Robert Christgau in a 1976 *Village Voice* essay entitled "Yes, There Is a Rock-Critic Establishment (But Is That Bad for Rock?)." Christgau's pantheon of influential critics consisted of writer John Rockwell of the *New York Times*; Paul Nelson, then editor of the record-review section of *Rolling Stone*; Jon Landau, critic, producer, and soon to be manager of Bruce Springsteen; Dave Marsh, then a free-lance writer and soon to be the first rock critic to land on the bestseller list with a biography of Springsteen (*Born to Run*, 1979); and Christgau himself.

Christgau—the only half-mockingly self-proclaimed "Dean of American Rock Critics" and one who had logged time at *Esquire* magazine and Long Island's *Newsday* and was well into a second reign as music editor of the *Voice*—used the issue of Bruce Springsteen's unprecedented media feat of appearing on the covers of both *Time* and *Newsweek* in the same week of October 1975 to discuss what rock criticism had become. Christgau summed up the usual prejudices against rock criticism with eloquent wit: "The first tenet of mass culture theory . . . is that the mass audience ineluctably stifles aesthetic worth; so, scratch rock. The first tenet of newsroom cynicism . . . is that hard-news 'digging' is a more blessed endeavor than feature writing, of which reviewing is the lowliest example; so scratch criticism."

But Christgau summed up in a phrase the characteristic that made rock criticism a compelling proposition: "the fannishness of rock criticism . . . when it works, evokes and analyzes good times simultaneously. . . ." In the late 1960s, Jon Landau had attempted to promulgate a rock-critic version of film criticism's auteur theory, attempting to locate the auteur in any given body of work by a musician, whether it was the singer, the producer, the songwriter, perhaps even the engineer of the music under discussion. This proved even more unwieldy and inaccurate than it does in film theory—so many people contribute to an album's success or failure that it is virtually impossible to pin down the plausible rock and roll auteur.

What critics such as Christgau, Greil Marcus (author of 1975's *Mystery Train: Images of America in Rock 'n' Roll Music*), Paul Nelson, and Dave Marsh brought to rock criticism was an understanding of mass-culture theory ranging from, as Christgau put it, "Adorno on the left and Ortega y Gasset on the right." Theirs was a ferocious defense of rock music as, as the 1970s progressed, a besieged art: attacked as muddled and noisy by high-art partisans, as decadent and exhausted by aging middlebrow ex-fans, and as mere mindless pleasure by the it's-only-rock-and-roll lowbrows within the ranks of fandom itself.

The rock critics' essential argument was summed up by Christgau in a 1978 essay he wrote for the Boston *Phoenix*: "That limited technical means are no bar to vigor, spirit, inventiveness, humor, or power [and] many of us prefer it—permanently, we believe—to whatever well-crafted twaddle happens to suit your fancy."

At its best, rock criticism in the 1970s produced writers who confounded all expectations of what a critic was supposed to be. Foremost among these was Lester Bangs, an editor at *Creem* magazine in the mid-1970s and a vastly prolific free-lancer for virtually every magazine that published anything dealing with popular culture. Bangs's prose style owed much to the Beats, from Jack Kerouac's endless roll of typewriter paper to Allen Ginsberg's motto, "First thought, best thought." Bangs's intensely personal, vehemently first person singular style denied the distance between writer and reader.

And, ultimately, it was Bangs who offered the most eloquent defense and caution for rock in the 1970s. Despite enormous misgivings and a contempt for most of what was being released as rock product, Bangs continued to find the music compelling because (capital letters his) "THE MAIN REASON WE LISTEN TO MUSIC IN THE FIRST PLACE IS TO HEAR PASSION EXPRESSED—as I've believed all my life." For Bangs, who died in 1982, this was the heart of rock's enduring appeal, something its explosion as a big business could never completely destroy.

THE MID-1970s

Rock music had always been a vehicle to express frustration, rebellion, and obloquy, but as the 1970s proceeded, these themes were often softened to achieve mass acceptance. The notion of rock as mainstream entertainment was gaining ground steadily. David Bowie, for example, who in an earlier era might have been considered too inaccessible a figure for television audiences, turned up as a smiling guest on Cher's variety show in 1975. Rock was becoming a common language, the reference point for a splintered culture. In March 1976, presidential candidate Jimmy Carter told a lecture audience that Bob Dylan, Led Zeppelin, and the Grateful Dead were among the artists who had inspired him to work hard as governor of Georgia, and once he won the election, Carter continued to court rock by inviting numerous musicians to the White House.

Rock was used increasingly as the subject for movies, as a common reference point for what was now a succession of generations. In addition to the huge mid-decade hit *Saturday Night Fever*, rock history was taught by the Band's farewell-concert film *The Last Waltz* (1977), directed with elegiac grandeur by Martin Scorsese, as well as *The Buddy Holly Story* (1978), featuring an Oscar-nominated performance in the title role by Gary Busey. In 1978, disco was inadvertently pilloried in the dreadful *Thank God It's Friday*, while the first interesting made-for-television movie about rock premiered: *Dead Man's Curve*, a surprisingly incisive look at the tumultuous surf-music careers of Jan and Dean. Even when some of this use of rock in other media yielded good art, it hammered home an unavoidable point: that rock's transformation into big-business entertainment was complete—it would never really rattle anyone again.

And indeed, oblivious to these aesthetic niceties, the major record companies were cultivating their own growth with great energy. By the end of the 1970s, the rock market would be controlled by just six major companies: CBS, Warner Communications, Polygram, RCA, MCA, and Capitol-EMI. By commandeering the marketplace and streamlining the path between artist and consumer, the industry would be able to reap maximum profits during the boom years 1977 and 1978, during which time the *Saturday Night Fever* sound track and Fleetwood Mac's *Rumours* sold more than fifteen million copies each.

As the bucks were rolling in, much of big-time, Establishment rock was proving efficient, ingratiating, and . . . dull. If ever there was a period when an aging rock fan might look at the record charts and say, "This is when I start listening to Grover Washington," the end of the seventies was it. The rise of the reggae/disco/punk underground coincided with the rise of what came to be called faceless rock—crisply recorded, eminently catchy, anonymous hits by bands such as Styx, REO Speedwagon, and Journey, none of whom established individual personalities outside their own large but essentially discrete audiences. Donna Summer might use her disco prominence to try for a movie career, for example, but REO Speedwagon's lead singer Kevin Cronin didn't have a chance at a similar cross-media move—nobody outside the REO fan club had any idea who he was.

This was an odd, disorienting period, a time during which, for example, Kiss was invited to place its eight hands in the wet cement of Grauman's Chinese Theater in Hollywood, and an Establishment figure no less than Mickey Rooney went on record as deploring this latest confusion of noise with art. This was a period in which some of the sharpest cultural commentary came not from rock but from rock parodists: "Saturday Night Live," the youth-oriented comedy-variety show that debuted on NBC-TV in 1975, regularly lampooned the preening excesses of big-name rock stars.

The most extraordinary example of this occurred on October 2, 1976, with John Belushi's merciless mimicry of Joe Cocker's spasmodic stage movements while the singer himself performed in earnest next to the burly comic. It was an amazing moment: hilarious, scary, in extremely poor taste, and yet so skillfully performed as to provoke nothing less than mesmerized admiration. This was the sort of on-the-edge art that rock artists were supposed to typify; instead, it was achieved during the savaging of a rock artist.

Rock music continued to claim lives: Phil Ochs, an exceptionally intelligent, complex folkie—who had spent the last few years making sporadic performances in a gold lamé suit as an homage to Elvis Presley—committed suicide on April 9, 1976; the Supremes' Florence Ballard had died six weeks earlier. Ballard's death was particularly poignant—she left the world penniless and bitter, the Supreme with the most technically accomplished voice who had been shunted aside by the star qualities of Diana Ross. Her death serves as a sour metaphor for Motown Records' suicidal slip into solipsism throughout the latter half of the decade.

In the midst of complacency, fat-cat profiteering, conservation, and death, rock needed some reinvigoration, and found it not at the top of the charts but in a series of lively underground movements. Disco, funk, reggae, and punk were all upstart phenomena; none had any claim to rock mass acceptability when they made their bids for prominence in the late 1970s.

As different as these genres were, they held one characteristic in common: All were grass-roots movements, would-be popular musics created by the same kinds of people who had invented rock and roll—the disenfranchised, the visionary, the eccentric, the despised but ambitious. Given their stylistic diversity, it's not surprising that these grass-roots subgenres affected mainstream rock in various ways. Disco, for example, offered itself as a further refinement of soul and as a pop genre that glorified the upward mobility reflected in the rise of rock as a big business. "You want conspicuous consumption?" disco seemed to say to the industry; "You got it."

Funk wanted to hit the consumer in the same place—in the hips, not the head; on the dance floor, not in the concert hall—but was intended as disco's garish older brother, a music as old as James Brown's earliest protosoul but decked out in 1970s finery, utilizing fully the 1970s technology.

Reggae was outsider culture, sailing up from Jamaica on the strength of an inveigling rhythm. Reggae took the biggest chance of all in attempting to introduce a new beat to the rock industry, and, though it never became a mass market success in America (it succeeded fully in England), it certainly made its presence felt as a musical influence on much American-made rock.

Punk offered the most explicit reaction to the mid-1970s rock industry, repulsed as it was by the complacency and cynicism it saw as the primary results of rock's commercial success. The 1970s would call into question everything assumed by the 1960s—this, in fact, would prove the 1970s' greatest achievement, since it prevented popular music from slipping into repetition and purposelessness. Just as early-1970s progressive rock was an inevitable result of the 1960s interest in legitimizing rock as an art form, so was mid-1970s reggae, disco, funk, and punk rock a series of invigorating alternatives for those people who yearned for a new sound and for the chance to be in on the ground floor of the Next Big Thing.

32

OUTSIDER ART: DISCO AND FUNK

T hree subdivisions of 1970s music—reggae, disco, and funk—were created primarily by black musicians at the edges of the rock industry. Although each genre would toss up its own share of eccentrics and cult artists, most of its practitioners were, first and foremost, pop artists—outsiders seeking a way in to the center of the industry. In each case, one artist achieved, or at least came close to achieving, that kind of success. Reggae's Bob Marley would take his place as an equal among the most influential 1970s rock performers; disco's Donna Summer became a mainstream entertainer transcending her discredited genre; and if funk's George Clinton did not attain his oft-stated goal—to become "the black Beatles"—the rhythms he refined represented the first substantial evolution in modern rhythm and blues since Sly Stone's work in the late 1960s.

With remarkable prescience, James Brown explained to an English interviewer why the course of black music in the 1970s took the turn it did: "We didn't want anything to do with progressive music. So we stayed with soul. And the kind of soul we wanted was fast dance things." Brown said this in 1975, as disco and funk were about to deluge—some rock fans would say pollute—the rock world. Brown himself nearly drowned in the flood; by 1979, backed into a commercial corner, he took to billing himself (quite accurately, of course) as "The Original Disco Man," and made a comeback with a single entitled "It's Too Funky in Here." Disco would be soul music's logical progression—it was the sound of urban rhythm and blues meeting the challenge of new technology (synthesizers, drum machines, etc.) as well as a new economy (a tight one, especially for the black audience that heard it most clearly).

Disco was the most self-contained genre in the history of pop, the most clearly defined, and the most despised. No other pop musical form has ever attracted such rabid partisans and fanatical foes, dividing audiences along racial and sexual lines, even as its function, paradoxically—as music designed to make you dance, dance, dance—was to turn the pop audience into one big happy family.

Of course, before the word came to signify a musical genre, a *disco*—or discotheque, to use the quaint full-length form of the word—was a place where you went to dance to records rather than live bands. In the early 1960s, discotheques were already established in America and Europe as venues for adventurous disc jockeys to test the potential popularity of new records with receptive audiences. However, by the late 1960s, discotheques were beginning to fade as live performances became the dominant form of evening entertainment for the pop music audience. In New York, for example, the Peppermint Lounge, famous in the early 1960s as the place where the twist became a hip dance craze, slipped into obscurity at roughly the same time that Bill Graham's Fillmore East, featuring a regularly shifting triple bill of live rock acts, became the new "in" spot for adventurous music. But during the eclipse, discotheques didn't completely disappear; instead they went underground, refining their purpose and developing their own, new aesthetic. By the time they reemerged in major metropolitan areas in the early 1970s, they were no longer playing pop and rock songs but a species of streamlined, designed-for-dancing music that would be labeled *disco* in the 1970s.

These new discos offered the disc jockey as a species of pop artist. Through skill, timing, and taste, the disc jockey used two turntables to segue between records with compatible beats—the idea was to build and build the tension of the music until it "peaked," provoking screams of pleasure from the sweaty, exhausted, second-winded revelers on the dance floor. When combined with an array of lights pulsing and strobing to the rhythm of the music, a disco set overseen by a master disc jockey could be a hypnotic, ecstatic experience.

In the early 1970s, discos became a haven for a few groups who had been closed out of the increasingly white, sexist, male-dominated business that rock and roll was becoming. Gays, blacks, and women found in the discos a sympathetic environment; moreover, the implicit sexuality of the disco experience—the building, peaking, and climaxing of the music—was appealing to an audience slightly older and more secure in sexual matters than was the teenage audience for rock and roll. Where so much rock music dealt with sex as anticipation and neurotic fantasy, disco approached sex as fun, pure and simple. Well, maybe also kinky.

Early disco music owed very little to rock and roll in its direct antecedents, country music and rural blues. Instead, disco found its paradigms in the suave, polished music of Kenneth Gamble and Leon Huff's Philadelphia International Records production style; in the most elaborate ballads of Stevie Wonder, post-Temptations Eddie Kendricks, and Marvin Gaye; in the lush and often campy orchestrations of Barry White; in the cool makeout music of Jerry "The Ice Man" Butler and Isaac "Hot Buttered Soul" Hayes.

The first major disco hits to be played widely on pop radio stations were the Hues Corporation's "Rock the Boat" and George McCrae's "Rock Your Baby," both released in the first half of 1974. The Hues Corporation—St. Clair Lee, Tommy Brown, Karl Russell, and H. Ann Kelly—emphasized its tight harmonies combined with a curt, sexy beat, and sold over two million copies of their hit single. McCrae was by 1974 a veteran rhythm-and-blues singer perennially in search of a hit. He certainly found it in "Rock Your Baby": Recorded at TK Records Studios in Hialeah (near Miami), Florida, and distributed by RCA Records, the song was a number-one hit in fifty-three countries, selling two million copies in America and a million in England alone. The song's appeal was obvious, sporting as it did an easy but insistent beat and McCrae's high, ethereal tenor voice, which merged in the chorus with a soaring synthesizer line. A year later, George's wife, Gwen, would have her own disco smash with "Rockin' Chair."

Is it a coincidence that all three of these early disco successes should have the word rock in the title and chorus of the songs? Not at all—in the beginning, disco sought to emphasize its similarities to rock and roll, to find a way to appeal to the vast audience that did not go to the discos.

"Rock Your Baby" had been written and produced by Harry Wayne Casey and Richard Finch, a former record retailer and bass player in pickup bands, respectively, who began working as engineers at TK Studios in 1973. With its success, they shot to prominence as disco's first auteurs and formed their own nine-man disco group, KC and the Sunshine Band. They recorded a couple of local disco hits, "Blow Your Whistle" and "Sound Your Funky Horn," but it was 1975's "Get Down Tonight," a far more hard-edged, vehement dance song than their previous work, that brought them nationwide success. "Get Down Tonight" emphasized the bass, drums, and the Latin-flavored percussion of cowbells and timbales to create a fierce, driving rhythm. Over this, Harry Casey, "KC," sang in a sharp blue-eyed-soul rasp. KC's musical approach was radical in its conservatism—he didn't bother using the instrument that came to symbolize disco, the synthesizer, opting instead to build a rich, thick, funky sound with a beefed-up, extra-large rock band. Nowhere are disco's roots in James Brown's and Otis Redding's danceable numbers clearer than in the irrepressible work of KC and the Sunshine Band, one of the few disco aggregations that released full-length albums that held up to repeated listening, with distinctive, adventurous songs rather than a hit single and four variations on the theme. Soon after "Get Down Tonight" hit number one in August 1975, their style would be dubbed the Miami Sound; and Casey and Finch followed up on their initial success with an even bigger hit, the sassy, abrasive "That's the Way (I Like It)," number one at the end of October 1975.

Casey and Finch's closest competition in early 1975 was Van McCoy, whose "The Hustle" was the first of the commercial disco hits to spawn, in a great pop-music tradition, a dance craze. A former songwriter for acts as disparate as Gladys Knight and the Pips, Mitch Miller, Peter and Gordon, Aretha Franklin, and Bobby Vinton, McCoy struck it big with "The Hustle," a cool, understated disco record that ended up selling over ten million copies in just two years. McCoy would never duplicate this early success; he died on July 6, 1979, at the age of thirty-five.

And 1975 also yielded disco's finest hit, one that actually summoned up wit as well as camp—"Shame, Shame, Shame," released in January 1975 by Shirley and Company. Shirley was Shirley Goodman, a New Orleans singer who, as a member of Shirley and Lee (her partner was singer Leonard Lee), had already made rock music history in 1956 with "Let the Good Times Roll." Goodman's high, girlish trill, rippling with an undercurrent of sexual excitement, was a great rock and roll voice, and it is her dry, sarcastic performance on "Shame, Shame, Shame" ("Shame on you/If you can't dance, too") combined with its irresistible, hipshaking melody, that made the song an immediate smash.

"Shame, Shame, Shame" was released on an album later in 1975 that bears mention for its cover: It was a crude, crayoned drawing of Shirley shaking her finger in admonition, as if to say "Shame, shame, shame," to Richard Nixon (then boogieing down at the Watergate hearings) who was looking extremely uncomfortable posing next to Shirley.

These early hits soon sparked a veritable disco explosion. By 1975, there were between two hundred and three hundred discos in New York alone, and at least ten times more than that across the country. Dance singles were selling upward of 100,000 copies, and there was growing evidence that consumers would be willing to buy disco in an album format—KC and the Sunshine Band had proved that. Yet, for a while at least, it remained an outsider's music, produced outside the recording industry mainstream. As critic Tom Smucker has pointed out, "Disco was not invented by the captains of monopoly culture so they could banish rock, soften brains, and snort cocaine at Studio 54. . . ." In fact, wrote Smucker in 1979, "Disco developed its own independent network for publicity and distribution, largely through the disco club d.j.s. with no help from the large record companies and no radio play."

Soon enough, however, it would inspire such cynical ripoffs as schlock society pianist Peter Nero's *Disco, Dance, and Love Themes for the '70s* (1975), former jazz flutist Herbie Mann's *Discotheque* (1975), and Percy Faith's *Disco Party* (1975), unlistenable albums all. Faith's album included a disco version of "Hava Nagilah." And Sir Monti Rock III, a charming no-talent and professional celebrity who had built a show-business career appearing on *The Tonight Show* moaning about his decadent, nonstop party of a life, reemerged in 1974 as Disco Tex and The Sex-O-Lettes and actually recorded a hit, a novelty single, "Get Dancin'," written and produced by the perennial hack Bob Crewe.

An important source of early disco was Europe: Producers and records emerging in 1974 and 1975 from Canada, Germany, Italy, France, and England had as much impact on the American disco audience as American records did. Disco projects were often multinational efforts; the Ritchie Family, for example, was a group of Philadelphia backup singers produced by a pair of Frenchmen, Jacques Morali and Henri Belolo, who in 1974 covered "Brazil," a hit thirty years before for South American–born North American bandleader Xavier Cugat. Many of these foreign-flavored disco songs were cast as novelty hits, such as Silver Convention's chirpy "Fly, Robin, Fly," released in October 1975, sung by three German women and winner of a 1975 Grammy Award for Best Rhythm and Blues Instrumental Performance.

The lush but peppy mock-symphonic sound of a record like "Fly, Robin, Fly" was soon tagged "Eurodisco," and the king of Eurodisco was Italian producer Giorgio Moroder, born in 1941 and settled in Germany by the late 1960s. Rising to studio session work as a bassist, he soon mastered the ultimate disco instrument, the synthesizer, and set about producing records with a frequent collaborator, lyricist Pete Bellotte.

In Munich in 1976, Moroder produced a major disco hit, "Love to Love You Baby," sung by an unknown American vocalist, Donna Summer. "Love to Love You Baby" earned its popularity via the churning, urgent instrumentation and Summer's searching, sexy vocal. Summer spent much of the song's eight-minutes-plus moaning the title phrase, and the immense popularity of "Love to Love You Baby" gave rise to the first jokes about disco being nothing more than mindless repetitions featuring orgasmic voices.

The story of the American breakthrough of "Love to Love You Baby" is telling about the almost inadvertent but inexorable rise of disco in America. Moroder brought his song to Neil Bogart of Casablanca Records in Los Angeles. Intrigued by this overblown but undeniably clever piece of music, Bogart tested its appeal by putting it on during a party he was giving in his home. "Love to Love You Baby" caused an immediate sensation, so the legend goes, with partygoers insisting that this early, four-minute version of the song be played over and over throughout the evening.

This reaction prompted Bogart to ask Moroder to lengthen the song, and Moroder complied with an exhausting twenty-minute version, which was soon shaved down to a sixteen-minute 50-second version that supposedly worked wonders throughout discos in Manhattan. New York discos being the ultimate tastemakers throughout disco's history, "Love to Love You Baby" took off and established Bogart's Casablanca Records, previously known primarily as the home of masked hard rockers Kiss, as an important disco record label.

"Love to Love You Baby" also changed the commercial format for disco records. With its extended length, it didn't fit onto a little seven-inch single, and soon the twelve inch-single format that had become common among disco disc jockeys would find its way into record stores. Artistically, this extended length meant that an inventive producer like Moroder could take the time to establish different moods and dramatic sections within a single composition. Disco thus held out the possibility for increased artistic expression on the part of the producer, and Moroder took full advantage of this even as he shamelessly exploited disco's crassest commercial possibilities: Among his all-instrumental disco albums were titles like *Battlestar Galactica* (music built around a semipopular science-fiction television show in the mid-1970s), *From Here to Eternity*, and *Knights in White Satin*, the latter a romanticization of the Moody Blues' already wildly romantic 1972 hit.

Moroder was producing state-of-the-art disco. Donna Summer, on the other hand, was widely viewed as little more than the producer's puppet, but she proved to be a much more tenacious, ambitious performer than that. Summer, born in 1948 in Boston, was trained both as a gospel singer in her family church and as a Broadway show music singer with extensive American and European road-company experience. Her ambition to become a pop singer led her to backup-vocal session work in Munich, where she met Moroder, who at that time was just starting up Oasis Records with his partner Bellotte. She recorded a couple of European hits with the pair, "Hostage" and "Lady of the Night," in 1973–74. "Love to Love You Baby," in 1975, was her American breakthrough, but, oddly enough, the song never became as much of a European success as her previous Moroder collaborations.

Summer followed up "Love to Love You Baby" with the predictable rip-off sequels, an album of variations bearing the same name as the single, as well as "Love Trilogy," a seemingly endless bit of vocal moaning and synthesizer noodling. Summer was in danger of becoming a novelty act in a genre that was breeding them like flies: By early 1976, there had already been a highly successful Summer imitation, "More, More, More," whose orgasmic yelps were emitted by an unassailable expert—pornographic film star Andrea True, fronting, as it were, the Andrea True Connection. Perhaps the most memorable novelty was the immortal "Kung Fu Fighting," (1974) Carl Douglas's prescient co-optation of the nascent kung-fu boom, deftly inserted into a disco beat. Actually, Carl Douglas's ambitions were even broader than this—he had hoped to turn "Kung Fu Fighting" into a dance craze in the manner of the Hustle, with well-dressed disco dancers chopping the air and letting out passionate *aieeee!*s on the beat. Alas, this did not come to pass.

In the midst of this, Donna Summer took stock of her situation and decided she had better make her ambitions known. She implored Moroder to give her something more than a series of terse come-ons and double entendres to sing, and he came up with *I Remember Yesterday*, a 1977 release that demonstrated Summer's range. Powered by "I Feel Love," a throbbing, quietly murmured declaration of passion, as the album's million-selling hit single, *I Remember Yesterday* suggested Summer's abilities as a pop crooner on the title track and "Back in Love Again," while "Love's Unkind" was nothing less than a rock song, clipped and passionate. Rumors immediately swirled within the disco community that Donna had sold out, of course—this was the disco version of Dylan going electric. With subsequent albums, the best of which was *Bad Girls* (1979), a double-record set that turned Summer's disco-hooker image inside out and used it to her advantage, Summer would go on to broaden her audience beyond the disco crowd and to establish herself as a pop artist of some distinction. But Summer was an exception: Most disco artists were anonymous acts, puppets of the producer—the true disco auteur—who usually had one big hit and then disappeared as quickly as they had surfaced.

By the mid-1970s, disco had established a substantial cult following, retaining its ties to the black and gay cultures that had been alienated by white rock music, one that was more mature than the audience for most rock acts. In most places, you had to be over twenty-one to gain admittance into the disco of your choice, and you probably had to adhere to a trumped-up dress code designed to winnow out youths in T-shirts, jeans, and sneakers—a rock concert uniform scorned by disco's increasingly pervasive snobbish attitude.

Around 1975, this situation began to change; disco's audience base became broader. What was needed was a white act that would attract the basic disco audience and also pull in the rock and roll teens, and the act that accomplished this most triumphantly was the Bee Gees. Australian brothers Robin, Maurice, and Barry Gibb had been around since the 1960s, recording infrequent pop hits (who can forget 1967's "New York Mining Disaster 1941"?). But it was only when they mastered the infectious drone of disco that they began to achieve a popularity that began inviting comparisons to the Beatles.

The Bee Gees' *Main Course*, released in May 1975 and produced by veteran rhythm-and-blues producer Arif Mardin, contained "Jive Talkin'," a disco smash that started the group on an unprecedented roll. *Children of the World*, released in September 1976 and produced by the Bee Gees themselves, followed Mardin's formula—prominent percussion, subtle synthesizers, an emphasis on Maurice's mousy tenor-soprano voice—and did even better, yielding "You Should Be Dancing" and "Boogie Child" as the dance-club hits as well as "Love So Right" as a ballad success. But the album that catapulted the Bee Gees to superstardom was the 1977 double-record sound track for *Saturday Night Fever*, which became one of the biggest blockbusters of all time. The movie *Saturday Night Fever*, a melodrama about a working-class New York kid who grows up to become a prizewinning disco dancer, would establish disco as a mass phenomenon.

The Bee Gees' cuts were not the only hit songs on the album. They sang the spunky, understated title song; they sang the anthemic "Stayin' Alive"; they sang the treacly ballad "How Deep Is Your Love?" *Saturday Night Fever* also broke the Tramps' incendiary "Disco Inferno"; Walter Murphy's synthesizer interpretation of Beethoven's Fifth Symphony, "A Fifth of Beethoven"; and—a smaller hit, but one of the collection's best, tightest rhythms—KC and the Sunshine Band's "Boogie Shoes." Nonetheless, it was the Bee Gees who thereafter had to perform in football stadiums, so massive had their audience become, and it was the Bee Gees who pushed disco to the forefront of American commercial music.

The Grammy award for 1977 in the Best New Artist category was given to the disco group A Taste of Honey, whose first (and to date only) hit single, "Boogie Oogie Oogie," was divined by the American Academy of Recording Arts and Sciences to be more worthy of merit than the whole of Elvis Costello's *My Aim Is True* album, which had also been nominated.

The year 1977 also spawned one of the few disco groups that operated as a self-defining unit: Chic, led by bassist Bernard Edwards and guitarist Nile Rodgers, wrote their own songs and produced themselves. Their initial hit, "Dance, Dance, Dance (Yowsah, Yowsah, Yowsah)," which was released in October and spent twenty-five weeks on the charts, was structured around an undulating bass line and an exaggeratedly comic vocal that threatened to turn the song into the disco version of "Winchester Cathedral."

Edwards and Rodgers had teamed up in New York in the early 1970s as part of the Big Apple Band and had also done extensive session work, but they were interested in disco as an expressive pop form right from the start—they played, for instance, on Carl Douglas's "Kung Fu Fighting," self-expression of an odd but undeniable sort. While working sessions in London, Rodgers had hatched the idea for Chic, and returning to New York, recruited Edwards, drummer Tony Thompson, and singers Alfa Anderson and Norma Jean Wright.

"Dance, Dance, Dance" was a solid hit, but a derivative one—it was just an exceptionally well played version of Philadelphia International–style disco. It was Chic's next hit, "Le Freak" (1978), that expressed Edwards's and Rodgers's originality. A cool, stark guitar-plus-bass riff, coupled with the female voices' frosty declamation of the chorus "Le freak, c'est chic," exerted a fascinating, erotic allure to listeners.

The members of Chic, attired on their album covers in tuxedos and evening gowns, represented disco's most idealized dreams of upward mobility. Chic's image was minimalist elegance; their mustic was high-tech pop—glistening, calm, and functional. Critic Stephen Holden described Edwards and Rodgers as "minimalistic aural interior decorators," and he meant the phrase as a compliment—if, as its detractors said, disco was wallpaper for the ears, Chic manufactured the most refined and minutely detailed wallpaper of all.

Risqué, released in 1979, contained the most influential Chic single of all, "Good Times," an achingly ironic anthem for the recession 1970s.

"Good times, these are the good times," the women sang with flat, emotion-drained voices, while Edwards, Rodgers, and Thompson laid down a stinging, persistent riff. In its brutal succinctness, "Good Times" located the common ground between disco and funk; the central riff of the song was an insinuating one that James Brown might have built an epic dance groove around. As it was, rap artists in the ensuing years did just that: Grandmaster Flash's "Grandmaster Flash on the Wheels of Steel" used the "Good Times" riff as its spine, and its bleak extension of Chic's neo-Depression lyric made that spine tingle.

Chic's commercial success peaked with Risqué. Real People, released in 1980, didn't fare nearly as well on the charts, and each subsequent Chic album did even worse. But in some ways, Real People was the group's most impressive collection for the way it sustains a mood of romantic disappointment by lacing it with stylish jokes and—a real breakthrough for these serene demidecadents—some undisguised emotion.

The album begins with "Open Up," in which Rodgers's guitar wobbles and splashes with stilted dignity, like a tipsy, tuxedoed host greeting you at the door with both hands full of champagne glasses. But this in no way prepares you for the next song, "Real People," on which Chic tries to deny the whole high-class, wittily disdainful image they'd spent the past few years establishing: "Real people/I want to live my life/With some real people."

This was silly, of course. Anyone who chatters on about wanting to meet "real people" is likely to be the most insufferable, un-real person imaginable; the song is Chic's best rich-people-talk-funny joke yet. The same premise underlies "Rebels Are We," the album's commercially unsuccessful single: If it's one thing Chic does not seem to be, it's rebels; in their high collars, tiny bow ties, and sultry strapless gowns, this was a group whose place in the Establishment was secure.

But implicit in all of Chic's chic was the understanding that, to most of their audience, this group's image was little more than a fantasy. The very real rebellion of Bernard Edwards and Nile Rodgers was that they were consummately successful in terms that even white power brokers would understand.

For instance, during this period, Edwards and Rodgers also became highly sought-after producers for other artists. Calling their production company The Chic Organization, they constructed hit singles for a tired disco act, Sister Sledge ("He's the Greatest Dancer"), a tired soul act, Diana Ross ("I'm Coming Out," in which Diana did not announce her homosexuality, and "Upside Down," in which Ross was thoroughly convincing singing about being upended and turned "inside out" by her latest "boy").

The high society to which Chic addressed much of its music had, all too pervasively, come to pass. In the public imagination, disco was a world of gleaming white suits (such as the one John Travolta modeled in Saturday Night Fever), admission to exclusive discotheques, and cocaine coming out of one's ears. The focus of many of these public dreams was Studio 54 in Manhattan. In the late 1970s, Studio 54 was the citadel of disco, overseen by co-owner Steve Rubell as a place to indulge fantasies and wield power.

Anyone who was anyone, from Mick Jagger to Henry Kissinger, wanted to be seen in Studio 54, and thousands of nobodies clamored to get in. Rubell played up to this by setting up velvet ropes and burly bodyguards outside the club's entrance, where the teeming but impeccably dressed rabble was held at bay as the Disco Select were permitted entry. Rubell's conviction for income tax evasion in 1982 put a sudden stop to this dream world, and it was a measure of disco's politics that one of Rubell's staunchest supporters was lawyer Roy Cohn, who had made his name standing by Joe McCarthy twenty-five years earlier.

This sort of pseudo–high society with a right-wing aura lowered what little esteem disco might have had with most critics and an increasingly vocal segment of the pop audience. A diverse coalition—AOR radio minions, hard core rock fans, homophobes, racists—united to up the stakes in the it-all-sounds-the-same antidisco crusade. And a crusade it had become. In its most emblematic moment, on July 12, 1979, Chicago disc jockey Steve Dahl mustered support from a crowd that had come to Comiskey Park for a White Sox–Detroit Tigers double header. To the chant of "Disco sucks!" Dahl, a jock for WLUP, then an archetypal AOR station, piled hundreds of disco albums into a wooden box in center field and set it on fire. It didn't take an astute social critic to draw the ugly inferences that could be drawn from this hyped-up spree.

By the following year, disco had peaked as a commercial blockbuster, reduced by the media and its own opportunists to the status of a novelty music. Among the supposedly authentic rock and rollers who contributed to disco's overexposure was Rod Stewart, who loudly professed to despise the crudity of punk rock but had no such disdain for disco, which revitalized his career in 1978 with the dance club smash "Da Ya Think I'm Sexy" and launched him on a new phase—from English rhythm-and-blues master to transplanted El Lay pop hack.

Disco was more wittily co-opted by Elton John, who squeezed one great single out of it, 1975's "Philadelphia Freedom" (a song that earned John an appearance on U.S. television's "Soul Train," a dance-music show that rarely showcased white performers) as well as one excellent hit, 1979's "Mama Can't Buy You Love," produced by soul veteran Thom Bell.

Ultimately, however, disco was a victim of its success in the face of racism and homophobia that would not abate. In the popular imagination, it became a bad joke, a sour parody of pop affluence. But true to its pervasive irony and gift for self-absorption, there was a disco group to embody the genre's last hurrah: the Village People.

No group was ever more aptly termed a sextet—these six beefy male singers offered themselves as cartoon homosexual pinups who dressed in strict character: Randy Jones was duded up as a cowboy; David Hodo was a construction worker; Glenn Hughes was the so-called leather man; Felipe Rose appeared as an American Indian; Alexander Briley donned a variety of military costumes, from Navy admiral to Army doughboy; and lead singer Victor Willis favored a policeman's uniform.

The Village People was a pop concept invented by producer Jacques Morali, who also co-wrote the group's material, which was little more than a series of cheery jingles set to a rigid disco beat: "In the Navy," "Y.M.C.A.," and above all, "Macho Man," were all platinum-selling hits between 1977 and 1979. As a live act, the Village People were even more outrageously artificial—they lip-synched their songs to prerecorded music, changing costumes onstage and wiggling to please like male strippers. After the initial mild scandal of their existence, the Village People went the way of rock shockers like Alice Cooper—they became domesticated threats, family fare, the stuff of Bob Hope television specials. Disco was dead.

Disco, with its sharp-dressed dancers and sleekly polished, intricately arranged songs, was absorbed into the pop mainstream all too quickly—its acceptance only increased the contempt many rock fans felt for it. Funk, on the other hand, was far less immediately accessible; it took pride in displaying the rough edges that disco assiduously smoothed over. Disco wanted you to think that this music had been invented yesterday; it took rock's urge for contemporaneousness to an extreme. Funk, on the other hand, wanted you to know it had a past—it harked back to early rhythm and blues and pre-Motown soul in its gritty instrumentation and studio production.

Funk at its creative peak in the mid-1970s was embodied in one man, George Clinton, who proffered an aggressively vulgar, brilliantly literate version of the discredited subgenre.

Born in 1940, Clinton was of the generation for whom funk began and ended with James Brown, whose greatest music deemphasized melody while exaggerating the polyrhythms that coursed around the beat with minimal, subtle shifts in emphasis—Brown's heart beat all the way back to Africa. In 1955, Clinton, training as a barber in Plainfield, New Jersey, formed a vocal group called the Parliaments who performed locally for well over a decade until in 1967, their single "(I Just Wanna) Testify" became a top-twenty pop hit on the Revilot label. "(I Just Wanna) Testify" seized on the chugging bass guitar lines that powered so many of James Brown's hits and added strong harmonies to a catchy, incessantly repeated chorus.

After the success of this single, the Parliaments became embroiled in a contract dispute that resulted in Clinton being legally prohibited from using the name. He then dropped out: he moved to Detroit, where he began hanging out with the local white hippie/rock-and-roll community, and, he said, "dropped a whole lotta acid." He also picked up a second idol: Jimi Hendrix, whose coalition of black and white rock fans was an audience Clinton decided he wanted too.

"Funk was for the future," said Clinton in 1976, "but it started to catch on because it was a total rejection of the smooth and slick Motown-type sound. Black people had become fed up with the dress-alike, dance-routine type of group. . . . The early days of Funkadelic were deliberately planned for three years in advance—we deliberately avoided the fancy dance routine stuff because there was no opportunity for improvisation." Clinton credited another musician, future collaborator Sly Stone, with providing the sort of musical/aesthetic role model he could use: "I'd say it was Sly who first cracked the barrier between white and black rock. He was slick! Jimi Hendrix could have been the first, but he was too way out for the masses. Sly was clever because he bridged the gap between Jimi and the Temptations."

To accomplish his goal, Clinton formed a large (twelve-plus players) band he dubbed Funkadelic, a name that encapsulated his interest in music and mind expansion. From the start, Funkadelic was brazenly provocative. The early 1970s saw the release of Funkadelic albums on the Detroit-based Westbound label, with titles like "Free Your Ass and Your Mind Will Follow," "Maggot Brain," "America Eats Its Young," and "Cosmic Slop." These records contained wild amalgamations of raw funk rhythm, Hendrix-influenced rock guitar (usually provided by Michael Hampton, Gary Shider, and the late Glen Goins), science-fiction plots, and Clinton's knotty, original variations on black street slang. Because the music was so sprawling and lengthy, it didn't receive much radio play—at the time, black stations were programming much more mannerly material, while white FM stations (in theory, the ideal home for Clinton's music) were beginning to show evidence of the racism and narrow-mindedness that would soon ruin rock radio. In any case, Clinton had a hard time getting heard on the airways.

Funkadelic thus made its reputation as a live act. The albums attracted a cult following, which rapidly expanded once audiences began to get a look at what the group was doing in concert. Clinton orchestrated stunning, crazily ambitious three- and four-hour affairs in which he would emerge from a coffin (an *homage* to 1950s rocker Screamin' Jay Hawkins) or descend from the roof of the hall in a massive cardboard spaceship or a golden pyramid. Clinton wore gaudy, sequined space suits and for many years favored a long blond wig onstage; the rest of the band dressed in extravagantly mismatching outfits that ranged from glittery superhero costumes to Gary Shider's extralarge, plain white diaper.

Clinton's "P-Funk Earth Tour" in 1976 featured a $260,000 stage set designed by Jules Fisher, who had performed similar overstatements for the likes of Kiss and David Bowie. As he commented to journalist Lisa Robinson, "Black [audiences] have never experienced a really loud group, let alone all these theatrics. It's never been done, except for Earth, Wind and Fire, and even they are kind of soft a lot of the time."

Clinton's ambitions were enormous. He wanted nothing less than to change the way people thought of black music; he wanted to express the idea that funkiness could be eloquent, in much the same manner as Richard Pryor was doing as a stand-up comic. "When rock came in, it wasn't respected by blacks," Clinton said to *Newsweek* magazine in 1976. "That's because blacks were into being cool. You didn't want to be funky like Richard Pryor is today because that kind of nigger really embarrassed you. But deep down inside, that's all of us." Thus the true meaning of a Clinton composition of that era: "Tear the Roof Off the Sucker (Give Up the Funk)" indeed.

Clinton's tactics as a businessman were nearly as outrageous as his onstage stunts. When his Parliaments contract dispute was settled in 1974, he took up the name again, lopping off the s on the end of it, and signed his band to Casablanca Records. Parliament, however, consisted of the same musicians as Funkadelic—Clinton's quite legitimate commercial strategy was that Funkadelic would record the wild material that he wrote and his guitarists embellished, while Parliament albums would contain comparatively concise songs with intricate plots. Parliament hits of this era included "Up for the Down Stroke," "Tear the Roof Off the Sucker (Give Up the Funk)," "Do That Stuff," "Aqua Boogie," and "Flash Light." In 1976, with the Parliament album *Mothership Connection* riding high on the charts, he crowed, "I have no doubt that one day we're going to be as big as the Beatles." For all this, his instincts were also munificent; at the height of his popularity in the late 1970s, for example, he was donating, from every ticket sold, 25 cents, to the United Negro College Fund.

Clinton ruled his bands like a benevolent despot ("Funk," he liked to say, "is its own reward"), overseeing the creation and production of his albums but also encouraging spontaneity and improvisation in performing the work. Clinton desired nothing less than a P-Funk empire, and to this end, he secured contracts for Parliament-Funkadelic musicians as spinoff acts with a variety of labels. Among these were Bootsy's Rubber Band (featuring bassist Bootsy Collins, who as a teenager had backed James Brown in his JBs band on such funk-defining hits as "Mother Popcorn," "Ain't It Funky Now," "Let a Man Come in and Do the Popcorn (Parts One and Two)"); the Horny Horns, led by trumpeter Maceo Parker, another Brown alumnus; the Brides of Funkenstein; Junie Morrison, once a member of the Ohio Players and author of their hit "Funky Worm," the song that brought him to Clinton's attention; keyboardist Bernie Worrell, who would later become part of the Talking Heads' touring unit; and Zapp, a group led by singer-guitarist Roger Troutman and his brothers.

Then, too, Clinton approached his work with the serene confidence of an avant-garde artist; much of his philosophy might come from the notebooks of Alfred Jarry. "You cannot make sense and be funky," he told *Rolling Stone* magazine. "We take the heaviness out of being profound." Given the profoundly conservative beast that the pop music audience had become by the mid-1970s, it is remarkable that George Clinton turned his provocative speculations into intermittently bestselling music.

Throughout this era black music pursued its own rhythmic variations. Disco and funk shared a black, primarily urban audience, even if those two genres were frequently antithetical. Funk's George Clinton even coined an implicitly antidisco slogan; he said that his brand of funk was "here to rescue dance music from the blahs."

It is the most tragic irony of 1970s rock music that its audience began to divide along racial lines at precisely the moment when its creators became most intensely involved in experiments that mixed black and white musical styles in fresh, different ways.

33

ROCK AND REGGAE

Reggae was supposed to be the new sound in pop music for America in the 1970s, the rhythm that would take a prominent place among all other pop music genres. Imported from its native Jamaica, the product of a desperately poor, despised underclass, and replete with a world view and a religion of which most Americans had never even heard, reggae certainly had its work cut out for it.

In fact, however, most pop fans in the United States were familiar with reggae's rhythm even if they didn't know it by that name. The music that accentuated the offbeat in every sense was a composite of Jamaica's invention and a deft amalgamation of various other genres—New Orleans rock and roll, Southern rhythm and blues, Trinidadian calypso, African polyrhythms.

Reggae had made a few tentative trips across the U.S. border in the form of novelty singles in the late 1960s. In 1963, the British heir to a Jamaican fortune, Chris Blackwell, produced a perky, ingratiating record by a fifteen-year-old Clarendon, Jamaica, singer called Millie Small. "My Boy Lollipop" had been written in 1956 and had existed in Jamaica in various recorded versions, some of them quite popular. What was immediately noticeable about Small's version, however, was her little-girl coo, which radiated sexiness while flirting with the Mann Act. But what kept listeners coming back to it was its undulating beat, a rhythm that accented the second and fourth beats of rock's steady ¼. (For trivia fans, it is also worth noting that Rod Stewart, of all people, played harmonica on this recording.) "My Boy Lollipop" went to number two on the American pop charts, and although she conducted a very successful career in her homeland, where she was known as Queen of the Bluebeat and appeared regularly on Jamaican radio, television, and stage, Millie Small did not resurface on the American charts.

After "My Boy Lollipop," the next big made-in-Jamaica reggae hit was Desmond Dekker's 1969 single "The Israelites," a mesmerizing chant that fully captured the lulling magic of reggae. After that, the reggae beat popped up here and there irregularly in American and British hits. An English novelty group, Mungo Jerry, employed a singularly clumsy version of reggae in its 1968 hit "In the Summertime"; Paul Simon, looking for a new rhythm after splitting up with Art Garfunkel, went to Kingston, Jamaica, in 1971 to record "Mother and Child Reunion" for his first solo album, *Paul Simon*. But the next legitimate Stateside reggae success was Johnny Nash's "I Can See Clearly Now," released in 1972.

Nash, an American singer who had been floundering for a style and a foot in the door, went down to Jamaica to record with local musicians in the late 1960s. There he recorded a moderate Jamaican and American hit, "Hold Me Tight," which charted in 1968, but it was the coursing, ethereal "I Can See Clearly Now" that made him, however briefly, a star.

The first true superstar of reggae, however, was Jimmy Cliff. Cliff was an altogether different sort of artist from Millie Small. He wrote and produced much of his own material and was a first-rate interpretive singer. His warm, earnest vocal style, which owed much to the soft sensuality of American singers like Sam Cooke and Smokey Robinson, was in marked contrast to the coyness of Millie Small or the chattering vehemence of Desmond Dekker.

Cliff hit it big in England before becoming widely known to American listeners. His "Wonderful World, Beautiful People" was a Top Ten hit in England, and the 1970 album of the same name, released in America by A&M Records, contained two other remarkable songs, the prayerlike "Many Rivers to Cross" and the quietly defiant, radical "Vietnam." The album sold poorly in America, and Cliff's fame in England was short-lived since, ironically, he soon began trying to make it as an American-style soul singer, with poor results. Nonetheless, it was Cliff who would become America's first and, until the rise of Bob Marley, foremost icon of reggae, when he starred in *The Harder They Come* in 1972.

The Harder They Come, shot in the slums of Kingston and directed by Perry Henzell, told the story of Ivan O. Martin, a good-hearted, destitute country boy whose goal is to become a famous reggae singer but who ends up Jamaica's most famous outlaw. This was a tale that had been told many times in rock history—Elvis Presley alone made at least two movies with roughly the same plot—but this one was told with a fresh eye for a new culture and was accompanied by the lurching beat of great reggae songs by not only Cliff but also Toots and the Maytals, the Melodians, the Slickers, and Desmond Dekker.

The Harder They Come became one of the most popular cult movies in America, playing to midnight audiences for years after its initial commercial run. The film also made Jimmy Cliff the most recognized reggae artist in the world, but Cliff resisted his own stardom. At the height of his mid-1970s international fame, in fact, he went into seclusion, a premature retirement from which the momentum of his career never recovered.

But the way had been paved. By the mid-1970s, reggae had become an au courant topic of investigation and celebration in America, receiving wide, enthusiastic exposure in mainstream news magazines and newspapers, on college campuses and on television, and on any radio station whose format and/or budget could afford to let at least one white ganja-head program his own Saturday morning reggae show. It seemed as if every rock fan in his or her late twenties/early thirties who had been searching for a bandwagon since the Beatles broke up loved this Jamaican music. How much this had to do with a true appreciation of the music or the increasing use of marijuana as the 1970s substitute for an after-work martini was impossible to gauge, but, one way or another, reggae had definitely become a subject about which everyone had to form an opinion.

Reggae was then about twenty years old, although it didn't take on its present name until late in the 1960s. By that time, it was virtually synonymous with the religion that grew up parallel to it: Rastafarianism, a millenarian, fundamentalist faith that believes that Ethiopian emperor Haile Selassie was the biblically predicted second coming of Jesus Christ. It was a hopeful, next world–looking religion that found enormous appeal among people who had nothing in this world. The practices of Rastafarianism rapidly became inseparable from those of reggae musicianship—most famously, for instance, the wearing of hair in matted tresses called dreadlocks, and the smoking of enormous quantities of marijuana (or "ganja," or "herb") as both a religious gesture of meditation and a creative inspirational tool.

At the same time, there was a contemporary, radical edge to Rastafarianism, an aspect of the faith inspired by the back-to-Africa teachings of Marcus Garvey. Journalist, teacher, union organizer, and theorist, Garvey embodied and articulated the most eloquent protest against the inhumane living conditions of the majority of the Jamaican population, and his writings inspired many reggae lyrics among the more politically aware musicians, most notably Bob Marley.

Reggae and Rastafarianism made those Jamaicans who subscribed to both even more alienated from the culture around them; the upper and middle classes in Jamaica—to say nothing of the conservative, frequently repressive government—had little more than contempt and fear for the Rastas and their music. Since they also ran the radio stations, reggae came to be disseminated primarily via "sound systems," the Jamaican term for the portable amplifiers and turntable hookups that disc jockeys set up at parties or on the street to play the latest hits to an appreciative, dancing audience.

Still, a recording industry emerged, dominated in the 1960s by such Jamaican kingpins as producers/label owners Coxsone Dodd, Prince Buster, and Leslie Kong, who were often musicians and producers as well as being businessmen. But the man who attempted to bring reggae to listeners outside Jamaica in the most ambitious way was Chris Blackwell.

Born in London in 1937, Blackwell was part of the family that had founded the enormously prosperous Crosse and Blackwell company. Blackwell's mother was Jamaican. Raised in Jamaica until he was ten, sent to England for his education, Blackwell was like a lot of rich kids—he enjoyed pop music, and when he returned to Jamaica as a cocky eighteen-year-old, he began to immerse himself in Kingston's nascent reggae scene.

By the early sixties, Blackwell had begun recording reggae music, and soon after, he founded Island Records, named for a then-popular novel, Alec Waugh's *Island in the Sun*. By 1964, he had his first worldwide smash: Millie Small's "My Boy Lollipop." Ambitious and well funded, Blackwell soon spread the interests of Island Records well beyond reggae music, signing and recording with spectacular success such 1960s stars as Steve Winwood and Traffic; Cat Stevens; Fairport Convention; Jethro Tull; Free; and Emerson, Lake, and Palmer. In fact, by 1971, Jimmy Cliff was the only reggae artist signed to Island Records; Blackwell's interests had gradually shifted almost entirely to English and American rock and roll.

But in 1972, Blackwell developed a fondness for one reggae band in particular—the Wailers and, even more specifically, the group's charismatic leader, Bob Marley. By then a seasoned pro, the twenty-six-year-old Marley had been performing for over a decade and had recorded a few moderately successful Jamaican records with producers Lee "Scratch" Perry, Leslie Kong, and Coxsone Dodd. Of these men, the most inventive and certainly the most eccentric was Perry, who had begun his career working for Dodd as a teenage disc jockey called Little Lee Perry. As a producer, Perry broke the rules, slowing down songs until they were impossible to dance to, turning such late-1960s singles as "Clint Eastwood" and "Return of Django" into the aural equivalent of Sergio Leone's spaghetti Westerns—vast, florid, romantic spectacles of sound.

Perry ruled the acts he produced with absolute power, and soon enough, he clashed with Marley, who had his own ideas about how his group should sound on record. Then, too, Perry claimed in a rancorous interview he gave to the British pop music newspaper *New Musical Express* in 1984 that he and Marley "worked like brothers until Chris Blackwell saw it was something great and came like a big hawk and grab Bob Marley up." Perry went so far as to blame Marley's 1981 death on his split with his old producer: "If he had listened to Scratch, the idiot, the shit, the madman, he wouldn't have died."

Bob Marley and his group, which included guitarist Peter Tosh, drummer Bunny Livingston, and bassist Aston "Family Man" Barrett, were Rastafarian family men by the time they came to Chris Blackwell's attention—Marley and his wife, Rita, for instance, had already had two children. Nonetheless, they were eager to leave behind the lulling complacency of a moderately successful Jamaican career if Blackwell could bring them to the attention of a much larger audience.

To this end, Marley and the Wailers recorded the album *Catch a Fire* in 1972. It proved to be a landmark record, at first because it was an album: Reggae until that time had been considered primarily a singles genre; albums were slapped together in the 1960s Motown manner—two or three hit singles plus a lot of filler. *Catch a Fire*, however, cohered as an album; the songs written by Marley and Tosh—"No More Trouble," "Concrete Jungle," "Kinky Reggae"—built in intensity to offer a unified statement of sharp political awareness and intense romantic longing.

Unfortunately, *Catch a Fire* was released in America not long after Johnny Nash's *I Can See Clearly Now*, and given the choice of Nash's alluring croon and Marley's scratchy yell, most listeners chose the former. *Catch a Fire* sold only fourteen thousand copies in its first year in release in America. However, the album did receive rave reviews in many important publications, and within the music industry, *Catch a Fire* was acknowledged to be an outstanding, even revolutionary, example of reggae record-making, far superior in its technology than most other reggae records, and far more eloquent in the power of its music.

Burnin', released in 1973, was filled with even more aggressive music—songs such as "Get Up, Stand Up," "Burnin' and Lootin'," "Rasta Man Chant," and "I Shot the Sheriff" (originally entitled "I Shot the Police," but even Marley couldn't go that far)—and unlike *Catch a Fire*, it found its intended audience. With Blackwell acting as the band's manager and utilizing Island Records' full-bore promotion process, *Burnin'* became the album to build a major North American tour around. In October 1973, Marley and the Wailers embarked on one that attracted substantial audiences, as they became the opening act for Sly and the Family Stone, then on the verge of Sly Stone's long slip into oblivion.

Four shows into the tour, Marley and his group were booted off the bill, some said because Stone's audience didn't respond to Marley's reggae, others said because Marley and his group were regularly making Sly and the Family Stone look like ragtag amateurs. But since they were already in America, Marley and the Wailers decided to capitalize on it, and proceeded to fashion their own scattershot tour of the West Coast, playing in small halls for little money. It was a gamble that paid off, for it brought them to the attention of Eric Clapton, who recorded "I Shot the Sheriff" in 1974 on his *461 Ocean Boulevard* album. The album, Clapton's sure, decisive move toward a relaxed, latterday blues style, was a tremendous success in England and especially in America, where "I Shot the Sheriff" became a number-one single. The result was increased visibility for Marley as the author of the song and a growing feeling among some American listeners that reggae was the hippest sound around.

A new American audience eagerly awaited the next Marley and the Wailers album, *Natty Dread*, released in 1975, and they were not disappointed. It contained some of the group's strongest material, in particular the agonizingly beautiful "No Woman, No Cry." On the strength of the excellence of *Natty Dread*, Marley and company set out on a long tour that included North and South America, Europe, and Africa. The tour was a success both as commerce and as symbol, gaining Marley a substantial cult following in America while confirming his constantly growing star/spiritual-leader status in the other countries.

Meanwhile, other reggae artists were plugging along with varying degrees of crossover attention. Toots Hibbert, certainly the most important singer and songwriter after Marley, might logically have seemed to be an even bigger star than Marley in America—after all, Hibbert's singing was rooted in the rough-and-ready sexiness of American soul vocalists like Otis Redding and Wilson Pickett. If there was a rather dismaying fatalism to some of Hibbert's music—in moments of greatest oppression, Toots began hymning to God that he was coming to join Him, where Marley would snarl that he was going to burn his earthly palace down to the ground—it was delivered in soul-gospel terms that any fan of Aretha Franklin and Sam Cooke could understand. Toots and the Maytals' *Funky Kingston*, released by Island in 1975, was a great reggae album—tuneful without compromising the mesmeric drone of the beat—but it barely made a dent in the American pop charts. Worse, the group never made another album equal to it, although *Reggae Got Soul*, whose title suggested Hibberts' ambitions, came close.

Still, a staggering variety of reggae music was pouring forth: the rough harmonies of the Mighty Diamonds, the ferocious polemics of Burning Spear, the gentle postsoul of the Heptones, the tense eccentricity of U Roy, the functional middle-of-the-road reggae-pop of Third World.

Peter Tosh, who played Keith Richards to Bob Marley's Mick Jagger, left the Wailers in 1973, when it had become clear to him that Marley was the one true star of this band. Working with the celebrated rhythm section of drummer Sly Dunbar and bassist Robbie Shakespeare, he recorded "Legalize It" in 1976. The title referred to marijuana: Although considered a religious sacrament among Rastafarians, "herb" was nonetheless still as illegal in Jamaica as it was in America. Even more so, in fact: in a country in which you could receive a life sentence for carrying a gun, you could get a lengthy jail sentence for getting caught with ganja in any amount. Later, Tosh would smoke a "spliff" onstage in front of a Kingston audience of 30,000 people that included Jamaican Prime Minister Michael Manley, a liberal supported by Bob Marley, and deliver a half-hour tirade against the country's drug laws and the oppression of poor people. The fact that Tosh and others were devoted to changing Jamaica's drug laws further limited their audience in America to little more than a cult, even though Tosh went on to record *Equal Rights* in 1977 and in 1978 signed with Rolling Stones Records, distributed by Atlantic, for *Bush Doctor*, which included a duet with Mick Jagger, "(You've Got to Walk and) Don't Look Back," that reached number eighty-one on the United States pop charts.

Influential as it was, reggae itself would remain a cult genre, the province of the independents. The two major disseminators of reggae in America were Island Records and the Jamaican-based Virgin Records, distributed in the United States by Columbia Records in the latter half of the 1970s. The major U.S. companies were extremely wary of signing and, even once they were signed, promoting reggae artists. This was, after all, a whole new rhythm—people in America had to learn how to dance to it. Why would they expend that effort when they could buy an Elton John album whose melodies stuck in their heads and got their toes tapping the first time they played it?

To a large extent, the majors were correct about reggae's limited commercial appeal, and Marley remained the only big star to emerge from reggae. But as much as even he was esteemed, he didn't represent boffo sales figures and sold-out American football stadiums. Part of the reason for this was racism and cultural condescension: The honchos in Los Angeles and New York, busy refining rock as a big business, had little use for these perennially stoned wild-hairs with their lackadaisical recording methods and invariably late-starting, Grateful Dead–length concerts. There was a cultural gap: Whereas American rock was largely a concert music (album sales promoted by extensive touring), reggae was almost exclusively a studio music in Jamaica. There, even major stars rarely performed in public, much less embarked on anything so organized as a tour; here, such tactics were essential to the dissemination of the product. So when many of the biggest reggae acts proved to be disappointingly uneven or ragged in their U.S. appearances, it only further discouraged American record companies from becoming enthusiastic about breaking reggae in the United States.

It also resulted in off-kilter evaluations of various reggae acts—Jimmy Cliff, who hadn't written or recorded a significant song since the early days of his career, became one of the more dependable reggae acts to tour America because he'd long ago mastered the slick stage-show format that made him attractive both to audiences and concert promoters. Toots and the Maytals, on the other hand, who offered an uneven live show at best even as they were recording some of their finest music, were rapidly downgraded to opening-act, and finally no-tour-at-all, status.

Nonetheless, Marley's importance to Jamaica continued to grow. He had steadily become the spokesman for a large number of poor Jamaicans, a role that was acknowledged even by Jamaica's government. In 1976, he was considered sufficiently dangerous by conservative elements to be the victim of an attempted assassination. With releases such as *Rastaman Vibration* (1976), *Exodus* (1977), and *Kaya* (1978), Marley sold millions of records throughout the world and promulgated his Marxism-as-mysticism philosophy.

Marley died on May 11, 1981, a victim of brain and lung cancer. His death was the occasion for national mourning in Jamaica, and Prime Ministers Edward Seaga and Michael Manley attended his funeral. He was buried in his birthplace, St. Ann, Jamaica. He had brought the message of Rastafarianism to unprecedented numbers of people all over the world and had inspired the establishment of countless reggae communities, in addition to his greatest legacy, his body of living music.

Probably the most important reggae artist to emerge after Marley's death was Augustus Pablo, born Horace Swaby in 1953 in Kingston. Pablo's instrument of choice was the melodica, the plastic combination wind and keyboard instrument that most people considered little more than a child's toy. From his melodica, however, Pablo coaxed stately, eerily beautiful sounds.

Pablo's first music business break came from Marley himself, who in 1969 and 1970 asked Pablo to play the melodica on such Wailers tracks as "Sun Is Shining," "Kaya," and "Memphis." Pablo also performed with Jimmy Cliff and Burning Spear before striking out on his own, releasing his first album in 1972. In 1974, he recorded *King Tubby Meets Rockers Uptown*, a definitive example of "dub" music.

Dub was the name given to the all-instrumental remix of the A side of a reggae single—the vocals of the song are "dubbed out" or stripped away. These rumbling, lengthy B sides frequently became more popular than the A sides of the singles. Some musicians, such as the King Tubby mentioned in Pablo's album title and especially Lee "Scratch" Perry as far back as the late 1960s, had been developing dub as its own genre, and at its best in the work of Augustus Pablo, dub is the most sensuous and radical of all reggae subgenres. In Pablo's hands, virtually any melody loaned itself to the improvisational elaboration of the dub process; he would rework such unlikely tunes as "Fiddler on the Roof," "Old Man River," and Rod McKuen's "Jean," and make shimmeringly beautiful music from them. Furthermore, Augustus Pablo would evince notable staying power in the here-today, gone-tomorrow world of reggae stardom. His early 1980s albums *King Tubby Meets Rockers in a Fire House* and *Earth's Rightful Ruler* would be every bit as inventive and lively as his early, acclaimed albums.

If Jamaican reggae failed to reach a mass audience in America, it profoundly affected all sorts of rock musicians, American and English alike. In England, at the height of punk fury in 1977, the Clash recorded "Complete Control," a single produced by Lee "Scratch" Perry, made to protest CBS Records' refusal to release the English band's "too crude" debut album in America. (*The Clash* ended up selling over 100,000 copies as an import.) The reggae boom also spurred a revival of ska, a form of Jamaican dance music popular in the late 1950s and early 1960s that emphasized a lighter, quicker beat. Ska made its British comeback in the late 1970s, particularly in the industrial city of Coventry, when bands such as the Specials, the Selecter, Madness, and the English Beat began updating the ska rhythm and started a whole fashion craze (tiny porkpie hats, big sunglasses, enormous brothel-creeper shoes) to go along with it.

Selecter leader Noel Davies formed the independent 2-Tone label in 1979; the label's name derived from two characteristics of the movement: ska's new devotees had a fondness for wearing black and white clothes, and, more significant, it was a thoroughly integrated pop form at a time when most rock genres were becoming strictly segregated. That same year 2-Tone released its first single, "Gangsters"; it landed in the British Top Ten. Madness became a star concert attraction for its neck-snapping "skanking" choreography and jaunty tunes sung in defiantly thick working-class accents, while the Specials' more serious, politically minded debut album was produced by an illustrious admirer, Elvis Costello. In America, the 2-Tone label was distributed by Chrysalis Records, but the ska revival never caught on here, and 2-Tone dissolved in 1981.

That same year, however, the Specials released what was probably the most important record of the ska revival, "Ghost Town," a bitterly explicit excoriation of deteriorating race relations and mounting unemployment in England. Banned by the BBC, "Ghost Town" nonetheless became the number-one single in England in the summer of the Brixton riots.

The one ska band that seemed capable of enduring commercial success and perhaps even an American breakthrough was the English Beat (called the Beat in England; the band added the *English* when a mediocre Los Angeles new wave band called the Beat was signed to CBS in the late 1970s). Emerging from Birmingham, the English Beat's first single was a bouncy ska version of Smokey Robinson's "Tears of a Clown," and the group spent its career alternating between witty romantic music and sharply phrased political songs. Among its members was a fifty-year-old Jamaican saxophone player named Saxa, who had performed on many of the earliest reggae hits recorded in Jamaica.

The English Beat made steady inroads in America, becoming a particular favorite on college radio stations and touring as the opening act for the Pretenders and the Talking Heads in 1980. The English Beat broke up, however, in 1983, to be replaced by General Public, a new group formed by Beat singer Ranking Roger and singer-guitarist Dave Wakeling.

In America, artists as diverse as Paul Simon, Stevie Wonder, and Blondie recorded singles with a heavy reggae influence, and popular ones at that: Blondie's "The Tide Is High" was a number-one song in 1980, and Stevie Wonder's "Master Blaster" received extensive radio play.

The rock band that would eventually parlay reggae to the greatest commercial success was the Police, the English-American new wave trio. Emerging in the late 1970s, the band was a stadium-filling superstar act by the early 1980s, and even in football arenas, the band regularly slowed their act to a crawl with lengthy reggae interludes and the exaggeration of the reggae elements in such hit songs as "Can't Stand Losing You," "Voices Inside My Head," and "Roxanne."

Ultimately, the Jamaican styles—reggae, ska, and dub—would prove too exotic, too odd, too rough to ingratiate themselves with the American mainstream. Nonetheless, they influenced a great amount of 1970s rock music, even if most of the Jamaican artists who originated the style were denied the stardom that usually accrues to such influence. Both reggae's rhythm and its status as an embattled subculture were noted and admired with great interest and typical ferocity by another new 1970s form, punk.

34

ALL SHOOK UP: THE PUNK EXPLOSION

Of all the grass roots subgenres of the seventies, punk came closest to exploding the complacent, conservative nature of the rock business. Punk attempted to restore to rock everything its success as a mass phenomenon was draining from it, most of all the now nearly quaint notion that anyone could make this music. Punk was a reaction to the increasing pride in technical virtuosity that was overrunning rock on every level, from the elaborate instruments used to create the music to the scientifically researched ways a major rock tour was mounted and executed.

Punk was rock's most notable attempt in the late 1970s to inject angry, rebellious, risk-taking notions into the music. But the tricks of provocation had to be learned somewhere, and the grandest example of a risky, aggressive, cynical yet ambitious sensibility worming its way into the rock world was the man many called a godfather of punk: Lou Reed.

Dour, sardonic, bitter, his perennial deadpan a blue mask of irony and despair, Lou Reed stands as a crucial figure in 1970s rock. In him, all things meet: As an artist, Reed is as apt a symbol of the noncommercial rock star as anyone could want; as a singer-songwriter, he combined conversational commonplaces with a profound cynicism to yield music that would make the likes of James Taylor blanch; as a performer, he maintained a highly adversarial relationship with his audience, challenging them one minute, insulting them the next. His influence, good and bad, can be heard in the work of rockers as various as David Bowie, the New York Dolls, Roxy Music, and the entire bloody corpus of punk rock.

547

Before there was Lou Reed, there was the Velvet Underground, a band that in the midst of the utopian, freedom-loving, feel-good 1960s, proffered apocalypse, addiction, and feel-bad. As one of the Velvet Underground's principal songwriters, guitarists, and singers, Reed embodied the band's fuck-you/nod-out attitude most succinctly. Reed's contributions to the band included the furious "White Light/White Heat" and the ultimate drug-rock songs "Waiting for the Man" and "Heroin." Although most rock histories have already settled on the image of the band as cold, intelligent, primitive artists, this neglects the fact that even at his most young and surly, Reed was writing beautifully detailed, emotionally and lyrically complex songs such as "Pale Blue Eyes" and "Beginning to See the Light."

The Velvet Underground was a peculiar, always-shaky alliance of clashing sensibilities. Nonetheless, when the band fell apart in 1970, Reed was at sea. For all his prodigious talent and hustler's ambition, he apparently hadn't been plotting the intricacies of launching a solo career in an increasingly commercial era. His first solo album, Lou Reed (1972), sounds as baffled and defensive as Reed claimed to have been during this post-Velvets period. The music is far less intentionally primitive—it's downright polished, in fact, something Reed must have been striving for when he asked members of the English art rock band Yes to contribute to the recording.

In fact, the initial phase of Reed's solo career was a depressing one. While his Velvet Underground work had been marked by pessimism trying heroically to express itself in vivid, precise terms, albums such as Transformer (1972), Berlin (1973), and Sally Can't Dance (1974) dressed that pessimism in fashionable glitter or reduced it to narcissism, decadence, and contempt. Reed shook off this self-indulgent dolor on his 1974 live album Rock 'n' Roll Animal, but parodied that revitalization with another live collection the following year, Lou Reed Live. In 1975, he became perverse in earnest, releasing Metal Machine Music, a two-record set of white noise without a single conventional pop music melody. It is a measure of just how severely Reed had breached the conventions of artist-audience trust that his record company, RCA—like all major labels, not known for their concern for the consumer—actually recalled the album, in effect apologizing for releasing it at all. Reed followed this spit in the eye with a kiss on the cheek—a warm (if by Velvets standards second-rate) collection of pop tunes called Coney Island Baby (1976)—but it was clear that something had to give.

Reed moved on to Arista Records that year, almost immediately releasing Rock and Roll Heart, a continuation of the generous-but-slight, pleasant-but-parodic compositions that had characterized Coney Island Baby. The emblematic Reed song of this period, for example, is Rock and Roll Heart's "I Believe in Love," whose title alone is a mockery of the sentimentality that Reed had always despised and whose lyrics included such is-he-kidding-or-isn't-he lines as "I believe in the Iron Cross," followed soon after by "I believe in good-time music."

From there, Reed's recordings would take a slow but steady upturn in quality. *Street Hassle* (1978) strove much too hard to be a masterpiece, but it did yield the dissonant, discursive pleasures of the title song and faced up to neuroses like "I Wanna Be Black" with humor and honesty. Yet another live album, *Take No Prisoners* (1973), was primarily a vehicle for the petulant cult rocker to savage two of his most vigorous supporters, Robert Christgau of the *Village Voice* and the *New York Times*'s John Rockwell, in a series of between-song insults. *The Bells* (1979) went even further than *Street Hassle* in making his bile more, ah, palatable. With jazzlike improvisational expansiveness, Reed discussed feelings of pain, doubt, and unrequited love.

In the 1980s, that love would become requited. *The Blue Mask* (1982) commenced what would eventually prove to be a trilogy of albums celebrating a new marriage and Reed's attempt to remain a questing artist without giving way to dissipation or depression. *The Blue Mask* is probably Reed's most perfectly realized work: a cogent, unified statement about sprawling, conflicted emotions and ideas. The album moves from the intensely personal ("Women," "Underneath the Bottle") to the grandly metaphorical ("The Day John Kennedy Died," "Waves of Fear"), employing forthright language and the extraordinarily blunt, succinct, powerful guitar work of Robert Quine to make its fiercest emotional points. Reed would follow this major masterpiece with minor ones, *Legendary Hearts* (1983) and *New Sensations* (1984), that elaborated upon the discussions of marriage, commitment, and art begun on *The Blue Mask*.

It was Reed's achievement to force his technical limitations—a flat monotone of a voice, rudimentary instrumental technique, and overreliance on Dylanesque confessional lyrics—to express his most intricate thoughts. His was a distinctly New York sensibility: Emerging from the depths of Manhattan's Lower East Side, the Velvet Underground and then Reed as a solo act embodied the street-smart cynicism of the Big Rotten Apple. Reed's example was followed by virtually every smart band in the city, and nowhere was his influence more vividly felt than in that great protopunk band, the New York Dolls.

Certainly neither *great* nor *punk* in any of its variations were words applied to the Dolls when they began performing late in 1971—*awful* and *ugly* were more like it. Moreover, at the time, the Dolls were associated with glam-rock and David Bowie in his most flamboyantly gay period, an understandable mistake, given that four out of five Dolls wore Spandex and platform boots, while the fifth, singer David Johansen, most often favored high heels and the occasional dress.

No, the sensibility of the New York Dolls was closest to that of Lou Reed's, and not just because the band's original drummer, Billy Murcia, died of a drug overdose in 1972 during the band's first tour of England, shortly before the band recorded its debut album. The mean wisecracks and impassioned cynicism that informed the Dolls' songs represented an attitude that Reed's work with the Velvet Underground embodied, as did the

Dolls' distinct lack of musicianship. But the Velvets had a few trained players in among the ringers; the Dolls were almost entirely self-taught, and their best musician, lead guitarist Johnny Thunders, emulated Keith Richards's willful primitivism.

The result was a band that looked like an exploding thrift shop and sounded like Chuck Berry's pepperoni-pizza-inspired nightmare. Loud, jangling, and insistent, the Dolls became stars at Greenwich Village's Mercer Arts Center on sheer strength of character, in which regard they were truly superstars. Moreover, they were a thoroughly "New York" band; as critic Robert Christgau wrote, "[The Dolls] articulated the noisy, brutal excitement the city offered its populace as nothing ever had, and so offered a kind of control over it."

New York Dolls, recorded in late 1973 and produced by wonderkid Todd Rundgren, featured such intentionally crude, alienated-from-the-self anthems as Thunders's and Johansen's "Personality Crisis," and Johansen's "Looking for a Kiss" and "Lonely Planet Boy," as well as an attempt to play up to their media image, "Trash," co-written by Johansen and guitarist Sylvain Sylvain. Rundgren, known for his own delicately textured recordings, seems to have taken a long lunch during the recording of *New York Dolls*—the album's sound may be kindly termed muddy, with Johansen's ragged roar rising up from the depths of the murk. In its sloppy, crude way, it was a thrilling record; in fact, it was thrilling in part because it was so sloppy and crude—in the face of an increasingly sophisticated record industry, the Dolls blew a big, wet Bronx cheer.

A year later, veteran girl-group producer Shadow Morton oversaw the Dolls' second and final album, *Too Much Too Soon*, which included Johansen's vehement version of Sonny Boy Williamson's blues rant "Don't Start Me Talkin'," as well as the Dolls' interpretation of Gamble and Huff's Philly-soul rocker "There's Gonna Be a Showdown" and a raucous updating of the novelty tune "Stranded in the Jungle," in which Shadow Morton applied his vaunted genius for witty sound effects by summoning up what sounded like a batch of wild animals hooting, chattering, and roaring while trapped in an IRT subway car.

The Dolls lusted after fame and did indeed become the darlings of a rock-and-roll underground society that included journalists Lisa Robinson and Danny Fields, who used every opportunity to plug the band in the various teenybopper magazines they edited with artful irony during this period. Yet neither of the Dolls' albums sold beyond their tiny local cult following, and the band floundered even as they served as a do-it-yourself example to many would-be, soon-to-be-punk musicians in New York and England. Under the leadership of Johansen and Sylvain, the duo managed to keep the Dolls a going concern until 1977; by that time, bassist Arthur Kane had succumbed to a drinking problem, and Johnny Thunders and drummer Jerry Nolan formed the Heartbreakers. The Dolls broke up just as the "new wave" of punk bands began to emerge from the Lower East Side, at once an ironic exemplar and a warning to the young bands of the commercial perils that awaited them in the pursuit of adventurously stripped-down music.

The most commercially successful acts to exploit the glam-rock ethos of makeup, musical primitivism, and sexual ambiguity were Alice Cooper and Kiss. Alice Cooper was born Vincent Furnier in Detroit, Michigan, in 1945. Forming a band consisting of high school chums, Furnier adopted the name Alice Cooper and moved the group to Los Angeles in 1968, where he attracted the attention of manager Shep Gordon, who got the band signed to Frank Zappa's new Straight Record label. Cooper's first two albums, *Pretties For You* (1969) and *Easy Action* (1970), were little more than obnoxious novelty items, lacking humor or punch.

Moving back to Detroit, the band came under the wing of producer Bob Ezrin, who oversaw *Love It to Death* (1970). Then the rock station CKLW, across the river from Detroit in Windsor, Ontario, began to play one song from the album, "Eighteen," over and over. This bit of walloping spitefulness became a local hit among Detroit listeners, who were beguiled by the growling guy with a girl's name who asserts he's just eighteen (Alice was actually a jaded twenty-five). Cooper's local appearances enhanced Alice-mania; with a stage show that featured mock hangings and an onstage electrocution, Alice Cooper became the hippest rock rebellion yet. "Sometimes half the audience would be up and out before we finished our first number," Cooper recalled in 1975. "A lot of them, though, were afraid to walk out. They were afraid to move. Do you realize what a feeling of power that can give you?"

For a while, Cooper was using his power wisely indeed, turning out more teen revenge fantasies, like "School's Out" (1972), featuring one of the most ferocious vocals ever recorded. He also padded his albums with crude crowd pleasers that stoked his bad-boy image: "Dead Babies" and "I Love the Dead" are typical titles. Cooper's shows began to take on the order of full-scale musical comedies, albeit ones in extremely poor taste. *Billion Dollar Babies* (1973) and *Welcome to My Nightmare* (1975) were both promoted by tours featuring elaborate props (Alice wearing a live boa constrictor around his neck) and stunts (Alice chopping up dolls with a chain saw). Soon enough, he slipped into self-parody and began talking wistfully to the press about how he, Alice Cooper, was just ordinary-guy Vince Furnier, whose greatest ambition was to play golf with Bob Hope. Even that wish came true.

Kiss managed, in a far more commercial and cynical way, to achieve the sort of success through crudity and street smarts that the New York Dolls had hoped for. Kiss, too, was a New York band, formed in 1972 by singer-bassist Gene Simmons (who in the early days supplemented his income by teaching at P.S. 75 in Manhattan) and guitarist Paul Stanley. Simmons and Stanley recruited drummer Peter Criss through an ad in *Rolling Stone* and guitarist Ace Frehley through an ad in the *Village Voice*. All had labored in a series of mediocre bands, but from the start, the concept behind Kiss was an attention-getter: The band appeared only in elaborate makeup and glittery costumes—no one was supposed to see the group's real faces.

The strategy, when combined with brutally simple, catchy hard rock, worked. The band gathered a large number of fans, dubbed the Kiss Army, who liked the riffs and the mystique, and the band's stage shows were enjoyably vulgar, highlighted by Simmons's most impressive feature, a long, pointy tongue that he waggled rudely at the audience while shaking his head in an approximation of a monster gone mad.

For a while in the mid-1970s, Kiss was a phenomenon, selling millions of copies of such albums as *Alive, Destroyer,* and *Rock and Roll Over.* The cartoonishness of the band's image gave way to the inevitable: In 1977, Marvel Comics published a Kiss comic book that depicted the band as superheroes; always up for some peculiar publicity, the band spread the word that the red ink in the comic contained blood from each of the band members' bodies. Crudely drawn and indifferently plotted, the Kiss comic book sold poorly and coincidentally signaled the end of the band's massive popularity.

But the experiments of the New York Dolls, Alice Cooper, and Kiss, updating the Velvet Underground, inspired a new wave of artists just beginning to emerge in the rock clubs of lower Manhattan. In the early 1970s, the New York rock scene had been tired and musty. Down on the Lower East Side, Bill Graham's Fillmore East had closed in 1971 after degenerating into a site for mediocre hard rock acts to ply their trade. The Fillmore's position as a medium-size hall for rock acts too big for Greenwich Village nightclubs and too small to fill Madison Square Garden had been filled by the Academy of Music on East Fourteenth Street. Overseen by promoter Howard Stein, the Academy (later renamed the Palladium under Stein's reign) had become a haven for heavy metal and art rock, the place to see Black Oak Arkansas or Gentle Giant or Renaissance or to score a Quaalude in the downstairs bathroom.

The smaller spots had been equally moribund, with such folk clubs as the Bitter End reduced to booking mild folk-rock or soft rock acts now that the bottom had fallen out of the folk music boom. If you had a hankering to see Brewer and Shipley, the Bitter End (soon to be renamed, by the mid-1980s, the Other End) was the place to go. The Mercer Arts Center, the decrepit site of the club the New York Dolls called home, collapsed, quite literally, in 1974. In short, Manhattan was dead as a rock and roll town.

The middle of the decade, however, brought the first stirrings of a nascent music scene. In 1975, Hilly Kristal, owner of a nondescript Bowery bar called CBGB and OMFUG (the name stood for "Country, Bluegrass, and Blues and Other Music for Urban Gourmets"), allowed a few local musicians to talk him into using the rear of his long, narrow bar as a stage on which to perform for free. Poet and protopunk Patti Smith moved in for a seven-week stint in mid-1975 and established CBGBs as a beachhead of the rock and roll avant garde. Before long, Kristal had a list of regular bands rotating at CBGBs—bands such as Tuff Darts, Blondie, Stumblebunny, the Ramones, Television, Talking Heads. Word was beginning to spread among hip arty types that CBGBs was the place to be—both to hear music that stood in stark contrast to the polished stuff that was coming to overrun the rock industry, and to be seen in the new "in" spot.

It was poet and rock star Patti Smith who would become presiding goddess of the growing "new wave" scene. Smith, raised in New Jersey, inspired equally by Rimbaud and Verlaine at one extreme and Jim Morrison and Jimi Hendrix at the other, had been a New York art world figure since the late 1960s. A thin waif with a gravelly mumble of a voice, Smith had started out as a painter, took up playwriting while enduring a liaison with writer Sam Shepard, and began writing poetry heavily influenced by the Russians (especially Mayakovski) and the New Yorkers (especially Frank O'Hara).

After a while, all her supposedly clashing influences began to coincide: She befriended rock critic–musician Lenny Kaye, who started accompanying her poetry readings with electric guitar music, and from there it was just a short leap to forming a band and commencing wild, surrealistic performances in places like CBGBs. In 1974, she released an independently produced single, "Hey Joe," a salute to culture heroes ranging from Hendrix to Patty Hearst, backed with "Piss Factory," a harrowing reminiscence of time spent working on an assembly line. The initial pressing of the single sold out quickly, proving that Smith's determinedly harsh poetic music had some sort of commercial appeal, and later that year she became the first of the so-called new wave artists to be signed to a major label: Clive Davis's brand-new Arista Records, his comeback to the record industry after being dismissed from the presidency of Columbia Records in 1973. Thus Patti Smith joined a big-time record company whose roster also included Eric Carmen and Barry Manilow.

The records Patti Smith made during the last half of the 1970s and the first years of the 1980s were sprawling, ambitious affairs that attracted a rabid cult following and had only one substantial commercial success, "Because the Night" in 1978.

If Patti Smith provided New York new wave with its first indelible image, Richard Hell gave it its anthem. Hell, the son of an English teacher and still another dabbler in the New York art scene, recorded "Blank Generation" in 1977 with his band the Voidoids. "Blank Generation," sneered by Hell to the accompaniment of guitarist Robert Quine's concise buzz-saw guitar riffs, limned the general air of hopelessness and hostility with which the members of this young New York rock scene viewed their world. Although much of his later music was self-indulgent and/or self-repetitive, Hell was also an important fashion setter for the new wave scene; his ripped clothing and just-fell-outta-bed hairstyle would soon become the trademarks of punk fashion.

Probably the most striking band to follow in the wake of Patti Smith,

Richard Hell, and the burgeoning CBGBs scene was the Ramones, formed in 1974 by four Forest Hills, New York, friends. Naming their group for a pseudonym Paul McCartney had used in his Silver Beatle days, the members then decided to drop their real surnames and to adopt "Ramone" instead. From the start, the Ramones distinguished themselves from the general run of loud, fast upstarts by becoming much louder and much faster than any group around. Johnny and Dee Dee Ramone whipped up deafening storms of sound with only two or three guitar chords; Tommy Ramone slammed the beat with metronomic precision. Joey Ramone—impossibly tall, limp haired, and ungainly—leaned into this hurricane and bleated songs with titles like "Beat on the Brat," "Gimme Gimme Shock Treatment," and "Now I Wanna Sniff Some Glue." Most of the Ramones' songs didn't last more than two minutes; their average performance clocked in at less than thirty minutes, but it was arguably the most exhilarating half-hour in rock and roll. In performance and concept, the Ramones were utterly new, and at their best, thrillingly good.

The Ramones were greeted with a mixture of awe and ridicule. The band was like a cartoon of a rock and roll group, and many considered them little more than a novelty act. But behind their amiable-dunce demeanor, the Ramones were hard workers: They were the first of the New York new wave bands to tour extensively, and their appearances in England in 1976 were later cited by many English punk bands as the original inspiration for that country's do-it-yourself rock revolution. The Ramones continued to refine and streamline their attack until it became a magnificent blur of sound. *The Ramones*, the band's 1976 debut disc, was recorded for a paltry $6,000 and stands as a definitive statement of punk/new wave music.

The band that came to symbolize New York new wave at its knottiest, though, was the Talking Heads, whose initially terse, squawking, demotic sound summed up all that was eccentric and anticommercial about the lower Manhattan scene. The band was formed by three graduates of the Rhode Island School of Design, David Byrne, Chris Frantz, and Tina Weymouth, who while still in school had performed in a quintet called, depending on their feelings that evening, either the Artistics or the Autistics.

In 1975, having moved to New York, Byrne, Frantz, and Weymouth became the Talking Heads and began performing a mix of original songs and campy covers at lower Manhattan clubs, eventually settling in at CBGBs as the minimalistic, ironic alternative to the heated pop of Blondie and the complex sobersidedness of Television. With his craning neck, big pop eyes, quivering Adam's apple, and ululating gurgle of a voice, David Byrne was Nerd Incarnate, and his signature song rapidly became "Psycho Killer," which was intended by Byrne as an impressionistic sketch of a murderer's thoughts, not as a stylistic credo. Nonetheless, it was an image that stuck; a decade later, reviewing the 1984 Talking Heads concert film *Stop Making Sense*, critic Carter Ratcliff would refer to the way Byrne had devised "a variant on his basic 'Psycho Killer' self for each song; he demonstrates over and over that a public self is a Frankenstein self, a monster put together from bits and pieces of image-tissue."

Similar experiments were taking place in England, although, as critic Jim Miller wrote for *The New Republic*, the New York punks were "older, cooler and artier" than their British counterparts, who were "young, angry, and hell-bent on fame, assaulting the pop scene head-on." The baptism of British punk was the first performance of the Sex Pistols at St. Martins College of Art in London on November 6, 1975. In the great tradition of rock and roll scandal, the social secretary of the school was obliged to cut off the band's electrical supply five songs into the Pistols' set. Nonetheless, the damage had been done: By the same time the following year, punk rock— the music made by the Pistols and literally hundreds of other bands in England—had become, depending on your point of view, either the most exhilarating thing to happen to rock music in a decade or the most vile abomination rock music had yet inspired.

For its fans in England, in America, and throughout the rest of the world, punk rock was a shared secret, an explosion of music and ideas and attitudes that not only weren't understood by the mass media and most people over forty; punk rock's implications weren't even understood by the vast majority of the rock audience itself. Punk rock's partisans immediately became, as English sociologist and critic Dick Hebdige called it, a sub-culture, characterized by "a guttersnipe rhetoric, [an] obsession with class and relevance that were expressly designed to undercut the intellectual posturing of the previous generation of rock musicians."

Or by their own lights, the Sex Pistols—lead singer Johnny Rotten, lead guitarist Steve Jones, bassist Glen Matlock, drummer Paul Cook—were single-mindedly bent on exposing what Rotten called "fucking cheap, shoddy rock and rollers." Which was to say, everyone except the Sex Pistols and, at their most convolutedly idealistic, the idea of rock and roll itself.

To consider their beginnings, there was no reason to think the Sex Pistols would be anything more than what their detractors always considered them: a bad joke. In one sense, the Pistols were as manufactured a rock band as the Monkees had been—the pioneers of punk rock were master-minded by Malcolm McLaren, veteran of the Paris riots of 1968, would-be artist involved in the French Situationist movement, with a healthy interest in both Dada and making money. McLaren's primary artwork, until his creation of the Sex Pistols, was his King's Road boutique, which regularly underwent changes of name: one month it was Let It Rock, the next it was Too Fast to Live, Too Young to Die; then it was just Sex, and finally it was Seditionaries.

McLaren was a glib wiseguy who'd already dabbled in pop Svengaliism by managing the New York Dolls in their final days. In a gesture that does a lot to suggest his outrageousness, his cynicism, and his stupidity, McLaren attempted to turn the Dolls into a profitable scandal by draping them in the

Communist flag as a stage set. The Dolls, mired in drugs and debt, did not last long under McLaren's guidance.

Deciding to build his own band, McLaren recruited John Lydon, a sarcastic, musically illiterate unemployed janitor, at a time when England's unemployment rate among youth was at an all-time high. Renaming him Johnny Rotten, McLaren tossed him in with Matlock, who was hanging out at the clothing store, and Cook and Jones, chums as well as professional rock musicians sick of their lowly lot in life. Cook, Jones, and Matlock had certain tastes in common—all three despised the fatuous complacency of the rock-star world above them and held critical favorites like David Bowie and Roxy Music to be, in Matlock's words, "very contrived . . . there was no rock and roll then at all." Lydon/Rotten, by contrast, hadn't sung professionally before and professed to have little use for rock music, which suited McLaren's purposes perfectly. Then, too, as Paul Cook told Fred and Judy Vermorel, "We was still learning to play at the time, so we wasn't really worried about whether he had a great voice or anything."

With Rotten sneering and jeering while the rest of the band emitted squalls of rhythmic noise, the Sex Pistols were immediately noticed, and followed. Indeed, what is most remarkable about the band was just how fast they rose to prominence. In the Vermorels' 1978 book *The Sex Pistols*, Dave Goodman, the band's earliest producer and sound man, is quoted as saying that "Joe Strummer of the 101ers [a post–pub rock, semiacoustic outfit], when he saw the Pistols . . . he just freaked and left the band immediately after the gig and formed his own punk rock group." That group, the Clash, would soon be competing with the Sex Pistols for the Most Famous Punk Rock Band title.

The Sex Pistols appeared regularly at the 100 Club, one of the few places in London that put up with the volume of the band and the rowdiness of the band's colorfully dressed followers. Other early punk venues included the Nashville, Dingwalls, and the Marquee, but the 100 Club was Punk Central for the first year of its initial explosion. It was there that Terry Slater of EMI Records saw the Pistols and began thinking that, judging from the rabid reaction of an increasingly large audience, the group should be signed to a recording contract.

McLaren, of course, was only too happy to agree to this, and the band was signed to EMI on October 10, 1976, less than a year after they had formed. Fans who had come to understand that the Pistols were meant to stand in opposition to everything the big-time rock industry represented were understandably appalled ("SEX PISTOLS JOIN ESTABLISHMENT" read the headline of the pop newspaper *Music Week* when the signing was announced), but it soon became clear that far from being co-opted by the big bad music business, the Sex Pistols were about to prove that they were more than any entrenched conventional industry could handle.

Less than two months later, the Sex Pistols released their first single, "Anarchy in the U.K.," which, years later, sounds like a classic rock record, vibrating with anger, energy, humor, and rhythm. But at the time, with Rotten snarling in its opening lines, "I am the Antichrist," these were precisely the terms on which the band was immediately attacked by people of good breeding all across England. EMI was shocked at how shocked everyone—the public, the straight press—seemed to be and sought to distance themselves from the band, at one point denying them the funds to proceed with a planned tour of England to promote the single. McLaren accused EMI of failing to distribute "Anarchy in the U.K.," saying to *Melody Maker* with a mixture of triumph and disgust, "EMI say they are behind us, but as far as I can see they seem to be about two miles behind us. Everyone seems to be backing away from us in the industry—promoters, agents, and all the businessmen."

McLaren wasn't exaggerating: In response to McLaren's comments, John Reed, chairman of EMI, all but admitted what was then considered the ghastly mistake of having signed the group: "We shall do everything we can to constrain their public behavior, although this is a matter over which we have no real control. Similarly, EMI will review its general guidelines regarding the content of pop records."

By "public behavior," Reed was doubtless referring to the Sex Pistols' instantly notorious December 1, 1976, appearance on a British television show, "Today," hosted by Bill Grundy. Grundy, dripping contempt for the surly rockers, had asked for trouble, baiting Rotten by taunting him to "say something outrageous." Rotten complied with, "You dirty sod; you dirty bastard." Asked what they'd done with the forty thousand pounds EMI had given the band as an advance, Rotten said, "Fucking spent it, didn't we?" The next day the *Daily Mirror* reported that a forty-seven-year-old lorry driver, James Holmes, shocked that his eight-year-old son had been exposed to such language, kicked in his television set. "It blew up and I was knocked backwards," he was quoted as saying. "I was so angry and disgusted with this filth that I took a swing with my boot . . . . I don't want this sort of muck coming into my home at teatime."

After the Grundy affair, which, while cast as a publicity stunt (as much for Grundy's benefit as for the Pistols'), truly rattled the whole of England, the band commenced a tour of the country in the company of the nascent Clash and other punk bands, and in the middle of it, were unceremoniously dumped by EMI. Soon after this, citing the disappointingly usual rock star reason—artistic differences with his colleagues—Glen Matlock quit the band, to be replaced by Sid Vicious.

On March 9, 1977, the Sex Pistols were signed to A&M Records, which announced the agreement with a corporate statement saying that "the Sex Pistols' becoming available presented us with a unique business opportunity. . . ."

One week later, with the band having just finished recording its next single, "God Save the Queen," A&M issued a statement that they would now "rescind the agreement between themselves and the Sex Pistols." In explanation, managing director Derek Green said, "I changed my mind."

By May, the band was signed to Virgin Records, which released "God Save the Queen" at the height of public interest in Queen Elizabeth's Silver Jubilee celebration. "God Save the Queen" was taken for what it was—as blunt an attack on the monarchy as could be imagined. "God save the Queen, the fascist regime," sneered Johnny Rotten, climaxing the song with what is at once one of the most dramatic (and on another level, most pathetic) threats ever uttered by a rock performer: "We mean it, man," he yelled, well aware of the fact that "God Save the Queen" was so extreme, so hostile, so blithely nihilistic, that tolerant people might interpret it as a joke.

Banned in Britain, "God Save the Queen" was an instant sensation, hitting Number One by mid-June. Again, it bears stressing that, as intriguing as the Pistols' style of outrage and disgust may have been, their music would not have survived being banned by the most powerful radio station in England if it didn't hold up awfully well as rock and roll.

This both "God Save the Queen" and "Anarchy in the U.K." certainly do, and the fact that the band accomplished this with only the most rudimentary form of musicianship was a profound inspiration to literally thousands of people disaffected with the mainstream rock scene, to say nothing of their own lives. Thus it was that a whole social scene sprang up with the emergence of the Sex Pistols—the band was merely the most visible symbol of a new era of youth subculture.

Amid a generation steeped in media savvy, England's punk scene offered ample visual signs for a salivating media to absorb and transmit around the world. The punks' metaphors for their depressed economic and mental states were torn and ripped fabric, the leather of bondage and S & M, the shaved heads of prisoners. Feeling no kinship for the white rock music of England and America, they found kinship with Jamaican reggae, music recorded primarily by an underclass with whom they could identify. As Dick Hebdige wrote in his 1979 book *Subculture: The Meaning of Style*, "Reggae attracted those punks who wanted to give tangible form to their alienation; it carried the necessary conviction, the political bite, so obviously missing in most contemporary white music."

Reggae's slow, stuttering beat and implacable rhythm was one of the clearest influences on the Sex Pistols' most well-known colleagues, the Clash. In the face of the Clash's eventual absorption into the corporate rock world, the Sex Pistols' tale seems like an abruptly ended anecdote. The Pistols released their first and only album, *Never Mind the Bollocks, Here's the Sex Pistols*, in late 1977; the record was distributed by Warner Bros. in America, and the company sent out pretorn promotional T-shirts to accompany the album. For Warner Bros., handling the Sex Pistols was both a risk and a logical move; the company had spent the preceding ten years as the hippest and most open-minded of the major labels, and punk was a challenge to rise to. Still, it took all the persuasive efforts of Warners A&R chief

Bob Regher to convince the company that this, unarguably the most exciting band in 1977 rock and roll, was worth the inevitable trouble.

For their part, the Sex Pistols and other punk bands weren't having an easy time of it. Rotten and Paul Cook were each assaulted in separate instances by people hostile to punk rock. Writing about the Clash, English rock critic Simon Frith cited an incident in Wales in which "local Christians had a service outside [the site of a Clash concert] and denounced punks as the Antichrist, though, as Joe Strummer said, 'They wouldn't know the Antichrist if he hit them across the face with a wet kipper.'"

Strummer was the son of a British diplomat who broke into show biz by "busking"—playing music in the London subways for whatever money passersby would toss into his open guitar case. Teaming up with guitarist Mick Jones, they formed the Clash with bassist Paul Simonon after the trio had attended an inspiring early Sex Pistols performance. Working first with Tory Crimes and subsequently Topper Headon as drummer, the Clash quickly established its prominence on the London punk scene as bitter idealists surrounded by nihilists of varying degrees of conviction.

The Clash's protest songs were both harsh and eloquent. If you listened closely you could understand exactly what Strummer was yammering about on early Clash songs such as "Career Opportunities" (pervasive British unemployment), "White Riot" (English racism), and "I'm So Bored with the U.S.A." (encroaching imperialism). On its 1977 debut album *The Clash*, the band made most explicit its admiration for Reggae with a murderously slow, pointed version of Junior Murvin's "Police and Thieves."

Significantly, CBS Records in London signed the Clash, but its American branch deemed *The Clash*, which had reached number two on the British pop charts, "too crude" to be released in the home of the brave. The embarrassing result of this was that over 100,000 imported copies of *The Clash* were sold before CBS gave it a formal U.S. release in 1979. In response to this situation, the Clash thumbed its collective nose at CBS by recording a single about arrogant corporations entitled "Complete Control." *London Calling* (1979) provided the Clash with its commercial breakthrough in America when the single "Train in Vain" cracked the U.S. top thirty.

Indeed, the Clash was one of the many adventurous bands helped commercially by the growing, loose network of college radio stations throughout America, which began offering its listeners an alternative to the rigid formatting of commercial radio. To college audiences in the United States, bands such as the Sex Pistols, the Clash, Siouxsie and the Banshees, and others represented the sort of rebellious, rough-edged music that was youth's birthright. The fact that the big stations didn't play this music, which had a large audience overseas, only increased its allure.

Hundreds of English punk bands sprang up in response to the lead of the Sex Pistols and the Clash. Some of them, such as X-Ray Spex, Generation X, the Buzzcocks, and the Damned, launched successful careers; others released a memorable single or two before breaking up or disappearing. The most dramatic example of the latter situation was Magazine's "Shot by Both Sides," a spectacularly powerful, dramatically compelling British hit single issued in late 1977. Magazine, led by singer-songwriter Howard Devoto, pursued a career through a quick succession of albums, but nothing the band (or Devoto as a solo artist) did ever matched the achievement of "Shot by Both Sides."

One important effect of British punk was the opportunity it offered women to participate fully in the rock world for the first time in the history of the music. Because it refused to accept the usual standards of rock, which along with other things by the 1970s had become ever more entrenched in a kind of reflexive sexism, punk's anyone-can-do-this attitude encouraged women who had heretofore been discouraged from trying to start a band, or write a song, or produce a record. The most exhilarating symbol of punk's open-mindedness was the triumph of Poly Styrene, a portly woman with braces who fit no one's clichéd idea of what a "chick singer" ought to be. With her soaring, wobbling voice and sharp, sarcastic phrasing, Styrene led X-Ray Spex through a series of thrilling performances, from their initial hit single "Oh Bondage, Up Yours!" (1977) on through the 1978 album *Germ-free Adolescents*.

The punk rock subculture yielded its own independent record labels (after the example of the Sex Pistols, very few major companies were willing to sign punk bands), as well as its own fanzines and music clubs. The most significant of the independent labels were Stiff Records, whose stars were Elvis Costello and Nick Lowe, and Rough Trade Records, whose tiny Portobello Road offices included its own small, makeshift record-pressing plant as well as a roster of artists who made uncompromisingly abrasive, intentionally crude, or hostile music.

As a sudden shock, as a brief innovation, as an abrupt series of new ideas about what rock music could include and what it could get rid of, punk was an enlivening force in mainstream rock and roll. In this sense, punk's commercial failure in America was not only irrelevant but, in a way, proof that it had succeeded: What punk did was clear the air—it completed a section of rock history by defining the big business of the rock industry and then condemning it. Punk inspired countless amateurs or even nonmusicians to take up guitars against a sea of mediocre professionalism and thus altered the terms by which rock music was discussed. It's probably safe to say that other, nonpunk performers—people like Prince, Michael Jackson, Cyndi Lauper, Bruce Springsteen—could not have made the radical gestures they did without the act of punk, which broadened the entire concept of what you could do—and what you could get away with—in rock.

35

THE POSTPUNK IMPLOSION

As a reaction to the bloodlessness of mid-1970s rock and roll, punk would influence a wide range of artists on both sides of the Atlantic. Eventually, too, it would provoke its own reactionary antidotes—the New Romantics, for example, who would emerge at the close of the decade. But punk itself would prove short-lived as an actual movement. The most symbolically apt, if highly artificial grave marker for the death of punk rock is the demise of Sid Vicious in Manhattan on February 2, 1979. Vicious represented punk rock at its bleakest, its aggressive pride in amateurism and nihilism brought to a stupid, ugly end. Hooked on heroin, accused of killing his girlfriend Nancy Spungen the month before, the former bassist for the Sex Pistols had thoroughly botched whatever was left of his career when the Pistols disbanded. With Sid Vicious, much of punk rock had become a sick joke to many people—indeed, to the ignorant and the hostile, Sid was what it meant to be a punk rocker.

But this is not unlike what Vicious's former band mate, John Lydon—the former Johnny Rotten—thought as well. After the Pistols' breakup, Lydon reverted to his legal name and began excoriating punk rock with all the fervor he'd originally brought to the condemnation of commercial rock and roll only a few years earlier. The Sex Pistols, Lydon announced, had "finished rock and roll"; he would, he said, proceed to show us what would come next.

Where Sid Vicious had chosen to turn himself into a sour parody of the Sex Pistols' pungent nay-saying—the high point of Vicious's post-Pistols career, for example, was a caterwauling cover of the Frank Sinatra hit "My

561

Way"—Lydon was smart, ambitious, and angry enough to extend his rebellion to a new musical format, one that denied the militant primitivism of punk rock. That format became Public Image Ltd.

This new band's initial album, *Public Image/First Issue*, was released in late 1978 in England but was denied an American release, and for once the staid U.S. record company standards were appropriate—*Public Image/First Issue* was a boring mess. Public Image Ltd., which consisted of Lydon as vocalist and theorist, Jah Wobble on bass, and Keith Levene on guitar and synthesizer, was making, announced Lydon, "anti-rock-and-roll"—a neat trick, and one very nearly achieved on the band's fascinating 1980 release, *Metal Box*, or, in its American title, *Second Edition*.

Once again, Lydon was trying to attack rock and roll where it lived—most immediately, in the matter of packaging. *Metal Box* in its original, English version consisted of three twelve-inch 45 rpm EPs wedged into a tin canister similar to a film can. It was difficult to remove the records from this contraption, and expensive to produce, so the album's American distributor, Island Records, decided to release the material in a more conventional format, as a two-record, 33 rpm set with the usual cardboard jacket. As Lydon commented with impish wistfulness at the time, "All our wonderful ideas—shattered."

Nonetheless, *Metal Box/Second Edition* had its impact. The music on this effort was certainly a species of rock and roll—you could hear it in the steady pounding of a series of anonymous drummers; in Wobble's bass lines, at their best influenced by reggae, at their worst by pretentious art rock; in Levene's positively Emerson, Lake, and Palmer—esque keyboard indulgences; as well as in Lydon's amelodic but definitely rhythmic vocalizing.

"Swan Lake," called more vividly "Death Disco" in its English single version, was hypnotic yet compelling dance music at a time when *disco* was a dirty word. "Poptones," which Lydon claimed in interviews was about male rape but whose lyric was unintelligible on record, was nonetheless a powerful, rip-roaring piece of music, powered by Lydon's sorrowful, furious whine and wail. The collection was by no means perfect—"No Birds," "Bad Baby," and "Graveyard" were particularly arty, pretentious, and dull—but the album peaked in triumph with "Careering," a composition whose melody bounced off Lydon's bellow and whose words turned the title into a loose pun. John Lydon's careering was both an impudent nose-thumbing and a brilliant solution to the dilemma of what to do after you've killed off punk rock.

Listening to *Second Edition* was like taking an idling stroll through a bad dream—if Alice Cooper hadn't already used it, Lydon might have entitled the project *Welcome to My Nightmare*. *Edition* commenced with "Albatross," in which Lydon moaned wearily about "Getting rid of the albatross," a phrase that stood for a lot: For Lydon, perhaps, the burden of the

Sex Pistols legend, and for the rest of his generation, rock history, rock stardom, and the very idea that rock lyrics might yield something called literature.

One reaction to Punk might almost have been predicted: Calling themselves the New Romantics, a group of British youths decided to turn the clock back a few hours to those halcyon days of . . . David Bowie and glam-rock. The New Romantics, overseen in Pierrot makeup by an English disc jockey and clotheshorse calling himself Steve Strange, tried to revitalize the idea of the discotheque as well as the notion of dressing up. Victorian gowns, billowy-sleeved pirate shirts, kabuki makeup, Edwardian high collars, spats and jackboots, derbies and turbans—anything went with the New Romantics, as long as it was neither sloppy-hippie nor aggressive-punk.

Although a few bands briefly allied themselves with the New Romantic movement—Spandau Ballet and Visage, among them—the trend didn't have much staying power, even in an increasingly escapist-minded, economically depressed England. In America, the New Romantics attracted even fewer fans; their one notable outpost was—where else?—fashion-mad Hollywood, where a semi-private club called The Veil met weekly in various Los Angeles nightclubs to strut odd fashions and be glimpsed by slack-jawed movie stars.

The New Romanticism was built upon an ironic artifice that was uninformed by history. Neither Steve Strange, whose banal concept for replacing rock concerts consisted of the revival of Italian-style "neo-realist theater," nor the rich kids who preened in Hollywood seemed to have any idea that art movements like Dada, surrealism, and futurism; painters like Picabia and Beardsley; writers like Huysmans and Firbank; and filmmakers like Buñuel and even Andy Warhol in his I-am-a-camera phase—that all these people had done what the New Romantics were trying to do, and with more control, class, and wit.

The English response to the collapse of punk rock was far more ambitious and radical. The inevitably dubbed "post-punk" bands were a reaction not only to the early punk groups but to the well-intentioned but essentially reactionary ska revivalism of the 2-Tone Records crowd; to mushrooming unemployment under Margaret Thatcher's reign; and to the fascist-skinhead racism and violence that was erupting all over England.

Bands such as the Gang of Four, the Raincoats, Essential Logic, the Mekons, the Au Pairs, Red Crayola, and Scritti Politti were making music that was dense in more ways than one. While each band evinced its own style, all held in common a suspicion of pop music niceties such as catchy melodies and mannerly crooning, as well as an interest in employing harsh, abrasive sounds to jolt the listener into rethinking the idea of what rock music was supposed to contain. In England, these bands' records achieved a certain amount of popularity; in America, they sank without a trace.

Popularity was not something these musicians courted, however. To them, popularity was achieved by working within a music industry of which they wanted no part. The Gang of Four was a quartet led by Jon King and Andy Gill, fine arts students at the University of Leeds. One of the few post-punk bands to be signed to a major label deal (Warner Bros. in America and EMI in England), the Gang of Four took its inspiration not from other musicians (the band members could barely be called that themselves) but from a painfully self-conscious postmodernist aesthetic. Describing the effect they hoped to achieve in their music to Greil Marcus in a 1980 *Rolling Stone* interview, for example, band member Hugo Burnham said, "It's very consciously like the split screens Godard used in *Numero Deux*." Burnham tossed this off as if it was the most logical comparison in the world, and, to the band, it was.

What the Gang of Four reacted to most aggressively was simplicity in rock music—simplicity of ideas, simplicity of structure. Most of all, the Gang of Four's hoarsely shouted, rhythmically blunt music was about distance— distance from the audience, and from the emotions called up by a song lyric. "You've got a description of events, not necessarily an emotional identification of those events, but a description, or, given the received ideas people bring to events, a re-description," King told *Rolling Stone*. "The music that goes with it attempts to re-create, to reinvent a form to accompany that redescription of the world."

Both the Raincoats, an all-woman quartet, and Essential Logic, led by eighteen-year-old saxophonist-singer Lora Logic, recorded their dissonant, prickly music for Rough Trade Records, a serenely independent record company housed in back of a small record store off Portobello Road in London. Working from the premise of its owner, Geoff Travis—"Changing things from the inside is nonsense. . . . It doesn't matter how much 'creative control' a band is given—you're still indentured [to a major label]"— Rough Trade kept its business on an intentionally small scale, pressing no more copies of a record than demand called for, distributing the marginal profits equally among its employees.

In America, post-punk fall-out tended to be far less serious and aggressive. For one thing, it was important for the mass media to turn punk into a joke, a trend that would pass—otherwise, punk might actually raise issues about corporate show business and, more broadly, corporate government that television, in particular, assumed the general public didn't want to hear.

In most cases, American punks were only too glad to comply. The New York punk–new wave scene had turned in on itself, yielding primarily repetition and cynicism in place of innovation and aggression.

Los Angeles, by contrast, spawned a particularly nasty post-punk scene, one in which punk was interpreted as a series of fashion decisions and surface gestures. In the land of sun and money, punk's original impulses weren't merely ignored—they weren't even comprehended by the middle-class teenagers who used punk rock as the latest excuse to get drunk and wrap the family Mercedes around a tree on the weekend.

The seeds of L.A. punk were planted by early English punk bands such as the Sex Pistols and the Clash, whose hostile stance toward the music industry struck a chord with many youthful Angelenos who were growing up despising Los Angeles' "laid-back" music scene. To the L.A. punks, the Eagles self-pitying crooning about "Life in the Fast Lane" seemed as hateful as Rod Stewart squawking "Da Ya Think I'm Sexy?" did to English kids.

The archetypal L.A. punk was Darby Crash, an upper-middle-class lout who founded a band called the Germs in the first flush of English punk. Crash sang in an anonymous caterwaul, throwing himself around the stage à la Iggy Stooge. He was by many accounts a charming brat who attracted a certain amount of loyalty and even talent: Joan Jett, for example, produced the first Germs album in 1979. In good Hollywood-decadent style, Crash was also addicted to heroin, and he apparently committed suicide using a particularly virulent and fashionable strain of the drug, China White, in 1980. (Within a month, a band called China White began performing around town.)

By then, the L.A. scene was becoming known as "hard-core punk," and concerts became all-out melees featuring "slam dancing," a move that consisted primarily of ramming into anyone in your general vicinity. Thus many hard-core concerts climaxed in a certain amount of painful, self-inflicted punk-bashing; and hard-core bands began to find it increasingly difficult to find concert halls that would permit this guff to occur. These punks looked like hell, and they sounded like hell, and since most of them had never heard of Céline or Genet, they thought their songs described hell in a new way, too.

One major rock band rose out of the stifling L.A. hard-core scene: X. X leaders John Doe and Exene had met in the late 1970s at a Venice, California, poetry workshop; soon enough they were living together and writing songs (in 1982, they would marry, an unusual and almost perversely heartening gesture to make in the context of the L.A. punk demimonde). They hooked up with a drummer named Don Bonebrake and a guitarist who called himself Billy Zoom who had once backed Gene Vincent and who played rockabilly riffs at a furious pace. Wedding Chuck Berry–style rock-and-roll guitar chords to an authentic West Coast poetics that combined Jack Spicer's surreal informality with Charles Bukowski's brutish vulgarity, X put their frustrations across to their listeners in a way that was both harsh and exciting, frothing up musical maelstroms you'd have been quite happy to drown in.

In the Midwest, punk flourished more benevolently, inspiring new bands and new independent labels. Ohio was particularly fertile ground for this sort of thing, with towns like Akron, Kent, and Cleveland yielding a striking amount of intriguing music that had nothing to do with mainstream, major-industry-based rock.

Pere Ubu, for example, was a Cleveland group that fully lived up to a name plucked from Alfred Jarry's early twentieth century dadaist play. This band spent the late 1970s and early 1980s recording albums featuring lurching, stop-start melodies, clanging percussion, and the gulping, yelping vocals of David Thomas, who once said, "My job in the band is to try to be the talking that goes on inside your brains, okay?" Okay: muttering, squawking, reciting blunt declarative sentences and then breaking them down to repeat single words or phrases over and over again, Thomas and Pere Ubu achieved a kind of fractured poetry. This was rock and roll in name and attitude only—by any conventional measure, it was an entertaining form of avant-garde art.

Pere Ubu and bands such as the Bizarros, Tin Huey, and Devo were abetted by independent labels like Clone and Blank Records, which pressed enough records to supply the loose coalition of locals, national press, and intrigued outsiders—five thousand copies per record usually did the trick, and amazingly enough in this era of million-plus superstar sales, five thousand got the bands noticed, both across America and across the pond (England took Ohio seriously).

Interesting as some of it was, most of these bands made music that was simply too weird for nationwide consumption. Devo landed a contract with Warner Bros. Records in 1978 and turned itself into a novelty act that made funny videos (directed by Chuck Statler) before videos had MTV for exposure. And one Ohioan, a woman named Chrissie Hynde, bypassed her state's odd take on punk altogether, emigrating to England to form the Pretenders. Inspired by the punks' anybody-can-make-music philosophy, Hynde began writing songs and singing with rockers as disparate as the Damned, Nick Lowe, and ex–New York Doll Johnny Thunders. She formed the Pretenders in 1978, releasing the Nick Lowe–produced "Stop Your Sobbing," the band's first hit, that fall. (Hynde would have a child by the author of "Sobbing," Kinks leader Ray Davies, in 1983.)

On the strength of "Stop Your Sobbing," the Pretenders were signed to Sire, a subsidiary of Warner Bros. Records and proceeded to release a series of albums highlighted by Hynde's prickly, precise lyrics and forceful lead singing. In June 1982, the band's guitarist, James Honeyman-Scott, died of a drug overdose. He was replaced by Nick Lowe colleague Billy Bremner.

Although Hynde took her original inspiration from the punks, the Pretenders' music was much more melodic and accessible than punk rock— Hynde's eloquent, atmospheric songwriting found more direct antecedents in the work of rockers as dissimilar as Bob Dylan and Van Morrison. Hynde was a charismatic figure as the group's leader—a woman who transcended the tough-cookie cliché to offer a far more detailed picture of a female rocker than was usually found in the Pretenders' hard-edged rock genre.

In the first rosy glow of mid-1970s punk rock, everyone with a snarl was assumed to be a punk; this was especially true of Americans observing the English, because who could tell those hostile players without a scorecard anyway?

Initially, albums like Graham Parker and the Rumour's *Howlin' Wind* (1976) and Elvis Costello's *My Aim Is True* (1977) sounded punk, with their sneered vocals, buzzing guitars, and hopped-up tempos. But soon enough, it became clear that these fellows had little in common with the Sex Pistols and the Clash. Instead of destroying all rock and roll, Parker and Costello wanted to deepen a tradition. They were the latest wrinkle in singer-songwriters, even as they wanted to explode the complacency and self-absorption of someone like James Taylor.

With his fondness for knotty wordplay and propensity for undisguised hostility, Costello was following in the bloody tracks of Bob Dylan. He disguised this debt, however, in the moody soul music rhythms of many of his songs and in his uniquely prickly image: gangly and splayfooted on the cover of "My Aim Is True," wearing heavy hornrims, he looked like Buddy Holly's dorky younger brother. But this was a heroic nerd; as a pop hero (which he became despite his contempt for the role), Costello was the Avenging Dork, out to rid rock and roll of facile emotion and thoughtlessness.

Born Declan Patrick McManus in England in 1955, he was the son of a jazz trumpeter and big-band leader who left the family to play small pubs when his Declan was just a child. Raised working-class genteel, the future rocker took a variety of jobs (the most legendary being one as a computer operator—what better employment for a would-be avenging dork?) before adopting his stage name and beginning to strum his guitar in a distinctly folkie-ish manner until he'd written a batch of songs that established his own identity.

In July 1977, still unknown and furious about it, Costello set himself up outside the London hotel where CBS Records was holding its international convention. With tinny amplifiers buzzing, he impressed someone at the company enough to land a contract, and he recorded a few months later with a last-minute pickup band of Marin County musicians who went by the group name Clover. Costello told Greil Marcus in a notably candid 1982 interview for *Rolling Stone*, "I didn't have the money to go down to the Roxy and see . . . the Clash, the Sex Pistols. I just read about them in *Melody Maker* and *New Musical Express* the same as anyone else. . . . I got up at seven in the morning and so I couldn't go. I was married with a son; I couldn't take the day off. I took enough time playing sick, taking sick time off my job, just to make *My Aim Is True*."

My Aim Is True was greeted with critical hosannas on both sides of the Atlantic. In England, the record made Costello a star; in America, it made him the guy who wrote Linda Ronstadt's "Alison." Although he would later revile Ronstadt's interpretation of his soft-hearted but hardheaded ballad, the wooden, earnest version of it that appeared on her 1978 album *Living in the U.S.A.* put much needed money in his bank account and upped his recognition factor beyond the audience of several thousand that would have bought *My Aim Is True* on advance word alone.

In one of his earliest stateside interviews, Costello announced that his primary inspirations were "revenge and guilt," and that not only did he dislike the term *artist* to describe himself, but "even the word *musician* I kind of balk at." This tune changed pretty quickly, for two reasons: Costello was far more ambitious than perhaps even he suspected in the Year of Punk 1977, and he was so prolific that he became a professional musician by, if nothing else, default.

My Aim Is True was quickly succeeded by *This Year's Model* (1978), which showcased his new British backing band, the three-man Attractions: keyboardist Steve Nason, bassist Bruce Thomas, and drummer Pete Thomas. The music on this album was at once stripped down and richer, and fully more aggressive. The songs ranged from the pure, stark, relentless pounding of "Pump It Up" to the complex, even delicate punning in "Lip Service." Aside from a funny, eloquent rant about the banality of radio (entitled, aptly enough, "Radio, Radio"), Costello shouted himself hoarse about the torture of love. It all boiled down to women—can't-live-with-'em-can't-live-without-'em, but the boiling-down process was truly scalding.

The (non-American) hits just kept coming: Six months later, he was back with *Armed Forces*, which featured softly crooned songs about fascism ("Oliver's Army," "Two Little Hitlers") as well as unknowable songs of a dense and distant beauty ("Accidents will Happen," "Busy Bodies"). The album seemed to extend the naked misogyny that Costello cultivated like a curse—the catalog of ol' debbil Woman's sexual lures in "Green Shirt" echoed the condemnation of makeup and the advertising world in *This Year's Model's* "Lipstick Vogue." But Costello had added a layer of meaning to his pop songs; the woman who teases and flirts in "Green Shirt" is shining the buttons on an Army man's uniform. The original title of the album was supposed to have been *Emotional Fascism*, and that would not have been too strong a phrase at all.

At his most audacious, Costello used rock and roll's traditional and pervasive sexism to illuminate ideas he was hatching about the rise of the National Front in the Year of Punk 1977. What, if any, were the connections to be made between punk outsiders and fascist ones? Was the British government siding with the men in the green (or brown, or black) shirts? What was the fascination held by Oswald Mosely, who had led the British fascist movement in England in the 1930s and whose continuing appearances on British television—his apparently enduring allure—inspired Costello first to rage and then to write songs that articulated his rage.

By the time he and his band arrived in America in early 1979 for what he'd dubbed the "Armed Funk Tour," Costello had transformed himself into both a master rock showman and an unbelievably hostile man. In a Columbus, Ohio, bar one night, he got into an argument with singer Bonnie Bramlett and members of the Stephen Stills Band. The widely publicized result was that in the course of the argument, Costello called Ray Charles a blind, ignorant nigger, and leveled similar insults at James Brown.

Later, speaking to Greil Marcus in the 1982 *Rolling Stone* interview titled "Elvis Costello Repents," he said, "It's become a terrible thing hanging over my head—it's horrible to work hard for a long time and find that what you're best known for is something as idiotic as this." Costello said that he was very drunk at the time, "and I suppose that in my drunkenness, my contempt for [Bramlett and the others] was probably exaggerated beyond my real contempt for them . . . they just seemed to typify a lot of things that I thought were wrong with American music."

Chastened by the embarrassing, almost unbelievable incident—this was, after all, the man whose great debt to soul music was made explicit in the homage *Get Happy* (1980) and who produced the first album by the integrated British band the Specials—Costello would tone down his aggressive demeanor for the rest of the tour, and, indeed, for the next few years. Whereas his first visits to the United States had been characterized by petulance and spite—yelling at the crowd when they didn't react as he wanted them to, refusing to play encores—the shows that followed what came to be called the Ray Charles incident on the "Armed Funk Tour" showed just how much Costello wanted to put his music across.

Now his demeanor was much less severe: He said good evening and numerous thank you's, no small courtesies for a man whose best songwriting increasingly took the form of finely wrought tantrums. He experimented with such punk-scorned theatrical touches as artful stage lighting. On every date of the tour, he closed his performance with a stinging version of his pal Nick Lowe's "(What's So Funny 'Bout) Peace, Love and Understanding."

Every night except, that is, February 17, 1979, when he opted to perform at the Palomino, a famous country music nightclub in a suburb of Los Angeles. There he began the evening with the Nick Lowe tune, and proceeded to astonish the crammed club of rock fans with seven pure country songs, wailed, deeply felt interpretations of such honky-tonk touchstones as Ray Price's "He'll Have to Go" and a recent George Jones hit, "(If I Put Them All Together) I'd Have You." Whereas his rock concerts found Costello pursuing his obsessions—never stop disrupting your own life; always fight for an impossible love—the Palomino performance offered Costello at play. It turned out that he was just as obsessive about playfulness as he was about everything else, right down to his meticulous homage to George Jones, the studied but sincere "Stranger in the House."

Out in the Palomino crowd was Nick Lowe, who had produced all Costello's albums thus far in between conducting his own career. Both Lowe and Costello had emerged from England's mid-1970s "pub rock" scene, an alternative network of musicians who had had enough of Genesis and Yes and Led Zeppelin and all their American counterparts. Pub rock was in a sense reactionary, doting on early rock styles and even country music, but its organizing principle was forward thinking: Well before the Sex Pistols began castigating Rod Stewart as a fatuous rock star, the pub rockers were playing small venues and sneering at stadium-size concerts.

The most successful—and therefore most paradoxical—of the pub-rock bands was Brinsley Schwarz, a group named for its portly lead guitarist and featuring the songwriting and singing of Nick Lowe. To Brinsley Schwarz, Lowe contributed a series of gentle country music tributes such as "Ebury Down" and "Country Girl," clearly influenced by the Byrds of the Gram Parsons era.

But pubs such as the Tally Ho and the Hope and Anchor were also the hosts for other bands such as Kilburn and the High Roads (featuring a polio-stricken art teacher named Ian Dury, who would in the late 1970s release a few garrulous, gleefully smutty records under his own name), Eggs Over Easy, Bees Make Honey, and Chilli Willi and the Red-Hot Peppers.

Nick Lowe proved to be the most durable of the pub rockers, cultivating a casual, let's-get-it-over-with approach to recording—he was the Dean Martin of pub. It was Lowe's first few singles that were the inaugural releases from Stiff Records, an independent label launched by former Brinsley Schwarz manager Dave Robinson and Jake Riviera. Stiff, which prided itself on the commercial eccentricity of its artists and such company mottoes as "If it's a Stiff, it's a hit," was but one of a slew of independent labels that sprang up to accommodate both pub and punk rock.

In 1978, Lowe launched his solo career with an album called *Jesus of Cool* in England and *Pure Pop for Now People* in America. A little masterpiece of rock pastiche, *Pure Pop* was remarkable for the diversity of its musical styles, from a lulling ballad called "Marie Provost," about a Hollywood silent-film star who gets eaten by her dachshund, to "Rollers Show," a perky pop song saluting the then-reigning teenybopper act in the world, a clutch of kilted Scottish lads called the Bay City Rollers.

Where Nick Lowe contrived "cool" to distance himself from both the pop industry and punk rock, Graham Parker fairly seethed with alienation—he never fit in anywhere, and he was steamed about it. Parker, born in the working-class London suburb of Hackney, grew up to become a gas station attendant while strumming an acoustic guitar in his spare time. He put in his own amount of time in pub bands but also began writing his own harshly eloquent, castigating songs, which he sang in a raspy croon.

Parker released his debut album, *Howlin' Wind*, in 1976, and filled it with tempestuous petulance like "Don't Ask Me Questions," in which Graham is addressed by God, and God is told to mind his own beeswax. Parker's band was called the Rumour and consisted of two ex-Brinsleys, Bob Andrews and Schwarz himself, as well as graduates from the pub-rock bands Bontemps Roulez and Ducks Deluxe. Oh yes: *Howlin' Wind* was produced by Nick Lowe in a rare spare moment.

Graham Parker found a fervent audience in England and a cult audience in America. His albums were invariably uneven, the best of them being 1979's *Squeezing Out Sparks*, a sustained rush of tuneful anger featuring one blistering, baffling masterpiece, "Discovering Japan," in which Parker's inamorata is compared to a map of Japan, and somehow the metaphor is sustained for the entire length of the song.

Another prominent member of the pub postgrad scene was Dave Edmunds, a Welsh guitarist who had studied at the speakers of Sam Phillips. Like Parker, Costello, and especially Lowe, Edmunds abhorred technical progress in rock and roll and strove to make records that were as simple and yet as magical as those Phillips had recorded at Sun Records. Edmunds painstakingly reproduced the tinniness and echoes of Chuck Berry and Jerry Lee Lewis in his early records, and was rewarded with a U.S. hit very early in his career, when his morose, mordant 1970 cover of Smiley Lewis's "I Hear You Knocking" went Top Ten.

Edmunds fits into the pub puzzle this way: He produced Brinsley Schwarz's last album, *New Favourites*, in 1974, and then formed a band called Rockpile, featuring pubbers Billy Bremner and Terry Williams. This band toured with Nick Lowe throughout most of the late 1970s, before breaking up quite acrimoniously during a United States tour in 1981.

Costello, Parker, Lowe, and Edmunds were the sort of singer-songwriters for a new, older rock audience, one that had given up on Dylan, perhaps enjoyed the clamor of the punks, but still yearned to "hear the words." Soon an American would come to prominence who addressed these same yearnings in a prototypically American fashion. Bruce Springsteen, born in New Jersey and raised working-class, confronted all the questions the punks and the new English singer-songwriters were raising simply by existing; his music may have initially seemed like a throwback to the rock and roll of earlier eras, but it ultimately proved to be a transcendence of it. More than any other rocker of the 1970s, Springsteen provided his audience not only with music and entertainment but also with the same sort of cultural and historical perspective that Elvis Presley had lent the 1950s and the Beatles had offered the 1960s.

Unlike Presley and the Beatles, however, Springsteen didn't burst upon the rock scene full-blown, an instant phenomenon. In fact, Springsteen's saga provides a telling glimpse of the rock-and-roll system of a different decade. Having built a reputation as an exciting live act playing up and down the New Jersey shore in the late 1960s and early 1970s, Springsteen was signed by John Hammond, the jazz, blues, and folk fan-businessman who had signed such luminaries as Billie Holiday, Benny Goodman, and Bob Dylan to Columbia Records in his capacity as artists-and-repertoire vice president for the company.

Springsteen was an odd mixture of influences. While his tumultuous stage shows frequently climaxed with raucous versions of rock oldies by the likes of Presley, Roy Orbison, Chuck Berry, Bo Diddley, and Buddy Holly, Springsteen's own compositions were thoroughly influenced by the poetic verbiage of Dylan and Van Morrison, from whom he learned that stuffing a line with too many syllables could, when emanating from the right mouth, yield revelatory, exciting music.

Springsteen's debut album, *Greetings from Asbury Park, N.J.* (1973), was the work of raw talent—so raw as to be underdone at times, but full of energy and more ideas than its author had melodies for. Its successor, *The Wild, the Innocent, and the E Street Shuffle* (1973), was an improvement on the same concepts—Springsteen's tales of Jersey street kids and adults caught in emotional or economic traps were more sharply observed but no less romantic or crazily ambitious.

Working within a music industry increasingly geared to releasing uniformly smooth, accommodating product, Springsteen dared to be uneven: One minute "New York City Serenade" would sink to the depths of self-pitying sentimentalism, as sure as a cross between *West Side Story* and James Taylor; the next minute, "Rosalita (Come Out Tonight)" would change your idea of what a great rock song could accomplish. Without ever using so pretentious a term or succumbing to its contradictions, Springsteen was writing the real rock operas.

Once Springsteen began playing hip towns like Manhattan and Boston regularly, it wasn't long before the cognoscenti began to chime in with praise. Springsteen sparked one of the most memorable incidents in the history of rock criticism in 1974, when Jon Landau, *Rolling Stone* critic and record producer (Jackson Browne, Livingston Taylor, MC5), caught a Springsteen revel in a Cambridge bar called Charley's and staggered back to his typewriter starry-eyed. Tapping out a review, he wrote the most advertised line any rock critic ever wrote: "I saw rock and roll's future and its name is Bruce Springsteen." As Dave Marsh wrote in *Born to Run*, his 1979 biography of Springsteen, "For the rest of his career, Bruce Springsteen will be judged not on whether he is good, but on whether he is great." Although it would take a few years for Landau's view to become a consensus, it was at this moment that Springsteen became the first rock star of the 1970s to challenge the reputation of every great rocker who had come before him.

Landau's effusive but well-grounded praise—there was a reasoned piece of criticism wrapped around that money quote, after all—rekindled the interest of Columbia Records in their own act. To them, Springsteen had become something of a burden: Neither of his albums had sold very well, and his manager, a roughneck named Mike Appel, was once described by John Hammond as being "as offensive as any man I've ever met, but utterly selfless in his devotion to Bruce." This made Appel irreplaceable but impossible to work with.

Then, too, 1974 found Springsteen in a creative bind: Always a painstaking craftsman and increasingly self-conscious about his work, he had spent nine months working on his third album and had only produced one cut,

"Born to Run." At an utter loss as to where to go with the project, he brought Landau in as co-producer, who pushed him to a conclusion. When the album, ultimately titled *Born to Run*, was released in late 1975, it was hailed as a rock tour de force and was the first Springsteen record to capture the grand recklessness of his live shows. It also inspired an unprecedented journalistic occurrence: The week of October 27, 1975, both *Time* and *Newsweek* magazines placed him on their respective covers, and Springsteen abruptly became both a household name and a figure ripe for scornful accusations of hype.

Judged strictly as music that has by now withstood the test of a little time, *Born to Run* does indeed sound like one of the finest, most eloquent and hard-edged statements in all of rock music. Its booming, cavernous sound owes something to Phil Spector and something to the up-from-the-South echoes of New Orleans records such as those of Fats Domino and Huey "Piano" Smith. On this album, Springsteen finally managed to compress his lyrical ideas into useful, memorable turns of phrase. A line like "Tramps like us, baby, we were born to run" connects Springsteen not only to rock and roll history—from Chuck Berry's "Promised Land" to Dion's "The Wanderer" to Van Morrison's "Into the Mystic"—but as it swells up from the massed guitars, saxophone, and keyboards of Springsteen's E Street Band, becomes a passionate cry that could hold its own against the swelling tide of punk rock (and virtually everything else) that would follow it.

Soon after all this hoopla, Landau would head off to produce singer-songwriter Jackson Browne's most effective studio album, *The Pretender*—once again, Landau played tough editor, helping an ambitious artist articulate and demystify his recurring themes. At the same time, however, Springsteen began to disagree with Appel about the direction his career was heading. According to Marsh in his *Born to Run* biography, Springsteen deplored the big-arena circuit to which Appel wanted to affix his client; coming as this did at a time when Appel's management contract with Springsteen was due to expire, tension mounted, culminating in a bitter split.

The lawsuits and countersuits that followed left Springsteen hamstrung—literally unable to release a record—for three years, when *Darkness at the Edge of Town*, a woefully somber, florid, even melodramatic effort, appeared in 1979. The album was greeted with mixed reviews and good but not spectacular sales, and left Springsteen-watchers in a state of uneasy anticipation. In concert, their man had proved himself the Great Rock Hope; on record, he was heroically ambitious. In him, all things seemed to meet: naturalism and self-consciousness; recklessness and professionalism; a sense of rock history and a vision of rock future. The promise of Springsteen would have to wait until the new decade to be fulfilled, though.

Artists such as Springsteen, Costello, and the Pretenders were doing much to provide the seventies with distinctive standard bearers, rockers who had the potential to mean as much to this decade's audience as the Beatles or Elvis Presley had to their respective decades. It had taken most of the seventies to arrive at this promising point, but here it was nonetheless.

It came as something of a shock, therefore, when the music industry went into a sudden tailspin. From a high point in 1978 of 726.2 million album sales, the number dropped to 575.6 million units in 1982. Even when the increased list price for albums and cassettes adjusted the sales figures by the Recording Industry Association of America, the music industry's gross revenues dropped from 1978's $4.31 billion to 1982's $3.59 billion.

Some blamed the abrupt music industry depression on the rise of video games, which were attracting many teenagers' pocket money; others cited the blandness of the corporate rock of the radio-dominating faceless bands. Cassette sales, which, by 1980, equaled sales of albums, was a new target for blame, fostering charges that recording an album a friend had bought on cheaper blank tape was killing business. Or perhaps it was all a case of greed coming home to roost: Presented with unprecedented profits in the middle of the decade, the major record labels had responded by upping the list price of albums, and tour promoters increased ticket prices for concerts.

Whatever the reason, by 1980 the *Wall Street Journal* was saying, "Concert promoters across the country report that business is down as much as 30% from 1979, which was also an off year. Even superstar acts are failing to fill arenas and are canceling tours or playing smaller halls." Record companies responded to the sudden drop in business by laying off large numbers of employees and cutting back on promotion and advertising. The *Wall Street Journal* quoted a director of artist development at Arista Records as saying that "a couple of years, or even a year ago, when a new band signed with Arista, it was assumed it would receive between $30,000 and $100,000 in tour support." But of the twenty Arista bands then signed to the label, the *Journal* reported, "all but two are self-supporting."

This sort of news must have been profoundly satisfying to diehard punk rockers, since it meant that their basic contention had been true all along: The rock industry could not keep getting bigger and fatter and ever more complacent about its importance to its audience.

While many doomsayers were predicting the death of the rock industry at this point, what eventually occurred as a result of the economic slump would pave the way for the revitalization of rock as a whole: New faces and new forms of technology would arouse the audience's interest again, as did the solid new work created by a considerable number of rock's established figures.

36

ROCK ENDURES

You might say that the most valuable lesson learned by rockers over the course of the 1970s was how to be professional without turning into hacks. That is, as the industry expanded, artists as well as businessmen had to figure out a way to reconcile the music with the commerce it had inspired. Many of the new acts emerging at this time took the big-business aspect of the industry for granted (or, in the case of the punks, rejected the industry entirely). More established artists as various as Jackson Browne, Bob Dylan, and Fleetwood Mac found ways to pursue their various visions while remaining mindful of the commercial sprawl that had grown up around them.

Other rock vets tussled with the industry's tendency to classify and stereotype artists to achieve easy marketing. Joni Mitchell, for example, indulged her eccentricities by pursuing an interest in jazz to a commercial standoff. Albums such as *Hejira* (1976), *Don Juan's Reckless Daughter* (1977), *Mingus* (1979—a collaboration with the great jazz bassist and composer, who died before its release), and—her finest work in ten years—*Wild Things Run Fast* (1982) were notable primarily for their overarching ambitions and the lengths to which Mitchell would go to deny her prodigious talent for pop-folk melodies and coolly simple singing.

Neither was the old James Taylor ethos entirely dead: Its chief late-1970s practitioner was Jackson Browne, sitting in the Hollywood Hills and taking his metaphorical pulse to the eloquent moan of David Lindley's pedal steel guitar. Although he had entitled a 1973 album *For Everyman*, Browne's interests were primarily personal and his fans loved him for it; because he had a gift for moonily memorable melodies and dreamily romantic word-play, his self-absorption invited identification, and a large audience, in-cluding a sizable number of critics, identified like mad.

It was on only two albums, however, that Browne's autobiographical musing became compelling for the entire length of the record—the Jon Landau–produced *The Pretender* (1976), which honed his standard themes of I-love-you, you-don't-understand-me into icicles of irony, and *Running On Empty* (1977), a live album that exploited his languor to create a wonderfully relaxed, meditative kind of antilive album.

To give him his due, Browne also had a social conscience. He was instrumental in organizing a 1979 concert to protest the building of nuclear power plants following the Three Mile Island incident. The "No Nukes" event, held in Madison Square Garden, was admirably diverse, with artists ranging from Bruce Springsteen to Chaka Khan, from Gil Scott-Heron to Bonnie Raitt, and if the music was mediocre—it was as if the deadly pop-boogie of another participating act, the Doobie Brothers, had infected the rest of the lineup—there was no doubting its sincerity. Nor was there in Browne's repeated early 1980s arrests for waging civil-disobedience dem-onstrations in front of California's Diablo Canyon nuclear power plant.

In 1976, Browne would also help a friend get signed to the label he was contracted to, Asylum, and produce his album. *Warren Zevon* introduced an original, quirky singer-songwriter whose primary inspiration seemed to be the coldblooded prose of Dashiell Hammett and the tragic romanticism of Ross Macdonald. This private eye/rocker had spent his youth playing piano behind the Everly Brothers on the road, but his own records were shot through with the exact opposite of the Everlys' willful guilelessness—Zevon's music was profoundly cynical.

Although Linda Ronstadt found and recorded the solace that murmured beneath his songs like "Hasten Down the Wind" and "Carmelita," Zevon found his true calling in such witty, meticulously observed, bloodily fa-talistic tunes as "Roland Headless Thompson Gunner" and "Lawyers, Guns, and Money," from his third and best album *Excitable Boy* (1978).

Zevon's raspy voice and downbeat worldview found little more than a cult audience, despite Jackson Browne's help and the esteem of many of his more popular colleagues. He burned up part of his record-industry good-will by succumbing to a well-publicized case of alcoholism, and after 1982, this prodigiously gifted musician found himself without a major label affiliation, a typical story in the increasingly conservative music business.

The kind of wizened despair that Warren Zevon wrote and sang about would instead be marketed through the far slicker, less detailed music of the Eagles, the prototypical California hedonists. The band reached its summit with *Hotel California* (1976), a tour of California good-life dec-adence unmatched in its arrogant candor. By the time of their next release, the exhausted, self-parodic *The Long Run* (1979), the rumors of a breakup of

Los Angeles' most famous country-pop-rock band were rife, and the dissolution occurred soon after the album hit the top of the charts. Each Eagle, in the grand tradition of 1970s supergroup breakups, left to pursue his own solo career, with highly uneven results.

Among the other Los Angeles bands, Lowell George and Little Feat would exert an influence on 1970s rock that considerably outstripped the group's commercial success. From the start—the band's debut album *Little Feat* was released in 1970—George's slurred, growly vocals and slide guitar playing had dominated the band. George, a former member of Frank Zappa's Mothers of Invention, who as a child had appeared on "Ted Mack's Original Amateur Hour" playing the harmonica, wrote much of the band's material, which combined rock, blues, gospel, and funky jazz in a novel manner. Many artists covered Little Feat material; acts as various as Bonnie Raitt and the Eagles professed to be influenced by Feat's laid-back-with-passion style. Linda Ronstadt recorded George's "Willin'" on her 1974 album *Heart Like a Wheel*.

Nonetheless, Little Feat remained a cult band, a status enhanced by George's increasingly obscure, knotty music on such albums as *Time Loves a Hero* (1977) and *Waiting for Columbus* (1978), even as keyboardist Bill Payne and guitarist Paul Barrère stepped up their contributions as songwriters. George broke with the group and released a solo album, *Thanks, I'll Eat It Here*, in 1979. Shortly after its release, on tour with his own band, he suffered a heart attack and died.

By now, Fleetwood Mac had settled in as bona-fide Los Angeles superstars, but the stability of the group was shaken when John and Christine McVie divorced in 1976 and lovers Buckingham and Nicks separated soon after. But unlike Fleetwood Mac's other dissensions, these rifts yielded unifying art: *Rumours*, released in 1977 at the height of punk-rock fervor, remains one of the landmark pop albums of the decade and one of its most impressive commercial successes, with over sixteen million copies sold.

At a time when too much of the rock world had succumbed to the slickness and smugness that punk rock was revolting against, *Rumours* suggested the finest possibilities of slick rock and roll. From the brooding sensuousness and precise details of Christine McVie on "Don't Stop" to Lindsey Buckingham's exuberant wail on "Go Your Own Way," this was middle-of-the-road rock for adult rock fans.

More than anyone, though, it was Lindsey Buckingham who kept the music interesting. "We are five very different individuals," Christine McVie would tell *Rolling Stone* in 1982. "Also very strong-minded. . . . But this is a good combination of musicians." For all that, however, it was Buckingham who became the group's chief arbiter, co-producing songs no matter who else was officially producing a session, adding sound effects and emphasizing various details no matter who was singing or had written the song.

A Californian with a fondness for the Clash and a reverence for the Beach Boys, Buckingham aspired toward eccentricity in the Brian Wilson manner: lush, beautiful, almost abstract eccentricity. When the guitars roar and the voices mass on the chorus of "Go Your Own Way," it is Buckingham's tenor that is memorably, intentionally ragged, and when it came time to record the follow-up to *Rumours*, it was Buckingham who took command of this intimidating task and produced the most original, quirky, and intriguing album any superstar band has ever released: *Tusk*.

You could say that *Tusk* was a failure because it didn't sell half as many copies as *Rumours* had; neither did it yield as many catchy songs as either *Fleetwood Mac* or *Rumours*—this despite the fact that *Tusk* was a sprawling two-record set. Nonetheless, *Tusk*, released in 1979 and featuring vocals Buckingham recorded on his hands and knees in the bathroom of his house, is a triumph of eccentricity. The title song featured African Burundi polyrhythmic drumming and a chorus sung by the entire University of Southern California Trojan Marching Band; another high point is "Not That Funny," an anti-pop song that is little more than Buckingham yelling, "Well, it's not that funny, is it?," over and over until his vocal cords fray and shred and finally give way. All this, and the other four "very strong-minded" members of the group still found it in their hearts to include a production credit that read, "Produced by Fleetwood Mac (Special Thanks to Lindsey Buckingham)."

Tusk was a magnificent response to the huge popularity of the group's two previous records: Yes, it was self-indulgent, but this was self-indulgence on a scale so vast that it became absorbing to the general listener; self-indulgence became both theme and method of Lindsey Buckingham's confrontation with mass taste. If one of Buckingham's liabilities was his Brian Wilson–ish obsession with banality—no song is ever "about" anything more than feeling sad or feeling happy—he is also far more mature than Brian Wilson ever was in acknowledging the excruciating pain of feeling sad (or, for that paradoxical matter, feeling happy). For a massively popular musician, Buckingham operated like a closeted avant-gardist, layering vocals and sound effects, regularly exceeding the public's limits of sonic ugliness to achieve a dense, revelatory sound.

There is a sense in which Buckingham probably intended *Tusk* to ruin Fleetwood Mac's commercial stature, to so alienate the band's newfound audience of housewives and teenyboppers that they'd never call out in concert again for "Rhiannon" or "Say You Love Me." Buckingham made no secret about wanting to make solo records, and a bemused Mick Fleetwood recalled that Buckingham constantly worried that the band's popularity would hem him in: "I think he was seeing this big shadow over him, like he thought Fleetwood Mac was going to potentially stop him . . . Lindsey was saying, 'I don't know how to ask you or John—what if I want to play drums or do something on my own?' I had to say, 'Well, if it sounds good, who gives a shit?' It doesn't say much for this situation if after fifteen years it can't take care of everyone within it."

Buckingham would go on to make solo albums, and one of them, *Law and Order* (1981), was even a popular success, eccentricities and all. The rest of the band, feeling just as constrained, would soon embark on their own projects as well. Nicks would become by far the most commercially successful, releasing *Bella Donna* in 1981 to such popular acclaim that it was rumored that she had tried to buy her way out of her contract with Fleetwood Mac. In 1982, the band would reunite to record *Mirage*—"Rumours II," as Buckingham wryly (or was that bitterly?) described it. Once again, Fleetwood Mac's audience proved faithful—the album went to the top of the charts and sold a few million copies within the first few weeks of its release.

Fans would also prove unexpectedly kind to the purveyors of the "other" California sound, the long-outmoded San Francisco acid rock of the Grateful Dead. After the 1970 success of *Workingman's Dead*, the bestselling album of their career, the band would persevere, even into the 1980s, with average record sales and minimal impact on the music world. The Dead were frequently accused of being self-indulgent, and they were, but the point of much of the group's music was that self-indulgence had its place, in art and in life, and the Dead's singularly benign, often witty version of self-indulgence was one of the qualities the band's fans treasured most.

These fans—the Dead Heads—were an underground society of their own, a legion spawned in response to the low-key garrulousness of the Dead's legendary four-, five-, six-hour-plus concerts. Long before Bruce Springsteen attracted admiration for lengthy shows and the devotion of his following, the Dead were offering their Heads maximum music for the ticket price, and devotees responded by following the band from town to town.

With this unshakable dedication sustaining the band, Grateful Dead concerts remained sold-out affairs around the world. Garcia, singer-guitarist Bob Weir, and drummer Bill Kreutzmann all embarked on solo ventures at one time or another, and in the early 1980s, Garcia attracted some rare mass-media attention for a minor drug bust, but the Dead remained intact, continuing to release records and make extensive tours attracting large, adoring audiences.

Among veteran rockers, the Rolling Stones fared better than many of their colleagues. The band spent the mid-1970s making lackluster music, hard rock, and a hard search for subject matter. Their emblematic song of this period was "It's Only Rock and Roll" (1974), which suggested that the Stones were getting a bit bored with their chosen genre. Certainly *Black and Blue* (1976), which introduced guitarist Ron Wood to the group, was one of the band's most half-hearted releases, its music a contemptuous response to the disco music of that period. The most controversial thing about *Black and Blue* wasn't its music but its ad campaign, which depicted a woman bound, gagged, and bruised. Many people considered that this transcended the Stones' usual flirtation with misogyny, and several feminist groups, most notably Women Against Pornography, pressured the group to stop its ad campaign, which it did. The Stones shook off their lethargy, however, with 1978's *Some Girls*, a collection of hard-edged, wittily observed hard-rock songs.

Bob Dylan's mid-1970s career was more uneven than the Stones'. In 1975, midway through a decade that would leave him creatively flummoxed, he released *Blood on the Tracks*, one of his finest, most mature efforts. Issued at a time when interest in his career could not have been lower, the album shocked and pleased long-time Dylan watchers for its precise emotional eloquence.

That same year Dylan's label, Columbia Records, released *The Basement Tapes*, a two-record collection of demonstration tapes that Dylan and the Band had recorded in 1967. Oft-bootlegged, *The Basement Tapes* fully lived up to their legend—wildly funny, tumultuously raucous, ferociously impassioned, there were songs here (eighteen by Dylan, six by the Band) as strong as any in the canon of American popular music. It is a measure of just how trend-conscious and conservative the American record-buying audience had become by mid-decade, however, that *The Basement Tapes*, despite being heralded as a great work by every critic in the area of a typewriter, was only a modest commercial success, wafting up to the number-seven position briefly and then fluttering rapidly down the charts.

This came as a stark contrast to *Blood on the Tracks*, which achieved a strong Number One position, and the album that followed it, *Desire*, which, despite its blatant inferiority to both *Blood* and *The Basement Tapes*, hit Number One on the strength of "Hurricane," its controversial salute to Rubin "Hurricane" Carter, a boxer accused of murder—falsely, thought Dylan and many other supporters. (Carter, in fact, was exonerated of the crime in 1985.)

Desire, which also included a somber hymn to gangster Joey Gallo, was said to represent Dylan's "return" to topicality and the protest song; actually both "Hurricane" and "Joey" prefigured the woe-unto-superstars-like-me songs that Dylan would write more and more frequently as the decade drew to an end. It was also around this time that he launched the "Rolling Thunder Revue," a tour that carried a massive band of well-knowns (including Joan Baez and Allen Ginsberg) and lesser-knowns (playwright Sam Shepard, not yet a movie star; witty Texas songwriter T-Bone Burnette) around the country performing drastically, sometimes perversely rearranged songs from the Dylan canon. It was his first tour in a decade, and a genial debacle. The album documenting the tour *Hard Rain* (1976) would be an aesthetic debacle. And having filmed the whole shebang, Dylan would eventually release a four-hour movie about it, entitled *Renaldo and Clara*, that would prove a tedious failure.

In 1978, Dylan issued one of his weakest efforts ever, Street Legal, in which the perversity of his Rolling Thunder style (white clown makeup and odd versions of famous songs) gave way to out-and-out self-parody or, perhaps, contempt for his audience. The album's songs were mediocre dirges, and the tour that followed it was a scandal. On the Street Legal tour, "My Back Pages" became a jazz ballad, while "Tangled Up in Blue" was slowed down and a saxophone solo inserted into its center.

The sentiments of the lyrics seemed to mean nothing to Dylan; he sang them with no heed to their conventional emphases. The words were simply metered noise for his now pleasantly ravaged voice to sing. But mashed verbiage had usually taken on great emotive force in Dylan's previous work—the style he adopted on, say, the Before the Flood tour expressed exactly what he wanted to convey: anger, isolation, confusion, boundless joy. But all that his performances in late 1978 conveyed was Dylan's assertion that this was his material and he could do anything he wanted with it, including butcher it.

Even more unnerving was the fact that Dylan was acting friendly—was acting, in fact, like a Vegas lounge singer, all unctuous charm. He told banal little anecdotes to introduce songs like "Ballad of a Thin Man" and "One More Cup of Coffee"; and during a performance at the Los Angeles Forum on November 15, 1978, he told the crowd that Phil Spector was in the audience, adding, "People call me a genius; well, Phil's a real genius." It was like a ghastly reincarnation of Ed Sullivan. Dylan later introduced "Forever Young" by saying, "I wrote this song for one of my babies when he was a baby."

What all this mid-1970s Dylan activity reveals, among other things, is that Bob Dylan was untouched by virtually all the musical developments unfolding around him. Of punk and its immediate predecessors, for instance, he took no notice. In fact, except for Blood on the Tracks, an album thoroughly of its time, Dylan responded to the 1970s with the instincts of many in his audience—that is, he simply echoed the music he'd been making in the 1960s.

The 1970s ended badly for a number of rock veterans. The most poignant tragedy of this period was the death of Elvis Presley. He had begun the 1970s rather promisingly. "Burning Love," a great rocker of a single, went to number two in 1972; a year later, his television special "Elvis: Aloha from Hawaii," was a spectacular ratings success, broadcast worldwide to an estimated audience of over a billion people.

But Presley was a troubled man. He had divorced his wife Priscilla in 1973 and was said to have been devastated by their separation. As the decade wore on, his weight ballooned, his recording work all but stopped, and his concerts sometimes verged on self-parody. Presley died on August 16, 1977, a victim of congestive heart failure and advanced arteriosclerosis.

Presley's passing was accorded the sort of mourning usually reserved for the death of a president. Thousands gathered outside Graceland, his Memphis mansion; President Jimmy Carter expressed his sorrow in a formal statement. True to his legend, however, Presley's career-long manager, Colonel Tom Parker, dispensed with sentimentality. Asked what he would do now that his greatest client had died, Parker remarked, "I'll keep right on managing him." And indeed, Parker proceeded to oversee an endless stream of Presley tributes, album reissues, and commercial projects dedicated to Presley's memory.

(By coincidence, on the heels of Presley's death, *The Beatles at the Hollywood Bowl* was released, the first official live Beatles album, taken from a decade-old concert. It was an album that reminded us all over again how rich and vital this ultimate rock band's music and example had been. With these two occurrences taken together, the 1950s and the 1960s had symbolically put pressure on the 1970s to put up or shut up.)

For another aging rock act, the late 1970s was a test beyond endurance. The Who had begun the decade at a pitch of triumph, with the release of *Who's Next* (1971), which contained some of the band's best-played hard rock, its most acute love songs, and much of Pete Townshend's most lucid thinking as a songwriter. The band's work grew more and more uneven as the 1970s wore on—Townshend would later admit that he'd spent much of the decade wrecked on liquor—but both 1973's *Quadrophenia* (eighty savage minutes in the life of a mod, and filmed as such six years later) and 1975's *The Who by Numbers* (which included "However Much I Booze") had their moments.

On September 7, 1978, drummer Keith Moon died from an overdose of an antialcoholism sedative ingested shortly before he'd gone to bed. The band had withstood the assault of the punks—for whom the Who was yet another example of musical rebellion gone tame—and now Townshend, Daltrey, and Entwistle would recruit drummer Kenney Jones to persist in what was becoming an increasingly irrelevant enterprise: bringing tried-and-true Who music to huge numbers of young fans packed into vast stadiums. Death intervened once more in this setting. On December 3, 1979, at the Riverfront Coliseum in Cincinnati, Ohio, eleven Who fans lost their lives in a stampede to get through the few doors opened by the coliseum staff and the show's promoters, Electric Factory Concerts of Philadelphia.

Presley's death had been a dull shock; Moon's death an almost predictable one—the drummer had cultivated a reputation for suicidal excessiveness. Soon after rock music hauled itself into the 1980s, however, it received the most jolting shock of all: the murder of John Lennon.

In September 1980, Lennon and Yoko Ono signed with Geffen Records and two months later released *Double Fantasy,* a Number One album with a Number One single, "(Just Like) Starting Over." Then on December 8, 1980, Lennon was shot seven times outside the Dakota, the apartment building he lived in, by Mark David Chapman, a twenty-five-year-old Beatle fan.

Lennon's death was a crucial event in rock culture. Unlike Elvis Presley (the only other comparable example in cultural outreach and musical importance), Lennon might easily have pursued a long creative career. Moreover, the fact that Lennon was murdered by a self-professed fan made horrifyingly true all the paranoid fantasies that both pop stars and their audiences might have about the love/hate nature of rock-and-roll prominence.

Lennon's death was the ultimate example of the era's fragmentation. All the media pundits repeated the same phrase—"The dream is over"—and it was: Rock fans were now forever separated from the myth of the Beatles. There was nothing left but to face the future.

THE 1980s

By the early 1980s, the rock industry had begun to right itself. New record company parsimoniousness, staff cutbacks, and a rise in album list prices would help, but more important was an infusion of new stars that revitalized the audience's interest in the music. It gradually became apparent that after the latter half of the seventies, spent searching for the new Beatles and trying to assimilate the new styles, eccentrics, and images tossed up by this period of confusion, crisis, and creativity, the eighties were to be a time of synthesis, regeneration, and rebirth. In a new form like rap music, rock had a subgenre that was able to penetrate the rock mainstream in a way that, say, reggae hadn't been able to do. In music videos, rock had a new format for the dissemination of the music, one that enlivened many tired rock star images. And in a star like Michael Jackson—as well as in Bruce Springsteen, Prince, Cyndi Lauper, and others—rock finally had figures that could unite a huge audience once again.

There were many reasons offered for how the record industry pulled itself out of its economic slump in the early eighties. Assertions about the state of the Reagan economy were crapshoots—one person's "resurgence" was another's "recession"—but it was clear that video games had indeed proved to be the fad their detractors had claimed (*Newsweek* even carried a "PINBALL IS BACK!" story), and that new ways of playing music, most significantly in the new compact disc (CD) technology, were piquing people's interest in music again. Music videos, used sporadically throughout rock's history (remember seeing the Beatles ramble through a murky "Strawberry Fields Forever" video screened on the *Ed Sullivan Show?*), became a broadcast staple in the eighties, drawing teens like flies with their cinema-school camera tricks and ostentatious displays of rock band fashions.

You could also hold another theory about the salvation of eighties rock, and it would center around one man, someone who sold an unprecedented number of records, revitalized the industry economy with one album release, and turned all media eyes upon himself, making rock the center of popular culture in a way it hadn't been since the Fab Four.

37

ROCK IN THE
VIDEO AGE

Michael Jackson's rise to the peak of superstardom had begun fairly inauspiciously. Freed from Motown in the mid-1970s, he and his brothers had found themselves encountering many of the same artistic constraints at their new label, Epic.

Not trusting the brothers to write and produce themselves, Epic assigned them to Kenneth Gamble and Leon Huff, the Philadelphia International kingpins whose label was, by no coincidence at all, distributed by Epic's parent company, CBS Records. The result, The Jacksons (1976), was a sorry piece of music-making, sluggish and awkward; it died a quick death on the record charts. None of the Jacksons was allowed to play so much as a single instrument on The Jacksons; that labor fell to Gamble and Huff's Sound of Philadelphia session men. Their next Gamble and Huff release, Goin' Places (1977), also went nowhere on the charts but did feature Tito Jackson on guitar and Randy Jackson on congas.

Despite their shaky record sales—or perhaps because of them—the Jacksons hosted a television variety show during the summer of 1976. Michael spent his spare time fending off rumors that he and singer-songwriter Clifton Davis were lovers and that he, Michael, had recently undergone a sex-change operation. In 1977, he whiled away his time making his first movie—the film version of the Broadway smash musical The Wiz. Directed by an odd choice—Sidney Lumet, known for his gritty, realistic New York films—The Wiz featured Michael as the Scarecrow and his old friend Diana Ross as a far-too-old Dorothy. The movie was a resounding flop; a bit more surprisingly, so was the sound-track album, a two-record affair overseen impeccably by Quincy Jones but made ponderous with mediocre material.

But finally, in 1978, the Jacksons hit it big with their third Epic release, *Destiny*. Was it a coincidence that this was the first record they were allowed to write and produce themselves? It's unlikely. Powered by the crisp, surging hit single "Blame It on the Boogie," the Jacksons established themselves as an act that offered an alternative to disco by making danceable rhythms disciplined by pop-song rigor and detailed by Michael's soul-gospel phrasing.

The major triumph of the album, however—the song that brought the Jacksons to the forefront of 1970s pop music—was "Shake Your Body (Down to the Ground)," written by Michael and Randy. The song went platinum. "Shake Your Body (Down to the Ground)" is a significant song for a couple of reasons. For instance, it is one of the first songs whose popularity was dramatically increased by the release of a "dance remix"—that is, a lengthened and enhanced version of the album cut.

The remix of "Shake Your Body" was executed by John Luongo, a veteran New York disco producer and dj. Luongo recalled that when he handed in his initial remix of the record, "the boys loved it, but Epic hated it—they weren't even going to release it. . . . It was an accident that it got pressed at all—for some reason, my version was submitted and they pressed up a few thousand copies. Well, that version was the one all the dance clubs jumped on; the djs that didn't get my version started complaining to Epic, which had to cave in. . . . Without any modesty at all, I'd say that that version of 'Shake Your Body' added another 500,000 in sales."

In late 1979, Michael released his first major solo album, *Off the Wall*, and promptly sold more than seven million records—this, compared with *Destiny's* supposedly triumphant one million. Michael solo was a whole new ball game.

Off the Wall, like the *Wiz* sound track a project guided by producer Quincy Jones, was a state-of-the-art pop record—slick yet passionate, cagey yet daring. Its fast numbers—"Don't Stop 'Til You Get Enough," "Working Day and Night," "Get on the Floor"—were thumping, screaming dance-club dreams, while its ballads—"She's Out of My Life," "It's the Falling in Love," and a song written by new chum Paul McCartney, "Girlfriend"—allowed Michael to croon with a maturity he had not evinced before.

But *Off the Wall* was more than music; it was a pop-cultural event. Michael's cover pose—grinning in a black tuxedo and bow tie, his too-short pants revealing glowing white socks—proved to be an eccentric, highly influential fashion statement. The Jacksons put out a record in 1980, *Triumph*, which continued the act's hot streak with hits such as "Can You Feel It," "Lovely One," and "Heartbreak Hotel" (not the Elvis Presley song but, as written by Michael, a prime example of his pop paranoia). But, increasingly, it was Michael who fascinated audiences and the media; try as he might to show solidarity with his brothers, this was more and more an act with one star and his talented accompanists.

The triumphs of *Triumph* were almost entirely Michael's, and he must have known it; the popular and critical acclaim for his contributions to the album seemed to coincide with a period of increased ambition and inspired creativity for him. As soon as the Jacksons had completed the requisite tour to promote the album, Michael holed up with producer and friend Quincy Jones to plot his next solo album. With the release of this one, public curiosity about Michael would give way to Michael-mania.

Thriller (1982) was greeted initially with hearty but not effusive praise as a first-rate album, a record that would enhance and further develop Michael Jackson's growing popularity. Its initial single, "Billie Jean," added considerably to the paradoxes of Michael's public persona. A song written from the point of view of a narrator accused by a supposedly deluded woman ("Billie Jean is not my lover") of siring a child he refused to recognize as his own, "Billie Jean" referred to things that Michael Jackson had spent his life avoiding (if you believe his publicity)—premarital sex and awkward romantic situations. Just as important as its odd, quixotic lyric was its rhythm, a chugging, insinuating riff written by Michael.

Thriller was an immediate hit, but Michael-mania didn't really commence in earnest until May 16, 1983, when a television special called "Motown 25" was shown on NBC. The show was a two-hour salute to Motown Records' twenty-fifth anniversary and, like any presentation of black popular culture on network television, it was hopelessly compromised. While it's true that both Marvin Gaye and Stevie Wonder were displayed in all their eccentric grandeur (Gaye was particularly fascinating, nattering on and on in stream-of-consciousness speechifying while noodling aimlessly at the piano), the network had managed to insert a pair of totally inappropriate yet, in theory, ratings-boosting white pop stars. One of them was Linda Ronstadt, selected, one supposes, because she had had occasion to make wooden pulp out of a few Smokey Robinson compositions over the course of her career; the other was Adam Ant, a British postpunk novelty act for whom there was absolutely no excuse.

"Motown 25" was a mediocre jumble of poorly edited old film clips of Motown acts at their zenith and pathetic latter-day performances by these same veterans. The exception was the performance given by Michael Jackson. At first, Michael appeared as just another Jackson brother, as the group rattled off rushed versions of their early Motown hits. It was supposed to be a big deal that Jermaine, long estranged from both the act and the family, deigned to perform as a member of the Jacksons for this pseudomomentous occasion.

But then pop history occurred. The brothers slunk offstage as Michael, one white sequined glove glittering from his right hand, looked into the camera to murmur in his soft, chalky voice, "I have to say, those were the good old days; I love those songs. Those were magic moments, with all of my brothers, including Jermaine [Oh God, people across the nation must have been moaning, is he going to rattle on like Marvin did?]. You know, those were good songs [yep, it sure looked like it] . . . I like those songs a lot [uh-huh, uh-huh—has he had a nose job or what?] . . . but especially, I like the new songs."

Suddenly the mean, low-down drumbeat of "Billie Jean" pulsed through TV sets across America; in the theater from which this show was being broadcast, the shocked, delighted screams of youngsters in the audience could be heard. Out of nowhere, Michael produced a black fedora of the kind that Fred Astaire used to cock jauntily over one brow; now Michael did the same.

And then Michael's body seemed to explode with rhythmic, tightly controlled convulsions. Combining Astaire's subtle soft-shoe grace with robotic break-dancing moves no one could have imagined he even knew about (how could he have heard of break dancing when he lived in a sealed universe of L.A., Katharine Hepburn, and boa constrictors?), Jackson thrilled and baffled millions of people, just as the Beatles had done two decades earlier and Elvis Presley had done a decade before that.

This was the pivotal moment of Michael Jackson's career; it irrevocably separated his career from that of his brothers. More significant, it was the first opportunity he'd had to show black America, which had long suspected it, and white America, which had been systematically shielded from it, that this was one complex, sexy postteen idol. The "Motown 25" TV special was crucial in the dramatic expansion of Michael Jackson's audience, because millions of people who hadn't yet heard of *Thriller*, who hadn't thought about Michael Jackson since his days as the pint-size front man for the Jackson 5, suddenly realized that this was a rock-and-roller they could get behind. In what would eventually prove to be Michael Jackson's greatest pop-cultural achievement and, ultimately, his biggest problem, parents and children knew that night that here was a rock star both generations could agree was the coolest.

After the "Motown 25" special, sales of *Thriller* increased dramatically, and Michael Jackson's position in the popular culture became a subject of daily discussion among fans and in the media. Eventually *Thriller* would yield six Number One singles—"Billie Jean," "Beat It," "Wanna Be Starting Something," "P.Y.T. (Pretty Young Thing)," "Human Nature," and the title song—more than any other album in pop-music history. "Thriller" eventually sold more than thirty million copies worldwide and spent thirty-seven weeks at Number One on the pop charts—and almost singlehandedly turned around the supposedly ailing music industry. The next logical move was . . . a tour. What then became the "Victory Tour," in honor of both Michael's vast success and the title of the at that time still-theoretical new Jacksons album, is one of the most infamous botches in the history of pop music.

It was said that Michael didn't want to tour at all, that he wanted to hibernate for a while in Encino and maybe consider a few movie offers. But, the legend goes, Michael relented to pressure from his father and to feelings of loyalty to his brothers. He knew that a tour at this point in his career would consist of a string of sold-out shows played to audiences as big as he chose to have. He gave in, with extreme reluctance.

Joe Jackson had recently survived a shake-up in his long-time management of the group—Michael in particular was unhappy with his father's aggressive manner, but he bowed, as always, to family loyalty. Joe struck a deal with boxing promoter Don King to oversee the "Victory Tour." King, with his criminal record and grandiose, self-promotional style, was everything Michael felt he did not need at this point in his career, yet he continued to swallow his objections; for his part, King was to receive 7.5 percent of the Jacksons' net profits from the tour.

King was an amateur at organizing rock concerts; he thought he could organize a pop music tour the same way he handled such massive prizefights as the Ali-Frazier "Thrilla in Manila." In the early stages, King was all talk about huge arenas, closed-circuit television broadcasts, and outlandish publicity stunts. It soon became clear, however, that King wasn't moving quickly enough and did not have the organization behind him to back up his bluster. After going through a succession of candidates, the Jacksons settled on an additional promoter: Chuck Sullivan, a New York lawyer whose family owned the New England Patriots and ran Sullivan Stadium outside Boston, in Foxboro.

Sullivan was nearly as green as King when it came to rock tours—although in the midst of the tour he would refer to Michael as the Mozart of our time, in private he opted to listen to the Clancy Brothers and Tommy Makem. Sullivan had promoted a few big rock concerts before in his family's Sullivan Stadium, featuring stars like David Bowie and the Police—but he had never overseen a nationwide rock tour. Worse, he underestimated the overwhelming demand for the Jacksons (or at least Michael) in 1984. From the first, everything went wrong: Some of the stadiums he began to book for the summer tour weren't big enough to hold the Jacksons' massive stage set; he set up a mail-order method of selling tickets that was complicated and open to charges of greed. To make a profit on the tour, he agreed to an outrageous ticket price—$30. All this left him open to much criticism.

When the troubled "Victory Tour" finally got under way in Kansas City on July 6, 1984, it proved to be a gigantic anticlimax. For $30 each, fans saw the Jacksons for a mere ninety minutes, lots of flashing lights, lasers, and miniexplosions, and an unadventurous song selection consisting of the most obvious greatest hits and a minimum of solo Michael. Before it was over, in Los Angeles in December 1984, Chuck Sullivan would suffer a mild heart attack brought on by stress, and Michael Jackson had announced that this would be his last tour with his brothers. What had begun as a celebration of Michael Jackson's ascendancy as the most popular pop star of the first half of the 1980s had ended with his squeaky-clean image tarnished as well as critically overexposed.

As the "Victory Tour" debacle makes plain, rock stars frequently remained at the mercy of the people who organized their daily business—managers, promoters, record-company executives. Many rock acts wanted more of a say in their own destinies, and though the role of the manager had increased over the course of the 1970s and early 1980s, it began to grow even more crucial. A new class of supermanagers was emerging, exemplified by Irving Azoff, who had established himself as a kingpin in the early 1970s, overseeing, at one time or another, the careers of such artists as Steely Dan, the Eagles, Jackson Browne, Jimmy Buffett, and Warren Zevon. Azoff, who began his management career handling the faceless Midwestern band REO Speedwagon, was known for his aggressive dealings with everyone—record companies, tour promoters, and critics alike. In the process, Azoff became a media figure himself—his frequent feuds with *Rolling Stone* founder and publisher Jann Wenner over what he thought was niggling treatment of his acts in the magazine's pages was widely reported in entertainment circles, for example. In 1982, Azoff became president of MCA Records.

Another example of the influential latter-day manager is Ken Kragen, who worked wonders for at least two of his clients. In the mid-1970s, Kragen took on Kenny Rogers, then a bearded, slightly paunchy has-been, the former lead singer for the 1960s folk-rock band the First Edition, and turned him into a bearded, very paunchy country music superstar. Then, in 1980, he performed his magic on Lionel Richie, who had just left the band he'd grown up in, the Commodores. As a prominent member of the Commodores, Richie had written a series of ballads in the late 1970s—"Easy," "Three Times a Lady"—that made him the star of the group. He had begun to break away from the group by recording a duet with Diana Ross, "Endless Love," and by writing material for country-schlock star Kenny Rogers. But it was under Kragen's ministrations that Richie made the transition from soul group member to the early 1980s' smoothest balladeer. Richie began recording as a solo artist, and his grainy, urgent voice found a huge audience among the so-called adult contemporary radio listenership. Polite, sincere, and ickily romantic, Richie was nonetheless a solid craftsman with a knack for a catchy chorus.

Kragen credited his achievements to his managerial style: He devoted all his attention to only a few clients at a time; he teamed his clients with better-known stars (Rogers sang a series of hit duets with established country singer Dottie West in order to give him credibility with the country music audience); and he orchestrated his clients' tours and public appearances to give them maximum media coverage and audience impact.

Indeed, media coverage was becoming more critical than ever in rock. Among the vague theories promulgated for the revitalization of the music business were: that video games had proved a fad, to be replaced by small portable tape recorders and the Sony Walkman; that punk/new wave or Michael Jackson had gotten people interested in music again; that sufficient corporate fat had been trimmed—and, especially, that the new rock videos that were coming to be featured on television, especially on special music networks, were piquing fans' curiosity.

The most important of outlets was MTV, or Music Television, a cable television network that began broadcasting on August 1, 1981. MTV's immediate precursor had been "Popclips," a music-video show dreamed up by former Monkee Michael Nesmith the year before. "Popclips," featuring standup comic/actor Howie Mandel as its sole video disc jockey, or "vj," was shown on Warner Cable's Nickelodeon cable television channel. Warner Amex Satellite Entertainment Company realized the possibilities of a considerably more toned down, demographics-minded version of this mating of rock music and television, and allotted $20 million in startup costs to give birth to what became MTV.

Video illustrations of rock music were, of course, nothing new. Rock musicians of the 1950s had appeared in many movies in self-contained concert sequences that amounted to protovideos, and by the late 1960s, bands like the Beatles and the Rolling Stones were filming short movies to illuminate their latest singles and having them broadcast on television programs such as *American Bandstand.*

The increasing sophistication and portability of video equipment in the 1970s made the idea of using videos as rock music promotional tools more and more attractive. Since the record companies and their artists financed these videos as promotional items, it was MTV's initial masterstroke to convince the major labels that allowing the cable channel to broadcast these minimovies at no fee to MTV amounted to invaluable free advertising for the labels and musicians. At its inception, MTV managed to persuade all but Polygram Records to donate the music clips free of charge. (Polygram soon capitulated too.)

MTV was designed to be perceived by a twelve- to thirty-four-year-old audience as the TV version of a radio station, offering programming twelve hours a day, every day of the year, and presented by a team of genial vjs. To this end, MTV immediately began using the techniques of modern radio to determine its format: From the start, the station employed five telephone operators to make five thousand calls a week to target homes containing potential viewers. These surveyors played snippets of new and familiar songs over the phone and queried listeners about their likes and dislikes and their familiarity with the videos of the artists under discussion.

From this research and a general philosophical-cum-commercial agreement with AOR radio stations' white hard rock policy, MTV devised its playlist. But early on, before videos became de rigueur for every act with a serious shot at the big time, the channel inevitably favored those few groups that were already experimenting with interesting, elaborate videos.

This meant that British acts had an advantage on MTV, since Britain's long history of rock music television shows had long provided a market for music videos in a way that was unheard of in America. Music industry analysts would later assert that the early-1980s popularity in America of such English bands as Duran Duran, Human League, Adam Ant, A Flock of Seagulls, and the Australian band Men at Work could be traced directly to MTV's broadcast of these bands' slick polished videos.

It was Duran Duran who won the dubious distinction of being the first rock band to achieve success largely on the strength of its videos. Duran Duran's videos looked like slick, high-fashion television commercials, stressing close-ups of the band members' soft, pretty features for the teen girls in the audience, and plenty of scantily clad models prancing in high heels for the teen boys to find absorbing. One especially cynical effort was their 1981 video for "Girls on Film," directed by former rock musicians Kevin Godley and Lol Creme. In Michael Shore's *Rolling Stone Book of Rock Video* (1984), Godley is quoted as saying, "Lol and I were told by Duran's management simply to make a very provocative, sexy video that had some sort of tenuous connection to the band and would be seen in clubs and cause people to talk." This the "Girls on Film" video did, featuring as it did the aforementioned scantily clad models engaging in pillow fights and tussling with sumo wrestlers. The video was so steamy, to say nothing of offensive, that it actually would be banned by many of the television outlets beginning to feature the new medium.

Despite this—or perhaps in part because of this—MTV was a considerable success early on in its career. Carried by 1,775 cable operators two years into its existence, MTV was by common consensus the fastest growing network in cable television history. Its vjs—former radio disc jockeys J. J. Jackson and Mark Goodman, actors Alan Hunter and Nina Blackwood, and Martha Quinn, whose chief claim to fame was the fact that she was the stepdaughter of economist Jane Bryant Quinn—became stars themselves. Within the first year of beginning broadcasting, MTV announced proudly, its vjs were attracting 100,000 letters a month.

The success of MTV had a palpable impact on the music business as a whole. Soon the major record labels began colluding with MTV in promoting acts through tour date information and contests (an executive told *Rolling Stone* that the station held contests—"Win a weekend with Van Halen," etc.—"to help build an emotional bond through the fantasies they develop"). The artists themselves were downright eager to accept the exposure MTV offered, with musicians as prestigious as Pete Townshend and David Bowie, among many others, filming commercials in which they urged viewers of commercial television to call their cable operators and shout, "I want my MTV!"

Initially, though, before videos were commonplace, MTV seemed to offer a slight alternative to more rigid rock-radio formats. It could give an oddball act like Devo, new-wave eccentrics from Akron, Ohio, who had made a series of startling, disturbingly surreal videos directed by Chuck Statler, extensive exposure in those early days, despite the fact that the band's experimental music was choppy and obscure. By offering glimpses of a few performers who hadn't been able to crack radio, it offered new success stories. Take, for example, Greg Kihn, a San Francisco pop-rocker stalled at cult status for nearly a decade, whose 1983 single "Jeopardy," when accompanied by a clever, self-spoofing video, suddenly gave him his first hit; when put into MTV's "heavy rotation" (three or four plays per day on the station), its sales tripled. And it was rock video, oddly enough, that would finally bring widespread exposure to Randy Newman, via the exceptionally witty video of his "I Love L.A.," directed by his cousin Tim Newman. The song even found a third incarnation as the sound track to a popular 1984 television commercial for Adidas running shoes.

The flip side of this was the station's continuing resistance to airing black music. It seemed obvious to the station's critics that if a white rocker like Greg Kihn could break through to a wider audience via this medium, so could a black rocker like Rick James, yet James's videos were denied entry to MTV's playlist. Indeed, as Steven Levy observed, writing about MTV in a December 1983 issue of *Rolling Stone,* "Of the over 750 videos shown on MTV during the channel's first eighteen months, fewer than two dozen featured black artists, even including such racially mixed bands as the English Beat."

Robert Pittman, who as executive vice president and chief operating officer of Warner Amex Satellite Entertainment Company was a regular spokesman for MTV's policies, shrugged off the charges of racism that cropped up almost immediately by saying that black artists simply weren't making rock and roll—they were making rhythm and blues, or disco. Speaking to Levy, Pittman went so far as to call the people who objected to MTV's exclusion of black artists as "little Hitlers or people from Eastern-bloc communist countries. . . . I don't know who the fuck these people are to tell people what they should like."

The most dramatic example of MTV's exclusionary policies occurred during the height of the popularity of Michael Jackson's 1982 *Thriller* album. The videos Jackson made to accompany these songs, in particular those for "Billie Jean," "Beat It," and "Thriller," did much to confirm the widespread use of videos as effective promotional tools. "Billie Jean," directed by Steve Barron, depicted Michael as a glowingly mysterious figure being shadowed by a private detective; while the video had little to do with the lyrics of the song, it successfully conveyed the feelings of paranoia and entrapment that pervade Jackson's music. "Beat It," directed by Bob Giraldi and costing the then-unprecedented sum of $150,000 (most videos at the time cost about a third of that), became Michael's version of *West Side Story,* with a prancing street gang snarling behind Michael and, under the direction of choreographer Michael Peters, matching him wiggle for wiggle, head snap for head snap.

The video for "Thriller" was something else altogether. It was directed by feature film director John Landis (Barron and Giraldi had come out of the TV commercial business), and Landis had been chosen because Michael was such a fan of Landis's *An American Werewolf in London*, a very gory, amoral movie for such a supposedly gentle, virtuous soul as Michael. Landis filled the small screen with lurid monster makeup on scores of extras, and turned Michael into a drooling werewolf who chomped on his girlfriend—again, something of a departure for Michael Jackson's image. So much so, in fact, that upon looking at the final results, Michael became alarmed that his more devoted followers would think he was advocating black magic or, heaven forbid, satanism, and he felt compelled to tack a disclaimer onto the beginning of the video.

"Thriller" eventually became an hour-long home videocassette entitled *The Making of Michael Jackson's Thriller*, which consisted of the video itself, bulked out with insufferably cute chat sessions between Jackson and Landis, plus footage of fans screaming during the filming of the video, rehearsals for the video, and scenes of the laborious effort it took to apply Michael's werewolf makeup. This was a vanity production to end all vanity productions—except, of course, it didn't: As the months and years went by, videos became the most self-indulgent of all rock star/record company self-indulgences. The bottom line was clear: *The Making of Michael Jackson's Thriller* sold over 350,000 copies in the first six months of its release.

As wildly popular as Jackson's videos were, however, none of them was being aired on MTV. The reason? This music, the cable station said, was "not rock and roll." Why not? The clear implication was: because the artist was black. But very quickly, demand for Michael Jackson in any media form grew so great that MTV bowed to public pressure and added the videos to its nearly lily white playlist. But that may not have been the sole source of pressure: It was rumored at the time that Columbia Records had threatened MTV that it would pull all its artists' videos (which, like every other label's, were donated free to the cable network in exchange for promotion) unless Jackson's videos were programmed on the channel. It seems likely that if they were faced with the prospect of losing such archetypal MTV acts as the hard-rock softies Journey, MTV might easily have caved in. Thereafter, "Billie Jean" was spoken of as having "broken the color barrier" in MTV—as if this were an achievement the channel should have been proud of, instead of ashamed of having established in the first place.

Beneath its slick, soothing surface, the underlying message of MTV was that rock and roll was merely entertainment, fun; its endless chains of surrealistic video imagery suggested that rock music had nothing to do with the real world. Pittman, never one to opt for subtlety, put it succinctly: "In the sixties, politics and rock music fused. But there are no more political statements [in rock]. The only thing rock fans have in common is the music—that's the coalition MTV has gathered." It was this attitude, combined with the apparently endless banality of all but the tiniest percentage of the videos being screened, that made the rise of MTV a fact to bemoan.

Yet as with any successful business venture, MTV was immediately copied. Ted Turner's so-called SuperStation in Atlanta, WTBS, reaching a cable audience of 22 million, began "Night Tracks," six hours of videos on Friday and Saturday nights, in 1983. Other video programs included the USA Network's "Night Flight" (more videos) and "1990" (a video plus rock interview show hosted by print journalist Lisa Robinson, whose droll wittiness was drastically held in check lest it become too apparent just how trite the show's format really was).

Network television was far more cautious: Only NBC launched a full-time video show—"Friday Night Videos," a ninety-minute anthology produced by Dick Ebersol, producer of "Saturday Night Live." The media in all its forms was eager to annoint video as the next and permanent development in the history of rock and roll, but by mid-1985, MTV's ratings were down 25 percent from the previous year.

MTV and the video revolution were just one aspect of the new technology being deployed in the modern rock era. If the 1960s was the period of the rock album, the 1970s saw the steady, inexorable rise of the cassette as the preferred medium for the dissemination of rock music. By 1983, half of the $3.78 billion in recorded music profits came from cassettes; a year later, cassette sales would inch past those of album sales for the first time in history.

The reason for this is simple: There were now more ways to play a cassette. In July 1979, Sony introduced the Walkman to America, and this small tape player with lightweight headphones changed the way the largest market in the world listened to its music. Within a year, it was not unusual to see a jogger thumping down the street to a rhythm heard only by the runner, or a commuter bouncing along on the morning train cut off from outside distractions with a pair of headphones clamped on, tuned in to a private universe of music. At the other extreme, large portable tape players—boom boxes, as they came to be called—were being manufactured with increasingly subtle sound quality.

You could assign to each decade of rock history its predominant recording medium: the 1950s—the single; the 1960s—the album; the 1970s—the cassette. The 1980s heralded the arrival of the compact disc, or CD. In CD technology, the music encoded on a disc is activated by a laser beam, not a mechanical stylus, and thus CDs had the instant advantage of never wearing out the way a record, with a diamond needle cutting into vinyl, inevitably did. CD champions asserted that the sound quality was superior to records and cassettes, and sales took off: During the December 1985 winter holiday season, traditionally the music business's busiest time, America's supplies of this new music format were completely sold out—even the most profit conscious of the major record companies had underestimated the demand that sprang up for CDs over the course of a mere two years.

A kind of consensus-through-consumption was emerging here: The public's desire to know and see more-more-more of Michael—the common reaction to any rock star throughout the history of the music—now had new mediums by which to slake its celebrity thirst. Think of MTV as a kinetic *Sixteen* magazine, of videos as live-action pinups, and the synthesis of the 1980s becomes apparent once more: new ways to experience the feeling of good old rock and roll.

38

THE BLACK ROCK REVIVAL

Cautiously at first, then with something approaching giddy abandon, music with a danceable beat—none dared call it disco—became popular again as the 1980s proceeded. The new dance music was much more varied than disco had been, and incorporated elements of punk/new wave and funk into its mix. When combined with the outreach of music videos, in which you could see your idols dancing as well as feel the beat yourself, much of the rhythm-based music that black artists such as George Clinton had been refining began to appeal to more and more people.

In 1983, Clinton began releasing a series of records under his own name—no more Parliament-Funkadelicizing for him—and hit pay dirt with the single "Atomic Dog," whose rough-edged, push-pull rhythm would be an influential sound over the next couple of years. Like anyone with a hit, Clinton made a music video to accompany "Atomic Dog," a particularly inventive one that combined animation and live action to make Clinton's funk cartoonishly accessible to a broad audience that might know little about funk. But MTV didn't program "Atomic Dog"—it didn't fit their format; a familiar refrain. However, the exposure the video received on other commercial televison outlets helped the single, which had reached Number One on *Billboard*'s Black Singles chart, to crack the pop chart as well.

Clinton was only the most well-established example in black rock music of a daring, almost experimental nature that managed to reach a wide audience in the 1980s. The other, even more brash and even more commercially successful example of this was rap music, the stripped-down, spoken-word variation on James Brown–style funk that survived slurs similar to those that had been leveled at disco (for example, "That noise isn't rock and roll!") to become an essential part of the roiling synthesis of 1980s rock.

George Clinton's success with funk provided black musicians with a way to revive the rowdy music that had not been heard on pop radio stations since the heyday of 1960s soul. Now such bands as the early Commodores ("Brick House") and the Gap Band ("You Dropped a Bomb on Me") scored hit singles with bass-heavy tunes that repeated a single, prominent riff in clever, catchy ways.

Out in Los Angeles, former pro footballer Dick Griffey organized Solar Records (the name was an anagram for "Sound of Los Angeles Records"), whose funk acts included Lakeside, an otherwise nondescript bunch whose wardrobe changed with every album—for one release they were cowboys, in the next they were pirates—and whose best funk steal was "Fantastic Voyage" (1980). Griffey wasn't primarily concerned with funk, however; he had intended Solar to compete with Motown by employing such polished vocal groups as Shalamar. His hits were few and far between, however.

Clinton felt much more direct competition from a Motown act: Rick James, the self-proclaimed "king of punk-funk." As the title suggests, James was a rock-music hustler in the grand manner—not content to steal from one hot trend (funk), he decided to align himself with another (punk) by fiat.

Actually, James's music had absolutely nothing to do with punk rock. He was a rhythm-and-blues player who had studied all Clinton's moves and grafted them onto his own stud/pimp image. James's hits in the late 1970s and early 1980s included "You and I," "Give It to Me Baby," and "Super Freak (Part 1)," good black radio fodder all.

The most important development in black music during this time, however, was the flowering of a pop genre whose elemental style and bleak bluntness was perfectly suited to a period of diminished expectations.

Rap music was one element of what became known as "hip hop" culture, an alternative, underclass expression of art that included break dancing and graffiti writing as well as rapping. As one of the subculture's guiding lights, musician and Bronx community organizer Afrika Bambaataa has said, "At that time [the late 1970s], the Bronx wasn't into radio music no more. It was an anti-disco movement. Like you had a lot of new-wavers and other people coming out and saying 'disco sucks.' Well, the same thing with hip hop, 'cause they was against the disco that was being played on the radio."

Although the pop music listeners did not become aware of rap as a fully developed genre until the Sugar Hill Gang's 1979 hit single "Rapper's Delight," released on the tiny New Jersey label Sugar Hill Records, rap had roots in black popular music as far back as you were willing to stretch them. Most people, including the rappers themselves, credit James Brown with the curt, choppy, minimally accompanied speechifying that characterizes rapping. Nonetheless, some commentators have made convincing cases for carrying rap back even further. In his 1984 book *The Rap Attack*, for example, David Toop compared rap's rhyming couplets and obscure street slang to Cab Calloway's "hi-de-hi-de-hi-de-ho" verbal scatting.

Rap's most immediate predecessors, however, were James Brown's anti-compositions such as 1971's implacable "Get Up, Get Into It, Get Involved," as well as Jamaican "toasting," the reggae-ized version of rap that had been popular since the late 1960s. In this regard, a rap pioneer was the fellow known as Cool Herc, a Jamaican who moved to the Bronx in the early 1970s and began applying reggae toasting to the American black hits of the day. As someone without a record contract, however, Herc was virtually a folk artist, laboring in obscurity except among those in his immediate area. Then, too, little reggae penetrated the Bronx, home of nearly all the early rappers. There, rap was quite literally a street music—rappers stood on corners improvising rhymes, either unaccompanied (post–doo-wop) or to the instrumental versions of well-known hits of the day.

The best rappers were called djs, for the way they commandeered the music as authoritatively as a disc jockey at a radio station, and by all accounts the most influential dj was DJ Hollywood, who, as rapper Kurtis Blow told David Toop, "could just blaze a crowd with the rhymes he said. I expected him to shoot right to the top—he had a chance before we did."

But with no major record label interested in this music—where were the melodies? where was the singing?—early rappers like DJ Hollywood were either ignored or treated ignorantly: Hollywood's brush with greatness, for example, came when Epic Records released one single in 1980. The company issued it as a seven-inch record when all other rap music was being released in a twelve-inch form, and added a cooing female chorus to Hollywood's rap; the single went nowhere.

No, rap's commercial breakthrough was 1979's "Rapper's Delight," a charmingly silly record fashioned by a group of Bronx street rappers and experienced New Jersey session musicians called the Sugar Hill Gang, overseen by Sugar Hill Records president Sylvia Robinson. Robinson was a veteran figure in black pop music: In the 1950s, billed as Little Sylvia, she replaced "Little" Esther Phillips on Savoy Records when the latter left the label. In 1955 she teamed up with guitarist Mickey Baker to form Mickey and Sylvia and had a top-twenty single with "Love Is Strange."

By the 1970s, Robinson had become a businesswoman in partnership with her husband, Joe Robinson.Their Sugar Hill Records was recording modest hits and outright bombs in the disco and post–Philly Sound styles when her son Joey played her bootleg tapes of Bronx rap parties. Intrigued, she asked Joey's friends what kind of music they liked, and when most of them described rap music, a genre no one had committed to record in any professional way, she decided it might be worth taking a chance on. Robinson assembled the Sugar Hill Gang as calculatedly as Don Kirshner formed the Monkees. For example, one member, Big Bank Hank, a bouncer in a Jersey nightclub, was chosen for his girth and genial smile; another was an unemployed friend of Joey's whom Robinson's son had overheard improvising rhymes.

"Rapper's Delight" went to number thirty-six on the pop charts, an impressive achievement indeed when you consider that most white rock stations—in fact, virtually all of them—wouldn't touch the record. Its success did not move many of the major record companies to get on the rap bandwagon, but it did send other independent labels scrambling for young rappers who would record big hits for little more than exposure and subway fare.

The hit that proved rap might be more than a one-shot novelty was Kurtis Blow's "The Breaks." Released in 1980 by Mercury Records, a once major but then floundering label, it was seven minutes of bad news that appealed to a huge audience. On "The Breaks," a guitar scratched out a coarse four-note figure in a high, sarcastic register; on top of this, some exotic percussion was applied—a stuttering steel-drum sound you could feel in the back of your sinuses. Then Kurtis Blow himself came sauntering in on the music like an uninvited, high-on-life house guest, launching into a torrent of rhyming couplets detailing all the bad luck in the world—universal problems like, "Ma Bell sends you a whopping bill/With eighteen phone calls to Brazil"—to which the only possible response was the chorus from an exhausted-sounding group of band members: "That's the breaks, that's the breaks." As pop music, this was brutally blunt stuff; as social commentary, it was sharp and sharp-witted.

After the success of "The Breaks" and "Rapper's Delight," there ensued a slew of fascinating rap records, all of them on Sugar Hill or tiny New York independents like Enjoy, Profile, or Jamtu: the Funky Four Plus One's "That's the Joint," Spoonie Gee's "Love Rap," the Fearless Four's "Rockin' It," and Grandmaster Flash and the Furious Five's "Superrappin.'"

The early 1980s was, then, a period of constant jostling for the kingpin position in rap; in any given month, one record would dominate the rap cult, would push the innovations of a previous hit into still further new, uncharted areas. This was how one of the most extraordinary records to come out of hip hop culture, "The Adventures of Grandmaster Flash on the Wheels of Steel," came about.

Grandmaster Flash, born Joseph Saddler, was a club dj who did not rap; his primary function was to work the dual turntables on which he intercut between various records in a rhythmic manner to achieve a collage of sounds. "The Adventures of Grandmaster Flash on the Wheels of Steel," released in 1981 on Sugar Hill Records, was a summation of turntable artistry, stitching together bits of Chic's disco hit "Good Times," the English art rock band Queen's "Another One Bites the Dust," a snippet of Blondie's Deborah Harry chanting, "Flash is bad, Flash is bad," a snatch of dialog from a children's record, and much more to create a pulsing, buzzing, whirring machine of sound that yielded new details every time you listened to it.

As the 1980s proceeded, it became clear that rap and hip hop were inspiring a new, postdisco dance music, a genre intent on not making the same mistakes that mired mid-1970s disco in mindless repetition and aesthetic enervation. Like disco, this new dance music sprang not from the corporate music business but from a network of small labels such as Sugar Hill Records in New Jersey and Tom Silverman's Tommy Boy Records in New York.

The fiercely competitive scene that arose yielded not only fresh performers but fresh technicians as well—producers and engineers who approached the music in ways that were far different from those of their rock music counterparts. By far the most important of these producers was Arthur Baker, a New Yorker by way of Boston who, with his shoulder-length hair and beefy physique, looked more like a Hell's Angel biker than a record producer.

Baker moved along the usual dance music route: club dj to engineer to remixer to producer. He made his mark producing a series of twelve-inch singles with Afrika Bambaataa and his group the Soul Sonic Force. Bambaataa singles such as "Jazzy Sensation," "Planet Rock," and "Looking for the Perfect Beat" established Arthur Baker's style—sharp, staccato percussion, dense layers of echo on the vocals and one or two prominent instruments, plus sound effects galore. While everyone around him was stripping music down to its barest bones (often just a voice and a beat), Baker was busy piling up sounds, creating the thickest, richest, productions since Phil Spector went overboard on "River Deep, Mountain High." In art terms, if most hip hop music was minimalist, Baker's productions were baroque—gloriously so.

For sheer formal daring, rap's greatest coup was effected by Run-DMC in 1983. This New York rap act established itself with one exceptionally tough, witty single, "It's Like That/Sucker MCs," and followed it up with the rap/rock synthesis that many music fans had been dreaming about: "Rock Box" combined a slamming beat, a crisp rap, and wildly lyrical hard-rock guitar work by Eddie Martinez that suggested both Jimi Hendrix and Eddie Van Halen. With innovations like this, rap had proved itself to be far more than a novelty—it was yet another sign of rock's continuing invention and revitalized spirit.

Rap also transcended its pleasures as music to stand as an example of the shift in attitude toward pop innovation in the 1970s versus the 1980s. All the 1970s upstart genres, from disco to punk, had met with immediate, fierce, and prolonged resistance from the mainstream. In the 1980s, rap developed on its own, thriving on its underground status, until it gradually but steadily seeped into mainstream consciousness. The shock of its newness and rawness was tempered by just enough familiarity to permit it access to the mainstream. So it was with much black music in the 1980s—resistance giving way to accessibility.

39

NEW FACES IN
THE 1980s

Everything had fallen into place: By the 1980s, rock was ready to emerge from the late-1970s period of doubt and confusion about its future; music videos, despite their controversial nature as TV commercials for rock, had done much to attract a new, young, and more broadminded audience; and by lucky coincidence, a small slew of 1960s rock veterans who had spent the 1970s in various forms of retreat (retirement, victims of the oldies syndrome, or at a loss for new ideas) reemerged to no small acclaim.

Thus, while the early eighties boasted variety coming out of its ears, this was not a matter of that old seventies fragmentation reasserting itself. On the contrary, both the new eighties acts and the revitalized veterans held a number of things in common. Foremost among these was a sense of rock music history: A new act like Cyndi Lauper was able to invoke the sobbing choke of Lesley Gore while emulating the funky chic of punk fashion; an old pro like John Fogerty was able to utilize eighties technology to achieve a more perfect version of what he'd wanted to be for ten years: a one-man band, overdubbing and playing all the instruments himself, but never before with such precision and conviction.

Among the more noticeable eighties acts was Culture Club, with a good example of the reintegrated rock star: Lead singer Boy George sang in a sweet tenor voice with the sure scholarship of a fellow who'd majored in Advanced Smokey Robinson. On such hits as "Do You Really Want to Hurt Me," "I'll Tumble 4 Ya," and "Karma Chameleon," he crooned with grace and power. What captured everyone's attention, though, was his sartorial flash: Affecting elaborate female makeup, fond of billowy frocks, and

603

cultivating a giggly, bitchy conversational style, Boy George became in 1982–1983 the latest reason for parents to wish rock and roll would just go away.

George turned out to be an articulate if petulant charmer, and he quickly became the English version of Alice Cooper—a supposedly outrageous, rebellious figure who was actually very comfortable hobnobbing with the show business figures of a previous generation. In George's case, for example, he struck up an inexplicable friendship with Joan Rivers.

Another fresh British-based act, the trio called the Police, also featured a lead singer who would transcend his status as a musician to become an object of fan magazine curiosity. In the case of Sting (born Gordon Sumner), it was not for reasons of obscure sexuality—quite the opposite. With his sharply chiseled good looks, his ferocious frown, and his interview small talk dotted with references to Nabokov and Gurdjieff, Sting became a pop idol for people who wanted their pinups to flaunt their gray matter.

The Police were rounded out by British lead guitarist Andy Summers and American drummer Stewart Copeland, and the band scored hits with songs such as "Roxanne," "Message in a Bottle," "Don't Stand So Close to Me," and "Every Breath You Take." The Police were interesting from a business point of view, as well. Copeland's brother Miles founded an independent label, the Illegal Records Syndicate (or I.R.S. Records), and the most successful booking agency for new wave acts, Frontier Booking, International, commonly known as F.B.I. (Both these acronyms were sly salutes to the Copeland brothers' father, a former CIA agent.) The Police, booked by F.B.I., advanced their early career by breaking with the usual pattern followed by young bands, which routinely go into debt to their record companies because of drawing an advance against royalties for touring expenses and promotion.

With F.B.I., the Police didn't take an advance from either I.R.S. or I.R.S.'s big-time distributor, A&M Records. Instead, the band toured on the cheap, sharing one hotel room, traveling from concert to concert in a van rather than a spacious tour bus. This was a throwback to the earliest days of rock, of course—it really wasn't a new idea—but when the Police started out in the late 1970s, at a time when rock stars felt it necessary to be treated lavishly as befitted a new pop royalty, the Police and other F.B.I.-booked acts were able to travel farther and save more money than many young bands that went broke trying to make it.

The Police's career was also aided by the suave videos the group filmed to promote their records. Then, too, Sting launched a successful acting career, securing increasingly larger roles in feature films such as *Quadrophenia* (1979), *Brimstone and Treacle* (1982), and *The Bride* (1984).

The only band from the original New York punk scene that went on to forge a strong commercial career in the 1980s was the Talking Heads. By the late 1970s, group leader David Byrne had refined his nerd image to offer himself to his listeners as the perennial outsider, alienated from everyday life, to be sure, but fascinated by it nonetheless. That's one reason the band's first two albums, *Talking Heads '77* (1977) and *More Songs about Buildings and Food* (1978), contained so many compositions about the workaday world, from "Don't Worry about the Government" to "Artists Only" to "The Big Country," the latter a grand, ambitious song meant to convey the feeling of flying over the United States close enough to the ground to peer into people's lives as they undertook their everyday routines. "When we started playing in clubs," Byrne told the *New York Times* in a 1985 interview, "the typical rock stance was aggressive—black leather and shades and all that. We were deliberately going against that. . . . We threw out the idea of costumes, of lighting, of any kind of movement or gestures onstage."

As the 1970s drew to a close and rock radio formats grew more and more racially segregated, the Talking Heads made its most important aesthetic decision, one born of both conviction and boredom. Tired of the harshly rhythmed music by which the punk/new wave scene was by then dominated, the entire band began to explore the ways their own music could accommodate the looser, sexier rhythms of contemporary black music. One result was a project created by band members Chris Frantz and Tina Weymouth (who had by then married), a studio band called the Tom Tom Club. This group recorded a self-titled debut album in 1981 that yielded "Genius of Love," a hit single whose sensuous, stuttering bass and drum pattern was enormously influential in the dance-rock music of other artists over the next twelve months; the basic riff in "Genius of Love" was incorporated into a number of records by rap groups.

The other result of the band's immersion in black music was *Speaking in Tongues*, a 1983 album that proved a substantial commercial success. The promotional tour for it found the band expanded to twice its normal size, with the addition of four black musicians who helped the Heads reproduce the thick, multirhythmed music they had achieved through dense multiple tracks in the recording studio. At about this period of the band's life, keyboardist Jerry Harrison has said, "[We] felt there was a growing racism in the United States and that, in a very quiet way, we made this big point. We were both male and female, black and white, on stage, having fun, no one in a particularly subservient role, and no one drawing attention to it." In this way, the Talking Heads stood, triumphantly, in implicit rebuke to the scores of white rock bands all around them who dominated the segregated album-oriented-rock–formatted radio stations while plundering the vast body of black popular music.

Out of the *Speaking in Tongues* tour came the 1984 concert film *Stop Making Sense*, directed by theatrical film director Jonathan Demme and widely hailed as the most elegant rock movie ever made. To its few detractors, it was this very elegance—its careful avoidance of crowd-reaction shots as vulgar pandering, its meticulous framing of the band (especially Byrne) as stylized art objects—that drained the music of much of its excitement.

In fact, what all the rave reviews from movie critics who otherwise disdained rock music suggested was that *Stop Making Sense* was a rock concert movie for people who never went to rock concerts. Nonetheless, it was an excellent promotional device for the band (that media monster MTV took to "sponsoring" the film, broadcasting theater locations where it was playing and thus giving this former artsy new wave band unprecedented exposure) as well as earning them considerable respect among an older audience that had abandoned rock and roll. By mid-1985, the Talking Heads was perhaps the most highly esteemed rock band in America, and Byrne found himself written about as the object of structuralist analysis in *Artforum* and interviewed about his work habits as "David Byrne: Thinking Man's Rock Star" for the *New York Times Magazine's* "The Creative Mind" series, a feature normally reserved for the most entrenched middlebrow art heroes.

By now there were other new artists, too—and some more venerable ones reborn—to claim the rock audience's adulation. Tina Turner had spent the 1950s and 1960s yelling out rhythm-and-blues songs and dancing up a storm for the Ike and Tina Turner Revue. But after divorcing Ike in 1975, she looked like another washed-up pop star—her solo albums were lackluster affairs, and her other media exposure was limited to an amusing cameo she made in the 1975 film of the Who's *Tommy*.

In early 1984, however, Turner staged one of the most spectacular comebacks in pop music history. *Private Dancer*, produced in England, brought a pop polish to Turner's rhythm-and-blues belting, and it went platinum. Suddenly, all the residual affection the public had felt toward the brassy, friendly Turner found an outlet in her fresh stardom—her bright smile and the leggy look she emphasized onstage found its way onto scores of magazine covers, where Turner reveled in her newfound fame and told of the ugly side of life with Ike. As Ike slipped into obscurity, unable to capitalize on the success of his ex-wife, Tina headlined stadium arenas, co-starred in the 1985 film *Mad Max Beyond Thunderdome*, sang a top-twenty duet with Canadian rocker Bryan Adams, "It's Only Love."

Another surprise success story of 1984 was Cyndi Lauper's debut album, *She's So Unusual*, which sold over three million copies. With her clear, strong voice and strikingly odd image—thrift-shop-elegant clothes, multicolor hair, exaggerated New Yawk speaking voice—Lauper seemed an exotic yet unpretentious figure. She employed this image to great effect in the videos filmed to accompany hit singles like "Girls Just Want to Have Fun," "Time after Time," and "She Bop." In these videos, bright, comic-booklike color schemes emphasized Lauper's own multihued persona, and the action invariably centered around her plucky ragamuffin-with-brains image.

For all her studied wackiness, Lauper offered a significant alternative to the other female rock stars of the day. She completely bypassed the woman-as-sex-object stereotype that virtually all female rockers must confront, while at the same time raising questions, however lightheartedly phrased, about women's sexuality. Thus newspaper op-ed pages across the country gassed on about the implications of girls just wanting to have fun, and "She Bop" was decried in conservative quarters for advancing a thinly disguised metaphor for masturbation.

In these and other matters, Lauper's aggressive eccentricity served her well. Amid the minor controversies, Lauper ignored the dimwitted hubbub and threw her audience curves—she displayed, for instance, an interest in show biz wrestling via her friendship with professional wrestler Captain Lou Albano. She would also pop up as part of the superstar chorus for the rock charity project "We Are the World."

Madonna, another mid-1980s star, didn't reject the woman-as-sex-object stereotype: In fact, she took it to new heights. She had been a favorite in disco circles for two full years before her cooing voice and commanding sartorial style (layered gypsy dresses, tons of bangles, exposed navel) attracted the attention of the mainstream pop audience. In 1982, her twelve-inch disco singles "Everybody" and "Burning Up" were popular requests at the New York music clubs that mattered, and the supporters she attracted there helped Madonna (born Madonna Louise Ciccone) secure a contract with Warner Bros. Records. Her debut album, *Madonna*, in 1983, yielded dance music successes that gradually became pop radio hits—"Holiday," "Borderline," "Lucky Star," and "Physical Attraction."

But it was with 1984's *Like a Virgin* that Madonna-mania hit in earnest. The ex–Alvin Ailey dancer launched a tour to promote the album and found herself singing to prepubescent audiences who dressed just like she did—a *Time* magazine story on the singer dubbed the fans "Wanna-Bes," and the name stuck. "Like a Virgin" and "Material Girl" were singles hits, but they also attracted criticism in some quarters for their supposedly retrograde attitude toward women—Madonna had never made any secret of the fact that her prime role model was Marilyn Monroe as a gold digger in *Gentlemen Prefer Blondes*. In 1985, Madonna became a movie star in the Susan Seidelman–directed comedy *Desperately Seeking Susan*, in which she stole the show from her more established co-star Rosanna Arquette.

It was movies that would revive the career of an older cult artist, Tom Waits, in the early 1980s. Waits had spent the 1970s releasing a series of albums that attempted to do for pop music what Raymond Chandler had done for fiction: His tales of urban lowlifes and fractured romances, told in hard-boiled language and mumbled for authenticity, attracted a cult following but limited his mass appeal. By 1980, his seventh album, *Heart Attack and Vine*, found him at a creative dead end reduced to repeating himself endlessly.

Waits's creative breakthrough occurred when he began composing music for movies such as Francis Ford Coppola's *One from the Heart*, which compelled him to move into new areas of subject matter and musical genre. When other artists "go Hollywood," it means that their work becomes soft and compromised. Waits's "gone Hollywood" adventures inspired his best albums, the stylistically diverse and ambitious *Swordfishtrombones* (1984) and *Rain Dogs* (1985), which owed as much to Brecht–Weill as Hammett–Chandler.

And in 1985, another kind of singer-songwriter, John Fogerty, would emerge from a decade-long silence with *Centerfield*, a collection of songs written, produced, and performed by Fogerty all by himself. This had been Fogerty's modus operandi since the dissolution of Creedence Clearwater Revival in the early 1970s. Creedence had been a nearly impossible act to follow—the group had scored, for example, seven Top Ten singles between 1969 and 1970—and Fogerty was not inclined to compete with his ex-band by forming a new one: Both *Blue Ridge Rangers* (1972) and *John Fogerty* (1975) had consisted of music made entirely by Fogerty and had fared significantly less well in the marketplace than had Creedence's music.

Centerfield was a different story. On songs like "The Old Man Down the Road," "Rock and Roll Girls" and "Big Train (from Memphis)," the album displayed renewed vigor—the headlong passion of these songs might be mistaken for the Creedence Clearwater Revival of old. *Centerfield* became a Number One album, and the reclusive Fogerty gave chipper interviews in which he told of his years-long crises of confidence, of looking around at stars like Michael Jackson and Prince and not knowing whether he "could cut it anymore." To millions of rock fans, for whom Creedence's old hits sounded fresh and vital, he still could.

The most popular 1980s heavy metal acts broke little new ground musically—the whole appeal of heavy metal is that it stays roughly the same, year after year, after all—but took advantage of rock videos and the most sophisticated stage set technology and recording techniques to develop distinctively naughty styles. They included Motley Crue (Kiss with dirtier lyrics), Ratt (young Zeppelin-ites), and Quiet Riot (metal with a sense of humor).

The most popular of such bands was Van Halen, a Los Angeles–based quartet led by flamboyant singer David Lee Roth and lead guitarist Eddie Van Halen. Eddie's technical virtuosity, displayed in the tumultuous cascade of precisely fingered notes he could summon from his homemade guitar, brought the band a certain grudging critical respect; Roth's bad-boy-on-the-make image, enhanced by a leering wit and uncommon gift of gab, brought the group mainstream media attention, something few heavy metal groups ever achieve. Roth left the band in 1985 to pursue a career in movies and as a solo music act; Eddie Van Halen continued his band without Roth, replacing the singer with Sammy Hagar, a singer-guitarist who had himself led a mediocre heavy metal outfit.

All these new acts, at one point or another in their ascent to stardom, seemed on the verge of transcending their respective genres to attain true mass stardom. Only a few actually accomplished this; the most unlikely—the most quirky and ostentatiously cocky—was Prince.

He had been around during the previous decade. Both *For You* (1978) and *Prince* (1979) were entirely written, sung, produced, and played by Prince, but these records suggested primarily that what we had here was a pretty good Stevie Wonder rip-off. Prince had Wonder's grainy, wavery tenor voice and loopy falsetto down pat; he had Wonder's goony romanticism coming out of his ears.

True, Prince seemed to have a talent for implied filthiness that Wonder lacked: the highlight of *For You* was a ditty called "Soft and Wet," and *Prince*, which featured the pop hit "I Wanna Be Your Lover," peaked with a song containing the line "I want to come inside you." On that one, Prince even implied that he might have a sense of humor, because he expected us (or at least radio programmers) to think he meant, "Come inside your head"—y'know, like, get to know you.

But all comparisons to Stevie Wonder, as well as his chances for extensive radio airplay, were destroyed in 1980, when Prince released *Dirty Mind*, a torrent of explicit sexuality unprecedented in a commercial rock record. *Dirty Mind* contained hymns to incest ("Sister": opening lines: "I was only 16, but I guess that's no excuse/My sister was 32, lovely and loose. . . . Incest is everything it's meant to be"), oral sex ("Head": Prince meets a woman on her way to her wedding ceremony who takes one look at our hero and says, "You're such a hunk, so full of spunk, I'll give you/Head. . . ."), and ménages à trois ("When You Were Mine": "I was never the kind to make a fuss/When he was there sleepin' in between the two of us").

More important than all this highly agreeable dirtiness, though, was the fact that Prince had found a way to bridge the ever-widening gap between black and white rock. Stinging hard rock guitar stylings were prominent in many of *Dirty Mind*'s arrangements, and while the bass playing was definitely on the funky side, much of the music had the forced slamming of late-1970s rock and roll. *Dirty Mind* was released to ecstatic reviews but only moderate sales—AOR was not about to let this scrawny shortie, who wore only a black jock strap and a raincoat on his album cover, onto its playlists.

So who was this guy, anyway? Born Prince Rogers Nelson in 1960 in Minneapolis, Prince was the son of a mulatto jazz musician father and an Italian mother, a pair whose pained relationship he later immortalized in the 1984 film *Purple Rain*.

After forming a band called first Grand Central and then Champayne, Prince hooked up with small-time Minneapolis agent Owen Husney, who managed to secure a first-rate deal for his client with Warner Bros. Records. Even in the money-mad mid-1970s rock industry, it was unheard of for a new artist to retain much creative control over his initial recordings, but Prince was permitted to produce himself, with Warner Bros. having the option to override his work if they didn't like the results. In one of his very rare interviews, Prince was asked by *Newsweek*'s Barbara Graustark in 1982 whether Warner Bros. had "flinched" when he put "Head" on *Dirty Mind*. "They flinched at just about everything," he replied.

For all his supposed shyness, Prince conducted his career with serene aplomb. He was especially good at manipulating the media to his own purposes and was fond of the put-on in the Bob Dylan manner. When Graustark asked him whom he hung out with in Minnesota, he dead-panned, "Prostitutes. Pimps. Drug dealers. Really bad people, and preachers' daughters." He didn't need a weatherman to know which way the wind blew.

After *Dirty Mind* came *Controversy* (1981). Its highlight was a 1:48 ditty called "Ronnie Talk to Russia," urging President Reagan to commence arms control talks over a thudding funk beat. Radical, you say? Downright left wing? Maybe, except that just a few months later, chatting to *New Musical Express* he blithely observed, "Thank God we got a better President now, with bigger balls than Carter. I think Reagan's a lot better. Just for the power he represents, if nothing else. . . ." Those crazy rock stars.

Prince was handling himself in a regal manner, issuing pronunciamentos with the flick of a sneer, but he wasn't a rock idol yet. In 1982, for example, signed on as the Rolling Stones' opening act, he was booed offstage at the Los Angeles Coliseum by a majority of the 100,000 white rock fans there who hadn't the vaguest idea who he was. To a hailstorm of beer bottles, Prince and his band the Revolution left the stage after only twenty minutes. For someone as sensitive to the merest slight as Prince had freely admitted he was, the shock must have been considerable.

Prince's commercial breakthrough was his next release, *1999*, which contained "Little Red Corvette," the true synthesis of funk and punk that Rick James had been trying in vain to concoct. "Little Red Corvette" was the single that even white rock radio couldn't deny; initially played only on black or "urban contemporary" stations, demand for it was so great among white listeners that AOR had to relent. In retrospect, "Little Red Corvette" was a record that helped signal the end of AOR's institutionalized racism.

If *1999* was Prince's commercial breakthrough, *Purple Rain*, in 1984, was his multimedia triumph. As both album and movie, *Purple Rain* got Prince's image across to a massive audience, and the surprise was that millions adored this petulant brat. Early in the year, he released the album's initial single, "When Doves Cry," whose stark instrumentation, dominated by a single, staccato percussion track and humorless hand claps, broke all the rules about what was "acceptable" on rock radio in the wake of Michael Jackson's impeccably produced recordings.

"When Doves Cry"—what did the title mean? did it matter?—went to Number One before the movie was released, but once the film hit the theaters, Prince's music became the sound of America. The film itself was nothing special; this tale of a sullen, introspective rocker named simply "The Kid" who rises to stardom had been told better through Elvis Presley two decades before in *King Creole* and *Jailhouse Rock*. But Prince proved special indeed. His black-olive-size eyes looked great on the big screen, and up there, his sullenness took on the allure of James Dean—Prince was a rebel with a purple cause.

Self-produced, self-written, directed by malleable novice Albert Magnoli and shot in Prince's hometown, *Purple Rain* introduced audiences to a new set of performers. Prince had surrounded himself with members of his Minnesota mafia: His chief nemesis in the film, the leader of a rival band, was played by Morris Day, in real life the leader of the Prince offshoot band the Time. With his bulging pop eyes and satyr's leer, Day stole a few scenes from his mentor; Day certainly possessed the one quality that had always prevented Prince from being a rock star you could admire: a sense of humor.

Nonetheless, Prince exerted a certain beguiling charm, a quality that established itself most forcefully whenever the film veered into a concert sequence. There Prince proved himself the proper heir to both Jimi Hendrix and Little Richard, pumping out songs such as "Let's Go Crazy," "Darling Nikki," "I Would Die 4 U," and the entirely apt "Baby I'm a Star," which in the movie climaxed with Prince throttling a guitar that with its final chord . . . ejaculated . . . something.

Within the first year of its release, the sound track to *Purple Rain* sold over 13 million copies; the score won the 1984 Oscar (Prince accepted wearing a purple cowl and murmuring thanks to God). The videocassette version of the film sold 500,000 copies in the six months after it was issued in December 1984.

All this for a sullen shrimp whose music gradually became obsessed with impending nuclear war. That is, after all, what the song "Purple Rain" referred to—"I only want to see you underneath the purple rain," that is, dead. The image refers back to a line in "1999," the one about "judgment day/The sky was all purple, there were people runnin' everywhere."

In Prince's mind, sex, guilt, and Armageddon were entwined; nowhere was this more clear than on his next release, *Around the World in a Day* (1985), a quixotic hodgepodge of 1960s pop styles, most obviously *Sgt. Pepper*-era Beatles and Jimi Hendrix. Where *Purple Rain* was Prince's ambitious amalgamation of hard rock and funk music, *Around the World* was a regressive experiment in pop nostalgia. The title song, set to a droning swirl of Middle Eastern and African instruments, implored us to "Open your heart/Open your mind," and offered the peculiarly phrased invitation, "The little I will escort you/To places within your mind." If ever there was a time for pop fans to know their own minds, this was it.

The prolific, perverse Prince followed this up less than a year later with *Parade*, the sound track to a new Prince-directed film containing one instant masterpiece: "Kiss," a song whose stuttering bass, crisp percussion, and muttered vocal link Prince's music to its finest influence—Sly Stone.

Along with Michael Jackson and Prince, the other musician dominating rock discourse in the 1980s was Bruce Springsteen. Springsteen had begun the decade with *The River* (1980), a rollicking two-record set with his E Street Band, but he followed it up with *Nebraska* (1982), a brooding solo album of hard-edged character studies. These ranged from a ghostly summoning-up of mass murder Charles Starkweather in the title song to an unemployed fellow whose only solace is his swiftly moving car on "Open All Night." Downbeat and relentless, *Nebraska* was a commercial long shot, to say the least; indeed, recorded at a time when flagging record sales were petrifying record companies into rigid conservatism, only an artist of Springsteen's potential drawing power could have released such an album for a major label. But *Nebraska* did well enough to justify its release by Columbia—briefly reaching number three on the charts—and it stands artistically as one of the richest, boldest albums in Springsteen's canon.

Then, in 1984, Springsteen would unwittingly provide fresh evidence of rock's vast cultural outreach. His 1984–1985 *Born in the U.S.A.* tour confirmed Springsteen's superstar status—sometimes in ways that worked against the principles implied in his songs. If *Nebraska* had demonstrated his artistic ambition, *Born in the U.S.A.*, his next album with the E Street Band, proved Springsteen's commercial strength. Like *Nebraska*, *Born in the U.S.A.* was concerned with dramatizing the lives of the working-class people who, increasingly, were not only closed out of rock and roll except as potential suckers for heavy metal bands, but out of the nation's economy as well. A big hit as soon as it reached the record stores, *Born in the U.S.A.* also achieved the dubious distinction of being the only rock album to be co-opted by both candidates, Ronald Reagan and Walter Mondale, in the 1984 presidential elections. Not only did the candidates invoke the grand old American spirit they—and their speechwriters—heard in the *Born in the U.S.A.* album, but conservative newspaper columnist George Will told of attending a Springsteen performance and coming away a classical-music snob born again into rock-and-roll fandom.

No matter that in songs such as the title track and "My Hometown" Springsteen was making points about government policies for the working class, Vietnam veterans, and women that were far to the left of anything the Republican and Democratic parties might support. By identifying with Springsteen, both Reagan and Mondale were able to associate themselves with his impeccable rocker-of-the-people image, and *Born in the U.S.A.* itself was redefined in a new context: a rabble-rousing hymn to patriotism. Springsteen rebuffed the strenuous efforts of both sides to enlist his endorsement, and on the American leg of this tour, showed his own political colors, in each city he played, by donating money to local food banks, shelters for the homeless, and union funds.

Ultimately, the ascendancy of Springsteen and Michael Jackson summons up the spirit of Elvis Presley. It is a measure of Presley's pervasive impact on rock music that his spirit has manifested itself in every period of the music's history. It was Presley who contained within himself the whole of rock in the 1950s. In the 1960s, the Beatles assumed that role: The

English quartet was Presley split into four. In the 1970s, his image trashed and his life wasted by drugs and self-indulgence, Presley prevailed as symbol. Elvis Costello, arguably the most talented songwriter to emerge in that decade, appropriated Presley's Christian name as an act of ironic defiance.

Springsteen and Jackson assumed different characteristics of Presley's public persona. In Springsteen, we could hear and see Presley's heroic humility, his regular-guy sense of humor, his implied spokesmanship for the American lower middle class. In Jackson, we could observe Presley's smoldering sexuality, his artful, sometimes disturbing eccentricity, his gospel-music roots, and his enduring love for the florid pop ballad. Together, they offered the very definition of the best of the 1980s: rock music imbued with a sense of history, but invigorated by fresh innovation.

40

ROCK INTO THE FUTURE

With the arrival of the 1980s, it was as if rock and roll had regained its memory after a decade-long sleep. A few good nightmares aside (punk rock was a particularly nasty one), the 1970s had been an almost total betrayal of rock's past as a tool for the expression of social consciousness. With the renewal of rock as an aesthetic force in the eighties, it seemed only natural that this era's rock would also turn, as it did in the sixties, to take positions on social issues, to dramatize political conflicts.

Except for some eloquent screeds from the punks, you'd be hard-pressed to find a good song about the Vietnam War in the whole decade of the 1970s, for example. But by the early 1980s, rock musicians were coming up with vivid, tough-minded work about the debacle of Vietnam and its aftermath in songs such as the Charlie Daniels Band's "Still in Saigon," Stevie Wonder's "Front Line," the San Francisco punk band the Dead Kennedys' "Holiday in Cambodia," and Billy Joel's "Goodnight Saigon."

Joel, in fact, is a perfect example of an artist revitalized by lifting his eyes from 1970s navel-gazing. The Long Island–born Joel had become a massively popular rock star on the strength of his energetic bathos. He'd been recording his coyly ironic slices of life since 1972, and he won a devoted cult following for such woe-is-me-and-you tales as "Piano Man" and "New York State of Mind," but he didn't really hit it big until 1977's *The Stranger*. Released during the height of punk rock, it is well to remember that the song gracing most pop fans' lips during that time was Joel's "Just the Way You Are," a song whose cultural/aesthetic paradox was typical of Joel's stardom: condescension perceived by fans as sympathy.

Even after the success of *The Stranger*, it took Joel a while to realize what his best talents were. He tried to be the poor man's Springsteen on 1978's *52nd Street* and was a disaster as a new-waver-come-lately on 1980's *Glass Houses*, but on *The Nylon Curtain* and especially 1983's *An Innocent Man*, Joel achieved his true calling: He reveled in his facility to mimic other pop styles and exploited this ability with heartfelt sincerity. *An Innocent Man* was a virtual survey of 1950s and 1960s pop music, and a highly enjoyable one at that, from the Four Seasons–style yearning of "Uptown Girl" to the doo-wop a cappella harmonies (multitracked with himself) of "The Longest Time."

Other long-time singer-songwriters recharged themselves by taking stock of what had occurred in the 1970s—in music and in the world. In 1978, Neil Young released a three-record retrospective of his work, *Decade*, that did full justice to his odd but powerfully original career. He topped this with *Rust Never Sleeps* (1979), his head-on confrontation with punk rock. "The King is dead, but he's not forgotten/This is the story of Johnny Rotten"; the couplet provided the invocation for this raw, ornery album, in which Young aligned himself with a younger generation even as he became more set in his ways. His point, of course, was that his old ways—guitars thrashing, vocals howling into the feedback—were among the true predecessors of punk, even if the punks weren't willing to give him the credit.

Young would fritter away the early 1980s mucking about with synthesizers and trendy gadgetry (*Trans*, 1981) and mocking old-fashioned rock and roll (*Everybody's Rockin'*, 1983). These records did not sell beyond Young's rapidly shrinking cult. He would appall many of his fans in October 1984 by telling Jason DeParle of the Omaha *World-Herald* that he admired Ronald Reagan: "So what if he's a trigger-happy cowboy? He hasn't pulled the trigger. Don't you think it's better that Russia and all these other countries think that he's a trigger-happy cowboy than think that it's Jimmy Carter, who wants to give them back the Panama Canal?" Young also said, "Americans need to stop being supported by the government and get out and work. You can't always support the weak."

And as if to prove he wasn't kidding, he took to playing country and honky-tonk music—straight, no irony—sporting original lyrics containing a distinctly conservative edge.

In 1980, the Clash had put out *Sandinista!*, a three-record set that nailed to the wall American and, in its tacit complicity, British foreign policy in Central America. Rock was even prepared to react quickly to Ronald Reagan's conservative revolution: The Dead Kennedys, whose lead singer Jello Biafra had run for mayor of San Francisco in 1980, released the anti-Reagan screed "Let Them Eat Jellybeans." In 1985, the Ramones watched on television as Reagan went to Germany to place a wreath in a graveyard containing the remains of Nazi soldiers; the New York punk band immediately rose from their couch to record "Bonzo Goes to Bitburg," so bitter and precise a protest that the group's American label, Sire, initially refused to release it. The song crept back over here as an English import.

Evidence of rock's renewed social conscience moved beyond individual gestures in 1984, when Bob Geldof, leader of the Irish rock band the Boomtown Rats, organized an all-star group of primarily British rockers called Band Aid, which recorded a single, "Do They Know It's Christmas?" Participants included members of bands such as the Police, Ultravox, and Spandau Ballet. The proceeds—some $13 million—went to the starving in Ethiopia, as did those of the American version of this gesture, "We Are the World," recorded by a group of predominantly American superstars calling themselves United Support of Artists for Africa, or more commonly, USA for Africa. On January 28, 1985, a crowd of stars including Michael Jackson and Lionel Richie (co-authors of the song), Stevie Wonder, Ray Charles, Bruce Springsteen, Cyndi Lauper, Bob Dylan, Willie Nelson, Journey's Steve Perry, and Diana Ross convened at A&M Recording Studios in Los Angeles shortly after the conclusion of the live television broadcast of Dick Clark's "American Music Awards" show. They sang, they posed for pictures, they ate donated food, they schmoozed, they networked—and, in producer Quincy Jones's oft-repeated phrase, they "checked their egos at the door." "We Are the World" was filled with an optimism phrased with the ebullient self-interest of Werner Erhardt's est: "There's a choice we're making/We're saving our own lives."

Bob Geldof's next and most massive project was Live Aid, two simultaneous concerts, one held in Philadelphia's JFK Stadium, the other in London's Wembly Stadium, on July 13, 1985. The overlapping shows lasted over seventeen hours and were broadcast in 140 countries (in America, on MTV), and donations—eventually over $85 million in pledges—were phoned in. For such a quintessentially 1980s event, the acts appearing in Philadelphia were dominated by 1960s legends—Crosby, Stills, and Nash; Bob Dylan; Led Zeppelin; Joan Baez (who gave the media its collective lead by walking onstage and shouting to the crowd, "This is your Woodstock!"); Mick Jagger; and Neil Young, who less than a year before had said, "You can't always support the weak; you have to make the weak stand on one leg, or a half a leg, whatever they've got." Go figure.

The stand-out performance in England was given by Ireland's U2, which over the past few years had emerged as a postpunk act of some consequence. The quartet's sound was big and booming—layered, fuzzy guitar tracks vibrated beneath the stentorian crooning of lead singer Bono Vox— and the band's politics were unfurled as ostentatiously as the flag of Ireland at many of their concerts. U2's left-liberal humanism—they pleaded for tolerance between England and Ireland and wrote hard-rock hymns to Martin Luther King—was explicit in the lyrics of their songs, but even more effectively conveyed by the band's stage shows, which were most concerned with breaking down the barriers separating artist and audience. During Live Aid at Wembley, Vox made a typical gesture of solidarity by jumping into the audience to hug a few fans made emotional by U2's emotional music.

Black acts at Live Aid, in keeping with the AOR tone of the event, were noticeably few, with most attention paid to Teddy Pendergrass (making his first concert appearance since a 1978 auto accident left the soul singer paralyzed from the waist down) and Tina Turner, who sang a few sassy duets with Jagger. Michael Jackson, widely rumored to make a surprise appearance, did not perform; a few days after the event, his manager said that Jackson had been busy planning a collaboration with film directors Francis Ford Coppola and George Lucas: a minimovie called *Captain Eo*, to be shown at Disneyland and Disney World. The English concert featured crowd-rousing performances by, among others, Dire Straits, joined midway through by Sting; Elvis Costello; David Bowie; Paul McCartney; and Elton John.

The next major media charity event, Farm Aid, came about as the result of a remark made by Bob Dylan during his desultory acoustic Live Aid appearance. Dylan mumbled something about how he wished some of the Live Aid money could go to failing farmers in the Midwest. As typically gnomic and querulous as they were, Dylan's words reached the ears of Willie Nelson.

By the 1980s, Nelson was the foremost exponent of what came to be called the outlaw movement, the style uniting country and rock music. This "movement" had occurred quite by accident when Nelson, a veteran songwriter who had written such modern country classics as "Night Life," "Crazy," and "Funny How Time Slips Away"—all hits for other artists— found his own Nashville-based performing career at a standstill. He took a 1970 fire that destroyed his Nashville home as a portent and, chucking it all, returned to his native Texas, falling in with a bunch of younger song-writers and letting his hair grow into a scraggly ponytail. In 1972, he held the first of his Fourth of July "picnics," a loose show of Austin-based country and rock performers, which rapidly grew in audience size and popularity.

In 1974 and 1975, he released *Phases and Stages* and *Red-Headed Stranger*, respectively, country-music concept albums with the hard edge of rock and roll. These albums were commercial successes and also earned Nelson enormous newfound respect as a songwriter within the music industry. In 1976, he made his biggest commercial breakthrough: *Outlaws*, a compilation album with selections by Nelson himself, Waylon Jennings, Jessi Colter, and Tompall Glaser, became the first country music album to go platinum.

After this, Nelson commenced a string of hit albums and singles and acquired a degree of popularity unprecedented for a country singer, managing to broaden his following to include the pop audience. His 1978 album *Stardust* was a project his Columbia Records employers thought doomed to failure—a collection of pop song standards crooned by Willie. Instead, it confounded all expectations by selling over five million copies and making Nelson familiar to an audience that didn't know Hank Snow from Kitty Wells.

Nelson used his newfound superstardom to his own purposes, recording a series of duet albums with friends and former legends who had fallen on hard times, such as Roger Miller, Ray Price, and Webb Pierce—the Pierce collaboration, *In the Jailhouse Now* (1982), is a particularly choice example of the old-fashioned honky-tonk country style that Nelson helped revitalize—and even appearing in movies, such as *Honeysuckle Rose, The Electric Horseman,* and *Songwriter.*

But he was also worried about the plight of farmers facing foreclosure, and Dylan had given him an idea—to unite country music and rock and roll in the service of an all-American cause. And so Farm Aid, co-organized by Nelson and Midwestern rocker John Cougar Mellencamp, was held September 22, 1985, in Champaign, Illinois.

Designed to make the general public aware of the severe slump in commodities prices and simultaneously skyrocketing production costs and interest rates for the average family farmer, Farm Aid was a tricky media proposition. For one thing, many of the committees formed by the farmers to provide relief—organizations to which Farm Aid money might conceivably be donated—had been infiltrated by right-wing extremists; for another, the concert ran the risk of turning into a jingoistic reaction to Live Aid, and indeed, a let's-take-care-of-our-own attitude crept into the statements of performers ranging from Charlie Daniels to Neil Young.

There were numerous other such pop-charity events in 1985, as individual groups of musicians in Mexico, Canada, and Australia banded together to record charitable all-star records. By far the most explicitly political such project was "Sun City," a single and an album recorded by Artists United Against Apartheid, a coalition consisting of the most diverse range of stars of all the pop charity projects—Miles Davis, Jackson Browne, Bruce Springsteen, the ubiquitous Bob Dylan, Afrika Bambaataa, Jimmy Cliff, Herbie Hancock, Pat Benatar, Kurtis Blow, and Ruben Blades were among the participants; former E Street Band guitarist Steve Van Zant and rap-music record producer Arthur Baker produced the record. The proceeds of the sales of "Sun City" went to the Africa Fund, a nonprofit organization giving aid to political prisoners and their families inside South Africa. But while Bob Geldof had spent the period around Live Aid saying that his project "transcended politics," the lyrics of "Sun City" came out against the South African policy of apartheid and said that the Reagan government's policy of "constructive engagement" (i.e., maintaining U.S. economic ties to South Africa while urging the latter government to abandon apartheid) was "nothing but a joke."

As might be expected in a time of conservative radio programming, "Sun City" fared less well commercially than "We Are the World." The latter rose quickly to Number One; "Sun City" struggled into the Top Forty. The rhythm-and-blues-powered song was deemed "too rough" and rejected by many of the same rock radio stations that normally would have jumped to play anything with Bruce Springsteen's voice on it.

Political or not, these charitable events contributed to an unprecedented wave of goodwill in the mass media toward rock music. Still, by mid-1985, a Washington, D.C.–based antirock committee called the Parents Music Resource Center was gathering steam. The PMRC was formed to combat what it deemed "blatant explicit lyric content" in rock records. Among the PMRC's founder was Tipper Gore, wife of Tennessee Senator Albert Gore; Susan Baker, wife of Treasury Secretary James Baker; Georgie Packwood, wife of Oregon Senator Robert Packwood; and Nancy Thurmond, wife of South Carolina Senator Strom Thurmond. These women's spouses are relevant information because it was their political clout that was at least partially responsible for the group's ability to get a September 19 Senate Commerce Committee hearing scheduled on the deleterious effects of rock music on its listeners.

The PMRC contended that rock music "has taken a radical turn . . . much of it is blatantly obscene and violent and projects activities, values, and behavior corrosive to young minds and a healthy population." The PMRC's targets included everyone from heavy metal acts such as Judas Priest and Motley Crue to mainstream pop stars like Madonna and Prince, all of whom, they contended, created "pornography in rock music." The ultimate goal of the PMRC was to institute a ratings system that would alert parents to what the committee heard as offensive material.

At the Senate hearing, an unlikely trio of pop stars—Frank Zappa, John Denver, and Dee Snider (lead singer of Twisted Sister)—testified against any such ratings system. After the hearing, Zappa launched a campaign against the PMRC that included nationwide appearances on TV and radio talk shows and college campuses, haranguing against what he saw as the PMRC's violations of free speech for the music industry.

This was Zappa's most mainstream appearance in years. He had spent the decade of the 1970s consolidating his reputation as an ornery oddball whose talents were, depending on your point of view, either squandered or used to decidedly avant-garde ends. Much of the goodwill Zappa had accumulated with the public and critics in the 1960s for his hard-edged, adventurous music dissipated in the 1970s as Zappa began to emphasize sophomoric humor in concert-audience rousers like "Don't Eat the Yellow Snow"; "Dancin' Fool," a swipe at disco; and "Jewish Princess," which provoked the B'nai B'rith Anti-Defamation League to file a complaint against Zappa with the Federal Communications Commission.

Zappa's work came to seem schizophrenic. On the one hand, he would release intricate, brazenly uncommercial but highly interesting efforts like the three-record, mail-order-only 1982 package *Shut Up 'N' Play Yer Guitar* (the title suggested what many of his once-and-future fans felt). On the other hand, Zappa pursued novelty hits with barely disguised condescension toward their intended pop audience. By far the most successful of this latter type of material was "Valley Girl," a parody of Southern California teenage slang enunciated with convincing vigor by Zappa's fourteen-year-old daughter Moon Unit.

When the PMRC launched its campaign, Zappa protested what he saw as an attempt at governmental censorship. "These ladies want to get laws passed that will prohibit you from being able to buy whatever kind of music you like," he stated, "especially if you have the bad luck to be a teenager." It seemed that the old battle, waged since the 1950s, about rock's effects on impressionable youth, had never truly been won: In November 1985, the PMRC scored a small victory when the Recording Industry Association of America, a music-industry organization that represents more than twenty record labels, including all the majors, agreed to place a sticker on records saying "Explicit Lyrics—Parental Advisory" on albums the individual record company involved deemed appropriate. Rock had, in effect, come full circle.

Even as the PMRC was mounting its antirock campaign, a group of music-industry figures was proposing to honor much of the same music that the PMRC was pillorying. Bigwigs such as Atlantic Records founders Ahmet and Nesuhi Ertegun, Warner Bros. Records president Mo Ostin, *Rolling Stone* publisher Jann Wenner, and concert promoter Bill Graham proposed creating a Rock and Roll Hall of Fame, in which rock's innovators would be enshrined. Numerous major cities across America vied as the site for the museum. In May 1986, Cleveland, Ohio, was announced the winner on the basis of sheer enthusiasm—the town whose primary claim to rock fame as the home of pioneer rock dj Alan Freed mustered hundreds of thousands of signatures on petitions imploring the Hall of Fame board to pick their fair town. It worked.

The 1980s had brought about a heightening of rock's most emblematic characteristics. By the middle of the decade, the music was known to a larger audience than any mass art had ever reached; nonetheless, in many quarters, it was perceived as every bit as controversial as it had been at its birth thirty years earlier. Rock was a big business that held within it a distinctly anticommercial, even avant-garde, aspect—it retained its power to alienate as many people as it attracted.

Which meant, ultimately, that 1980s rock had regained much of the power, mystery, and edginess that it had lost momentarily in the 1970s. By mid-decade, the music was making a series of exciting reconnections to its past. The rigid categories of the 1970s were breaking down, allowing for vigorous, healthy cross-pollination. The 1980s dance music, to take just one example, could be recognized as disco with a rock-and-roll influence; its mechanistic drone had been humanized, enlarged by a vast range of styles: the Talking Heads reintroduced the music to both artiness and Africanness; Madonna suggested that dance music could be sung with the quietly humorous implacability of one of her unacknowledged influences, Lesley Gore.

The dominance of AOR, which gave rock a white face and robbed a generation of rock fans of its rhythm-and-blues roots, gave way to the latest version of Top Forty: CHR, or Contemporary Hits Radio, in which a Lionel Richie ballad could be followed by a ZZ Top boogie, and both songs benefited from the recontextualization.

The richest rock in the 1980s possessed the most important thing a now-thirty-year-old art form could: a sure sense of its own history. What made Bruce Springsteen so exciting to such a broad range of listeners in the mid-1980s was not only the fact that he was writing moving music that spoke to the immediate concerns of his audience, but that this highly contemporary music also invoked the vivid examples of everyone from Woody Guthrie to the Drifters to Phil Spector. Similarly, in Michael Jackson, it is possible to trace the entire course of entertainment in America, and not just in music, either: a pop star who names Walt Disney, Sam Cooke, and Fred Astaire as among his forebears has a lot to tell us about the history of popular culture in our time. And this, finally, is what the best rock music will always do: give root to our past while describing our present, and thus suggest the sound of a possible future.

INDEX

About the Authors

Ed Ward writes for the Austin *Chronicle* and is the author of *Michael Bloomfield: The Rise and Fall of an American Guitar Hero*. He has been a contributing editor to *Crawdaddy*, *Rolling Stone*, *Creem*, *Oui*, *Chic*, *City* (San Francisco), *Music Sound Output*, and *Third Coast*. Former music columnist and critic for the *Austin American-Statesman*, he has written for nearly every pop music publication in this country.

Geoffrey Stokes writes on the media and the pop scene for *The Village Voice*. He is the author of many books, including *The Beatles*, *Sex and the American Teenager* (with Robert Coles) and *Pinstripe Pandemonium: A Season with the New York Yankees*, and was editor of *The Village Voice Anthology: 1956–1980*. His book *Star-Making Machinery: Inside the Business of Rock & Roll* won the ASCAP–Deems Taylor Award.

Ken Tucker is the pop music critic for *The Philadelphia Inquirer*. His criticism has appeared in *The New York Times Book Review*, *The Village Voice*, *Rolling Stone*, and *Esquire*. He contributed to *The Rolling Stone Illustrated History of Rock & Roll*, edited by Jim Miller, and to *The Rolling Stone Record Guide*, edited by Dave Marsh. He was also a finalist for the 1984 Pulitzer Prize for Criticism.